Migration and Public Policy

The International Library of Studies on Migration

Series Editor: Professor Robin Cohen
Department of Sociology, University of Warwick, UK

1. Theories of Migration
   Professor Robin Cohen

2. Geography and Migration
   Dr Vaughan Robinson

3. Sociology of Migration
   Professor Robin Cohen

4. Migration in European History (Volumes I and II)
   Professor Colin Holmes

5. The Politics of Migration
   Professor Robin Cohen and Professor Zig Layton-Henry

6. Law and Migration
   Selina Goulbourne

7. Migration and Social Cohesion
   Dr Steven Vertovec

8. Migration and Public Policy
   Dr Vaughan Robinson

Future titles will include:

Migration, Diasporas and Transnationalism
Dr Steven Vertovec and Professor Robin Cohen

Gender and Migration
Dr Katie Willis and Dr Brenda Yeoh

Wherever possible, the articles in these volumes have been reproduced as originally published using facsimile reproduction, inclusive of footnotes and pagination to facilitate ease of reference.

For a list of all Edward Elgar published titles visit our site on the World Wide Web at
http://www.e-elgar.co.uk

Migration and Public Policy

Edited by

Vaughan Robinson

Reader in Geography, Director of the Migration Unit,
University of Wales, Swansea, UK

THE INTERNATIONAL LIBRARY OF STUDIES ON MIGRATION

An Edward Elgar Collection

Cheltenham, UK • Northampton, MA, USA

Published by
Edward Elgar Publishing Limited
Glensanda House
Montpellier Parade
Cheltenham
Glos GL50 1UA
UK

Edward Elgar Publishing, Inc.
6 Market Street
Northampton
Massachusetts 01060
USA

A catalogue record for this book is available from the British Library

Library of Congress Cataloguing in Publication Data

Migration and public policy / edited by Vaughan Robinson.
(The international library of studies on migration: 8)
1. Migration, Internal. 2. Migration, Internal—Government policy. 3. Emigration and immigration. 4. Emigration and immigration—Government policy. I. Robinson, Vaughan. II. Series.
HB1952.M538 1999
304.8—dc21 99–17120
CIP

ISBN 1 85898 922 1

Printed and bound in Great Britain by MPG Books Ltd, Bodmin, Cornwall

Contents

Acknowledgements

The editor and publishers wish to thank the authors and the following who have kindly given permission for the use of copyright material.

Blackwell Publishers, Inc. for article: Keith H. Halfacree (1996), 'Out of Place in the Country: Travellers and the "Rural Idyll"', *Antipode*, **28** (1), January, 42–71.

Cambridge University Press for article: Hazel Flett, Jeff Henderson and Bill Brown (1979), 'The Practice of Racial Dispersal in Birmingham, 1969–1975', *Journal of Social Policy*, **8** (3), July, 289–309.

Carfax Publishing Limited for articles: Alan Mabin (1992), 'Comprehensive Segregation: The Origins of the Group Areas Act and its Planning Apparatuses', *Journal of Southern African Studies*, **18** (2), June, 405–29; Mike King (1993), 'The Impact of Western European Border Policies on the Control of "Refugees" in Eastern and Central Europe', *New Community*, **19** (2), January, 183–99; Wolfgang Seifert (1997), 'Admission Policy, Patterns of Migration and Integration: The German and French Case Compared', *New Community*, **23** (4), October, 441–60; Kimberly A. Hamilton (1997), 'Europe, Africa, and International Migration: An Uncomfortable Triangle of Interests', *New Community*, **23** (4), October, 549–70.

Center for Migration Studies for articles: Alejandro Portes (1978), 'Toward a Structural Analysis of Illegal (Undocumented) Immigration', *International Migration Review*, **12** (4), Winter, 469–84; Saskia Sassen-Koob (1979), 'Economic Growth and Immigration in Venezuela', *International Migration Review*, **13** (3), Fall, 455–74; Gertrud Neuwirth and Lynn Clark (1981), 'Indochinese Refugees in Canada: Sponsorship and Adjustment', *International Migration Review*, **15** (1), Spring-Summer, 131–40; Nasra M. Shah (1983), 'Pakistani Workers in the Middle East: Volume, Trends and Consequences', *International Migration Review*, **17** (3), Fall, 410–24; Xiushi Yang and Sidney Goldstein (1990), 'Population Movement in Zhejiang Province, China: The Impact of Government Policies', *International Migration Review*, **XXIV** (3), Fall, 509–33; James Jupp (1995), 'From "White Australia" to "Part of Asia": Recent Shifts in Australian Immigration Policy Towards the Region', *International Migration Review*, **XXIX** (1), Spring, 207–28; Graeme Hugo (1996), 'Environmental Concerns and International Migration', *International Migration Review*, **XXX** (1), Spring, 105–31; Myron Weiner (1996), 'Ethics, National Sovereignty and the Control of Immigration', *International Migration Review*, **XXX** (1), Spring, 171–97.

Elsevier Science Ltd for articles: A.M. Findlay (1988), 'From Settlers to Skilled Transients: The Changing Structure of British International Migration', *Geoforum*, **19** (4), 401–10;

William T.S. Gould (1988), 'Government Policies and International Migration of Skilled Workers in Sub-Saharan Africa', *Geoforum*, **19** (4), 433–45; Thomas R. Leinbach (1989), 'The Transmigration Programme in Indonesian National Development Strategy: Current Status and Future Requirements', *Habitat International*, **13** (3), 81–93; Vaughan Robinson (1995), 'The Changing Nature and European Perceptions of Europe's Refugee Problem', *Geoforum*, **26** (4), 411–27.

Geographical Association for article: Vaughan Robinson (1989), 'Up the Creek without a Paddle?: Britain's Boat People Ten Years On', *Geography*, **74**, 332–8.

International Organization for Migration for articles: Sharon Stanton Russell (1992), 'Migrant Remittances and Development', *International Migration*, **XXX** (3/4), 267–87; Nicholas P. Glytsos (1995), 'Problems and Policies Regarding the Socio-Economic Integration of Returnees and Foreign Workers in Greece', *International Migration*, **33** (2), 155–73; Tamar Horowitz (1996), 'Value-Oriented Parameters in Migration Policies in the 1990s: The Israeli Experience', *International Migration*, **XXXIV** (4), 513–35.

James H. Johnson and John Salt for their own article: (1981), 'Population Redistribution Policies in Great Britain', *Nordia*, **15** (2), 77–92.

Oxford University Press for articles: Michael M. Cernea (1990), 'Internal Refugee Flows and Development-Induced Population Displacement', *Journal of Refugee Studies*, **3** (4), 320–39; Roger Zetter (1991), 'Labelling Refugees: Forming and Transforming a Bureaucratic Identity', *Journal of Refugee Studies*, **4** (1), 39–62.

Population Studies for article: Judith A. Fortney (1970), 'International Migration of Professionals', *Population Studies*, **XXIV** (2), July, 217–32.

Rivers Oram Press for excerpt: Allan Findlay (1994), 'An Economic Audit of Contemporary Immigration', in Sarah Spencer (ed.), *Strangers and Citizens: A Positive Approach to Migrants and Refugees*, Chapter 6, 159–201, 386–90.

Routledge for article: Akbar S. Ahmed (1995), '"Ethnic Cleansing": A Metaphor for Our Time?', *Ethnic and Racial Studies*, **18** (1), January, 1–25.

Sage Publications, Inc. for article: Barry N. Stein (1983), 'The Commitment to Refugee Resettlement', *Annals of the American Academy of Political and Social Science*, **467**, May, 187–201.

University of California Press for article: Joost R. Hiltermann (1991), 'Settling for War: Soviet Immigration and Israel's Settlement Policy in East Jerusalem', *Journal of Palestine Studies*, **XX** (2), Winter, 71–85.

John Wiley and Sons Limited for article: Paul Boyle (1995), 'Public Housing as a Barrier to Long-Distance Migration', *International Journal of Population Geography*, **1** (2), December, 147–64.

Every effort has been made to trace all the copyright holders but if any have been inadvertently overlooked the publishers will be pleased to make the necessary arrangment at the first opportunity.

In addition the publishers wish to thank the Library of the London School of Economics and Political Science, the Marshall Library of Economics, Cambridge University and B&N Microfilm, London, for their assistance in obtaining these articles.

Introduction

Vaughan Robinson

In what has been termed the 'Age of Migration' (Castles and Miller, 1993) we take mobility and migration for granted. In any one year over 4 million people become international migrants by crossing an international boundary and settling in a new country for more than one year (Weiner, 1995). At any one point in time there are 60 million international migrants in the world (Castles and Miller, 1993), of which perhaps 17 million are refugees (UNHCR, 1997). Temporary international travel for business, leisure and education has also mushroomed of late, with the availability of ever-cheaper airfares and new international opportunities for collaboration and competition. Nor does international migration dominate mobility. Within Developing Countries there are 20 million Internally Displaced Persons who have been forced from their homes (Bennett, 1998). In the 'North' there is the 'normal' continual churning of populations as families not only adjust their housing to new demographic, social, economic or marital status, but also seek out more desired environments within which to live and socialise (Boyle, Halfacree and Robinson, 1998). Even for those who do not seek a permanent change of residence, mobility is commonplace, with longer commutes to work, a greater willingness to travel to use facilities and a general belief that personal mobility can be equated with freedom. In short, an increasing proportion of the world's population now finds itself in the final stages of Zelinsky's (1971, 247) Mobility Transition, within which:

> 'participants are in almost non stop daily, weekly or seasonal oscillation across and within spatial and social zones'.

Migration and Different Models of Nationhood

Although migration has become a commonplace, it should not be taken for granted. Migration is inextricably linked to how the nation-state defines and reproduces itself. Smith (1991) argues that there are two main models of the nation; the ethnic or pre-Western model, and the civic or Western model. In the former, the nation was defined by

> 'Genealogy and presumed descent ties, popular mobilization, vernacular languages, customs and traditions: these are the elements of an alternative, ethnic conception of the nation, one that mirrored the very different route of 'nation-formation' travelled by many communities in eastern Europe and Asia' (Smith, 1991: 12–13).

What is significant about this earlier conception of the nation is that it depends upon descent not residence. Membership of the ethnic nation cannot be acquired through immigration into its territory, nor can emigration sunder the bonds that make individuals members of the nation for life. In short, migration represents no threat to national identity and therefore need not be closely regulated. Groups such as nomads need not be dissuaded from crossing international boundaries since they cannot gain membership of the nation (and the benefits which this confers) simply through living on one side of a border rather than the other.

The Western model of nation is however based upon different principles, summarised by Smith (1991: 9) as follows:

> 'it is in the first place, a predominantly spatial or territorial conception. According to this view, nations must possess compact, well-defined territories. People and territory must ... belong to each other'.

He argues that such nations require 'homelands' within which can be situated an historical national memory. Those who gain legal access to this homeland and reside there, are offered legal membership of the nation, which carries with it certain benefits (eg being afforded protection by the state and the right to exploit the land) in exchange for certain obligations (eg submitting to the laws of the community). And within this homeland, the educational system and the mass media ensure that common values are widely disseminated and adhered to.

This alternative conception of the nation creates a very different perception of migration. Unregulated migration challenges the nation, directly. Such migration would allow individuals to circumvent the usual membership procedure, thereby potentially threatening the homogeneity of the nation. It implies that control of who can and who cannot become a member has been lost. And it further implies that the benefits of membership are available to all, regardless of whether they agree to shoulder the associated obligations. For these reasons, the civic model of the nation requires precisely defined territorial boundaries which are made impermeable to unwanted migration, and within which ethnic, racial, religious and linguistic homogeneity can be encouraged.

Not surprisingly, then, as the civic model of the nation has become more entrenched so, too, has migration control. As Carens (1996, 158) puts it, 'every state has the authority to admit or exclude aliens as it chooses since that authority is widely acknowledged to be one of the essential elements of sovereignty'. Dowty (1987) lists the various reasons why states now feel that they have to control immigration and, to a lesser extent, emigration. These include: the desire not to let criminals escape domestic law; a wish to protect citizens from public health threats (see Malkki's 1998) description of the popular demonisation of Africa and Africans through their association with AIDS and Ebola); the fear of political and military activists operating within their boundaries and destabilising the nation's security; the imperative of avoiding cultural contamination; popular fears about the impact of migrant workers upon the livelihood of indigenous workers; and the more general fear of allowing entry to potentially dissenting groups of 'others'.

Dowty (1987) also outlines the countervailing reasons why the rights of the individual in respect of mobility should not be over-ruled by the needs of the state. He argues that the right to stay or go is a basic human right, albeit 'the forgotten right'. That the right of escape from persecution is also a fundamental right. That migration is not simply an end in itself, but is also often a prerequisite of other human rights, such as the right to marry someone of your own choosing, the right to an acceptable standard of living, the right to access education and appropriate employment opportunities, and the right to practice whatever religion you choose. Dowty argues that the right to migrate is intrinsic to democracy, since it allows citizens to show their disapproval of a regime by emigrating. Finally, he argues that there has to be a symmetry to intervention in migration since it would be unreasonable to allow countries the right to expel citizens without citizens themselves having corresponding rights of entry to another country.

The Structure of the Book

Despite Dowty's explication of the reasons why states should be wary of closing their borders, many governments have chosen to intervene in both emigration and immigration, and others have chosen to use internal migration to engineer particular social, economic, political, religious or security outcomes. This collection brings together a selection of papers on this theme and is designed to indicate the many ways in which states have tried to shape migration flows and patterns for ulterior motives, and also some of the intended and unintended outcomes of such manipulation. The book is organized into four main sections, each of which focuses on a different dimension of public policy towards migration and migrants. The first looks at some of the issues raised in debates surrounding open borders, thereby developing the argument beyond that outlined above. The second concentrates upon state intervention in migration, and is divided into three separate subsections. The first is concerned with direct and deliberate state management of migration, providing examples of discouragement, encouragement, prevention and repatriation. It also demonstrates the way in which certain regimes have introduced policies designed to infringe the rights only of certain potential migrants. The second subsection focuses upon the way in which other state actions can have indirect, and often unintended, but severe, implications for mobility. And the third subsection looks briefly at how the direct intervention of one state can have indirect consequences for the migration regimes of others. The third section then describes how states engineer the settlement and integration of migrants so as to achieve particular national objectives. And the last section briefly demonstrates the impact of migration upon sending and receiving societies and the way in which states might intervene to maximize perceived benefits or minimize perceived disadvantages of a particular scale, type or flow of migration. A brief commentary on each of these issues follows in the remainder of this introduction to allow the reader to contextualize each of the subsequent papers and see why individual papers have been selected for reproduction.

Debating Intervention in Migration Issues

Until recently, migration policy tended to rely upon a series of unstated but implicit assumptions which were never exposed to rigorous debate or scrutiny. Migration policy tended just to be that way, with exceptions (such as the admission of particular groups of quota refugees) being justified in isolation and on very simplistic grounds. More recently, however, as the mobility of people across international boundaries has become both easier and more threatening in its scale and its dissimilarity, and as policies have shifted inexorably from laisser-faire to interventionist, key actors have felt the need to justify their own actions or scrutinize those of others. A debate has therefore developed about the advantages and disadvantages of immigration and also about what is the most appropriate basis upon which to construct immigration policy.

In several countries authors have tried to educate the public and change the attitudes of legislators by presenting the 'facts' of immigration and drawing up balance sheets which weigh the positive advantages to be derived from further (or less restricted) immigration against the costs. Findlay (1994) (Chapter 1), for example, has produced an economic audit of contemporary immigration to the UK. He weighs the labour market contribution of immigrants against their welfare costs and concludes that 'current British immigration policy lacks clear economic objectives and ... that an economic argument exists for a more pro-active stance on immigration' (Findlay, 1994: 159). In particular, Findlay argues for greater skilled migration to meet skill shortages in the British labour market, for a relaxation of rules that prevent Transnational Corporations moving some of their staff through British branch offices, and for further encouragement of entrepreneurial immigration. His views can be compared with those of Coleman (1992) who sees little need for, or benefit from, further mass immigration into the EU. Parallel work to that of Findlay includes Spencer's (1994) *Immigration as an Economic Asset: the German Experience.* Spencer concluded that her contributors' empirical studies:

> 'provide(s) a sound basis for debate on future immigration policy. They show that it would be mistaken to underestimate the positive impact which immigration has had, and the extent of demand for immigrants which may exist in the future'. (Spencer, 1994; xxvi)

Gieseck, et al. (1994), for example, estimate that the net fiscal gain from immigration to Germany in 1992 was DM14 billion, to which has to be added the higher economic growth made possible by immigrant labour. And Ulrich (1994) describes how in 1989 foreigners contributed 7.8 per cent of all pension contributions in Germany but drew only 1.9 per cent of all pensions paid.

Europe has not been the only part of the world to have engaged in such balance sheet exercises. Wooden, Holton, Hugo and Sloan's (1994) *Australian Immigration: A Survey of the Issues* contains a similar analysis for Australia. Wooden's (1994) chapter on the economic impact of immigration concluded that immigration does offer economic benefits but that these might be quite small. In particular, immigration has had a beneficial impact upon the construction industry and upon government finances, has provided economies of scale which have probably increased output, and has introduced skills to the Australian labour force. There is little countervailing evidence that it increases unemployment, as has often been claimed.

While some authors have therefore been content to appeal to the self-interest of the public in receiving countries by demonstrating that immigration is (economically) beneficial, others have sought to argue their case on a higher plane, referring instead to notions of morality, ethics or social justice. Carens (1996), for example, suggests that migration policy and practice can be constructed from two different perspectives, the idealistic and the realistic. These two positions are often in tension, but need not be in conflict. He argues that the idealistic perspective has been the more common in the academic literature, with writers being independent, challenging, and willing to ask the most fundamental questions. An idealistic perspective always seeks to achieve the highest ideals and is unfettered by current practice or apparent constraints. Idealistic migration policy would thus begin with such profound questions as 'what are the rights of the individual?' and 'should the state have the power to deny entry to certain individuals?' and then move on to matters such as 'should humanity be divided into separate states?', and 'what is absolute justice?' Carens (1996) then goes on to outline his alternative 'realistic' perspective. This, he argues, focuses on what is possible, given existing realities, thereby trying to avoid too large a gap between the 'ought' and the 'is'. Realistic approaches to migration policy would thus recognize that the state exists (without necessarily accepting this as a good thing), and that policy has to be in line with public behavioural and attitudinal realities. Realistic approaches also focus attention on how moral outcomes can be made more palatable to the common 'man'. Carens suggests there are three ways of achieving this. Getting people to emotionally identify with 'others' encourages them to set aside their own narrow self-interest, and treat others better, but emotional identification is easily 'overloaded'. Arranging for a coincidence of self-interest with morality also makes morality more effective, with for example, people being willing to bear short-term costs if they think there is a long-term return for them or their children. And, lastly, contemporary morality can be given greater appeal by rooting it in the moral tradition of the target community, with its unique social and historical characteristics. In short, a migration policy derived from a realistic approach to morality would 'focus moral discussion on issues that are actually up for debate in society, and thus ... maximize the opportunity for reasoned moral reflection to have an impact on public life' (Carens, 1996: 164).

The question of the morality of migration policy can be pursued from the abstract to the concrete. We would begin by acknowledging that, whereas the rights of the state with regard to migration have been well-defined and tested over a number of centuries, only recently has a concern developed about the right of the individual to leave or enter countries of their choice. With the development of a global economy, global communications and a global labour market, the demand from individuals to move has risen sharply, especially from low-wage and low-labour demand areas to high-wage and high-labour demand areas. The historic rights of the state to regulate migration are thus increasingly being challenged in the modern era by individuals who press for their own rights. Moreover the state is also forced to recognize that potential migrants will use legal means of entry where possible, but are sufficiently well-informed to use illegal methods to circumvent restriction, if necessary. Consequently, therefore, advanced industrial states are faced with a moral dilemma. How do they balance the needs and well-being of their existing populations with the desires of potential immigrants and the need for cheap labour? How are the rights of one group of people to be weighed against the rights of another? Moreover this dilemma is further complicated by the perception that the rights of certain potential immigrant groups should be privileged over those of others. Those who are experiencing infringements of their basic human rights through torture, harassment or persecution are seen as more deserving of entry than those who simply wish to gain a better standard of living. Weiner (1996) (Chapter 2) therefore sees the crux of the matter as:

> is 'migration a basic human right or (are) the claims of outsiders ... superseded by the principle of national sovereignty – the moral obligation of states to do the best for their own citizens'. (Weiner, 1996: 171)

Weiner then goes on to apply moral reasoning to several questions. Should states have open borders? Should states select to whom they offer entry? Should the moral claims of refugees be privileged over those of others? Should states intervene in the internal working of other states in order to prevent unwanted migration? Should migration policy lead, respond to, or mirror public opinion? He argues that these questions and othere related to migration policy need to be exposed to analysis from the perspective of the developing field of applied ethics. Such analyses would need, however, to bear in mind four things. Firstly, that there is a distinction between personal morality and the application of moral principles to public policy. Secondly, that the ethics of ultimate ends differ from the ethics of responsibility. Thirdly, that there is a difference between fundamentally unjust policies and injustices of implementation. And finally, that migration debates cannot be resolved solely by invoking principles of absolute justice, since they involve conflicting rights, claims and values. Weiner (1996, 195) concludes that 'migration and refugee issues cannot simply be reduced to moral questions, but neither ... are they solely questions of national sovereignty in which moral judgements play no role'.

Whilst Carens and Weiner have sought to apply general principles of morality and ethics to the whole migration debate, other writers have, instead, focused upon particular dimensions of migration. For example, Shacknove (1985) tries to define what constitutes a refugee from first principles. And Hathaway (1990) looks at how international refugee law (and practice) is not grounded in the concept of humanitarianism or orientated towards the protection of basic human rights, as it ought to be. 'Its purpose is not specifically to meet the needs of the refugees themselves ... , but rather is to govern disruptions of regulated international migration in accordance with the interests of states' (Hathaway, 1990: 133). Hathaway's suggestion for how this paradox could be resolved focuses upon regional solutions to refugee crises in which states could offer asylum, knowing that applicants would be from the same racial (even ethnic) group as the indigenous population. Humanitarianism need not therefore threaten social homogeneity.

Intervention in Migration

Direct

For reasons already identified above, states often feel it is important to regulate the flow of people into or within their territory. This regulation can take several forms. It may involve regulating immigration, emigration or internal migration, and various combinations of encouragement, discouragement, prevention, or expulsion. Mechanisms include economic incentives, legislation or military force.

INTERNATIONAL MIGRATION

International migration is perhaps easier to regulate than internal migration. States have clearly defined boundaries, historically recognized powers to determine who enters and leaves, and the right to use legal instruments and physical means to prevent entry or egress.

Discouraging emigration: Historically, the emphasis was upon preventing emigration, in line with a mercantilist perspective that viewed population as a resource to be hoarded alongside other resources such as precious metals. This mindset saw population as a source of economic wealth, both through its direct productive capacity and through its action as consumers. Larger national populations created more and consumed more. For this reason, states often tried to prevent their citizens emigrating. The Isle of Man (Robinson, 1990), for example, had strict laws in the eighteenth century which not only saw emigrants being prosecuted, but also enforced the confiscation of any vessels used to carry them. Even in the twentieth century, mercantilist attitudes have persisted in transmuted and more sophisticated form. Adams (1968) martials the arguments used within the Developing World against the 'brain drain' of uncontrolled emigration of highly skilled labour. More, recently, however, the emphasis has shifted to hoarding populations for non-economic reasons. Central amongst these has been the production and reproduction of the nation-state. Glass (1967) provides a detailed account of how the fascist state in Italy in the inter-war years reversed decades of population loss through international emigration. From 1927 onwards, the goal of the state was to retain its existing population and attract Italians overseas back to Italy. Illegal emigration became much more difficult, border guards were given swingeing powers, emigrants were required to sign a contract which prevented them subsequently being joined overseas by relatives, and emigration was not permitted without a pre-existing guarantee of work overseas. Not surprisingly, population loss through net migration fell from 58,000 in 1931 to 9000 in 1936. Nor have such policies been unique to right wing administrations. As late as 1988 Soviet citizens were effectively prevented from emigrating to the West because of the difficulty of getting an international passport.

Encouraging emigration: In other cases, governments have sought to do the opposite. They have encouraged their populations (or more usually fragments of their populations) to migrate overseas. Bean and Melville (1990) document the case study of state-sanctioned child migration from Britain to Empire between 1618 and 1967. Some 150,000 children aged 4–14 years of age were sent from Britain to Australia, Canada, New Zealand and South Africa. Underlying this managed migration was a desire to ensure the economic development of the Empire, whilst simultaneously ensuring its Anglicization. As one Catholic agency put it in 1938:

> 'Those who are co-operating in this great and noble project of transplanting poor children who are without means, influence, and parentless in many cases, from congested and unpromising surroundings, to a land rich in natural, but undeveloped resources which are awaiting the correct type of people to render them productive, are doing much to strengthen and extend the Empire'. (in Bean and Melville, 1990: 6)

The furtherance of empire was thus elevated above the needs of the children themselves. Many were given no choice in their migration, a fair proportion had only been placed in homes temporarily yet were still sent overseas without their parents' permission, and most were exploited in their new lands, even brutalized and abused.

The desire to ensure racial purity also underpinned another notorious planned emigration. Marrus (1985) documents the efforts of the Nazi authorities to rid Germany of the Jewish population, prior to the decision to exterminate it. He describes how Jews faced ever-tighter restrictions and more virulent harassment in the run-up to the Second World War, and how many responded by emigrating. Seventeen thousand fled to Shanghai in 1939 alone, with many more seeking sanctuary in British Palestine or the UK itself. But beyond this active encouragement of individual emigration, Hitler was also seeking to resolve the problem more rapidly by the forced expulsion of Jews to overseas reservations. An international solution was sought as part of appeasement. Madagascar, Kenya and Northern Rhodesia were all considered as possible sites of reservations, although in the end, the outbreak of the Second World War led to the Nazis adopting an alternative 'Final Solution'.

The encouragement of emigration need not only be sought to expel 'others' who are deemed to threaten societal homogeneity. Increasingly, and very much in contrast to the mercantilist tradition, labour is now being seen by many developing countries as a commodity which can profitably be exported. Bangladesh provides one example of a country which actively set out to export workers for national economic gain. In the 1970s they established a Bureau of Manpower, Emigration and Training to put foreign employers in touch with suitable Bangladeshi workers and then to facilitate the departure and travel of emigrant Bangladeshis to the 'North' (Ali et al., 1981). As Shah (1983) (Chapter 3) notes, similar policies were in place in Pakistan. There, the Overseas Pakistani Foundation even trained labour for specific overseas placements. As a consequence, 1.2 million Pakistani workers had found work in the Middle East by 1981. In return, Pakistan gained considerably from the flow of remittances, which at one time netted the government 40 per cent of its total foreign exchange earnings and some 8 per cent of gross national produce.

Forced emigration: Although it is difficult to distinguish between actively encouraged emigration and forced emigration, the latter does form a discrete category (see Peterson's 1958 typology of migrations for example). Here, residents within a country are given no choice about whether they stay or go. Whilst economic issues might cause some of these forced movements, many more are stimulated by the desire for societal homogeneity. Zolberg (1983) was one of the first to offer an holistic explanation for refugee movements arguing that they were triggered by political rather than economic forces, especially the crystallization of nation-states out of defunct multi-ethnic empires. The latter often leave a legacy of 'misfit groups' in former colonies. Such misfits are of two types. 'Minorities' are people of one identity finding themselves in a country with a different identity. The 'stateless' are peoples with an identity that does not correspond to that of any current nation-state. Zolberg went on to argue that refugee movements are created when newly emerging nation-states seek to homogenize their populations, cultures and identity by expelling minorities or the stateless. The literature abounds with examples of such refugee expulsions. Twaddle (1975) has described the expulsion of the racially-defined Asian minority from Uganda in 1973, and van Hear (1998) illustrates the discussion of the creation of new diasporas with a number of expulsions.

Encouraging immigration: Whilst state intervention in emigration has been very important, concern has shifted more in the post-war period to the issue of immigration. Initially, in the post-war economic boom of the 1950s and 1960s, many advanced industrial economies found themselves short of labour, and therefore intervened to stimulate mass labour migration. Such intervention sought not only to rectify imbalances in gross quantitative labour supply, but also to reshape the skills-mix within the labour force. Rising aspirations in post-war Europe and greater opportunities for meaningful social mobility meant that indigenous labour was increasingly unwilling to undertake the less well-paid and unpleasant unskilled jobs in manufacturing and low-level services. In addition, in certain industrial sectors, jobs were being degraded as employers either sought to extract greater profit from new investment or drive down labour costs as a substitute for capital investment (Fevre, 1984). As a result, there was a need for cheap unskilled labour in growing economies such as Germany and the UK. The response to this varied between countries. Britain turned to its colonies and former-colonies for workers, and sought spontaneous unassisted migration (although there was some direct recruitment). The outcome has been to produce an ethnic minority population that now numbers some 3 million or 5.5 per cent of the nation's population (Peach, 1996). Germany, instead, opted for a guestworker system in which young men were rotated through the German economy on short-term contracts, recruited directly, and processed and transported by the government (Castles, 1985). At its peak, Germany employed some 2.6 million foreign workers (Castles, Booth and Wallace, 1984). In Britain, West Indian and Asian migrants were given settlement and welfare rights, and were entitled to political participation. In Germany, these rights were not accorded to the Turks and Yugoslavs who fulfilled similar industrial functions. Nor were labour shortages unique to Europe in the aftermath of the Second World War. In Australia, Arthur Calwell, the first Minister for Immigration called, in 1945, for the country to 'populate or perish' and sought annual population growth of 2 per cent, of which half was to come from net immigration. This would require net immigration of 70,000 per year, and Calwell set about achieving this target by offering free transportation to Australia for British ex-servicemen and miners, and subsidized £10 passages for other migrants. These, and other incentives, ensured that between 1946 and 1970 net annual gain through immigration never fell below 70,000 people, and in some quinquennia exceeded 80,000 and even 100,000. In other countries, different strategies were employed to attract replacement labour. Portes (1978) (Chapter 4) describes how the shortage of cheap labour in the agricultural sector of California was met by the state deliberately choosing to ignore the illegal seasonal migration of Mexicans across the border, and Jenkins (1978) argues the state also denied the border patrols the wherewithal to make the border impermeable. And finally, labour shortages have not been unique to 'northern' countries. Sassen-Koob (1979) (Chapter 5) recounts how from 1973 onwards the Venezuelan government sought to recruit foreign labour both from the Iberian peninsula and from neighbouring countries of the Andean Pact to add up to a million workers to its labour force.

States have not only sought to encourage immigration for economic reasons. In other cases there have been attempts to reunite ethnic or religious groups that have come under threat in certain of their diasporic satellites. Israel's evacuation of Falasha Jews from Ethiopia in May 1991 is a case in point. Israeli military personnel were used to airlift some 16,000 Falasha from Addis Ababa to Israel when they came under threat from a prolonged civil war. Germany's reunification of the ethnic German people through the staged immigration of Aussiedler is another. Jones (1996) estimates that some 4 million people have been involved in this migration since the beginning of the 1950s, with an average of 71,000 people entering Germany each year between 1950 and 1993 from countries such as Poland, Romania and Russia. Prior to the end of the Cold War, Germany even paid other governments to allow ethnic Germans to emigrate, with Romania receiving 8800DM per head. But Israel's attempts to liberate and attract Soviet Jews is perhaps one of the most studied migrations of this type. The rationale for this intervention in migration is two-fold. Firstly, Israel wishes to see Jewish people escape from persecution or infringements of their civil liberties. But it also wishes to strengthen its own strategic position in the Middle East by shifting the demographic balance in Israel through the augmentation of the non-Arab population. Birman (1979) charts this migration and the characteristics of those who have participated in it. Cohen (1992: 122) outlines the rationale for stimulating immigration, both in his own words: 'Jewish immigration is instrumental to "reclaiming" the land for exclusive Jewish use, and the promise of great numbers of new immigrants necessarily means the acceleration of this process' and in those of Prime Minister Yitzhak Shamir who simply said 'Big immigration requires Israel to be big as well'.

Discouraging immigration: The sorting and re-grouping of ethnic and religious groups has undoubtedly continued to stimulate migration - or even intensify it - in the post-Cold War period, with governments actively promoting the immigration of members of certain chosen groups. But, in parallel, the changed economic circumstances of the 'North' have led to radical shifts in government attitudes there to migration, with states actively dissuading mass immigration. There have been several reasons for this change of policy. First, the economic shock occasioned by the 'oil crisis' of 1973 and subsequent economic restructuring has reduced the need for further mass migration of unskilled labour (but see Sassen's 1991 counterarguments about Global Cities). Second, the rise of the ultra-competitive Pacific Rim economies has seen the development of a New International Division of Labour, with menial manufacturing employment being relocated to these countries from Europe and North America. Third, economic restructuring has led to persistent mass unemployment and sluggish economic growth in the North. Fourth, partly because of the previous points, but also because of latent racism, public opinion in the North has moved away from further immigration of visible minorities (Simon and Alexander, 1993). Moroever as public opinion changed, so it has become apparent that ethnic minority populations cannot be as easily absorbed as had once been hoped. Inner city disturbances in the United States and Europe (see Joshua, Wallace and Booth, 1983 on the UK and Hargreaves, 1996 on France) heightened this perception. And finally, as the moral panic about further mass immigration rose to a crescendo, so the European populations of the North began to express their fears through the ballot box (see Hainsworth, 1992) and through physical attacks on racial minorities and non-conforming groups.

Particularly since the 1960s, then, we have seen increasing state intervention designed to restrict immigration in general, but particularly the movement of unskilled labour from the developing world to the developed world. In the UK this process had begun in 1902 with the Aliens Act, which was introduced to exclude Jewish immigration from East Europe, but it acquired an explicitly racial dimension in 1962 with the Commonwealth Immigrants Act. William Deedes, the then Prime Minister for Immigration was candid when he acknowledged that 'the real purpose was to restrict the influx of coloured immigrants. [although] We were reluctant to say as much openly' (Deedes, 1968: 10). Nevertheless the Act had the desired result, with immigration from the West Indies, for example, falling from 66,000 in 1961 to 5,000 in 1968. Subsequent legislation in the UK has tightened immigration restrictions further, effectively limiting primary labour migration to Europeans and those who have patrial links with the UK, since, as Mrs Thatcher famously remarked in 1978 'people are really rather afraid that this country might be swamped by people of a different culture'. And whilst unskilled labour migration has been choked off, professional and skilled migration has been maintained in the interests of the British economy. Nor has the UK been alone in its restrictionist stance. Australia has, for most of this century, employed a 'White Australia' policy, first introduced in the 1901 Immigration Restriction Act. The purpose of this was not to reduce the scale of immigration (for reasons outlined above), but to ensure that all immigrants were drawn from a common racial/ethnic stock which would reinforce WASP dominance, rather than challenge it. Jupp (1995: 208) (Chapter 6) comments on how the exclusion of non-European immigrants was never written into law but how the 1901 Act allowed 'absolute discretion to prohibit undesirable immigrants, without specifying the basis of such undesirability'. He goes on to describe how, prior to 1958, all immigrants had to take a dictation test and how 'undesirables' would deliberately be given the test in a language they could not understand. The White Australia Policy was only eventually dismantled between 1966 and 1973, but authors such as Blainey (1984), and the Great Migration Debates of 1984 and 1990 demonstrate that the attitudes which underlay it were slower to dissolve, with some arguing that Australian culture and heritage are under threat from large-scale Asian immigration.

Elsewhere, countries have adopted alternative explicit and implicit bases for their intervention in immigration. The US has recently demonstrated how its refugee admission policy is driven by the troika of foreign policy considerations, domestic political factors and cost (Zucker and Zucker, 1996). They describe how Cuban and Haitian migrants to the US have received diametrically opposed treatment, with the former being classified as refugees, given assistance in reaching the US, and offered asylum, and the latter being interdicted by the US Coast Guard, offered minimal screening, being classified as economic migrants and being returned to Haiti. For the Zuckers, this difference in treatment is not caused by the Cubans having a larger lobby group in the US or being cheaper to resettle, but by the fact that Haitians are fleeing a pro-American capitalist regime whilst the Cubans are trying to leave an anti-American communist state. US foreign policy demands that friends of America should not be embarrassed, but that enemies of America should be publicly and repeatedly humiliated as a way of confirming the moral superiority of capitalist democracy.

But whilst countries such as the UK, Australia and the US have allowed their immigration policies to be shaped by non-economic factors, very few countries can ever genuinely escape from the fact that migration is also an economic transaction, which can offer considerable benefits. Hence, as countries have moved towards greater control of migration most have been prepared to allow continued movement of skilled and professional workers. Fortney (1970) (Chapter 7) was one of the first to consider this group of migrants in any detail. She describes the number of professional migrants entering the US in the 1960s and considers their impact upon Ameican science and medicine, as well as upon the economies of those countries from which they have migrated. She concludes that professional migration nearly always benefits the receiving country but that its impact upon the sending country is much less clear. More recently, Findlay (1988) (Chapter 8), has charted the scale of professional immigration to the UK and demonstrated how skills-selectivity is changing the whole composition of British immigration.

Exclusion: In many cases the trend towards control has developed a momentum that has culminated in exclusion. Perhaps one of the best contemporary examples of this has been the development of 'Fortress Europe'. Robinson (1995) (Chapter 9) traces the historical development of exclusionary policies towards asylum seekers in Europe, noting that from the 1980s onwards generosity of spirit has given way to ever more restrictive policies. Asylum seekers are now denied access by a raft of mechanisms which include visa requirements, the first country asylum rule, carriers' liability acts, intergovernmental agreements, and punitive restrictions on those who do not follow prescribed application channels. Others, such as Scheinman (1983) have bemoaned similar trends elsewhere in the world.

Repatriation: Associated with the move towards exclusion of potential immigrants has been the desire to return immigrants who had previously gained entry. The rate of repatriation gathered pace quickly in the 1990s, such that 2.4 million refugees were repatriated in 1992, an unprecedented average of 6600 per day (UNHCR, 1993). In some cases this has involved the summary expulsion of populations, occasionally by force (eg the removal of Vietnamese economic migrants from Hong Kong prior to the Colony's return to China). In others, NGOs and national governments have co-operated to engineer planned voluntary return. Research on interventions of this type includes Simon and Preston's (1993) study of the repatriation of 42,000 Namibians from Angola and Zambia in 1989. And Glytsos (1995) (Chapter 10) has looked at the policies put in place by the Greek government to reintegrate returnees, who numbered some 628,000 people between 1971 and 1986. These include the Pontians who have left the Former Soviet Union, former political refugees, and ex-labour migrants and their families.

INTERNAL MIGRATION

Governments have also sought to influence internal migration for a variety of reasons, and again it is possible to distinguish intervention seeking to encourage, force, and discourage general or specific population movements.

Discouraging internal migration: One of the major problems faced by governments – especially in Developing Countries – has been the spontaneous movement of population from rural to urban areas, as the urban industrial economy develops along a different trajectory to the remainder of the country. Gugler (1988) has estimated that perhaps two-fifths of the growth of Third World cities arises from rural-urban migration, with much of this being directed towards primate cities. Khartoum, for example, saw its population rise from 1.34 million in 1983 to 3.0 million in 1987 as migrants moved to the city to build a better life in the wake of famine, drought and civil war elsewhere in the country (El-Bushra, 1989). Whilst much rural-urban migration in Developing Countries is undoubtedly economically motivated in the narrowest sense (Findlay and Findlay, 1987), mobility is also encouraged by the collective consumption role of the city (Gilbert and Gugler, 1992). Cities do not just attract migrants because they offer employment opportunities, but also because they possess an undue proportion of the nation's educational and training opportunities, better quality housing, and healthcare facilities. Moreover, once migration streams develop, their chain nature and the dissemination of idealized portrayals of urban life by the media ensure that they acquire a momentum that is difficult to counteract.

Although many governments in the Developing World might wish to control rural-urban migration, few have the power to do so. The exceptions are the planned socialist states where populations have become used to greater degrees of state control and management. In some of these countries, policies have been introduced to curb the flight to the cities. In China, potential migrants were prevented from moving by a migration registration system that denied unregistered migrants access to legal forms of employment or official grain supplies. Yang and Goldstein (1990) (Chapter 11) provide a case study from Zhejiang Province, China. They describe how planners there have sought to prevent rural migrants moving permanently to the largest cities and have instead directed them to small towns and small cities in an effort to fill-out the urban hierarchy. However the labour needs of urban employers have still been met by allowing large-scale temporary migration to cities in a system akin to the European guestworker model. Yang and Goldstein estimate that 15–20 per cent of the population of most large cities in their study area are now 'floating workers' who contribute to the urban economy but are allowed to make few demands on its social infrastructure or resources.

Encouraging internal migration: Rather more common have been state policies to encourage internal migration. Some of these, such as the UK's post-war New Towns policy have been driven by social objectives. In the wake of the Second World War successive British governments sought to provide better living conditions for the British people, both through the large-scale building of modern council houses in existing towns and through the decanting of populations from the cores of conurbations to New Towns built on greenfield sites. Underlying this state-managed migration was the belief that low-density living in semi-rural areas was inherently socially, morally and physically superior to high density living in inner-cities, a belief first codified in Ebenezer Howard's (1898) celebrated 'Three Magnets' diagram. In this diagram Howard juxtaposed the 'beauty of nature', 'fresh air', 'low rents', 'abundance of water', and 'bright sunshine' found in rural areas with the 'fogs and droughts', 'slums and gin palaces', 'murky skies', 'high rents and prices', 'isolation of crowds', 'excessive hours' and 'closing out of nature' found in urban areas. 'Garden Cities' were Howard's preferred solution to the problem of how to offer the economic benefits of urban living and the social and environmental benefits of rural living. The British New Towns movement tended to agree. Between 1945 and the mid 1980s 28 New Towns were created. They housed 2 million people by the end of the 1980s, of which 1.1 million had migrated from other metropolises (Cherry, 1988). And social engineering was even practiced in their internal layout with deliberate mixing of house types and sizes so as to ensure the mixing of the social classes.

Frequently state encouragement of internal migration is driven by less idealistic considerations and seeks instead to improve economic efficiency. A wide variety of examples of such policies exist. Luling (1989) describes the villagization programme introduced by President Mengistu of Ethiopia in the late 1980s and early 1990s, which sought the migration of the entire Ethiopian rural population (some 38 million people) into planned centralized settlements. Once under state control and supervision, farmers could be given productivity targets and these could be enforced. Johnson and Salt, 1981 (Chapter 12) describe the various measures taken by the UK government to stimulate inter-regional migration of labour. For example, they note how governments have sought to overcome the traditional reluctance of the unemployed to engage in long distance migration by offering financial incentives. But they conclude that policy was uncoordinated and that often individual policies conflicted with each other.

Elsewhere the stimulation of internal movements has been promoted by a desire to achieve a particular demographic outcome. Indonesia's transmigration programme is one of the most reported examples of this thinking. Leinbach (1989) (Chapter 13) describes how 65 per cent of Indonesia's population lives on the island of Java at densities exceeding 2000 persons per square kilometre, and how the outer islands of Sumatra, Sulawesi and Kalimantan have much smaller populations living at low densities. As a result, between 1969 and 1987 the Indonesian government has used $439 million of World Bank money to move 2.5 million people onto 6000 square kilometres of newly cleared land. Leinbach notes both the successes and failures of the programme, commenting that it had reduced the primacy of Java but that this had been achieved at considerable human, environmental and social cost.

Strategic considerations can also underlay state-sponsored internal migration. Clarke (1994) recounts how successive Beijing governments sent ethnic Han settlers west into Tibet progressively to populate the area. Settlement in garrison towns, along lowland valleys, and beside the key transport routes secured territory and ensured control of the local population. But Israel has perhaps had one of the most deliberate and overt strategies of altering the ethnic/racial balance of areas for strategic geopolitical purposes. Cohen (1992) argues that the struggle for land has always been at the heart of the relationship between Israelis, Arabs and Palestinians, with the Israeli government progressively annexing land to expand the state of Israel eastwards in an effort to create a strategically viable unit. Immigration policy has then been used to acquire settlers for this land. As Cohen (1992: 122) puts it, 'Jewish immigration is instrumental to "reclaiming" the land for exclusive Jewish use, and the promise of great numbers of new immigrants necessarily means the acceleration of this process'. Thus internal migration policies have been used to funnel Israelis and newly arrived international migrants (eg Soviet Jews discussed earlier) into contested spaces so that these become both demographically and perceptually Jewish, not Arab, territory. Hiltermann (1991) (Chapter 14) outlines the policies that have been employed by Israelii authorities to achieve this, including the moves by Jerusalem City Council to attract migrants.

Forced internal migration: Where power is very clearly in the hands of a particular group in society, the encouragement of migration can be so strong that the outcome is forced migration or internal displacement of other groups within society. Apartheid provided a powerful example of such policies, driven by the desire of whites not to have to experience social interaction with members of the other races. Grand Apartheid therefore sought to separate the races regionally into discrete homelands, and Urban Apartheid then zoned cities by race to ensure limited inter-racial mixing within residential neighbourhoods (Mabin, 1992) (Chapter 15). The 1959 Promotion of Bantu Self-Government Act sought regional separation of the races, with the black population being subdivided into ten separate 'national units' on the basis of language as a supposed surrogate for tribal membership. Each was then allocated a homeland or Bantustan, with the boundaries being prescribed in such a way as to exclude any natural resources, yet still provide white employers in neighbouring areas with a supply of cheap black labour. Blacks were then moved to the Bantustan to which they had been assigned, with over 1.7 million people being relocated between 1960 and 1983 (Christopher, 1994). The Group Areas Act of 1950 sought to achieve the same separation within cities. Estimates of how many people were forced to migrate because of racial zoning are very ambiguous, but Christopher suggests that over three-quarters of a million blacks were forced out of inner-areas alone. The impact of these policies upon cities and families has been recorded by Christopher (1987), Reintges (1992) and Western (1981), amongst others.

Ethnic cleansing: When power is concentrated in the hands of people who are ruthless and have the military capabilities to enforce their prejudices, forced migration can become part of a broader project of ethnic cleansing. Bell-Fialkoff (1993) provides a chronology of events of ethnic cleansing and Ahmed (1995) (Chapter 16) offers a wider account of the rationale and symbolism of ethnic cleansing in the contemporary world. As events in Rwanda and the Former Yugoslavia have shown all too graphically, ethnic cleansing can produce massive population displacement, often at very short notice, as well as terrible human rights violations (see Gutman, 1993). For example, 250,000 refugees are known to have fled from Rwanda into Tanzania in a 48-hour period in Spring 1994.

Unintended

Whilst many governments pursue intervention in migration issues to achieve specific national goals, the consequences of intervention in the migration regime of one country can have significant impacts upon other countries. This is not really surprising given that the process of international migration necessarily involves two separate states. Hamilton (1997) (Chapter 17) has recently considered the interlinkages between sending society, receiving society and migrant communities. She uses the example of migration between Africa and Europe to argue that all three of these interest groups need to be seen as, and act as, partners in policy, and that state-centred policy has probably become historically obsolete. King (1993) (Chapter 18) provides an alternative example when he catalogues how the policies of Western Europe towards migration from the east have impacted heavily, but unintentionally, upon Hungary, which has now become a 'waiting room' for migrants seeking entry to the 'greater inner Europe'. He also describes the irony of the situation. Previously, the border between Austria and Hungary had been policed by the Hungarians who wished to prevent emigration. Now it was policed by the Austrians who wished to deter immigration, leaving Hungarian forces free to close the formerly open borders with Romania, the Ukraine and Yugoslavia.

Indirect

A wide range of state interventions that were never intended to impact directly upon migration often do so indirectly. Economic policy, housing policy, educational policy and military activity all have specific objectives, but they also change the world within which people make decisions about whether to migrate or remain where they are. Cernea (1990) (Chapter 19) itemises a range of development projects which have the indirect consequence of creating what he terms 'oustees'. Cernea focuses upon one type of oustee, peoples affected by dam construction. He estimates that between 1979 and 1985 between eight and fifteen million people were so affected, and goes on to argue that this figure could have been substantially reduced with pre-planning and minor modifications to projects. In a later article, Cernea (1995) reviews the impacts that development-induced displacement has had upon people and proposes strategies to ameliorate these. Gould (1988) (Chapter 20) exemplifies a constrasting trend. He shows how social policy that would be fairly universally acclaimed can indirectly generate conditions conducive to an emigration perceived to be deleterious in its impacts. His specific case study is the educational policies of sub-Saharan African states. There, he argues, educational policy has been out of tune with the needs of the labour market. Too many highly-skilled graduates have been produced by local universities, when the local labour market really requires only medium-grade skills. This has produced simultaneous skills shortages and unemployment of skilled workers. And countries have used their higher education policies as part of their foreign policy, accepting offers of scholarships, places and fee-waivers from friendly foreign governments, without considering whether students will wish to return home after graduation or remain in the donor country. In both cases, education policy creates a demand for international migration. Housing policy also has an indirect impact upon migration. If affordable housing is readily available throughout the country, if information systems exist that allow purchasers to find out about properties elsewhere, and if house prices do not vary greatly across a country, then migration will be made so much easier. If the converse is true, migration propensities can be sharply reduced. The last UK government even went so far as to try to resuscitate the moribund privately rented sector in an effort to facilitate the temporary mobility of labour between regions. Boyle (1995) (Chapter 21) considers another sector of the housing market, namely state-subsidised social housing. He analyses the extent to which the presence of a substantial social housing sector in the UK acts as a deterrent to long distance internal migration. The absence of a 'market' in social housing which might let people exchange a property in one part of the country for a property elsewhere has long been thought to dampen migration, as have the in-built biases in favour of 'local' applicants for housing. Boyle uses statistical data to demonstrate that this is the case.

In a series of publications, Van Hear (eg 1993, 1995) has reviewed how military intervention designed to achieve strategic objectives often generates collateral migration, both within and between countries. He used the Gulf War of 1990–91 to illustrate the point, describing how four to five million migrants fled the region in several waves. In the first wave, a million foreign workers left occupied Kuwait in fear of their safety, and a further 850,000 Yemenis were expelled from Saudi Arabia. In the second wave, two million Kurds tried to leave Iraq to avoid persecution. And in the third, after the expulsion of Iraqi forces, workers who were thought to represent security risks by the reinstated Kuwait government were encouraged to leave. Thus, while Iraq sought to annexe Kuwait and its oil, it actually achieved the flight of up to five million people, and the associated dislocation of families, societies and economies (Van Hear, 1995).

Settlement and Integration

State intervention in the lives of migrants does not stop after their arrival in a new country. Many states elect directly to shape national patterns of integration and settlement, in order to meet specific, if often implicit, national objectives. In addition, states can shape the outcomes of migrations in other countries with which they have no direct association through their participation in the international community. Bodies such as the United Nations are increasingly intervening in matters that were previously considered to be the sole preserve of national sovereign governments.

The international community has various means at its disposal of influencing policy. These include: granting or withholding funding; diplomatic pressure and the threat of ostracization; public praise or condemnation; trade sanctions; brokering deals where the receipt of assistance is tied to certain outcomes being achieved; or even military intervention to ensure or prevent the implementation of particular policies.

As the means at the disposal of the international community have grown and as the community has become more confident, so supra-national organizations have intervened more. Stein (1983) (Chapter 22) takes the specific example of how the international community has evolved policies for the resettlement of refugees, and how these have become known as the 'durable solutions'. He defines a durable solution as meaning that 'refugees ... become self-sufficient, enabling them to integrate and participate fully in the social and economic life of their new country, or their homeland if they repatriate' (Stein, 1983: 190). Prior to the late 1980s, the three durable solutions favoured by the international community were settlement in the first country of asylum (usually a neighbour of the country generating refugees), voluntary repatriation once conditions in the sending society have improved, or permanent resettlement in a third country (often an industrial country in the North). All these policies depended upon a temporary or permanent 'exilic bias' by which refugees were thought to be better off outside their own country. The extent to which these different policies have been employed has varied over time, with third country resettlement becoming less popular in the 1980s and two new durable solutions being widely advocated in the 1990s (Robinson, 1998a). The first of these is forced repatriation. The second is containment of potential migrants in their country of origin, a policy based upon the renunciation of the exilic bias and its replacement by what Robinson (in Boyle, Halfacree and Robinson, 1998) has termed the new 'Hollywood bias'.

As the international community has intervened more in resettlement outcomes, so academics have tried to specify what conditions are conducive to 'successful' resettlement. Kunz (1981) suggests that success depends upon: whether the receiving country is a traditional country of immigration; whether there is any cultural compatibility between migrants and the local population; public opinion; and whether the receiving society aspires to assimilation or pluralism. Neuwirth (1988) adds to this list. She regards resettlement outcomes as being also dependent upon the occupational and social skills possessed by migrants. And Rogg (1971) argues that resettlement will be much more successful if a concentrated community of fellow nationals already exists in the new country.

The extent and type of intervention by sovereign governments in the resettlement of immigrants/asylum seekers within their borders critically depends upon attitudes towards national identity. Governments that feel their national identity should be defended will seek to ensure that it is imposed upon and adopted by all immigrants through assimilationist policies. Administrations that feel there is benefit to be had from the mixing of cultures and the evolution of national identity will favour integrationist policies. And governments that are truly multi-cultural in their thinking will celebrate diversity through pluralist policies. Castles (1992) describes how thinking and policy on these matters in Australia has changed over time, as that country has moved to become truly multicultural in its outlook and policies. He also assesses the extent to which the Australian model could be applicable to the EU. Seifert (1997) (Chapter 23) compares and contrasts the different models of citizenship and nationality which underpin French and German migration and integration policy in the late 1990s, with France still being assimilationist and Germany pursuing targeted immigration and rigid monoculturalism. Jones (1996) and Marshall (1992) consider German policies and outcomes in more depth, indicating how the selectivity of migration has made resettlement easier and more successful. And Horowitz (1996) (Chapter 24) reviews the Israeli government's attitude and policies towards immigrant 'absorption'.

One of the ways in which states intervene in the resettlement of migrant groups is through manipulation of settlement patterns and internal migration flows. Democracies do not have the power to intervene directly in these matters since freedom of movement and choice of place of residence are basic rights enjoyed by the vast majority of citizens. Democratic governments can therefore only intervene in these matters when they can either a) demonstrate that it is in the target group's best interests to have its rights suspended, b) show that the target group has forfeited its rights to be considered insiders, by demonizing them as non-conforming outsiders who do not 'deserve' the same rights as other citizens, or c) manipulate public opinion to the extent that the public believes there is some greater common good that overrides the rights of specific population fractions. Usually, therefore, the recipients of state manipulation of settlement patterns are the powerless, the ignorant, or the non-conforming. Halfacree (1996) (Chapter 25) takes the example of gypsies in the UK, and shows how the 1968 Caravan Sites Act and the 1994 Criminal Justice and Public Order Act have deliberately restricted the settlement and movement patterns of that group. Sibley (1981) shows how such intervention is steeped in assimilationist thinking and how it has been 'justified' by the unfavourable comparison of contemporary gypsies in the UK with an idealised notion of 'True Romanies'. Flett, Henderson and Brown (1979) (Chapter 26) demonstrate parallel policies at work targeted at ethnic minorities. They describe how Birmingham City Council pursued a deliberate, but covert, policy of ethnic residential mixing on its council estates. Whilst this may have been introduced to engineer greater social contact between different groups in order to reduce ignorance and prejudice it could only be operationalized by denying black applicants a full choice of properties and estates. Flett, Henderson and Brown argue that, in this case, the ends did not justify the means. Robinson (1989 and 1998b) (Chapters 27 and 28) has revealed how state intervention has been critical to the settlement and subsequent mobility of refugees in the UK. He demonstrates how successive governments sought to 'spread the burden' by deliberately dispersing refugees across the entire country, and how this task was then sub-contracted to NGOs so that the government would be distanced from any political backlash resulting from further ethnic minority settlement (Robinson, 1998b). Robinson (1989) then assesses the impact of this forced dispersal by quantifying the scale of subsequent secondary migration of refugees from locations which had been prescribed by the state to locations chosen by the refugees themselves. Hammar (1993) has undertaken parallel analyses of the Swedish government's dispersal of refugees. And Horowitz (1996) (Chapter 24) outlines the debates that have taken place in Israel about immigrant concentration versus dispersion.

Impacts of State Intervention

This last section briefly demonstrates how state intervention in migration and settlement produces consequences that can be beneficial or deleterious in their impacts, and how states can or should manage these impacts to advantage.

Russell (1992) (Chapter 29) looks at one particular economic impact of migration, namely remittances. Others take a broader definition of the potential economic impact of immigration, seeing it as a catalyst of more general economic regeneration. Kotkin (1993) focuses upon those 'tribes' that have used their ethnicity as an economic resource to create transnational economic networks. He shows how these networks are then used as conduits for the movement of capital, market and investment information, components and finished goods. He then contrasts the different methods used by ethnic groups to create and maintain such networks, with the Chinese generating networks through permanent dispersed settlement overseas and the Japanese using temporary professional sojourners as 'missionaries' from centralized corporate headquarters. He goes on to describe the Chinese as follows:

> 'Their background leads (Chinese) spacemen ... to think not so much in terms of nations or states but of a seamless global network connecting communities nevertheless united by a common ethnic identity ... (M)uch like the great Jewish businessmen ... Chinese entrepreneurs remain, in essence, arbitrageurs, their widespread dispersion a critical means of identifying prime business opportunities and developing the means to exploit them. It is the diaspora itself - not any nation-state or group of corporate entities - that underlies the emergence of Chinese economic power'. (Kotkin, 1993: 169)

For Kotkin, then, transnational ethnic groups should be seen as alternatives to single-country companies and Transnational Corporations as organizers of economic activity and creators of wealth, and they should therefore be courted like any other potential inward investor. Cohen's (1997) reformulation of the notion of diaspora and his development of a typology of diasporas implies similar attitudes towards economically successful transnational ethnic migrants. So, too, does work on the economic success of particular national fragments of global diasporas such as Robinson's (1993) study of the occupational mobility of East African Asians in the UK.

A different school of thought argues that state intervention in migration should not be motivated by the drive for greater economic wealth, but by a desire to ensure environmental sustainability. In his review of the relationship between environment and migration, Hugo (1996) (Chapter 30) describes how the environmental impact of further immigration has become a key element in the debate about future immigration policy in Australia. Large scale immigration is now perceptually associated with rising consumption of scarce national non-renewable resources, increased environmental degradation, and greater pressure on sensitive and fragile habitats. Clear pressure is therefore being exerted on government to restrict further immigration on environmental grounds. Nor are impacts recognized only in developed countries. Ghimire (1994) has shown how the presence of refugee populations impacts upon the environment. Using evidence from around the developing world he argues that refugees can contaminate water, clear forests, degrade pastures, and cause soil erosion. The UNHCR (1995) concurs, noting how Mozambican refugees in Malawi cut over half a million cubic metres of wood per annum for cooking and heating. Again such evidence could be used to justify restrictionist policies.

State intervention in immigration also has a profound impact on public attitudes, both towards further immigration and towards immigrants. On the one hand, open discussion of how best to prevent the entry of a particular group problematizes that group and in turn justifies subsequent restrictive acts. Thus, the discussion that took place in the 1950s of whether to deny black immigrants access to the UK (Holmes, 1991) helped form the popular perception that blacks were associated with social problems and problems of law and order. Consequently, when black people became the victims of racial violence in the disturbances in Notting Hill (London) and Nottingham in 1958, white racism was not blamed. Rather, opinion polls showed that black people were blamed, with over 75 per cent of white respondents wishing to see further 'coloured' immigration into the UK halted. Immigration policy had thus been racialized. On the other hand, a willingness on the part of the public to participate directly in assisting immigrants can positively influence public policy. Neuwirth and Clark (1981) (Chapter 31) consider the private sponsorship scheme in Canada, through which the number of Vietnamese refugees admitted was linked directly to the willingness of Canadian groups to take responsibility for their settlement. They note how sponsors got involved for a variety of personal reasons, but how sponsorship was an 'overwhelming success' that allowed Canada to resettle more refugees than would otherwise have been the case.

Finally, individual and institutional responses to state intervention in migration can trigger further intervention. Zetter (1991) (Chapter 32) describes how, once the Greek Cypriot government had admitted and taken responsibility for refugees from the north of the island, officials reacted by characterizing and labelling these migrants in a particular way. Policy towards housing and repatriation was then drafted with these perceived characteristics in mind, much to the annoyance of the refugees who felt they were being misunderstood and ill-provided for. A recent case study in the UK has found parallel misunderstandings about who refugees are, and what their needs are, and this was explained in terms of cultures of 'ignorance', 'disbelief' and 'denial' (Robinson, 1998c).

Conclusion

This essay has attempted to achieve two things. Firstly, justify and explain what is inevitably an idiosyncratic choice of papers to be included in this reader. And secondly, indicate that state intervention in migration is a complex and multi-faceted phenomenon that deserves considerably greater study than it has hitherto received. Much of the work completed to date has either been of a descriptive or applied nature, seeking only to chart the extent to which states have intervened, or evaluate interventions and their intended and unintended outcomes. Whilst there is no doubt that this is highly valuable, there is also a need for work that seeks to understand why states intervene, upon what assumptions they intervene, what outcomes they desire from intervention, and how each of the preceding decisions is arrived at. If work of this type could be completed alongside the more applied projects, then both our understanding and our ability to assist in decision making would be considerably strengthened. There are already signs that this may be happening in the allied field of Refugee Studies, where, at a recent conference, two papers were devoted to arguing the ethics of intervention in general, and different forms of intervention in particular (Weiner, 1998: Carens, 1998).

References

Adams, W. (1968) *The Brain Drain*, Macmillan, New York

Ahmed, A. (1995) 'Ethnic cleansing: a metaphor of our time?', *Ethnic and Racial Studies*, **18** (1), 1-25

Ali, S., Habibullah, A., Hossain, A., Islam, R., Mahmud, W., Osmani, S., Rahman, Q. and Siddiqui, A. (1981) *Labour Migration from Bangladesh to the Middle East*, World Bank, Washington

Bean, P. and Melville, J. (1990) *Lost Children of the Empire: the Untold Story of Britain's Child Migrants*, Unwin Hyman, London

Bell-Fialkoff, A. (1993) 'A brief history of ethnic cleansing', *Foreign Affairs*, **72** (3), 110-121

Bennett, J. (1998) *Rights Have No Borders: Worldwide Internal Displacement*, Norwegian Refugee Council, Oslo

Birman, I. (1979) 'Jewish emigration from the USSR', *Soviet Jewish Affairs*, **9** (2), 46-64

Blainey, G. (1984) *All for Australia*, Methuen, North Ryde

Boyle, P. (1995) 'Public housing as a barrier to long distance migration', *International Journal of Population Geography*, **1** (2), 147-64

Boyle, P., Halfacree, K. and Robinson, V. (1998) *Exploring Contemporary Migration*, Longman, London

Carens, J. (1996) 'Realistic and idealistic approaches to the ethics of migration', *International Migration Review*, **30** (1), 156-70

Carens, J. (1998) 'The ethics of refugee policy: the problem of asylum in Western states', unpublished paper presented at the 'Growth of Forced Migration: new directions in research, policy and practice' conference, Oxford, March 25-7

Castles, S. (1985) 'The guests who stayed - the debate on 'foreigners policy'' in the German Federal Republic', *International Migration Review*, **19** (3), 517-33

Castles, S. (1992) 'The Australian model of immigration and multiculturalism', *International Migration Review*, **26** (2), 549-67

Castles, S. Booth, H. and Wallace, T. (1984) *Here for Good: Western Europe's New Ethnic Minorities*, Pluto, London

Castles, S. and Miller, M. (1993) *The Age of Migration: International Population Movements in the Modern World*, Macmillan, Basingstoke

Cernea, M. (1990) 'Internal refugee flows and development-induced population displacement', *Journal of Refugee Studies*, **3** (4), 320-339

Cernea, M. (1995) 'Understanding and preventing impoverishment from displacement: reflections on the state of knowledge', *Journal of Refugee Studies*, **8** (3), 245-64

Cherry, G. (1988) *Cities and Plans: The Shaping of Urban Britain in the Nineteenth and Twentieth Centuries*, Edward Arnold, London

Christopher, A. (1987) 'Apartheid planning in South Africa: the case of Port Elizabeth', *Geographical Journal*, **153** (2), 195-204

Christopher, A. (1994) *The Atlas of Apartheid*, Routledge, London

Clarke, G.E. (1994) 'The movement of population to the west of China: Tibet and Qinghai', in J.M. Brown and R. Foot (eds) *Migration: the Asian Experience*, Macmillan, Basingstoke, 221-58

Cohen, B. (1992) 'Israel's expansion through immigration', *Middle East Policy*, **1** (2), 120-35

Cohen, R. (1997) *Global Diasporas*, UCL Press, London

Coleman, D. (1992) 'Does Europe need immigrants? Population and workforce projections', *International Migration Review*, **26** (2), 413-62

Deedes, W. (1968) *Race Without Rancour*, Conservative Political Centre, London

Dowty, A. (1987) *Closed Borders: the Contemporary Assault on the Freedom of Movement*, Yale University Press, London

El-Bushra, E. (1989) 'The urban crisis and rural-urban migration in Sudan', in R. Potter and T. Unwin (eds) *The Geography of Urban-Rural Interaction in Developing Countries*, Routledge, London, 109-40

Fevre, R. (1984) *Cheap Labour and Racial Discrimination*, Gower, Aldershot

Findlay, A. (1988) 'From settlers to skilled transients: the changing structure of British international migration', *Geoforum*, **19** (4), 401-10

Findlay, A. (1994) 'An economic audit of contemporary migration', in S. Spencer (ed.) *Strangers and Citizens*, Oram Rivers Press, London, 159-201
Findlay, A. and Findlay, A. (1987) *Population and Development in the Third World*, Routledge, London
Flett, H., Henderson, J. and Brown, B. (1979) 'The practice of racial dispersal in Birmingham 1969-75', *Journal of Social Policy*, **8**, 289-309
Fortney, J. (1970) 'International migration of professionals', *Population Studies*, **24** (2), 217-35
Ghimire, K. (1994) 'Refugees and deforestation', *International Migration*, **32** (4), 561-70
Giesek, A., Heilemann, U., Dietrich, H. and von Loeffelholz (1994) 'Economic implications of migration into the Federal Republic of Germany 1988-1992', in S. Spencer (ed.) *Immigration as an Economic Asset: The German Experience*, Trentham Books, London, 15-39
Gilbert, A. and Gugler, J. (1992) *Cities, Poverty and Development: Urbanisation in the Third World (2nd edn)*, Oxford University Press, Oxford
Glass, D. (1967) *Population Policies and Movements in Europe*, Frank Cass, London
Glytsos, N. (1995) 'The socio-economic integration of returnees and foreign workers in Greece, *International Migration*, **33** (2), 155-77
Gould, W. (1988) 'Government policies and international migration of skilled workers in sub-Saharan Africa', *Geoforum*, **19** (4), 433-45
Gugler, J. (1988) *The Urbanization of the Third World*, Oxford University Press, Oxford
Gutman, R. (1993) *A Witness to Genocide*, Element Books, Shaftesbury
Hainsworth, P. (1992) *The Extreme Right in Europe and the USA*, Pinter, London
Halfacree, K. (1996) 'Out of place in the country', *Antipode*, **28** (1), 42-72
Hamilton, K. (1997) 'Europe, Africa and international migration', *New Community*, **23** (4), 549-71
Hammar, T. (1993) 'The Sweden-wide strategy of refugee dispersal', in R. Black and V. Robinson (eds) *Geography and Refugees: Patterns and Processes of Change*, Belhaven, London, 104-18
Hargreaves, A. (1996) 'A deviant construction: the French media and the "banlieues"', *New Community*, **22** (4), 607-18
Hathaway, J. (1990) 'A reconsideration of the underlying premise of refugee law', *Harvard International Law Journal*, **31** (1), 129-81
Hiltermann, J.R. (1991) 'Settling for War: Soviet emigration and Israel's settlement policy in East Jerusalem', *Journal of Palestine Studies*, **20** (2), 71-85
Holmes, C. (1991) *A Tolerant Country? Immigrants, Refugees and Minorities in Britain*, Faber and Faber, London
Horowitz, T. (1996) 'Value-orientated parameters in migration policies in the 1990s', *International Migration*, **34** (4), 497-510
Howard, E. (1988) *Garden Cities of Tomorrow*, Faber, London
Hugo, G. (1996) 'Environmental concerns and international migration', *International Migration Review*, **30** (1), 105-32
Jenkins, J. (1978) 'The demand for immigrant workers: labour scarcity or social control?', *International Migration Review*, **12** (4), 514-36
Johnson, J. and Salt, J. (1981) 'Population Redistribution policies in Great Britain'., *Nordia*, **15** (2), 77-92
Jones, P. (1996) 'Immigrants, Germans and national identity in the new Germany: some policy issues', *International Journal of Population Geography*, **2**, 119-31
Joshua, H., Wallace, T. and Booth, H. (1983) *To Ride the Storm: the 1980 Bristol Riot and the State*, Heinemann, London
Jupp, J. (1995) 'From "White Australia" to "part of Asia": recent shifts in Australian immigration policy towards the region', *International Migration Review*, **29** (1), 207-28
King, M. (1993) 'The Impact of Western European border policies on the control of "refugees" in Eastern and Central Europe', *New Community*, **19** (2), 183-99
Kotkin, J. (1993) *Tribes: How Race, Religion and Identity Determine Success in the New Global Economy*, Random House, New York
Kunz, E. (1981) 'Exile and resettlement: refugee theory', *International Migration Review*, **15** (1-2), 42-51
Leinbach, T. (1989) 'The transmigration programme in Indonesian national development strategy',

Habitat International, **13** (3), 81-93
Luling, V. (1989) 'Wiping out a way of life', *Geographical Magazine*, July, 34-7
Mabin, A. (1992) 'Comprehensive segregation: the origins of the Group Areas Act and its planning apparatuses', *Journal of Southern African Studies*, **18** (2), 405-29
Marrus, M. (1985) *The Unwanted: European Refugees in the Twentieth Century*, Oxford University Press, Oxford
Marshall, B. (1992) 'German Migration Policies', in G. Smith, W.E. Paterson, P.H. Merkl, and S. Padgett (eds) *Developments in German Politics*, Macmillan, Basingstoke, 247-63
Malkki, L. (1998) 'Envisioning African futures: dystopia and the social imagination of political disorder', unpublished paper presented at the 'Growth of Forced Migration: new directions in research, policy and practice' conference, Oxford, March 25-7
Neuwirth, G. (1988) 'Refugee resettlement', *Current Sociology*, **36** (2), 27-41
Neuwirth, G. and Clark, L. (1981) 'Indochinese refugees in Canada: sponsorship and adjustment', *International Migration Review*, **15** (1-2), 131-40
Peach, C. (1996) *Ethnicity in the 1991 Census: Volume 2 The ethnic minority populations of Great Britain*, HMSO, London
Peterson, W. (1958) A general typology of migration, *American Sociological Review*, **23** (3), 256-66
Portes, A. (1978) 'Toward a structural analysis of illegal (undocumented) immigration', *International Migration Review*, **12** (4), 469-84
Reintges, C. (1992) 'Urban (mis)management? A case-study of the effects of orderly urbanisation on Duncan Village' in D. Smith (ed.) *The Apartheid City and Beyond*, Routlege, London, 99-111
Robinson, V. (1989) 'Up the creek without a paddle? Britain's boat people ten years on', *Geography*, **74**, 332-8
Robinson, V. (1990) 'Social demography', in V. Robinson and D. McCaroll (eds) *The Isle of Man: Celebrating a Sense of Place*, Liverpool University Press, Liverpool, 133-59
Robinson, V. (1993) 'Marching into the middle classes? The longterm resettlement of East African Asians in the UK', *Journal of Refugee Studies*, **6** (3), 230-48
Robinson, V. (1996) 'The changing nature and European perceptions of Europe's refugee problem', *Geoforum*, **26** (4), 411-27
Robinson, V. (1998a) 'Security, migration and refugees', in D. Graham and N. Poku (eds), *Redefining Security: Population Movements and National Security*, Greenwood Press, Connecticut, in press
Robinson, V. (1998b) 'The development of policies for the resettlement of quota refugees in the UK, 1945-91', in M. Kenzer (ed.), *Under Threat, An Atlas of Refugees and Forced Displacement*, Toronto University Press, in press
Robinson, V. (1998c) 'Cultures of ignorance, disbelief and denial; refugees in Wales', *Journal of Refugee Studies*, in press
Rogg, E. (1971) 'The influence of a strong refugee community on the economic adjustment of its members', *International Migration Review*, **5** (4), 474-81
Russell, S. (1992) 'Migrant remittances and development', *International Migration*, **30** (3/4), 267-87
Sassen, S. (1991) *Global Cities: New York, London, Tokyo*, Princeton University Press, Princeton
Sassen-Koob, S. (1979) 'Economic growth and immigration in Venezuela', *International Migration Review*, **13** (3), 455-74
Scheinman, R. (1983) 'Refugees: goodbye to the Good Old Days', *Annals, American Academy of Political and Social Sciences*, **467**, 78-88
Seifert, W. (1997) 'Admission policy, patterns of migration and integration', *New Community*, **23** (4), 441-60
Shacknove, A. (1985) 'Who is a refugee?', *Ethics*, **95** 274-84
Shah, N. (1983) 'Pakistani workers in the Middle East: volume, trends and consequences', International Migration Review, **17** (3), 410-24
Sibley, D. (1981) *Outsiders in Urban Societies*, Blackwell, Oxford
Simon, D. and Preston, R. (1993) 'Return to the promised land: repatriation and resettlement of Namibian refugees, 1989-90', R. Black and V. Robinson (eds) *Geography and Refugees: Patterns and Processes of Change*, Belhaven, London, 47-64
Simon, R. and Alexander, S. (1993) *The Ambivalent Welcome. Print Media, Public Opinion and*

Immigration, Praeger, London
Smith, D. (1991) *National Identity*, Penguin, Harmondsworth
Stein, B. (1983) 'The commitment to refugee resettlement', *Annals, American Academy of Political and Social Science*, **467**, 187-201
Twaddle, M. (1975) *Expulsion of a Minority: Essays on Ugandan Asians*, Athlone Press, London
Ulrich, R. (1994) 'The impact of foreigners on the public purse', in S. Spencer (ed.) *Immigration as an Economic Asset: The German Experience*, Trentham Books, London, 65-93
UNHCR (1993) *The State of the World's Refugees: The Challenge of Protection*, Penguin, Harmondsworth
UNHCR (1995) *The State of the World's Refugees: In Search of Solutions*, Oxford University Press, Oxford
UNHCR (1997) *The State of the World's Refugees: a Humanitarian Agenda*, Oxford University Press, Oxford
Van Hear, N. (1993) 'Mass flight in the Middle East: involuntary migration and the Gulf conflict, 1990-91', in R. Black and V. Robinson (eds) *Geography and Migration*, Belhaven, London, 64-83
Van Hear, N. (1995) 'The impact of involuntary mass return to Jordan in the wake of the Gulf crisis', *International Migration Review*, **29** (2), 352-74
Van Hear, N. (1998) *New Diasporas: the Mass Exodus, Dispersal and Regrouping of Migrant Communities*, UCL Press, London
Weiner, M. (1995) *The Global Migration Crisis: Challenge to States and to Human Rights*, Harper Collins, New York
Weiner, M. (1996) Ethics, national sovereignty and the control of immigration', *International Migration Review*, **30** (1), 171-96
Weiner, M. (1998) The clash of norms: dilemmas in refugee policy', unpublished paper presented at the 'Growth of Forced Migration: new directions in research, policy and practice' conference, Oxford, March 25-7
Western, J. (1981) *Outcast Cape Town*, Allen and Unwin, London
Wooden, M., Holton, R., Hugo, G. and Sloan, J. (1994) *Australian Immigration: A Survey of the Issues (2nd edn)*, Australian Government Publishing Services, Canberra
Wooden, M. (1994) 'The economic impact of immigration', in Wooden, M., Holton, R., Hugo, G. and Sloan, J. (eds) *Australian Immigration: A Survey of the Issues (2nd edn)*, Australian Government Publishing Services, Canberra, 111-58
Yang, X. and Goldstein, S. (1990) 'Population movement in Zheijiang Province, China: the impact of government policies' *International Migration Review*, **24** (3), 509-33
Zelinsky, W. (1971) 'The hypothesis of the mobility transition', *Geographical Review*, **61**, 219-49
Zetter, R. (1991) 'Labelling refugees: forming and transforming a bureaucratic identity', *Journal of Refugee Studies*, **4** (1), 39-62
Zolberg, A. (1983) 'The formation of new states as a refugee-generating process', *Annals of the American Academy of Political and Social Sciences*, **467**, 24-38
Zucker, N. and Zucker, N. (1996) *Desperate Crossing: Seeking Refuge in America*, M.E. Sharpe, New York

[1]

AN ECONOMIC AUDIT OF CONTEMPORARY IMMIGRATION

Allan Findlay

Is immigration good for the British economy in the 1990s? British immigration policy has become progressively more restrictive since the 1960s. Cultural and political considerations have been strong influences on policy formulation in this area, but the economic basis for the policy trend is less clear. The objective of this paper is to conduct an economic audit of immigration to Britain in order to re-examine the economic implications of allowing, or conversely restricting, further immigration. At a time when government has been eager to advocate policies in other areas of economic activity which favour liberalisation and international competition, it is particularly appropriate to investigate whether an economic basis exists for restricting the operation of international market forces with regard to labour supply.

This chapter commences by considering a range of issues concerned with the definition of labour immigration. It then proceeds to investigate a range of economic arguments which might be made for relaxing immigration controls. Attention then turns to evaluating the economic basis for existing immigration policy and considers the consequences for the British economy of persisting with current policy tools. The paper concludes that current British immigration policy lacks clear economic objectives and suggests that an economic argument exists for a more pro-active stance on immigration.

Numerical arguments

Confusion in economic arguments concerning immigration arises because of differences in the definitions and terms used to describe the phenomenon.

Consider for example Tables 6.1, 6.2 and 6.3 which follow three different conventions in the identification of 'immigrants'. Table 6.1

defines persons entering the UK for more than a year. Table 6.2 defines migrants relative to the concept of nationality, while Table 6.3 is concerned with one aspect of Britains's ethnic minority population, many of whom are second or third generation migrants and would not be included as a result in the statistics collated in Tables 6.1 and 6.2. Issues of statistical definition are discussed further in Appendix 6.1.

Of particular relevance to this paper is the fact that economic problems associated with immigration are nearly always presented relative to data for Britain's ethnic minorities (consider for example the tendency of the Labour Force Survey (LFS) to report annually on unemployment amongst ethnic minorities) rather than tabulations for first generation immigrants. The result has been the re-inforcement of the false image that all immigration has been similar to the economic experience of certain ethnic minorities. It can be argued that unemployment levels (Table 6.3) or wage rates for second or third-generation migrant populations are of little relevance in considering the economic implications of contemporary immigration. Instead such data should be treated as being of significance primarily in reporting the levels of social and economic discrimination which have operated over time against certain minority populations.

Historical patterns of immigration may have led to local impacts which have been to the disadvantage of the non-migrant population. Complaints about immigrant communities occupying scarce housing stock, filling jobs or depressing wages to the detriment of the so-called 'British' population are nearly always based either on experience from the early part of the twentieth century (prior to the introduction of the Aliens Act of 1919) or on circumstances surrounding second or third-generation immigrant groups. In the former case there is evidence of local competition between immigrants and non-migrants for access to limited job opportunities as reported for example in association with the 1919 dockland riots in Glasgow over the use of 'colonial labour'.[1] In the latter case, the spatial concentration of 'visible' ethnic minorities in the central areas of many English cities has undoubtedly contributed to tensions with 'white' unemployed youths who have perceived second and third-generation immigrants as one reason for their own difficulties in finding jobs. Peach[2] has examined the role of ethnicity and unemployment in accounting for the English urban riots of the early 1980s.

In practice, as Table 6.3 shows, it is the 'visible' ethnic minorities which have borne the brunt of unemployment during times of

Table 6.1 International Immigration by Citizenship, UK (1988–90) (numbers in thousands)

	British *No.*	*(%)*	*Old Commonwealth*	*New Commonwealth*	*Foreign*
1988	89	41	21	32	74
1989	104	42	24	42	79
1990	106	40	32	38	91

Source: OPCS, *International Immigration*, 1992.

Table 6.2 Foreign (non-EC) Population (1989)

Country	*Number*	*% Total Population*	*of which in 1989*
Belgium	332,000	3.3	45% North African
Denmark	115,000	2.3	30% Yugoslavs and Turks
France	2,102,000	3.8	65% North African
Germany	3,520,000	5.7	65% Yugoslavs and Turks
Greece	123,000	1.2	
Holland	464,000	3.1	40% Turks, 30% Moroccans
Ireland	17,000	0.5	40% Americans
Italy	236,000	0.4	
Portugal	74,000	0.7	
Spain	165,000	0.4	
Britain	1,025,000	1.8	16% Indians, 13% Americans

Source: Eurostat Demographic Statistics 1992, Luxembourg, EC; *Labour Force Survey*, 1993.

recession. The fact that certain ethnic minorities are geographically concentrated in certain places in Britain has served to heighten the popular misconception that the descendents of former immigrant groups occupy jobs or housing stock to the disadvantage of the rest of the population. In relation to this view two points must be noted. First, it must be stressed once again that the nature of historical migration patterns associated with Britain's 'visible' ethnic minorities bears only a very limited relation to the pattern and type of immigration permitted under current British immigration policies. Second, most of the jobs occupied by the 'visible' ethnic minorities are ones which are shunned by the rest of the population. Far from there having been resentment against the recruitment of ethnic minorities to these jobs, 'staff-hungry' local authorities were often most appreciative of the services offered by these groups.[3]

A final definitional issue is the distinction between stocks and flows. Table 6.1 presented flow information about immigrant entry to the United Kingdom. It therefore reflects the outcome in migration terms of Britain's position within the contemporary international migration system. Tables 6.2 and 6.4, by contrast, refer to migration stocks. Stocks reflect the cumulative outcome of historical migration processes. It is apparent from comparison of Tables 6.1 and 6.4 that current foreign national immigration is very different from the patterns which operated in the past. Some of the differences may be due to differences in the data sources for the two tables, but there is widespread evidence that the primary reason for such differences is the fundamental switch which has occurred in the way in which the international migration system is organised. For example, immigrants from the Indian sub-continent made up 10.0% of the inflow of migrants to Britain in 1990, yet the same region accounted for 14.3% of the immigrant stock.

The implications of these contrasts for economic analysis are clear: immigration policy recommendations stemming from economic statistics relating to Britain's migration stock are of limited value since Britain's position in the world economy has fundamentally changed over the last thirty years. Economic analysis of immigration should be based on data relating to current migrants or to those who have arrived in the recent past, since it is these groups that reflect Britain's current economic position in the world and it is to groups such as these that policy should be addressed. It should be remembered that an economic analysis of this kind of data relates only to those allowed to enter the UK and not to the much larger number of people wishing to migrate to Britain.

Flow statistics and statistics relating to recent cohorts of immigrants are therefore the ones which are of greatest relevance. Immigrant flow statistics present a very different and much more favourable picture of the potential economic benefits of migration than do statistics for the least well assimilated ethnic minority populations. This point leads naturally to discussion of the nature and quality of data relating to the economic dimensions of immigration.

Economic data on immigration to Britain

Given the comments of the previous section, it can be stated that, ideally, economic data should relate to migration flow information and to the experience of cohorts of migrants arriving in immigration flows over recent years. Systematic and detailed information of this kind on the economics of immigration does not exist in Britain, nor in many other West European countries. By contrast, ample and much fuller economic data sets are collated in countries such as Australia and Canada.

The contrast is starkly evident if one compares the nature of the data sets used in two recent International Labour Office (ILO) analyses of discrimination against immigrants. The volume on Australia is replete with statistics on immigrant salaries, immigrant occupational status and employment by industrial sector, immigrant levels of educational attainment and on job training tabulated relative to place of birth and immigrant generation.[4] By contrast the volume on immigrants to Western Europe,[5] appears to rely either on piecemeal economic surveys or on data such as the Labour Force Survey's ethnically defined migrant stocks.

Since 1984 the Labour Force Survey has permitted migration to be viewed from other perspectives, but with a few notable exceptions[6] analysts have stubbornly ignored these opportunities. From 1984 the Labour Force Survey has asked about nationality and about place of residence a year earlier, and since 1985 there has been the possibility of information about migration flows. The value of the Labour Force Survey with regard to these questions is, however, limited due both to the absence of key economic variables and to the fact that the LFS is a sample survey, making it difficult to achieve statistically significant data for many immigration flows because of the smallness of the total sample size.

It should be noted that some of the specialised academic surveys which have been undertaken on the economic impact of immigration do produce interesting conclusions pertinent to this paper. For example a National Institute Survey of the 1960–66 Commonwealth influx to the UK concluded that this immigrant cohort had, on balance, helped to meet the aspirations—existing amongst policy makers and the wider public—to promote higher standards of living in Britain.[7]

Given the limited recent economic data available on immigration to Britain (at least until after the publication of the full results of the 1991 census) inferences have to be drawn about the economic implications of immigration based largely on the demographic information contained in the Labour Force and International Passenger Surveys (IPS). Useful evidence also emerges from consider-

Table 6.3 Unemployment Numbers and Rates by Ethnic Origin and Sex (Persons of working age, Great Britain 1991)

Ethnic Origin	*All Persons*	*Men*	*Women*
Unemployment numbers: ILO definition (men 16-65, women 16-60)-(thousands)			
All persons working age	2,263	1,417	846
Whites	2,068	1,291	777
Ethnic minority groups	179	115	64
of which			
West Indian/Guyanese	37	23	15
Indian	46	29	17
Pakistan/Bangladesh	47	36	11
All Others	48	28	20
Unemployment rates (% economically active persons of working age)			
All persons of working age*	8.3	9.1	7.3
Whites	8.0	9.0	7.0
Ethnic minority groups	15.0	16.0	14.0
of which			
West Indian/Guyanese	15.0	18.0	12.0
Indian	12.0	12.0	11.0
Pakistan/Bangladesh	25.0	25.0	24.0
All Others	14.0	14.0	14.0

* Includes those who did not state ethnic origin

Source: Labour Force Survey, 1991.

Table 6.4 All Persons working in the UK by Nationality (1988-90) (thousands)

	1988	*1989*	*1990*
All nationalities	25,540	26,417	26,658
UK nationals	24,315	25,201	25,541
Foreign nationals	871	960	933
EC countries (excl Eire)	460	497	473
Eire	307	325	323
Non EC foreign	411	463	460

Source: Labour Force Survey, 1991.

ation of the economic implications of immigration which have been charted for other developed countries where fuller economic data sets exist.

Culture versus economics in the analysis of immigration

Thus far the word 'economic' has been used extensively in this paper without the question being raised as to whether economic dimensions of migration can be studied meaningfully in isolation from other dimensions. Migrants may or may not sell their labour and they may or may not consume different goods and services in their host country. These impacts of migration have undoubted economic implications, but the cultural impact on the host society and for the migrant community is harder to assess. What weight should be placed on these cultural and social issues?

This matter is perhaps best explored by considering the contrasts which exist between different parts of the developed world with regard to the issue of immigration. Countries which share many common economic characteristics appear to hold starkly different views on the economic desirability of immigration. The history books will record how, from the mid 1970s onwards, most West European states sought vigorously to close their boundaries to many forms of labour immigration, establishing what may be described as a 'fortress mentality'.[8] The former British Prime Minister, Baroness Thatcher, declared in a television interview in the 1970s that the British fear 'being swamped by people of a different culture. [Britain] must hold out the clear prospect of an end to immigration'.[9]

John Major has vocally re-inforced these arguments in the context of the debate over the Maastricht treaty and has pointed to immigration as one of the key issues on which Britain wishes to maintain independent policies from Europe in order to 'double-bolt' the doors against immigrants. Britain therefore continues to refuse to sign the Schengen accord which would end intra-EC passport checks. Britain's suspicion of Schengen is presumably based on the unsubstantiated fear that it will lead to the inflow of large numbers of migrants who will contribute little to Britain's economic prosperity. The matter of whether certain migrant groups such as refugees could become a significant economic burden is taken up later in this paper.

While Britain has moved to make immigration more difficult, in North America, both the USA and Canada have re-defined their immigration policies to permit an increase in immigration. This has been done in such a way as to boost the immigration of highly skilled and professional staff, but certain categories of refugees have also been welcomed. This difference in strategy has been analysed by a range of academics[10] who conclude that the positive North American ideology towards immigration is fundamentally based on the belief that immigration contributes to the vitality of the nation by infusing new life blood into a multi-cultural nation, while in Western Europe resistance to multi-culturalism is strong. This has produced political tensions that have in turn generated a series of discussions about the perceived 'burden' to the welfare state associated with further immigration. Urbani and Granaglia[11] and others have shown that even within Western Europe significant differences exist in terms of the degree of openness or closure sought by both immigration and emigration policies, and the extent to which different nations have sought to restrict citizenship.

This is not the place for an extended review of European attitudes to ethnic minorities and immigration. They have only been introduced briefly to make the point that if national variations exist in terms of political responses to immigration, then it is not unreasonable to expect cultural factors to produce different interpretations of what is meant by the economic costs and benefits of migration.

To summarise the conclusions of the paper so far, differences of definition, lack of data, and contrasts in what is culturally interpreted to be the economic impact of migration, go some way to explaining why so many apparently paradoxical positions are held with regard to immigration policy.

Discussion now turns to a more detailed evaluation of trends in labour migration in relation to economic growth and to the possible labour market impacts of immigration to Britain.

West European labour migration and economic growth

It is extremely difficult to establish the nature of the relationship between labour migration and economic growth. Logic might suggest that a state will permit labour immigration to occur when economic circumstances are favourable and when labour resources within the state are scarce. The historical record shows that this is not necessarily the case. It is also difficult to establish lines of causality. For example, should one ask 'Does immigration affect rates of economic growth?' or is it more appropriate to start by asking 'Does economic growth stimulate immigration?'

The problem may be illustrated by considering patterns of economic performance in Western Europe in the 1970s. The decade began well with countries averaging between 4% and 6% growth per annum in their domestic products.[12] Böhning[13] and others have described how these rapidly expanding economies during the 1960s and early 1970s were threatened by labour shortages, resulting from the relatively low levels of labour market growth which, in turn, had been affected by the slow growth of their labour forces from natural population increase. The tight labour market situation fuelled fears of wage inflation acting as a check on economic growth. In this context labour immigration from labour surplus economies resulted. Within national labour markets upward social mobility attracted nationals away from the less desirable jobs leaving vacancies to be filled by immigrants.

The 1973 oil crisis undoubtedly brought to an end the period of continuous economic growth which most Western European countries had been enjoying, with recession affecting their economies in 1974 and 1975. However, by 1976 economic recovery was obvious, with Great Britain recording economic growth of 3.9%, and West Germany and France moving ahead even more strongly with growth rates of 5.6% and 5.2% respectively. Economic growth was sustained across most of Western Europe during the rest of the 1970s with recession not returning to most countries until 1980.

The reversal of economic fortunes in 1974/5 was associated with rising unemployment in most Western European countries, but what was significant was that these trends continued in the latter part of the decade despite the return to economic growth. Both unemployment and economic growth rates rose in the mid 1970s. Unemployment rates also soared in the late 1970s and early 1980s as the next recession made its impact. The fact that rising unemployment in 1974/5 was associated with the introduction of a range of policy measures to halt further immigration is not surprising. From 1976 onwards, renewed economic growth did not bring down unemployment and there were moves to strengthen policies on repatriation.[14]

White,[15] in a detailed analysis of immigration policies in Western Europe, notes in fact that attempts to halt labour immigration in many countries actually preceded the economic crisis. In Britain the Immigration Act was passed in 1971, while in West Germany steps were taken to stabilise immigrant stocks in the summer of 1973, before the oil crisis had occurred. Switzerland adopted a restrictive policy on immigration from 1970. Algeria banned emigration to France from September 1973 in outrage at racial attacks on Algerian migrants. Salt[16] and other academics agree that in the early 1970s restrictions on immigration were primarily initiated in response to social concerns over the size of certain immigrant communities, rather than in relation to the economic crisis. Once in place it was, however, the economic situation, and in particular the scale of domestic unemployment, which was cited as the reason for justifying the extension of restrictive immigration policies.

What conclusions can be drawn from the experience of Western Europe in the 1970s? First, it would seem that from 1974 onwards national economic growth no longer translated into labour market demand in such a way as to reduce unemployment levels and to create labour shortages of the kind which had encouraged labour immigration in the 1960s and early 1970s. Second, the introduction of restrictive immigration policies pre-dated economic decline in some countries, suggesting that social factors may be critical in initiating the political contexts in which further immigration is perceived as undesirable. Third, politicians in Western Europe cited rising unemployment as a reason for sustaining restrictive immigration controls. Rising unemployment in the 1970s and 1980s was not caused by immigration but by other internal and international forces.

Immigration and economic performance of selected non-EC states

If the European experience suggests that economic growth no longer guarantees conditions in which labour demand will grow and immigration become a desirable policy option in order to avoid wage inflation, this does not prove the inverse case: it does not prove that immigration is an undesirable labour market policy option. Indeed since it is a policy which has not been attempted since the 1960s in Britain, it becomes pertinent to ask if there is evidence from other parts of the globe that immigration can benefit advanced economies.

Table 6.5 presents a range of economic indicators and immigration flows for three non EC countries. In recent years British politicians have often looked to North America for inspiration on economic policy rather than following European models. It is therefore interesting to note from Table 6.5 that both the USA and Canada have followed much more positive strategies towards immigration. They have adopted new legislation to favour high quality immigration and have introduced policy measures which have encouraged increased levels of immigration amongst those categories of immigrant deemed to be of greatest value to their economies. The consequences of the positive ideologies on immigration held by these countries is evident in terms of the rising numbers of immigrants accepted for settlement. This is most dramatic in the Canadian case where numbers almost doubled between 1986 and 1989. Australia also supports a selective pro-immigration policy and has endorsed (1991) a new plan to expand further immigration flows.[17]

No one would suggest that the UK economy is similar in all respects to those of the three other countries listed in Table 6.5. It is however interesting to note from Table 6.5 that Britain can not excuse itself from following the immigration stance of these nations in terms of statements about Britain's weaker economic performance. OECD[18] figures show quite clearly that over the 30 year span, 1960–90, Britain experienced a very similar rate of growth in real GDP per caput as the USA and Australia, and over the last decade, 1979–90, enjoyed more rapid economic growth than any of these three states. At the same time the UK experienced lower levels of population growth and much slower rates of labour force increase than the other countries. Few would suggest that immigration to the USA, Canada and Australia has had damaging effects on these advanced economies and it is apparent from the new pro-immigration legislation of these countries that their governments certainly do not view immigration as a negative economic influence.

To summarise the debate, positive economic growth is not a sufficient condition to justify a policy favouring immigration on economic grounds. However, having examined Table 6.5 it is equally important to stress that large scale immigration should not be viewed as inconsistent with substantial economic growth in modern western societies. Even during periods of recession Canada, the USA and Australia have held to their pro-immigration stances, maintaining the view that positive selective immigration is to do with nation building and future economic well-being. Despite the introduction of highly restrictive immigration policies, British politicians continue to portray immigration as a phenomenon associated primarily with labour flows from Britain's former colonies of the kind which occurred in the first

Table 6.5 Economic Indicators and Immigration: A Comparison of UK, USA, Australia and Canada

	—Annual Growth Rate—				*—InFlows of— Permanent Settlers (thousands)*			
	Population Growth (%)	*Labour Force Growth (%)*	*Real GDP p.c. Growth (%)*					
	1960-90	*60-90*	*60-90*	*79-90*	*1986*	*1987*	*1988*	*1989*
UK	0.3	0.5	2.1	1.9	47	46	49	49
USA	1.1	1.9	2.0	1.6	602	602	643	1091
Australia	1.6	2.4	2.3	1.6	103	128	151	131
Canada	0.8	2.5	2.9	1.8	99	152	162	192

Source: OECD, 1992, *Economic Outlook 1960-90;* OECD, 1991, *SOPEMI, 1990.*

half of the twentieth century. In practice so-called 'skilled transients' have replaced 'settler migration'.[19] British politicians need to consider very carefully why their stance on immigration has not shifted in line with changes in the international migration system and why their view of immigration is so different from that of countries like Canada. A significant number of western economies with satisfactory levels of economic growth certainly view immigration as making a positive economic contribution.

British labour market trends and the implications for migration

Analysis of recent statements by the British Government on immigration issues (made in the context of the debate over granting new passports to a small number of skilled people from Hong Kong and in the wake of concern from European neighbours over the possible consequences of an influx of migrants from Eastern Europe), suggest that two economic worries are paramount; first that large scale immigration might exacerbate unemployment and second that it might place an insurmountable burden on the social services and social security systems. It is therefore pertinent to examine what trends are likely to emerge in the British labour force over the next few years, as well as extending the investigation to consider the wider economic costs of supporting a flow of immigrants.

Labour supply

Table 6.6 shows the labour force estimates used by the British Department of Employment along with labour force projections to the year 2001, based on the most recent finding of the 1991 Labour Force Survey. There has been a steady growth in the size of Britain's labour force over the last two decades from 24,895,000 in 1971 to 26,242,000 in 1981 and 28,081,000 in 1991. The 1982–91 growth which produced a net increase in the size of the labour force of 2,039,000 persons was particularly strong by European standards. Between 1985 and 1990 Britain had the third-highest average annual rate of employment growth, after Spain and Luxembourg. By contrast the Government's official labour force projections to the year 2001 show a much slower rate of growth, with nearly all the increase coming from increased female participation. Between 1992 and 2001 the male labour force is expected to grow by as little as 104,000, with net reductions in the most active male cohorts of the labour force. A reduction of 841,000 in the number of men in the labour force in the age cohort 20–34 years is anticipated by the year 2001, representing one of the most significant alterations in the supply of labour which the British labour market has experienced in recent decades.

Trends in labour force size and structure are dependent on:

- the size and structure of the total population (which in turn is determined by mortality, fertility and migration) and
- the activity and participation rates in each sex and age group.

It is useful first of all to consider the effects of demographic trends on labour supply. Table 6.7 shows the size and age distribution of the British population of working age. Population growth was the dominant force accounting for the increased supply of labour to the labour force in the 1970s and the early 1980s, but from 1983 a significant trend towards demographic decline in the number of young people entering the labour force altered this effect. By 1991 there were 769,000 fewer people in the 16–19 age cohort than in 1982. The continued effect of low birth rates will produce further reductions in the number of young people in this age cohort by the year 1994,when there will only be 2,602,000 16–19 year olds (nearly a million less than a decade earlier). It is statistics such as these which have fuelled speculation about a 'demographic time-bomb' creating fierce labour market pressures and perhaps introducing circumstances in which labour immigration might once again become an attractive policy option.

Table 6.6 Estimates and Projections of the Resident Population of Great Britain aged 16 years and over (thousands)

Age	*Estimates*		*Projections*	
All persons	*1990*	*1991*	*2000*	*2005*
16–19	3,109	2,943	2,829	2,844
20–24	4,419	4,364	3,368	3,430
25–34	8,571	8,717	8,144	7,890
35–44	7,699	7,718	8,443	8,589
45–54	6,335	6,441	7,519	7,538
55–59	2,867	2,852	3,152	3,279
60–64	2,828	2,809	2,793	2,769
65 and over	8,793	8,837	9,024	9,024
All ages	44,621	44,680	45,255	45,363
Working age (Men aged 16–64, women aged 16–59)	34,362	34,389	34,822	34,923

Source: OPCS.

Table 6.7 Estimates and Projections of the Civilian Labour Force in Great Britain (thousands)

Age	*Estimates*		*Projections*		*Change*
All persons	*1990*	*1991*	*2000*	*2005*	*1992–2001*
16–19	2,268	2,129	2,009	2,021	3
20–24	3,581	3,462	2,620	2,679	-698
25–34	7,049	7,142	6,914	6,722	-541
35–44	6,593	6,614	7,441	7,594	1,112
45–54	5,204	5,271	6,173	6,186	674
55–59	1,944	1,918	2,128	2,215	287
60–64	1,074	1,083	1,059	1,054	-10
65 and over	477	461	380	377	-58
All ages	28,206	28,081	28,724	28,847	768
Working age (Men aged 16–64, women aged 16–59)	27,398	27,270	27,978	28,102	802

Source: Labour Force Survey 1991 and *Employment Gazette*, April 1992.

The economic effects on the labour market of demographic change extend far beyond the crude impact on overall labour force size. Long-run financial implications of continued low birth rates and the associated ageing of the population include changes in patterns of consumption, investment and saving. Concern has arisen over how future pensions are to be financed; how career mobility is to be sustained; and how flexible employment policies are to be maintained.

It is important to note that while government population projections are based on fertility and mortality rates which are unlikely to change greatly over the short term (and where the effects take some time to impact upon the labour market), they also depend upon assumptions about international migration. For example, the British population projections prepared in 1985 assumed that Britain would continue to experience net emigration of about 17,000 persons per year, rather than having emigration and immigration held in balance. The result was the prediction of a population of working age by the year 2000 which would be 200,000 lower than without the net emigration effect.

Changes in participation rates were noted above as the second major influence affecting labour force trends. Comparison of Tables 6.6 and 6.7 indicates that demographic influences are only one dimension of labour force change. Participation rates are much more variable over time and are much harder to project with accuracy. For example, the increases which occurred in Britain's labour force in 1983–4 and 1988–9 may be explained largely by fluctuations in activity rates. In the 1980s participation rates tended to rise for women and to fall for men. It is expected that reductions in male participation rates will produce a decline of the male labour force in the years 1992–4.

Projections of participation rates of the British population are produced by the Department of Employment based on assumptions about how economic, demographic and social factors will affect activity rates. For example, an attempt is made to project the influence of changes in unemployment levels on the number of people participating in the labour force. The net effect of the Department of Employment's projections about participation rates is to produce increases in the number of women in the labour force. These increases will greatly outweigh the effect of small reductions in male participation rates. The consequence of labour force projections is first to dampen greatly the impact of demographic processes over the next decade and second to produce a further important redistributive effect on the structure of the labour force. Not only will there be fewer young people, with all the economic consequences that ensue from this, but there will also be a higher proportion of women in the labour force by the year 2001.

Comparison of current (1991) labour force projections with previous ones is particularly important for the analyst concerned with immigration issues. The 1990–1 fall in the labour force of 125,000 was double the projected figure of 67,000. This has been attributed to the fact that many fewer young people than expected entered the labour force, with a larger number staying on in full-time education. These statistics illustrate the relative uncertainty of the projection process, and indicate something of the scale of error which could arise in projections which already forecast a fairly stagnant picture in terms of labour supply.

The analysis of trends in the structure of Britain's labour force point to the 1990s as being very different from those of earlier decades. The decline in fertility levels and the subsequent reduction in the number of young people entering the labour force has been a significant influence on labour force structure. It has not, and will not of itself, create a demand for higher levels of immigration, since participation rates and the restructuring of labour demand intervene to affect labour force size and composition. Therefore, neither economic growth nor demographic shrinkage are sufficient conditions *in themselves* to *necessitate* an increase in immigration in the 1990s. Other labour supply options exist. The 1990s will however be a decade when a reduced level of new entries to the labour market from the younger cohorts of the population will oblige employers to consider all the options including immigration if they are to maintain current capital to labour ratios and to avoid wage inflation and a loss of flexible workforce practices.

Labour demand

Change in the demand for labour in Britain over the last two decades has been very great indeed. Between 1971 and 1981 employment declined by 2.5% even although positive rates of economic growth were recorded in all but three years. Reduction of demand was greatest in manufacturing (–24.3%) while service employment grew by 13.5%. The equivalent figures for 1981 to 1989 are 4.3% overall growth, but with a further 14.3% decline in manufacturing jobs and a 17.9% growth in services. The reasons for these very significant changes in employment demand have been analysed in detail by Massey[20] and more recently by Champion and Townsend[21] and Owen.[22] They include the effects of industrial restructuring in the face of increased international competition, resulting in the shedding of manufacturing jobs due to plant rationalisation, re-organisation and re-investment in more capital intensive production systems. An increase in the internationalisation of production systems has seen companies redistribute certain types of jobs across the globe to locations where wage levels were more advantageous. In particular this meant a reduction in the number of jobs in Britain in the older established labour intensive industries. While production jobs were internationalised, managerial and professional jobs remained in Britain creating Britains's contribution to what some have described as the 'new international division of labour'.[23]

The Labour Force Surveys of the 1980s show a consistent shift over the 1980s towards a lower proportion of manual and semi-skilled jobs and towards a proportional increase in professional and managerial posts. An interesting corollary to this has been the trend for job-related migration within Britain to be increasingly associated with professional and managerial staff. Owen[24] has shown that regional variations exist, but that in the case of the south of Britain job-related migrants were between 4 and 5 times more likely to be managerial or professional staff than manual workers (defined to include craft, skilled manual workers and plant and machine operators).

It seems probable that in the 1990s structural changes in the British economy will continue, although they may affect the demand for labour in a different fashion from in the past. Green[25] has suggested that employers and governments will continue to seek to raise standards of living. This will only be possible if British firms remain internationally competitive. On the one hand they must avoid undue wage inflation, and on the other hand ensure adequate investment in new technologies and in human resources. Skills appropriate to these new technologies must be acquired and an ability developed to adapt to the new patterns of work organisation which will emerge. One aspect of new work patterns will be increased job mobility, not just at a local scale, but at the international level.

The Institute of Employment Research (University of Warwick) estimate that in the UK there will be a 1.3 million (15%) increase in higher level non-manual occupations by the year 2000. By the turn of the century professional, associate professional and managerial and administrative occupations are projected to account for over one-third of all jobs (compared with under one quarter in 1971). Not only does this represent a very significant increase in specific skill and occupational categories, but the effect is increased by the spatial concentration of demand in the south of England (which incidentally also faces the tightest constraints on labour supply in terms of the supply-side processes discussed above).

The concentrated pattern of selective demand for certain types of labour leads according to Green,[26] to the key question of 'whether pressures arising from economic and geographical imbalances between prosperous centres and the rest of the community will encourage the mobility of economic activity and jobs and/or the mobility of labour.'

The reason why this international mobility arises more strongly as an option in relation to this trend than to other forces affecting the relation between labour supply and demand, is that matching labour demand for highly skilled jobs cannot be achieved in a situation of demographic decline simply by raising participation rates. Filling skilled jobs requires time for education and training potential employees. Consequently, failure to identify future needs for particular specialised and highly skilled functions well in advance may create a situation in which short- or even long-run skill shortages will arise. Such gaps can only be filled by immigration. It is in this context that the situation may well arise (and already has done) whereby a labour market experiences labour surpluses at one level (for example, of semi-skilled and certain white collar jobs) while at the same time facing severe skill shortages at other higher levels which can only be filled by some form of immigration.

This situation has been identified in a useful labour market model proposed by Lonnroth.[27] In discussing appropriate labour market policies to 'squeeze the supply and demand curves at various skill levels closer together', Lonnroth[28] advocates not only a policy of continuous upgrading of labour skills on the domestic labour market, but also international labour mobility. 'Paradoxically the gross migratory flows within free labour market areas may be too modest to meet the needs of internationalisation and labour force development. Policies should therefore promote temporary international mobility of key personnel, international trainee exchanges, education and training abroad.'[29] Before the nature of these and other possible policies can be considered in further detail, it is necessary to consider whether there is any evidence from the recent UK migration experience of need existing within the country for immigration of certain skill groups. This task is undertaken in the next section of this paper. The analysis which has been presented of Britain's labour market, has shown that demographic trends will continue to reduce the scale of new entrants to the labour market over the next decade. This effect will, however, be partly offset by rising female participation rates. Labour demand has shifted considerably over the last two decades. The restructuring of the economy which has followed is in part responsible for some of the mismatches which have occurred between patterns of labour supply and labour demand.

In the long run new skills can and should be produced as a result of adaptations to the education and training systems of the country, but in the short run and in the medium term it is possible, and indeed probable, that skill shortages may occur in certain professional and managerial positions which could be filled to the benefit of the economy by qualified immigrants. From this conclusion it follows that the issues which policy makers should address, prior to developing a migration stance, are not whether there is any domestic unemployment or whether participation rates are likely to compensate for demographic shrinkage, but whether there are selective skill shortages and how these can best be filled in the interests of economic growth and the standards of living of the resident population.

Rising demand for skilled foreign labour

The clearest empirical evidence supporting the labour demand argument for immigration can be found in trends in the number of work permits issued by the British Government to allow foreign labour to work on a short or longer term basis in the country. The work permit system is useful in demonstrating the existence of a clear economic demand for foreign labour in Britain because a work permit application should only be granted by the Department of Employment if it considers that there is no 'suitable' resident labour. The term 'suitable' is of great importance and we shall return to considering its meaning later.

Seymour[30] in a review of the UK work permit system has identified the precise objectives of the scheme. These are primarily to protect the resident labour force rather than to serve the economic interests of the economy. This prioritisation of the interests of the indigenous labour force helps to explain why so little attention is paid within the scheme to identifying the labour market needs of the economy as a whole. Although lip service is paid under the scheme to 'the interests of the

UK as a whole by assisting inward investment'[31] there is neither recognition of the possibility that the wider economy might benefit from immigration of entrepreneurs (independently from major capital transfers) nor of the economic stimulus which immigration of certain skills might produce.

The Department of Employment needs to be convinced by the employer who applies for a work permit for a foreign employee that reasonable attempts have been made to recruit a resident or EC worker (NB work permits are not needed for EC citizens) before looking elsewhere. Another significant control which seeks to ensure that foreign labour is not recruited to the detriment of resident workers is that the job must be offered at wages and under conditions which are not less favourable than those which would be granted to British staff.

Despite these many controls there has been a sustained and substantial rise in the number of both short- and long-term work permits granted over recent years (Table 6.8). The number of long-term permits granted rose by 29% in 1988 over the previous year, by 28% in 1989 and by 21% in 1990. To quote from the SOPEMI report; 'prior to 1990 the increase in permits reflected the stronger performance of the national economy. However during 1990 numbers of unemployed rose by 227,000, so the rise in work permits granted occurred despite a deterioration in labour market conditions. This suggests that either there is some fundamental mismatch between the characteristics of supply and demand, and/or that some lag effect exists between labour market conditions at home and employers' use of overseas workers'.[32]

The types of jobs for which the permits were most sought were in insurance, banking and finance, and professional services. Professional and managerial staff account for 81% of long-term work permits. Work permit data also serves to illustrate the changing nature of work organisation which has been alluded to above. This is so because it lists permits offered to persons making inter-company transfers (that is transfers within an international organisation from one location to another). Around 40% of all work permits are granted for inter-company transfers reflecting the strength of large international employers in stimulating and sustaining the system of international mobility.

Previous work by this author using the results of the International Passenger Survey[33] has researched this issue, and has shown the growing significance to Britain of skilled transient movements of staff within large companies. Japan and the USA are the two non-European countries with which Britain is most closely linked by this

Table 6.8 Work Permits Issued, UK (1987–90)

Year	Long-term permits	Short-term	Trainee	Total
1987	8063	9385	2900	20348
1988	10391	11793	3790	25974
1989	13268	12234	4228	29730
1990	16055	13760	4812	34627

Source: From J. Salt, 1992, 'International Migration and the United Kingdom' (SOPEMI) report to the OECD.

new form of international migration. Transferring staff from branch to branch in large international companies for periods of two or three years has become a major (arguably the major) element of the British migration system and one which contrasts strongly with the historical processes of settler immigration. Skilled transient movements are favoured by large companies as part of their internationalisation strategies. This not only reflects the way that strong economic forces operate within the internal labour markets of large companies to fill vacancies by internal transfers within the company (albeit by international relocation of an employee) rather than by external recruitment. It also reflects the benefits which the large company perceives to exist from promoting the circulation of human capital between different branches in order to sustain corporate identity as well as to facilitate communication between different branches of a firm. All these reasons may constitute for the firm one facet of why local labour may not be considered 'suitable' and it helps to explain why international skill mobility may seem to be highly desirable for reasons quite separate from the international matching of specific skill shortages with potential sources of qualified manpower.

There would seem to be at least two reasons why one would expect skilled transient international moves to continue to increase in the near future. First, it seems highly likely that throughout most developed and developing countries linkages between economies will grow stronger as policies favouring selective integration occurs. Nowhere is this trend more evident than in the states of Western Europe in the 1990s as they commit themselves to greater monetary and political integration. Research by Kritz and Caces[34] suggests that by the mid-1980s 4.6% of all professional and administrative workers in Belgium were foreign born, while in the UK the proportion was 6.0% and in Sweden 7.2%. An even more startling statistic is that, according to the UK 1981 census, 40% of all people defined as 'foreign born' (i.e., excluding second generation ethnic minorities) were employed in professional or administrative jobs.

The brief analysis presented here of the skilled transient immigration to Britain has shown first, that skill gaps do exist within the British economy, which employers and the Department of Employment judge to be best filled by skilled immigration. Second, analysis of work permits and complementary information from the International Passenger Survey (revealing similar trends with regard to skilled immigration to, and emigration from, EC countries) underscores the need to see immigration as fulfilling more than the simple need to match specific skill shortages. The internationalisation of both production and service activities has necessitated the increased mobility of certain types of human capital. This is so, not only because of the need of certain national labour markets to access international skill specialisms, but also to facilitate the needs of the internal labour markets of global corporations to circulate some of their highly skilled manpower between the different states in which they are operating. Third, the discussion points to the need to consider British immigration policy in the light of these new types of labour migration which differ considerably in their economic character from the settler immigration patterns of the past. In practice this switch in immigration behaviour has been recognised in part by the government in its recent review of the work permit scheme (Summer 1991).

The revised work permit scheme involves the creation of a two tier work permit system to facilitate the circulation of highly qualified staff, particularly those who are involved in corporate transfers. In the first tier, applications are dealt with fairly quickly because a simplified procedure has been introduced for dealing with those cases which are deemed clearly to merit approval by the Department of Employment. It is claimed that 75% of all applications are dealt with within eight weeks of receipt. These cases include senior transfers within Trans National Corporations (described as Inter Company Transfers), such as board level transfers, moves associated with inward investment and occupations considered to be in acute short supply. The Department of Employment does not however issue a list of short supply occupations since it is claimed that this list varies over even very short time periods. To quote Onslow-Cole[35] 'This list is amended on an almost daily basis and in view of the recession is currently very short.' All applications not falling under the first category require fuller documentation and are treated at greater length as Tier 2 applications.

In 1993 a set of parliamentary questions were posed to the Secretary of State for Employment concerning the operation of the revised work permit scheme. It emerged that no comparative statistics were available to evaluate whether the introduction of a second tier had been to the disadvantage of applicants other than those making internal company transfers. Of greater significance in response to the question 'what research and data collection is carried out by the Department (of Employment) to assess which skills are in short supply in the UK in order to guide officials who are dealing with work permit applications?' it emerged that no systematic data collection existed and that work permit requests were researched on an individual and ad hoc basis.

It should be stressed that the work permit scheme relates to temporary immigration. Although some work permit holders do apply to extend their permits or to settle more permanently, the vast majority (86%) leave before or on expiry of their work permit.[36] It is not therefore a system which in any way can be thought of as analagous to the types of skill recruitment achieved by the immigration quotas and point system schemes operated in certain other countries, which relate to permanent settlement of skilled workers.

The significance of market demand for labour immigration

The previous section of the paper used work permit data to argue the case that there is a clear economic demand for immigrant labour in Britain. Those who contest this view will inevitably suggest that work permits account for only a small proportion of all immigration. It is important therefore to consider in more detail precisely how significant is market demand for labour immigration. This is achieved here first, by further consideration of work permit data and second, by pointing to other indicators of demand.

In 1992, the number of work permit holders and their dependants permitted to enter Britain numbered 52,000 persons. This compared with 52,600 persons accepted for permanent settlement.[37] The numbers involved are therefore highly significant. Furthermore, amongst those admitted for permanent settlement in their own right on completion of four years residence, work permit holders were the single largest category (and almost twice the number of the next most important group—those in permit free employment). As noted earlier, work permits offer only a limited insight into the demand for immigrant skills. This is so because large flows of Irish labour as well as workers from EC countries (and from 1994 from EFTA) enter the UK without requiring work permits. It is for this reason that the analysis in this paper has frequently referred to the International Passenger Survey and the Labour Force Survey. These other sources substantiate the view that (a) skilled transient migration is now by far the dominant form of migration affecting Britain; and (b) a very significant market demand for immigrant skills exists within the British economy.

These views are supported by survey work of individual professions and skill groups. One example suffices here to make the point. Buchan, Seccombe and Bull[38] in an extensive survey of UK nurses show that the *annual* number of nurses entering the UK professional register who had previously been registered abroad was between 2,400 and 3,500 in the period 1984–91. An upward trend was identified with the importance of non-UK sources of nurses (as a proportion of all new admissions to the UK professional register) rising to one in ten in 1990/91. In nursing this strong demand for foreign nurses reflects the combination of increased demand for healthcare at a time when intake to domestic nurse training has been on the decline. Such a level of dependence on foreign nurses serves as only one example of the demand which exists in Britain for specific immigrant skills.

Other labour market dimensions of immigration

The case which has been presented in the preceding part of this paper suggests that selective labour immigration is both necessary and desirable relative to the needs of the British labour market. This has been shown to be true in terms of Britain's economic needs in relation to specific skill shortages which can best be met in the short term by temporary immigration. It is also true in relation to needs created by a switch in the organisation of the labour market which has required an increased international mobility of professional and managerial staff moving within large organisations.

Another argument, and one which is not developed in detail in this paper because it probably does not involve very large numbers of immigrants, is that immigrants create jobs rather than filling them. The USA and Canada have specialised in recruiting entrepreneurs and investors and have specifically recognised this category of migrants. Britain too has a facility within immigration regulations to allow the entry of very wealthy immigrants, but seems much less successful than its North American rivals in attracting this category of investor migrant. In Britain's case people are allowed to enter as business persons if first, they are bringing to the UK a minimum of £200,000 of their own money to be invested in a business, second they are to be occupied full-time in running the business, and third the business will provide new, full-time employment for persons already settled in Britain. Trott[39] has described the other conditions attaching to this mode of entry.

While attracting entrepreneurial immigrants is clearly desirable in economic terms, the British rules on this type of immigration have a number of problems. Trott[40] points out that it is not easy to determine what money belongs to the migrant. Does it include loans? What is the Home Office definition of a person being occupied full-time in their own business? Perhaps the greatest problem is that many businesses do not require £200,000 to be successful or may start very adequately on lower levels of capital and later expand. The government's own criteria in the 1980s and early 1990s for a British person to be seen as a successful entrepreneur, certainly did not involve a cash threshold of £200,000 for new business start-ups.

Historical evidence shows from around the globe that immigrants are often highly successful as entrepreneurs but that their success lies not in their capital stock but in their skills and motivation. For instance, one example of modern day free market success was the transfer of textile entrepreneurs from Shanghai to Hong Kong following the Communist take-over of mainland China. The entrepreneur refugees from Shanghai were deemed to have been responsible, at least in part, for the development of Hong Kong's successful textile industry in the 1950s. Many other examples could be quoted which reinforce the point that it is skills and motivation rather than capital which are the key characteristics determining the entrepreneurial success of refugee and voluntary migrant moves. The USA, in revising its current immigration policy in 1991, moved to try to increase the number of entrepreneurs coming to the US each year. In so-doing it has given more weight not only to inward investor groups, but also to those potential migrants with high inventive and creative capacities such as key scientists and leading professionals.

The difference in outlook and strategy between Britain and other countries is well illustrated by returning to the case of Hong Kong, and in contrasting the approaches taken to encourage Hong Kong skills to seek foreign passports in the run-up to 1997. In Hong Kong the number of 'immigration agencies' expanded from under ten in 1980 to over 120 by 1990. The main task of such agencies was to offer advice to the Hong Kong elite on how to gain visas and passports for immigration to other countries. The USA, Canada, Australia and New Zealand have actively developed these agencies in order to recruit potential investors and highly skilled immigrants. By contrast the UK's negative ideology on immigration and the outcry which surrounded the legislation to offer passports to a small number of highly placed Hong Kong citizens sent the inverse message to Hong Kong. While Canada emerged as the favoured destination for Hong Kong's elite, Britain found that its offer of a limited number of passports was initially not even taken up in full.

In brief, immigration can serve as a means to create jobs and investment. In Britain's case this strategy has not been pursued successfully by comparison with the results achieved in other countries.

The case for encouraging entrepreneurial migration needs to be balanced by a comment on the development implications of a 'brain drain' from less developed to more developed nations. Clearly it is unacceptable to recommend that a more developed country like Britain should seek to prosper by recruiting skills from the least developed countries of the world, where the most skilled nationals clearly have a key responsibility in helping in the development of their own country. However, where skilled persons seek entry to a country as refugees, as was the case for many East Germans fleeing to former West Germany in the 1940s and 1950s, or where migration is between countries of approximately the same level of development (as between Hong Kong and the UK—GNP *per capita* in Hong Kong and Scotland are similar) then no accusation of favouring a 'brain drain' can be sustained.

Immigration to Britain is of course permitted on non-economic grounds. No one would want to suggest that refugees should only be admitted if they have desirable skills. It is quite legitimate that migration policy should facilitate a degree of immigration associated with both the granting of asylum to a controlled in-flow of refugees and also to permit family re-unification. It is important to note that such forms of migration also have an impact on the labour market and that the nature of the impact of these forms of immigration need not be perceived as negative. This paper has argued that this form of immigration may not result in major positive economic gains, but it also does not have net negative consequences. Indeed some refugees may in fact be economically highly desirable, because of their entrepreneurial potential for the host economy. At present very little is done to foster this potential. Undoubtedly, investment in language training and similar support facilities to promote the integration of refugees would yield significant economic gains for the UK through promoting a more rapid achievement of the significant economic potential of these groups.

In the absence of detailed economic statistics by migrant cohort it is difficult to provide an overall audit of the impact on the labour market. Lack of appropriate economic data also makes it difficult to estimate with any accuracy what would be the impact of an increase in unskilled immigration. Such data is needed in order to judge whether further immigration of this kind would simply swell the ranks of the unemployed, or whether it would improve Britain's gross operating surplus (the difference between value added and wage bills). At present Britain lags way behind its competitors on this key measure of rates of return on capital (Spain 20.3%; USA 18.0%; Netherlands 17.2%; UK 10.8%). The Government should be able to assess the effect of further immigration on key economic measures such as these, and should be urged to collect adequate economic data on immigration in order to be able to make well substantiated judgements about what level and kind of immigration is appropriate to the economy. At present economic data of this kind is not available, hence precluding the possibilities of making detailed impact statements based on different immigration scenarios (of the kind produced in Canada and Australia).

Straubhaar and Zimmermann, Zimmermann and Rivera-Batiz et al.,[41] conclude that immigrants often complement native workers resulting in an increase in productivity and wages—a finding not incompatible with some of the models proposed by Borjas and Simon.[42] Straubhaar and Zimmermann's[43] work is also significant in identifying short-term adjustment costs as one of the key issues associated with immigration. They propose that the net benefits of migration can only be enjoyed if the host population is assured that adjustment costs are being fully covered. One solution is to offset short-run costs associated with immigration by imposing entrance fees and migration taxes. A substantial body of academic work exists in Germany to support the contention that net economic benefits accrue from immigration, even after short-run costs have been taken into consideration.[44]

The Labour Force Survey allows one only a few interesting comparisons between the labour characteristics of foreign nationals employed in Britain and the rest of the British work force. Table 6.9, for example, shows that foreign nationals are on average more highly skilled. The 1990 LFS suggested that 21.7% of UK nationals were in professional or managerial jobs. By contrast 23.8% of immigrants from the EC (excluding Eire) were in this socio-economic group and an impressive 28.3% of those from the 'rest of the world' were professionals or managers. The contribution to the labour force of immigration must therefore surely be interpreted as a positive one in terms of skill levels and qualifications. At the other end of the labour market, male foreign workers were less likely to be in manual jobs than UK nationals (50.4% and 52.6% respectively). It was only among female workers that foreign nationals were more likely to be involved in manual jobs. Immigrants are shown by Table 6.9 to be much less likely to fall in the 'other non-manual' category covering most white collar and semi-skilled jobs. This data suggests that for all foreign nationals, and not just those with temporary work permits, Lonnroth's pro-immigration labour market model has some validity in describing the British case.

An economic audit of immigration to West Germany has recently produced some interesting findings which bear serious consideration. A study produced by the Rheinish-Westfälische Institute (RWI) in 1991 provided a range of evidence to support the view that the immigrant community contributed substantially to the state's affluence. The 3.5 million immigrants who entered West Germany between 1988 and 1991 would not be described as skilled transients of the kind discussed earlier in this paper. Instead they were made up of refugees, economic migrants and family members seeking re-unification. Baron[45] reviewing the report notes that the new labour supply enabled German firms to extend their productive capacity and far from taking up jobs which otherwise would have been occupied by West Germans the wealth generated as a result of the immigrants created a net increase in employment (i.e., in addition creating extra jobs to match the jobs taken by the immigrants) of 20,000 jobs. The RWI also calculated an increase in economic growth of between 0.5% and 1.0% per annum which was attributed to the increase in foreign labour.

One reason that greater economic returns are not achieved as a result of immigration in countries such as Britain is the negative influence of discrimination. Racial discrimination in the labour

Table 6.9 Socio-economic Grouping of the Workforce by Nationality, UK (1990)

	Professionals Employers Managers	*Other Non-manual*	*Manual*	*Other*	*Total*
Total					
All Nationalities	21.7	33.2	44.4	0.7	100.0
UK	21.6	33.3	44.3	0.7	100.0
Foreign Nationals	24.7	28.7	45.7	0.9	100.0
EC (exc Eire)	23.8	28.5	47.7	0.0	100.0
Eire	19.9	29.8	49.1	0.2	100.0
Rest of the world	28.3	28.0	42.4	1.3	100.0
Men					
All Nationalities	28.3	18.3	52.5	0.9	100.0
UK	28.2	18.3	52.6	0.9	100.0
Foreign Nationals	31.7	16.7	50.4	1.2	100.0
EC (exc Eire)	32.9	15.2	51.9	0.0	100.0
Eire	23.8	14.9	59.1	2.2	100.0
Rest of the world	37.1	18.5	44.0	0.4	100.0
Women					
All Nationalities	13.2	52.6	33.8	0.4	100.0
UK	13.1	52.9	33.6	0.4	100.0
Foreign Nationals	15.5	44.1	39.7	0.7	100.0
EC (exc Eire)	15.1	42.5	42.5	0.0	100.0
Eire	14.1	48.6	36.6	0.7	100.0
Rest of the world	16.7	41.4	40.9	1.0	100.0

market results in 'visible' immigrant groups being unable to access the jobs for which they are trained. This results in some immigrant groups consistently occupying jobs for which they are over-qualified, and as a result reduces their productive contribution relative to what would have been achieved in the absence of racial discriminiation. Phizacklea and Miles and Miles[46] have paid particular attention to the employment conditions of immigrants at the lower end of the labour market. They have noted the concentration of immigrants in certain industries—notably vehicle production, textiles and hotels and catering. The types of jobs which they take up often share the unfortunate characteristics of unsocial hours or an unpleasant working environment. Many researchers suggest that immigrant labour in these types of jobs provide a replacement workforce for positions in socially undesirable jobs vacated by the national workforce.

There is a considerable literature on the extent to which discrimination operates against immigrants, and in particular against certain ethnic groups seeking work or promotion in the British labour force. Undoubtedly unemployment rates are higher for certain ethnic minority groups (Table 6.3), and a considerable body of research suggests that this can largely be attributed to racial discrimination.[47] Amongst the positive results of this indictment on British society are the facts that 1) immigrant young people are more likely to stay on in education than their national peer group, and 2) social pressures may be responsible for the greater entrepreneurship of immigrants. De Beijl[48] reports that no less than 16% of immigrants were self-employed compared with 12% of nationals, with entrepreneurship being particularly high among Pakistani and Indian ethnic groups. Encouraging evidence is produced by Robinson[49] from the LFS to show that amongst Pakistani, Indian, and East African Asian ethnic minorities the percentages of the population experiencing upward social mobility has exceeded that of the population of UK origin.

Finally, in relation to the labour market impact of foreign immigration it is important to discuss a 1989 survey of British employers of foreign labour.[50] The survey was concerned to establish the reasons given by British companies for using foreign labour. The survey focussed on four sectors: electronic engineering, financial services, health, and hotels and catering. Most of those included in the survey confirmed that a major reason for employing foreign staff was the existence of a local skill shortage. To quote 'either skills were not available (e.g., in software or nursing) or indigenous labour had proved reluctant to migrate'.[51]

The survey reached the very important conclusion that there was little evidence of foreign labour being introduced as a substitute for training British nationals. Employers suggested that British nationals often shunned the jobs occupied by immigrants on account of the low wage levels of these jobs or their anti-social hours. In the South East, where most of the immigrant labour was found, tight labour market circumstances during most of the 1980s ensured that other better paid work was available for local labour, while many job seekers from other parts of the UK were dissuaded from coming to the region to poorly paid jobs because of the high cost of finding accommodation. This was not true of better paid jobs.[52] Another reason given for the use of immigrant labour[53] was that some companies saw international staff transfers as part of staff training and career development, and therefore looked favourably both on temporary emigration of British staff and temporary transfer into the UK of foreign staff.

This section has shown, therefore, that there is considerable evidence that immigration has beneficial effects for the British labour market. This is not to say that all immigration which occurs should be geared to this objective, and it remains true that many second and third-generation immigrants of certain ethnic groups remain at a disadvantage within the labour market through inadequately developed language skills, lack of relevant occupational training, discriminatory recruitment policies and other factors. On average, however, the evidence suggests that immigration (and not just those on short-term work permits) has served to increase the pool of skilled labour and to relieve skill shortages in other parts of the labour market. The involvement of foreign labour has not been a substitute to training the local population nor is there any body of evidence to suggest that immigration has cost jobs for the indigenous population.

Migration and dependency burden

It has been noted earlier in this paper that one of the main reasons advanced by policy makers for minimising immigration is the dependency burden which it might impose upon the state in terms of the costs of providing services and support to the immigrant community. Increased dependency is an issue of broader concern to the British Government because of the ageing of the indigenous population and consequently the adverse shift in the ratio of active to dependent people in the population. If migration were to be shown to add to the costs of servicing and supporting the dependent population, disproportionately relative to the tax contribution made by immigrants, then this concern would have some justification.

Green[54] has compared dependency ratios across the EC for 1985 and the projected populations of the EC states in 2025. Britain stands out uniquely in this analysis as the one state which has less than 30% of its population under 15 and less than 30% over 65 (both in 1985 and 2025). By the year 2025 there will be a small increase in the population over 65 relative to the numbers of elderly in 1985 and there will also be a drop in the number of under 15s. But the key point is that, of all EC countries, Britain should have less concern than any other over the issues surrounding increased dependency because of demographic ageing.

Table 6.10 Education Expenditure by Age Group, UK (1984-5)

	Total Spending (£m)	*Spending per head (£)*
Schools		
3-4	500	775
5-10	4300	1090
11-15	5500	1465
16-18	900	2275
Non-Advanced Further Education		
16-24	1300	2015
Higher Education		
16-24	3500	5325

Source: Pearson, Smith and White, 'Demographic Influences on Public Spending', Fiscal Studies, 1989.

It is of course true that dependency ratios are a very crude basis for measuring the economic impact of demographic influences. It has been shown that in Britain the highest expenditure groups for local government bodies are teenagers (11–15 years) during their secondary school years and the very elderly (over 75 years), because of the high costs of health and social services support.

Pearson, Smith and White[55] have illustrated these expenditure costs in terms of their calculations of cohort specific expenditure on the education and health services (Tables 6.10 and 6.11). *Per capita* expenditure on education of those in higher education is very great, but the overall cost to the state is not so high since participation rates in higher education are only 13% for those aged 19 or 20 years, compared with 94% participation for 11–15 year olds in secondary education. These rates are calculated in terms of FTEs (full-time equivalent staff) as a percentage of persons in the relevant age cohorts. The details of pension costs in relation to demographic ageing is another important issue, but one which is not addressed in this paper.

Turning to the migrant population in particular, with reference to the service costs which have been presented, there is one important point which needs to be made from the outset. It is that emigration (of both British and non-British citizens) must to some extent offset any effect of immigration in terms of the net costs of service provision. If for the moment the differential characteristics of immigrants and emigrants are put on one side, then it becomes important to ask to what extent immigrants simply replace emigrants in terms of housing costs, education costs, health service costs etc. The

Table 6.11 Spending per Head on Health and Personal Social Services (1989–92) (£ per head: figures rounded to nearest £)

Births	1300
0–4	400
5–15	300
16–64	200
64–74	600
75+	1600

Source: Pearson, Smith and White, 'Demographic Influences on Public Spending', Fiscal Studies, 1989.

Table 6.12 Summary Age Structure of Immigrants and Emigrants, UK (1990)

Age cohort	*Immigrants (thousands)*	*Emigrants (thousands)*
Under 15	41.3	41.1
15–24	85.5	67.9
25–44	118.9	104.5
45–59/64	16.3	14.2
60/65+	4.8	3.0

Source: OPCS (1991), *International Migration*, 1990. For more details see Bailey.[56]

time series information made available from the International Passenger Survey shows that Britain experienced net emigration throughout the 1960s and 1970s (except 1979). Between 1980 and 1990 net emigration occurred on four occasions.

If emigrants depart having received an investment from their country of origin in the form of previous education or training, or for example medical support, and end up working elsewhere and paying taxes elsewhere, then the net benefits in terms of the economics of the welfare system will accrue to the country of destination rather than of origin. Thus it must be argued that for most of the last three decades the British economy has been a loser through the migration system, because of net emigration from Britain—the familiar spectre of the 'brain drain'. It is ironic that, now this effect has ceased, the economic arguments have been forgotten and net immigration has been portrayed as imposing a dependency burden. No substantiated evidence has ever been produced to support this view.

Given that most emigrants and immigrants are in the most active age cohorts (in 1990, 81% of emigrants from Britain were between 15 and 59–64 years of age) it can generally be accepted that a situation of net emigration (other things being equal) will mean a net loss of resources from the welfare system, while net immigration should have the inverse effect.

A more detailed examination of British emigration and immigration flows in 1990 (using IPS data published in the OPCS monitor on *International Migration*) confirms that the migration system led in that year to a net out migration of persons under 10 years of age: a small inflow of 10–14 year olds, totalling a net gain of about 3,000 (the expensive cohort for education services): a large gain of persons aged 15–34 and 40 to 44 (the most active age cohorts in labour market terms, and in terms of tax raising—including poll tax paid by the economically inactive elements of the population): a net loss of persons in the 35 to 39 cohort and an almost even balance amongst the small number of older members of the population involved in immigration.

On the basis of this data it can be concluded that in Britain migration flows yielded an increase in that section of the population due to pay more in tax than they would expect to receive in educational, health and social benefits. Thus increased tax yield more than covers the cost of the small net gain of teenagers (still assuming that immigrant and emigrant populations have the same characteristics). The same net gain to financing the welfare system appears to have occurred in the majority of years in the 1980s through net immigration. By the same logic, in the 1970s, when net emigration was taking place, the age specific character of the migration process is likely to have had a negative effect in terms of the balance of investments made in British people who became migrants.

It is now relevant to relax the assumption that immigrants and emigrants share the same characteristics. Clearly activity rates, unemployment rates, birth rates, education costs and health and welfare costs vary by ethnic group and by immigrant nationality. No recent systematic data set exists, however, to inform the researcher of the current, or recent, tax receipts versus costs of supporting immigrants and their families. In the absence of such data it is impossible to robustly argue either that immigrants impose a net dependency burden on the UK economy or that they make a net contribution to the welfare services through direct and indirect taxation and through taxation to both central and local government. As mentioned earlier in this paper, the last study of this kind known to the author was undertaken by the National Institute in relation to the 1960–6 Commonwealth influx. The conclusion was that the net impact was likely to be positive. To quote from Jones and Smith:[57]

> There is some evidence that average income per employed New Commonwealth worker is lower than the national level, but we also know that labour force participation rates are higher for the New Commonwealth than for the indigenous population, so total household income may well not deviate much from the national average....While it is not practicable to estimate the relative contributions of immigrants in the form of national insurance contributions and tax payments, it seems unlikely that, if New Commonwealth immigrants do pay less, the difference would more than outweigh their smaller share of the social services.

Since the 1960s the migration system, as has been shown, has shifted considerably towards the acceptance of a lower proportion of immigrants for settlement and an increase in the proportion of entrants on short- or long-term work permits. The implications of this must be a shift away from immigration flows with long-term cost implications as settlers age, become inactive, and look increasingly towards welfare services and retirement benefits. Current immigration involves increasing numbers of skilled transients, who contribute to the tax base of the economy during their limited stay in the UK, but make relatively little demand on the so-called 'welfare state'. In addition the suggestion made in relation to Table 6.9 on the skill levels of the immigrant stock of the UK would point to immigrants having a greater potential to pay taxes than the local population, given their higher proportional respresentation amongst professional and managerial staff.

Much more detailed information is available about the so-called 'dependency burden' and tax contributions of immigrants to Canada and Australia.[58] A study carried out by the Economic Council of Canada in relation to Canada's published Immigration plan concludes that new immigrants, through paying extra taxes, make a small net contribution towards reducing Canada's demographic dependency burden. However, the 'reduction of the tax burden for the rest of the population is quite insignificant'.[59] In other words immigration as a policy measure would not be justified solely on the basis of reducing the dependency burden on the rest of the population, but on the other hand immigrants to Canada certainly are not expected to add to that burden. The National Population Council for Australia[60] in addressing the same issues concludes that the impact of migrants on government revenue and expenditure is much the same as for other Australians except for three important areas:

- Most migrants enter Australia after having completed their education. Thus net transfers by migrants over a lifetime are likely to be higher than for other Australians.
- Because the average migrant is younger than the average Austrialian-born person, immigration over the next forty years will act to bolster numbers at working age when the large baby boom generations are in aged dependency.
- There are significant costs to governments in providing ethno-specific services, such as English language training.

Similar arguments seem valid in the UK situation. In both Canada and Australia it is also argued that the increased investment in physical infrastructure associated with population growth by immigration favours a larger overall population size on economic efficiency grounds. This last argument seems less appropriate in a UK context where, first, the overall population is already much greater, second the nature of infrastructural investment has followed a very different economic history, and third there is a stagnant or perhaps declining population situation.

This section of the paper has sought to present the fragmentary evidence which exists concerning the economic dependency burden which might be imposed by immigration. It is concluded tentatively that migrants to the UK are likely to make a very small net contribution to the economy in terms of the balance between the taxes paid relative to the extra expenditure required to support them. For most of the 1970s and part of the 1980s the main problem for the UK welfare system relative to migration was its position relative to a system of net emigration. The situation of net immigration which has emerged in recent years should not be a cause for economic concern. Net immigration, under the present conditions, is not likely to impose any net-costs on the British economy (in terms of the taxes versus services trade-off) and may even produce small net gains. In these economic circumstances politicians should consider very carefully the arguments for a more liberal immigration policy, not only of those persons who have valuable skills to contribute to the British economy but also of those migrants who are seeking to enter the country as refugees and on other bases.

Policy issues

This chapter has sought to examine the economic basis for Britain's position on immigration. It has been argued from evidence relating to the work permit system that there is clear evidence that British businesses need a certain level of immigration of certain skill groups. As pointed out in an earlier section of this paper, work permits are granted for a significant number of immigrant entries to the UK each year. The full scale of labour market demand for immigration cannot, however, be judged from the number of work permits issued. First, many applications made for labour permits by employees are turned down by the government. Second, very large numbers of Europeans enter Britain to work, yet need no work permit under EC law. Hence demand is much greater than shown by work permit data. For this reason the paper referred frequently to data from the International Passenger Survey to substantiate the views that there is a broader demand from the British economy for skilled transient migration from a range of destinations. Third, independent surveys of specific occupational groups such as nurses,[61] have been referred to to illustrate the point that the British economy could benefit substantially from selective immigration of a range of skilled labour.

In addition to selective labour immigration it has been noted that entrepreneurial migration could have significant economic benefits for Britain, just as it has had for other advanced economies. It has also been argued that refugees and immigration of less skilled labour does not result in significant net costs for the economy and may in the long run result in net gains. The question which this section of the paper addresses is whether government policy on immigration maximises the economic benefits which could be achieved.

Many of the skilled transient migrants, of the kind identified earlier in this paper as being of the greatest economic benefit to the United Kingdom, enter the country under the work permit system. Up until 1991 there were long delays in dealing with applications for work permits and the revision of the work permit system has been welcomed by most members of the business community. However, it is important to ask whether the system serves the British economy as a whole or only certain privileged groups. An analysis of work permits by Salt[62] shows that by far the majority are issued to skilled workers from only two countries—Japan and the USA and that most of these permits are for people who gain employment in the South East of

England. This undoubtedly reflects the high proportion of permits which are allocated for inter-company transfers by trans-national corporations from Japan and the USA. It is only a slight exaggeration to say that the current work permit system exists primarily to serve trans-national employees wishing to enter the South East.

Why do skilled workers from other countries, and to other parts of the UK, gain so few work permits? The answer to this is complex, but includes the following elements. First, immigrants from the EC (and from EFTA countries from January 1994) are not required to have work permits. Therefore the work permit system does not fully reflect the substantial demand for foreign labour which exists in Britain, since many of the most important countries are not covered by the scheme, but International Passenger Survey and Labour Force Survey data show that substantial skill exchanges of similar types of immigrants (in professional and economic terms) take place with the EC.

Second, work permits are granted on the basis of applications by employers rather than by immigrants. Consequently, skills are more likely to be introduced from those countries with which employers have strong contacts, irrespective of whether this is the most appropriate source in terms of the benefits to the British economy. The system does not serve well those immigrants who have skills needed by the British economy, but who are not well linked to potential employers.

Third, there is no clearly established basis by which the Department of Employment determines those skills which are in acute short supply in the UK and, as noted earlier, the list of occupations appear to change very frequently and without explanation or notice. Some commentators would suggest that employers are in a better position to judge their labour requirements than the Department of Employment, and would therefore question the level of work permit refusals. The lack of transparency in the decision making process opens the system to criticism by those who fail to receive work permits. Fourth, the scheme is not designed to assist entrepreneurial immigration of persons who may be self-employed. As noted earlier, a separate channel does exist for business immigration but this is defined on the basis of applicants proving that they have a large capital sum available for investment in job creating opportunities, rather than on evidence of entrepreneurial potential.

Fifth, one effect of the streamlining of tier one applications for work permits may simply have been to create longer delays for tier two applicants, although it is still too early to be sure about the long-term effects of the switch in the policy.

Sixth, the revised work permit scheme no longer has a section on the application form (as under the old scheme) which permits potential migrants and their employers to present economic arguments for being granted entry to the British labour market. Only the Department of Employment is effectively given the right to judge which skills are needed, with no opportunity for applicants to demonstrate their economic value.

Finally, the revised system has made it much harder for work permits to be extended than under the old scheme. Currently employers need to promote full documentation to obtain an extension to a work permit, for an employee which the Department of Employment has already judged to be of economic value in relation to the initial application. As a result the costs to a company of sustaining foreign labour has risen as a result of the revision to the work permit scheme. In summary, the work permit system used by Britain seems to serve primarily as a form of entry control, of blocking or delaying the temporary immigration of would-be migrants from outside the EC who do not have strong contacts with a large scale employer in the UK. It is not primarily a system which seeks, on a rational economic basis, to achieve labour market adjustments through immigration to meet the broader needs of the British economy.

If the needs of the economy were to be met, then a much lower priority should be assigned within the work permit scheme to protecting the resident labour force. In place of this the scheme should 'rely more on employers' judgement of their own needs',[63] implying a much lower rejection rate of work permit applications by employers. In 1991 the refusal rate for the main scheme was 19.6%; in 1990 it was 20.8%. For Commonwealth nationals, however, the refusal rate in 1991 was 35.3%, for foreign nationals only 13.5%. Initial data for 1992 suggests that the new procedures may have reduced the number of refusals.[64]

In addition greater investment would be required to research systematically the skilled needs of the British economy so that appropriate migrants could be actively encouraged to come to UK, in contrast to the current system which remains purely reactive to limited requests.

Perhaps the greatest problem for Britain is that the work permit system is concerned with temporary migrants and consequently involves work permits of limited duration. No clear migration channel exists to permit immigration of persons who are capable of making a contribution to Britain's economy on a permanent basis other than the rather exclusive business scheme for persons with £200,000 or more. Permanent settlement is assumed to relate to cases of family re-unification or persons seeking asylum in the UK. While such entrants may make a significant economic contribution, the nature of immigration legislation for these two latter categories tries to separate out 'genuine' cases from so-called 'economic' migrants, thus implying (without any evidence to support the case) that refugees and spouses are 'uneconomic' and that all other categories of permanent immigrants are to be dissuaded from entering the country, regardless of any economic contibution which they could make.

Thus, if Britain were to adopt an immigration policy which was to truly serve the needs of the economy, it would require not only an improved work permit system to cope with short-run fluctuations in demand but also a longer term strategy. Other countries operate a range of schemes selectively to recruit key workers. Most notorious are the quota systems used in North America. Poorly managed or misinformed systems run the risk of promoting permanent immigration of skills not required by the economy, but Britain's lack of any scheme for meeting the economy's long-term labour needs is equally unsatisfactory. More adequate labour market research and long-term skill needs is required, coupled to a pro-active rather than re-active system of selecting persons for permanent settlement.

If evidence from countries as disparate as Germany and Canada is to be believed, advanced economies have much to gain from permanent immigration of certain skill groups. These countries have adopted very different policies on immigration from the UK. Two aspects are highlighted here. The first is the information base on which decisions about immigration are taken. The second is the machinery used to select migrants.

The quality of cohort data for immigrant groups in Australia has already been discussed. This data has been used to good effect in advising government on alternative scenarios for future immigration, making it possible to estimate the social integration and contribution of different groups over time.[65] In Canada, cohort data is also available for immigrants by place of birth and period of immigration to Canada cross-tabulated by key variables such as language proficiency, labour force participation rates adjusted for age, unemployment levels and duration, earnings and occupational status, occupational distribution by gender, and receipt of government welfare assistance. Analysis of this detailed information makes it possible to make informed policy decisions about immigration options for Canada.[66] In Britain the Labour Force Survey gives only limited insights on some of these issues and no systematic monitoring of immigrant cohorts has been attempted in recent years to examine the overall economic impact of immigrant groups.

The second main distinction worthy of note here is that countries such as the USA and Canada select immigrants on the basis of a migration policy which decides migration quotas for each year, and selects immigrants for these quotas on the basis of a points system. Such an approach faces a range of problems, such as determining accurately in advance which skill categories should be encouraged to migrate and which should be discouraged. Another oft cited difficulty is that, while migrants may enter under one part of the quota system, (e.g. in relation to a particular skill group) it is not easy to ensure that they remain in this category after being granted entry. What is important however is that the system signals to potential immigrants the desire of the host country to mould their labour market in a positive fashion.

Britain seems to see immigration as a threat to an existing social or economic order. Immigration policy appears to be constructed largely to protect an established identity by limiting immigrant entry to privileged economic and social relations. By contrast Canadian, US and Australian immigration policy seems to view immigraton as of much greater economic benefit to the host society. Immigration is perceived as a means to build the future and immigration policy is used to select those migrants which are most likely to participate in the building of the new identities of the future.

This paper has not argued that Britain should model itself in migration terms on any other country, whether European or North American. Britain has experienced specific historical and geographical circumstances which have positioned it in a particular location in relation to the world labour market and relative to international labour migration systems. Its migration policies need to be tailored to this context. What the paper has argued, however, is that a selective immigration policy which takes greater account of the economic dimensions of international skill transfers would be rather different from the current policy. It would consider new ways to facilitate entrepreneurial immigration. It would see positive economic potential in many of the persons who apply to enter as refugees and it would switch from a philosophy of excluding potential migrants to 'protect' the status quo, to a system of positive selection of those immigrants with most to contribute to Britain.

Conclusions

This paper has tried to explore certain economic aspects of immigration. It has argued that immigration statistics should not be confused with data on certain ethnic minorities. An economic case for immigration cannot rest purely on evidence of economic growth outpacing labour force growth, nor on labour force projections which identify a reduction or stagnation in labour supply. It has been shown that these are not sufficient conditions to argue for immigration.

Three aspects of labour demand do, however, provide grounds to suggest that labour market benefits for Britain could arise from encouraging selective immigration. First, it has been argued that certain skill shortages exist within the UK economy which, in the short run at least, should continue to be overcome through immigration of persons via the British work permit scheme. Second, it has been argued that changes in the organisation of labour, in particular within large international companies, necessitate the international circulation of staff. Third, it has been mentioned briefly that there may be grounds for encouraging entrepreneurial immigration as a device which generates jobs rather than filling jobs by immigration. In the absence of robust data sets it is difficult to judge the overall economic impact of less skilled immigration to the UK. The limited survey material which is available would suggest that this type of immigration is not at the cost of the indigenous workforce, neither causing job losses nor job displacement.

Throughout this paper evidence has been produced in relation to virtually every aspect of the immigration system to show that inadequate research by government and a poor statistical base is a source of misinformation and weak policy making. Evaluation of British labour market trends led to the conclusion that policy makers need to determine urgently whether there are selective skill shortages which are damaging the UK economy and how best these can be met. In relation to the British work permit scheme it has been argued that the government has failed to invest in adequate data collection mechanisms to meet the short-run needs of the economy. In relation to the economic costs of immigration it has been shown that no comprehensive survey has been undertaken since the 1960s. In short, government immigration policy has no adequate research data base to justify its economic objections to higher levels of immigration. Nor does data exist to support the application of policy tools such as the work-permit scheme in its present form. Providing an adequate statistical base should be a pre-requisite to any further policy developments on immigration, regardless of their objectives or political orientation.

It has been argued that Britain holds a negative ideology towards immigration and may as a result gain much less in economic terms from immigration than might otherwise be achieved. It would seem that the government's current stand on immigration is not determined primarily on economic grounds. If it is to sustain its current policies, a stronger economic argument against immigration needs to be made and to be supported by economic data. In the absence of such data and in the face of the economic arguments which have been presented in favour of immigration in this paper, one is forced to conclude that current British immigration policy is governed primarily by political and cultural considerations. If Britain is to avoid the accusation of being racist in its immigration stance, then a serious economic investigation of the grounds of immigration policy seems long overdue.

NOTES

1 B. Maan, 'The New Scots', Edinburgh, Donald, 1992.
2 Peach, 'Immigrants and the 1981 Urban Riots in Britain', *Contemporary Studies of Migration*, ed. P. White and B. Vander Knaap, Geobooks, pp.143–54.
3 Maan, op.cit.
4 L. Foster, A. Marshall and L. Williams, 'Discrimination against Immigrant Workers in Australia', *World Employment Programme Discussion Paper*, no.34, Geneva, ILO, 1991.

Notes

5 R. de Beijl, 'Discrimination of Migrant Workers in Western Europe', *World Employment Programme Discussion Paper*, no.49, Geneva, ILO, 1990.
6 J. Salt and J. Kitching, 'Foreign Workers and the UK Labour Market', *Employment Gazette*, no.98, 1990, pp.538–46.
7 K. Jones and A. Smith, 'The Economic Impact of Commonwealth Immigration', Cambridge University Press, 1970.
8 T. Hammar, 'Comparing European and North American International Migration', *International Migration Review*, no.23, 1989, pp.631–7. A. Zolberg, 'The Next Waves: Migration Theory for a Changing World', *International Migration Review*, no.23, 1989, pp.403–30.
9 Population Reference Bureau, *Intercom*, May 1978.
10 B. Heisler and M. Heisler, 'From Foreign Workers to Settlers', Sage, Beverley Hills, CA, 1986. L. Bacci, 'South-North Migration: A Comparative Approach to North American and European experiences', Conference paper presented to the OECD International Conference on Migration, Rome, 13–15 March, 1991.
11 G. Urbani and E. Granaglia, *Immigrazione e diritti di cittadinanaza*, Rome, Editalia, 1991.
12 P. White, 'International migration in the 1970s', *West European Population Change*, ed. A. Findlay and P. White, Croom Helm, Beckenham, 1986.
13 R. Bohning, *The migration of workers in the United Kingdom and the European Community*, London, Oxford University Press, London, 1972.
14 R. Lawless, A. Findlay and A. Findlay, *Return migration to the Maghreb*, London, Arc, 1982.
15 White, op.cit.
16 J. Salt, 'Europe's Foreign Labour Migrants in Transition' *Geography*, no.70, 1985, pp.162–8.
17 'Population Issues and Australia's Future', National Population Council (Australia), Canberra, 1991.
18 *Economic outlook 1960–90*, Paris, OECD, 1992.
19 A. Findlay, 'From Settlers to Skilled Transients', *Geoforum*, no.19, 1988, pp.401–10.
20 D. Massey, *Spatial Divisions of Labour*, London, Macmillan, 1984.
21 A. Champion and A. Townsend, *Contemporary Britain*, London, Arnold, 1990.
22 D. Owen, 'Migration and employment', *Migration Processes and Patterns*, no.2, ed. J. Stillwell *et al.*, London, Belhaven, 1992, pp.205–24.
23 F. Frobel *et al.*, *The New International Division of Labour*, Cambridge University Press, 1980.
24 Owen, op.cit., p.223.
25 A. Green, 'Changing Labour Processes and Internal Migration', *Migration Processes and Patterns*, no.1, A. Champran *et al.*, London,

Belhaven, 1992, pp.105–18.

26 Green, op.cit., p.6.

27 J. Lonnroth, 'Labour Market Policies for the 1990s', unpublished paper presented at the OECD International Conference on Migration, Rome, 13–15 March 1991.

28 Ibid, p.13.

29 Ibid. p.15.

30 J. Seymour, 'Labour Migration and the UK Work Permit Scheme', unpublished paper presented at the IPPR/Frierich Ebert Foundation seminar on The Economic and Social Impact of Migration, London, 6–7 March 1993, p.7.

31 Ibid.

32 J. Salt, 'International Migration and the United Kingdom', report of the United Kingdom SOPEMI correspondent to the OECD, 1992 (unpublished), p.10.

33 Findlay, op.cit., J. Salt and A. Findlay, 'International Migration of Highly Skilled Manpower', *The Impact of International Migration on Developing Countries*, ed. R. Appleyard, OECD, Paris, 1989, pp.159–82.

34 M. Kritz and F. Cases, 'Science and Technology Transfers and Migration Flows', *International Migration Systems*, ed. M. Kritz *et al.* Oxford, Clarendon Press, 1992, pp.221–43.

35 J. Onslow-Cole, 'Work Permits, A Review of Changes to the Scheme', *Immigration and Nationality Law and Practice*, no.5, 1991, pp.50–2.

36 Written answer, 5 February 1993.

37 *Home Office Statistical Bulletin*, issue 14/93, London, Government Statistical Service.

38 J. Buchan, I. Seccombe and J. Ball, 'The International Mobility of Nurses', *Institute of Manpower Studies Report*, no.230, Brighton, IMS, 1992.

39 P. Trott, 'Practical Problems for Businessmen', *Immigration and Nationality Law and Practice*, no.4, 1990, pp.73–4.

40 Ibid., p.111.

41 T. Straubhaar and K. Zimmermann, 'Towards a European Migration Policy', *Munchener Wirtschaftswissenshaftliche Beitrage*, 92/2, Ludwig Maximilians University, Munich, 1991. K. Zimmermann, 'European Migration Policy', *International Economic Insights*, no.3, p.9, 1992. F. Rivera-Batiz, *et al.*, 'US Immigration Policy Reform in the 1980s', New York, Praeger, 1991.

42 G. Borjas, *Friends or Strangers?*, Basic Books, New York, 1990. J. Simon, *The Economic Consequences of Immigration*, Oxford, Blackwell, 1989.

43 Straubhaar and Zimmermann, op.cit.

44 A. Gieseck, V. Heilemann and H.D. von Loeffelholz, 'Economic and Social Implications of Migration into the F.R. of Germany', paper presented to the IPPR/Friedrich Ebert Foundation Seminar on the

Notes

Economic and Social Impact of Migration, London, 6–7 March 1993. R. Ulrich, 'The Impact of Foreigners on the public purse in Germany', paper presented to the IPPR/Friedrich Ebert Foundation seminar on the Economic and Social Impact of Migration, London, 6–7 March 1993. K. Zimmermann, 'Labour Market Impacts of Immigration', paper presented to the IPPR/Friedrich Ebert Foundation seminar on The Economic and Social Impact of Migration, London, 6–7 March 1993.

45 S. Baron, 'Blut und Boden', *Wirtshaftswoche*, no.44, 25 October 1991.

46 A. Phizacklea and R. Miles, *Labour and Racism*, London, Routledge and Kegan Paul, 1980. R. Miles, *Capitalism and Unfree Labour*, London, Tavistock, 1990.

47 M. Cross, *Vocational Training of Young Migrants in the United Kingdom*, Luxembourg, Official Publications of the EC, 1986. A. Newnham, *Employment, Unemployment and Black People*, London, Runnymede Trust, 1986. J. Brennan and P. McGeevor, *Ethnic Minorities and the Graduate Labour Market*, CRE, London, 1990.

48 de Beijl, op.cit.

49 V. Robinson, 'The Internal Migration of Britain's Ethnic Population', *Migration Processes and Patterns*, ed. A. Champion *et al.*, New York, Belhaven, no.1, 1992, pp.188–200.

50 Salt and Kitching, op.cit.

51 Ibid., p.545.

52 A. Fielding, 'Inter-regional Migration and Social Change', *Transactions*, IBG, no.14, 1989, pp.24–36.

53 Salt and Kitching, op.cit.

54 A. Green, op.cit.

55 M. Pearson, S. Smith and S. White, 'Demographic Influences on Public Spending', *Fiscal Studies*, no.1, 1989, pp.48–65.

56 J. Bailey, 'International migration', *Population Trends*, no. 67, 1992, pp.29–34.

57 Jones and Smith, op.cit.

58 F. Hawkins, *Critical Years in Immigration: Canada and Australia Compared*, Montreal and Kingston, McGill-Queens University Press, 1989.

59 Economic Council of Canada, *Economic and Social impact of Immigration*, Information Canada, Ottowa, 1991, p.51.

60 National Population Council (Australia), op.cit.

61 Buchan, Seccombe and Ball, op.cit.

62 Salt, op.cit.

63 CBI, 'Review of the Work Permit System', *Employment Affairs Report*, no.29, 1989, pp.12–15.

64 Department of Employment unpublished data reproduced in Salt, op.cit.

65 National Population Council (Australia), op.cit.

66 Economic Council of Canada, op.cit.

67 J. Haskey, 'The Ethnic Minority Population of Great Britain', ***Population Trends***, no.60, 1990, pp.35–8.
68 Robinson, op.cit.
69 Immigrant Statistics Unit, 'Population of New Commonwealth and Pakistant Ethnic Origin', ***Population Trends***, no.16, 1979, pp.22–8.

[2]

Ethics, National Sovereignty and the Control of Immigration

Myron Weiner
Massachusetts Institute of Technology

This paper examines the debate as to whether migration is a basic human right or if the claims of outsiders are superseded by the principle of national sovereignty – the moral obligation of states to do the best for their own citizens. In evaluating migration and refugees it focuses on issues of open borders, migration selectivity, the capacity of sovereign states to control entry, the claims of refugees, the relationship between sovereignty and justifiable intervention, and the role of public opinion and morals throughout migration policies.

In a world of global inequalities, persecution, and violence, are states ethically obligated to open their borders as wide as is economically feasible and politically acceptable to their citizens? Is migration a basic human right or are the claims of outsiders superseded by the principle of national sovereignty that the moral obligation of states is to do the best for their own citizens (*see* Weiner, 1993:1–35)? How should we weigh these conflicting moral claims? This article examines the debate between these two positions, focusing on the issues of open borders, migration selectivity, the capacity of sovereign states to control entry, the moral claims of refugees, the relationship between sovereignty[1] and justifiable intervention, and the role of public opinion in migration policies.

Underlying much of the debate over migration and refugee policies is the fundamental moral contradiction between the notion that emigration is widely regarded as a matter of human rights (for a liberal view on the right of emigration, *see* Whelan, 1981:636–653) while immigration is regarded as a matter of national sovereignty (*see* Sohn and Buergenthal, 1992:3). The United Nations Universal Declaration of Human Rights and the Helsinki Accords assert a universal right of emigration; yet all governments and international organizations agree that governments have the right to determine those to admit and to whom citizenship should be granted. But if people are free to leave, where are they to go? Are states then obliged to take in migrants from poor countries? Refugees in flight? Are they obliged to grant citizenship to guestworkers and to regularize the status of illegal migrants? Underlying many of these policy questions are fundamental moral issues posed, on the one hand, by the conflicting claims and rights of those who seek admission and, on the other, by the concerns of governments and their citizens to control their borders and

[1]The concept of state or national sovereignty is used here not only in the familiar sense of legal or political freedom by a government from external control – though obviously bounded and contingent in numerous ways – but also in the sense of the obligations of a state to its citizens.

protect themselves against what they regard as threats to their security, economic well-being, political stability, and cultural identity. Political theorists have traditionally been concerned with defining the rights and duties of citizens and of those who live within national boundaries, only recently with the claims of outsiders who seek admission. Over the centuries, political theorists have defined and expanded our conception of the rights of individuals, but they have done so within the framework of the state. As a result, in liberal democratic societies the right to move within the country has become as much of a right as freedom of speech, assembly or religion, but international law does not guarantee the right of people to move from one country to another. The question is whether the moral justification for freedom of movement within countries can and should be extended to freedom of movement among countries.

Migration and refugee policies raise moral issues because, directly or indirectly, they involve the exercise of coercion. Within countries, restrictions on the movement of people are decried because they are coercive. However, it is also coercion that prevents people from freely moving across international boundaries. Coercion takes place when ships carrying would-be refugees are halted at sea and sent home, guards prevent undocumented migrants from crossing a border, refugees are confined to camps or forcibly repatriated, illegal migrants are rounded up by the police, employers are fined for hiring illegal migrants, and individuals are arrested for providing sanctuary to unsuccessful refugee claimants. Whenever coercion is employed by the state to prevent people from doing what they want to without apparent harm to others – both within and outside the state – a moral issue arises.

Migration policy also raises the issue of fairness. Citizenship is determined by country of birth or by the citizenship of our parents, not by choice. Consequently, one's life chances depend upon being born in a prosperous country or to parents who are citizens of a prosperous country, where there are opportunities for advancement and there is no persecution. Individuals born in a poor, autocratic country, where there are few opportunities, and where those who have particular beliefs or belong to particular ethnic or religious communities are treated badly, are truly unfortunate. The fact that one's opportunities can so strongly and permanently be constrained by the simple chance of birth seems unfair.

RESTRICTIVE ENTRY

To most citizens, however, the argument in favor of national sovereignty with respect to control over migration appears to be commonsensical. Let us consider what the consequences might be if a country had completely open borders to anyone who wished to enter. While this approach seems to take the moral high ground by avoiding coercion, it clearly jeopardizes the well-being of the host population and threatens politicide. A safe and prosperous country that declares its borders open risks being overwhelmed by a massive influx of immigrants from poor and/or violent countries. If the country then provides these immigrants with the same benefits it offers its own citizens (education for children, healthcare, unemployment benefits, etc.), its social services and welfare services may be stretched to the limit. The country's own poor may find themselves pushed aside by migrants prepared to work at lower wages. If the number of migrants is large enough, the local population may find itself outnumbered by people who speak another language, belong to another culture, and perhaps seek to change the political system. As the number of migrants grows, the local population may become xenophobic, resulting in the growth of antimigrant political organizations, violence, and social disorder. Poor countries might also be at risk if their borders are open. Peasants from densely populated neighboring countries might freely enter in search of land and employment, thereby putting pressure on the local population. Refugees from civil conflict might cross the border and damage the local ecology by cutting firewood, consuming water, generating waste, and destroying grasslands. The indigenous population might become acutely afraid of domination by the intruding ethnic group, especially if the community is one with which it has a history of enmity.

Any country, rich or poor, that opened its borders might soon find other states taking advantage of its beneficent policy. A neighboring country whose elite wanted a more homogeneous society could now readily expel its minorities. A government that wanted a more egalitarian society could dump its unemployed and its poor. An authoritarian regime could rid itself of its opponents; a country could empty its jails, mental institutions, and homes for the aged. In an extreme case, an overcrowded populous country could take over a hypothetically generous country simply by "transferring" a large part of its population, and an aggressive country would no longer need tanks and missiles for an invasion.

Notwithstanding these objections, some political theorists argue that liberal democratic societies ought to have open borders, or that, short of open borders, a liberal democratic country should take in as many migrants and refugees as its citizenry will allow. The primary criterion for admission, these theorists insist, should not be the needs of the host country but the plight of those who seek admission.

THE DEBATE OVER OPEN ADMISSIONS

The philosopher John Rawls (1971) provides the starting point for theorists who take this position. Rawls argues that people, not knowing anything about their own personal situation (*e.g.*, their class, race, or ability) who could choose the kind of society in which they wanted to live from behind this "veil of ignorance," would follow self-interest and choose to live in a society in which institutions were constructed to benefit those who were the least well off (what Rawls calls "the difference principle"). Inequalities of wealth and power and income, in other words, would be acceptable only insofar as they ultimately benefited those in the society who were least well off. In this aspect, Rawls' theory stems from the assumptions of classical liberalism, with its notions of liberty, justice as fairness, and the right to equality.

For Rawls, the "original position" (starting from a "veil of ignorance") is necessary for thinking about the issues of justice within a given society, but others have argued that this approach should be applied universally across different societies. Joseph Carens has systematically expounded this position in a number of articles (1992a:25–47, 1988a:207–230, 1992b:31–44, 1991:18–29, 1987a:413–443, 1987b:251–273, 1987c, 1988b:41–60). Others who also argue for a universal theory of justice include Peter Singer (1988:111–130), Charles Beitz (1979), Henry Shue (1980), Brian Barry (1973), and two British legal scholars, Ann Dummett and Andrew Nicol (1992).

These philosophers and legal scholars argue that, since it is purely a matter of chance whether we are born in a country that is peaceful, democratic, and prosperous or in a country that is poor, authoritarian, and torn by civil conflict, starting from the original position we would all clearly prefer to be born in the peaceful, democratic, prosperous society. From a liberal egalitarian perspective there are, therefore, no grounds for limiting membership in any society to those who happen to be born there. Birthplace and parentage are, as Carens writes, "arbitrary from a moral point of view" (1987b:261).

Free migration across open borders would enable those who were born in disadvantaged countries to improve their position by moving to a place where they would have greater opportunity. If, by moving, the worse-off can thereby improve their position, Carens argues, the well-being of current citizens is irrelevant. Carens also says that it is irrelevant if open borders generate an influx of a people from another culture or if the numbers of migrants are large enough to undermine the dominance of the existing culture. The claims of locals, Carens asserts, should not be given priority over the claims of others simply by virtue of their citizenship.

> The best immigration policy from a utilitarian perspective would be the one that maximized overall economic gains. In this calculation, current citizens would enjoy no privileged position. The gains and losses of aliens would count just as much. Now the dominant view among both classical and neoclassical economics is that the free mobility of capital and labor is essential to the maximization of overall economic gains. But the free mobility of labor requires open borders. So, despite the fact that the economic costs to current citizens are morally relevant to the utilitarian framework, they would probably not be sufficient to justify restrictions. (Carens, 1987b:263)

The moral argument for free migration thus grows out of the reality that there are gross economic inequalities between states. When differences are vast, freedom of movement would enable individuals to avail themselves of opportunities to improve their income and general well-being and to increase their freedom and safety. From this point of view, both notions of *jus sanguinis* and *jus solis* are fundamentally unfair, for they deny freedom of choice. Why should citizenship rights automatically be conferred on individuals who, through no act of their own, happen to be born in a particular place or to parents who are citizens of that country?

Yet, while the arguments put forth by Rawls, Carens and others make open borders and free movement seem morally clearcut, there are contending moral considerations which suggest that open borders may generate great injustices. Michael Walzer, in his 1983 book, asserts that it is also moral to develop policies which preserve a particular way of life (*see also* Sidgwick, 1891; Schuck and Smith, 1985). Walzer distinguishes between "members" and "strangers," *i.e.*, those who belong to our political community and those who do not, and he writes that "the theory of justice must allow for the territorial state, specifying the rights of its inhabitants and recognizing the collective right of admission and refusal" (Schuck and Smith, 1985:44). Countries, writes Walzer, are somewhat like clubs which can (and should) regulate admissions (Walzer, 1983). We, who are members of a community, define who we are, what kind of community we want to have, and whom we should admit into it. We can give membership to strangers, but we are not obliged to except under special circumstances.

If someone is in urgent need and the risks and costs of giving aid are low, we ought to help the injured stranger – not on the basis of justice but on the basis of charity. But giving help – which may lead us to offer the hospitality of our home (or our country) – does not necessarily require that we admit the stranger to membership in our community.

Walzer further argues that people who belong to a community will defend their local politics and culture against strangers, and that if the state did not take on this responsibility, we would not have a world without walls but rather we would "create a thousand petty fortresses. . . . The distinctiveness of cultures and groups depends upon closure and, without it, cannot be conceived as a stable feature of human life. If this distinctiveness is valued, as most people seem to believe, then closure must be permitted somewhat" (p. 39). Walzer therefore finds value in the sovereign state not because it is exclusive, but because it provides for greater inclusiveness than would be possible if it did not exist. Building upon Walzer, then, the debate over open borders and the broader issue of whether governments have greater obligations to their own citizens than to others has grown to involve the philosophers who call themselves "communitarians." The issue is whether "community" is valued and, therefore, whether members of a community have rights and obligations toward one another that transcend those toward individuals who do not belong to the community. For our purposes, "community" can be defined as coterminous with nationality, and "nationals" can be defined as citizens of a political institution known as the state.

Global egalitarians dismiss the idea of community as an impediment to a just world. "The socialist tradition," explains David Miller, "has been overwhelmingly hostile to nationality as a source of identity, usually regarding it merely as an artificially created impediment to the brotherhood of man" (1992:87). Like the socialists, the globalists (and many with this view would regard themselves as socialists) place the highest value on egalitarianism. Consequently, those who subscribe to the ideals of global justice put aside notions of community and the value which a community places upon itself – which may be liberty, a sense of common identity and mutual obligation to one another.

The global egalitarian position is thus in opposition to those who want to improve the well-being of the population within their own country and who, therefore, weigh proposals for immigration against such considerations as its impact on the welfare system, employment, the delivery of educational benefits and healthcare, the environment, and intergroup relations. From this perspective, migration should be permitted only when it best serves the interests of the country and its citizens rather than serving the interests of the migrants. Many global egalitarians advocating immigration seek to avoid this conundrum by stressing the compatibility of migration with national well-being, for example by pointing to the contribution migrants make to economic growth, the taxes they pay in return for social benefits, and the benefits of cultural diversity. However, those who take this latter position in effect have conceded the argument that whether a country should or should not have migrants needs to be based upon an empirical consideration of costs and benefits, rather than a philosophical position in favor of global equality.

For globalists, the highest moral value is distributive justice. The preservation of a nation's existence, its political order, political institutions, and cultural identity, and of the well-being and interests of its citizens are subordinate to the goal of global distributive justice.[2] Global redistribution – through open borders or foreign aid – is regarded not as a humanitarian act, but as a moral imperative. Globalists thus pay little attention to whether the adoption of their principles in a world comprised of sovereign states would lead to an improvement or a worsening of the human condition in any specific country. The adoption, for example, of a globalist position on migration by a single country puts that country at risk when other countries choose not to open their borders. As we suggested earlier, migration can then become an act of aggression against the country with open borders as one country disposes of its unwanted upon another. Under such circumstances, an open door to migrants might very well

[2]Indeed, Rawl's focus on distributive justice within a society does not take into account other legitimate moral objectives, such as enhancing opportunities for individuals and creating a social and economic order that will increase national wealth.

do more harm than good to large numbers of people. Moreover, if a state chooses not to give preference to the well-being of its own citizens over the well-being of citizens of other countries, then, as Walzer suggests, local communities and regions within the country might protect themselves by imposing restrictions upon entry or discriminating against foreign residents, generating the very opposite result from what the globalists intend (for a forceful statement of this view, *see* King, 1983:525–536).

There are, of course, many sensible reasons why governments might welcome immigrants: they may meet labor-force needs in industry, the service sector, or agriculture; they may bring cultural diversity and cosmopolitanism to countries whose citizens would like to be less parochial; they may provide entrepreneurship and other needed skills and talents; the country may regard itself as a "home" to people with whom its citizens have historic, cultural or religious ties; and families of immigrant origin may want to bring in their relatives and other members of their ethnic community. A government may also choose to open its borders to one or more neighboring countries with which it shares free trade and similar living standards. But these policies fall within the normal framework of a state's domestic and foreign policies. None implies moral obligation.

In addition, there may be ideological reasons for a country to encourage migration. For traditional immigrant countries such as the United States, Canada and Australia, there is a popular ideological presumption in favor of continued migration. Many Americans, for example, see immigration as a way of reasserting the image of America as a land of opportunity, still capable of offering success and fortune to those admitted. For Israel, the admission of Jews from anywhere in the world is essential to the Zionist conception of the state as a haven for world Jewry. The costs of absorption, the availability of housing and employment, the potential social dislocations are not relevant considerations in deciding whether Jews should be admitted.

However, though there are numerous reasons a country might support and encourage immigration, many governments choose to severely limit or even close their borders to migration. The reasons given for restricting migration, as previously noted, are numerous. In some countries local inhabitants are fearful that a large influx of immigrants will overwhelm them, reducing them to a demographic minority and threatening their cultural and political dominance. Other countries fear that migration will exacerbate problems of overcrowding, poverty, unemployment, and xenophobia. And in some countries citizens have such a strong sense of an exclusive cultural identity that the incorporation into citizenship of even a small number of outsiders is unacceptable.

The moral stance that global justice can be served by a world of open borders in which individuals are free to move wherever they wish presumes a world without borders, without states, without repressive regimes, without vast differences in the health, education and welfare services offered by governing authorities, and without vast differences in incomes and employment. In the absence of these conditions the noble vision becomes a nightmare, for the consequences of opening the borders of a country in extreme situations can be the erosion of the institutions and values that liberal societies have created for themselves and which make them attractive to outsiders. In the real world of states, governments are morally responsible to their own citizens and to those who legally reside within their territory.

MIGRATION SELECTIVITY

For societies that do admit migrants, few issues have generated more public debate than the morality of admitting one class of migrants and not another. Does the principle of national sovereignty permit states to discriminate on the basis of race, religion or ethnicity in choosing whom to admit? The White Australia policy, the prewar U.S. policy of excluding Asians, and the reluctance of contemporary Germany and other Western European states to admit Gypsies and Muslims have all come under criticism. Today, such policies are widely regarded as morally unacceptable. Somewhat more morally acceptable are preferential policies – by Israel for Jews, by Germany for people of German origin, by India for Hindus, by Pakistan for Muslims, by Arab countries for fellow Arabs, by Nepal for people of Nepali origin, and so on. There are also other kinds of preferences for people with certain skills, educational levels, local relatives, or financial resources. While some would argue that a country has the right to determine admission qualifications, liberals feel justifiably uncomfortable when the preferences are based on religion, ethnic origin or, especially, race.

The line between preferences and discrimination, though it has some merit, is a morally thin one that is easily crossed. A White Australia policy reflects not simply a preference for whites, but hostility to blacks, Asians, and other nonwhites. In contrast, a national preference for one's ethnic group (Germans, Jews, Nepalis, Arabs, etc.) is to some degree justified by the need or desire to maintain a sense of community. Yet even ethnic preferences are not always moral; a multi-ethnic society which gives preference to one ethnic community over another is, in effect, making a moral distinction among its own citizens. States can more easily justify preferences in admission policy when their security is at risk. Israelis, aware of the long history of persecution of Jews in countries in which they are a minority, regard their country as a place of refuge for Jews throughout the world and legitimately fear that their country would cease to be a homeland for Jews were its borders open to all Arabs who wished to come.

A similar concern for ethnic survival shapes the immigration policies of Bhutan, a small Tibetan kingdom located northeast of India and east of Nepal. For many years, immigrants from the densely populated region of eastern Nepal migrated into Bhutan, eventually leading to concerns that the local Tibetan population might soon be outnumbered. Moreover, if citizenship is granted to the Nepalis and democracy is extended, then the Nepalis may vote to overturn the monarchy and the country will cease to be an independent Tibetan state. The king, with support from his Tibetan subjects, has therefore imposed a series of restrictions on the non-Tibetan population with the intention of halting the flows of Nepalis into the country, as well as to ensure the cultural, political and demographic hegemony of the indigenous Tibetan population. The government announced that the Tibetan language would be taught in all the schools, that Tibetan dress should be worn by everyone, and that those who entered the country after the late 1950s would not be admitted into citizenship.

The great variation in government policies toward migration reminds us of how closely tied questions of who should be admitted into the community are to conceptions of national identity, as well as to economic issues. A policy of excluding individuals on the basis of their group identity is morally unacceptable. But whether a country's migration policies should give preferences to ethnic kin, to the spouses, children, parents, or siblings of citizens or resident aliens, to individuals with specified skills or levels of education, or to unskilled low-wage workers or to individuals of financial means, or indeed whether a country should have an immigration policy at all is not a matter of general moral principles but of politically defined national interests and values, that is, in the broadest sense, national sovereignty.

DO GLOBAL MARKETS MAKE MIGRATION INEVITABLE AND UNCONTROLLABLE?

Some opponents of the notion that national sovereignty should shape migration policies argue that national sovereignty is itself an anachronistic conception. According to this argument, the world economy and global communications are such powerful forces for international migration that states are essentially powerless to effectively control who enters. There is now a global labor market which largely determines the flow of people so that attempts to restrict entry simply result in the growth of an illegal migrant population living without the benefit of rights. Under these circumstances it is best to allow the market to work, to reap its benefits and mitigate its costs.

The argument for this view is as follows: developed countries find it difficult to prevent illegal migration because many employers want the low-skilled, low-wage workers that they are unable to find in the local labor market. A number of factors have contributed to this demand. Employers can no longer recruit from the now absent rural hinterland or among the urban poor who reject low-wage employment when they can often do better on welfare entitlements. Declining fertility and population aging in industrial societies also leads to an increase in the demand for imported labor. Faced with a tight labor market for low-wage labor, employers of labor, like users of capital, turn to the global market to meet their needs. Employers in the United States have found low-wage workers in Mexico and the Caribbean; German employers have turned to Turkey, Yugoslavia, Greece and, more recently, to Eastern Europe; French, Italian, and Spanish employers find their workers in North Africa. Even when employers can find workers on the local market they often prefer foreign workers, who are pliable, unlikely to join unions, willing to work long hours, tolerate conditions that local labor finds unacceptable, and can readily be dismissed when they are no longer needed.

The emergence of a global labor market is made possible by advances in information technology and transportation. Mexicans, Turks, Chinese, Algerians, Filipinos, Jamaicans, Tunisians, Croatians, Serbs are now familiar with the labor markets of Europe, the United States, and Canada. They have friends and relatives abroad who inform them of changing market conditions and of the opportunities for employment and housing. Transportation costs, moreover, have declined, and brokers have now organized the international market in labor. Potential migrants also have learned entry regulations and how best to get around them, *e.g.*, by entering a country as tourists and staying to find jobs. They also know they can claim political asylum and, while their cases are reviewed, find work or live at government expense. Employment opportunities abound in the less-regulated secondary labor market – in restaurants, small businesses, and domestic service. Forged documents are readily available for purchase. Meanwhile, circumstances in their home countries are often dire. In developing countries an estimated 38 million people join the labor force every year, and as many as 700 million people are already unemployed or underemployed (UNDP, 1992:54). Consequently, the risks of illegal migration are relatively low and the rewards, in terms of finding employment and obtaining higher wages than at home, are high. Indeed, it is surprising that only a small fraction of employment-age individuals in developing countries has thus far attempted to migrate.

Since, it is further argued, illegal migration and nonjustifiable claims for asylum are strongly employment-and employer-driven, policy instruments to significantly reduce the flow are not likely to work. Government penalties against employers who hire illegal migrants in the United States appear to have had only limited effects. Studies of the 1986 U.S. Immigration Reform and Control Act, for example, report that the legislation has not halted illegal migration and may have only marginally reduced the flow (Cornelius, 1989:689–705; also *see* Bean *et al.*, 1990, especially pp. 33–76). Western European guestworker programs to rotate workers and prevent permanent settlement also have not had their intended effects. Japan, in spite of imposing large fines on employers for the employment of illegal aliens, has been unable to prevent the growth of an illegal labor force (Cornelius, 1992; Cornelius, Martin and Hollifield, 1995; Sassen, 1988, 1991).

Moreover, notwithstanding efforts by countries in the European Union to tighten their immigration and asylum policies, the annual flow of irregulars has been increasing since the mid-1980s. The number of annual asylum seekers (excluding displaced persons from the former Yugoslavia) increased from 165,000 in 1985 to 314,000 in 1989 to 690,000 in 1992; in the same years the estimated number of illegal immigrants increased from 50,000 to 150,000 to 370,000. The number of annual registered migrants to Western Europe also reportedly increased – from 650,000 in 1985 to 1,380,000 in 1993 (ICMPD, 1994:10). This can be partly attributed to the result of family reunion but also reflects the growth in the number of asylum seekers in previous years who were subsequently granted residence permits.

Liberal democratic political systems are particularly constrained from adopting policies to tightly control immigration – partly by their liberal ideology which leads governments to provide entitlements to legal and illegal immigrants and claimants for asylum and which prevents them from engaging in large-scale expulsions, and partly by the influence of lobbyists (*e.g.*, business, ethnic groups, migration lawyers and civil libertarians) on behalf of illegal migrants and asylum seekers (*see* Hollifield, 1991). In the United States the introduction of a counterfeit-proof identity card that would be required as a condition of employment, for example, is opposed by civil libertarians. Many members of the middle class employ illegal domestic servants, a lifestyle on which government is reluctant to intrude. Furthermore, many people in Western Europe and North America do not regard the overstay of a visa or an illegal entry as a crime but rather as an understandable effort of someone attempting to improve his or her position at no cost to others – a "victimless crime."

Less-developed countries also find it difficult to control unwanted entries. Market forces play a role here as well. Migrants move from one Third World country to another when opportunities are available for employment or for gaining access to land. Border control is made more difficult by the arbitrary character of many postcolonial borders, which cut across ethnic communities and divide lands customarily used by cattle farmers and shifting cultivators. In addition to market forces, moreover, civil conflicts and natural disasters have led millions of people, especially in Africa, to move across international borders within the Third World. Finally, new states often lack the military and administrative capacity to halt movement across their borders and are therefore even less capable than industrial societies of imposing restrictions and penalties on employers for using illegal aliens.

Given these realities, it is argued, both market and political forces are now so powerful that traditional conceptions of state sovereignty, which rest upon notions of borders and state capacity to define membership, have become or are becoming an anachronism. If this argument is correct then states must develop new approaches to address migration issues. If states, especially advanced industrial democracies, cannot control who enters, they should turn instead to the question of how best to deal with the consequences of such entries.

Proponents of policy changes to address the consequences do not suggest that governments should announce that their borders are open, but rather that they should expand the amount of legal migration and quietly accept illegal, *i.e.*, "unauthorized" or "undocumented," migration. An analogy can be drawn with free international markets in goods and the globalization of capital markets. If the free market in trade and capital is beneficial to all countries, proponents of this approach assert, so is a free market in labor. Furthermore, just as it has become difficult, as well as undesirable, for countries to prevent the free movement of goods and capital (legally or through smuggling), so too is it difficult and undesirable to prevent the globalization of labor.

Such a policy conclusion draws on the views of neoclassical economists, who point to the economic benefits of the free movement of the factors of production. Everyone gains, they argue, if communities produce what they can make most efficiently and then trade their goods with others. Capital would move to where it could be most efficiently (and profitably) utilized, and every country would be better off if money and goods could move freely. Neoclassical economists have applied this same logic to the free movement of labor within a country: individuals would move to where their labor was most needed and the price paid would be the highest, making the country, as well as individuals, better off. Given this economic rationale, would it not be desirable to permit as much free movement of labor across international boundaries as is politically acceptable? Labor-exporting countries would gain by earning remittances from their overseas workers, while receiving countries would gain by employing unskilled foreign workers for jobs that locals do not want and by compensation for domestic labor shortages.

> The absorptive capacity of Western European countries, though not as great as that of America or Australia, is still bigger than timid people think. European politicians who run scared of racist or anti-immigrant feeling will be doing their countries no favors. Their guiding principle as they map out Europe's immigration plans should not be 'How few can we get away with letting in?', but rather, 'How many can we possibly take without creating unbearable social strain?' (*The Economist*, "The Would-be Europeans," Aug. 4, 1990, p. 15)

The argument of the global egalitarians and the neoclassical economists thus converges on matters of migration, both arguing in favor of increasingly open borders as an instrument for achieving greater worldwide economic equality. The question of what drives migration flows and to what extent they are beneficial to receiving countries is, of course, central to the argument of the neoclassical economists. It is first necessary to note that the consequences of the free movement of labor across international borders are not the same as the consequences of the free movement of capital and goods across these same borders. The logic of free trade between countries is that it finds its own equilibrium – a country that bought more than it sold would see the value of its currency decline, the cost of imports go up, and the price of its exports go down until a trade balance was established. No such simple mechanism operates with respect to the free movement of people across national boundaries. A world without borders might indeed be one in which the free movement of people and the free movement of capital and goods would benefit all; but in a world in which states and boundaries do exist, the free movement of people, unlike the free movement of capital and goods, would damage those countries that chose to have unregulated borders. Indeed, much the same argument is used by those who advocate some form of managed trade in conditions in which there is no free movement of the factors of production since governments provide subsidies or impose costs upon their own producers and place a variety of tariff and nontariff restrictions on imports.

A relatively free international labor market is not without its costs. Migrants can displace some local labor; a large-scale influx can put a burden on housing, education, and social services and depress wages. Refugees can impose heavy costs upon the government and upon local people, push up food prices, crowd urban settlements, and damage the local ecology; some – though by no means all – societies are threatened if there are large numbers of immigrants from another culture. And ethnic conflicts between migrants and locals, especially between migrants and indigenous minorities and among different migrant communities, can be politically destabilizing and violent and hence injurious to economic growth. There are also opportunity costs. In a tight labor market employers have an incentive to seek ways to make labor more productive. Technological and managerial innovations are more likely to occur when labor costs go up. Unemployment will decline. Previously excluded or restricted groups – the disabled, women, minorities – are likely to be pulled into the labor force.

Demographers have argued against a widely held view that declining fertility rates and aging population will create a need for importing labor. For one thing, fertility rates have not been declining in all advanced industrial countries; since the mid-1980s fertility rates have risen in Germany, the United States, and Canada. More significantly, unemployment rates are high – over 10 percent in Western Europe and about 6 percent in the United States. Workers have been losing jobs in rust belt industries, and in many sectors of the economy the demand for low-skilled labor has declined. If there is an unmet demand for low-skilled workers in sectors of the economy it is because the welfare system removes some low-skilled workers from the labor force and many young people are unwilling to do manual work that is considered dirty, socially undesirable, and pays low wages. It seems unlikely that the labor market in developed countries, especially for low-skilled workers, will be tight during the next ten or twenty years, given the growth of labor-displacing technologies, the movement of low-cost labor-intensive industries from developed to developing countries, the growing capacity of the service sector to transfer computer and telecommunication functions from high-wage to low-wage economies, increased opportunities for female participation in the labor force, and the continued availability of young people in a labor force that has a persistent high level of unemployment (Coleman, 1985:413–461).

Particularly telling is the growth in international migration to developed countries even in the midst of a recession and high unemployment, suggesting that either supply is creating its own demand or that ease of access rather than the structure of the labor market is shaping the flow. The large increase in the number of migrants to Germany – the stock of foreigners increased from 4.5 million in 1988 to an estimated 6.5 million by 1994 – had little to do with a growth in demand for labor. During this same period, the United Kingdom experienced no significant increase in the size of its foreign population. The difference clearly has to do with ease of access. The United Kingdom's insular position enabled it to keep down the flow of illegal migrants, while Germany's location on the borders of Eastern Europe made it more vulnerable than Britain to claimants for asylum. Moreover, Britain adopted a more restrictive asylum policy than Germany. Similarly, the presumed globalization of the labor market did not prevent Japan from choosing not to have a guestworker program when Western Europe did, nor has it prevented Japan from keeping down the number of asylum seekers and illegal migrants by imposing tighter controls than have most Western governments.

The comparative evidence suggests that states have been able to control entry, though never completely. Germany does not have an illegal alien problem of the magnitude of the United States. But, then, Germany requires all citizens and aliens to register when they take up a new residence; a Central Aliens Register compiles information on foreigners living in Germany, and all residents carry national identification documents which they must produce when they seek employment. Similar identification systems exist in most of the Scandinavian countries with the result that these countries have relatively few illegal residents compared with the United States. A national ID card may be politically unacceptable in the United States, where it is regarded as an infringement on civil liberties, but its use elsewhere suggests that control over migration is possible.

A variety of other types of controls have been used to prevent unwanted migration and to reduce the number of claimants for asylum. Australia requires that all visitors (except those from New Zealand) apply for visas. The government keeps records of which country's nationals fail to leave and then tightens visa controls on the countries that produce visa overstayers. Germany, the Czech Republic, and Poland have established cooperative policing of borders, and in many other countries, including the United States, more resources are being allocated to improve border controls. European governments have devised policies aimed at reducing the number of asylum claimants: sanctions against carriers of individuals without papers, accelerated asylum reviews, restrictions on entry of asylum claimants from third countries, the preparation of lists of "safe" countries whose citizens cannot claim asylum, the establishment of safe havens in third countries, and deportations of individuals whose asylum claims have been rejected. Critics correctly note that some of these policies as presently implemented are violations of the U.N. Refugee Convention. The point, however, is that governments have successfully controlled migration notwithstanding the demand for low-wage labor by many of their own employers and the growth of global communication, global transportation, and global markets – all of which facilitate international migration. Indeed, in the absence of such controls it seems likely that international migration would be far higher than it is. According to U.N. estimates, the annual flow of migrants across international boundaries is approximately 4 million persons, plus episodic refugee movements – a small number in a world of 5.7 billion people, with an annual worldwide population increase of 90 to 100 million. The inability of states to have total control over who enters and who overstays their visas is no more an argument against control than the persistence of crime is an argument for ending the enforcement of criminal law.

THE MORAL CLAIMS OF REFUGEES

Most governments agree that refugees are in need of protection – but who is a refugee? The well-known distinction is between the definition offered by the 1951 United Nations Refugee Convention and the 1967 Protocol relating to the Status of Refugees, of refugees as persons "with a well-founded fear of being persecuted for reasons of race, religion, nationality, membership in a particular social group, or political opinion" and the broader definition of the Organization of African Unity (OAU) of refugees as persons compelled to leave their place of residence because of events seriously disturbing public order (Organization of African Unity Convention Governing the Specific Aspects of Refugee Problems in Africa, adopted September 10, 1969).

Although the United Nations Refugee Convention limits the notion of refugee to individuals who are persecuted or fear persecution and the OAU definition includes individuals who flee from generalized violence, both definitions view refugees as individuals who lack the protection of their own government. Neither definition, however, applies to displaced persons within a country, irrespective of whether there is persecution or violence, or to individuals fleeing from natural disasters such as floods, droughts, or earthquakes. And neither definition includes individuals who flee from a tyrannical regime unless they are personally persecuted or their society is torn by life-threatening violence.

Some human rights activists, therefore, see both the U.N. and the OAU definitions as too narrow. Andrew Shacknove asserts that a moral claim to refugee status arises whenever a state fails to protect the basic needs of its citizens (1985:274–284; *see also* 1988). Consistent with such a broad moral definition, some human rights activists argue that liberal democratic countries ought to admit all individuals whose human rights are violated by their government. Thus, a Saudi woman is justified in seeking asylum in Canada because of her views on the status of women. A woman from Mali may legitimately flee to France rather than permit her daughter to undergo a clitoridectomy. A homosexual fearing persecution in his homeland, Brazil, because of his sexual preferences may claim asylum in Canada. A Chinese couple is justified in claiming asylum in the United States because they have had more children than are permitted by the Chinese government. A Gypsy may claim asylum in Germany because the Gypsy community suffers from discrimination in Romania. In each case there is a plausible claim for asylum based on human rights violations.

There are, however, several practical objections to broadening the definition of refugees. If acts of discrimination, short of "persecution," are the basis for claiming asylum, a large part of the world's population could do so. Asylum on the basis of discrimination could plausibly be claimed, for example, by over 100 million Indian Muslims whose mosque at Ayodhya was destroyed and who were fearful after many Muslims in Bombay and elsewhere were killed by Hindus. Millions of women around the world could similarly point to discriminatory restrictions imposed by their state or society as justification for seeking asylum. Moreover, a country that does not want its minorities could engage in systematic discrimination and impel countries that embrace a liberal conception of refugees to admit all whose human rights have been violated. The more liberal democratic states and international agencies become in granting asylum to persecuted minorities, the greater the inducement for a nationalist regime to engage in some form of "ethnic cleansing."

Thus, a broader definition of refugee would, in effect, offer refugee status to entire populations in societies with civil conflicts, authoritarian regimes, or weak governments that fail to protect human rights. Refugee policies would move from a consideration of individual cases to an assessment of regimes. Given the number of countries that could be classified as violators of human rights, liberal democratic countries would have to open their borders to much of the world. This shift has moral implications both for sending countries, which might have incentives to increase injustices against their minority population, and for receiving countries, which would be faced with the dilemma of accommodating the humanitarian needs of an increasing migrant population while responding to the needs of its own citizens.

Refugee status is, as one scholar put it, a scarce resource (Martin, 1991). Individuals who have been granted refugee status are in a privileged category; it is an entitlement that allows one to move to a safe country for protection and assistance. Governments must decide to whom these entitlements should be given and how generous they should be. The broader the definition and the greater the entitlements, the more refugees will come. Citizens of a poor country with an authoritarian regime who have the option of moving permanently to a more prosperous democratic country will readily do so. Even the narrower definition of a refugee as "having a well-founded fear of persecution" has problems when there are so many claimants that there can no longer be proper adjudication of their claims. How can government adjudicators readily distinguish among those who are seeking better economic opportunities, who are fleeing from violence, or who have a personal well-founded fear of persecution? How might governments create enforceable criteria for admission that would be morally defensible? Alas, no simple test can reveal who is at risk and who is not. We enter into the realm of intangibles – judgments about the motivations of claimants, problems of evidence when the burden is upon claimants to demonstrate they are at risk of persecution, and more general judgments about conditions in the home country which threaten the lives of individuals on account of their race, religion, ethnic identity or political beliefs.

At times the advocates and the policymakers shout at one another. Human rights activists accuse government officials of callousness and of failing to recognize their responsibility to people at risk; government officials, in turn, accuse human rights activists of insensitivity to the needs of home countries – particularly its poor and its social and political stability – and to the impact generous asylum and refugee policies can have on the behavior of countries eager to unburden themselves of their own poor and their minorities.

Faced with the prospect of a large refugee influx, many governments have argued that refugees should remain in the country of first asylum. Several justifications are offered for such policies, including: 1) the adjustment of refugees is likely to be easier when economic and social conditions are more similar; 2) the costs of maintaining refugees are lower if they remain in Third World countries than if they are settled in developed countries; 3) refugees are more likely to voluntarily repatriate when conditions change at home if the country of asylum does not provide them with material advantages. When the first-asylum rule is put into effect, governments of refugee-receiving countries are often angry not only at the country that generates refugees but at countries that are unwilling to share the refugee burden. Thus, Germany has been irritated by the unwillingness of other members of the European Community to readily admit Bosnians, Croatians, and Romanians; Thailand and Malaysia were insistent that they would accommodate refugees from Indochina only if the United States, France, and other countries took some of the refugees. The United States tried, with very limited success, to persuade Caribbean countries to take in some of the Haitian refugees; Japan annoyed many of its Asian neighbors by accepting only a handful of refugees from Indochina.

Whatever the criteria, there is the matter of how to adjudicate claims – whether there should be in-country refugee reviews at embassies and consulates in the country of origin, whether airlines should be required to check the visas of individuals before transporting them, whether interdiction and adjudication on board ships can provide an adequate review, and whether governments should have lists of safe countries where democratic practices presumably make it unnecessary for individuals to seek asylum. For good reason human rights advocates have objected to many of these practices, arguing instead that those who seek asylum should be allowed to enter a country where their claims can receive a full and fair legal review under the guidance of legal counsel. Furthermore, they argue, pending the resolution of their claims asylum seekers should not be detained and should be allowed to work or receive public benefits. Human rights advocates insist that rejected claimants should have full rights of appeal and not be sent home if they are at risk. Governments should also monitor the fate of those who are repatriated after their claim for asylum is rejected.

Yet, even while taking the high moral ground, human rights groups create another moral conundrum. Liberal democratic states, in adopting the protections proposed above, then become the ultimate guarantors of human rights: first, by admitting those whose rights have been violated by their home government; and second, by monitoring human rights conditions so as to determine whether it is safe for rejected asylum claimants to return home. The right of asylum is thus elevated to being the mechanism by which liberal democratic states guarantee human rights to all individuals in repressive societies, assuring those individuals who are able to escape that the rights they seek can be obtained elsewhere if they cannot be obtained at home. If, however, it is beyond the capacity of liberal democratic states to provide protection to all whose rights are violated, then the goal must be the more modest one of providing protection to those whose rights and lives are the most egregiously threatened while deterring and rejecting others. At the end of the day it may not be possible for any individual government to provide protection to all who seek it.

NATIONAL SOVEREIGNTY AND INTERVENTION

According to the principles of realpolitik, sovereign states ought not to concern themselves with the ways in which other states treat their own citizens. What matters is their foreign policies. But the concern by the Western powers during the cold war that militarily strong autocratic regimes constituted a threat to world peace has in part given way to the present concern with the disintegration of states. The war in Bosnia, the threat of Islamic fundamentalism in Algeria, ethnic conflicts in Rwanda and Burundi, warlordism in Somalia, deteriorating economic and political conditions in Cuba and Haiti, a secessionist movement in Chechnya, civil wars in Tajikistan and Afghanistan, and an irredentist war between Azerbaijan and Armenia have forced policymakers to address the issues of human rights violations, ethnic cleansing, genocide, stagnant economies, deteriorating environments, and refugee protection. Conflicts within states, once falling within the purview of traditional conceptions of state sovereignty, are now regarded as an issue for the larger international community – in part because of humanitarian concerns over the loss of civilian lives, in part because of the risk that violent disputes within states may spill across international borders, and in part because these conflicts generate refugee flows across borders that impose a burden on others.

It is beyond the scope of this paper to suggest the range of policies that governments might use to deter or halt aggression by a government against its own citizens or the kinds of incentives that might be employed to strengthen democratic institutions and respect for individual rights, including that of minorities. The main point here is that the claim of national sovereignty is no longer regarded, at least by the Western powers, as grounds for noninterference in how governments treat their own citizens. Many Third World governments, most notably China but other governments as well, do not accept this view, insisting that human rights and democratic procedures are largely Western not global, for they do not take into account national values and conditions.

However, the large-scale flight of refugees and internally displaced persons has invoked a response by international institutions and by national governments. Though the mandate of the UNHCR is to protect refugees, over the years it has become increasingly involved in providing protection for internally displaced persons. Governments faced with a large influx of refugees may consider intervention, including armed intervention, to halt the flow, as India did in the Pakistan-Bangladesh conflict of 1971. As the global media reports the devastating conditions which put people to flight, governments and their citizens are often driven by a humanitarian impulse to intervene. At the same time, governments recognize that many interventionist policies are costly. Trade restrictions on countries that violate human rights, for example, harm exporters, increase unemployment, and raise prices at home. The use of military power to separate contestants in an internal war is problematic, highly risky and for many governments politically unacceptable; humanitarian assistance can be financially costly and, as the Bosnia conflict demonstrated, may require costly military protection. The current quest, therefore, is for politically and financially low-cost policies that will change conditions within countries that generate unwanted flows of refugees and migrants. The international community is particularly ambivalent and indecisive when a civil war erupts as a result of a secessionist movement that threatens to break up an existing state. And the slaughter of one people by another in a fratricidal ethnic conflict may make ineffective the kind of limited short-term intervention that governments and their military forces prefer, particularly when the international community is unwilling to support one side or another in a conflict. Coercion to compel a settlement is ordinarily difficult, even more so when regional and international armed forces are poorly coordinated and individual states make their own assessment of what level and type of forces they are prepared to provide and how high a risk to take. The amount of ground forces needed to halt genocide or to force the separation of opposing armies is generally greater than the international community is collectively prepared to provide, air strikes are not without risk, and it is rarely clear as to what targets would compel a determined armed group to halt their attacks. Even as the principle of justifiable intervention wins adherents, the question of how to intervene effectively and collectively is now one of the most difficult unresolved questions for policymakers and scholars of international relations.

MIGRATION POLICIES AND PUBLIC OPINION

In dealing with these issues, democratic governments must take into account the views of their own citizens; but to what extent should a government base its immigration and refugee laws on public opinion? What if a substantial part of the electorate is xenophobic? Should the U.S. Congress, for example, have imposed national quotas on immigration after World War I because an anti-immigrant lobby sought to halt the influx of migrants from Eastern and Southern Europe? Should the British government have passed restrictive immigration laws in the 1970s after Enoch Powell, a Member of Parliament, won support for his antimigrant views? Should French politicians have adopted a restrictive stance toward refugee admission and migration as a result of the rise of popular support for Jean-Marie Le Pen's right-wing antimigrant party? Should the German government have revised its generous asylum laws because of violent attacks against foreigners? Was it wrong for the governments of Southeast Asia to refuse to accept Vietnamese refugees because of widespread opposition? And was it wrong for the government of Pakistan to refuse to admit "stranded Pakistanis" (as they call themselves) left in Bangladesh after independence because local people in the Karachi region opposed the further influx of immigrants?

Government leaders often take the position that they must be responsive to public sentiments even if the public is irrationally xenophobic. Political leaders fear, moreover, that opposition politicians will use antimigrant sentiments to win electoral support. A somewhat more sophisticated version of this argument is that unless responsible policymakers take heed of deeply felt public sentiments, extreme right-wing parties will grow and threaten the democratic system. This fear has particular credibility in countries with authoritarian traditions and fragile democratic structures. Moreover, the migrants and refugees themselves may be at physical risk.

Yet, if the proposed policies are morally unjust then they should not be adopted, no matter how strong public sentiment may be, even in a democracy. Consequently, a complex balance must be struck between catering to the wishes of a citizenry and protecting the rights of migrants and refugees. Antimigrant, antirefugee sentiment may come from a relatively small though vociferous group of citizens. It is generally within the power of a government to seek public support for existing policies if it is clear that these policies are sensible ones. The Swiss government was able to resist a widespread popular demand that its guestworkers be expelled by demonstrating that workers were engaged in occupations for which Swiss workers were not available and that the country's economy would suffer if the guestworkers were expelled. The Australian government was ahead of Australian public opinion in its support for a nondiscriminatory immigrant admissions policy. The French government has successfully resisted demands that locally born children of migrants could not readily acquire citizenship. There are times, too, when a public has been willing to accept extraordinarily large numbers of refugees, as was the case of the Pakistani willingness to accommodate millions of Afghans, and the American and French willingness to take in many Indochinese. When there is public opposition, moreover, it may be for good reasons. The concerns expressed by many Americans and Europeans that their governments should take steps to halt illegal migration, establish more rigorous procedures to prevent foreigners from entering under false asylum claims, repatriate rejected asylum seekers, and reduce immigration during a period of recession, should not be dismissed – no matter how unsavory some of the antimigrant rhetoric. For a country to have an acceptable immigration policy, it must be able to effectively control illegal immigration. For a country to have an acceptable refugee policy, it must be able to prevent large numbers of immigrants from entering and remaining on the basis of unjustifiable asylum claims. The unwillingness of governments to take steps to halt an unwanted influx of foreigners can erode immigration and refugee policies, strengthen right-wing parties, and generate xenophobic fears and violent behavior that may put democratic societies at risk.

THE LIMITS AND USES OF MORAL REASONING IN PUBLIC POLICY

As with most issues of public policy, conflicts over immigration and refugee policies typically reflect group and institutional interests. Behind debates over these policies, however, often lie fundamental issues of public values and of conflicting moral considerations that are rarely made explicit. With the end of the cold war, there is emerging a greater moral and political consensus on universal human rights than ever before and a willingness to at least consider what international regimes might be created to embody and institutionalize this consensus. But there is also a widespread recognition that international population movements create major problems for states and that states have a legitimate right to limit these flows when their interests are affected. Thus, there is a need to balance state interests with moral considerations in the formulation of migration policies.

There is not – and to restate the thesis of this paper – there cannot be an international consensus on the question of whether governments should admit migrants. Indeed, if an international consensus is emerging, it is that no government is obligated to admit migrants, that migration is a matter of individual national policy, that most governments need more effective control over their borders, that more forceful measures are needed to halt illegal migration and the growth of worldwide migrant smuggling, that improved procedures are needed to distinguish genuine asylum seekers and refugees suffering from persecution and violence from individuals who use these procedures to migrate, that "temporary" guestworker policies do not work. Also, in formulating migration policies government should give increasing importance to whether the skills and education levels of migrants strengthen the economy, rather than to the needs of the migrants themselves. There is a consensus that refugees and asylees are in need of protection, but disagreement on who should be granted protection, how best to adjudicate asylum claims, and where and what kind of protection is desirable. There is a widespread view among the Western powers and many governments in the Third World that states cannot retreat behind the principle of national sovereignty if their mistreatment of their own citizens or their inability to maintain internal order results in massive flights. Disagreement exists, however, over what steps – if any – should be taken by the international community.

In some policy areas – mostly notably in the field of health, biogenetics, and in policies relating to the use of nuclear weapons – explicit attention has been paid to moral questions. The development of the field of applied ethics has been directed not at offering moral solutions to complex policy issues but rather at identifying the moral questions and specifying the trade-offs among alternative moral principles. Similarly, the task in the migration and refugee field is to extract the moral assumptions from the policy debates, to identify the dilemmas posed by conflicting moral principles, and to suggest how an explicit examination of moral issues can clarify policy choices. The moral issues with respect to migrants and refugees have been transformed in recent years by the emergence of a movement in support of universal human rights which transcend international boundaries so that many citizens feel they have moral obligations to those who live outside their boundaries. But citizens in liberal societies also wish to weigh these claims against the needs and claims of their own citizens.

Moral reasoning differs from other kinds of reasoning about public policies. Typically, policy decisions are based on weighing costs and benefits, evaluating effectiveness, and considering political consequences – all of which have moral implications – but this is not the same as employing moral reasoning. Efforts to apply moral reasoning often flounder in a quagmire of conundrums and moral contradictions. While these often cannot be resolved, one must at least understand what they are.

There is, first of all, the need to distinguish between personal morality and the application of moral principles to public policy. The moral choices we make as individuals need not, and often should not, be the same as the moral choices made by policymakers. A woman may have a moral objection to aborting her fetus, but that is not an argument for a public policy that bans abortions. One may be a pacifist, but that is not an argument for a public policy of disarmament. One may have a moral aversion to pornography, but that is not an argument for censorship. One may be willing to accommodate a poor immigrant in one's home, but that is not an argument for a policy to admit poor people from other countries. Personal ethics are a poor basis for public choices because they do not take into account the costs such policies impose upon others. Similarly, personal benefits from previous policies that permitted the migration of one's parents, for example, are not justification for a liberal migration policy, either past or present.

It is also important to distinguish, as Max Weber did, between two kinds of ethics: the ethics of ultimate ends, which pursues an absolute ideal; and the ethics of responsibility, which requires that political leaders choose courses that are often less than ideal. Policymakers must not consider simply whether policies are in some abstract sense moral, but also whether there is a reasonable likelihood that morally desirable objectives can be achieved. The morality of an act should be judged by its probable consequences, not by its intent; good intentions are not a sufficient basis for choosing moral policies since many well-intended policies have had bad results. A policy, for example, that induces people to take hazardous risks for desirable ends (*e.g.*, a policy that leads individuals to flee their country in unseaworthy boats) may have morally unsound consequences.

An apparently morally justifiable policy, moreover, can sometimes lead to costly results and imprudent actions. Policymakers may have to make the difficult judgment of whether military action to provide protection for internally displaced persons will lead to a more costly war that will inflict even greater loss of human life. Support for a persecuted ethnic minority demanding self-determination, for example, might lead to a civil war and large-scale violence. Military intervention in another country to halt persecution or stop violent conflict also, if soldiers are killed, may lead to premature withdrawal that could result in greater harm to those originally intended to receive help. Similarly, policies intended to reduce the numbers of people who fall into a particular category targeted for aid (poor, disabled, refugees, etc.) may inadvertently increase their numbers. As economists point out, we get more of what we subsidize. When, for example, governments offer entitlements to the disabled, the number of people who find ways to get themselves classified as disabled increases. The more benefits we offer asylum seekers (legal aid, free housing, medical care, food, employment), the more people are likely to seek asylum. This is not an argument against helping the disabled, the poor, single parents, asylees, refugees, etc., but a warning that the greater the entitlements the narrower the definition must be of who is qualified to receive them. Migration and refugee policies are based upon definitional distinctions as to who are beneficiaries. For each category (asylees, refugees, guestworkers, permanent migrants) there must be precise rules as to who qualifies for what benefits. Both the criteria and the entitlements must be clear and the logic behind them morally defensible as well as administratively practical; poorly defined criteria combined with generous entitlements are an invitation to abuse.

Moral reasoning also requires that we distinguish between unjust policies and injustices in the implementation of policies. While juries and judges may render unfair verdicts, it does not necessarily follow that the laws upon which these verdicts are based are unjust. Similarly, those who review asylum cases may unjustly send someone back home to cruel treatment or even death, but the criteria for granting asylum may be reasonable. Incorrect judgments are often a regrettable effect of just policies and can be addressed by improved adjudication procedures and better trained personnel. Advocates of open borders who use instances of unjust decisions as arguments for admitting all who claim asylum are, therefore, just as misguided as advocates of total exclusion who point to abuses by asylum claimants as grounds to admit no one. Abuses either by those who administer laws or by those who are its beneficiaries should not be grounds for adopting policies or procedures that are less just.

Confusion over the morality of policies, as distinct from the morality of implementation, often stems from uneven application of the rules. Policies, and their implementation, should not be arbitrary; they should be reasonably consistent and they should be seen as based upon principles that people recognize as being fair. Just as individuals should not be arbitrarily arrested for a crime or arbitrarily freed, so individuals should not be arbitrarily admitted into a country or arbitrarily rejected. Much of the unease over migration and refugee policies is the result of inconsistent, often arbitrary, acts by policymakers or by those who administer policies. For example, individuals are sometimes granted asylum if they come from one authoritarian state, but not from another. Individuals in identical circumstances were treated automatically by the United States as refugees, for example, if they came from Cuba, but as economic migrants if they came from Haiti. A consular official may arbitrarily give an entry visa to one person but not to another, or may grant asylum to one claimant while denying it to another. Policies that are inconsistent, arbitrary or patently unfair generate cynicism and become a legitimate basis for public outrage.

Not all the difficulties of applying moral reasoning to public policy are generated by confusion over what aspects of policy – outcomes, implementation, or the policy itself – must be just. Incorporating morality in public policy often entails making difficult choices among divergent values. It is morally attractive to treat all human beings equally without regard to their nationality, but is a military commander morally wrong to adopt a military strategy intended to minimize deaths among his own troops at the cost of increasing deaths among his enemies, including their civilians? Is it morally wrong for a government to be concerned with the effect of the size and composition of a migrant or refugee influx upon the well-being of its own population, or to give preference to immigrants with whom its own citizens have ties of kinship and culture? These judgments often offend those who would apply universalistic criteria, but one ought not to render morally meaningless their basis in the ties of affection that bind families, communities, and citizens. Issues of moral choice are particularly complex when we try to decide which strangers require our help and how we balance our own needs and self-interests against those of strangers and even enemies. These difficult moral choices arise because resources are always limited and because one person's gain often entails someone else's loss.

Finally, the incorporation of moral reasoning into public policies requires that we recognize that we cannot resolve debates over migration with reference to principles of absolute justice. The issues are difficult to resolve in large part because there are conflicting claims, conflicting values, and conflicting rights. No principles of absolute justice can help us decide how many migrants should be admitted, whether preferences for admission should be given to people with skills and high levels of education or to the unskilled, whether preferences should be given to the spouses, parents and minor children of citizens but not to their siblings, whether or not a country should admit guestworkers, whether refugee status should be granted to anyone whose human rights are violated or only to those who are persecuted or are threatened with violence, and what kinds of controls are appropriate for dealing with illegal migrants. The moral questions posed by each of these issues cannot be resolved without consideration of the impact of one policy upon another and upon the effects of policy decisions upon the larger society. If immigration is not a basic human right – and it cannot be as long as there are states – then each country must weigh conflicting claims and consider the consequences of alternative policies for their own citizens. It is important that we not conflate issues of public interest, public values, and fundamental human rights. Migration and refugee issues cannot simply be reduced to moral questions, but neither, as we have suggested throughout this essay, are they solely questions of national sovereignty in which moral judgments play no role.

REFERENCES

Barry, B.
1973 *The Liberal Theory of Justice.* Oxford: Clarendon Press.

Bean, F. D. *et al.*, eds.
1990 *Undocumented Migration to the United States: IRCA and the Experience of the 1980s.* Washington, DC: Urban Institute Press.

Beitz, C. R.
1979 *Political Theory and International Relations.* Princeton, NJ: Princeton University Press.

Carens, J. H.
1992a "Migration and Morality: A Liberal Equalitarian Perspective." In *Free Movement.* Ed. B. Barry and R. Goodin. London: Harvest Wheatsheaf.

———
1992b "Refugees and the Limits of Obligation," *Public Affairs* Quarterly, 6(1). January.

———
1991 "States and Refugees: A Normative Analysis." In *Refugee Policy: Canada and the United States.* Ed. H. Adelman. Toronto: York Lane Press.

———
1988a "Immigration and the Welfare State." In *Democracy and the Welfare State.* Ed. A. Gutmann. Princeton, NJ: Princeton University Press.

———
1988b "Nationalism and the Exclusion of Immigrants: Lessons from Australian Immigration Policy." In *Open Borders? Closed Societies: The Ethical and Political Issues.* Ed. M. Gibney. Westport, CT: Greenwood Press.

———
1987a "Who Belongs? Theoretical and Legal Questions About Birthright Citizenship in the United States," *University of Toronto Law Journal,* 37.

———
1987b "Aliens and Citizens: The Case for Open Borders," *The Review of Politics,* 49(2). Spring.

———
1987c "Moral Realism vs. Moral Idealism: The Ethics of International Migration," American Political Science Association. September.

Coleman, D.
1985 "Does Europe Need Immigrants?" *International Labour Review,* 26.

Cornelius, W.
1992 *Controlling Illegal Immigration: A Global Perspective. The Case of Japan.* Research project of the Center for U.S.-Mexican Studies, University of California, San Diego.

———
1989 "Impacts of the 1986 U.S. Immigration Law on Emigration from Rural Mexican Sending Communities," *Population and Development Review,* 15(4). December.

Cornelius, W., P. Martin and J. Hollifield, eds.
1995 *Controlling Immigration: A Global Perspective.* Stanford: Stanford University Press.

Dummett, A. and A. Nicol
1992 *Subjects, Citizens, Aliens and Others: Nationality and Immigration Law.* London: Weidenfeld and Nicolson.

Hollifield, J. F.
1991 *Immigrants, Markets and States: The Political Economy of Immigration in Postwar Europe.* Cambridge, MA: Harvard University Press.

International Centre for Migration Policy Development (ICMPD)
1994 *A Comparative Analysis of Entry and Asylum Policies in Selected Western Countries.* Vienna, May 1994. The report is by the director, Jonas Widgren.

King, T.
1983 "Immigration from Developing Countries: Some Philosophical Issues," *Ethics.* April.

Martin, D.
1991 "The Refugee Concept: On Definitions, Politics and the Careful Use of a Scarce Resource." In *Refugee Policy: Canada and the United States.* Ed. H. Adelman. Toronto: York Lane Press.

Miller, D.
1992 "Community and Citizenship." In *Communitarianism and Individualism*. Ed. S. Avineri and Avner de-Shalit. Oxford: Oxford University Press.

Rawls, J.
1971 *A Theory of Justice*. Cambridge, MA: Harvard University Press.

Sassen, S.
1991 *The Global City: New York, Tokyo*. Princeton, NJ: Princeton University Press.

———
1988 *The Mobility of Labor and Capital: A Study in International Investment and Labor Flows*. Cambridge: Cambridge University Press.

Schuck, P.H. and R. M. Smith
1985 *Citizenship without Consent: Illegal Aliens in the American* Polity. New Haven, CT: Yale University Press.

Shacknove, A.
1988 "American Duties to Refugees: Their Scope and Limits," In *Open Borders? Closed Societies*. Ed. M. Gibney. New York: Greenwood Press.

———
1985 "Who is a Refugee?" *Ethics*. 95.

Shue, H.
1980 *Basic Rights: Subsistence, Affluence, and U.S. Foreign Policy*. Princeton, NJ: Princeton University Press.

Sidgwick, H.
1891 *The Elements of Politics*. London: Macmillan.

Singer, P. and R. Singer
1988 "The Ethics of Refugee Policy." In *Open Borders? Closed Societies? The Ethical and Political Issues*. Ed. M. Gibney. Westport, CT: Greenwood Press.

Sohn, L. B. and T. Buergenthal, eds.
1992 *The Movement of Persons Across Borders*. Washington, DC: American Society of International Law.

United Nations Development Program (UNDP)
1992 *Human Development Report 1992*. New York: Oxford University Press.

Walzer, M.
1983 *Spheres of Justice: A Defense of Pluralism and* Equality. New York: Basic Books.

Weiner, M.
1995 *The Global Migration Crisis: Challenge to States and to Human Rights*. New York: Harper Collins.

———
1993 "Security, Stability and International Migration." In *International Migration and* Security. Ed. M. Weiner. Boulder, CO: Westview Press.

Whelan, F.
1981 "Citizenship and the Right to Leave," *American Political Science Review*, 75(3). September.

[3]

Pakistani Workers in the Middle East: Volume, Trends and Consequences

Nasra M. Shah
East-West Population Institute
Honolulu, Hawaii, East-West Center

Temporary international migration for employment is not a new phenomenon and much has been written about 'guest workers' to European countries. Labor migration to the oil producing Middle East countries is, however, a relatively recent occupation—one that is likely to have far reaching impacts on both labor importing and exporting countries. Serageldin *et al.* (1983) have estimated that from about 1.6 million migrant workers in 1975 the number would increase to about 4.3 million in 1985 in the major capital rich labor importing countries.[1] In some oil producing countries, such as Qatar, Kuwait and the United Arab Emirates, non-national workers comprise over seventy percent of the total labor force. In recent years, the relative proportion of non-Arab migrant labor has increased, proportionately more South and South East Asian and East Asian workers are now employed in the Middle East than in the mid-seventies.

Pakistan has become one of the major labor exporters as a result of the shift in labor importation preferences. While there is some disagreement about the precise number of Pakistanis who are currently employed in the Middle East, the various estimates suggest that somewhat more than one million is a plausible number. Research based on the 1981 Census and household surveys during the late 1970s indicates that the number of workers in the Middle East ranges somewhere between 1 to 2 million. A minimum estimate based on the total number of workers who went for employment through the Bureau of

[1] These figures are likely to be an underestimate as discussed later.

Emigration and Overseas Employment and were registered with it during 1971-81 is given as (776,174) (Table 1). Over 95 percent of these registered workers were employed in the Middle East. These figures approximate the stock of migrants since the Bureau estimates that only about 5 percent of those who left returned to Pakistan permanently during this period (Akbar, 1981). The Bureau figures, however are likely to be an underestimate since the Manpower Division (which is the source for the data) did not collect information on "direct" emigrants (*i.e.*, those who obtained visas through their friends or relatives) prior to 1977. Furthermore, the Table does not include illegal emigrants who may have emigrated without any clearance through the Bureau of Emigration and Overseas Employment, the agency which is responsible for processing all such migrant workers. Finally, the Table does not include persons who emigrate for reasons other than employment, but later take up jobs. While the above factors are likely to result in an underestimation of the stock of workers, it is not clear whether an emigrant is counted by the Bureau each time he goes abroad on a new contract. If this is the case, the Bureau figures should probably not be used to estimate the stock of migrants since they may overestimate it. In general, data collection in Pakistan suffers from several weaknesses; emigration data is unlikely to be an exception.

Other estimates of the total number (stock) of migrants range between 1.12 and 1.79 million (Gilani *et al.*, 1981a), about 70 percent of whom were working in the Middle East. The 1981 Census also provides a figure close to Gilani *et al's* estimate of 1. 7 million (Kahn and Karim, 1983). The 1981 Census asked whether any members of the respondent's household left Pakistan during the previous ten years and were still abroad. The total number of persons thus reported was 1. 7 million.

Note that all the estimates discussed so far are based on data collected within Pakistan itself. Another estimate made by Serageldin *et al.*, (1983) as part of a World Bank project offers a much more conservative figure. They believe that the stock of Pakistani workers in the nine major oil exporting countries[2] was 205,700 in 1975. They project this number to increase to 555,100 by 1985 under a high economic growth assumption and only 446,000 under a low economic growth assumption. It is not clear whether these calculations were based on data available within the importing countries or on estimates provided by the labor exporting countries. Their base figures for 1975, however, seem to be a clear underestimate when compared to estimates provided by various researchers within the country. The Pakistan government also estimates a much larger magnitude to have taken place. The government has estimated that there are about 1.4 million Pakistanis

[2] Algeria, Bahrain, Iran, Kuwait, Libya, Oman, Qatar, Saudi Arabia and United Arab Emirates.

currently working and living abroad, a large majority in the Middle East. It is expected that the number of Pakistani workers abroad would have risen by an additional 0.4 million during the current Five Year Plan period, 1977-78 to 1982-83 (Finance Division, 1982:8). The government has an active policy of encouraging labor emigration and has instituted a crash program for training skilled and semi-skilled workers for overseas employment.

TABLE 1

ANNUAL FLOW OF EMIGRANT WORKERS FROM PAKISTAN, 1971-81 BY CHANNEL

Year	Private (overseas employment[a] promoters)	Public[b]	Direct[c]	Total
1971	3,340	194	–	3,534
1972	3,359	1,171	–	4,530
1973	7,654	4,646	–	12,300
1974	14,652	1,676	–	16,328
1975	21,766	1,311	–	23,077
1976	38,516	3,174	–	41,690
1977	77,664	2,606	60,175	140,445
1978	78,685	3,246	47,602	129,533
1979	80,615	3,058	34,586	118,259
1980	91,482	17,114	24,801	133,397
1981	119,711	821	32,549	153,081
Total Number	537,444	39,017	199,713	776,174
Percent	69.3	5.0	25.7	100.0

Source: Finance Division 1982, p. 8.

Notes: [a] About 400 overseas employment promoters have been licensed by the government to recruit workers on behalf of foreign employers. The work of these promoters is regulated and controlled by the regional protectorates of emigrants which work under the Director General, Bureau of Emigration and Overseas Employment.

[b]Emigrants who are supplied by the government upon the request of a foreign government.

[c] This includes individual work visas obtained through relatives and friends.

For details of the process of emigration, *See*, Akbar, 1981:25-35.

CHARACTERISTICS OF MIGRANTS

While the debate on the actual number of Pakistani workers in the Middle East is not yet over, it seems safe to conclude that more than one million workers are currently employed in the Middle East. The migrants constitute about 6-8 percent of the total labor force of Pakistan and consist largely of males aged 25 to 40 years (Akbar, 1981). It has been estimated by Gilani *et al.*, (1981) that about 70 percent of the migrants are married, but only 4 percent are accompanied by their families.

In terms of destination of migrants, Gilani *et al.*, found that about 70 percent of all emigrants they interviewed were destined for the Middle East. They estimated that 34 percent of all emigrants were going to Saudi Arabia and 20 percent to the United Arab Emirates. Comparable data from the Bureau of Emigration indicates that between 1971 and 1980, 38 percent of those who emigrated through the Bureau went to Saudi Arabia, a figure quite close to Gilani's (Akbar, 1981:33-35).

Of all the Middle East emigrants in Gilani's study, two-thirds came from rural areas. At least some of these rural migrants are likely to have come to urban areas to land a job in the international market, thus contributing to the rural-urban internal migration within the country. Furthermore, at least some of the emigrants are likely to settle in urban areas once they return to Pakistan after having experienced an urban way of life and with higher aspirations for their children's education (Shah and Karim, 1982).

With regard to the occupational structure of migrants, Gilani *et al.* found that 83 percent of the migrants in their sample were production workers—43 percent unskilled laborers and 40 percent skilled workers. The skilled workers consisted of drivers (8%), carpenters (6%), masons (6%), tailors (4%), etc. Of the 17 percent non-production workers, 4 percent were professional (*e.g.*, engineers, teachers and nurses), 6 percent were businessmen and 2 percent were service workers (Gilani *et al.*, 1981a:28-30). Compared to the figures from Gilani *et al's* study the Bureau of Emigration data show the share of production workers among those who emigrated to the Middle East through the Bureau during 1971-77 to be 71 percent, about 12 percent less than Gilani's figures. Regardless of the source, however, production workers do comprise a large majority of all migrants to the Middle East. The impact of such heavy out-migration of these workers is discussed later.

The Gilani *et al.* analysis further indicates that the proportion of unskilled labor has gone up over time compared to the proportion of skilled labor (Table 2). The percentage of unskilled migrants had increased from 30 percent six years ago to 51 percent during the year of survey (*i.e.*, 1979). This pattern is contrary to that in other countries, and to the general trend toward increased importation of skilled (rather than unskilled) workers by the host countries. The increasing proportion of unskilled workers has been viewed as a cause for concern by some researchers (*e.g.*, Ahmad, 1982). The increase in unskilled workers implies that the training facilities within the country have not been able to produce the desired amount and quality of skilled workers which could fulfill the demand in the Middle East; such demand is, therefore, being met from countries other than Pakistan.

TABLE 2

INTERTEMPORAL COMPOSITION OF THE MIGRANT OCCUPATIONS

	The Date of Migration				
Occupation	Within a year	Between last 1 and 2 years	Between last 3 and 4 years	Between last 5 and 6 years	Above 6 years
Unskilled Labor	50.6	46.4	39.3	39.6	30.2
Agriculture	3.0	8.1	3.7	0.0	3.9
Non-Agriculture	47.6	38.3	35.6	39.6	26.5
Skilled Labor	38.2	44.6	48.6	45.3	47.0
Carpenters/Masons	11.6	14.6	16.1	11.8	11.7
Technicians/Mechanics	17.9	19.5	20.8	15.2	17.4
Tailors	4.6	4.0	3.9	7.5	9.3
Drivers	4.1	6.5	7.8	10.8	8.6
Clerical Workers	0.6	0.7	2.7	3.8	3.5
Professional/Managerial Workers	4.4	2.6	2.7	2.8	3.1
Business Workers	4.4	4.6	5.8	6.6	10.9
Service Workers	1.8	1.1	2.9	1.9	5.1
Total	100.0	100.0	100.0	100.0	100.0

Source: Gilani *et al.*, 1981:33.

POLICIES AND THE PROCESS OF EMIGRATION

As mentioned above, the government has an active policy to encourage labor migration to the Middle East. It has set up several training institutions to develop a skilled manpower which would cater to the needs of labor. importers. A crash training program was started in 1975-76 by the Manpower Division which aimed at producing about 50,000 skilled and semi-skilled workers annually. The program was, however, able to train only 11,100 workers during the first three years of its operation. Another training program was started in January, 1980 by the Overseas Pakistanis Foundation (OPF), an autonomous body which was set up by the government in 1979. The OPF imparts training through 44 institutions and had trained close to 10, 000 persons during the first 21 months of its operation (Ahmad, 1982:26).

While several facilities are in existence, this training capacity is not being fully utilized at present. At the three major institutes set up by the government, there is a 12 percent enrollment deficiency; furthermore, 37 percent of all enrolled do not complete the training (Ahmad, 1982:27). Some of the reasons for the underutilization of such facilities are the shortage of adequately trained instructors, the long duration of courses, and inappropriateness of the training, etc. The inadequacy of training facilities requires immediate attention and concerted effort to remedy the situation.

Skill development as a general policy is a desired goal. It is nowhere specified what the desirable characteristics of the trainees in terms of age and sex are. Cultural values (in Pakistan as well as host countries), however, restrict most of the jobs to men. One category of female workers where the Pakistan government has put a restriction in terms of age is that of maidservants. The Emigration Ordinance, 1979, states that "the minimum age for employment of women as maid-servants shall be forty-five years...". While the intent of the law is to discourage the exploitation of young female domestic servants, it is not clear whether this restriction has discouraged the export of workers in this category.

The process of emigration has been quite tightly regulated during the last few years. The Emigration Ordinance, 1979, has provided an administrative structure as well as rules and penalties designed to regulate emigration. An overview of the administrative structure is given in Figure I. An agency, known as the Bureau of Emigration and Overseas Employment, had been set up as early as 1972. The Emigration Ordinance, 1979, (Government of Pakistan, 1979) regularized the positions in the Bureau and established the positions of Director General of the Bureau, protectors of emigrants and Labour Attaches in host countries. There are at present five Protectorates of Emigrants which work under the Bureau. The Protectorates oversee and regulate the work under the Bureau. They oversee and regulate the work of 400 Employment Promoters—private individuals who have been granted licenses to recruit workers.

There are three channels which may provide overseas workers as indicated in Table 1 earlier—private, public and direct. Private migration takes place through the employment promoters; public migration is handled by the Overseas Employment Corporation; direct migration results from issuance of a visa directly to the employee, arranged usually through a friend or relative. The private channel provides close to 70 percent of all workers registered by the government. The figures in Table 1, are however, an underestimate of all workers, as discussed above; the actual proportion of workers supplied through promoters is in fact probably not as high. In the study by Gilani *et al.* (1981), only about one-fourth of the respondents said they had obtained their jobs through recruiting agents (*i.e.*, promoters); the rest had managed to find jobs through friends or relatives or through their own efforts (Gilani *et al.*, 1981). The discrepancy in the findings of the two reports could have resulted from factors such as the inclusion of illegal migrants in the Gilani study or a nonrepresentative sample for that study. No conclusions about this are possible, however.

The Emigration Ordinance, 1979, laid down various rules to ensure the welfare of the migrants. Severe penalties (such as imprisonment up to 14 years) for forgery of documents, false representation of government authority, charging fees in addition to the prescribed amounts, have been laid down. Labor attaches who are stationed in the host countries are responsible for safeguarding the interests of emigrants and promoting overseas employment. Finally, certain agencies such as the OPF have been set up with the objectives of promoting the welfare of overseas Pakistanis and their dependents and to deal with various problems arising from emigration. The government has also established a Welfare Fund and all emigrants are required to make a small contribution to this fund.

CONSEQUENCES OF MIGRATION

In a very broad sense, the consequences of labor migration may be classified into economic and noneconomic ones. Reseachers and policymakers within Pakistan have begun to pay attention to both of these consequences, but particularly the economic ones. On the positive side, perhaps the major reason why international labor migration has become so significant is the increased amount of remittances associated with such migration. From an insignificant level of about $15.5 billion in 1972-73, the volume of remittances rose to 1.7 billion in 1979-80. During the period 1977-78. During the period 1977-78 to 1980-81, remittances grew at a rate of 22.5 percent per year and exceeded $2.1 billion during 1980-81 (Pakistan Embassy, 1981b). Gilani *et al.* (1981:72) have estimated that "valued at current market prices, remittances now comprise 8 percent of the GNP and 40 percent of the total foreign exchange earnings and finance 86 percent of the trace deficit". The

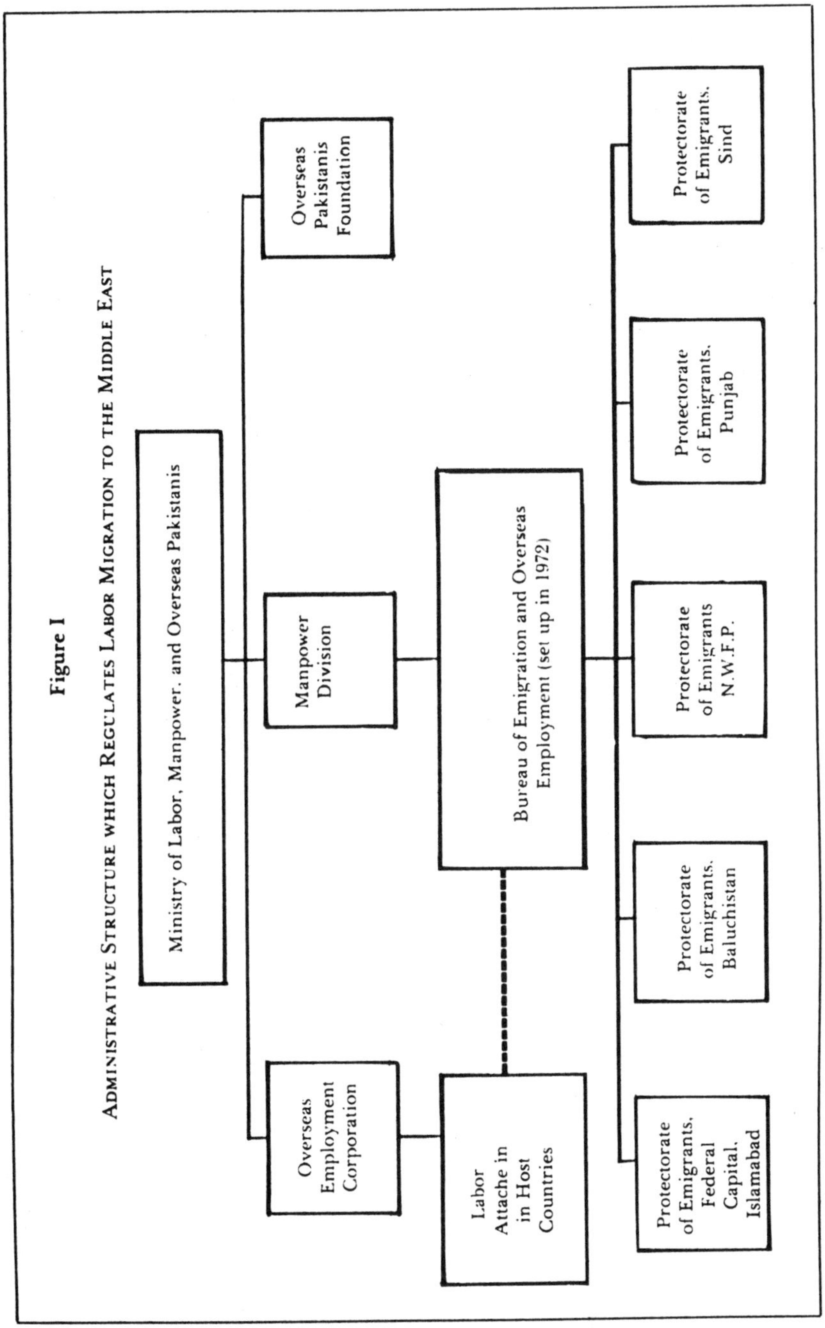

Figure I

ADMINISTRATIVE STRUCTURE WHICH REGULATES LABOR MIGRATION TO THE MIDDLE EAST significance of remittances for the economy of Pakistan is highlighted by the fact that a slow down in the inflow of home remittances during the fiscal year 1981-82 is considered as one of the major factors which has negatively affected the international trade and balance of payments situation in the country during this period (Finance Division, 1982:99). The Finance Division has not provided any data on the amount of remittances received during 1981-82. One factor which could have negatively affected the inflow of remittances received during 1981-82 is the deduction of 'zakat' (obligatory charity, equivalent to 2½% on the savings as required by Islamic laws) from private bank accounts; this possibility needs to be studied. While remittances currently form an extremely significant factor in the Pakistan economy, they are not necessarily being used in the most economically efficient manner at the present time. It was found by Gilani *et al.* (1981) that a large proportion (62%) of remittances received by the families of migrant workers was spent on consumption of food, clothing and accommodations. etc. rather than on direct investment (Table 3). Another 22 percent was spent on real estate including housing, real estate for commercial purposes and agricultural land. Finally, only 13 percent of remittances was spent on direct investment such as agricultural machinery or other industrial or commercial investment. While the increased expenditure on food is likely to raise nutritional levels of the family, thereby reducing morbidity and increasing productivity, it is desirable that a larger proportion of the remittances should be used for productive investments in the future. Furthermore, policies which would reduce the inflationary impact of remittances need to be instituted.

Among the possible negative economic consequences, the one that has been most thoroughly discussed relates to the skill loss and the concommittant shortages of labor in certain skill categories (ILO-ARTEP, 1983; Gilani *et al.*, 1981; Ahmad, 1982). By comparing the local demand for certain occupations within Pakistan with the number of migrants in that occupation, Gilani *et al.* (1981) concluded that certain occupations such as carpenters, electricians and plumbers were suffering from a labor shortage within the country. In another study commissioned by the Pakistan government, large shortages among certain categories of workers were reported. For example, there was a domestic shortage of 33,000 carpenters, 26,000 bricklayers and masons, 23,000 welders and 22,000 plumbers and pipe fitters (Pakistan Government, 1981). Such large shortages are bound to affect the domestic productivity negatively.

Another point that has been repeatedly emphasized concerns the apparently better quality of emigrants compared to workers who are left behind Domestic productivity is likely to suffer because the most qualified and experienced workers have emigrated. A serious consequence of the emigration of the more experienced workers consists of the loss of the best teachers or *ustads* who have traditionally taught many skills to their students or *shagird* in the informal sector. In a survey of informal living

TABLE 3

USES OF REMITTANCES IN PAKISTAN

Expenditure	Amount (000 Rs.)	Percent
Consumption	18,012	62.19
Recurring consumption	16,512	57.00
Marriages	680	2.35
Consumer durables	820	2.84
Real Estate	6,280	21.68
Construction/purchase of residential house	3,516	12.14
Improvement in house	658	2.27
Commercial real estate	1,658	5.72
Agricultural land	448	1.55
Investment/Savings	3,752	12.95
Agricultural investment	957	3.30
Industrial/commercial investment	2,378	8.21
Financial investment/saving	417	1.44
Residual	922	3.18
Total	28,966	100.00

Source: Gilani *et al.*, 1981:144.

arrangements in Islamabad and surrounding areas, Ahmad (1982) found that the quality of workmen who are now employed in construction projects is very low. A steep drop, quantitatively as well as qualitatively, has occurred in the output of skilled workers from the informal sector. The absence of qualified and experienced trainers has significantly reduced the trainer/trainee ratio. Thus, the present state of "the blind leading the blind" is likely to incur a serious deterioration of skill standards in construction trades. Based on his research, Ahmad (1982) concludes that at present "Pakistan faces a quality crisis in the manpower at its disposal". It is essential to improve the quality of the manpower in order to meet the specialized demand for foreign emigration as well as prevent a negative impact on the growth of the nonagricultural sector within Pakistan.

Among the noneconomic consequences, the likely impact on the status of women and children has drawn some attention. As mentioned above, the majority of workers to the Middle East are males who move without their families. Policies of the host countries discourage migration of dependents by placing certain restrictions; only college educated workers can bring dependents to Saudi Arabia, while in Kuwait a minimum salary is necessary before dependents are allowed to join the worker (Addleton, forthcoming and 1981). Thus, more than a million households in the country have to cope with the absence of one or more male members. Data on social impacts of such male absence are being collected by a team of researchers including Ijaz Gilani (the author of the first comprehensive study on the phenomenon) at Islamabad, with funding from the Overseas Pakistanis Foundation. The study is being conducted in the five districts which have experienced unusually high emigration, namely Kohat, Gujrat, Larkana, Turbat and Mirpur. Detailed information on migrants, their families and return-migrants is being collected.

Findings from two small case studies of villages are as follows. Bilquees and Hamid (1981) concluded from their study in a village in Gujar Khan that in terms of nutritional levels, the standard of living of emigrant households has certainly improved. The absence of male members has, however, had an adverse impact on agricultural production. Increased incomes in the migrant households has not led to any positive change in attitudes towards girls' education and about 16 percent of women still do not want to educate their daughters. One other aspect which is viewed negatively by the authors is the relative laxity in sexual morality (what they term corruption) among women resulting from their husbands' long absence and a knowledge of contraception. Needless to say, the findings from this one village may or may not be generalizable to the country as a whole and the question of such impacts must await additional research.

Shaheed (1981), in her study of three villages, made an attempt to study the impact of the absence of men, and of remittances on women in terms of the amount of work done, decision making power and changes in the status of women, if any. She found that the standard of living for most women improved in terms of food and clothing. Male absence, however, meant added responsibilities and in the case of poorer households, it implied heavier workloads for the women. There was minimal gain in actual decision making power since women rarely had direct and personal control over remittances. Women seldom had bank accounts in their own names where they could receive money from their husbands/sons, etc. Some male relative usually acted as an intermediary between the bank and the woman; thus, in some cases, she was the *de facto* but unrecognized household head. Female members of the family gained in terms of the social status which a family unit as a whole acquired through its increased consumption, but most families were not able to improve their economic status enough to maintain their women in *purdah* (seclusion). The majority of rural women continued to engage in farm activities as they had done prior to the male member's migration.

Other noneconomic consequences such as changes in the social and political structures of communities, regional variations in the gains from migration, long term aspirations for self and children, etc. have not been adequately studied so far. The study by Islamabac researchers mentioned above will answer some of the institutional level questions. Also, data from a study currently under way at the Pakistan Institute of Development Economics should add to existing information (for scope, *See,* Irfan, 1981). Yet another study is planned by the Statistics Division, in collaboration with the U.N.'s Economic and Social Commission for Asia and the Pacific. Thus, over the next few years, satisfactory information on various aspects of labor migration is likely to become available.

CONCLUSIONS

The phenomenal increase in labor migration from Pakistan to the Middle East has positive as well a negative aspects. Remittances provide 40 percent of the foreign exchange earnings in the country. Remittances have apparently led to improvements in the nutritional levels of migrant households and probably fulfill many of the basic needs of such households. A high level of consumption expenditure has, however, contributed to a high rate of inflation estimated to be over 20 percent per year (ILO/ARTEP, 1983), thus dampening the gains from increased household incomes. Emigration has lessened the problem of unemployment and underemployment within the country, but has resulted in shortages of certain skills. In fact, skill shortages in certain industries are beginning to affect the quality of work and productivity within Pakistan. The quality of the labor force is likely to suffer a long term impact due to the inadequacy and shortage of trainers in the informal sector.

The human cost resulting from the process is also considerable, as reported by the Director General, Bureau of Emigration and Overseas Employment, Pakistan. In spite of all the measures taken by the government to eradicate malpractice and exploitation of workers, the expatriate labor is treated with prejudice in the host countries. The emigrants are offered substandard wages and living conditions and are compelled to work overtime without extra payment. Sometimes the employers unilaterally deport emigrants in breach of contract. In cases of injuries and death, the workers or their dependents are not paid due compensation. In short, "emigrants are treated like slaves and even worse than that" (Akbar, 1981). With the promulgation of the 1979 Emigration Ordinance and stricter controls, these conditions should improve.

The social and political costs of migration are not yet well understood. The process of labor migration has certainly resulted in a revolution of rising expectations. The continued high import of consumer goods is a clear demonstration of the society's changing tastes; a certain amount of competition to acquire the latest in terms of televisions/VCRs and other goods exist among those who can afford it. The impact of increased wealth on corruption and bribery are also not fully understood or quantified; they, however, seem to have increased over the last few years. The traditional 'fatalism' and complacency with one's lot has been corroded and emigration is probably one of the significant elements in such corrosion.

Labor migration has helped the country by easing the foreign exchange problem. It has been beneficial to the migrant and his family and has led to an improved standard of living for them. It is likely to have positive impacts on the future investment in human resources if aspirations for children's education can be realized more easily. Several other social and demographic impacts are likely to occur. Together with the positive consequences, it is also important to be aware of the possible negative ones so that the process can be regulated in a manner which minimizes the cost and maximizes the benefits to both the sending and receiving countries.

REFERENCES

Addleton, J.

Forthcoming. "The Impact of International Migration on Economic Development in Pakistan", *Asian Survey*.

1981 "The Role of Migration in Development: Pakistan and the Gulf". *The Fletcher Forum*. 4(2).

Ahmad, M.

1982 "Emigration of Scarce Skills in Pakistan, ILO International Migration for Employment, Working Paper No. 5, Geneva. Mimeo.

Akbar, M.

1981 Country Paper: Pakistan: *Emigration for Employment*. Report on ARPLA Symposium on overseas recruitment procedures for senior officials of South Asian Countries. ILO, Islamabad, May, 1981.

Bilquees, F. and S. Hamid
1981 "Impact of International Migration on Women and Children Left Behind: A case study of a Punjabi Village". Research Report Series, No. 115. Islamabad: Pakistan Institute of Development Economics.

Finance Division
1982 *Pakistan Economic Survey 1981-82*. Islamabad: Government of Pakistan, Economic Advisor's Wing.

Gilani, I., M. Khan and I. Munawar
1981 *Labour Migration from Pakistan to the Middle East and Its Impact on the Domestic Economy.* Two parts. Research Report Series, Nos. 126 and 127, Islamabad: Pakistan Institute of Development Economics.

Government of Pakistan
1978 "The Gazette of Pakistan Extraordinary", Ordinance No. XVIII of 1979 (Emigration Ordinance, 1979), Islamabad: Law Division.

ILO-ARTEP
1983 *Employment and Structural Change in Pakistan—Issues for the Eighties: A Report for the Pakistan Planning Commission for the Sixth Five Year Plan (1983-88).* Bangkok: The Asian Employment Program (Prepared by Rashid Amjad and others).

Irfan, M.
1981 *An Introduction to Studies in Population, Labour Force and Migration: A PIDE ILO-UNFPA Project.* Research Report Series, No. 118. Islamabad: Pakistan Institute of Development Economics.

Khan, A. H. and M.S. Karim
1983 "Migration Patterns in Pakistan during 1970s: Evidence from the 1981 Census Data". Paper presented at the Conference on "Recent Population Trends in South Asia" held in New Delhi, February 2-8, 1983.

Pakistan Embassy
1981 *Pakistan Affairs.* Vol. 34(18), Washington, D.C.

Pakistan Government (Manpower Division)
1981 *Occupational and Educational Manpower Requirements and Supply of the Fifth Year Plan (1978-83), Islamabad.*

Serageldin, I. *et al.*
1983 *Manpower and International Labor Migration in the Middle East and North Africa.* New York: Oxford University Press.

Shah, N.M. and M.S. Karim
1981 "Migration, Urban Growth and Development: Pakistan's Experience", *Asian and Pacific Census Forum,* 9(2).

Shaheed, Farida
1981 *Migration and It's Effects on Women in the Village pf Provenance.* Paper presented at the Tripartite Asian Regional Seminar, Rural Development and Women" held at Mahabaleshwar, India, April 6-11.

[4]

Toward a Structural Analysis of Illegal (Undocumented) Immigration

Alejandro Portes
Duke University

In his introduction to this issue of *IMR* which attempts to understand more fully different aspects of undocumented immigration, the guest editor situates the articles in the present context of research and policy, and complements them by summarizing some of the ideas common to all and by analyzing, on their basis, the significance of the current Administration's plan to deal with the illegal flow.

RESEARCH AND POLICY

The recent wave of interest on the topic of illegal immigration has given rise to a growing scholarly literature which examines various aspects of the problem. Much of this literature is prescriptive, that is it attempts to persuade readers to support one or another solution to the problem. The reasons for this emphasis are not difficult to determine. Illegal immigration is one of those issues in which the interests of scholars and of government agencies converge. Hence, much of the recent literature aims primarily at an audience composed of decision-makers: officials of the Justice and Labor departments, members of the Judiciary committees and Immigration sub-committees in Congress, and the like.

While much pressure has been applied to the social sciences to produce "policy-relevant" results, the experience in this particular case has not been encouraging. Observing from the outside the on-going controversy, one would not fail to note the bewildering array of proposed solutions to the problem. This controversy takes place not only among policy-makers, but among scholarly investigators as well. Among the solutions proposed by experts on the problem are: "closing the border" and preventing further illegal entry; "opening the border" and allowing anyone who wishes to come to the United States to do so; organize a contract foreign labor program patterned along Western European lines; support a rural industrialization program in Mexico to attack the "roots of the problem"; offer amnesty to illegals already in the country, while closing the border to future ones; penalize employers for hiring illegal workers; concentrate on apprehension of smugglers of illegal aliens as a way to reduce the flow; and so on.

While commendable in principle, the emphasis on policy-relevance of the current literature is not without drawbacks. To engage in this policy advisory role with government officials, social scientists must perforce accept certain assumptions. First, they must accept that illegal immigration is indeed a "problem". Second, they must accept the government's intentions of solving this problem in behalf of the best interests of the majority. Third, they must assume that government agencies are indeed capable of carrying out the proposed recommendations, even against resistance.

Each of these assumptions is based on a questionable view of the relationships between government and civil society and collectively they represent a surprising departure from an extensive scholarly literature on the nature of the state in advanced industrial societies. By adopting the official perspective, rather than the social science perspective as a point of departure, researchers deliberately surrender important theoretical tools of analysis. Though it might be argued that this is the price to pay for involvement in the "real world", the truth is that studies which examine the problem within officially pre-established limits yield a constrained and impoverished product.

A thorough scholarly analysis of illegal immigration cannot take the popular and governmental definitions of the subject for granted, but must subject them to scrutiny as integral components of the object of study. Such scrutiny begins by the very definition of the phenomenon as a "problem". It can be argued that, from the perspective of studies of the functioning of the Mexican economy and the structure of U.S. labor markets, illegal immigration has represented not a problem, but a solution to the problem. The flow of illegal labor effectively met problems confronted by sectors of the dominant classes and by the state in both sending and receiving countries (Bustamante, 1976; Barrera, 1977; Portes, 1974). The sudden redefinition of an otherwise established pattern as a "problem" and its instant prominence in the public mind is itself one of the most important issues to be investigated.

Similarly, the assumptions of governmental commitment to the interests of the less favored classes and of full capacity to implement the recommended policies are unacceptable in any serious analysis of the situation. Understanding the meaning of illegal immigration and the role it has played in sending and receiving societies, is also understanding the structural constraints which governmental agencies have faced and the ultimate goals of the state in preserving the dominant economic order.

These constraints and goals exist despite the good intentions of particular officials.

The articles presented in this issue of the *International Migration Review* do not defend any particular policy position, nor do individual authors adopt an advisory role with respect to governmental policy. They represent, instead, attempts to understand more fully different aspects of illegal immigration, including the role of the state and the structural conditions to which it must respond. Each of the articles included here are revisions of papers presented at the panel on "Mexican and Central American Immigration", held during the 1977 meetings of the Latin American Studies Association in Houston. Two of the papers deal primarily with Mexico and two with the United States.

The Dinerman article is a close-range study of conditions leading to illegal migration from a rural village in Mexico. It is one of the few available studies of illegal migration at its point of origin. In the classic tradition of anthropology, its primary concern is not individual psychological traits, but the social network of relationships and mutual obligations conditioning the decision to migrate.

The paper by Francisco Alba summarizes, in concise form, the view on the broader structural determinants of the illegal flow held by Mexican scholars concerned with the problem. The study by J. Craig Jenkins offers an empirical test of two apparently related, but contrary hypotheses on the nature of the "pull" attracting illegal migrants to the United States. The paper documents a point of strategic importance: that the dynamics of the illegal movement cannot be reduced to the simple terms of supply and demand of labor. Finally, the essay by Robert L. Bach represents an attempt to place the contemporary situation in historical perspective, showing how the American state permitted and indeed had to permit illegal immigration to meet its various commitments to different sectors of capital and labor. The paper outlines the historical dialectics which made illegal immigration the direct consequence not of the weakness, but of the strength of U.S. organized labor.

Taken together, these papers contain fundamental points for extending our current understanding of the phenomenon. The remainder of this introduction will be dedicated to complement them by summarizing some of the ideas common to all and by analyzing, on their basis, the significance of the current Administration's plan to deal with the illegal flow.

THEORETICAL PROPOSITIONS

Contemporary illegal migration is not a phenomenon limited to Mexican workers. The overwhelming representation of Mexicans among captured aliens in the United States is, in part, a function of the deployment practices of enforcement agencies (U.S. Department of Justice, 1978). Illegal migration from other countries, especially the Dominican Republic and others in the Caribbean, appears to have gained increasing importance in recent years, though they figure less prominently in apprehension statistics. Illegal immigration to the United States is also identical in its structural form and origins to migration movements from the European periphery to industrialized West European nations. It is in this broader context where the specific instance represented by Mexican migration must be placed. Whatever their origins, contemporary illegal migrations across national borders share three characteristics: 1) they occur between countries, both of which are inserted in the capitalist international economy; 2) they originate in "peripheral" areas of the system and move toward "core" areas; and 3) they are migrations of labor, that is of individuals who move with the sole purpose of selling their work capacity.

This latter characteristic differentiates contemporary illegal movements from political or religious migrations or from "colonizing" initiatives designed to exploit resources in an unsettled hinterland. It also points to the fundamental premise for a comprehensive analysis of the phenomenon. That is, the causes of illegal immigration are ultimately found in the use and control of labor in different areas of the international economy.

This general proposition must be specified by examining concrete structural characteristics of both sending and receiving countries. The set of propositions that follow appears to be in agreement with the underlying theoretical premises of each of the ensuing articles. These propositions do not attempt to provide a comprehensive analysis, but only to serve as introduction to more detailed studies.

CONDITIONS IN THE UNITED STATES

Concerning the receiving "core" countries, there are two initial propositions: 1) other things being equal, the rate of return to capital is inversely related to the costs of labor; and 2) advanced capitalist societies tend to be characterized by scarcity of labor, either in the absolute sense of exhaustion of the domestic labor supply or the relative one of exhaustion of labor willing to work for low wages.

Relative scarcity is a product of past organization of the working-class and the approval of social security and welfare legislation which effectively places a "floor" under wages and reduces the vulnerability of the unemployed (Bonacich, 1976). Germany and Switzerland approach the conditions of absolute scarcity; the United States, England, and France are examples of relatively scarce labor (Castells, 1975; Castles and Kosack, 1973).

A third initial proposition is that the defense of the rate of profit against labor scarcity and higher labor costs takes two historical forms: (a) increasing the productivity of labor per worker; and (b) finding new supply sources of low-cost labor.

Larger enterprises in the United States and elsewhere in the industrialized world have evolved a pattern of meeting increases in labor costs with technological innovation and reduction in the size of the labor force. In addition, those in the "oligapolistic" sector—controlling substantial shares of their respective markets—are able to pass on the costs of labor increases as price increases to consumers (O'Connor, 1973). Smaller industrial and service firms cannot readily pass on their labor costs. In addition, many continue to be labor intensive since there is no available technology to increase labor productivity or it is beyond their means. In this situation, the only available alternative is to seek a reduction of the share of the product going to labor as wages.

The search for new sources of low-cost labor takes two major forms: 1) exporting the production process to where such labor sources are found; and 2) importing low-cost labor to replace or supplement the domestic work force.

The export of labor intensive production abroad accounts for the rapid industrial growth in recent years of places such as Korea, Taiwan, Hong Kong, Singapore, and some Caribbean nations (Jalée, 1973; NACLA, 1976). In the particular case of Mexico, the *maquiladoras*—U.S. industries which settle on the Mexican side of the border under a custom-and-tax agreement with the Mexican government—constitute a well-documented instance of cheap labor production abroad for re-export back to the United States. Labor intensive industries, such as electronics and textiles, have been particularly prominent among the maquiladoras (NACLA, 1976; Urquidi and Villarreal, 1975).

There are a number of firms which, by their very nature, cannot easily export themselves abroad. Agricultural enterprises are the most obvious and best publicized examples, although certainly not the only ones. A wide variety of urban services cannot be "produced" except in-place and, hence, require a readily available supply of low-cost labor. Conversely, the historical function of labor immigration has been to defend the rate of profit by increasing the supply of available workers.

Usefulness of immigrant workers to domestic firms does not depend solely on the quantitative increase they produce on the supply of labor, but on their qualitative characteristics as well. Immigrant labor is usually low-cost labor which can be used to replace more expensive domestic workers, or to weaken the latter's bargaining position. The greater exploitation of immigrant workers is a fact which has been repeatedly documented (Rosenblum, 1973; Castles and Kosack, 1973; Mohl and Betten, 1972), though it has been often attributed to the greater "docility" of immigrants or to their lower aspirations (Lipset and Bendix, 1959).

The greater exploitation of immigrant workers, however, is not a consequence of their docility or compliance, but of their objective vulnerability. Such vulnerability is a direct result of having crossed a political border. As a new and foreign group, immigrant workers are more easily subject to threats and repression by employers and the state than citizen workers. Their protesting work conditions can be easily defined as the work of "foreign subversives" (Rosenblum, 1973), rather than one involving legitimate labor revindications. It is the political status of immigrants and the legal relationship it entails with the state, which accounts for their objective position of weakness *vis-à-vis* their employers. From this proposition it follows, however, that the more rights immigrants acquire and the more they come to resemble the native proletariat, the less useful they are as a defense against labor demands. It is for this reason that the objective interest of firms for which profit depends on a low-wage labor force is to import immigrants in the most legally tenuous position. Thus, illegal immigrants become the most vulnerable of workers. Their juridical situation deprives them of most civil rights and prevents their effective organization for making demands.

The act of surreptitiously crossing a political border places the worker in a still weaker position than legal immigrants, since it formally confronts him with the enforcement apparatus of the receiving state. The status of violator of legal codes prevents open challenge to work conditions and creates serious barriers in efforts to involve the immigrant in organizations of the domestic working class. This juridical weakness is "appropriated" by employers in the form of a higher rate of profit. The rate of exploitation of these workers is thus in direct relationship to their condition as a legally defenseless group.

The advantages of hiring illegal labor are not limited, however, to wages paid by individual employers. For the receiving economy as a whole, illegal labor saves the cost of rearing the worker and supporting him during his early unproductive years. This is a trait which illegals share with all immigrants. In addition, however, the juridical conditions of illegals prevent them from claiming or taking advantage of benefits such as old age pensions, unemployment compensation, disability payments, and the like. As available studies indicate, illegal Mexican workers respond to long term unemployment by simply returning home (Cornelius, 1976; Dinerman, 1977). For the class of employers as a whole, illegal aliens save the cost of production of the labor force and its reproduction during unproductive periods and old age.

A corollary of this proposition is that, during periods of high unemployment such as in recessions, illegals return or are returned to their country. This shifts the costs of supporting an idle labor force from the core to the periphery of the international economy. The experience of mass returns and deportations of Mexican workers during the years following the Depression, during "Operation Weback" in 1954, and the campaign during the recent (1974-76) recession provide historical evidence of this pattern (Cardenas, 1976).

The above propositions might suggest, however, a teleological argument in which illegal immigration is deliberately brought about by the class of employers most affected by high domestic labor cost. The fact that they have made use of this movement and found it advantageous does not mean that they deliberately instigated its emergence. Illegal immigration is not the only means of meeting a condition of labor scarcity in advanced capitalist societies, as the experience of labor programs in Western Europe show. More importantly, Southwest growers—perhaps the most prominent class of employers of Mexican labor—opposed throughout the twentieth century attempts to enforce the border, since they regarded such regulation as a threat to the free movement of their labor (Barrera, 1977). It was only later that growers and other employers perceived the advantages of surreptitious entry in terms of increasing the legal vulnerability of immigrants without significantly decreasing their numbers.

Reasons that led the American state to restrict legal immigration but, later on, to allow illegal immigration as a form of providing labor to threatened enterprises are the subject of Robert Bach's article. His analysis begins, in a sense, where the above propositions end. To round this introduction, one final point, concerning the concrete case of Mexican immigration, must be made:

Illegal Mexican immigration is not a new phenomenon, but a historical movement transformed in its legal character by deliberate political decision. Criminalizing this pre-established migratory flow was a decision originally taken against the migrants and their employers and on the basis of events involving interests of capital and organized workers in the center of the American political economy (Barrera, 1977; Bach, 1977).

CONDITIONS IN MEXICO

Concerning the situation of peripheral societies, three initial propositions must be advanced: 1) international labor immigration does not tend to originate at present in societies which are rural and stagnant, but in those which are urbanizing and industrializing within a capitalist framework; 2) contrary to the situation of advanced nations, peripheral countries tend to be characterized by an abundance of labor, either in the absolute sense of unemployed individuals or in the relative one of individuals who can be easily shifted from their present activities for minor increases in remuneration; and 3) because of the absence of alternatives, industrialization proceeds in peripheral capitalist societies on the basis of technologies developed for the conditions of labor scarcity in core nations.

The labor needs of capital intensive industries in peripheral countries can be easily met by the abundant domestic labor supply. Around the employed industrial sectors, there develop a vast network of informal activities which survive by providing for the needs of employed workers and simultaneously cheapening the cost of their consumption (Portes, 1978). Even labor absorption by the informal sector, however, is not enough. Conditions of labor oversupply in peripheral countries are also aggravated by the trend of capitalist industrialization in peripheral countries to be regressive in terms of income distribution. A positive correlation may be found to exist, between the growth of the product and the growth of income inequality among the classes.

The specific case of Mexico (*see*, Eckstein, 1977; Blair, 1974) and others, such as Brazil (Baer, 1975; Bacha, 1976), show that the success of the import-substitution strategy of industrialization, while leading to aggregate economic growth, tends to increase the already vast disparities in wealth between the small managerial and capital owning minority and the mass of the population. Reasons for this pattern are complex and could not be adequately treated here. The fundamental point, however, is that the progressive expropriation of the majority of the population removes it from access to the standards of living regarded as minimally acceptable in the advanced countries. This situation is aggravated, in turn, by two other developments. Initially, the industrial transformation of a peripheral country tends to diffuse among the mass of the population the reality and benefits of "modern" standards of consumption. Efforts by consumer-goods industrial firms to expand the internal market lead to constant and widespread use of the media in an effort to reach all sectors of the population. This includes vast layers of population whose economic situation scarcely permits considering the purchase of advertised products (Delacroix, 1977).

The second development aggravating the situation is that industrial expansion progressively weakens the bonds of rural subsistence economies mobilizing their population toward the cities. This, in turn, increases the over-supply of labor in urban areas.

From the standpoint of the state, the combination of an unemployed and underemployed labor force, regressive income distribution, exposure of the population to unattainable modern consumption standards, and mobilization of the peasantry toward cities adds up to an explosive situation. Frequently, the only recourse left to the state is systematic repression (Cardoso, 1973). From this perspective, it becomes clear why the Mexican government, like similar governments in other peripheral countries, has not been particularly keen in discouraging emigration of part of the domestic labor force abroad.

Peripheral capitalist nations benefit from labor emigration in two ways: 1) politically, migration alleviates the tensions created by growing inequalities and the demonstration effect of modern standards of consumption; and 2) economically, it strengthens the fiscal position of the state through remittances of hard currency from emigrants.

It must be stressed, however, that such benefits are associated with the fact of migration and not with the fact that migration is illegal. Peripheral governments have, in fact, a vested interest in legalizing international labor immigration for two reasons: first, legal agreements tend to insure the continuity and predictability of the movement; second, they increase, in time, the rate of home remittances by decreasing the exploitation to which workers are subject abroad. For these reasons, the Mexican government has repeatedly proposed re-establishment of a contract labor program. In 1972, for example, bilateral study commissions were established by the presidents of the United States and Mexico to study problems relating to illegal immigration. Final reports were issued in 1973 with different conclusions. The Mexican Study Commission recommended re-establishment of the Bracero Program in a modified form. Predictably, this recommendation was rejected by the U.S. Commission (Cardenas, 1976).

Illegal or not, the fundamental point, however, is that international labor immigration responds to structural determinants in both sending and receiving countries. Such determinants exist independent of the apparatus of legal regulation, the national pride and culture of the exporting society, and the intentions of political leaders.

International labor migration also establishes a symbiotic bond between countries in different positions in the capitalist economy. It simultaneously alleviates labor scarcity and high labor costs in core areas and conditions of labor over-supply, capital scarcity, and difficulty in controlling the labor force in peripheral ones.

The simultaneous transfer of labor and capital and the convergence of needs met by illegal immigration should not be taken to mean that the movement consists of a one-way flow into the "promised land" of advanced societies. From the point of view of individual workers, migration is a strategy to maximize economic opportunities distributed unequally in space. The specific opportunity attached to illegal entry is access to highly paid (in terms of the peripheral country) manual work.

In the specific case of Mexican immigrants, permanent stay in the United States does not maximize, however, all economic opportunities. Investments based on accumulated savings during stays in the U.S., can be made more easily in places of origin or elsewhere in Mexico. Greater familiarity with the social and economic context, the help of relatives and friends, and the greater yield of money savings in Mexico encourage significant return investments by illegal migrants. As the article by Ina Dinerman suggests, the consumption value of U.S.-accumulated savings also acquires greater social significance and has a greater yield in places of origin. While, from the point of view of U.S. employers, Mexican illegals represent a low-cost and tractable labor force; from the point of view of the migrants, employers and the work they offer may be a simple way of replenishing family cash or acquiring the means to start and expand a business. As such, illegal labor migration cannot be conceptualized as a simple demographic displacement, but as a process of network-building through which individuals adapt to the uneven spatial distribution of economic advantage. The process may involve return migration and a cyclical pattern in which "commuting" across the border is timed to coincide with changing economic opportunities and family needs.

PROPOSED POLICIES

In August 1977, President Carter announced the Administration's proposals to deal with illegal immigration to the United States. At the time of this writing, the proposals were still in Congress where extensive hearings have been held. The purpose of analyzing these proposals is to clarify their meaning in the light of the objective situation they aim to modify. The language of humanitarianism in which they are couched does not fully convey their implications for the American economy and for those nations where immigration originates. The theoretical perspective outlined by the above set of propositions is useful in guiding analysis of what these implications might be.

Major points of the Administration's proposals are well known and do not need detailed restatement. In essence, they consist of amnesty for illegal immigrants who can prove continuous residence in the United States before January 1, 1970; a partial amnesty for those who can prove residence in the United States prior to January 1, 1977; and a renewed enforcement effort to prevent further illegal immigration. Illegal aliens in the first category will be eligible for permanent residence status; once this is granted, they will enjoy the same social security rights as citizen workers and will be eligible for citizenship after a three-to-five year period.

Illegal immigrants in the country before 1977 will be eligible for a change of status to the newly created category of temporary resident alien (TRA); they will have the right to reside and work in the United States for a period of five years, though they will lack access to both major Federal social security benefits and eventual citizenship.

The new border enforcement effort will consist of significant increases in the personnel of the Border Patrol and other enforcement agencies; the creation of task forces to capture and prosecute smuggling rings; and, most importantly, the application of stiff civil fines to employers who engage in a "pattern or practice" of hiring illegal aliens (U.S. Department of Justice, 1978). In addition, the legislative proposals mention unspecified efforts to work jointly with the governments of the countries from which illegal immigration comes.

The Administration has made efforts to present these proposals as stemming from humanitarian and populist concerns: illegals already in the country will be integrated into American society, thus preventing the creation of an "underclass" of exploited workers; effective enforcement of the border will prevent further unfair competition with the American labor force. While these explanations are in part valid, they fail to clarify the ultimate politico-economic intent and implications of the proposals.

Consider first the full pardon provision. Despite the importance attributed by the Administration to this humanitarian measure, its significance is likely to be quite limited for the actual number of beneficiaries is a relatively small minority. Apprehension data from the Immigration and Naturalization Service (1977) and all other available figures indicate that the flow of illegal immigrants reached truly massive proportions only during the present decade. In relative terms, those coming before 1970 are but a small fraction of total illegal immigration.

Two additional trends point in the same direction. First, early illegal immigrants wishing to settle permanently in the United States have often managed to legalize their situation via "family reunification" and other provisions of the 1965 Immigration Law. Details of these provisions have been spelled out elsewhere (*see*, Briggs, 1975). While the proportion of pre-1970 illegal immigrants who have legalized their situation is unknown, there is evidence that a substantial percentage of legal Mexican immigration in recent years is composed of former illegal immigrants. An ongoing study of a sample of 822 Mexican legal immigrants first interviewed at entry points in Laredo and El Paso in 1973, found that over 60 percent could be reliably estimated to have lived earlier in the United States as illegals. Over ninety percent of the sample had obtained resident visas under family reunification provisions as spouses and relatives of U.S. citizens and permanent residents (Portes, 1977).

Finally, there is the particular character of illegal labor migration, as described at the close of the preceeding section. The scare rhetoric during the recent recession (1974–75) and much scholarly discourse as well portrayed the flow as a oneway exodus from hunger and want. Contrary to this, all available evidence for Mexican immigrants indicates that the process is a complex one, frequently involving temporary stays, return migration, and a cyclical re-entry pattern. The illegal population in the United States at any given time might be best characterized as those in the process of consolidating an economic position in the United States or in their country of origin, rather than those who once crossed the gates of the "land of plenty" never to return.

It is not probable that many of the pre-1970 illegal immigrants are still in the U.S. as illegals at present. Those wishing to stay frequently managed to legalize their situation; many others have undoubtedly returned to their country to live or reinvest savings accumulated during their northbound trips. Thus, the category of "fully amnestied" under the Administration's proposals is likely to represent the exception, rather than the rule among the current illegal population.

More important are the proposed regulations affecting the bulk of illegal immigrants: those arriving during the present decade. It was noted above that illegal immigration was not the only means of channelling low-cost foreign labor to threatened enterprises in the competitive sector. The contract-labor program utilized by Western European countries offers the best known alternative. Assuming that the intention is to transform the illegal labor flow into a regulated program, the Administration faces two alternatives.

The first, and simplest, is to repatriate as many illegals as possible, effectively control the border, and then organize the regulated entry of foreign labor. Such strategy would meet insurmountable obstacles beginning with the opposition of churches, ethnic organizations, civil rights groups, and the Mexican government to massive arrests and repatriations and ending with the historic opposition of the AFL-CIO to any contract foreign labor program. Fortunately, there is a second strategy. This consists of converting illegal workers already in the country into a *de facto* contract labor force. Current official estimates of the number of illegals already in the United States are three-to-five millions (U.S. Department of Justice, 1978). This is a sizable figure comparable to the total number of foreign contract workers for all of Western Europe in recent years (Castells, 1975).

How can this transformation be carried out? By legalizing the status of illegal aliens and their right to work, while withholding permanent residence and social welfare services available to citizens. Crucial among the latter are the rights to unemployment and welfare payments since these would place the same "floor" under new contract workers as now exists for citizens and permanent residents.

The Administration's proposed legislation would accomplish precisely this. It will give illegal workers temporary work permits without access to permanent residence and citizenship—which would strengthen their capacity for organization; without the right to bring their families—which would force increases in salaries and social costs for the state; and without a "flow" of social security benefits—which would eventually render their labor as expensive as that of domestic workers. Temporary resident aliens will be ineligible for such benefits as Medicaid, food stamps, aid to families with dependent children, and supplemental security income. They will receive a five year residence permit, after which their situation is to be reviewed by the Justice Department.

Thus, while these proposals will reduce the vulnerability and exploitation of illegal workers, they will still preserve many of the features which have made immigrant labor attractive in the past. The U.S. economy will continue to save the "indirect costs" of social welfare required for citizens and permanent resident workers. Temporary workers will also lack access to political rights and will remain under a vulnerable legal situation given the precarious nature of their residency permits.

Passage of the Administration's proposals will mean that the United States will have a recognized foreign contract labor force, thus approaching the situation of other Western industrialized nations. The strategy adopted has the advantage of neatly by-passing organized labor's opposition to any renewed bracero or immigrant workers' program by creating this category out of workers who have already managed to enter the country. This is justified in the name of humanitarian concerns which disarm labor opposition.

The most important question for the future, however, lies in the third part of the Administration's proposals: enforcement of the border to prevent further illegal immigration. The issue here is whether the government will indeed be willing and able, in the face of sustained internal and external pressures, to implement the necessary measures. If it does not, what the present legislative package would have accomplished is essentially to stratify the illegal labor force into an elite of permanent and pardoned immigrants, a stable mass of recognized temporary workers, and a rapidly growing sub-stratum of new illegals. The situation would be similar to that of several Western European countries, where legal and illegal immigrants co-exist and fulfill different functions for different layers of firms. This outcome is not unlikely, since the newly legalized temporary labor force is bound to be progressively absorbed by the larger enterprises, thus generating renewed demand for low-cost labor among farmers and small urban employers.

If, on the other hand, the illegal flow is stopped, a series of predictable consequences would follow. Enterprises for which the production process is not tied to a particular location can be expected to continue exporting themselves abroad, especially to peripheral low-cost labor countries. Other firms in services, industry, and agriculture would step up pressures for some formalized access to foreign sources of labor. Since the economic situation in Mexico is not likely to change in the near future, these employers would have a major ally in the Mexican government. Stopping labor immigration would mean doing away with a symbiotic relationship which today fulfills important needs for capitalist economies at different levels of development. Affected interests on both sides of the border can be expected to put pressure on the Administration to find a suitable alternative.

A "guest" immigrant worker program patterned after the Western European model is one of the most likely outcomes. The proposed transformation of illegals already in the country into a temporary work force might be regarded as a first step in this direction. Barring this, the federal government would be forced to decrease costs of enterprises depending on access to cheap labor through some form of subsidy. While the survival of many enterprises in the competitive sector is not essential to the functioning and growth of U.S. capitalism, they are still politically powerful in local government and in Congress (O'Connor, 1973). The tenacious resistance offered by Southwest growers, first to the end of the Bracero Program and then to enforcement efforts against illegal workers (Stoddard, 1976), is only a partial example of the reaction to be expected if border enforcement is not followed by substitute access to other sources of foreign low-cost labor.

Recent events, including the proposals of the Carter Administration, offer vast evidence that illegal labor immigration is neither a conjunctural nor a regionally-circumscribed phenomenon, but a process which is structurally central to both the receiving and exporting economies. The flow of labor from peripheral to core nations constitutes one of the most important defining features of the contemporary world economy. Those in the United States who insist on regarding illegal immigration as a purely domestic phenomenon are confronted with the evidence of a Mexican government acting like a veritable lobby group on a piece of American legislation. If nothing else, these recent developments have brought light on a previously obscure process where, protected by public indifference, interests on both sides of the border benefited for many years from the plight of the most defenseless workers. It is our hope that the tentative propositions presented above and the four papers which follow would contribute to the understanding of this complex phenomenon.

REFERENCES

Bach, R.L.
1977 "Mexican Immigration and the American State". Paper presented at the session on

Mexican and Central American Immigration, meetings of the Latin American Studies Association, Houston. November.

Bacha, E.
1976 *Os mitos de uma decada: ensaios da economia brasileira.* Rio de Janeiro: Paz e Terra.

Baer, W.
1975 "La reciente experiencia brasileña de desarrollo: una interpretación", *Revista Paraquaya de Sociología* 34:7-39. Sept.-Dec.

Barrera, M.
1977 *Class Segmentation and Internal Colonialism, A Theory of Racial Inequality Based on the Chicano Experience.* Unpublished book manuscript, Department of Political Science, University of California at San Diego.

Blair, C.P.
1974 "Mexico in the World Economy", *Current History,* 217-230. May.

Bonacich, E.
1976 "Advanced Capitalism and Black/White Relations: A Split Labor Market Interpretation", *American Sociological Review,* 41:34-51. February.

Briggs, V.M.
1975 "Labor Market Aspects of Mexican Migration to the United States in the 1970s". Paper presented at the Conference on Contemporary Dilemmas of the Mexican-United States Border. San Antonio: The Weatherhead Foundation.

Bustamante, J.A.
1976 "Espaldas mojadas: materia prima para la expansión del capital norteamericano", *Cuadernos del CES,* 9.

Cardenas, G.
1976 "United States Immigration Policy Toward Mexico: A Historical Perspective". Unpublished manuscript, Department of Sociology, University of Texas at Austin.

Cardoso, F.H.
1973 "Associated Dependent Development: Theoretical and Practical Implications". In *Authoritarian Brazil,* Edited by A. Stepan. New Haven: Yale University Press.

Castells, M.
1975 "Immigrant Workers and Class Struggles in Advanced Capitalism: The Western European Experience," *Politics and Society,* 5:33-66.

Castles, S. and G. Kosack
1973 *Immigrant Workers and Class Structure in Western Europe.* London: Oxford University Press.

Cornelius, W.A.
1976 "Mexican Migration to the United States: The View from Rural Sending Communities". Unpublished manuscript, Department of Political Science, Massachusetts Institute of Technology.

Delacroix, J.
1977 "The Permeability of Informational Boundaries and Economic Growth: A Cross-National Study", *Studies in Comparative International Development,* 12:3-28. Spring.

Dinerman, I.
1977 "Patterns of Adaptation among Households of U.S.-Bound Migrants From Michoacán, Mexico". Paper presented at the session on Mexican and Central American Immigration, meetings of the Latin American Studies Association, Houston. November.

Eckstein, S.
1977 *The Poverty of Revolution, the State and the Urban Poor in Mexico.* Princeton: Princeton University Press.

Immigration and Naturalization Service
1977 Special Tabulations to be included in the *1976 Annual Report.* Washington, D.C.: U.S. Department of Justice.

Jalee, P.
1973 *Imperialism in the Seventies.* New York: Third Press.

Lipset, S.M. and R. Bendix
1959 *Social Mobility in Industrial Society.* Berkeley: University of California Press.

Mohl, R.A. and N. Betten
1972 "Ethnic Adjustment in the Industrial City: The International Institute of Gary", *International Migration Review,* 6:361–376. Winter.

NACLA
1976 "Hit and Run: U.S. Runaway Shops in the Mexican Border", *Latin America and Empire Report,* 9:(5). November.

O'Connor, J.
1973 *The Fiscal Crisis of the State.* New York: St. Martin's Press.

Portes, A.
1974 "Return of the Wetback", *Society,* 11:40–46. March-April.
1977 "Recent Latin American Immigrants to the United States". Progress Report Submitted to the National Institute of Mental Health and National Science Foundation. (mimeo.)
1978 "The Informal Sector and the World-Economy, Notes on the Structure of Subsidized Labor", *Bulletin of the Institute of Development Studies* (University of Sussex). Forthcoming.

Rosenblum, G.
1973 *Immigrant Workers, Their Impact on American Labor Radicalism.* New York: Basic Books.

Stoddard, E.R.
1976 "A Conceptual Analysis of the 'Alien Invasion:' Institutionalized Support of Illegal Mexican Aliens in the U.S.", *International Migration Review,* 10:157–189. Summer.

U.S. Department of Justice
1978 "Illegal Immigration: President's Program". Special document issued by the Office of the Attorney General. February.

Urquidi, V.L. and S. Mendez Villarreal
1975 "Importancia económica de la zona fronteriza del norte de México". Paper presented at the Conference on Contemporary Dilemmas of the Mexican-United States Border. San Antonio: The Weatherhead Foundation.

[5]

Economic Growth and Immigration in Venezuela[1]

Saskia Sassen-Koob
Queens College of the
City University of New York

Changes in immigration flows and policy in the last three decades are linked to differences in the level and types of economic growth in Venezuela. This provides an historical context within which to locate the post-1973 rise in immigrant entries and policy changes which have led to a definition of immigration as the import of foreign workers. These changes were generated by the unusually high economic growth rates made possible by the increase in the international price of oil, Venezuela's major export.

Between 1972 and 1974 state revenues in Venezuela increased by 250 percent as a result of the rise in international oil prices. The consequent expansion in the government's financial capacity and the decision to use this potential for the implementation of a vast development plan (*Gaceta Oficial*, 1976a) created the conditions for a pronounced jump in the demand for labor. Responding to this context of an increase in government expenditures, economic growth and labor needs, Venezuela initiated an aggressive pro-immigration policy in 1973. The distinguishing feature of post-1973 immigration has less to do with quantitative levels, though these were significant, than with a redefinition in government practice and policy regarding the place of immigration in the economic development of the country.

Before 1973, Venezuelan immigration was viewed as a factor contributing to 1) overall population growth, especially in rural areas; 2) the improvement of cultural values and social organization by the incorporation of Europeans; and 3) the agricultural development through the settlement of European farmers (Thompson and Caliman, 1977:43–68; Kritz, 1975:517–519; Chi-Yi-Chen and Urquijo, 1974). In practice, however, immigration before 1973 only further stimulated population growth

[1]I wish to thank the Social Science Research Council for a grant supporting this work and the many persons in Venezuela who made the research possible, most especially Luis Lander and Daniel Asuaje. I am most grateful to Dean B. Savage for comments and suggestions.

in a few already rapidly growing cities and provided a labor supply for the urban labor market, at least partially displacing Venezuelans. Until 1958, Venezuela had fairly non-restrictive entry regulations for foreigners. After 1958 immigration was curtailed, partly in recognition of both its failure to fulfill the expected functions and the preponderance of foreigners in jobs that could have been performed by consequently unemployed Venezuelans.

After 1973, immigration began to be viewed more specifically as a factor which contributed directly to production. There is a recognition at the policy level that foreign labor is needed in all sectors of the economy if oil revenues, representing over 70 percent of all state revenues, are to be transformed into productive capacity (*Consejo Nacional de Recursos Humanos,* henceforth National Council on Human Resources, 1977; *Gaceta Oficial,* 1976b; 1978).

In the last few years Venezuela has officially stated that it has a problem of labor scarcity in semi-skilled, skilled, technical and managerial occupations, and that it would have a very serious shortage in its rural labor supply if it were not for the large undocumented work force (National Council on Human Resources, 1977:3-50;138). To alleviate labor scarcities, the government has implemented a number of new measures and programs. The three most important measures form the core of the post-1973 immigration policy and practice and include: 1) creation of an agency within the Ministry of Planning (CORDIPLAN) charged with the recruitment of foreign workers; 2) signing of labor import agreements with Spain and Portugal, to be followed with other such agreements; and 3) signing of the agreement on international labor circulation among the countries of the Andean Pact which has as one of its implicit aims the regularization of the undocumented rural workers in Venezuela.

The post-1973 immigration policy and practice emerge from processes rooted in a broader political and economic context and in the history of immigration in Venezuela. This paper provides a brief overview of this historical process but focuses primarily on two factors: the increase in undocumented immigration during the restrictive immigration period of the 1960s and the change in both immigration and immigration policy following the 1973 economic boom.[2] The pro-immigration phase of the

[2]The data are mostly drawn from three sources: 1) published data, especially by the Venezuelan Bureau of the Census and the *Dirección de Identificación y Extranjería* (henceforth DIEX); 2) processed data available in mimeograph form for internal circulation, especially data by the *Ministerio de Fomento,* the *Consejo Nacional de Recursos Humanos* and the DIEX; and 3) processed data available in data-banks, especially in the *Ministerio de Fomento,* the DIEX and the CENDES (*Centro de Estudios del Desarrollo*).

1950s has been studied extensively (Paez Celis, 1973:41 ff.; Chi-Yi-Chen, 1973; Kritz, 1975) and is only summarized here.

IMMIGRATION AND ECONOMIC GROWTH

Since the 1940s when the entry of foreigners first became a significant demographic factor, Venezuela's immigration record shows a fluctuating pattern. The massive immigration phase in the 1950s was followed by restrictions and officially negative net flows in the 1960s, shifting after 1973 to a rapid inflow of foreigners (Venezuela, *Ministerio de Fomento,* 1975, IV:93–95; 1965, IV:333–335). However, what actually took place was not a change from a positive net immigration flow in the 1950s to a negative one in the 1960s, but rather a transition from one kind of immigration to another with the absolute number of entries and positive net balance remaining fairly high even during the restrictive period. The difference was that the immigrant flow of the 1960s consisted almost wholly of undocumented workers directed predominantly to the rural sector rather than the cities as had been the case in the 1950s. Furthermore, the 1960 immigrants originated in other Latin American countries rather than the traditional European emigration countries (Spain, Portugal, Italy) which dominated the 1950s immigration. Thus, the implementation of a pro-immigration policy after 1973 represents not so much a reopening of the country to immigration *per se,* as a reopening to legal immigration and to the traditional European nationalities.

Not surprisingly, there is a relationship between these different kinds and levels of immigration and types of economic growth (Sassen-Koob, 1978; Mármora, 1972). The massive immigration of the 1950s corresponds to a period of unusually high economic growth rates in the secondary sector. It was in this decade that large-scale industrial development began, made possible in part by the huge increases in state revenues which started in the late 1940s when Venezuela became the main oil exporter in the world. Between 1945 and 1957, oil production increased by 300 percent and state revenues, as a result showed an eightfold increase (*Banco Central de Venezuela*: various years). Between 1950 and 1957, industrial production grew at an average of 12 percent a year; the average yearly investment rate in fixed capital represented over 25 percent of the gross national product; and the value of industrial production at constant prices increased by 240 percent (*Banco Central de Venezuela,* various years; Aranda, 1977:125–163; Sassen-Koob, 1979; Araujo, 1969). The consequent growth in secondary and tertiary sector jobs caused both a large scale immigration from Europe and massive internal migration (Paez Celis, 1973:41 ff.; Chi-Yi-Chen, 1973; Laxague and Paez Celis, 1975).

The vast majority of the immigrants stayed in a few large cities, particularly Caracas, because of the easy access to a large supply of jobs requiring few skills especially low-level tertiary sector jobs (Kritz, 1975: 524-529).

During the restrictive immigration decade of the 1960s there was a slowdown in industrial growth but a significant increase in agricultural production. At the same time there was a progressive depletion of the rural labor supply due to migration to urban areas during the 1950s. By 1961, less than one-third of the labor force was employed in farming, a share much lower than that typical of the Third World (Handelman, 1978:3). This depletion, along with the high growth rates in the agricultural sector, gave rise to labor scarcities and hence to a growing demand for workers from neighboring Colombia. Because of the closing of the borders, the entry and recruitment of Colombians had to be illegal and the imposition of even minimal entry controls was excluded. Indeed, the estimated number of entries and balance for the decade were similar to the figures for the legal immigration of the 1950s.

The huge jump in state revenues after 1973 and the implementation of a large five-year development plan created the conditions for a massive growth in the demand for labor—between 1976 and 1980 some 900,000 to 1,000,000 workers will be added to a labor force which in 1976 numbered only 37 million.[3] The Council on Human Resources has estimated that up to one-half of these workers will have to be imported, with the remainder to be provided by the national manpower training program. Thus the high growth rates in all sectors of the economy pushed the government toward the implementation of labor import policies.

UNDOCUMENTED IMMIGRATION AFTER 1960

There are no precise figures on the numbers of undocumented workers who came, left, or stayed. However, most estimates suggest that there was a total number of entries for the decade of about one million, and that by the early 1970s total net illegal immigration was about one-half million.

Although there are undocumented workers from a growing number of Latin American and Caribbean countries, it is generally agreed that up to 90 percent are from Colombia. Because of this, most estimates concern Colombians alone. The Colombian Bureau of Statistics (D.A.N.E.) has calculated that the net emigration of Colombians to Venezuela, both legal

[3]The severity of the labor shortage is brought out by the expansion of the national manpower training program, the *Instituto Nacional de Cooperación Educativa* (INCE). Its budget was increased by over 300% between 1976 and 1977 and its enrollment grew from little over 100,000 to over half a million in that same period (*Gaceta Oficial,* 1978).

and illegal, exceeded 441,800 persons between 1963 and 1973 (Colombia, *Ministerio del Trabajo y Seguridad Social,* 1978:18). As the balance of legal entries for that decade was about 70,000 persons, this would leave 371,000 undocumented Colombians. According to the Venezuelan Bureau of Statistics there were almost 400,000 undocumented immigrants by 1971. However, local authorities in the border states have estimated that by the early 1970s there were about 400,000 undocumented persons in one state alone, Zulia (Thompson and Caliman, 1977:78n). The Director General of the Immigration Office indicated that there were between 800,000 and 900,000 undocumented persons by 1976 (*El Nacional,* September 30, 1976; Interview with Dr. Ramon Velasquez). In 1971, President Caldera mentioned the figure of "several hundred thousands of undocumented Colombians" (*El Nacional,* January 29, 1971). Based on fieldwork, G. Rochcau, head of the International Catholic Migration Commission, calculated that there were 500,000 undocumented persons in 1971 (1972). The National Council on Human Resources (1977:125–138) showed how figures on the rural labor force which contain incongruencies can be explained if the presence of undocumented workers is considered. The Council estimated that by 1976 there were at least 700,000 undocumented Colombians and significant numbers of Brazilians and Ecuadorians, as well as a growing number of other Latin American and Caribbean nationalities. The Council expects the share of foreign workers in the rural labor force to increase over the next few years, especially if the growth rates foreseen by the five-year plan (1976–80) are fulfilled. According to a study done for the Ministry of the Interior and for the Council (Thompson and Caliman, 1977), recent experience demonstrates that the undocumented labor force is a needed labor supply in the rural economy which represented at least ten percent of the total labor force in 1976 (83–84) and well over half of the rural labor force. (*See also,* Gall, 1972).

Since the vast majority of undocumented workers in the 1960s were part of the rural labor supply, this raises a question about the capacity to absorb these workers in the agricultural sector.

During the 1960s this sector experienced high growth rates. While investment rates for the economy as a whole fell by 50 percent, from a yearly average of 26 percent of GNP in the 1950s to 14 percent in the 1960s, investment rates in agriculture remained constant as a percentage of GNP and increased by 56 percent in constant monetary values (*Banco Central de Venezuela,* 1970). Various facts indicate that there was an internal market capable of absorbing an increase in national food production. In the 1950s, agriculture's share of the GNP was less than half the respective share in Argentina or Mexico and about one-fourth that of Brazil or Colombia (Handelman, 1978:3). In that same decade, food imports increased at a higher rate than food production, reaching over 40 percent of total consumption by 1957 (*Banco Central de Venezuela*, 1970:192–193). Taking the 1952–1956 years as a base period and comparing Venezuela's agricultural production record up to 1970 with that of other countries, we find a very high rate of 135 percent for Venezuela in contrast to 47 percent for Western Europe, 24 percent for the U.S.A., and 58 percent for Latin America as a whole (Food and Agriculture Organization, various years; Handelman, 1978: Table 3). These pronounced differences are only in part explained by Venezuela's low level of mechanization in agriculture during the base period considered. Central is also the priority given to agricultural growth by the new government in 1958 which reflected itself in a 31 percent increase in agricultural production from 1958 to 1960. Between 1957 and 1969, cultivated land increased by 62.8 percent (*Banco Central de Venezuela*, 1970:1). Throughout this decade growth rates in agricultural production were consistently higher than in the officially recorded population.

Parallel to this growth in the rural economy, the large internal migrations to the cities continued. By 1960, two-thirds of the population was urban and less than one-third of the labor force was employed in farming, both very low shares by Third World standards. The rural labor force declined by a further 10 percent between 1960 and 1970. These figures probably underestimate the actual number of Venezuelans who left rural employment because they include foreign undocumented workers in the 1970 computation of the rural work force. Yet, even allowing for this inclusion, the official tally of the rural labor force in 1970 must be a considerable underestimate since the juxtaposition of agricultural growth rates and the numbers of workers would point to an increase in productivity of over 200 percent for this decade (an average of 12 percent a year). If we compare this figure with the already high 8 percent growth in productivity foreseen by the 1976–1980 Plan for the agricultural sector to be attained through a huge increase in investments, then we can see that the 12 percent figure is probably inadequate. That is to say, given the growth in agricultural production, the official figure for the rural labor force in that decade must be a serious underestimate of the actual number of workers employed in the sector. The additional workers went unrecorded because they were undocumented. That undocumented rural workers are filling a void rather than displacing Venezuelans (Council on Human Resources, 1977:138) in a growing agricultural sector indicates that mechanization alone could not outweigh the labor needs created by agricultural expansion.

In sum, the closure of immigration, the rise in agricultural production and the high rate of urbanization of the Venezuelan population in the

1950s and 1960 created the conditions for a labor shortage in rural areas and hence for the absorption of a rapidly growing undocumented immigration. It was in this context that undocumented workers came to constitute a needed labor supply for agricultural production.

POLITICAL AND ECONOMIC CONTEXT FOR THE REOPENING OF IMMIGRATION

The context within which the post-1973 changes in immigration policy and practice took place was characterized by the existence of objective conditions fostering labor scarcities. Just as important were structural and ideological factors which made labor imports an acceptable solution to such scarcities. We have already mentioned the enormous increases in state revenues, which went from 16,432 million *Bolivares* (B.) in 1973 to 42,834 million B. in 1974, where they have remained. Such an increase in state revenues represents a significant growth in the financial potential of the economy in view of the importance of public enterprise in Venezuela which accounted for 30 percent of total investment at the time of the increase.

The second aspect which needs to be emphasized is the decision, at the level of governmental policy, to transform this financial potential into actual productive capacity instead of, for example, placing revenues in the international credit market as private capital throughout Latin America has often done.[4] Thus, the government's capital investments grew by 300 percent between 1973 and 1976. The share of these investments going to industry grew more than ten-fold between 1973 and 1976 and more than four-fold for agriculture (Venezuela, *Ministerio de Hacienda,* various years; Venezuela, Presidente de, 1977: Table 26). For the years of the Fifth Plan (1976–1980) public investment is scheduled to grow by 250 percent, at constant prices. Private investment is expected to remain constant in the first two years and then to experience a jump once the initial phase of the government's industrial plans are carried out (*Gaceta Oficial,* 1976:18, Table II-8). The growth rates foreseen by the Fifth Plan range from a low of 6 percent for the tertiary sector to a high of 13 percent for manufacturing and 15 percent for construction (*Gaceta Oficial,* 1976:15, Tables II-1 and II-2). Another indicator of the rate of expansion is the growth in imports of raw materials and auxiliaries, and machinery and tools for industry and agriculture. In all these categories

[4] Nonetheless the jump in state revenues was so large it could not be fully absorbed by the existing investment structure. To this end the government created an Investment fund and in 1974 placed 31% of state revenues in it. As investment opportunities expanded, this share declined to 6% in 1976.

there have been increases of well over 100 percent and in some cases over 300 percent (Venezuela, *Ministerio de Fomento,* various years; Venezuela, Presidente de, 1977: Tables 40 and 41). In contrast, the value of imports of non-luxury consumption items did not grow and its share of total imports declined from 11.4 percent to 5.2 percent, suggesting an increase in economic activity aimed at import substitution. All indicators point to pronounced growth trends in the productive capacity of all sectors of the economy (*But see also,* Blanco *et al.*, 1977).

Third, the well defined and loudly voiced position of private enterprise on the existence of labor scarcities and the need for their alleviation through immigration must also be considered (FEDECAMARAS, 1977; various years). Throughout the 1960s, several of the producers' associations passed recommendations in their annual assemblies demanding such policy changes from the government. These complaints about labor scarcities continue today even though immigration has been reopened. According to private enterprise, the entry restrictions imposed in 1977 after two years of massive immigration, are an obstacle to the formation of the needed labor supply. The newspapers carry regular complaints by various kinds of producers about the inadequate and/or insufficient labor supply. Employers have used a number of tactics, including panels, study commissions and the creation of a special office, to promote the visibility of the issue. In informal interviews with members of the business elite, the answer to a general question on obstacles to expanded or new investments and ongoing projects was, typically, "an insufficient labor supply". It has, of course, historically been the view of capital that a plentiful labor supply and a certain level of unemployment are necessary for economic growth, and this fact should be seen as informing the position of employers in Venezuela on the issue of labor scarcity. Because these complaints have been raised repeatedly over a long period of time (Cordova and Silva Michelena, 1974; Chi-Yi-Chen and Urquijo, 1974:29) and are found in all sectors of the economy, they have lent a certain political weight and ideological homogeneity to the position of private enterprise on the immigration issue. Immigration has become a central component in the overall political and ideological stance of private enterprise to a much larger extent than in other developing countries.

The fourth aspect is that the labor unions have also lent support to a selective immigration policy after field research showed labor scarcities. This is a politically sensitive issue because in the past Venezuelan unions were against immigration. The present position of labor cannot be seen in isolation from its past victories and defeats. Very briefly, this history is marked by two successful but short-lived class alliances which overthrew dictatorships and imposed populist regimes. In 1945 and then again in

1958 an alliance between, on the one hand, progressive factions of the bourgeoisie and, on the other, organized labor and populist factions of the working class imposed governmental administrations which implemented a number of measures aimed at redirecting power away from the financial-commercial sector of the bourgeoisie and toward the industrial sector and the working class. The contradictions inherent in such alliances help to explain not only their short existence (1945–1948; 1958–1964) but also the highly repressive regimes that followed. As a result of the often bloody struggles of the 1960s, working class militancy had become muted by 1970. These facts explain both why the present government (1974–1978), which considers itself populist, gave union representatives a voice in policy making and implementing bodies and why there were no objections to union participation on the part of private enterprise. There is both the "tradition" of such participation by the unions while at the same time as a result of the defeat of the militancy in the 1960s and, possibly, the incorporation of unions into the status quo after the post-1973 economic boom (Sassen-Koob, 1979) that participation is not threatening to capital.

THE REOPENING OF IMMIGRATION AFTER 1973

Since 1973 there has been a pronounced increase in the numbers of permanent residents, registered entries of foreigners, naturalizations, and legalizations of undocumented workers. By October 1977, the total number of foreigners in Venezuela with residence permits had reached almost 1.2 million in a total population of 13 million. This figure is quite high considering that, in 1961, after a decade of massive immigration, there were only about half a million such foreigners and that by 1971 their number was only slightly higher./Although the 1960s saw the addition of almost 80,000 foreigners, there was also a loss of 57,800 persons with permanent residence permits. With the exception of 1969, each year of the 1960s recorded a loss of permanent residents. The reversal of this trend toward large increases in the number of permanent and temporary residence permits granted occurred over a rather short period of time, doubling the resident population between 1971 and 1977.

In 1976, Spanish migrants constituted the largest group of registered foreigners, followed by Italians, Colombians and Portuguese (*See*, Table 1).

Although the traditional nationalities still dominate, the largest rates of increase were for migrants from other Latin American countries. In the five years between 1971 and 1976, the "other Latin American" share of the Venezuelan population doubled in size. These figures of course exclude

TABLE 1

MAIN NATIONALITIES OF RESIDENT FOREIGNERS IN VENEZUELA 1976

Nationality	n
Spanish	270,700
Italian	223,411
Colombian	187,422
Portuguese	107,753
U.S.A.	79,672
Other	236,842
Total	1,105,800

SOURCE: DIEX, Ministry of the Interior.

the undocumented, who are overwhelmingly Latin American. The differential increase rates for the various Latin American countries point to the diversity of push and pull factors operative in these flows. Thus, the 257 percent increase rate for Uruguayans is clearly related to political push factors, while the 114 percent increase rate of Colombians and the 72 percent increase of Ecuadorians respond more directly to economic push and pull factors (*See*, Table 2).

The number of registered entries experienced a large jump after 1974. In 1975 there were about 570,000 and in 1976, well over 600,000 entries of

TABLE 2

REGISTERED MIGRANTS FROM LATIN AMERICA IN VENEZUELA: DIFFERENTIAL GROWTH RATES 1971–1976

Country	1971	1976	% Increase
Colombia	87,691	187,422	113.7
Ecuador	6,609	11,366	72.0
Peru	3,627	6,481	78.7
Bolivia	1,741	2,513	44.3
Chile	4,646	11,876	55.6
Argentina	7,951	12,111	52.3
Uruguay	1,201	4,286	256.9
Paraguay	208	325	52.3
Brazil	2,214	3,052	37.8
Total	115,888	239,432	106.6

SOURCE: DIEX, Ministry of the Interior.

this type (*See*, Table 3). In the past, the return rate for registered foreigners has been about 50 percent (Thompson and Caliman, 1977:158), but this rate is declining due to the economic boom. A share of registered entries consists of persons who do not intend to stay and who are on short term assignments with foreign or Venezuelan firms.

The declared occupational distribution of registered foreigners at time of arrival for 1976 shows that well over one-fourth of these migrants were clerical or sales workers and between 10 and 15 percent were professionals (*See*, Table 3). There are some marked differences between foreigners from the traditional emigration countries such as Portugal and Spain, and those from the U.S. and England. Thus, well over 15 percent of U.S. and English entries declared managerial and administrative occupations as compared with 4.6 percent of Italians and less than 2 percent of Colombians and Portuguese. Similarly, migrants from the traditional emigration countries were underrepresented in the professions while those from other Latin American countries, including Colombia, were overrepresented (11.5%). A large share of these Latin American professionals are political refugees. It is also the traditional emigration countries which have the largest share of sales and clerical workers, a fact which will tend to reinforce the considerable concentration of these nationalities in small scale commerce and services.

The annual number of naturalizations almost doubled between 1973 and 1974, and then doubled again between 1974 and 1975. Throughout the 1960s and up to 1973 the yearly naturalization level was about 5,000. In 1973 it reached 7,000, in 1974 it rose to 12,000 and in 1975-1976 it jumped up to 45,000. About one-third of all naturalizations (185,862) occurring between 1940 to 1976 took place in the last four years.[5]

There has also been a significant increase in the numbers of foreigners acquiring permanent residence. Thus, in the decade of massive immigration, 1950-1958, there was an annual average of 53,000 permits granted, summing up to a total of 453,000. Between 1959 and 1973, there was a yearly average of 25,400 permits granted; although most of these permits must have gone to persons who entered in the prior decade, the lower figure does in part reflect the negative immigration balance of this decade. Between 1974 and 1976, the annual average increased to about 50,000 (*See*,

[5]The incidence of naturalization varies significantly according to country of origin. Eastern Europeans have high rates of naturalization, ranging from 99.7% for Rumanians to 44% of Poles. In contrast, the traditional emigration nationalities have very low rates of naturalization: 11.6% of Italians, 11.4% of Portuguese, and 25.3% of Spaniards. These rates are still much higher than that of the U.S. (0.5%). Political push factors, the expectation to return to the home country and the comparative attractions of home and immigration country are all factors influencing naturalization rates.

TABLE 3

DECLARED OCCUPATION OF REGISTERED FOREIGNERS UPON ENTRY, VENEZUELA, 1976

Nationality	Manager/ Admin.	Professional	Clerical Sales	Farmer Farmworker	Minors Students	Other	Total
Total (N)	58,942	68,239	224,577	2,223	58,031	296,781	708,793
(%)	(8.3)	(9.6)	(31.7)	(0.3)	(8.2)	(41.9)	(100%)
Colombia	786	4,693	11,271	183	5,142	18,535	40,610
	(1.9)	(11.5)	(27.8)	(0.5)	(12.7)	(45.6)	(100%)
Other	3,996	14,532	25,653	432	13,885	38,666	97,164
South America	(4.1)	(15.0)	(26.4)	(0.4)	(14.3)	(39.8)	(100%)
Central America	2,219	6,008	17,043	199	6,896	27,199	59,564
(includes Caribbean)	(3.7)	(10.1)	(28.6)	(0.3)	(11.6)	(45.7)	(100%)
U.S.A.	30,682	18,294	40,240	—	12,592	74,050	175,858
	(17.4)	(10.4)	(22.9)	—	(7.2)	(42.1)	(100%)
Portugal	338	281	8,965	707	2,244	9,553	22,088
	(1.5)	(1.3)	(40.6)	(3.2)	(10.2)	(43.2)	(100%)
Italy	2,537	3,244	20,593	275	2,974	25,134	54,757
	(4.6)	(5.9)	(37.6)	(0.5)	(5.4)	(45.9)	(100%)
GFR	2,688	3,948	7,566	11	931	10,561	25,705
	(10.5)	(15.4)	(29.4)	(.04)	(3.6)	(41.1)	(100%)
France	2,350	3,552	5,820	37	1,373	9,600	22,732
	(10.3)	(15.6)	(25.6)	(0.2)	(6.0)	(42.2)	(100%)
Netherlands	2,155	1,946	12,285	7	4,320	18,382	39,095
	(5.5)	(5.0)	(31.4)	(.02)	(11.1)	(47.0)	(100%)
England	3,284	2,723	4,513	23	1,408	884	20,792
	(15.8)	(13.1)	(21.7)	(0.1)	(6.8)	(42.5)	(100%)
Other	7,907	9,018	70,628	349	6,266	56,260	150,428
(Spain not included)	(5.3)	(6.0)	(46.9)	(0.2)	(4.2)	(37.4)	(100%)

SOURCE: DIEX, Minestry of the Interior.

Table 4). This is a significant addition for such a short period of time if we consider that between 1941 and 1975 one million permanent residence permits were granted and that 30 percent of such permit holders left the country leaving a balance of 744,000 by 1975. (The 30% departure rate is an overestimate since as many as 77,800 were granted to persons, from countries such as the U.S.A., who never intended to be permanent residents but were simply on short-term assignments).

TABLE 4

ACQUISITION OF PERMANENT RESIDENCE, VENEZUELA, 1950–1976

Years	Total	Yearly Average
1950–1958	453,010	ca. 53,300
1959–1973	381,922	ca. 25,400
1974–1976	147,460	ca. 50,000

SOURCE: DIEX, Ministry of the Interior.

With the growth in entries, naturalizations and acquisitions of permanent residence, there has been a concomitant increase in deportations and legalizations of undocumented workers. Although deportations and legalizations represent only a small share of all undocumented persons, they are significant in that variations in their figures are usually indicative of variations in the size of the total undocumented population. While deportations between 1960 and 1970 averaged about 1,000 annually, in 1975 alone they reached 15,851 and in 1976, 48,172. A similar trend is visible in the case of legalizations. In the twelve years from 1960 to 1972 there was a total of 38,128 legalizations, while in 1976 alone there were 38,334. After 1973 it became quite easy for individuals in certain occupations to legalize their status since the only requirement was demonstration of employment, not difficult given the labor scarcities.

TABLE 5

LEGALIZATIONS AND DEPORTATIONS OF UNDOCUMENTED WORKERS, VENEZUELA, 1960–1976

Years	Legalizations	Deportations
1960–1971	31,093	10,337
1972	7,035	8,290
1973	13,818	3,324
1974	25,848	4,287
1975	36,152	15,851
1976	38,334	48,172

SOURCE: DIEX, Ministry of the Interior.

The increase in legalizations of undocumented workers since 1974 and the massive jump in registered entries of foreigners in 1975 and 1976 pointed to the need for implementing a selective immigration program. The economic boom was attracting a rapidly growing and almost completely unregulated flow of foreigners which was beginning to generate serious problems in terms of the capacity of existing infrastructure to absorb this additional population.

CHANGES IN IMMIGRATION POLICY AND PRACTICE AFTER 1973

Venezuelan immigration policy of the last forty years is based upon the Immigration and Colonization Law of 1936 and the Alien Act of 1937. In practice, it was the latter which covered the overwhelming share of foreign entries. During the massive immigration decade of the 1950s only 73,201 foreigners out of a million came with an immigrant visa. The 1937 Alien Act and its 1943 *Reglamento* define the rights and duties of all foreigners in the country. Immigration itself was actually regulated by the circulars and resolutions emitted by the *Direccion de Identificacion y Extranjeria* (Identification Bureau) of the Ministry of the Interior. Although a number of other agencies were created throughout the last four decades to control or stimulate immigration, in practice the DIEX alone processes the vast majority of all entries.

Since 1976 three additional bodies have been set up to control and regulate immigration. This has had two obvious consequences. First, it has shifted control away from the DIEX, that is to say, away from a body whose main concern is with legalistic issues and national security. Second, insofar as this control has been placed in bodies concerned with economic issues, it has led to a view of immigration in which economic pull factors acquire primary importance. Besides the DIEX, the bodies involved in the immigration process are the National Council on Human Resources, the Tripartite Selective Immigration Commission and the Program for Human Resources, all of which were set up in 1976. Furthermore, the recent ratification of Decision 116 on free labor circulation by the countries of the Andean Pact has added an important new element to immigration policy, particularly for Venezuela as it is the main labor receiver in the region.[6]

[6]Its stipulations include the development of an institutional support structure for international migrant workers, the extension of basic rights to migrants, including the right to unionization, and the implementation of an elaborate set of procedures aimed at regularizing the status of undocumented workers from member countries. (*Comisión del Acuerdo de Cartagena*, especially articles 25, 27 and 29). Though it is not part of the formal document, it

The Reopening of Immigration: Phase One, 1974-1976

Notwithstanding the recency of the immigration changes, it is already possible to distinguish two phases. From 1974 to 1976, there was a large and basically uncontrolled influx of foreigners. The official policy after 1974 was to promote selective immigration and to legalize undocumented workers, both of which measures were aimed at alleviating the acute labor scarcities created by the economic boom. After 1966 the government had implemented a selective immigration program under the control of the Department of Labor to facilitate the recruitment of needed technicians and professionals. The numbers involved, however, were very small: between 1966 and 1974 only 12,000 professionals and technicians came to Venezuela, and only 10 percent of these came through the Selective Immigration Office. After 1974 the purpose was to maintain selectivity, but to promote an accelerated increase in immigration. The increase took place, but the implementation of selective controls did not. Until the end of 1976, entry regulations were such that it was fairly easy to obtain a tourist visa and, upon finding employment, change to a residence permit. This ease is reflected in the large increase in the number of registered entries.

The fact that in 1975 and 1976 alone there were as many entries as there had been during the decade of the 1950s led to a number of measures intended to control these flows. After 1976 all requests for entry had to be processed through the DIEX thereby withdrawing the right of consular offices to grant permits. Since 1976 it has become virtually impossible for persons from other Latin American countries to obtain even a four-day tourist visa to Venezuela. In the three previous years, many Latins entering the country on tourist visas had obtained employment and changed their status to permanent resident. By 1976 a resolution was passed which froze the granting of such changes of status. Finally, in 1976 the planning and implementation of an effective selective immigration program was initiated. The urgency for this program was such that by the end of 1976 the first new agency, the National Council on Human Resources, was set up, and by the end of 1977 the new immigration program was launched.

---

is generally agreed that these provisions would affect Venezuela most importantly, since it is the main immigration country in the region and has the largest undocumented population. (*See also*, Marmora, in this issue). Two recent meetings have examined how the free labor circulation system would affect the large number of undocumented workers in Venezuela. The first, held in Cucuta, Colombia in March 1978, led to a second, more general meeting in Medellin, Colombia in May 1978 with government representatives from several Latin American countries with growing numbers of undocumented workers in Venezuela (*Seminario Latinoamericano sobre Politícas de Migraciones Laborales,* 1978).

The Reopening of Immigration: Phase Two, 1977 Onwards

The core of the new immigration policy is a provision of a work permit to accompany the entry visa. This permit contains information on the level of training of the holder and the kind of job for which entry was allowed. The work permit remains in possession of the employer and is sent to the Department of Labor for transfer to a new employer if the worker changes jobs.

A second element in this policy is that employers have to submit their requests for foreign workers to the recently created Program for Human Resources, an agency within the Ministry of Planning (CORDIPLAN). The Program has to publish such requests and consult with the labor unions and professional schools to make sure that no Venezuelan workers with the required skills are available. The Program then passes this information and the result of its inquiries to the Tripartite Selective Immigration Committee. The latter may request the Program to make additional inquiries or efforts before authorizing the recruitment of the foreign workers. Any work contract which does not meet the minimum requirements set by the Program and which has not been approved by it will be invalid. Once the requests for foreign workers are approved, they are passed to DIEX which checks on national security matters and issues the necessary visas.

The specific functions of each of the bodies involved in the immigration process are the following:

a) The National Council on Human Resources is a planning and consulting body created in the context of the Fifth Plan by direct order of the President and is responsible to him. It is in charge of the overall planning, orientation and control of all issues related to the labor supply and the labor market. It is also in charge of the planning, orientation and control of selective immigration through the Tripartite Selective Immigration Committee.

b) The Tripartite Selective Immigration Committee is composed of representatives from Government, the federation of labor unions (*Confederación de Trabajores de Venezuela*) and federation of producers' associations (FEDECAMARAS). Representatives from the Program on Human Resources, from the DIEX and from the Economy and Employment Bureau of the Department of Labor also have to be present at the meetings of the Tripartite Committee. This is the body actually charged with the practical control and regulation of the immigration process. It reviews all requests for foreign workers sent in by employers and obtains information on all immigration cases for inclusion in the data bank of the Council on Human Resources; it decides on the processes controlling the entry of foreign workers and the quantity and origin of the latter for the different sectors of the economy. It oversees the fulfillment of all regulations in the selective immigration process.

c) The Program on Human Resources operates as a dependency of the Ministry of Planning (CORDIPLAN) although there is considerable pressure to move it to the Department of Labor. It functions as the operational arm of the selective immigration process by: receiving and processing all requests for workers from employers; inquiring as to the availability of native workers; processing the work contracts of foreign workers; obtaining information about the labor availability in foreign countries; and validating the qualifications of foreign workers. In this last function, the Program is assisted by international agencies, most particularly the Intergovernmental Committee for European Migration (ICEM). The Program signed an agreement with ICEM whereby the latter is charged with the recruitment of semi-skilled and technical workers from various European countries. The Program is, furthermore, charged with the processing of workers coming to Venezuela under the labor transfer agreements signed between the governments of Venezuela and Spain (1977) and Portugal (1978). The operations of the Program are overseen by the Tripartite Committee. In brief, there is a single work contract through which foreign workers are hired, and this contract is processed by the Program.

d) The Identification Bureau (DIEX) of the Ministry of the Interior is charged with the implementation of the work permit as a document that is a necessary complement to the entry visa or for a change of visa. These visas are granted after approval by the Tripartite Committee. The latter are informed through the Program of any application by a foreigner in the country with a tourist visa for a change to temporary residence, a kind of permit allowing for short-term work assignments. In general the DIEX is charged with processing the documents required for entry, but it has to do so in close collaboration with the Program.

CONCLUSION

The implementation of the selective immigration program and the effectiveness of its operation have to be seen in the context of accelerated growth and, more narrowly, as a manpower issue. Manpower and immigration policies are being formulated under the pressure of economic growth. Given the subordination of immigration policy to manpower issues, the chances that such a program of selective immigration will work are greater than they were in the past.

There are, however, a number of larger issues which may have significant consequences for the immigration program. On the most general level is the question about whether or not a country such as Venezuela can carry out the industrialization plan it has undertaken. This plan has run into various kinds of problems ultimately rooted in the inadequacy of existing patterns of investment and infrastructure to absorb large increases in financial potential and economic activity. The social and economic structure of the country poses objective constraints to an accelerated industrialization plan that far surpasses that structure. One instance of this is the manpower training program. The availability of revenue meant that the government could triple the program's budget and incorporate, as one of the elements of the Fifth Plan, the expectation that this program would train a needed labor supply of one-half million persons in a labor force of 3.7 million. Can a program, even if it counts on a large budget, carry out this kind of a qualitative and quantitative leap?

Another instance with as yet undefined consequences, is the process of class recomposition that is taking place as a result of accelerated industrialization and the large influx of foreign workers, most of whom come from countries with longer traditions of working class mobilization and participation of professional cadres in economic and governmental activity. A further element in this process is the undeniable fact that the economic boom has not meant the incorporation of the marginal population nor the elimination of poverty.

REFERENCES

Aranda, S.
1977 *La Economía Venezolana.* Bogotá, Colombia: Siglo Veintiuno.

Araujo, O.
1969 *Situación Industrial de Venezuela.* Caracas: Edición Biblioteca Universidad Central de Venezuela.

Banco Central de Venezuela
Various years *Informe Económico.* Caracas.

———
1970 *La Economía Venezolana en los últimos Treinta Años.* Caracas

Blanco, C., *et al.*, eds.
1977 *Proceso Politico,* 4–5. Jan. Special Issue.

Chi-Yi-Chen
1973 "Distribución Espacial de la Población Venezolana". Dirección General de Estadística, Ministerio de Fomento: Serie Temas Contemporáneos. Caracas.

—— and J.I. Urquijo, S.J.
1974 *Condiciones del Trabajador Immigrante en Venezuela.* Caracas: Instituto de Investigaciones Económicas y Sociales. Universidid Católica A. Bello. Mimeo.

Colombia, Ministerio de Trabajo y Seguridad Social
1978 *Política de Migraciones Laborales en Colombia.* Bogota. Dirección General del Servicio Nacional de Empleo. Mimeo.

Comisión del Acuerdo de Cartagena
1977 *Instrumento Andino de Migración Laboral.* Decisión 116. 17o. Período de Sesiones Extraordinarias de la Comisión. Lima, Peru: Feb. 14-17. Mimeo.

Consejo Nacional de Recursos Humanos (National Council on Human Resources)
1977 *Informe sobre la Situacion General y Perspectivas de los Recursos Humanos.* Caracas. Mimeo.

Córdova, A. and H. Silva Michelena
1974 "Aspectos Teóricos del Subdesarrollo". Caracas: Edición Facultad de Ciencias Económicas y Sociales de la Universidad Central de Venezuela. Third printing.

Dirección de Identificación y Extranjería
Various years *Estadísticas.* Caracas: Ministerio de RelacionesInteriores.

Food and Agricultural Organization (FAO)
Various years *Monthly Bulletin of Economic and Agricultural Statistics.*

FEDECAMARAS (Federación Venezolana de Cámaras y Asociaciones de Comercio y Producción).
1977 *Situación de los Recursos Humanos.* Maracay. Mimeo.

——
Various years *Asamblea Anual.*

Gaceta Oficial de la República de Venezuela
1976 No. 1860 Extraordinario. March 11.

——
1976a No. 31.012. June 29.

——
1978 No. 2.129 Extraordinario. Jan. 17.

Gall. N.
1972 "Los Indocumentados Colombianos". *American Universities Field Staff Reports,* 16. Dec.

Handelman, H.
1978 "Scarcity Amidst Plenty: Food Problems in Oil Rich Venezuela". *American Universities Field Staff Reports,* 42. Sept.

Kritz, M.M.
1975 "The Impact of International Migration on Venezuelan Demographic and Social Structure". *International Migration Review,* 19:513-543. Winter.

Laxague C., G. and J. Paez Celis
1975 "Ensayo de un modelo Demo-Económico para describir algunas causas de la migración rural-urbana en Venezuela". *Estradística Venezolana,* 5:9-22. Oct.

Mármora, L.
1972 "El Estudio Histórico Estructural de los Movimientos Poblacionales en América Latina". In *Imperialismo y Urbanización en América Latina.* Madrid: Gili. Pp. 57-95.

Paez Celis, J.
1973 *Ensayo de Demografía Económica de Venezuela.* Caracas: Ministerio de Fomento.

Rochcau, G.
1972 *La Inmigración Colombiana a Venezuela.* Geneva, Switzerland. Mimeo.

Sassen-Koob, S.
1978 "The International Circulation of Resources and Development: The Case of Migrant Labor". *Development and Change,* 9:509-546. Oct.

―――
1979 "The Limits to Capital Accumulation in the Periphery: Venezuela". Unpublished.

Seminario Latinoamericano sobre Políticas de Migraciones Laborales.
1978 *Conclusiones y Recomendaciones.* Bogotá, Colombia: Ministerio de Trabajo y Seguridad Social. Mimeo.

Thompson, S. and H. Hernández Caliman
1977 Estudio Analítico de la Política Inmigratoria en Venezuela. Caracas: Consejo Nacional de Recursos Humanos y Ministerio de Relaciones Interiores. Mimeo.

Venezuela, Dirección General de Estadística y Censos Nacionales.
various years *Censo de Pobación y Vivienda.* Caracas: Ministerio de Fomento.

Venezuela, Dirección Nacional del Presupuesto
Various years *Presupuesto Nacional.* Caracas: Ministerio de Hacienda.

Venezuela, Presidente de
1977 *Tercer Mensaje al Congreso de la República.* Caracas. Anexo Estadístico. March.

[6]

From 'White Australia' to 'Part of Asia': Recent Shifts in Australian Immigration Policy Towards the Region

James Jupp
Center for Immigration and Multicultural Studies

This article examines the impact on Australia of population movements in the Asia-Pacific region since 1945, with special reference to the period since 1975 that marked the termination of the restrictive 'White Australia Policy.' That policy, which had its origins in racist theories popular at the end of the nineteenth century, isolated Australia from its immediate region and kept it tied to its European and, more specifically, British origins.

The impact of population, trade and capital movements in the region has been such as to make Australia 'part of Asia.' Nevertheless, public opinion has yet to accept these changes fully, especially when they involve changing the ethnic character of the resident population. It is concluded that the generation which has grown up since 1945 and which is now starting to dominate politics and intellectual life will find it easier to reorient Australia than did the previous generation, despite continuing ambivalence in public attitudes. The presence in Australia of large numbers of permanent residents and citizens of Asian origin is a necessary factor in expediting change.

Between the 1880s and the 1960s, Australia deliberately insulated itself from its geographical region by adopting the White Australia Policy (Willard, 1967). Officially known as the restrictive immigration policy, under the Commonwealth Immigration Restriction Act of 1901, the effective exclusion of non-European immigrants formed part of a wider ideology based on fashionable theories of racial superiority. These had their greatest currency in the English-speaking and Germanic cultures and were often supported by sophisticated 'scientific' theories as much as by popular prejudice. Thus, White Australia was not simply advocated by crude populists but by well-educated statesmen such as Alfred Deakin (1856–1919), an otherwise progressive and enlightened liberal. Nor was White Australia espoused only by the conservative side of Australian politics. On the contrary, it was most actively pursued by the Australian Labor Party, founded in 1891 and forming the first national social-democratic government in the world as early as 1904. The largest trade union, the Australian

Workers' Union, was among the most enthusiastic supporters of White Australia into the 1960s (Palfreeman, 1967; Price, 1974; Yarwood, 1964).

The objectives of White Australia were assimilationist, creating an ethnically homogenous society. The Aboriginal population was expected to die out, with those of 'mixed race' (now the majority) assimilating into the majority population to the point of eventual invisibility. This latter objective was vitiated by a battery of state laws which discriminated against Aborigines, denied them citizenship and the franchise, and confined them to reservations. These laws, which in some states included control of marriage and children, were ideologically related to similar laws in the southern United States and South Africa. The national government did not assume control over Aboriginal affairs until 1967 and the civil status of Aborigines – though not their economic conditions – was equalized as a result. Less draconian prohibitions were imposed on non-European residents, including prohibition on the acquisition of citizenship, without which they were often barred from property ownership or certain occupations. The major victims of these state laws were Chinese Australians, who constituted the largest Asian component of the population from the 1850s. All such restrictions have now been removed and racial discrimination is outlawed under a variety of state and federal laws, starting with the South Australian Act of 1966.

The most famous aspect of White Australia was its exclusion of non-European immigrants. This was never written into law despite preceding colonial legislation directed specifically against Chinese. Rather, the 1901 Act permitted absolute discretion to prohibit undesirable immigrants, without specifying the basis of such undesirability. The mechanisms for implementing the policy included a dictation test and fines on carriers bringing unacceptable immigrants. This latter device still remains. The dictation test was based on one introduced in Natal (South Africa) in 1897. It was normally given in a language not understood by the intending immigrant and was not a test of literacy. Under Japanese pressure on the British government, the original stipulation that the language must be European was modified, but in fact the language always was European. Altogether, between 1901 and the end of the test in 1958, there were 1,932 exclusions resulting from failing the test. This number was small because shipping companies would simply not issue tickets to non-Europeans who, in any case, were unlikely to attempt to settle in the knowledge that it would not be allowed. This very devious but highly effective technique avoided upsetting the British government, most of whose imperial subjects were non-Europeans, and their allies the Japanese. At this stage virtually all of Asia was under colonial domination or, as in the case of China, was not regarded as very influential because of internal disorder.

Immigration restriction was extremely effective in insulating Australia from its neighbors. While business, student, and distinguished visitors were allowed temporary entry, these were few in numbers until the admission of students (mainly from Malaysia and Singapore) under the Colombo Plan of 1951. Temporary workers, such as Japanese in the pearl diving industry, were only allowed in on contract. In the 1940s, all Japanese were deported after World War II internment, refugees from Asia were returned home after the war, and Japanese and other Asian brides of Australian servicemen were refused entry until 1952. These draconian measures were implemented by a Labor government; the Liberals, who were returned in 1949, were slightly more permissive. Gradual modifications allowed categories such as Anglo-Indians or Ceylon Burghers to be admitted from the former British Empire in the 1960s. The virtual prohibition of citizenship to non-Europeans was gradually relaxed. The most important changes under the Liberals were made in 1966 (London, 1970).

The White Australia Policy became dysfunctional in several respects: it limited the scope of immigration intake to European societies which eventually lost any strong incentive to move to Australia because of their growing prosperity; it alienated newly independent Asian states; it restricted the thinking of Australians to a world view unduly focused on distant regions such as Britain; it was based on theories and attitudes which became intellectually unfashionable; and it could be shown pragmatically not to be in the economic, social or political interests of Australia. The opponents of the policy emerged largely from the expanding tertiary educated sector, starting with the creation of the Immigration Reform Group at Melbourne University in 1959. The universities had experienced significant intakes of overseas Chinese students in the 1950s and were attuned to changing attitudes towards racism in the other English-speaking societies. Many of their staff were recruited from Britain, and liberal ideas were coming increasingly from the United States (London, 1970; Rivett, 1975).

An important factor eroding support for White Australia was the painless integration of large numbers of non-English-speaking Europeans under the mass migration programs launched in 1947. Originally these were intended to sustain White Australia by supplementing British immigration from Europe. However, Europeans were not the same as the British in many cultural respects. Governments moved away from assimilationist towards multicultural approaches, though this was not effective at the national level until 1973. These approaches no longer expected immigrants to become invisibly indistinct from Anglo-Australians. With the sources of immigrants extending towards the Middle East and the completion of an agreement with Turkey in 1967, the cultural arguments for White Australia became untenable, leaving exposed the crude racism which underlay the policy but which was officially denied. Recruiting campaigns in Latin America in the early 1970s did little to replenish the declining European intake. It became absurd to exclude professional Indians and Chinese while still encouraging the arrival of Balkan, Middle

Eastern, and Latin American unskilled workers. Pressures to change the policy came from the Department of Foreign Affairs rather than from within the Department of Immigration. Between 1966 and 1973, the policies of racial exclusion and immigrant assimilation were abandoned by the Liberal and Labor governments with surprisingly little political resistance. This paralleled changes in Canada and the United States but moved in the opposite direction from Britain, which was tightening its controls at the same time in the face of immigration from the Commonwealth (Freeman and Jupp, 1992).

BECOMING PART OF ASIA

The historic traditions of Australia had become an obstacle to adjusting to its geographical and economic situation. As a predominantly British society 12,000 miles from its origins, Australia was protected from reality by the British Empire until 1942 and by the White Australia Policy until 1973. Trade, investment, immigration, education, language and travel all bound Australia to Britain until well into the 1960s. Some key turning points include: the fall of Singapore at the beginning of 1942; the attraction of students under the Colombo Plan from 1951; the Japanese trade agreement of 1957; the involvement in Vietnam from 1965; the modification of restrictive immigration in 1966 and its termination in 1973; the shift from sea to air travel by the 1970s; and subsequent declines in British trade, investment and immigration. From the British side, important events were the passing of restrictive immigration acts in 1962 and 1968; entry into the European Community in 1973; and withdrawal from all Asian and Pacific possessions except Hong Kong between 1947 and 1980. While some of these events served to increase American influence, most of them emphasized the pre-eminence of geographical proximity as a factor in Australian reorientation. The maintenance of effective links with such a distant partner as Britain was only possible while that partner controlled the world's largest empire.

The relevance of proximity to strengthening ties with Asia can be indicated by air travel time between Sydney and various destinations by direct scheduled Qantas[1] flights. Destinations within four hours flying time of Sydney include New Zealand, Fiji and New Caledonia; within eight hours are Indonesia, French Polynesia, Papua New Guinea and Singapore; within twelve hours one can fly to Thailand, Hong Kong, Malaysia, the Philippines, Japan, Taiwan, South Korea, and Hawaii; it is sixteen hours to California.

Destinations such as Beijing, Colombo, or Delhi, can be reached directly within this timeframe by other carriers. Vancouver, Johannesburg, and

[1]Qantas is the Australian national carrier and transports over 40 percent of those traveling to and from Australia. Qantas itself has rescheduled its flights to diminish its European operations, although its premier flight, QF1, still goes to London.

Buenos Aires are at or near the sixteen-hour periphery. Australian travel links are now effectively within the Asia-Pacific region, a vital factor in tourism, immigration, and business. This does not mean that major movements do not still occur to Britain or Europe, but rather that these are more expensive and time-consuming. The leisurely days of sea travel, when Australians thought nothing of spending a month reaching England have now disappeared, as has the lack of British immigration restriction on which such long-distance movements were usually posited.

The severance of Australia from its British origins was not deliberate on either side. Queen Elizabeth still remains Australian head of state, despite growing republican sentiment. British immigrants still form the largest single element as they have done in every year since 1788, though they have not been far ahead of New Zealand, Vietnam or Hong Kong at various times in the past few years. Over 2 million Australians are entitled to a British passport because they or their parents were born in the United Kingdom. British investment is still the most important element in overseas investment, though U.S. and Japanese sources are increasingly important and there is growing interest from New Zealand and the Overseas Chinese. English is still the native tongue of 82 percent of the population, though this has dropped from about 97 percent in 1945. Mass and elite culture is still expressed largely through the English language, although American influence is very strong and dominates the commercial television channels watched by about 90 percent of Australians in preference to the much more 'British' ABC and the 'multicultural' SBS. Thus, despite the growth of Asian studies and the current popularity of Japanese as a school subject, the severance from Britain has not involved a massive shift in cultural orientation. A contradiction exists between the British historical tradition, the current Anglo-American cultural dominance and the Asia-Pacific geographic and economic location (Australia, 1977; 1979; Boyce and Angel, 1992; Evans and Grant, 1991).

IMMIGRATION

Historically, the issue which has been most sensitive in Australian-Asian relations has been immigration. The tradition of rebuilding a 'British' nation in the South Pacific dominated popular and official thinking between 1788 and 1945. Convict transportation (1788–1868) was overwhelmingly from the British Isles. Immigration assisted from public funds (1831–1982) was almost exclusively British and Irish until 1947, though Queensland extended support to 'Nordic cousins' from Germany and Scandinavia between the 1870s and 1914. This exception merely serves to underline the racial basis of population building, as racial theories fashionable by 1880 stressed the close relationship between the English and

Germanic peoples. Passage fares paid from public funds were deliberately used in the nineteenth century to reproduce the ethnic and religious character of the United Kingdom, an objective which also served to limit applications from the Catholic Irish who were much more willing to emigrate and much more dependent on public funds than the English or Scots. By 1914, the great majority of the population were of British Protestant origin. Irish Catholics formed the only major ethnic minority, and Aborigines and Chinese were seen as dying races which would eventually disappear. Although Catholics had far more political power than in Britain, Canada, or the United States, the drastic reduction of the population of Ireland by the 1880s meant that Catholic numbers were actually declining and were not being replenished from elsewhere. Apart from a brief interlude of Labor rule between 1929 and 1931, politicians of Irish Catholic origin were in opposition until the wartime Curtin and Chifley Labor governments (1941–1949). Thus, Australia was not only conceived of as 'White' but also as Protestant and British, especially by the ruling conservatives (Jupp, 1988; 1991).

Today Catholics form the largest nominal and by far the largest practicing denomination at 27 percent of the population. About 25 percent of the population are of non-British origin, while over 15 percent were born overseas in non-English-speaking countries. Most significantly, the national origin of over 900,000 might normally have meant their exclusion under the White Australia Policy prior to 1966, although not all of these were non-Europeans. Over 4 percent of the population were born in Asia and 1.6 percent in the Middle East and Africa. The relevant figures for Northeast, Southeast and South Asian birthplaces are shown in Table 1.

These figures indicate the extent to which the Asian-born population of Australia has increased between the censuses of 1981, 1986, and 1991. In the first five-year period, numbers increased by 150,000 and in the second by over 250,000. However, these numbers were very unevenly distributed between different sources and bore little relationship either to source country populations or their overall rate of emigration. Major countries of emigration such as Pakistan or Bangladesh scarcely influence the Australian intake. The largest populations, in order of size, are now from Vietnam, Malaysia, Philippines, Hong Kong, India, and Mainland China. Four of these six are countries in which English is a widely used second language, while the Vietnam figure represents family reunion for former refugees under 'orderly departure' programs. Numbers from Laos and Cambodia are much lower, and emigration from them to Australia has tapered off markedly. Many Australians do not effectively distinguish between Asians and other non-European people. The small Islamic population, many of whom are from southeastern Europe and Turkey, suffer from feelings of discrimination as much as do those from further east. In colloquial Austra-

TABLE 1

ASIAN BIRTHPLACES OF THE AUSTRALIAN POPULATION: 1981, 1986, AND 1991

Birthplace	1981	1986	1991
Bangladesh	n.a.	1,211	2,289
Burma	7,294	7,610	8,260
Cambodia	3,589	13,237	17,555
China (Mainland)	26,760	37,468	77,799
Hong Kong	15,717	28,293	57,510
India	41,657	47,816	60,958
Indonesia[a]	16,166	17,721	32,688
Japan	8,060	11,191	18,441
Korea	4,515	9,284	20,383
Laos	5,352	7,424	9,537
Malaysia	31,598	47,802	71,665
Pakistan	2,527	3,605	5,806
Philippines	15,431	33,727	73,144
Singapore	11,990	16,434	24,021
Sri Lanka	16,966	22,516	37,263
Taiwan (Republic of China)	n.a.	2,056	12,427
Thailand	3,346	6,994	13,756
Timor[a]	n.a.	6,559	n.a.
Vietnam	41,097	83,048	121,813
Other Asia[b]	4,546	1,658	n.a.
Total	256,611	405,654	665,315

Sources: 1981, 1986, and 1991 Census of Australia.
[a]Timor is included with Indonesia after 1986.
[b]Other Asia is mainly Afghanistan (2,674 in 1991).

lian, 'Asian' refers to east and southeast Asians; in practice this distinction is often not made. Nor is there always an acknowledgement that an increasing number of 'Asian appearance' persons are born in Australia.

Despite the prominence of the Vietnam born, the 1991 Census shows that people of Chinese origin form the largest Asian born category, as they did in the nineteenth century. They come from a variety of sources, including some less obvious such as Timor or Papua New Guinea (Choi, 1975; Kee, 1988). Table 2 indicates the origins of Cantonese-speakers (now and historically the largest Chinese language group in Australia) in 1991. A traditional objection to Asian immigration was that it would bring into Australia people of lower educational and living standards who would depress working and living conditions. It was this argument which was often strongest with the trade union and labor movement. However, because of rising qualifications for admission since 1975, this has not proved to be the case except for refugee intakes from Indochina. In general, Asian immi-

TABLE 2

BIRTHPLACES OF CANTONESE-SPEAKERS IN AUSTRALIA: 1991

Birthplace	Number
Hong Kong	48,611
China	34,009
Malaysia	21,512
Vietnam	21,186
Australia	14,888
Singapore	4,136
Cambodia	1,902
Papua New Guinea	1,606
Macau	1,357
Indonesia	849
England	465
Christmas Island	462
New Zealand	401
Taiwan	401
Fiji	368
Brunei	292
Solomon Islands	246
Thailand	217
All Others	3,068
Total	155,976

Source: 1991 Census

grants have had higher qualifications and have found more prestigious occupations than the native born. This is indicated in Table 3.

There are clearly two quite different categories of Asian immigrants. Those who came as refugees from Vietnam, Cambodia, and Laos are much less qualified and much more likely to enter the traditional manual jobs than those who came voluntarily (Lewins and Ly, 1984; Viviani, 1984; Viviani, Coughlan and Rowland, 1993; Coughlan, 1993). As official policy has sought highly skilled migrants in recent years, this means that national objectives are well served by a high level of Asian immigration. This fact has not, however, always informed public debate, which has been dominated by two stereotypes: that Asians are poorer and less skilled than Australians and that immigrants go into factory employment. These stereotypes may be true for many from Indochina, but are quite misleading when applied to others. Migration from most of Asia is basically middle class (Inglis, 1993; Mak, 1993).

A currently relevant indicator of disadvantage is level of unemployment, which has ranged between 6 percent and 11 percent of the workforce for

TABLE 3

PERCENTAGE IN WORKFORCE WITH PROFESSIONAL OCCUPATIONAL STATUS FOR SETTLER ARRIVALS BY ASIAN BIRTHPLACE: 1988–1989, 1989–1990, 1990–1991

Birthplace	1988–1989 (%)	1989–1990 (%)	1990–1991 (%)
Cambodia	2.4	6.5	10.6
China, Mainland	18.2	35.9	30.2
Hong Kong[a]	45.5	51.6	49.1
India	31.3	37.8	44.3
Indonesia	32.3	34.5	25.4
Japan	48.2	49.5	22.1
Korea	34.8	27.6	21.9
Laos	11.3	11.3	12.6
Malaysia	53.3	65.1	46.2
Philippines	9.5	22.9	27.9
Singapore	46.0	52.9	35.7
Sri Lanka	32.2	44.1	22.3
Taiwan (Republic of China)[a]	14.5	36.6	11.6
Thailand	35.7	35.2	17.9
Vietnam	2.9	3.7	4.2

Source: Bureau of Immigration Research: *Settler Arrivals.*

[a]The percentages from Hong Kong and Taiwan in the Managers and Administrators category were exceptionally high.

the past twenty years, a level much higher than when European and British immigration was at its height in the 1950s and 1960s. The unemployment levels for Vietnam born are consistently high, as Table 4 indicates.

Public perceptions of Asian immigration are confused by the large and growing number of Asian tourists arriving for short visits, concentrating especially in Sydney and Queensland. In 1992, expenditure by visitors from Japan and other Asian nations accounted for 41 percent of the total. Tourism is now a major element in the foreign exchange balance, exceeding the returns on most primary produce. In 1992, tourists spent $A4.3 billion in Australia, apart from fares and packages purchased outside the country. The relevant figures for 1991 and 1992 are shown in Table 5.

A consistent concern about ghettoes can be traced back for more than a century in Australia, having its origins in fears of the largely male Chinese concentrations which developed not only in Australia but also in California and other parts of the English-speaking world. This concern was later revived as small numbers of southern Europeans and East European Jews began to appear in Australian cities in the 1920s. Small Chinatowns persisted in Melbourne (the oldest), Sydney (the largest), Brisbane, and Perth despite the severe 1901 restrictions on immigration. These formed a

TABLE 4

UNEMPLOYMENT RATE BY BIRTHPLACE, GENDER, AND YEAR: 1986–1991

Year	Vietnamese Male (Percentage)	Vietnamese Female (Percentage)	Overseas Male (Percentage)	Overseas Female (Percentage)	Australian Male (Percentage)	Australian Female (Percentage)
1986	18.5	n.a.	8.3	9.0	7.5	8.2
1987	24.7	23.5	8.3	9.5	7.3	8.0
1988	25.6	24.2	7.0	8.1	6.4	7.0
1989	14.9	8.5	5.7	7.2	5.3	5.9
1990	20.3	15.7	7.4	8.1	6.7	6.8
1991	28.2	29.2	12.7	10.3	9.2	8.1

Source: Viviani *et al.*, 1993: Table 4.9.

natural focus for Overseas Chinese students arriving under the Colombo Plan in the 1950s. With the official ending of White Australia, the arrival of refugees from Indochina and the growth of Asian tourism, there has been a rapid expansion of these districts into rich commercial centers comparable in size to those in some North American cities.

Perhaps more controversially, the placing of Indochinese refugees in suburban reception centers on arrival led to their subsequent spread into adjacent outer suburbs which had not previously been characterized by Asian settlement. These included Cabramatta, Bankstown and Ashfield in western Sydney, Springvale and Footscray in Melbourne, and Darra in Brisbane. The placing of many refugees in public housing compounded this development in such places as Richmond in Melbourne. These areas began to develop the very public shopping and entertainment centers once confined to the inner city Chinatowns, with the widespread display of shop signs in Chinese, Vietnamese, or Cambodian. Some smaller Korean centers, such as in Canterbury (Sydney), also developed from nonrefugee settlement. However, there was no parallel to the large Indian settlements found

TABLE 5

INTERNATIONAL VISITORS BY REGION OF ORIGIN: 1991 AND 1992

Region	1991	1992
Japan	510,800	604,900
Other Asia	350,700	436,600
New Zealand	441,500	412,300
United States and Canada	309,800	295,200
United Kingdom and Ireland	258,200	282,300
Other Europe	247,000	264,100
All Other Countries	98,600	130,400
Total	2,216,600	2,425,800

Source: Bureau of Tourism Research, 1992 International Visitor Survey.

in British cities (Jupp *et al.*, 1990). The tourist industry took a major role in developing some Asian commercial centers but did not usually publicize those in outer suburbs.

POSITIVE AND NEGATIVE ATTITUDES

An important characteristic of public debate in Australia has been the confusion of attitudes towards Asian immigration with those toward immigration in general and towards Asian tourism, investment, or business links. Official attitudes towards tourist, investment, or business links have been very positive. A number of institutions have recently been created to advance economic links, especially with Northeast Asia (defined in Australia as Japan, China, Korea, Taiwan, and Hong Kong). These include the East Asia Analytical Unit within the Department of Foreign Affairs and Trade, the Australian National Korean Studies Centre, the Australia-China Council, the Australia Japan Foundation, the Australia-India Council, the Australia Indonesia Institute, and the Asia-Australia Institute at the University of New South Wales, headed by a former ambassador to Mainland China, Dr. Stephen Fitzgerald. These centers have not, however, shown the same interest in immigration as they do in business and cultural interchange. The major institution with such an interest is the Centre for the Study of Australian-Asian Relations at Griffith University, Queensland (Australian National Korean Studies Centre, 1992; East Asia Analytical Unit, 1992).

All these centers are enthusiastic about the Asian connection, and influence official and community attitudes favorably. At the national government level, one of the most important influences came from the report *Australia and the Northeast Asia Ascendancy*, produced for the Prime Minister and the Minister for Foreign Affairs and Trade in 1989. This report concluded that: Australia carries many assets into its relations with Northeast Asia; Australia must rely on persuading other countries, and influential groups within those countries, to move in directions that are consistent with their own interests; the disciplined force of economic diplomacy should be placed behind efforts to secure open, nondiscriminatory trade; it is important to develop professional excellence in managing relations with Northeast Asia; progress in domestic economic reform must accelerate to build a flexible, internationally-oriented economy; and there is a need to press ahead with trade liberalization, to maintain a strong economic orientation in nondiscriminatory immigration, and to continue with a liberal, nondiscriminatory policy toward foreign investment (Garnaut, 1989:6–7).

There can be little doubt, following the Garnaut report, that official Australia is strongly committed to building effective links with Asia and to maintaining an immigration program with a large Asian component. In a democracy, public debate is not determined by official attitudes alone.

Popular attitudes are much less enthusiastic about an Asian-dominated future than is suggested by many official statements. There are a number of crucial factors causing the Australian government to modify or slow down its otherwise strong drive towards building further Asian links. These include: a growing opposition to immigration; a continuing repetition of some themes derived from the White Australia past; suspicion of foreign investment; lingering hostility towards Japan based on wartime experience; conservationist arguments against further growth; and criticism of Asian political systems and practices. Fear of communism, so dominant a motif in the 1960s, seems no longer to be influential (Renouf, 1979; Dunn and Fung, 1985; Wang, 1992).

These inhibiting factors are often hard to disentangle; nor do they cluster around traditional liberal-conservative partisan polarities. One interesting example of their impact was in the now largely aborted plan to build, in Australia, a Multifunctional Polis (MFP) in cooperation with the Japanese. While this scheme was never completely clarified, it essentially proposed a 'city of the future' with a highly trained workforce concentrating on high technology development in ideal working and residential surroundings. As such, it was immediately attractive to the Department of Industry, Technology and Commerce. However, fears that the MFP would become an ethnic enclave were sparked by a consultant's report favoring a large majority of immigrant workers, presumably from Asia. Politicians on both sides began to back off from the scheme when fear of Asian mass immigration moved into the center of the argument. Eventually, the site of the new city was allocated to Adelaide, and there has been little further progress.

While the MFP was not completely destroyed by arguments over Asian immigration and concentration, these were very influential during the election year of 1990. The Leader of the Liberal Opposition, Andrew Peacock, in rejecting the proposal, said:

> Our immigration policy is well understood. We reject the notion of any development which would establish an enclave. This would be socially divisive and risk a backlash against foreign investment and immigration generally.

A similar position was taken by the Returned Services League, whose president called it "just another way of overcoming the immigration program and getting people in through the back door" (*Canberra Times*, March 17, 1990).

The MFP idea was muddled and showed up the weakness of overenthusiasm for links with Japan which had not been properly thought through. At the same time, there was growing opposition to other influences from Japan or the Overseas Chinese. These included criticism of a proposed Japanese retirement village in Western Australia, which was abandoned in 1988. In the same year, Professor Geoffrey Blainey, one of the most influential critics of Asian immigration and multiculturalism, argued that

Japanese investment in Queensland had become too evident and was damaging Japanese interests (*Courier Mail*, April 22, 1988). A movement against Japanese influence, Heart of a Nation, was launched in Queensland after a local opinion poll on the Gold Coast had shown 75 percent were alarmed at Japanese influence (Yencken, 1989:128). These manifestations of concern were resisted by the Queensland government and media and by many interests that have made considerable profit from Japanese involvement in Australia. They faded away again but left behind a commitment to register foreign-owned land by the Labor and Democrat parties. A continuing anti-Japanese strand of feeling has been sustained by some leaders of the Returned Services League, though certainly not by all of them (Japanese Embassy, 1988).

The importance of opposition to Asian influence, investment, tourism, and immigration is hard to gauge because media coverage revives the story from time to time and by doing so encourages public reaction that might otherwise remain dormant. Some journalists in talk-back radio and the tabloids have been quite irresponsible in this regard. Normally, public opinion polling does not show immigration to be a major concern, except when media campaigns are in progress. None of the major political parties is interested in a debate about Asian influence, which all support in varying degrees as do national and state governments. Nor are openly racist organizations of much significance in Australia, despite media exaggeration of their following from time to time. The most violent such group, in Perth, attracted much hostile criticism in Hong Kong and elsewhere. However, its members are now mostly in prison for violent offenses, and it has ceased to exist. A similar fate befell its Sydney counterpart. The most influential arguments against Asian immigration at present do not indicate a lingering influence from White Australia. Rather they are based on two concerns: that the economy cannot employ new arrivals and that the environment cannot support a continuing increase in the population. There is an undercurrent of suspicion about official multicultural policies, which often has a racist tinge. These recent developments parallel changes in attitudes towards immigration in both Canada and the United States and may be influenced from there. They are more directly traceable to periodic media interest in stories suggesting tension and prejudice (Goot, 1991).

PARTY POLITICS AND MULTICULTURALISM

There have been rapid shifts in many basic Australian attitudes over the past twenty years, but these have rarely been instigated by the political parties (Jupp and Kabala, 1993). Since the celebration of the bicentenary of British settlement in 1988, there has been a steadily rising support for republicanism, as measured in public opinion polls. A clear majority of

Australians currently seem willing to follow the road to a republican Australia within the Commonwealth, a status pioneered by India in 1950 and now adopted by the majority of former British colonies. Such a status need not alter the existing political institutions and international orientations of Australia. Indeed, it seems probable that any Australian government would move cautiously by changing the existing governor-generalship into a presidency with minimum constitutional rearrangement, following precedents already set by Sri Lanka and Malta, among others. Even such a cautious change requires constitutional amendments passed by a majority of voters in a majority of states (four out of six). It is unlikely to succeed unless the major political parties endorse such a change.

The move toward a republic would not necessarily change attitudes towards Asia. But these, too, are changing quite rapidly and are part of an overall change whereby Australians definitively turn their backs on the so-called 'settled policies' of the past that were beyond partisan debate. Among these were the exclusion of non-European immigrants and a cultural, ideological, and economic orientation towards the United Kingdom. The adoption of a republic (if it eventuates) would mark a very decisive break with 200 years of tradition and make it much easier to gain public acceptance for an effective reorientation towards Asia. For that reason alone it is unlikely to be achieved without some public controversy, especially from the conservative parties. At present, the Australian Labor Party and the Australian Democrats seem firmly and fairly unanimously committed to the republic; the Liberals are divided but many have unexpectedly appeared warm towards the idea since their election defeat of March, 1993, including the premier of the largest state, New South Wales; while the rural-based National Party is opposed. Support for a republic is greatest among the young.

Attitudes toward Asia are much more complex and difficult to categorize. All the major parties accept the importance of the Asian connection, but often for different reasons; neither has there been much debate within the partisan area on relevant issues. Even the conservative National Party, which represents farming and mining interests, is very conscious of the importance of markets for primary products in Japan and China. Its competitors come from North America and Western Europe rather than from Asia, though there is some minor importation of processed tropical products. Its major concern is for the ending of import restrictions by Japan, especially on beef. But against this enthusiasm for trade with Asia, many National Party activists and supporters have been hostile to Asian immigration and investment, especially in Queensland where the strongest party branch is located. As noted above, the Nationals are the most hesitant about breaking the British connection. National Party politicians normally represent electorates where the vast majority of voters are Australian born of British and Irish descent. The ethnic background of National politicians has been varied, especially in Queensland, and includes the only politician of Asian origin in the federal parliament, Senator Bill O'Chee who is of partly Chinese origin. The electoral and organizational base of the party however is strongly Anglo-Celtic, and rural conservatism is the strongest basis for resistance to the Asianization of Australia.

Except in Queensland (where it has been out of office since 1989), the National Party always rules in combination with the Liberals. Representing the urban professional classes, business and commerce, and some rural interests, the Liberal Party has a very ambivalent history in terms of its attitudes towards Asia. The founder of the party, the late Sir Robert Menzies, declared himself "British to the bootheels" and was an exceptionally enthusiastic admirer of Queen Elizabeth. His reluctance to visit Asia was always contrasted by critics with his willingness to visit England and to accept British imperial honors such as a Knighthood of the Thistle. Until Menzies retired in 1966, it was virtually impossible for Liberals to deny the validity of either White Australia or the British connection. Yet immediately afterwards there were quite rapid shifts, especially in the more liberal branches in Victoria and South Australia. The new party leader, Malcolm Fraser (prime minister from 1975 to 1983), was a strong advocate of multiculturalism and a strong opponent of racist attitudes towards immigrants and Aborigines. At the state level, the New South Wales Liberal government of Nick Greiner (who was born in Hungary) maintained a strong ethnic affairs commission and refused to readopt the imperial honors system abolished by its Labor predecessors.

Neither were these new attitudes uniformly adopted in the Liberal Party nor are they necessarily as influential today as in the 1980s. The growth of an economic rationalist trend among conservatives accompanied an increasing hardening of resistance to what were seen as trendy issues such as multiculturalism. The Liberal leader, John Howard, criticized both multiculturalism and Asian immigration in 1988, creating a furor which, among other things, contributed to his eventual loss of the leadership in 1989. He did not, however, condone outright calls for a reduction in Asian immigration made by the leader of the National Party in the Senate, John Stone. The rise of hard-line rationalists among the conservatives led to the defeat within the party of such progressive liberals as Ian Macphee, a former minister for immigration.

The combination of economic rationalism with conservative attitudes in noneconomic areas was confirmed by the election of John Hewson in 1990 as Liberal leader. Hewson, like Howard, criticized multiculturalism to the Western Australian Liberals at their annual conference in 1992, but he did not extend this argument to an attack on Asian immigration, trade, or investment. The Liberal program Fightback, on which they fought and lost the 1993 national elections, contained a number of punitive attitudes towards immigrants but not on an ethnic or racial basis. A postmortem analysis of the election defeat of March 1993 forced the Liberals to reconsider their attitudes towards multiculturalism and their failure to cultivate ethnic communities, including Asians. Hewson was replaced as leader by Alexander Downer during 1994 and he began to mend fences publicly with ethnic community leaders. The party under Howard and Hewson had gained a reputation of being unsympathetic to ethnic variety, and this was damaging it with the large part of the electorate of non-British background (Liberal and National Parties, 1991; Liberal Party of Australia, 1991).

The Australian Democrats have taken a limited role in debating issues relating to Asia and had turned around against mass immigration under their former leader, Senator John Coulter. However, Coulter's objections had been based on ecological rather than ethnic grounds, as he was originally an advocate of zero population growth. The participatory structure of the Democrats, their limited media coverage, and their varied strength from state to state makes it difficult to assess their position on many major issues. However, in origin they represent the more liberal wing of the Liberal Party, combined with 'Greens' and others unwilling to fit into a party system dominated by economic interests and issues. In South Australia, where they are strongest, they have opposed the Multifunctional Polis in the state parliament, but on ecological grounds rather than because of its Japanese origins. On immigration, their leader has advocated drastic reductions, but this does not seem to have been the attitude of the previous party spokesman on immigration, Senator Spindler. Other parties complain that they never know what position the Democrats will take up, and this seems true of their position on relations with Asia. However, it seems very unlikely that racist attitudes would have much credence in a party which is usually seen as on the more progressive and liberal side of Australian politics.

The oldest, strongest and currently dominant party in Australia is the Australian Labor Party (ALP). Historically the ALP, with its affiliated unions, was the strongest advocate of White Australia, and this continued until the resignation of its leader, Arthur Calwell in 1967. As with the retirement of Sir Robert Menzies from Liberal leadership, the passing of Calwell allowed a rapid reversal of previous attitudes. The new leader, Gough Whitlam (prime minister from 1973 to 1975) was determined to reverse support for White Australia, to reduce the British connection, and to oppose racist ideas and practices. His brief government officially ended White Australia, declared Australia to be a multicultural society, created a Community Relations Commission and a Racial Discrimination Act, granted independence to Papua New Guinea in 1975, recognized the Chinese Communist government in Beijing, and withdrew Australian troops from Vietnam.

Since the Whitlam government, the ALP has become identified with multiculturalism, with reorientation towards Asia, with republicanism, with equal opportunity programs, and with the full range of liberal attitudes on race relations also found on the reforming side of politics in other democracies.This is an almost complete reversal of traditional Labor party attitudes, though certainly not the only one. Indeed, it is often argued that the ALP simply continues an organizational name but has discarded virtually all its historic traditions. This is not entirely true, since a socialist element remains in the party and it is still based strongly on trade union affiliations and working class voters. This support base might suggest that opposition to immigration and multiculturalism still lurks beneath the surface of the party. However, its elected leadership is now almost completely middle class and tertiary educated – yet another departure from the fairly recent past.

CONCLUSIONS

Australia is no longer an isolated British outpost nor is it still wedded to the idea of White Australia based on fear of Asia. Officially Australia is a multicultural society, an active participant in the economics and politics of the Asia-Pacific region, and a fully independent state on the verge of severing its remaining constitutional links with the United Kingdom. Vital changes in outlook have taken place within the lifetime of the dominant generation aged between 40 and 60. Substantial shifts in cultural and ethnic background have resulted from mass immigration. Shifts in knowledge and beliefs followed the explosion of higher education which began in the 1960s. Television (introduced in 1956) brought American influences into every home, while the relative ease and cheapness of international travel greatly increased personal contact with, and experience of, neighboring peoples. The opening up of the Australian economy through liberalization of financial markets and the reduction of tariffs diversified the sources of investment and the location of markets. The rise of northeast Asia to comparable economic strength with Western Europe and North America compounded the relative decline of the United Kingdom as an imperial and economic power (Fynmore and Hill, 1992; BIE, 1978).

These changes have been relatively painless, although Australia (like New Zealand) is now suffering from the effects of undue dependence on primary produce markets, isolation from major industrial centers, and slow readjustment of a previously protected society. Mass immigration from universal sources has caused no serious tensions. Mass tourism from Asia has been welcomed even in a relatively conservative area like Queensland. Australian perceptions of Asia, while still tinged with fear of overwhelming numbers, no longer rest on notions of mass poverty and ignorance. The first foreign contact point for most Australians is no longer the impoverished waterfront of Colombo and Bombay but the affluence and cleanliness of Changi airport.

In many respects, then, the dilemmas of adjusting to Asia are no more threatening than the comparable adjustments which Britain must make as a member of the European community. Moreover, Australia has no binding constitutional links with Asian states and its only significant military commitment outside the Pacific islands is with Malaysia. Australia does not yet need to consider the cultural or political implications of its growing economic links with the region since, unlike Europe, the region has no formal political structure. Even were immigration from Asia to continue at higher levels than currently, settlers of Asian origin would constitute no higher a proportion of the population at the start of the next century than in Canada or the United States. There is no likelihood of English being displaced as the completely dominant medium of communication. Those who still argue from fear of Asia are a small and diminishing minority, appealing to the less well educated. This does not mean that they are politically irrelevant, but only that they are fighting for a lost cause.

Despite this fairly steady adjustment to the real world of the Asia-Pacific Rim, there are still problems waiting to be resolved in the new relationships and orientations. Australians are not going to become Asians in any sensible definition of the term. They may eat Asian food, learn Asian languages and take Asian holidays, none of which was true less than 40 years ago. But five times as many immigrants look to their origins in Britain and Europe as look to the whole of Asia and the Middle East. Nearly twenty times as many Australians look back to roots in Europe (predominantly the British Isles) as can claim an Asian inheritance. Australia is still not as cosmopolitan as two other major Pacific rim societies, Canada and the United States. This means that there will always be a degree of domestic suspicion towards greater Asianization as well as a degree of Asian suspicion toward Australia a European outpost.

These mutual suspicions may not matter too much if it is accepted that there are wide cultural differences within Asia as well as between the region and Australia. An unfortunate feature of recent Australian debate and popular perceptions has been the tendency to see Asia as homogenous and different. Yet in practice there are common links between Australia, Singapore, Malaysia, and the Philippines through the widespread use of the English language and a history of British or American influence. There are significant links between educated Indians and Sri Lankans and their Australian counterparts. Indeed, most immigrants to Australia from these two countries are English-speaking Christians. There are also, of course, important actual or potential links between Asian minority communities in Australia and their former compatriots. The Chinese-speaking minority in Australia already has important links with Hong Kong and Singapore, as with other such minorities in Canada, the United States, and Britain. The 1991 Census shows that 250,000 Australians are fluent in a Chinese language. This is a great potential resource which business and government is just starting to discover. The permeation of the business and professional classes by immigrants from Overseas Chinese, Indians, Sri Lankans, Filipinos, Vietnamese and their children will continue into the next century to the great potential benefit of Australian links with major Asian societies (Lever-Tracy, *et al.*, 1991).

Most public debate in Australia on the Asian connection tends to put the onus for change on Australians. They are enjoined to abandon the prejudices of the White Australian past as well as the orientations of the British imperial past. Many are reluctant to move rapidly along these roads, but they are a diminishing and aging element, if one which still strikes resonant chords in mass public opinion. Any deterioration in ethnic relations to the level now common in Western Europe would strengthen the conservative forces who resist necessary changes. However, such deterioration has yet to happen despite the jeremiads of some journalists and academics (Blainey, 1984; Markus and Ricklefs, 1985; Milne and Shergold, 1984; Monash University, 1988). The forthcoming debate about republicanism might also raise the salience of conservative appeals to a non-Asian past. But influential Australians have no need to feel ashamed or guilty about the pace of changing attitudes. The Australian relationship with Asia has been accepted by public opinion much more readily than the comparable changing relationship with Europe has been accepted in Britain.

REFERENCES

Adelman, H., A. Borowski, M. Burstein, and L. Foster, eds.
1994 *Immigration and Refugee Policy: Australia and Canada Compared*. Melbourne: Melbourne University Press.

Australia: Committee on Australia's Relations with the Third World
1979 *Australia and the Third World*. Canberra: Australian Government Publishing Service (AGPS).

Australia: Parliament of the Commonwealth
1991 *Business Migration Program: Report 310 of the Joint Committee of Public Accounts*. Canberra: AGPS.

Australia: Senate Standing Committee on Foreign Affairs and Defence
1977 *Australia and the Indian Ocean Region*. Canberra: Commonwealth Government Printer.

Australian Council on Population and Ethnic Affairs
1982 *Multiculturalism for all Australians*. Canberra: AGPS.

Australian National Korean Studies Centre
1992 *Korea to the Year 2000*. Canberra: East Asia Analytical Unit, Department of Foreign Affairs and Trade.

Blainey, G.
1984 *All for Australia*. Sydney: Methuen Haynes.

Boyce, P. J. and J. R. Angel, eds.
1992 *Diplomacy in the Marketplace: Australia in World Affairs 1981–90*. Melbourne: Longman Cheshire.

Bureau of Immigration and Population Research
1994 *Community Profiles: 1991 Census: Viet Nam Born*. Canberra: AGPS.

Bureau of Immigration Research
1991a *Community Profiles: Malaysia and Brunei Born*. Canberra: AGPS.

______
1991b *Community Profiles: Philippines Born*. Canberra: AGPS.

______
1990a *Community Profiles: Vietnam Born*. Canberra: AGPS.

______
1990b *Indochinese Refugees in Australia: Library Bibliography Series*. Canberra: AGPS.

Bureau of Industry Economics (BIE)
1978 *Industrialisation in Asia – Some Implications for Australian Industry*. Canberra: AGPS.

Choi, C. Y.
1975 *Chinese Migration and Settlement in Australia*. Sydney: Sydney University Press.

Coughlan, J.
1993 "Vietnamese Immigrants in Australia: A Socioeconomic Profile of the Ethnic Chinese and Vietnamese in Australia a Decade after the Beginning of the Long Journey." In *The Vietnamese Refugee Crisis: Reception and Resettlement Around the World*. Ed. P. Rutledge. Lansing: Michigan State University Press.

Dunn, H. A. and S. K. Fung, eds.
1985 *Sino-Australian Relations: The Record 1972–1985*. Griffith University, Centre for the Study of Australian-Asian Relations.

East Asia Analytical Unit, Department of Foreign Affairs and Trade
1992 *Australia and North-East Asia in the 1990s: Accelerating Change*. Canberra: AGPS.

Evans, G. and B. Grant
1991 *Australia's Foreign Relations in the World of the 1990s*. Melbourne: Melbourne University Press.

Freeman, G. P. and J. Jupp, eds.
1992 *Nations of Immigrants*. Melbourne: Oxford University Press.

Fynmore, R. and H. Hill, eds.
1992 *Australia's Business Challenge: South-East Asia in the 1990s*. Canberra: AGPS.

Garnaut, R.
1989 *Australia and the North-East Asian Ascendancy*. Canberra: AGPS.

Goot, M.
1991 "Public Opinion as Paradox: Australian Attitudes to the Rate of Immigration and the Rate of Asian Immigration, 1984–1990," *International Journal of Public Opinion Research*, 3:277–294.

Inglis, C. *et al*., eds.
1993 *Asians in Australia: The Dynamics of Migration and Settlement*. Singapore: Institute of Southeast Asian Studies.

Japanese Embassy
1988 *Survey of Australian Attitudes towards Japan*. Canberra: Embassy of Japan.

Jupp, J.
1991 *Immigration*. Sydney: Sydney University Press.

Jupp, J., ed.
1988 *The Australian People*. Sydney: Angus and Robertson.

Jupp, J. and M. Kabala, eds.
1993 *The Politics of Australian Immigration*. Canberra: AGPS.

Jupp, J., A. McRobbie, and B. York
1990 *Metropolitan Ghettoes and Ethnic Concentrations*. Wollongong: Centre for Multicultural Studies.

Kee, P.-K.
1988 *Chinese Immigrants in Australia: Construction of a Socio-Economic Profile*. Canberra: Office of Multicultural Affairs.

Lever-Tracy, C. *et al.*
1991 *Asian Entrepreneurs in Australia*. Canberra: AGPS.

Lewins, F. and J. Ly
1984 *The First Wave*. Sydney: Allen and Unwin.

Liberal and National Parties
1991 *Fightback! It's Your Australia*. Canberra: Liberal/National Parties.

Liberal Party of Australia
1991 *Australians Speak: Australia 2000*. Canberra: Liberal Party of Australia.

London, H. I.
1970 *Non-White Immigration and the 'White Australia' Policy*. New York: New York University Press.

Mak, A.
1993 *Pre-Departure Concerns of Prospective Migrants from Hong Kong to Australia*. Hong Kong: Institute of Asia-Pacific Studies.

Markus, A. and M. C. Ricklefs, eds.
1985 *Surrender Australia?* Sydney: Allen and Unwin.

Milne, F. and P. Shergold, eds.
1984 *The Great Immigration Debate*. Sydney: Federation of Ethnic Communities' Councils of Australia.

Monash University
1988 *Asian Immigration: Assessing the Issues*. Melbourne: Monash University Centre for Migrant and Intercultural Studies.

Palfreeman, A.
1967 *The Administration of the White Australia Policy*. Melbourne: Melbourne University Press.

Price, C. A.
1974 *The Great White Walls Are Built: Restrictive Immigration to North America and Australasia 1836–1888*. Canberra: ANU Press.

Renouf, A.
1979 *The Frightened Country*. Melbourne: Macmillan.

Rivett, K., ed.
1975 *Australia and the Non-White Migrant*. Melbourne: Melbourne University Press.

Sloan, J. and S. Kennedy
1992 *Temporary Movements of People to and from Australia*. Canberra: AGPS.

Viviani, N.
1984 *The Long Journey: Vietnamese Migration and Settlement in Australia*. Melbourne: Melbourne University Press.

Viviani, N., J. Coughlan, and T. Rowland
1993 *Indochinese in Australia*. Canberra: AGPS.

Wang, G.-W.
1992 *Community and Nation: China, Southeast Asia and Australia*. Sydney: Allen and Unwin.

Willard, M.
1967 *History of the White Australia Policy to 1920*. Melbourne: Melbourne University Press.

Wooden, M., R. Holton, G. Hugo, and J. Sloan, eds.
1994 *Australian Immigration: A Survey of the Issues*. Canberra: AGPS.

Yarwood, A. T.
1964 *Asian Migration to Australia*. Melbourne: Melbourne University Press.

Yencken, D.
1989 *Multifunction Polis: Social Issues Study*. Canberra: Department of Industry Technology and Commerce.

[7]

International Migration of Professionals*

JUDITH A. FORTNEY

The international migration of professional people and people with special skills is not a new phenomenon. What is new is the extent of the migration, the large number of people involved, and their proportion relative to other migrants. The character of mid-twentieth century migration to the U.S.A. and to other countries of the New World is unique in history. During the nineteenth and early twentieth centuries much larger numbers were involved than in the present migration, but the characteristics of the migrants were different. The uniqueness of to-day's migration stems from the high percentage of migrants who are professionals or are employed in other occupations involving a high degree of training.

In 1967 the U.S. received more than 360,000 immigrants (i.e. persons admitted with immigrant visas; the number of visitors admitted with non-immigrant visas usually exceeds the number of immigrants). Of these, 41,652 were in occupational category 'professional, technical and kindred workers', representing a 77% increase in this category over a ten-year period. In the still more highly skilled category of scientists, engineers and physicians there were 15,272 immigrants.[1,2] An additional 30,697 professional non-immigrants were admitted in 1967; an unknown proportion of these will remain in the U.S. to work and eventually change their status to that of immigrant. More than 63,000 persons were admitted in the same year as students and, as will be discussed later, many of these will change their status to immigrants and remain permanently in the U.S.

These numbers are not large when compared with migration statistics of earlier years, but, as we shall see later, their effect on American science and medicine is not negligible.

In the fiscal year 1907 more immigrants were admitted than in any other year of American history. But less than 1% of these 1,285,349 immigrants were professionals.[3] In the fiscal year 1967, 361,972 immigrants were admitted, and 11·5% of these were professional, technical and kindred workers.[4] Since 1960 the percentage of professionals has increased slightly though irregularly. (See Table 1, Column 3.) The large increase between 1966 and 1967 is partly accounted for by a change in the Immigration and Naturalization Law which came into effect on 1st December 1965 (that date is half-way through the fiscal year 1966). The new law abolished the national quota system which had been in existence since the early part of the century, and instead gave preference to persons with skills which might be 'especially advantageous' to the U.S. The only semblance of a quota remaining is that no more than 10% of immigrants may come from any one

* I am most grateful to Joseph J. Spengler for helpful comments on an earlier draft of this paper, and to Dr. Ernest Croft Long of the Duke Medical Center for assistance in the section on medicine. Since this article was written it has been brought to my attention through a news brief in *Science* that the number of scientists, engineers and physicians who migrated to the U.S.A. in 1969 was 21% less than in 1968 (13,000 in 1968, 10,300 in 1969). *Science* attributes this to a change in the immigration laws, (**167**, p. 1470) but changes in the scientific labour market are a more plausible explanation.

[1] United States Congress, Senate, March 1967, Subcommittee on Immigration and Naturalization of the Committee of the Judiciary, Hearings: *International Migration of Talent and Skills*, 90th Congress, p. 3.

[2] 'Scientists' does not include 'social scientists', and 'physicians' includes surgeons and dentists.

[3] United States, Department of Commerce and Labor, *Annual Report of the Commissioner General of Immigration to the Secretary of Commerce and Labor, 1907*, pp. 100–105.

[4] United States, Department of Justice, Immigration and Naturalization Service, *Annual Report, 1967*.

TABLE 1. *Immigration of Professional, Technical and Kindred Workers, Fiscal Years 1907, and 1961 and 1967*

Year	Total number of immigrants (1)	Number of Professional, technical and kindred workers (2)	Col. (2) as per cent of Col. (1) (3)
1907	1,285,349	12,600	0·98
1961	271,344	21,455	7·90
1962	283,763	23,710	8·35
1963	306,260	27,930	9·11
1964	292,248	28,756	9·83
1965	296,697	28,790	9·70
1966	323,040	30,039	9·29
1967	361,972	41,652	11·50

SOURCE: Immigration and Naturalization Service, *Annual Indicator of In-Migration to the United States of Aliens in Professional, and Related Occupations*, 1967.

country. Immediate effects of the new Immigration and Naturalization Law were to increase the percentage of professionals among the immigrants, and also to increase the percentage coming from the developing countries. The old law discriminated severely against all residents of 'coloured' countries, especially those of Asia. Immigrants from Asia in the professional, technical and kindred worker category more than doubled between 1965 and 1966 (2,078 to 5,628) and again between 1966 and 1967 (5,628 to 12,382). The number of scientists immigrating from Taiwan rose from 47 in 1965 to 1,321 in 1967; scientists immigrating from India increased from 100 to 1,425 in the same period; and from the Philippines from 90 to 1,066.[5] Immigrants from Africa in the professional and technical category also increased substantially although numbers remain small, 352 in 1965, 441 in 1966, and 668 in 1967.

The large percentage of professional, technical and kindred worker immigrants from Asia is shown in Table 2, from which it is also clear that more than 90% of all immigrants in this category come from Europe, North America and Asia.

TABLE 2. *Number of professional, technical and kindred workers who immigrated to the United States by region, and regional percentages of total, fiscal year 1967*

Region	Number	Per cent
Europe	13,119	31
North America	12,835	31
South America	2,126	5
Asia	12,382	30
Africa	668	2
Oceania	522	1
All Countries	41,652	100

SOURCE: Immigration and Naturalization Service, *Annual Indicator of In-Migration to the United States of Aliens in Professional and Related Occupations*, 1967.

[5] United States Congress, House, 28th March 1968, House Report No. 1215 of the Committee on Government Operations, *Scientific Brain Drain from the Developing Countries.*

Table 3 shows that regions vary in the percentage of migrants that are in the professional and technical category, and that developing countries lose relatively more emigrants in this class than do the already developed nations. Only 7·5% of the immigrants from other North American countries are professional and technical workers, but 22·7% of Asia's immigrants fall into this category.

TABLE 3. *Percentage of all immigrants who were professional, technical or kindred workers, by region, fiscal year 1967*

Region	Total number of immigrants	Per cent professional, technical or kindred workers
Europe	139,514	10·34
North America	140,138	7·50
South America	16,517	11·67
Asia	59,233	22·66
Africa	42,360	21·08
Oceania	2,328	19·71
All countries	361,972	11·5

SOURCE: Immigration and Naturalization Service, *Annual Indicator of In-Migration to the United States of Aliens in Professional and Related Occupations*, 1967.

A particular group of professional and technical immigrants that arouses special interest is the highly qualified category of scientists, engineers and physicians. In 1967 more than one-third of professional and technical immigrants fell into this élite group. Table 4, giving these figures, also shows that engineers are by far the most important group numerically, but if we group all health personnel together their number exceeds that of engineers.

TABLE 4. *Numbers of immigrant professional, technical and kindred workers in specified occupations, and percentages in specified occupations, fiscal year 1967*

Occupation	Number	Per cent
Natural scientists[(a)]	2,369	5·68
Social scientists[(b)]	459	1·10
Physicians, surgeons and dentists	3,557	8·53
Nurses	4,944	11·86
Other medical fields[(c)]	1,944	4·66
Engineers	8,682	20·84
Other technology and related fields[(d)]	5,400	12·96
Editors and reporters	268	0·64
Lawyers and judges	257	0·61
Professors and instructors	1,941	4·66
Religious workers and clergymen	1,754	4·21
Social and welfare workers	355	0·85
Teachers (elementary and secondary, n.e.c.)	5,280	12·67
Other (n.e.c.)	4,442	10·66
Total	41,652	100·00

SOURCE: Immigration and Naturalization Service, *Annual Indicator of In-Migration to the United States of Aliens in Professional and Related Occupations*, 1967.

(*a*) Includes 1,284 chemists, 455 physicists.
(*b*) Includes 193 economists.
(*c*) Includes 1,078 medical and dental technicians, 206 dieticians.
(*d*) Includes 1,701 accountants and auditors, 1,724 technicians (n.e.c.), 968 draftsmen.

A large percentage of the immigration of scientists from the developing countries consists of students who do not return home after completing their studies in the U.S. According to the annual report of the House Subcommittee on Research and Technical Programs, in 1967, 7,913 scientists, engineers and physicians immigrated from the developing countries; almost half (48%) of these were students already in the U.S. who had changed to immigrant status after graduation. For some countries the percentages were even higher; for Taiwan it was 89%; for Korea, 80%; for India, 78%; and for Iran, 71%. Scientific immigration from these four countries is almost entirely the result of student non-return.[6]

The figures given above refer to the proportion of immigrants who are student non-returnees. More difficult to estimate with precision is the proportion of students who do not return to their own countries. Analysis of Institute of International Education records indicates that 15 to 25% do not return, but the often quoted 'semi-official' figure is 8 to 10%.[7,8] This varies, of course, from country to country; in 1967 Taiwan had 4,299 students enrolled in science and engineering in American educational institutions; and in the same year Taiwan lost, through student immigration, 1,137, or 26%. By the same token Taiwan, India, Pakistan and Israel lost more students through non-return than they gained in that year by increased enrolments.[9]

The rate of student non-return varies both by field and level of training. It is largely students in the natural sciences and engineering, rather than the humanities or social sciences, who do not return home. Of the 3,772 students from developing countries who changed their status, 90% were either scientists or engineers who had entered the country with student visas.[10]

Perhaps it is helpful to note here that students normally enter the U.S. with either a F-visa (student visa) which is easily exchanged for an immigrant visa; or a J-visa (exchange visitor visa) which requires the visitor to leave the country for two years before he can receive an immigrant visa. However, he does not necessarily have to return to his own country; many go to Canada.

Foreign interns and residents who study in American hospitals are usually required to have J-visas, so after completion of their internship or residency they must leave. Many return after spending the requisite two years out of the country, but then, of course, they are recorded as new immigrants and not as students who have changed their status.

The very highly specialized sciences have the highest rates of non-return. Jobs are not available in these specialties in the developing or indeed in many of the developed countries. The Adlai Stevenson Institute for International Affairs surveyed two specialties and found a 45% non-return rate for foreign residents in neuro-surgery; 49% of students earning a master's degree and 73% of students earning the Ph.D. in nuclear engineering did not return home after graduation.[11]

The higher the level of training, the higher is the rate of student non-return. John C. Shearer (Professor of Economics, Oklahoma State University), testifying before the House Subcommittee on Immigration and Naturalization, said that a National Academy of Science study showed that 51% of foreign students receiving Ph.D.'s in the U.S. plan to remain in the country after graduation. For doctoral candidates from the developing countries the figure is over 60%.[12] Ex-President of

[6] *Ibid.*, p. 7.

[7] United States, Department of State, March 1967, *Some Facts and Figures on the Migration of Talent and Skills*, p. 5.

[8] United States Congress, House, 23rd January 1968, Subcommittee of the Committee on Government Operations, Hearings: *The Brain Drain of Scientists, Engineers and Physicians from the Developing Countries into the United States*, 90th Congress, p. 17.

[9] U.S. House, *Scientific Brain Drain from the Developing Countries*, pp. 7–8.

[10] *Ibid.*, p. 7.

[11] *Ibid.*, p. 9.

[12] *Ibid.*, p. 8.

Cornell University, James A. Perkins, estimates that more than 90% of Asian students who come to the U.S. do not return home.[13] And the Director-General of the International Labour Office estimates that fewer than 15% of students from South Korea and Iran return home.[14]

CONSEQUENCES FOR AMERICAN SCIENCE

Since the late 1950's, when the United States began its great post-Sputnik drive to develop science and technology, American educational institutions have not produced scientists and engineers fast enough to keep pace with demand. Immigrant scientists and engineers help to fill the gap, although the demand is still great. The relationship between the number of immigrants and the number of new graduates of American institutions is shown in Table 5. This table shows that immigrants comprise nearly 10% of engineers newly entering the profession in 1966. Thus, although the total number of immigrant engineers was less than 5,000, this is a significant number considering the specialized character of this profession. According to the National Science Foundation's national register of scientific manpower, there were only 416,800 scientists and 996,000 engineers employed in 1966.[15] So total numbers are relatively small. A little over 5% of the persons with doctorates in science in the United States in 1960 had foreign doctorates; the largest number were in chemistry, followed by physics and astronomy, then mathematics.[16]

TABLE 5. *Scientists and engineers who immigrated to the United States as a percentage of graduates in science and engineering of American institutions: Fiscal years 1956 and 1966*

	1956	1966
Scientists:		
Graduates of American institutions	45,948	99,145
Immigrants	1,022	1,852
Immigrants as percentage of graduates	2·2%	1·9%
Engineers:		
Graduates of American institutions	31,646	51,785
Immigrants	2,804	4,921
Immigrants as percentage of graduates	8·9%	9·5%

SOURCE: U.S. Government, *The Brain Drain into the United States of Scientists, Engineers and Physicians*, Staff Study for the Research and Technical Programs Subcommittee, 1967.

If we look at the élite of scientists in the United States we find that the percentage of foreign-born and trained increases. In 1961 there were 631 members of the National Academy of Science; 473 were born and trained in the United States, seven were born in the United States and trained abroad, 42 were born abroad and trained in the United States, and 109 were born and trained abroad. Relatively, 24% were born and 18% were trained abroad. Germany, Canada and England in that order head the list for both birth and training.[17]

By 1968 a total of 52 Americans had received the Nobel Prize for physics or chemistry. 21 of them were of foreign origin: eight received the prize as nationals of a foreign country

[13] U.S. Senate, *International Migration of Talent and Skills*, p. 87, testimony of Senator W. F. Mondale.

[14] International Labour Office, 1967, International Labour Conference, Fifty-first session, Report of the Director-General, *Non-Manual Workers: Problems and Prospects*, Geneva, p. 29.

[15] National Science Foundation, 1968, *Employment of Scientists and Engineers in the United States*.

[16] National Science Foundation, 1962, *Scientific Manpower from Abroad: United States Scientists and Engineers of Foreign Birth and Training*.

[17] *Ibid.*

and came to the United States afterwards. By the same date, 18 Americans had received the Nobel Prize in medicine and physiology; six of these were immigrants, and three more immigrated after receiving the prize.[18]

In addition to these illustrious scientists the United States has benefited incalculably from the 568 Hungarian engineers and natural scientists who arrived as refugees in 1957 (and there were others who first went to other countries, such as England and Canada, and later migrated to the United States); and also from 'Operation Paperclip' in which Wernher von Braun and his Peenemünde scientists were brought to the United States in late 1945, and an additional 169 engineers and natural scientists who arrived in the United States in 1948 as displaced persons.

Considering the qualifications of immigrant scientists and engineers, it appears that the immigrants are better qualified than the natives. The comparisons are made in Table 6, which unfortunately refers only to immigrants from the developing countries. It will be seen in Table 6 that whereas 53% of immigrant scientists have a Ph.D., only 38% of the United States total have that degree; and whilst 32% of the United States have only a Bachelor's degree, only 12% of immigrants are at that level. For engineers, the differences are even more pronounced; the percentage of immigrants with a Ph.D. is three times that of the United States total (15% and 5% respectively). As far as employment is concerned, 69% of immigrant scientists are involved in teaching and research compared with 48% of the United States total; for engineers the figures are 18% and 10% respectively.[19]

TABLE 6. *Qualifications and employment of natural scientists and engineers from the developing countries compared with the United States total of scientists and engineers, 1964*

	Scientists		Engineers	
	Immigrants	U.S. total	Immigrants	U.S. total
Degree held:				
Ph.D.	53%	38%	15%	5%
Master's	32%	27%	28%	17%
Bachelor's	12%	32%	38%	63%
Other	3%	2%	19%	15%
Employment:				
Teaching	19%	18%	6%	4%
Research	50%	30%	12%	6%

SOURCE: U.S. Government, *The Brain Drain into the United States of Scientists, Engineers and Physicians;* Staff Study for the Research and Technical Programs Subcommittee, 1967.

[18] The following eight men were awarded the Nobel Prize and later migrated to the United States: Albert Einstein and James Franck (Germany), Victor Hess and Wolfgang Pauli (Austria), Enrico Fermi (Italy), Chen Ning Yang and Tsung Dao Lee (China), and Peter Debye (born in Holland, awarded the prize for work in Germany). The following twelve men and one woman were born and trained abroad but were awarded the prize after migrating to the United States: Albert Michelson, Otto Stern, Polycarp Kusch, Rudolph Mossbauer, Maria Goeppert Mayer and Hans Bethe (Germany), Isador Isaac Rabi (Austria), William Ciaque (Canada), Felix Bloch (Switzerland), Emilio Segre (Italy), Eugene Wigner (Hungary) and Lars Onsager (Norway). The following three men were awarded the Nobel Prize for medicine and later migrated to the United States: Otto Meyerhoff (Germany), Otto Loewi (born in Germany, worked in Austria), Albert von Szent-Gyorgi (Hungary). The following five men and one woman were born and trained abroad and received the prize while in the United States: Alexis Carel (born in France, worked in United States, later returned to France), J. J. R. Macleod (Canada), Karl Lansteiner (Austria), Henrik Dam (Denmark, was in the United States only during the war years but received the prize while in the United States), Carl F. and Gerty T. Cori (Czechoslovakia).

[19] United States Congress, Senate, July 1967, Research and Technical Programs Subcommittee of the Committee on Government Operations, *The Brain Drain into the United States of Scientists, Engineers and Physicians*, p. 11.

Thus, although it would be exaggerating to say that American science depends on immigrants for ideas and talent, it is indebted to them to a very large extent. The number of immigrants is quite small, but in an area where total numbers are not large, immigrants form a significant percentage. Immigrant scientists and engineers contribute more to American science than their numbers might indicate, for they are over-represented in élite groups as measured by membership in the National Academy of Science, and being Nobel laureates. They also contain a higher percentage of Ph.D.'s.

TABLE 7. *Sources[a] of immigrant scientists and engineers, by region, fiscal years 1965, 1966 and 1967*

Region	1965	1966	1967
Western Europe	2,868	2,945	4,384
Eastern Europe	110	467	639
North America (Canada)	762	617	738
Central America	508	473	778
South America	384	343	382
Asia	566	2,175	5,237
Africa[b]	—	110	239
Other[c]	147	75	126
Total	5,345	7,205	12,523

The seven countries sending the largest number of scientists and engineers:

United Kingdom	2,293	Philippines	507
India	1,541	Germany	503
China[d]	1,359	Cuba	412
Canada	738		

SOURCE: National Science Foundation, *Scientists, Engineers, and Physicians from Abroad*, 1969.
(*a*) Country of birth.
(*b*) In 'other' in 1965.
(*c*) Mainly Australia and New Zealand since 1965.
(*d*) There were 408 from Taiwan in addition to these from Mainland China.

CONSEQUENCES FOR AMERICAN MEDICINE

It is not exaggerating to say that American medicine depends on immigrants. Fully 15% of all physicians practising in the United States are graduates of foreign medical schools.[20] This percentage has increased; it was only 6·3 in 1959, and appears to be still increasing. Of new physicians and dentists entering American practice (i.e. new graduates plus immigrants) in 1966, more than one-quarter were immigrants. These figures are shown in Table 8. If dentists were excluded, the contribution of immigrant physicians jumps to about 40% of the gross increase in 1967.[21]

At the end of 1967 there were 309,483 graduates of medical schools in the U.S. (not all of these were active physicians). Of these, 6,600 were graduates of Canadian medical schools, and 46,347 were graduates of other foreign medical schools. These figures are obtained by the American Medical Association and include among the graduates of foreign medical schools Americans who received their degrees abroad, and exclude foreign nationals who qualified in American schools. Nor are Canadian medical schools included among foreign schools for this purpose.

[20] American Medical Association, 1968, *Medical School Alumni*, 1967, Statistical Series, A.M.A. Chicago, Illinois, p. 26.

[21] National Science Foundation, 1969, *Scientists, Engineers and Physicians from Abroad*, p. 7.

Willard Wirtz (then Secretary of Labor) in his testimony before a House Subcommittee said that between 1952 and 1961 the U.S. had benefited from the immigration of 14,000 physicians and 28,000 nurses. Without this immigration the U.S. would be even more acutely short of medical personnel than is presently the case. Wirtz also gave a list of occupations for which there is an acute shortage in the U.S. This list includes physicians, surgeons, dentists, nurses and veterinarians.[22] Table 9 shows the number of immigrants in these and other health fields in 1967.

TABLE 8. *Physicians and dentists who immigrated to the United States as a percentage of graduates of American medical and dental schools, fiscal years 1956 and 1966*

	1956	1966
Graduates of American medical schools	9,862	10,580
Immigrant physicians	1,547	2,761
Immigrants as percentage of graduates	15·7%	26·1%

SOURCE: U.S. Government, *The Brain Drain into the United States of Scientists, Engineers and Physicians*, Staff Study for the Research and Technical Programs Subcommittee, 1967.

TABLE 9. *Immigrants in the health fields, fiscal year 1967*

Occupation	Number of immigrants
Physicians and surgeons	3,326
Dentists	231
Professional nurses	4,784
Student professional nurses	160
Other medical and related fields:	1,944
Chiropractors	(13)
Dieticians	(206)
Optometrists	(34)
Osteopaths	(2)
Pharmacists	(338)
Medical and dental technicians	(1,078)
Therapists and healers	(176)
Veterinarians	(26)
Total all health fields	10,445

SOURCE: Immigration and Naturalization Service, *Annual Indicator of In-Migration to the United States of Aliens in Professional and Related Occupations*, 1967.

Migration of health personnel is concentrated on particular areas, and also, oddly enough, particular medical schools. Thus, about 80% of immigrant physicians from Latin America come from nine medical schools in six countries. There are more than 6,000 Filipino nurses in the U.S., and more than 300 Iranian nurses in New York City alone.[23]

Table 10 shows the major sources of the *stock* of foreign physicians, the seven countries having the largest number of medical graduates practising in the U.S., and the contribution of the several regions of the world to the number of physicians practising in the U.S. It will be seen from Table 10 that almost half the foreign graduates comes from European medical schools.

[22] United States Congress, House, 1964, Subcommittee No. 1 of the Committee on the Judiciary, *Hearings to Amend the Immigration and Nationality Act*, H.R.7700, 88th Congress, July and August.

[23] I.L.O., p. 30.

Table 11, on the other hand, shows the source of immigrant physicians for the most recent year for which there are statistics – the fiscal year 1967. A comparison of the two tables shows the trend toward an increasing proportion of immigrant physicians coming from the developing countries. It should be noted that the I.N.S. figures used in Table 11 include dentists and Canadians, the A.M.A. figures of Table 10 do not include these groups.

While some of the numbers shown in Table 11 are not large relative to American medical personnel, they are large relative to the numbers of medical personnel in the country of origin (see next section); and perhaps small numbers that are not shown in Table 11 are even more significant. For example, eight physicians from Ghana and five from El Salvador immigrated in 1967; so did 15 nurses from Nigeria and eight from Nicaragua. The Ghanaian doctors may be more important to Ghana than are the 460 emigrant Canadian doctors to Canada.

TABLE 10. *Sources of immigrant physicians: the seven nations having the largest number of medical graduates practising in the United States; and percentage coming from each region of the world, 1967*

Nation	Number	Per cent
Philippines	5,927	12·8
West Germany	3,289	7·1
Italy	2,966	6·4
Switzerland	2,460	5·3
United Kingdom	2,418	5·2
Cuba	2,352	5·0
India	2,345	5·0
Total seven nations	21,757	46·9
Total all graduates of foreign schools[(a)]	46,347	100·0
Graduates of European schools		49·2%
Graduates of Asian schools[(b)]		32·4%
Graduates of Latin American schools		17·0%
Graduates of African schools		1·4%
Graduates of all foreign schools[(a)]		100·0%

SOURCE: *Medical School Alumni, 1967*, A.M.A. 1968, p. 23.

(*a*) Except Canadian.

(*b*) Including Australia and New Zealand.

Demographically the graduates of foreign medical schools show some differences from graduates of American schools. Foreign graduates are younger and a larger percentage are still in training. They are more likely to reside in metropolitan areas and more likely to be female. Nearly one-third of all woman doctors in the U.S. graduated from foreign medical schools.[24]

There are also differences with respect to professional status. These are, however, largely accounted for by the greater percentage of foreign graduates who are still in training as interns and residents in American hospitals. There is virtually no difference in the percentage engaged in patient care – about 90% for each group. The detailed figures are given in Table 12.

In terms of money, the 3,557 physicians and dentists who immigrated to the U.S. in 1967 represent a considerable financial gain. They were the equivalent of the output of the fifteen largest medical schools in the U.S. If we use the very conservative estimate of $20,000 as the cost of training a physician, this represents annual foreign aid to the United States of more than $70 million,

[24] A.M.A., p. 23.

TABLE 11. *Sources of physicians, surgeons and dentists, and professional nurses immigrating in fiscal year 1967*

Region	Physicians, Surgeons, Dentists	Per cent	Professional Nurses	Per cent
Europe	908	25·5	1,587	32·1
North America	928	26·1	2,276	46·0
South America	393	11·0	189	3·8
Asia	1,217	34·2	792	16·0
Africa	87	2·4	41	0·8
Oceania	24	0·7	59	1·2
All countries	3,557	100·00	4,944	100·00

The seven countries sending the largest number of physicians, surgeons and dentists

Philippines	612	Colombia	122
Canada	460	Turkey	114
United Kingdom	211		
Argentina	133		
Iran	125		

The seven countries sending the largest number of professional nurses

Canada	1,217	Ireland	214
United Kingdom	752	Germany	155
Jamaica	533	Trinidad and Tobago	132
Philippines	455		

SOURCE: Immigration and Naturalization Service, *Annual Indicator of In-migration to the United States of Aliens in Professional and Related Occupations*, 1967.

TABLE 12. *Medical school graduates by major professional activity and country of graduation, 31st December, 1967*

	U.S.A.	Canada	Foreign	Total
	%	%	%	%
Patient care	89·0	86·0	90·7	89·2
Solo, partnership, group and other	65·7	59·2	40·1	61·7
Interns, residents, fellows	12·2	13·6	32·0	15·2
Hospital staff	11·2	13·2	18·5	12·3
Other professional acitivities	6·4	9·1	7·2	6·6
Medical school faculty	3·7	4·9	3·6	3·7
Administration	1·5	1·8	0·7	1·4
Research	1·3	2·3	2·9	1·5
Inactive	4·6	4·9	2·2	4·2

SOURCE: *Medical School Alumni, 1967*, A.M.A. 1968, p. 24.

much of it from the developing countries to which the U.S. is sending financial assistance. Charles V. Kidd, Executive Secretary of the Federal Council for Science and Technology, discussing the contribution of immigrant physicians from Latin America, estimated that it would cost the U.S. about $60 million to build three new medical schools, each graduating 100 students a year, and $15 million a year to maintain them just to replace the 300 physicians who immigrate each year from Latin America. Again these are quite conservative estimates.[25]

CONSEQUENCES FOR THE COUNTRY OF ORIGIN

The effect of the migration of talent and skills on the country of origin tends, in general, to be greater than its effect on the country of destination. For example, 62 physicians from the Dominican Republic migrated to the United States in 1962. This number is small compared with approximately 300,000 (1967) doctors practising in the United States. But the number is quite large when compared with the number of doctors practising in the Dominican Republic and is the equivalent of one-third of their new medical graduates.

Similarly in the same year 18 Chilean engineers entered the United States, the equivalent of one-fifth of the newly graduating engineers in Chile; 30 Israeli doctors immigrated, the equivalent of 40% of Israel's new medical graduates.[26]

In 1965, 82 Colombian physicians migrated to the United States. Colombia graduates only 442 doctors a year and has a physician/population ratio of 1/2400 compared with 1/670 for the United States.[27] Karachi has a physician/population ratio that matches that of the developed countries, but Pakistan as a whole has a very poor ratio, and physicians (in common with other professionals) are unwilling to move to rural areas; yet Pakistan is proud of the number of doctors she exports, not only to the industrialized nations but also to the Arab world.[28]

The effect of emigration is far greater on the developing countries than it is on the industrialized nations where out-migration of professionals is largely compensated for by in-migration of professionals from developing countries. But although emigrants may be replaced in terms of numbers, it does not follow that they are replaced in terms of quality.

Argentina has for some time been, and still is, a country of large net immigration. However, in general, immigrants to Argentina have been of low educational standard and emigrants have had a high educational standard. Of the Argentinians migrating to the United States 35% are professional, physicians and engineers being the most common. The numbers are sufficiently large for 2·7% of all engineers immigrating to the United States to be Argentinian.[29]

The case of Britain is perhaps unique. Britain is also a country with a net gain in migration, and many of the immigrants are professional. In 1964 the major immigrant categories were 3,300 teachers, 1,600 engineers, 1,300 nurses and 800 doctors. Health personnel form the largest immigrant category into Britain, so that one-third of all hospital personnel are immigrants; 30 to 40% of nurses are foreign-born, although not necessarily foreign-trained.[30] In 1965–66 there were nearly 16,000 foreign-born nursing students in the United Kingdom.

The United Nations Institute for Training and Research estimated that in one year (the report does not say which year), Britain lost 3,000 professionals and gained 5,000 professionals through immigration. However, it is still estimated that Britain will be short of nearly 100,000

[25] U.S. Senate, *International Migration of Talent and Skills*, p. 77.

[26] U.S. House, *Scientific Brain Drain from the Developing Countries*, p. 5.

[27] U.S. Senate, *International Migration of Talent and Skills*.

[28] U.S. House, *Scientific Brain Drain from the Developing Countries*.

[29] Enrique Oteiza, 1965, 'Emigration of engineers from Argentina: A case of Latin American "brain drain", *International Labor Review*, **92**, 6.

[30] United Nations, 5th November 1968, General Assembly, Report of the Secretary General, *Outflow of Trained Personnel from the Developing Countries* (mimeographed).

persons with advanced training by 1970.[31] Emigration from Britain tends to be to the United States and to the developed countries of the Commonwealth, Australia, New Zealand, South Africa and Canada. Immigration tends to be from the developing countries of the Commonwealth.

The Royal Society of London, alarmed at the extent of emigration of scientists, commissioned a study of the problem. The study was restricted to scientists with a Ph.D. and covers the decade following 1952. The survey found that about 140 scientists leave the United Kingdom permanently each year, the equivalent of about 12% of the annual output of Ph.D.'s. About 60 of these go to the United States,[32] more than 20 to Canada, 35 to other Commonwealth countries and 25 elsewhere. The annual number of emigrant Ph.D.'s tripled during the decade. An additional 260 emigrate temporarily each year. The permanent emigration of university staff amounts to about 60 persons a year, or 1% of the total staff in science. Nine Fellows of the Royal Society emigrated permanently in the second half of the decade, and there are 20 Fellows now permanently residing in the United States. About half the emigrants leave in the year that they obtained their degree.

The sciences losing the greatest numbers are chemistry (32% of all scientific emigrants), physics (18%), geology (10%), metallurgy (6%), and biology, botany and zoology (each about 5%).

Several respondents commented that Britain seems to be losing her best scientists; a higher proportion of Ph.D.'s emigrate than scientists with only a bachelor's degree. It should be remembered that the Royal Society's study does not include those scientists who emigrated with a bachelor's or master's degree and subsequently earned a doctorate in their country of destination (and a large number of these do not return after receiving their degree).

This large-scale emigration of scientists has caused a major deficiency in Britain; the emigration of senior scientists is particularly serious, for these kinds of men are not replaced by immigration from the developing countries.[33]

The loss of physicians is also serious to Britain. In 1967, 206 physicians and surgeons from Britain entered the United States as immigrants (I do not have the figures for the number leaving Britain for other destinations). An additional unknown number entered the United States with temporary visas to work for a few months or years in American hospitals. In the same year Britain lost 752 emigrant nurses to the United States and 101 people in other medical fields.[34] As mentioned above the loss of these people is more than compensated for by immigrants from the Commonwealth, but the question of quality must inevitably be raised. Charles V. Kidd testifying before the House Subcommittee hearings said that Britain suffered more in terms of standards of medical care from emigration of doctors than the Philippines, although physician emigration from the Philippines is proportionately greater.[35]

Although the non-return of students does not represent as serious a financial loss to their home country as does the loss of persons who have already completed their training before emigrating, there is nevertheless a loss in terms of creativity and leadership potential, and other non-measurable characteristics. Again the numbers are not insignificant. For example, in 1965, there were only about 80 scientsts with Ph.D.'s in Korea, but there were more than ten times as many Korean scientists with Ph.D.'s working in the United States. However, Korean government officials evidently view the situation with equanimity, and say that when Korea is able fully to develop her universities there will be a large reserve of educated Koreans in the United States who will be able to staff them.[36]

[31] *Ibid.*

[32] Where they constitute 20% of all immigrant scientists (I.L.O.).

[33] Royal Society of London (no date), *Emigration of Scientists from the United Kingdom.*

[34] United States, Department of Justice, Immigration and Naturalization Service, *Annual Indicator of In-Migration to the United States of Aliens in Professional and Related Occupations*, 1967. See also, on the emigration of British doctors, B. Abel-Smith and K. Gales, *British Doctors at Home and Abroad* (London, 1964).

[35] U.S. House of Representatives, *The Brain Drain of Scientists, Engineers and Physicians from the Developing Countries into the United States*, p. 46.

[36] U.S. Senate, *International Migration of Talent and Skills*, p. 112.

REASONS FOR THE MIGRATION OF PROFESSIONALS

Enrique Oteiza, in discussing the case of Latin American engineers, suggests several reasons why professionals migrate readily. These reasons apply equally well to all nationalities in all fields. The five reasons follow:[37]

1. Advanced training is readily usable without adaptation.
2. Professionals usually know at least one other language well in addition to their mother tongue.
3. Communications between professionals in different countries is good because professionals often travel for business.
4. Demand for professionals is great in most countries, and usually exceeds supply.
5. Cost of transportation is minor in relation to salary.

These reasons explain only why professionals find it relatively simple to migrate, permanently or temporarily; they do not explain why professionals flock in large numbers to the industrialized nations of the world despite the urgent need for them in the underdeveloped countries. Walter Adams suggests the following reasons (which I have re-grouped and re-ordered) for this:[38]

I. Salary differentials.

II. (*a*) Professional opportunities, especially in research.
(*b*) The technology gap.
(*c*) Political balkanization, a disunited Europe, drive for independence in the African nations.

III. (*a*) Relevance of foreign training, especially of foreign students in the United States.
(*b*) Lack of realistic manpower policies.

IV. Monopolistic restrictions in the advanced countries.

V. Traditionalism in the country of origin, especially the hierarchies weighted against the young.

VI. Discrimination on non-economic grounds.

Again these reasons do not tell the whole story. Following is an expansion of them, and examples where appropriate.

I. Salary differentials: many professionals like to belittle this factor and stress professional opportunities more, but it is nevertheless significant. There is little evidence on relative incomes; Charles V. Kidd gave the following figures in his testimony before the Senate Subcommittee Hearings: Before migration to the United States three-fourths of immigrant scientists, engineers and physicians from Chile earned between $150 and $300 a month, and in the United States three-fourths of these immigrants earned more than $400 a month, and 40% earned over $800 a month.[39] University staff in many Latin American countries are paid so poorly and irregularly that most take an additional job to support themselves.[40] Very generally, British scientists, engineers and physicians at least double their salaries after migration to the United States, and perhaps to Canada, too. Salary differentials are perhaps more often a reason for failure to return rather than for emigrating in the first place.

[37] Oteiza, *loc. cit.*

[38] Walter Adams (ed.), 1968, *The Brain Drain* (New York: Macmillan Company), Introduction.

[39] U.S. Senate, *International Migration of Talent and Skills*, p. 79.

[40] Moysés Nussenzveig, 26th September 1969, 'Migration of scientists from Latin America', *Science*, pp. 1328–1332.

II. A more popular reason given by the immigrant professionals is the greater professional opportunity available in the developed countries. Professional opportunities are greater in the United States than in the other developed countries, and greater in the developed countries than in the developing countries. There are many reasons for this. One is the so-called 'technology gap'. The United States has a greater ideological commitment to research and development, and spends enormous sums of money on them. In the case of Europe, Iffland and Rieben comment that although the United States and Europe have nearly equal populations, the United States spends four times as much money on research ($24 billion in 1966), two-thirds of which is paid for by public authorities. Another reason for the limited research spending in Europe is the lack of corporate giants which spend a great deal of money on research in the United States. The United States has 400,000 persons engaged in research compared with only 150,000 in the six countries of the Common Market and Britain.[41]

A common situation in developing countries is that the large cities have adequate numbers of physicians and good hospitals, and there are not enough jobs in the cities for all new medical graduates. But the new doctors are unwilling to move to rural areas where salaries may be extremely low and professional opportunities negligible. (This is often the situation in the United States, also.) Thus arises the paradox of unemployment of doctors in a country that badly needs doctors. The Philippines provide an excellent example of this situation. One witness before the House Subcommittee Hearings said that certain medical schools in the Philippines train doctors who are better suited to work in the United States than at home, and are in fact training medical students for export.

III. Unemployment of professionals. This arises for two main reasons: irrelevant training of students and unrealistic manpower policies. Many foreign students in the United States discover that they have been overeducated, and the possibility of their finding a job in their field after returning home is very slim. The more specialized the science, the fewer the job opportunities in developing countries. For example, Ghana needs general practitioners more urgently than neuro-surgeons. Medical students in the United States receive more training in the degenerative diseases of old age than in means of lowering infant mortality: the latter training would be more appropriate for most developing countries.

In 1967 the Director-General of the International Labour Office made a report on problems of non-manual workers.[42] He stated that unemployment of non-manual workers is a serious problem in many countries, and suggested the following reasons:

(*a*) Educational and vocational training systems are not adapted to employment opportunities.
(*b*) Unawareness of the position of the occupation on the employment market.
(*c*) Distaste for technical occupations, even where there is certainty of employment.
(*d*) Preference for non-manual work, especially office jobs.
(*e*) Preference for urban areas and reluctance to move away from them.

There is considerable waste of money in training people for occupations in which there is unemployment, when at the same time there are manpower shortages in other occupations. There is also the problem of underemployment, when professionals are taking jobs that are 'beneath' them. The situation is most serious in Asia, less so in Africa and the Near and Middle East. In India there are half a million educated (high school or college) persons registered with employment agencies; most of these are looking for clerical jobs although they do not have the skills required (shorthand, typing, etc.). The Indian Census of 1961 showed that 10·4% of persons classed in scientific and technical occupations were unemployed, this was 16·3% for science graduates, 3·7% for engineering graduates, and 8·6% for physicians. Senator Mondale of Minnesota in a *Saturday Review* article presented as evidence before the Senate Subcommittee Hearings, quotes a university dean as

[41] Adams, *op. cit.*
[42] I.L.O.

saying, 'It is difficult to advise an Indian engineer to return home if there is a high risk that he will be a clerk-typist for the next ten years'.[43]

In the Philippines unemployment rates are high among arts graduates, up to 45% in some specialties. The problem is least serious in engineering, teaching, and business administration. The Japanese are excessively attracted to office jobs while there is a manpower shortage in manual and technical fields. It is feared that Japan will develop a surplus of college graduates.[44]

IV. Monopolistic restrictions. Probably the most significant factor in the large-scale immigration of physicians to the United States is the failure of American medical schools to keep up with demand. Table 13 shows the number of graduates of American medical and dental schools for several years up to 1967.

The restriction on available medical school places and restriction of output of medical schools is usually attributed to the monopolistic practices of the American Medical Association and its desire to keep the supply of physicians limited. Certainly these aims are fulfilled, but the effect is also to encourage immigration of physicians from abroad.

V. Traditionalism in country of origin. It is difficult to estimate how much of a problem traditionalism is considered to be; perhaps quite a lot of what is interpreted as traditionalism is really due to lack of funds. However, Dr. Donald F. Hornig (Special Assistant to the President (Johnson), and Director of the Office of Science and Technology of the Executive Office) feels that academic immigration from Europe is almost entirely due to the rigidity of academic life in Europe and especially the lack of freedom of junior staff.[45] Nobel Laureate Rudolph Mossbauer reportedly left the University of Munich for this reason.[46] Discrimination against junior staff is a common complaint, especially of British doctors migrating to the United States.

VI. Discrimination on non-economic grounds. The United States has been the beneficiary of persecution policies in other countries, particularly in the case of European Jews who left Europe in the 1930's. Other immigrants came, not because of personal persecution, but because of political upheaval, and this includes German scientists following World War II, Hungarian scientists following the 1957 uprising, and Cuban scientists and physicians following the Castro takeover in 1959.

The United States is often accused of deliberately draining other countries of their professionals. Professionals are expensive to produce and the United States saves vast amounts of money by not training these people themselves. Professor Richard Titmuss accuses the United States of deliberate recruitment of 100,000 engineers, scientists and doctors between 1949 and 1967, and thereby saving $4 billion by not paying for their training.[47] The Federal Government does not actively recruit, but in so far as many foreign graduate students are paid by federal research and development monies the government is responsible for the financing of some students. According to Charles Frankel (Assistant Secretary of State in the Johnson Administration), by far the largest part of the migration of professionals involves recruitment by American industry, universities, hospitals and research organizations (many of these last three are wholly or partly financed by the Federal Government).[48]

Although the Federal Government may not actively recruit abroad, State and local governments do. The Livermore School District (California) advertises for teachers in London newspapers. In addition there is at least one company founded for the sole purpose of recruiting

[43] U.S. Senate, *International Migration of Talent and Skills*, p. 94.

[44] I.L.O., p. 28–30.

[45] U.S. Senate, *The International Migration of Talent and Skills*, p. 107.

[46] U.S. House, *The Brain Drain of Scientists, Engineers and Physicians from the Developing Countries into the United States.*

[47] Adams, p. 59.

[48] U.S. Senate, *The Brain Drain into the United States of Scientists, Engineers and Physicians.*

scientists and engineers from abroad for American companies. Careers Incorporated was founded by William Douglass immediately after graduating from Yale. Douglass visits London several times a year, and after one visit in 1966 he put 1,400 researchers and engineers in touch with 30 American companies, mainly airplane manufacturers or electronic and atomic science concerns. It is not known how many of these 1,400 actually emigrated. The sales pitch included doubled or tripled salaries, moving expenses, promises of fast promotion, and easy housekeeping for wives. The British government is considering forbidding this kind of recruitment as West Germany has already done.[49] Perhaps it does not hurt to remember that British companies (e.g. Imperial Chemical Industries) recruit on American and Canadian campuses, and several companies advertise in North American professional journals for British scientists to return to Britain.

This recruitment by American companies is not only at the professional level; Dravo Corporation (Pittsburgh) imports Europeans through Canada for pipefitting and carpentering jobs. Kaynar Manufacturing Company (Fullerton, California) brings in Japanese machine tool operators.[50]

TABLE 13. *Graduates of American medical and dental schools, 1956 to 1967*

Year	Number of Graduates
1956	9,862
1962	10,392
1963	10,469
1964	10,538
1965	10,482
1966	10,580
1967(a)	10,610

SOURCE: United States Government, *The Brain Drain into the United States of Scientists, Engineers and Physicians*, p. 3.

(*a*) The number for 1967 is from United States Government, *Scientific Brain Drain from the Developing Countries*, House Report No. 1215, p. 12.

CONCLUSION

This paper has given a statistical evaluation of the extent of professional migration into the United States. I have also commented on the effects of this migration on American science and medicine, and the effects on the country of emigration. There appears to be general agreement that effects on the receiving country are almost entirely beneficial. The effects on the country of origin are harder to evaluate. In the long run extensive migration of talent and skill over a long period of time will have adverse effects on economic development. However, short-run effects may be beneficial in that unemployment of professionals is alleviated. But even this advantage may be a disguised disadvantage if necessary social, structural or occupational reforms are delayed.

The ethical questions the emigrating scientists must face are: (*a*) shall he maximize his contribution to the total development of world science and migrate to where he can work better? or (*b*) shall he stay in his own country and contribute to its development although his total contribution to science may be smaller. The best discussion of the national/international controversy appears in Adams, *The Brain Drain.*

Large-scale migration of professional and technical personnel has been identified as a problem. It is a problem that has caused concern to the United States government, and to the governments and learned societies of some developed countries. Ironically, it appears to cause less concern to the developing countries who are the chief losers.

[49] *London Observer*, 11th December 1966.

[50] *Time*, 9th May 1969.

[8]

Geoforum, Vol. 19, No. 4, pp. 401–410, 1988
Printed in Great Britain

0016–7185/88$3.00 + 0.00

From Settlers to Skilled Transients: the Changing Structure of British International Migration

A. M. FINDLAY,* Glasgow, U.K.

Abstract: This paper examines trends in British emigration using the results of the International Passenger Survey. Settlement emigration has declined in importance while in the early 1980s temporary skilled labour transfers have become dominant. Two parallel mechanisms are proposed to explain the regional patterns of skilled emigration, with particular emphasis being given to the role of international recruitment agencies in controlling which skills are sought in certain regional labour markets.

Introduction

The U.K. has a long tradition of emigration. Nine million people are estimated to have left the country between 1851 and the end of the nineteenth century; during the first half of the present century a further 7 million departed. The bulk of these emigrants left with the intention of settling permanently abroad. In the 1930s, and in the immediate post-war years, there was a brief interlude when immigration to Britain exceeded emigration (OPCS, 1985b), but during the 1960s and 1970s outflows once again became dominant. Between 1980 and 1985 no less than 835,000 British citizens emigrated from the country.

Recent British emigration is, however, very different in character from that of the nineteenth and early twentieth centuries. During the 1960s and 1970s the well-established process of 'settler' emigration went into decline and was progressively replaced by temporary emigration of skilled workers. This new phase of emigration, reflecting Britain's changing position in the world economy, is the subject of analysis of this paper. Since this new form of emigration is impermanent in nature, it cannot be studied in isolation from immigration. The return of temporary skilled migrants after relatively short spells of employment abroad has changed the composition of immigration flows to the country as much as that of emigration flows. Paradoxically, at the same time as Britain was becoming increasingly concerned to control immigration as witnessed by the introduction of the *British Nationality Act* 1981, immigration statistics showed a continued rise in the numbers of persons entering the U.K. This rise was caused by a steady increase in the circulation of British citizens at an international level, leading as a result to a growth in the 'immigration' of British citizens. In 1975, for example, 85,300 British citizens were recorded as entering the U.K. as migrants, and by 1985 the inflow had risen to 109,400.

Since this paper seeks to examine the distinctive character of recent trends in British emigration using a unique and unpublished data source in the form of special tabulations prepared by the Office of Population Censuses and Surveys (OPCS) for the Institute of British Geographers (IBG) Working Party on Skilled International Migration, it commences with an empirical analysis of this data set. It then proceeds inductively to establish generalisations about the new era emerging in British emigration and to relate them to existing theory.

Definitions

In order to analyse the character of this new era of

* Department of Geography, University of Glasgow, Glasgow G12 8QQ, U.K.

British emigration it is necessary to define more precisely the terminology being used, as well as to describe the chief source of data on British international migration—the International Passenger Survey (IPS). Throughout the remainder of this article the internationally agreed United Nations definition of *emigrant* is adopted. That is, "a person who has resided in the United Kingdom for a year and who on leaving has declared the intention to reside abroad for a year or more" (OPCS, 1985a, p. viii). The threshold of 1 year is inevitably arbitrary, but remains a useful yardstick for comparative research.

The emergence of temporary skilled labour migration as an important element in the British migration system has led to some tensions between the technical and academic definitions of migration. For example, the return of emigrants after a period of more than 1 year abroad boosts the number of immigrants as technically defined by the IPS. In some respects, these migrants merit the term 'return migrants', yet their return is different in nature from that of failed returnees or retirement migrants of the type that characterise the counterflows of traditional settler emigration (APPLEYARD, 1962; PRICE, 1981). The term 'transilient' has been used to describe this migrant group "whose outstanding characteristic is their readiness to move from one country to another and back again" (RICHMOND, 1968, p. 263), while more recently, in the context of the international circulation of staff within multinational organisations, the term 'skilled transients' has been used (APPLEYARD, 1985). In the case of Britain, skilled transients also need to be distinguished from another group of British-born 're-entrants' to the U.K., which consists of members of families of New Commonwealth origin who have temporarily returned abroad before re-entering Britain for a second or subsequent time (DEVIS, 1985). Only a small part of the international circulation of British citizens with professional and managerial skills is drawn from the population of New Commonwealth origin.

The term 'skilled migrant' also requires qualification. In a British context only a tiny proportion of actively employed persons interviewed by the IPS on departure from the country were technically defined as 'unskilled'. The IPS does, however, make a distinction between emigrants whose skills are of a managerial or professional type from those which are manual and clerical. In this article the term 'skilled' is applied to managerial and professional emigrants, but this should not be taken to imply that all other emigrants are 'unskilled'.

The IPS

The annual results of the IPS are published in aggregate form by the OPCS. The IPS was designed originally to produce information about financial transfers associated with the movement of population on the main air and sea routes to and from the U.K. Generation of international migration statistics is only a secondary objective of the survey. From 1964 onwards the IPS offers a systematic sample coverage of all major international routes except those to Eire. A detailed discussion of the statistical basis of the survey and the way in which it has evolved through time has been reported by DEVIS and WILSON (1981) as well as in several OPCS publications (OPCS, 1976, 1978, 1985a).

For the purposes of this paper it is sufficient to note here that in order to achieve its objectives the IPS interviews only a small portion of all emigrants and immigrants. For example, in 1985 the *estimate* that 108,495 British citizens emigrated was based on 578 interview contacts. Consequently, figures obtained from the IPS are "subject to sampling and non-sampling errors which can make the estimates for small categories unreliable" (OPCS, 1986, p. viii). This is the main reason for the high level of aggregation evident in the published tables of the IPS, which reduces their value to the geographer interested in both regional details and occupational cross-tabulations of migration flows. To overcome this difficulty, the IBG Working Party on Skilled International Migration requested OPCS to prepare special disaggregated tabulations for each year between 1980 and 1985. This paper produces new tables from this data source, but with reaggregation of the time series in order to maintain the regional and occupational details while at the same time reducing the risk of making false inferences as a result of the sampling errors associated with the small number of annual interview contacts.

From Settlers to Skilled Transients

During the 1970s temporary skilled labour migration became the most important single component of the stream of migrants leaving the U.K. Pointers to this switch in the character of British emigration can be found even in published IPS material (BULUSU, 1986). Professional and managerial staff, taken as a proportion of all actively employed emigrants, increased steadily from 37% of the total in 1973 to 59% in 1985. The temporary nature of emigration is made evident by the large number of British-born

Geoforum/Volume 19 Number 4/1988 403

Table 1. Migrants entering the U.K. in 1984 who were born in the U.K.: by citizenship, place of last residence and year of departure*

	Total		Year of departure		
	Number (thousands)	(%)	Before 1975 (%)	1975–1979 (%)	1980–1983 (%)
Citizenship					
All	83.1	100	14.4	22.6	63.0
British	79.1	100	13.5	22.1	64.3
Non-British	4.0	100	33.3	33.3	33.3
Place of last residence					
Old Commonwealth	11.7	100	33.3	22.2	43.6
New Commonwealth	13.1	100	26.7	6.9	66.4
Foreign†	58.3	100	7.9	26.2	66.0

* Source: adapted from OPCS (1986, p. 26).
† OPCS defines 'foreign' as all non-Commonwealth countries.

'immigrants' to the U.K. in 1984 (Table 1). Many of these re-entrants to the U.K. had been abroad for only a few years. For example, 64% of the 79,000 British citizens who returned to the U.K. in 1984 had been abroad for 3 years or less. The likelihood of a short stay abroad was greater for emigrants to New Commonwealth and foreign destinations (defined by OPCS as non-Commonwealth) than for persons departing to the traditional countries of British 'settler' migration in the Old Commonwealth. The published IPS tables also indicate very clearly that the number of emigrants to Canada, Australia and New Zealand has dropped sharply in the last 10 years, while other destinations such as the EEC have increased in importance (Table 2).

Table 2. Migrants leaving the U.K. for selected destinations by place of next residence and year of departure (percentages: British and non-British citizens)*

	Year of departure		
Place of next residence	1975	1980	1985
All Commonwealth	46.0	43.0	37.3
Old Commonwealth	34.0	28.5	20.0
New Commonwealth	12.0	14.5	17.3
All foreign†	54.0	57.0	62.7
EEC	11.8	14.7	16.9
U.S.A.	9.3	12.5	13.8
Middle East‡	n.d.	10.3	10.3

* Source: adapted from OPCS (1986).
† OPCS defines 'foreign' as all non-Commonwealth countries.
‡ The Middle East includes Israel and Iran, but excludes Turkey and Egypt under OPCS definitions.

The nature and scale of British skilled transient migration becomes even clearer from an examination of the unpublished IPS data referred to above and reproduced in summary form in Tables 3–7. It should be stressed that Tables 3–7 are based on relatively small sampling numbers in relation to the grossed-up totals and one should not put too much emphasis on individual cell entries. The reader should refer to them to identify trends and general patterns. Table 3 shows that between 1980 and 1985 there was a steady rise in the proportion of immigrants to the U.K. who were re-entrants. Amongst re-entrants there was a steady increase in the number who were in the professional and managerial categories. By comparison, the volume of manual and clerical workers re-entering the country oscillated considerably from year to year. There is a substantial increase in professional and managerial staff as a proportion of all actively employed migrants within the flow of re-entrants, rising from 56% in 1980 to 73% in 1985. Not only did highly-skilled persons come to represent a higher proportion of all international labour circulation, but they also appeared to be involved in a migration cycle of relatively short duration. Forty-one per cent of the professional and managerial group had been abroad for 2 or less years. There were, however, significant regional variations in the pattern and timing of skilled emigration. For example, 51% of professional and managerial migrants returning to Yorkshire and Humberside had been abroad for 2 or less years, while in the Northern region (of England) only 23% had been away for such a short period. These variations point to the importance of geographical variations in the mode of access to foreign labour

Table 3. Migrants* re-entering the U.K. by occupational status and year of entry (return)†

Year of entry (return)	Number of re-entrants (thousands)	Professional and managerial re-entrants (thousands)	Manual and clerical re-entrants (thousands)	Re-entrants as a percentage of all immigrants	Professional and managerial as a percentage of all actively employed re-entrants
1980	72.0	21.0	16.4	41.4	56.1
1981	71.2	22.5	13.8	46.4	62.0
1982	104.6	28.9	21.4	51.8	57.4
1983	101.7	32.5	22.0	50.4	59.7
1984	105.3	36.0	16.8	52.4	68.2
1985	116.7	38.9	14.6	50.3	72.7

* British and non-British citizens.
† Source: calculated from unpublished IPS data.

markets as well as to regional differences in the structure of the labour markets from which the migrants are drawn.

Regional Skills on the Move

More than a quarter of a million professional and managerial workers left the U.K. between 1980 and 1985 (Table 4). A further 230,000 manual and clerical employees emigrated during the same period. Regional participation in these flows varied considerably, both in terms of volume and skill mix. Three regions dominated the system: Greater London, Scotland and the rest of the South East. Table 4 standardises regional labour migration flows in terms of the size of the population in the active age cohorts. Greater London, the rest of the South East and Scotland made such large contributions to British labour migration that they alone had emigration rates above the national average. By contrast, the Midlands and Northern Ireland had much lower levels of labour

Table 4. Emigration of British citizens by region of last residence and occupational status (1980–1985)*

Standard regions	Emigration rate† per 1000 persons‡			Volume of professional and managerial emigration (thousands)	Professional and managerial as a percentage of all employed emigrants
	All employed emigrants	Professional and managerial emigrants	Manual and clerical emigrants		
Greater London	19.7	11.8	7.8	52.0	60.2
Scotland	17.0	9.0	8.1	28.8	52.7
Rest of South East	15.0	8.2	6.7	52.4	54.9
North West	13.5	6.0	7.4	24.4	44.9
North	13.3	5.8	7.5	11.4	43.6
South West	13.2	7.2	6.0	17.5	54.7
East Anglia	12.9	6.6	6.4	7.6	50.8
Wales	11.7	5.9	5.9	9.9	50.0
Yorkshire and Humberside	11.7	4.9	6.8	15.1	42.1
West Midlands	9.3	4.7	4.6	15.3	50.5
East Midlands	8.8	5.1	3.6	12.4	58.3
Northern Ireland	7.0	3.5	3.4	3.2	50.6
Total U.K.§	14.0	7.3	6.7	252.5	52.3

* Source: calculated from unpublished IPS data.
† In a strict sense the term 'emigration rate' should not be used since the statistics include some migrants who departed more than once during the years 1980–1985.
‡ The rate was calculated relative to the population in the active age groups at the beginning of the period. Active age groups for men 15–64, for women 15–59.
§ Regional totals do not sum to the U.K. total because of rounding and the exclusion of the Isle of Man and the Channel Islands.

Geoforum/Volume 19 Number 4/1988 405

emigration than might have been anticipated. In the case of Northern Ireland, this may be because some emigrants depart by air and seaports in the Republic of Ireland. Professional and managerial skills were drawn disproportionately from the South East and Scotland, but, while in the South East migrants with these skills greatly outnumbered manual and clerical emigrants, this was less true of Scotland which supported the highest rate of manual and clerical emigration in the country and had almost an even mix from these two major occupational groupings. Table 4 shows that in most regions professional and managerial emigration equalled or exceeded outflows from manual and clerical categories, but a geographical cluster of the three northern regions of England deviated significantly from this national pattern. The North of England appears still to be dominantly a source of less-skilled migrant workers.

It is worth noting that during the 1980s there was a rapid drop in the volume of manual and clerical emigration from the U.K. The level was almost halved if one compares the years 1980–1982 with the years 1983–1985. Decline was most rapid in the Northern region where in 1983–1985 the level was less than a quarter of that of the earlier period. By contrast, professional and managerial workers continued to emigrate in considerable numbers throughout the 1980s and decline was mainly limited to two destination regions: the Old Commonwealth and the Middle East. Emigration of British citizens with a high-skill status remained buoyant to European destinations and increased significantly to countries outside the EEC.

Where Are All the Skills Going?

The skill mix of emigration varies by destination zone as well as by region of origin (Table 5). Excluding skill flows of less than 2000 persons (which because of their small numbers tend towards extreme ratios) two groups of countries attracted the least skilled emigrants. The '*Auf Wiedersehen* Pet' phenomenon is evident in the low-skill input of emigration to France and the Federal Republic of Germany, while traditional settler emigration destinations such as Australia, New Zealand and the Republic of South Africa also received high proportions of manual and clerical migrants. At the other end of the spectrum, the results are perhaps more surprising. The most skilled outflow of British citizens was to the African Commonwealth, followed by a number of other Third World regions (which because of the relatively small size of the flows are not shown in Table 5). Significant proportions of professional and managerial migrants were also present in the flows to the U.S.A. and the Middle East.

Table 6 ranks destination regions for professional and managerial emigration in terms of the magnitude of flows during the years 1983–1985. The Middle East emerges ahead of the Old Commonwealth countries, displacing them from the premier position for the first

Table 5. Professional and managerial emigration of British citizens to selected destinations* 1980–1985†

Destinations	Professional and managerial as a percentage of all actively employed emigrants	Emigration volume (thousands)		
		Professional and managerial	Manual and clerical	Total actively employed
Highly-skilled emigration streams				
African Commonwealth	74.8	16.9	5.7	22.6
U.S.A.	63.8	30.7	17.4	48.0
Middle East	62.8	49.5	29.3	78.8
Europe excluding EEC	61.5	15.4	9.7	25.1
Least skilled emigration streams				
New Zealand	49.0	8.7	9.1	17.8
Federal Republic of Germany	39.1	12.9	20.0	32.8
South Africa	37.7	15.5	25.7	41.2
Australia	37.4	30.4	50.8	81.2
France	37.2	4.1	7.0	11.1

* Migration flows (actively employed persons) of less than 2000 persons were excluded from the table.
† Source: calculated from unpublished IPS data.

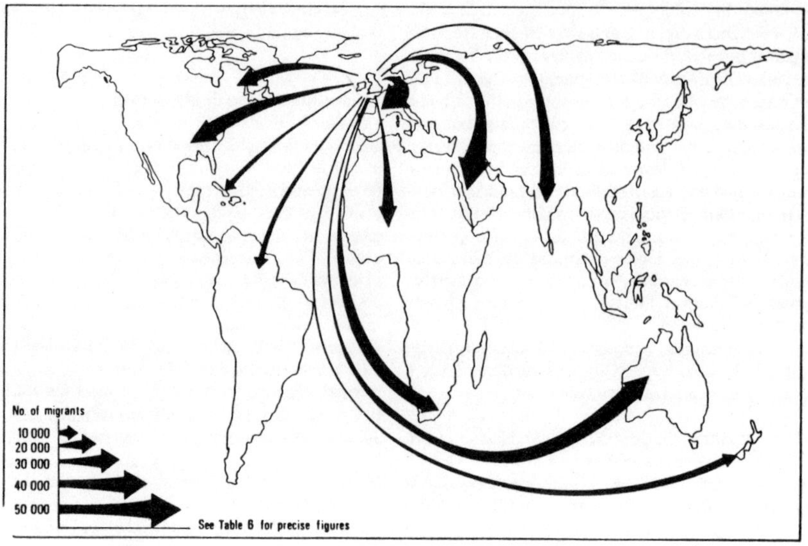

Figure 1. Professional and managerial emigration of British citizens, 1980–1985.

time in many centuries of British emigration (Figure 1). Similarly, it is noteworthy that the EEC countries proved more attractive than the U.S.A. Comparison of flows from 1980–1982 and 1983–1985 shows that the EEC was one of the most stable destination regions for British professional and managerial migrants. Perhaps as striking as the strong linkages are the regions of the world which remained weakly associated with Britain in terms of skilled labour migration. Japan, for example, does not feature in Table 6, since the IPS estimated that only about 1000 British professional and managerial workers emigrated there between 1980 and 1985. Emigration to large parts of the world such as China and the Soviet Union was practically absent from the skilled migration system monitored by the IPS.

Because of the small-cell problem it is hard to present a reliable table of origin–destination movements. Nevertheless origin–destination specific flows were present and identifiable in the data set. For half of Britain's standard regions the Old Commonwealth remained the main destination for skilled emigration. The pattern of association is strongest with those

Table 6. Professional and managerial emigration of British citizens by place of next residence* and year of departure (thousands)†

Place of next residence	Year of departure 1980–1982	1983–1985
Middle East	28.5	21.0
Old Commonwealth	39.0	17.8
Australia	19.9	10.5
Canada	13.9	3.9
New Zealand	5.2	3.4
EEC	15.5	15.1
Federal Republic of Germany	4.8	8.1
U.S.A.	17.4	13.3
Africa‡	13.1	9.9
Europe excluding EEC	6.7	8.7
South Africa	10.1	5.4
Other Commonwealth§	10.2	11.2
Other non-Commonwealth	5.6	4.0

* Cells of less than 2000 were amalgamated with 'other' destinations.

† Source: unpublished IPS data.

‡ Includes both Commonwealth and non-Commonwealth, but excludes South Africa.

§ I.e. other Commonwealth not included elsewhere in the table.

regions lying in the south of the country, as well as the North West and Yorkshire and Humberside. Regions such as the North of England, Wales and East Anglia were more involved with emigration to the Middle East, while the "Auld Alliance" appears to have bonded Scotland with the EEC. Scotland and Greater London could claim not only the highest emigration rates, but also the broadest emigration base in terms of the relative strengths of their flows to many different destinations. By contrast, regions such as the West Midlands, Yorkshire and Humberside and the North had very specialized emigration patterns concentrating almost exclusively on the Middle East and the Old Commonwealth.

Professional and Managerial Emigrants: Managers and Artists from London, Engineers and Nurses from Scotland

Not only do British regions differ by the destinations to which skilled emigrants depart, but they also vary remarkably in the types of professional and managerial expertise which they provided between 1980 and 1985. At a national level, approximately one-third of the 25,000 professional and managerial emigrants were scientists, engineers and skilled technicians, and a further third were professionals from education, health and welfare sectors. Three out of four were men, with the greatest male dominance in science, engineering and technical skills, but there were some emigrant skill categories and regions in which women were numerically more important. There were 5 times as many women as men in the emigration flow of education, health and welfare workers leaving Scotland, while from the South East (excluding Greater London) there were more women than men departing with professional expertise in the arts, literature and sport.

Table 7 shows the composition of professional and managerial skills emigrating from the three regions with the strongest involvement in highly-skilled emigration. The skill composition of professional emigration from Northern England is also included to illustrate the pattern found in a region with a much weaker tradition of this kind of emigration. Greater London and the rest of the South East had roughly the same number of highly-skilled emigrants, but these were drawn from very different backgrounds. This selectivity reflects on the one hand the locational structure of certain types of economic activities in relation to the London conurbation and on the other hand the varying residential capabilities and preferences of different skill groups. For example, 33% of professional and managerial emigrants from Greater London were drawn from the education, health and welfare sectors (they accounted for a fifth of the national total), while relative to the rest of the South East relatively few scientists and engineers left from Greater London.

In contrast with the other three regions shown in Table 7, the North had most of its small numbers of highly-skilled emigrants concentrated in just one category—science, engineering and related technical skills. Concentration in this category does not reflect a particularly large number of emigrants with these skills, but merely an absence of professionals from other backgrounds. By comparison, Scotland had a lower proportion of emigrant scientists and engineers, but the actual number departing between 1980 and 1985 (11,200) was of the same order of

Table 7. Characteristics of professional and managerial emigration from selected British regions, 1980–1985*

	Regions (figures as percentages of regional total)				
Occupational category	All U.K.	Greater London	Rest of South East	Scotland	North
Scientists, engineers and professional technical skills	36.2	24.0	37.4	39.0	59.8
Professionals in education, health and welfare	30.1	33.0	21.0	34.0	23.2
Professionals in administration	17.3	23.9	23.5	14.2	7.2
High-level and general managers	11.6	10.8	12.1	10.9	8.1
Professionals in literature, arts and sport	4.8	8.3	6.1	2.1	1.7
Total number (thousands)	252.5	52.0	52.4	28.8	11.4

* Source: calculated from unpublished IPS data.

magnitude as from the whole of Greater London. The pattern which once more emerges is therefore of a diverse and more balanced range of skills departing from the major emigration regions and a narrow skill base feeding the smaller flows from other regions of the country.

Generalisation and Theory

While this paper has intentionally aimed to provide a description of a previously unavailable data source, it remains valuable to conclude by seeking to establish generalisations and theory. The data have illustrated that emigration from the U.K. remains significant in volume, but it is different in character from the 'settler' emigration with which Britain has traditionally been associated. The new processes which seem to have emerged involve the circulation of highly-skilled persons who stay abroad for relatively short periods before returning once again to the U.K. These skilled transient flows seem to be particularly associated with certain (but not all) Third World destinations, the Middle East and the U.S.A., and to originate disproportionately from the South East of England and Scotland. It seems probable that in the remainder of the 1980s these patterns will become even more marked as emigration of manual and clerical workers *to* most destinations (with the possible exception of the EEC) and *from* other areas of the U.K. declines further, perhaps to the point of total insignificance. Outside the main emigration regions, migration of professional and managerial workers appears to be highly specific both in terms of destinations and skills.

How can these generalisations be reconciled with existing migration theory? It is evident that a certain level of explanation can be achieved using PETRAS' (1981) classification of labour migration in relation to a world economy approach. The decline of the empire and the increasing interaction of British capital and labour flows in a hierarchically organised global system of production has reduced the need and the opportunities for settler emigration and has promoted new forms of international labour transfers. FRIEDMANN's (1986) classification of cities in terms of their global control functions provides one model of a possible system within which these transfers might be expected to occur. In terms of global control functions Friedmann identifies the London conurbation as one of only four 'world cities' with a population of over 10 million. On this basis it might be expected to have the ability to generate on the one hand substantial 'brain exchanges' (SALT, 1984) with Tokyo, New York and Los Angeles, and on the other hand to be the focus of skilled labour flows moving in order to control and supervise capital and technology transfers from London to those cities located at lower levels in the world hierarchy within London's 'hinterland'. The empirical evidence presented above shows very small flows of skilled labour from London to Japan, but much stronger links with the U.S.A. It is difficult, however, to determine from IPS sources what proportion of Britain's skilled international migration to the U.S.A. is truly a brain exchange and what proportion is a continuation of settler emigration in the guise of a British 'brain drain'. Explanation of skilled migration flows between the most advanced industrialised economies in terms of theories derived from the concept of an international hierarchy of production necessitating the international transfer of skilled labour is not therefore entirely adequate. It seems possible that developments in telecommunications combined with an increase in the volume of short business trips may have been sufficient to obviate any substantial increase in skilled labour migration to fulfil these functions.

The British emigration experience of the 1980s does, however, present interesting evidence of strong interaction with some parts of the world in a fashion which might be compatible with a world economy approach. For example, Table 6 indicates that significant flows of professional and managerial workers left Britain for the Middle East, Republic of South Africa and parts of the African Commonwealth such as Nigeria, all of which might arguably be claimed to lie for historical reasons in the British-dominated hinterland of the world economy. PETRAS (1981, p. 48) has described this type of flow as involving no more than a "small number" of highly-skilled workers accompanying capital flows to "locations of production in low wage zones". Clearly, in terms of British emigration to Third World destinations, Petras' statement would seem to underestimate the significance of these flows, but it nevertheless offers one explanation for why they should occur.

Part of the reason that flows to the middle East and to the Third World destinations have been so large is that the flows have not only been stimulated by the core regions of the world economy but have also been brought into existence by the desire of certain countries of the Third World to create an indigenous industrial and service infrastructure (as well as to install and maintain complex modern military machinery). For example during the 1970s the Arab oil states had sufficient capital to launch the most ambitious of development plans. Achievement of these plans necessitated the transfer of foreign technology and managerial expertise in the form of skilled expatriate labour in order to establish and service newly-created institutions and enterprises. The demands for skilled labour were met mainly through a system of short-term contract migration using the services of international recruitment agencies.

The resulting skilled labour flows have been different in character from the international staff transfers occurring within the internal labour markets of multinational companies, and the presence of a parallel mechanism for skilled international labour migration helps to explain elements of the regional pattern of British emigration. British regional labour markets, with their specific traditions of industrial specialisation and faced with difficult problems of industrial restructuring, have been easy targets for international recruitment agencies seeking certain types of technological expertise and managerial skills. In the U.K. context these recruitment agencies are mainly located in central London, within the zone of the city specialising in international business services, but for their labour recruitment activities they have looked outside the high-wage zone of the capital. The perceptual map of regional labour markets held by these agencies has been critical in moulding the structure of skill specific flows emanating from many of the older industrial regions of England (ROBERTS, 1986).

Certain anomalies are evident between the empirical generalisations presented earlier in this article and the explanatory devices which have been briefly reviewed above. The most striking of these is the very high level of professional and managerial emigration from Scotland. Certainly this region has a long and glorious industrial history as well as moderately high levels of unemployment, but these factors have not proved sufficient to generate equally high levels of skilled migration from other regions such as Teesside or the West Midlands. Nor is it entirely convincing to argue that the phenomenon can be interpreted as a perpetuation of Scotland's heritage as an emigrant nation since there is no evidence that other sending regions involved in settler emigration have adapted to Britain's new position in the world economy in the same way.

A number of possible explanations present themselves which it is beyond the scope of this paper to evaluate in any detail. Firstly, Scotland has become host to more foreign-owned branch plants than any other region in the U.K. apart from the South East and North West. (Is it a coincidence that the North West ranks next after the South East, Scotland and the South West in the volume of professional and managerial emigration recorded in Table 4?) Foreign-owned branch plants provide the opportunity to professionals working outside the core economy to enter into the internal labour market of a multinational company. In the case of Scotland many American multinationals opened their first European plant there, followed by subsequent expansion into Europe, thus providing a path for career promotion and international migration. This might help to explain Scotland's relatively strong migration links with the EEC.

A second line of argument is based on the proposition of an Anglo-Scottish cultural divide. Scotland, more than any other of the standard regions of mainland Britain, maintains a distinct cultural identity. This may make the prospect of migration to London and to the labour markets of the South East less different from the prospect of temporary emigration abroad than would be the case for potential migrants departing from other regions. This raises the poignant question of whether international migrants choose or are chosen to move. Conceptual frameworks such as the 'career path' as well as empirical evidence (such as the Scottish case) demand that migrants are also given an active role in the moulding of migration systems.

Inevitably the questions asked and answered in this paper have been limited by the nature of the data set. Other theories and data are needed to understand the behavioural mechanisms which govern who migrates and for what reasons. Nevertheless, the macro-scale analysis presented in this article makes a specific contribution in highlighting the fact that emigration remains a key economic and demographic feature of the U.K.

Acknowledgements—The author is grateful to the Department of Geography, University of Glasgow, and to Black Horse Relocation who provided financial assistance to obtain special tabulations of IPS data from OPCS. All data included in Tables 3–7 are Crown Copyright and may only be reproduced with the permission of the OPCS.

References

APPLEYARD, R. T. (1962) The return movement of United Kingdom migrants from Australia, *Popul. Stud.*, **15**, 214–225.

APPLEYARD, R. T. (1985) Processes and determinants of international migration, Paper presented to the IUSSP seminar on Emerging Issues in International Migration, Bellagio, May 1985.

BULUSU, L. (1986) Recent patterns of migration from and to the U.K., *Popul. Trends*, **46**, 35–39.

DEVIS, T. (1985) International migration, *Popul. Trends*, **41**, 13–20.

DEVIS, T. and WILSON, P. (1981) UN recommendations on statistics of international migration: their use in the International Passenger Survey, Paper presented to the Expert Group on the Improvement of International Migration Statistics, New York, 21–25 September 1981.

FINDLAY, A. (in press) The impact of international migration on British localities, In: *Captive Britain*, P. Cooke and N. Thrift (Eds). Cambridge University Press, Cambridge.

FRIEDMANN, J. (1986) The world city hypothesis, *Dev. Change*, **17**, 69–83.

OPCS (1976) *International Migration*, 1975 (Series MN, 2). OPCS, London.

OPCS (1978) *International Migration*, 1976 (Series MN, 3). OPCS, London.

OPCS (1985a) *International Migration*, 1983 (Series MN, 10). OPCS, London.

OPCS (1985b) *International Migration, Spotlight*, 4. OPCS, London.

OPCS (1986) *International Migration*, 1984 (Series MN, 11). OPCS, London.

PETRAS, E. (1981) The global labour market in the modern world economy, In: *Global Trends in Migration*, pp. 44–63, M. Kritz *et al.* (Eds). Centre for Migration Studies, New York.

PRICE, R. (1981) Migration to and from Australia, In: *Commonwealth Migration*, pp. 11–49, T. E. Smith (Ed.). Macmillan, London.

RICHMOND, A. (1968) Return migration from Canada to Britain, *Popul. Stud.*, **22**, 263–271.

ROBERTS, R. (1986) Historical development of labour recruitment agencies in Britain, Presentation to the Workshop on Skilled International Recruitment, University College, London, November 1986.

SALT, J. (1984) High level manpower movements in Northwest Europe and the role of careers, *Int. Migration Rev.*, **17**, 633–652.

[9]

Pergamon

Geoforum, Vol. 26, No. 4, pp. 411–427, 1995

0016–7185/95 $9.50+0.00

The Changing Nature and European Perceptions of Europe's Refugee Problem

VAUGHAN ROBINSON,* Swansea, U.K.

Abstract: Many in Western Europe regard it as being in the grip of a refugee crisis. This paper considers this contention. It describes the main stages in the development of the current refugee crisis and argues that having established the agenda in the 1940s, Western Europe has been able to progressively distance itself from refugee episodes and define them as essentially problems of the Third World. The end of the Cold War and the growth in numbers of spontaneous, rather than quota, refugees have been considerable shocks to the West, which can no longer contain and distance itself from refugee flows. Shock has led Europe to overreact and become myopic in its view of refugee matters. In reality, figures demonstrate that Wetern Europe is not the centre of refugee generation, applications or resettlement. Despite this, governments have taken draconian unilateral and multilateral action to exclude not only Third World asylum seekers but also those from the East.

Introduction

Few would doubt that there is now a global refugee crisis. Authoritative sources suggest that the number of refugees in the world may be as many as 18.2 million (U.N.H.C.R., 1993) and that the total is rising by 3300 per day. However, the issue which this paper addresses is the more contentious question of Western Europe's status within this global crisis and its attitude towards it. More particularly, the paper seeks to outline how European involvement with refugees has changed over time, since the nineteenth century and how Europe has been gradually able to distance itself from the problem to the extent that a common view emerged, casting refugees as a problem created by others, located elsewhere and in need of local solution. The paper then describes recent changes which have shattered such an illusion and it outlines how European governments have responded to their new perception of the problem. Finally, it considers whether this new perception that Europe is facing a refugee 'crisis' is grounded in fact.

The Development of Europe's Involvement with Refugees

The recent history of European involvement with refugees can be divided into six major phases which are summarized in Table 1. Each of the time-periods will be discussed in turn.

Exiles and gentlemen: the early and mid nineteenth century

The major features of the pre-1880 period were that refugees did exist within Europe but that they were small in number (but see Zolberg, 1983 on the period

*Migration Unit, University of Wales Swansea, Singleton Park, Swansea SA2 8PP.

prior to the nineteenth century). They were largely European political exiles or dissidents who had left their countries of origin voluntarily and had travelled as individuals or with their immediate families to a neighbouring country. Since many dissidents were from well-to-do families they tended not to be economic burdens upon their adopted countries and governments were therefore not overly concerned with regulating the flow of such people. Porter (1979) notes, that as a result, exiles were treated generously by European governments and how, for example, in mid Victorian Britain none were either blocked at a port of entry or expelled from the country. In contrast, for the more ordinary members of society, the opportunities for flight from persecution were stark. 'Given that the majority in these agricultural societies lived perilously close to subsistence . . . it was simply not possible for masses of them to survive for long as refugees' (Marrus, 1985, p. 8).

The Pogroms: 1880s to 1914

With the increasing frequency and intensity of Pogroms in the Pale of Settlement, Europe experienced its first major refugee episode of recent times. This differed in several important respects from what had gone before. It has been estimated that between the first pogrom of 1881 and the outbreak of the First World War, over 2.5 million Jews fled the Pale. Most arrived destitute and dishevelled and by virtue of their numbers and their different language; lifestyle; culture and religion; were highly visible. Marrus (1985) argues that, whilst they were undoubtedly persecuted, many also left the Pale for economic reasons, a view he supports by citing return migration rates of up to 20%. In addition, many Jews did not wish to remain in Europe but preferred to seek a new future in the U.S. Europe was therefore absolved of the need to address its own refugee problem, which was conveniently displaced onto a willing ally. For those who chose to remain, or were unable to travel further, their welfare was taken care of by Jewish charitable organizations rather than by the state, another first in European refugee affairs. Lastly, whilst the migration was sizeable, it elicited no great response from European governments. Whilst some, such as the U.K. introduced legislation to restrict entry from East Europe (the 1905 Aliens Act) this was only applied in a very desultory fashion and had little real impact upon the scale and timing of the movement. As Marrus (1985, p. 39) put it, 'so long as America received virtually everyone who came, Europeans seldom had to define refugees, worry about their responsibilities, and ponder who qualified for aid and who did not'.

Internationalizing Europe's problems: the First World War and its aftermath

The First World War and its aftermath brought about a profound change in the refugee problem which faced Europe and the solutions available to it. The westward flood of 1 million refugees fleeing civil war and communism in Russia, the forced eviction of 600,000 Jews from the Pale and hundreds of thousands more Jews from Austria, the retreat of 1 million ethnic Germans to the newly-defined post-war Germany and the parallel gathering of Hungarians within the new Hungary, all shifted the scale of the refugee problem, and widened its geographical extent. By 1926, for example, there were 9.5 million refugees in Europe. However, at the same time that demand for asylum was increasing, the onset of economic depression meant that many of the traditional destinations for European refugees became less receptive, with Canada introducing restrictions in 1923 and the Johnson Act of 1924 imposing quotas on entry to the U.S. As a result and in contrast to the earlier period, Europe was increasingly forced to find alternative solutions to its domestic refugee problem. These took three forms. Firstly those European countries which had suffered the greatest losses during the First World War were able to absorb large numbers of refugees in order to make good their populations and workforces. In the 1920s France thus became the second most important country of immigration after the U.S., with refugees being positively recruited in places such as Greece. Secondly, the European colonial powers turned their gaze to their imperial possessions as possible alternative resettlement destinations: the number of Jews in Palestine trebled between 1918 and 1929, for example. And thirdly, Europe attempted to mobilize international assistance and forge new supra-national refugee organizations to manage the refugee problem, rather than rely upon *laissez-faire*. In 1921 the League of Nations appointed a High Commissioner with special responsibility for Russian refugees. Fridjof Nansen established several principles which have been retained in modified form until today. He argued for a coordinated international response to national refugee crises, for voluntary repatriation as the preferred long-term solution to refugee episodes and for the principle of 'non-refoulement' (see Goodwin-Gill, 1986), by which refugees would not be repatriated to their countries of origin against their wishes. He also believed and popularized the view that the refugee problem in Europe was a temporary one, arising from simple causes and capable of being resolved permanently within the decade.

Despite the remarkable achievements of Nansen and the League of Nations High Commission he headed, the movement of Europe towards the Second World War meant that the refugee issue was not resolved as Nansen had predicted, but again became prominent during the 1930s. The Spanish Civil War created some 450,000 refugees; 400,000 Jews left Poland between 1921 and 1931; and 150,000 Jews left Germany between 1933 and 1938. Again, Europe looked abroad for salvation in the face of depression and increasing popular resistance at home: at an international conference in Geneva in 1933, for instance, the French, Dutch and Belgian government representatives all complained of the impact which refugees were having upon their labour markets. In 1929 the U.S. further tightened its immigration legislation; and France from 1936 onwards began to summarily reject refugees at its borders, expel them, refuse them residence permits and strip them of the French nationality they had only just been given. In response, those in charge of resettling refugees looked even more towards empire. As Marrus (1985, p. 88) put it 'the world map was scoured repeatedly for resettlement possibilities . . . (as) . . . government leaders and civil servants warmed to the image of young Jews tilling the soil of sunny, distant lands, improving their lives immeasurably in the process'. Madagascar was touted as an additional possible Jewish homeland, as were Kenya, Northern Rhodesia, Ethiopia, British Guiana, the Dominican Republic, Cyprus and Surinam. Unable to resolve its own refugee problems through domestic resettlement or resettlement in one of the great countries of immigration, Europe was seeking to displace them onto what we now term Less Developed Countries (LDC). In addition, the interventionist strategy was further developed, with such initiatives as the League of Nations Greek Refugee Settlement Commission (1923), the new Nansen Office of the League of Nations (1931), the High Commission for Refugees Coming from Germany (1933) and the additional High Commission for Refugees (1939).

Europe at the epicentre: the Second World War and its aftermath

The Second World War was another significant turning point in refugee matters, for the allies had to accommodate and resettle some 14 million refugees and 11 million displaced persons in Europe. Their response was to use military personnel for day-to-day resettlement work under the loose direction of the newly-founded U.N. Relief and Rehabilitation Agency and then to replace this in 1947 with the International Refugee Organization, and then in 1951, with the United Nations High Commission for Refugees (see Proudfoot, 1957). The latter body has remained the core agency for refugee matters to this day.

These organizations pursued very similar policies. They sought to negotiate exchanges of population stranded on the wrong side of new international borders, to repatriate other displacees as quickly as possible (even if this was against the wishes of those concerned, as it was with many of those returned to Russia), to recombine ethnic populations wherever possible (such as the 8 million Volksdeutsche returning to West Germany) and to negotiate the onward movement of refugees whose skills were in demand either in Europe; North America; Israel or Australia.

Arising from the situation in post-war Europe, the U.N. proposed a formal legal definition of a refugee in 1951. This has been used ever since, albeit with subsequent modification. The original 1951 definition applied only to those refugees generated within Europe. Non-Europeans were not officially added to the legal definition until the 1967 Bellagio Protocol, and some countries have yet to sign this.

Thus, in the period prior to the 1960s, in which institutions, responsibilities and definitions were being formulated and codified, Europe was at the heart of the global refugee problem and Europe was both the instigator and beneficiary. Definitions applied to European refugees only and agencies were formed specifically to rehabilitate and resettle those dislocated by wars and persecution in Europe. Intervention and management came increasingly to be seen as the norm and non-European countries were expected to assist as part of international burden-sharing initiatives. Both this and local initiatives were, however, greatly assisted by the need to make good wartime damage and to satisfy acute labour shortages in many countries. For most of the period, European nations thus enthusiastically recruited and resettled refugees as a means of satisfying their demand for pliable and non-unionized labour (e.g. Britain's European Volunteer Workers scheme, Tannahill, 1958). Such synergy of refugee and immigration policy was predicated on the fact that refugees were overwhelmingly white and European and often Christian and skilled.

Globalisation and the moral high ground: 1960s and 1970s

Whilst the earlier phases had seen Europe addressing what was thought to be a European problem, the fifth phase saw a marked shift in the locus of refugee production. Whilst Europe continued to generate and resettle refugees (witness the Hungarian and Czech exoduses of 1957 and 1968 respectively) the major characteristic of this period was the growth in refugee numbers in the Third World.

The period witnessed the collapse of European empires and the associated creation of new, militarized and often multi-ethnic, nation-states (see Zolberg, 1983). At the same time, population growth began to accelerate to its 1960s peak (of 2.05%) and when this was combined with the debt crisis in the Third World, dependence upon volatile world markets for sales of staple products and the shock waves of the first energy crisis of 1973, the wealth gap between First and Third Worlds increased markedly. So too, did the rate of land degradation and the decline in average agricultural landholdings in the LDCs (Harrison, 1993). This powerful mix contrived to create conditions conducive both to human rights violations and the wholesale marginalization of population group. And the playing out of superpower rivalries in LDCs certainly did not help. Refugee flows from Bangladesh, Ghana, the Congo, Burundi, Nigeria, Uganda; Vietnam, Laos and Cambodia were the consequence.

The changing nature of the refugee 'problem' prompted other changes. In 1969 the Organization of African Unity proposed an alternative and broader definition of a refugee, based more upon the experience of Third World countries than post-war Europe. Equally, as the plight of refugees in the 'South' became more widely known and more graphically portrayed by the media, a public consensus began to develop in advanced societies that there needed to be an international response to such episodes, orchestrated by the West. The Vietnam War marked a high-water mark, with Western countries not only agreeing to fund reception and resettlement in first countries of asylum, but also agreeing to extend the concept of burden sharing out from its European roots, so that for the first time Europe was participating in burden-sharing by accepting refugees rather than providing them. Countries such as the U.S., France, Canada, Australia, Germany and the U.K., agreed to accept 1.25 million South East Asian refugees for permanent resettlement (Gold, 1992), often through private sponsorship schemes motivated by public humanitarianism (see Lanphier, 1993; Indra, 1993). However, whilst Europe honoured burden-sharing, it did so on its own terms. Countries such as the U.K. accepted refugees, but they were in numerically limited quotas and within these, individual refugees were selected according to strict criteria.

Knocking on the door: the 1980s

What makes the sixth phase a distinct period is the shift from refugees being accepted in pre-planned quotas to them arriving spontaneously. Whereas in the 1970s the West had regulated all aspects of the flow by selecting refugees (often on the criteria of labour market skills and assimilability) and agreeing to resettle them in predetermined quotas at specific times, the situation in the 1980s was very different. The spread of cheap air travel (see Miles, 1993), the progress of the mass media in the Third World and the chain effect of previous labour migrations served to empower many refugees, who travelled to the West and claimed asylum immediately at the airport or port, or after a period as a visitor or student. In some countries the realization that Third World refugees could no longer be kept at arm's-length was such a profound shock that it brought about a complete rethink of refugee admission policy, e.g. in Australia (Robinson, 1993a).

The second distinctive feature was that whereas in another decade the arrival of spontaneous refugees might have been tolerated, this was not the case in the 1980s. As Scheinman (1983) put it 'the age of innocence is over'. The economic downturn resulting from the two oil shocks and the rise of the Pacific Rim economies had left most Western economies suffering from unprecedented structural as well as cyclical unemployment. Labour migration had been sharply curtailed through progressively more restrictive legislation (e.g. the 1973 Anwerbestopp in Germany or the 1962 and 1968 Commonwealth Immigration Acts in the U.K.) and the extreme right had begun to re-emerge in countries such as the U.K. and France. The arrival of migrants from overseas colonies or Southern Europe in the previous two decades had stoked racism, which was increasingly being expressed, not only through discrimination but also racial harassment and violence. More than ever, 'the granting or withholding of refugee status . . . (became) . . . an instrument of the receiving state's diplomacy toward the sending state' (Scheinman, 1983, p. 80).

In response to the compassion-fatigue and latent racism of electorates, European governments began to redefine the discourse. Refugees were increasingly described as economic migrants, and distinctions were drawn in the media between 'genuine' and 'bogus' refugees. Legislation moved towards the harmonization of many aspects of refugee and immigration policies and the media and governments began to play the 'numbers game'. Deterrence came to the fore (e.g. the change from open to closed camps in the Crown Colony of Hong Kong). On an international stage, the concept of burden-sharing was increasingly usurped by policies which would keep Third World refugees in the Third World and prevent them from seeking asylum in the West; local resettlement, safe havens and prevention through military intervention became much more popular. The U.N.H.C.R. even sanctioned and condoned compulsory repatriation from Hong Kong.

Squaring the circle: 1990s

No sooner had the policy of arm's-length containment been formulated than circumstances rendered it obsolete for Europe. The rapid and unexpected melting of the Cold War, and the global law and order deficit that followed, changed the perceived source of refugees yet again. East–West migration took on much greater salience and threatened to overwhelm certain countries (see Salt, 1991). Significant numbers of refugees are now seeking asylum from the explosive rebirth of ethnic nationalism in the East and the attendant process of ethnic sorting, personified by the Yugoslavian civil war but also evident in internal migration patterns within the Former Soviet Union (Zayonchkovskaya *et al.*, 1993) in the migration of Aussiedler (who incidentally enjoy a different legal status in Germany to asylum seekers) back to the reunited Germany (Hofman and Heller, 1992; Jones and Wild, 1992) and in the return of ethnic Hungarians from Romania (Poulton, 1992).

However, although these new asylum seekers were European, circumstances were no more positive for them than they had been for the previous wave of spontaneous refugees from the Third World. Western Europe had been plunged into a deep recession by the close of the 1980s and unemployment levels had risen further. The former guest worker groups throughout Europe had entered a period of family creation and reunion which translated into growing ethnic minority populations (Penninx, 1984). The extreme right was resurgent throughout most of Western Europe (Hainsworth, 1992), not only in the polls but also in direct street action such as the attacks upon refugee hostels in former East Germany. Ethnic nationalism and the migration of 'preferred ethnics', such as the Aussiedler, also intensified the ingroup–outgroup distinctions which had been implicit in previous periods.

The result of this coincidence of circumstances is that Europe is again faced with dislocated peoples of its own and with spontaneous refugees who have only to travel relatively short distances to cross international boundaries and enter the industrialized core of Europe. However, unlike the 1940s, there is neither the demand for their labour, nor is there the humanitarian desire to assist their resettlement or the geopolitical kudos to be gained from hosting those fleeing

Communist regimes. What has resulted, has been the redefinition of 'deserving' and 'undeserving' refugees and the application of many of the restrictions which had previously been devised to limit the access of Third World (black) asylum seekers to fellow Europeans. The policies of containment and exclusion have been extended to cover not only the Third World, but also parts of Europe and Western Europe's refugee myopia has become even more pronounced.

Reactions to the Perceived Threat

As the refugee problem has revisited Europe, after a period in which it was contained, held at arm's-length and typified as a problem experienced by others, so national governments and supra-national bodies in Europe have responded to what they perceive to be a rising threat of inundation by refugees from the Third World and from the East. An atmosphere bordering on hysteria has developed about immigration from the Third World. In March 1994 in the U.K., for example, the *Daily Mail* said that a senior immigration officer had 'warned that huge numbers of Asians, Turks and North Africans are gathering in Europe waiting for an opportunity to invade Britain'. Edouard Balladour, the new Prime Minister of France said he was "extraordinarily determined' to respect the anti-immigrant feeling expressed by the electorate in the March 1993 General Elections' (Runnymede Trust, 1993). In February 1993 the Austrian Freedom Party presented a petition signed by 417,000 people asking for a halt to immigration. Throughout 1991 and 1992 sections of the British media undertook a concerted campaign against asylum seekers, describing them as 'cheats', 'dole cheats', 'bogus refugees' and describing the migration as an 'invasion of Europe', or a 'refugee invasion' (see Runnymede Trust, 1992). When Germany revised its constitution, Wolfgang Schauble, the parliamentary leader of the Christian Democrats justified it by saying that 'Our citizens are frightened by the unchecked refugee influx. We owe them a social order that allows Germans and foreigners to live peacefully side by side' (quoted in the *Guardian* 27 May 1993); and 'in Denmark, the media debate centres both on refugees as 'freeloaders' on the welfare state . . . and as thieves and criminals. . . .' (Fekete, 1993). Views and representations such as these have stimulated a wide range of measures to combat this perceived threat.

Unilateral action

Until recently most of the developments on refugee admission within the E.C. were unilateral actions by individual governments, albeit in close contact with each other. These unilateral actions can be grouped as follows:

Prevention of access. This may take the form of giving border patrols greater powers to determine who should be allowed to make an asylum claim. Examples of this include Austria in 1990 and Switzerland, where over 100,000 applicants were turned away in 1992 alone. Alternatively, states may physically tighten border security. Spain has, for example, spent 520 million pesetas on C.C.T.V., barbed wire and monitoring equipment to strengthening the frontiers of its North African enclave, Melillà (Webber, 1991). Eventually these unilateral actions lead to bilateral or multilateral agreements on border security and access. King (1993), for instance, notes the web of agreements which now exist between Denmark; Finland; Iceland; Norway; Sweden; Germany; Austria; Switzerland; former Czechoslovakia; and Poland. Morocco has even been drawn into the defence of the outer perimeter. Three other methods of preventing access have also been widely used in Europe. First, most countries have now introduced progressively lengthier lists of states from which asylum seekers will not be accepted without visas. Second, Carriers Liability Acts mean that airlines are fined if they carry passengers without visas (see Feller, 1989). The British government, for instance, had imposed fines of £74.87 million between 1987 and the end of 1994. Third, states have sought to introduce the concept of 'safe countries' whether these be 'safe countries of return' or 'safe countries of transit' (see E.C.R.E., 1993). The new Article 16a of the German Constitution, for example, states that 'travellers coming from a Member State of the European Communities or from a third State which implements the Convention relating to the Status of Refugees and the Convention for the Protection of Human Rights and Fundamental Freedoms may not claim asylum on account of political persecution.' Article 18 of the Law on Asylum Procedure mandates border guards to refuse entry to any potential applicant from such a 'safe' country. In parallel to these developments, steps have also been taken in some countries to retreat towards a narrower definition of a refugee. Nobel (1990) notes how Sweden has traditionally accepted *de facto* refugees such as war deserters but how, between 1989 and 1991, this broader definition was suspended.

Discouragement of asylum seekers. Many countries have engaged in active deterrence even of those applicants who have managed to gain entry to a country. Britain (see Cohen, 1989), Sweden and Denmark have housed asylum seekers on old ferryboats, whilst both Switzerland and Sweden have used tent encampments to accommodate those awaiting the outcome of the decision making process. Some countries have chosen instead to limit the rights and welfare benefits of those awaiting a decision. France no longer allows applicants to work during the determination procedure, Switzerland prohibits employment for the first three months after an application has been made and Sweden has reduced the daily welfare allowance by 5–10%. In November 1993 Germany passed new legislation on social benefits which had the effect of reducing the monthly allowance of adult asylum seekers by 82%. In some cases, countries are also making preliminary decisions about the likely outcome of an application and according different treatment to those considered unlikely to be granted asylum: the January 1992 amendments to the Aliens Act in the Netherlands thus allows the state to detain those with 'manifestly unfounded' claims in a secure unit. Finally, several countries have introduced legislation making it more difficult for refugees to later bring their relatives over to join them.

The decision making procedure. Under pressure from the growing backlog of applications (up from 159,000 in 1985 to 900,000 in 1991 according to Salt, 1991), all European countries have reviewed their refugee determination procedures, with a view to speeding them up. In December 1993, the upper house of the Dutch parliament approved a new aliens bill which will reduce the length of the refugee determination procedure from 15 months to 4. Strict time limits and fast-track procedures were also introduced in the U.K. under the Asylum and Immigration Appeals Act, 1993. Most have also reviewed their procedures so as to distinguish between 'economic migrants' and 'refugees' and others have sought to put in place accelerated procedures for applications which are deemed, at the outset, to be manifestly unfounded (e.g. Denmark). Recognition rates have thus fallen across Europe from 65% in 1980 to 10% in 1990 (Webber, 1993). Instead a growing proportion are being granted conditional refugee status such as 'Exceptional Leave to Remain' in the U.K.; 'Asilo' in Spain; 'Assimile a Refugie' in Belgium; and 'B' and 'C' status in Scandinavia. Such status usually limits and disadvantages the individual, yet in 1993 47% of all decisions in the U.K. were to grant Exceptional Leave to Remain (Home Office, 1995). A growing share of applicants are now also experiencing an initial outright rejection of their asylum claims. In the U.K., this proportion has climbed from 18% in 1989 through 53% in 1992 to 79% in 1994 (Home Office, 1995).

Return of unsuccessful applicants. As was noted above, in the 1980s many European countries did not take action against those who had failed to acquire Convention status and deport them. In the 1990s this position has changed somewhat. A number of European countries have reneged on their 1951 commitment to non-refoulement. Italy returned 24,000 Albanians in 1991, France has deported recognized Convention Refugees (Joly and Nettleton, 1990) and in 1992 Belgium even chartered aircraft to deport people in bulk. In May 1993 Germany entered into an agreement with Poland whereby the former would pay the latter $76.4 million compensation during 1994 if the latter would take back rejected asylum seekers.

Multilateral action

Although some argue that European refugee policy is dominated by unilateral rather than multilateral developments, there are examples of countries coming together to take joint action.

The end of the exilic bias. The prime multilateral action has been the ideological retreat from an exilic bias. During periods when refugees from the east were few in numbers and symbolic in nature, permanent resettlement in a western country was the preferred outcome. Increasingly, in the 1990s, Europe is switching its emphasis towards direct humanitarian and peacekeeping intervention in the source area in order to anchor potential refugees and forestall flight. The safe-havens in northern Iraq and Yugoslavia are clear examples of this tendency, as is the French government's current view that resettling former Yugoslavians overseas is to aid and abet ethnic cleansing.

The Dublin Convention. Other multilateral actions taken by the E.C. countries have been more formal. One of the first priorities was seen as putting in place a regime in which asylum seekers could make only one application for asylum within the E.C. and in which it would be clear which country was responsible for processing this. The Dublin Convention of 1990 achieved this. It eradicated the phenomenon of the 'refugee in orbit'. Instead, asylum seekers can now only make an application to that country which allowed entry or issued a visa, although another country can opt to process the application if it involves family reunion or extenuating circumstances.

The Schengen group. Certain states have come together to harmonize some aspects of policy. In June 1985 Belgium; Luxembourg; the Netherlands; Germany; and France signed the Schengen Agreement which was later ratified after negotiation in 1990. Italy joined the group in 1990, Spain and Portugal in 1991 and Greece in 1992. Many see the group and the treaties as a potential model for the remainder of Europe (Loescher, 1989). The Treaties aim to open internal borders for goods, services and people whilst at the same time introducing shared immigration and asylum policies. Visa policy would be harmonized (a common list of 129 countries requiring visas now exists) (Webber, 1993), Police controls at external borders tightened and a new Schengen Information System would collect and collate immigration and asylum data to allow the common exclusion of individuals. Even those third state aliens with visas would have a very limited duration of stay and might have to prove they possessed a return ticket and means of financial support. Finally, refugees would either have to submit their asylum applications at an external border of Schengen territory or within it. Given the Dublin Convention and Carriers Liability Acts, neither of these possibilities seems viable. What concerns some commentators most about Schengen, however, is the lack of accountability of the group (see Rudge, 1990).

Is the Panic Justified?

The raft of measures outlined above would suggest that Western Europe is in the grip of an unprecedented refugee crisis, requiring immediate and undemocratic responses. However, even the brief historical account presented earlier in this paper suggests that this is not the case and that Western Europe is facing a refugee problem which is smaller in scale and significance than those existing immediately prior to and after the Second World War. Is Western Europe really at the epicentre of a global refugee crisis as politicians and the media would have us believe?

The source of the world's refugees

Figure 1 maps the main sources of those 15.5 million refugees in need of protection on 1 January 1994, as defined by the United States Committee for Refugees (1994). Their definition of refugees is in some respects broader than the 1951 Convention definition but in others narrower. They define refugees as those 'who require international protection and/or assistance . . . (and are) . . . unable or unwilling to repatriate due to fear of persecution and violence in their homelands'. However they specifically exclude 'refugees permanently resettled in other countries'. Figure 1 demonstrates that the Yugoslavian crisis (and therefore Europe) had generated only 8.5% of all refugees in existence at that time. This is a far cry from the proportion of refugees generated by other parts of the world. Africa, for example, created some 37.6% of the global total, Afghanistan 22%, and the Middle East 19%. Whilst Europe undoubtedly has a significant part to play in the contemporary world refugee crisis it is by no means central to the crisis as a source of refugees. This point is underscored by the fact the U.S.C.R. did not even list Europe as a significant source of refugees until the close of the 1980s.

Europe as a destination

If, despite the current crises in Yugoslavia and the Former Soviet Union, Europe still only generates less than one in 10 of the world's refugees, does it have a more significant role to play as a destination for asylum seekers from elsewhere? Figure 2 collates

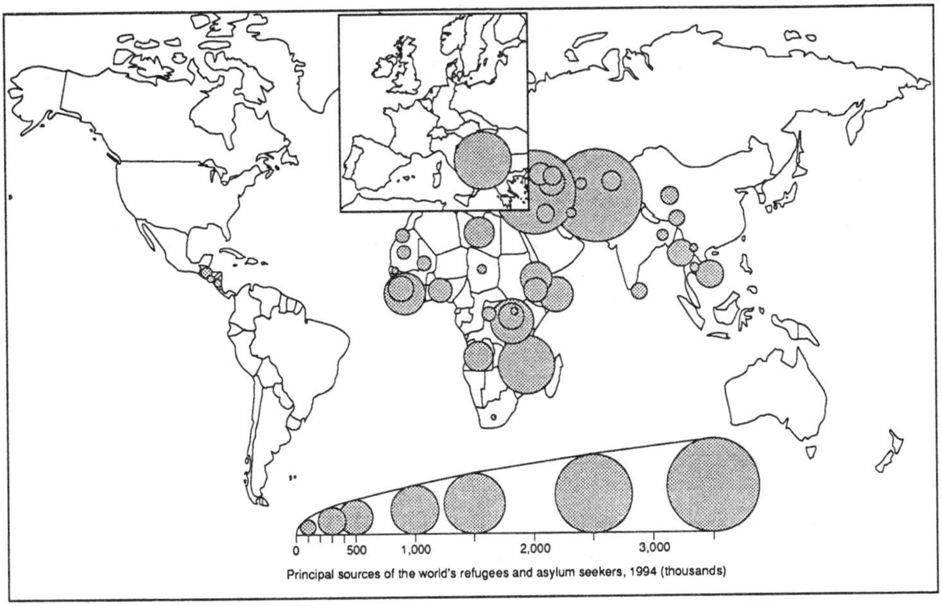

Figure 1. Principal sources of the world's refugees and asylum seekers, 1994.

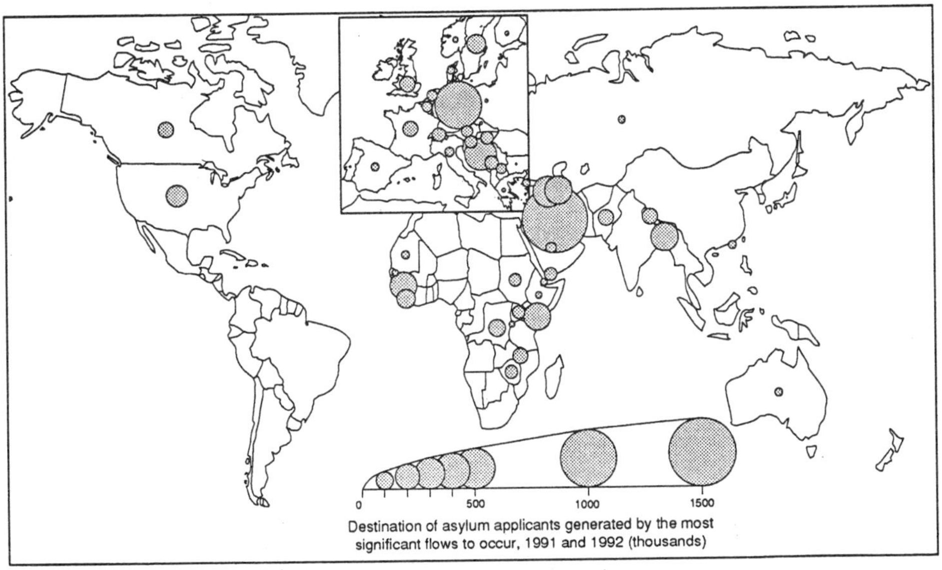

Figure 2. Destination of asylum seekers generated by the most significant flows to occur, 1991 and 1992.

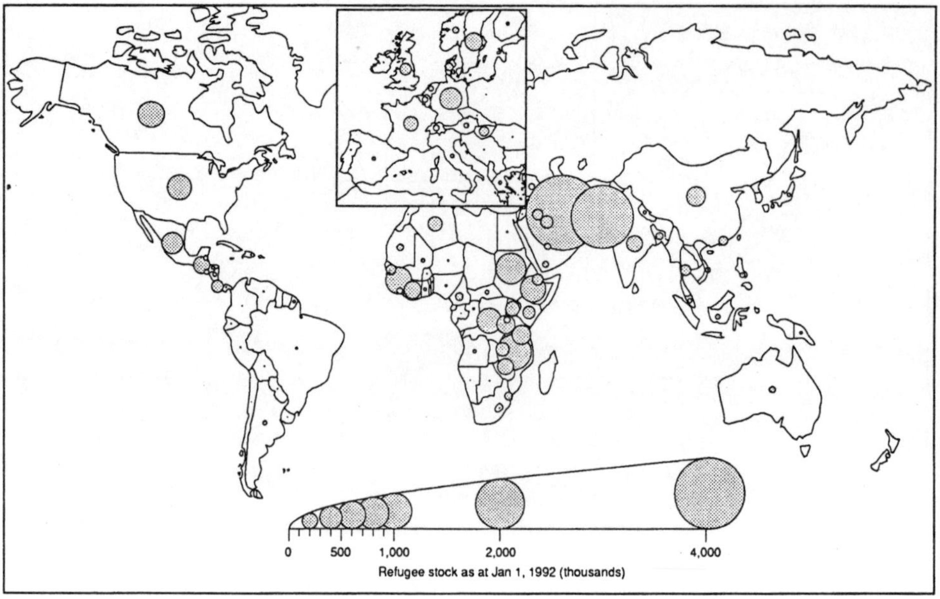

Figure 3. Refugee stock by country, 1992.

1993 U.N.H.C.R. data and charts the destination of asylum seekers created by the most significant refugee flows to occur in 1991 and 1992. It reveals that countries within Europe — especially West Germany (with 694,000 applicants) — *have* been important as destinations over this period, particularly when compared with other industrialized nations such as Canada (68,000), the United States (160,000), Australia (20,000) or Japan (500). Nevertheless a number of less affluent countries have fared much worse in relative terms, with Iran receiving 1.4 million refugees, and Guinea, Kenya and Bangladesh accepting nearly a quarter of a million refugees each.

The early years of this decade have been exceptional for Europe and it is therefore perhaps more useful to look at the cumulative total of refugees accepted for settlement in each country. Figure 3, which is based upon U.N.H.C.R. collation of individual government estimates (often including those in refugee-like circumstances) for the period up to 1 January 1992, indicates how, within Europe, Germany again stands out as having granted a relatively large cumulative total of people the right to permanent settlement (383,900). Most other Western European nations have totals of well under 50,000 with the exceptions of France (170,000), Sweden (238,400) and the U.K. (100,000). All of these figures are, however, dwarfed by those of a range of African and Asian countries such as Ethiopia (527,000); Guinea (548,000); the Sudan (729,200); Malawi (981,000); Iran (4.4 million); and Pakistan (3.1 million), let alone the United States (482,000) and Canada (538,100)

It is also important to set these totals into their domestic contexts. Table 2 compares the number of resettled refugees in 12 European countries with the size of their foreigner population. With the exception of the three Nordic countries, typically less than 5% of each country's foreign population are refugees. Furthermore, these figures need to be set against the forecasts (see Van der Knaap and Ode, 1992) that in the medium term, Western Europe faces falling fertility rates and therefore ageing and declining populations.

The data above suggest that whilst Europe is playing an increasing role as a generator of refugees and a significant role as a destination for asylum seekers, its plight is not unique or even exceptional. Indeed

Table 1. The main stages of Europe's involvement with refugees since the mid 19th century

Phase	Dates	Source and destination of refugees		Numbers	Migrant selectivity	Spontaneous or quota	Characteristics of refugees	Individual or group migration	Cause of flight	Perceived duration	Degree of control	Organizational structure	Government response
1.	19th century	Europe	Europe	small	self	S	European, exiles, well-to-do	I	political	continuous	nil	nil	nil
2.	1880s on	Europe	outside Europe	average of 71k pa	self	S	Europeans, Jews, impoverished	G	ethnic economic	finite	limited	community based NGOs	legislation
3.	1914 on	Europe	outside Europe Europe	average of 380 k pa	no	S	Europeans Jew/Russian cross-section	G	genocide political	finite	numerical	*ad hoc* Eurocentric International	intervention restriction
4.	1945–1950s	Europe	outside Europe Europe	average of 2.5 m pa	no	S	Europeans Jews/Germans impoverished	I/G	aftermath of war	finite	limited	Eurocentric International	active recruitment
5.	1960s and 1970s	LDCs East Europe	Europe by invitation	13 k pa in early 1970s	yes	Q	non-European impoverished	G	decolonization ethnic political	finite	numerical/ selection	*ad hoc* governmental brokered by UN	intervention
6.(a)	1980s on	LDCs	Europe	70 k in 1983	self/no	S	non-European impoverished	I	political war famine ethnic economic	infinite	numerical/ selection	Pan European/ NGOs	exclusion
6.(b)	1990s	Europe	Europe outside Europe	600 k in 1993	self	S/Q	Europeans impoverished skilled	I	political war ethnic	infinite	numerical/ selection	Pan European/ NGOs	panic exclusion

Table 2. Comparison of the number of refugees in 15 European countries with the size of their foreign populations, in thousands

	A Foreign Pop. 1989	B Refugee Pop. 1991	B as % of A
Austria	322.6	18.7	5.8
Belgium	880.8	24.1	2.7
Denmark	136.2*	44.0	32.3
France	3752.2*	170.0	4.5
Germany	4845.9	383.9	7.9
Greece	155.2*	9.0	5.8
Italy	407.0*	12.2	3.0
Luxembourg	104.0	0.7	0.7
Netherlands	641.9	21.3	3.3
Norway	140.3	29.1	20.7
Portugal	79.6†	1.0	1.2
Spain	334.9‡	9.2	2.7
Sweden	456.0	238.4	52.2
Switzerland	1040.3	27.6	2.7
U.K.	1948.0	100.0	5.1

Source: Refugee figures from U.N.H.C.R. (1993). Foreign totals for Italy, Denmark, Greece, Spain and Portugal from Van der Knaap and Ode (1992). Foreign totals for other countries from Salt (1991).
Notes: *1988 figure. †1985 figure. ‡1987 figure.

relative to its wealth and population size, Europe has until recently managed to avoid a proportionate share of the human fall-out from the world refugee crisis, although its financial contribution is much more impressive (Robinson, 1995).

The source of Western Europe's asylum seekers

If Western Europe is playing a growing part in the world refugee system, it remains to see whether this contribution is outward looking (and philanthropic) or myopic and self-serving.

As the Yugoslavian crisis has made plain, refugee episodes develop rapidly, and, as a result, there is great temporal volatility in the source of refugees seeking asylum in resettlement countries. This has been particularly true of Western Europe which has received several 'waves' and many 'vintages' (Kunz, 1973) of refugees over the last two decades. Figure 4 shows the main sources of refugees applying for asylum in 10 leading European (E.C. and E.F.T.A.) countries over the period 1988–1992. Even this short time-period demonstrates how at any one point in time Europe is experiencing the final vintages of previous waves as well as the first vintages of newly breaking waves. In Europe's case we can identify waves from a variety of directions. Taken together, these have produced a five year pattern (1988–1992 inclusive) in which between 40–50% of applicants are from Europe; 10% are from Africa; very few are from Latin America or South East Asia; and a declining proportion are from the Middle East (ca 10% in 1988–1990 falling to 2% in 1992). Comparison of these percentages with Figure 1 demonstrates that Europe is addressing its own problems at the expense of the larger problems which exist elsewhere in the world and that there is a clear geographical bias to Europe's contribution.

However, whilst Europe is undoubtedly looking after its own, it would be wrong to suggest that Western Europe, or the E.U. is yet following a common line on refugee acceptance and resettlement. Figure 5, for example, demonstrates that whilst there is a certain shared perspective that exiles from former Communist regimes are 'deserving', there is little European agreement on what is an appropriate response. Hence, whilst all 10 countries in Figure 5 have received significant numbers of applications for asylum from former Yugoslavians, Figure 6 indicates that forced migrants created by the disintegration of Yugoslavia have been very unevenly distributed within Western Europe. Within the old international boundaries of Yugoslavia 1.183 million former inhabitants have been displaced; and a further 556,000 have become refugees by virtue of crossing an international border. As Figure 6 shows, there is a clear geographical dimension to the pattern of flight underpinned by distance decay. However, other factors are also at work. Switzerland's response has been shaped by the existence of a sizeable number of Yugoslavian labour migrants within that country. The same could also be said for Austria and Germany. The latter has also been pivotal to the overall pattern for additional reasons: prior to the May 1993 amendments, Article 16 of the constitution guaranteed access to the asylum system for all; Article 19 guaranteed a legal right of appeal; the decision making procedure could often take years and few of those who failed to win asylum were ever deported (8% in 1989 according to Kemper, 1992); and 'Germany provides the most generous public support for asylum seekers in all of Europe' (U.S.C.R., 1993, p. 122) comprising housing; clothing; food; schooling; medical care; and a

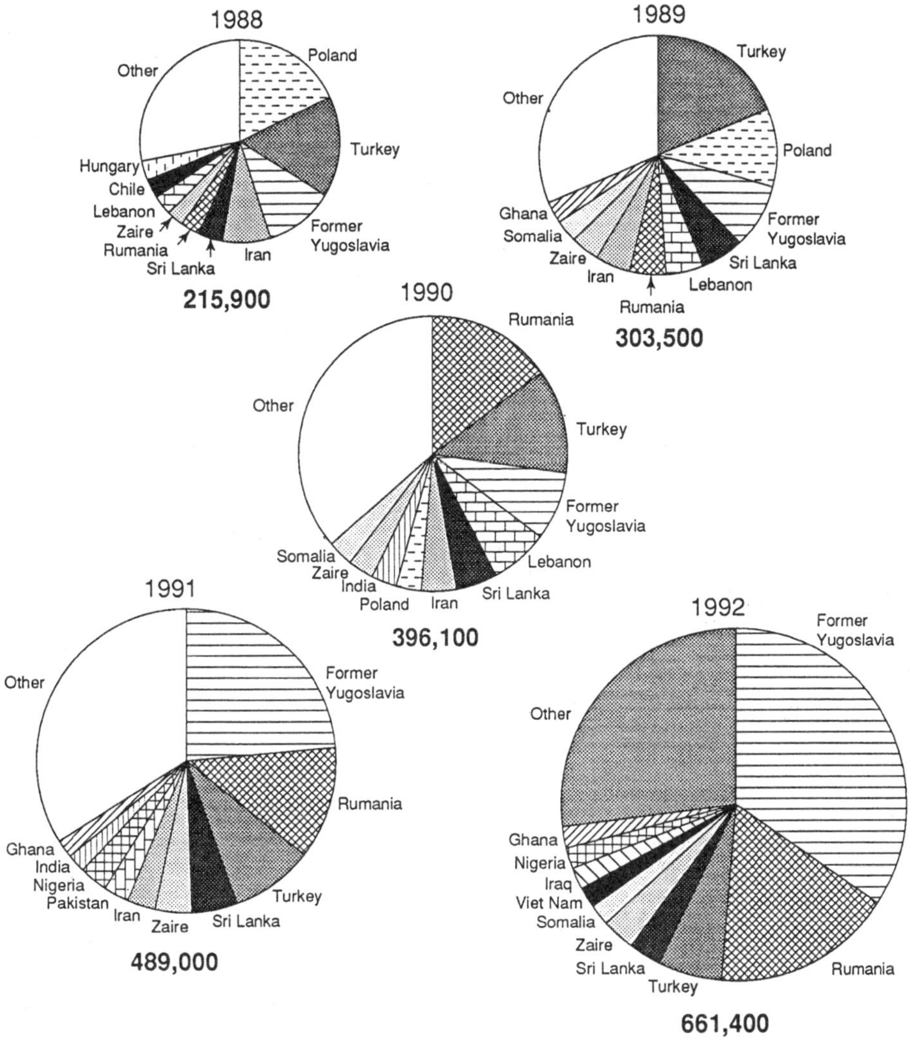

Figure 4. Source and number of refugees making asylum applications in 10 European countries, 1988–1992.

social allowance which averages $325 per adult per month. Not surprisingly, therefore, Germany proved highly attractive not only to asylum seekers fleeing directly from Yugoslavia but also to those who had already escaped to a third country. In 1991, over 10% of asylum seekers in Germany had arrived in that country from another European state. Figure 6 indicates that there are also countries which might be expected to have resettled significant numbers of Yugoslavians because of their geographical proximity, but which have failed to do so. Italy is a case in point. As a country with a tradition of emigration rather than immigration, Italy had never ratified the Bellagio Protocol and had therefore historically

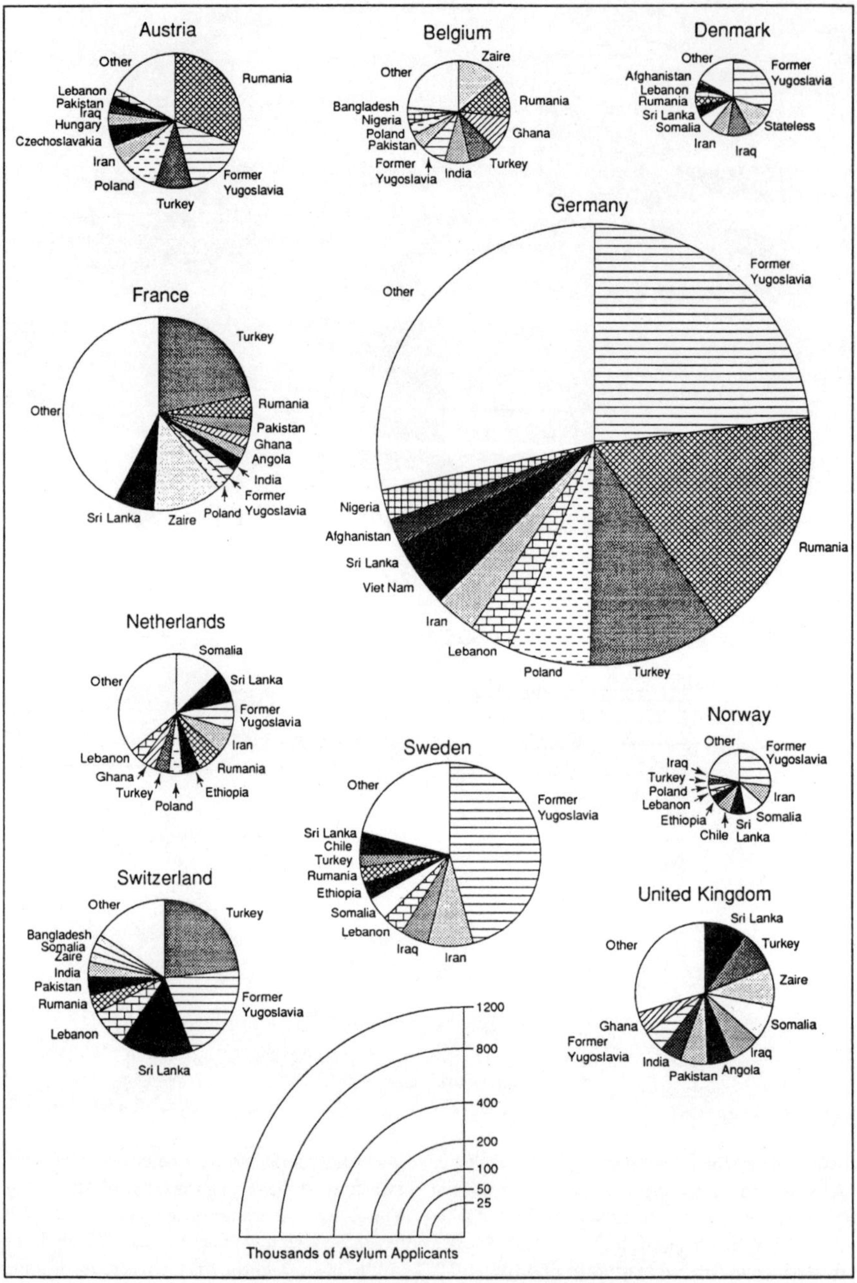

Figure 5. Source and number of refugees making asylum applications to 10 European countries, 1988–1992 disaggregated by individual country.

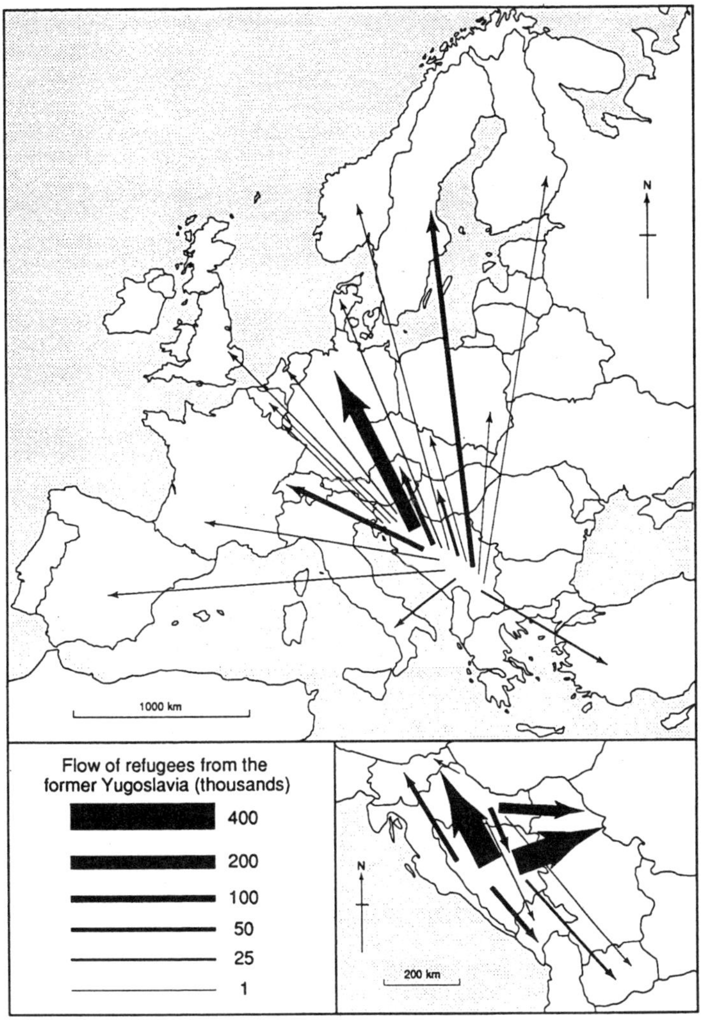

Figure 6. The human fall-out from the Yugoslavian crisis: outward flows and destinations.

accepted only small numbers of European refugees for settlement. However, during the 1970s the migration balance shifted markedly and for the first time, Italy became a destination for immigration, from Africa; the Middle East; and South East Asia. One commentator has described how the shock of this turnaround and the competition immigrants provided in the informal economy together led immigration to be seen as a 'social emergency' (Campani, 1993) and one which was perceived as a threat to Italy's relations with its northern European partners. In combination with the rapid growth of racist sentiments and violence at the end of the 1980s (see Martiniello, 1991) and the increase in political influence of the Leagues, these factors encouraged Italy to take an unusually hard line on refugees. The Martelli Law of 1990 consequently introduced a highly restrictive admissions policy, police patrols at borders were intensified, Albanian asylum seekers were expelled in August 1991 and Italy has committed itself to a policy of zero immigration. Finally there are those countries which are not intrinsically attractive to refugees but which have become major destinations because of their strategic geographical locations as 'waiting rooms' for access to the west. Hungary would be the best example (King, 1993).

Thus, whilst Europe as a whole has been concerned with looking after its own, there are significant variations in the specific nationalities which seek and are granted asylum in different European countries, with variations being driven by domestic and foreign policy considerations and historical linkages.

Conclusion

This paper has considered the view which is prevalent in Western Europe that the continent is presently experiencing an unprecedented refugee 'crisis' which requires (and mandates) governments and groups of governments to take radical and in some cases unconstitutional, measures in order to resolve it. The paper has described the sense of hysteria which has developed within Western Europe over the issue and has outlined some of the many measures which have been put in place in the last 5–7 years to stem the perceived 'flood' of spontaneous refugees. Two alternative perspectives have also been presented, both of which suggest rather different interpretations of current circumstances.

Firstly, basic statistical information has been presented which demonstrates that whilst Western Europe does play a part in the global refugee system, its position is by no means as central as current European hysteria would suggest.

Secondly, an historical review of European involvement in the global refugee problem since the nineteenth century suggests that the current position facing Western Europe is not exceptional in scale or intensity. Rather, it may appear so, because in the past Europe could — and invariably did — call on assistance from allies, empires and countries starved of labour. In so doing, it managed to isolate itself from many of the consequences (and potential consequences) of the refugee problem, a policy continued in the recent past through restricted refugee quotas and the creation of 'safe' havens in source countries. The current hysteria over refugee matters in Europe could thus be said to arise more from collective amnesia and the realization that Europe now has to find its own solutions to its refugee problems, than upon the intrinsic distinctiveness of present circumstances. In addition, the historical review demonstrates that whilst, in 1995, Europe may *regard* itself as being at the heart of the global refugee crisis, in the past that actually was the case. The main legal definition of a refugee was framed in Europe to accommodate European people and European circumstances. The first international efforts and organizations designed to assist refugees were created to solve European problems and often headed by European diplomats. Numerically, Europe's refugees formed the majority of the world's refugees.

Finally, despite the critical nature of this review of Europe's reaction to the global refugee problem, it has to be said that Europe's response has not been unique. Japan, as a comparator, merits particular attention (see Sellek, 1994 for a discussion of Japan's changing attitudes to immigration and pluralism). According to the U.S.C.R. (1994) Japan granted refugee status to only six people in 1993 and was considering the applications of only a further 47 persons, despite having a G.N.P. which lies in the world's top ten. Why each country, or even culture, responds in such different ways to the same global problem can, however, only ultimately be understood by detailed comparative study, case by case (see e.g. Robinson, 1993a, b).

References

Campani, G. (1993) Immigration and racism in Southern Europe: the Italian case, *Ethnic and Racial Studies*, **16**, 507–55.

Cohen, R. (1989) The detention of asylum-seekers in the U.K., In: *Reluctant Hosts: Europe and its Refugees*, D. Joly and R. Cohen (Eds). Avebury, Aldershot.

E.C.R.E. (1993) *Asylum in Europe*. European Consultation on Refugees and Exiles, London.

Fekete, L. (1993) Inside racist Europe, In: *Statewatching the New Europe*, T. Bunyan (Ed.). Statewatch, London.

Feller, E. (1989) Carrier sanctions and international law, *International Journal of Refugee Law*, **1**, 48–66.

Geoforum/Volume 26 Number 4/1995 427

Gold, S. (1992) *Refugee Communities*. Sage, London.

Goodwin-Gill, G. (1986) Non-refoulement and the new asylum seekers, *Virginia Journal of International Law*, **26**, 897–915.

Hainsworth, P. (1992) *The Extreme Right in Europe and the USA*. Pinter, London.

Harrison, P. (1993) *The Third Revolution*. Penguin, Harmondsworth.

Hofman, H. J. and Heller, W. (1992) Social and economic dimensions of the migration of Aussiedler into the former West Germany, Migration Unit Research Paper No. 2, Department of Geography, University College, Swansea.

Home Office (1995) *Statistical Bulletin on Asylum Statistics, 1994*. Government Statistical Service, London.

Indra, D. (1993) The spirit of the gift and the politics of resettlement, In: *The International Refugee Crisis: British and Canadian Responses*, V. Robinson (Ed.). Macmillan, Basingstoke.

Joly, D. and Nettleton, C. (1990) *Refugees in Europe*. Minority Rights Group, London.

Jones, P. N. and Wild, M. T. (1992) Western Germany's third wave of migrants, *Geoforum*, **23**, 1–11.

Kemper, F. (1992) New trends in international migration in Germany, unpublished paper presented at the International Geographical Union Population Congress, Los Angeles.

King, M. (1993) The impact of Western European border policies on the control of refugees in Eastern and Central Europe, *New Community*, **19**, 183–199.

Kunz, E. (1973) The refugee in flight: kinetic models and forms of displacement, *International Migration Review*, **7**, 125–146.

Lanphier, M. (1993) Host groups: public meets private, In: *The International Refugee Crisis: British and Canadian Responses*, V. Robinson (Ed.). Macmillan, Basingstoke.

Loescher, G. (1989) The European Community and refugees, *International Affairs*, **65**, 617–636.

Martiniello, M. (1991) Italy: racism in paradise? *Race and Class*, **32**, 79–84.

Marrus, M. R. (1985) *The Unwanted. European Refugees in the Twentieth Century*. Oxford University Press, Oxford.

Miles, R. (1993) Europe 1993: the significance of changing patterns of migration, *Ethnic and Racial Studies*, **16**, 459–466.

Nobel, P. (1990) What happened with Sweden's refugee policy? *International Journal of Refugee Law*, **2**, 265–273.

Penninx, R. (1984) Immigrant populations and demographic development in the member states of the council of Europe, Council of Europe Population Studies Paper No. 12, Strasbourg.

Porter, M. (1979) *The Refugee Issue in Mid-Victorian Politics*. Cambridge University Press, Cambridge.

Poulton, H. (1992) *The Balkans: Minorities and States in Conflict*. Minority Rights Group, London.

Proudfoot, M. (1957) *European Refugees: 1939–52*. Faber and Faber, London.

Robinson, V. (1993a) North and south: resettling Vietnamese refugees in Australia and the U.K., In: *Geography and Refugees*, R. Black and V. Robinson (Eds). Belhaven, London.

Robinson, V. (1993b) *The International Refugee Crisis: British and Canadian Responses*. Macmillan, Basingstoke.

Robinson, V. (1995) Redefining the front line: the geography of asylum seeking in the New Europe, In: *Migration in the European Community*, P. Rees, J. Stillwell, A. Convey and M. Kupiszewski (Eds). Pinter, London.

Runnymede Trust (1992) *Runnymede Bulletin*, 260, November.

Runnymede Trust (1993) *Runnymede Bulletin*, 269, October.

Rudge, P. (1990) Europe in the 1990s: the Berlin Walls of the mind, In: *World Refugee Survey, 1989*, United States Committee for Refugees (Eds). United States Committee for Refugees, New York.

Salt, J. (1991) *Current and Future International Migration Trends Affecting Europe*. Council of Europe, Strasbourg.

Scheinman, R. (1983) Refugees: goodbye to the good old days, annals, *Annals of the American Academy of Political and Social Science*, **467**, 78–88.

Sellek, Y. (1994) Illegal foreign workers in Japan: change and challenge in Japanese society, In: *Migration: the Asian Experience*, J. M. Brown and R. Foot (Eds). Macmillan, Basingstoke.

Tannahill, J. A. (1958) *European Volunteer Workers in Britain*. Manchester University Press, Manchester.

U.N.H.C.R. (1994) *The State of the World's Refugees*. Penguin, Harmondsworth.

U.S.C.R. (1994) *World Refugee Survey, 1994*. United States Committee for Refugees, New York.

Van der Knaap, G. and Ode, A. (1992) Population dynamics and interregional flows in Western Europe, unpublished paper presented at the Institute of British Geographers' Conference, Swansea

Webber, F. (1991) From ethno-centrism to Euro-racism, *Ethnic and Racial Studies*, **32**, 11–17.

Webber, F. (1993) The new Europe: immigration and asylum, In: *Statewatching the New Europe*, T. Bunyan (Ed.). Statewatch, London.

Zayonchkovskaya, Z., Kocharyan, A. and Vitkovskaya, G. (1993) Forced migration and ethnic processes in the former Soviet Union, In: *Geography and Refugees*, R. Black and V. Robinson (Eds). Belhaven, London.

Zolberg, A. (1983) The formation of new states as a refugee-generating process, *Annals of the American Academy of Political and Social Science*, **467**, 24–38.

[10]

Problems and Policies Regarding the Socio-economic Integration of Returnees and Foreign Workers in Greece[1]

Nicholas P. Glytsos*

INTRODUCTION

The integration of repatriating Greek migrants, ethnic Greeks and foreign workers has individual and macroeconomic aspects, both of which must be addressed within a dynamic perspective. The former concerns accommodation in general of the incoming population; the latter is related to the productive combination of their well-being and contribution to the country's economic development. While policies of integration necessarily involve both a costly short-term phase, as well as a long-term phase when the adjustment of newcomers is complete, the initial costs of accommodation and adjustment are recovered and their contribution to economic growth can be substantial. This article analyses the problems involved, and the policies and programmes adopted (or the lack of policies), for the integration of incoming workers to the Greek economy. Wherever possible, the suitability and effectiveness of measures taken are evaluated against the experience gained.

GREEK EMIGRANTS RETURNING HOME

Data collected by the National Statistical Service of Greece show that about 1 million Greeks, i.e., 12 per cent of the population, emigrated during the period 1960-1973, of which 300,000 went to Australia, the United States and Canada and 600,000 to West Germany. Then, between 1968 and 1977, 240,000 former emigrants (of which 185,000 were of working age – 15-64 years) returned home. About 50,000 came from the above three overseas countries and 140,000 from West Germany. Of the returnees, 15,000 settled in Eastern Macedonia and 14,000 in Thrace.

*Centre of Planning and Economic Research, Athens, Greece.

Return actually increased after West Germany imposed restricting entry policies in 1973, and democracy was restored in Greece, ending the regime of dictatorships between 1967 and 1973.

A micro census survey conducted in 1985/86 for the project, Emigration - Repatriation of Greek Population, shows that between 1971 and 1986 about 628,000 Greeks returned home, 61 per cent having come from Western Europe (44 per cent from West Germany). Not all these persons were "former emigrants", about one-third had been born abroad, most of them to Greek parents. About 42 per cent of returnees had been abroad for more than 10 years (Petropoulos, 1990: 90; GSGA, 1992) and slightly more than half the returnees were males, of whom 52 per cent were in the productive age group 15-44 years; the corresponding figure for females was 60 per cent. The proportion aged over 65 (4.5 per cent) was about the same for males and females (Table 1, page 173).

Because the overwhelming majority of returnees were economically active, they placed some pressure on the job market. Their unemployment rate was 10.4 per cent (8.7 per cent for males and 13.9 per cent for females) compared with 6.9 per cent for non-migrants. Sixty per cent of the unemployed were in the 30-64 age bracket compared with 34 per cent for non-migrants (Petropoulos, 1990: 96). A survey among six nationalities of migrants in West Germany in 1985 showed that 36 per cent of their savings had been used to purchase houses, apartments, building sites or household equipment, compared with only 7.3 per cent to purchase machinery, including agricultural machinery, or small businesses (Kondis, 1990: 221).

In the late 1950s and 1960s, the Greek Government reacted to high rates of unemployment in the rapidly increasing non-agricultural labour force by encouraging emigration. Between 1950 and 1979 bilateral agreements were signed with France, Belgium, West Germany, The Netherlands, Switzerland, Sweden, Australia, Libya and Cyprus. One aim of these agreements was to prepare prospective Greek emigrants with vocational training and language instruction; another was to ensure that they had social security protection in the host countries (Moussourou, 1991: 179-180).

Then in the mid-1970s, when West Germany stopped receiving foreign workers, and Greece was experiencing a rapidly decelerating rate of national population growth, the Greek Government reversed its policy and tried to induce the repatriation of migrants and their accumulated savings with new policies of investment incentives, subsidization for resettlement, schools for returning children and bilateral agreements on various issues. A package of measures designed to facilitate the housing of returnees included provision of mortgages and tax allowances if houses were purchased with foreign exchange. Also, the establishment and support of cooperatives in regions of high emigration were given priority for attracting migrants and their savings (Moussourou, 1991: 193-194), but during the period 1975-1980 only 5 production co-operatives in various industrial activities were created, summing 311 returnees. Both for the investment of remittances and for the employment of returnees, these measures were at the time judged inadequate. As a result, in 1982 the incentives were strengthened to include higher subsidization and more tax and depreciation allowances (Moussourou, 1991: 194). Other policies were directed to bilateral agreements for the transfer of social insurance rights and the granting of unemployment benefits. Those relating to training and legislation to establish companies for investing migrant savings were not deemed to be successful (Fakiolas, 1994: 587).

Although no special service was available for attracting investment by migrants, interested investors had access to government services that offered assistance to prospective investors whether migrant or non-migrant. The Office for the Promotion of Investment, established in 1987 in the Ministry of the National Economy, identified investment opportunities by industry and locality and explained available incentives as well as changes in investment policies. Services were also provided by the European Centre of Information and industry-specific centres of information. These centres advise small and medium-size enterprises on community projects, and assist in the establishment of enterprises, organizing market research, undertaking quality control, planning for new products, guidance on marketing and cost accounting for new entrepreneurs. The Agricultural Bank of Greece also has a special service for the promotion of migrant investment which offers technical, economic and financial assistance to prospective migrant investors in agriculture (Kondis, 1990: 225).

In setting investment incentives, Greek governments usually make favourable provisions for the investment of Greeks from abroad if this investment is financed from accumulated savings. In fact, these incentives are similar to those given to cooperative enterprises and the enterprises of local authorities, which generally receive higher investment subsidization (Kondis, 1990: 216). Between mid-1982 and mid-1984, investment of Greeks from abroad totalled only 5.9 million drachmas (US$ 66,000). But over the longer period 1982-1987 the volume of investment was 26.7 billion drachmas, or US$ 235 million. Sixty-four per cent of these investments were in the tertiary sector, 27 per cent in the secondary and 8.6 per cent in the primary. The average age of investors was 39 years and their average stay abroad was 14 years

(Kondis, 1990: 219). During the same period, migrant remittances to Greece totalled US$ 5,800 million. In other words, only 4 per cent of the accumulated flow of migrant savings was invested.[2]

On a more practical level, the returnees brought used household equipment and automobiles free of customs duties and other taxes, and were also entitled to free transfer of their foreign deposits between Greece and host countries. Other subsidies included a lump sum for settling in the countryside, as well as monthly allowances for children attending vocational training and adjustment courses. The maximum amount of allowance was 100,000 dr. (1991) and a two-year rent of 5,000 dr. per month. Those who registered as unemployed could receive benefits amounting to a maximum 135,000 dr. for 18 months. Training and retraining courses were also offered by the Organization of Employment (OAED). Seminars to help returnees integrate into Greek economic life and the Greek labour market were provided by the Productivity Centre (ELKEPA).

By 1993/94, 26 programmes of education and training of three to six months duration were addressing the needs of repatriating Greeks and migrants of Greek ethnic origin, including some Pontians. The total cost of these programmes is estimated to be 1.5 billion drachmas (5.3 million ECU) and the number of beneficiaries 2,266.

In addition to these training courses, provision has been made for the general education of second-generation children. For English speaking children, one elementary and one high school in Athens with both lower and upper levels accepts children with Greek citizenship or Greek ethnic origin. There are also two elementary and two high schools that are bilingual in Athens, mainly for returning youth from English speaking countries, and one elementary and one high school in Thessaloniki for English, French and German speaking students (GSGA, 1993a). After-school tutorials of up to 6 hours per week are also offered in regular schools. These include courses in Greek language, physics, mathematics, chemistry and history. The tutorials are for 3-9 students. If 10-20 students are interested, regular classes are created. Those attending the tutorials are subsidized. GSGA also provides information on such practical issues as customs regulations, social security, labour relations, investment, loans and mortgages. This information is sent to embassies, consulates and various migration agencies in host countries and to the countries of residence of ethnic Greeks.

A new set of bilateral agreements has been signed with Switzerland, Sweden, Norway, Austria, Cyprus, Canada, Australia, Libya, Brazil and Argentina for the purpose of transferring social security benefits and maintaining the social security rights of returnees (Moussourou, 1991: 194-195). A number of institutions have also been set up to assist repatriating migrants in resolving various problems, including the Centre of Psychic Hygiene of the Ministry of Health and Social Security, and special offices for migrants in the International Organization for Migration (IOM) and in OAED in Athens and Thessaloniki. In addition, private agencies include the Centre for Assistance of the World Council of Churches, also situated in Athens and Thessaloniki, and the Associations of Migrants and Greek Political refugees (Fakiolas and Dimitropoulou, 1988: 286).

International migration literature is generally negative in its evaluation of the effectiveness of repatriation policy; the experience of Greece seems to be no exception. In fact, the overwhelming majority of both Greek refugees and Greek migrants returned during the period 1976-1980 before most of these measures were introduced (Petropoulos, 1990: 102). This suggests that factors other than repatriation policies, such as the economic recession in host countries and the fall of dictatorship in Greece or, for the target migrants, fulfilment of their aims, were more effective determinants of return than measures adopted for encouraging them to return to Greece (Petropoulos, 1990: 102).

With the benefit of hindsight, one can see that certain policies aimed at helping returnees may have actually harmed them. For example, many migrants rushed to take back their social security contributions, thus giving up their social security rights (Emke-Poulopoulou, 1986: 436). Lack of policies or bureaucratic hindrance may have also led to the "undesirable" utilization of returnees' savings as well as their work experience and skills acquired during employment in the foreign country (Fakiolas, 1994: 588).

The educational policy for repatriating second-generation Greeks from European and overseas countries has been criticized as ineffective: e.g., the requirement of a minimum of more or less homogeneous classes of 10-25 students for the preparatory classes of the first two years of school established in the early 1980s, for students from Germany and the English speaking countries, was hard to justify unless many students travelled long distances to attend. Furthermore, the separation of students from their Greek counterparts, leading to their isolation, should have been avoided if their integration to Greek society was to be eased. These problems were subsequently overcome through the establishment of remedial classes of 3-9 children, after which they were integrated with Greek students. However, critics have claimed that teachers were inadequately qualified and there was a lack of audio-visual equipment. Whole special schools established in the mid-1980s in Athens for

English speaking children, and in Thessaloniki for English, French and German speaking children, were also judged inappropriate because an even larger number of these students were separated from the regular Greek educational system (Moussourou, 1991: 197-199).

GREEK POLITICAL REFUGEES RETURNING HOME

Greek political refugees are persons who were transferred to Eastern European countries during the 1946-1949 civil war and until 1974 were not permitted by the Greek government to return to Greece. Since that year, the first of restoration of democracy in Greece after seven years of a dictatorship, and especially since 1982, these refugees were free to repatriate. Returnees of this category number about 40,000, of whom about half settled in Macedonia and Thrace and many in Athens. Only 30 per cent had been born in Greece, the others were their foreign-born children.

A survey on the integration of these refugees commissioned by the General Secretariat for Greeks Abroad (GSGA) and conducted by Pantheion University showed that 38 per cent held degrees of third-level education. A high proportion were university graduates in engineering and medicine. About 30 per cent of the returnees had completed secondary technical education. Thirty-three per cent were unemployed and two-thirds of these were women. As for Greeks, unemployment was relatively higher for those with third and secondary level education. Lack of fluency in the Greek language was a problem, especially for many of those who had not been born in Greece. Over two-thirds of the returnees indicated that their economic situation in Greece was worse than it had been in their countries of former residence (Kassimati et al., 1993: 162). Forty-six per cent said that their adjustment to Greek society had been "difficult" and 28 per cent said it had been "easy".

The survey identified twelve associations of Greek political refugees which had helped the returnees by organizing seminars on Greek language and intermediating in the solution of bureaucratic problems. An institutional mechanism has been established to assist in the reception and reintegration of refugees to the Greek society and economy. This mechanism includes such organizations as the Committee of Repatriation and Reception of Political Refugees in Thessaloniki, established in 1983, and the Centre of Psychic Hygiene in Athens, established in 1984, to which returned pensioners, part-time employees and unemployed persons aged over 25 years are accepted for assistance (Soultania, 1990: 349-350). In 1986, a research project for action was initiated by the National Welfare Organization in Athens and Thessaloniki.

Returning political refugees are entitled to temporary relief assistance. A lump sum is allocated to help cover the cost of relocation and initial accommodation and subsistence. Confiscated property is also returned to them whenever possible. Some allowance is also made concerning military service; they may be excluded altogether or have their enlistment postponed, or be financially charged for their military duty (Soultania, 1990: 351). They are also eligible for free medical and hospital care in the National Health System, and they are given priority for mortgages by the Agricultural Bank of Greece in case they wish to live in the countryside and engage themselves exclusively in agriculture (Soultania, 1990: 352).

Until 1986, the ex-Soviet Union and East Germany continued to pay the pensions of returnees as did Bulgaria following a bilateral agreement with Greece signed in 1978. Bilateral agreements were also signed between Greece and eastern countries for the transfer of pensions and social security rights of repatriated political refugees after 1977.

On arrival in Greece, the refugees were registered with the Greek social security system which had been financed by the reimbursement of social security contributions from host countries. These funds were paid into a special account from which the pensioners receive the lower pension provided by the legislation of the Greek Social Security System (IKA) (Soultania, 1990: 353, Emke-Poulopoulou, 1986: 437). For unemployed returning refugees the Organization of Employment (OAED) provides not only unemployment benefits but also offers programmes of vocational training and retraining during which the refugees are subsidized. OAED also pays for their resettlement as well as two years' rent if they move to any region other than Athens and Thessaloniki.

Qualified returnees under 50 years of age may register retrospectively from the time they receive their degree for appointment to teaching positions in primary and secondary schools[3] (Emke-Poulopoulou, 1986: 359). Returnees who are students in the third level education may transfer to corresponding Greek higher education institutes at a rate of 10 per cent of new entrants in each department once they pass an examination. Finally, special tutoring is provided in all geographic departments for the integration of returning political refugees in the country's educational system, including subsidized programmes of Greek language instruction and professional training.

One programme of eight months duration is available to both Greek political refugees and to Pontians. In 1991 it was attended by 1,000 Pontians and 200 repatriating Greek refugees. A second programme of four months duration on information technologies is for Greek political refugees and other repatriating Greeks with high school diplomas or university degrees in economics who speak a foreign language. In one year, the 120 students who attended this programme received a stipend of 45,000 drachmas per month. Sixty-five per cent of the cost of the programmes (600 million drachmas – 2.6 million ECU) was met by the EU social fund.

FOREIGN MIGRANTS OF GREEK ETHNIC ORIGIN - PONTIANS

Although ethnic Greeks come from various parts of the Greek diaspora, in recent years many have come especially from the ex-Soviet Union, the Pontians, and from Albania. The Pontians were historically Greeks who moved to Pontosin, the north-eastern part of Asia Minor, between the eighth and sixteenth century A.D. By the end of the eighteenth and the beginning of the nineteenth century, the Pontians moved gradually towards Georgia in the then Russian Empire. This migration was at its peak between 1915 and 1923 as a result of undesirable conditions generated in their territories.

In 1937 Stalin banned Greek language instruction in all Greek Pontian schools. This and other repressions forced many of them to move again to Kazakhstan, Uzbekistan and Turkmenistan where they lived in deplorable conditions. Their situation improved slightly after 1956 when they were permitted to return to Georgia, and some took advantage of this possibility. The national identity of Pontians was respected after *perestroika* and the Greek language was taught in schools to about 10,000 children. Pontians are now free to move in the ex-Soviet Union; others are assisted in moving to Greece (Vergeti, 1992: 29-54). Over 40,000 Pontians now live in Greece which they enter at a rate of 10,000 to 15,000 a year, a flow that the Greek Ministry of Foreign Affairs believes may continue for several years.

A survey recently conducted on the Pontians in Greece (similar to the survey of Greek political refugees commissioned by the General Secretariat of Greeks Abroad of the Ministry of Foreign Affairs and elaborated by the Pantheion University) concluded that the most important reason why the majority of Pontians settled in Athens (60 per cent) and Thessaloniki (15 per cent), was that they had relatives in those places. The assistance provided by relatives may have negated, to some extent, the attractions of Macedonia and Thrace where about 20 per cent of the Pontians were found (Glytsos, 1992: 372).

This survey also showed that the educational level of Pontians was much higher than for indigenous Greeks: 27 per cent of Pontians hold third-level education degrees compared with 6.5 per cent (1981) of Greeks, and 36 per cent were secondary education leavers compared with 15 per cent of Greeks. A relatively high proportion had qualifications in civil and mechanical engineering (33 per cent) and medicine (13 per cent). A further 14 per cent had qualifications in literature and 13 per cent in economics. Graduates from technological institutes had concentrated in engineering technology, business administration and nursing (Kassimati, 1992b: 169-184).

About one half of economically active Pontians are unemployed; of those employed, 79 per cent are production and related workers, 9 per cent service workers and 4.7 per cent professional and technical workers (Ragoussis, 1992: 212). Not only are many highly qualified Pontians unemployed, but many also have low quality jobs in relation to their education. Among the unemployed, two-thirds are women of whom 28 per cent are in the 15-24 age group. Thirty-two per cent of male unemployed are also in the youth bracket (Ragoussis, 1992: 332). The share of the secondary education leavers in corresponding unemployment is very high for both men (45 per cent) and women (37 per cent). For third-level education graduates the rate is 22 per cent for men and 38 per cent for women.

While Pontians living in Macedonia and Thrace evaluate their economic situation as better than it was in the ex-Soviet Union, residents of Athens and Thessaloniki consider that they are worse off than before their coming (Kassimati, 1992c: 393).

Pontians and Albanians of the Greek minority are granted special treatment as if they are Greek citizens, compared with non-ethnic foreigners (Petrinioti, 1993: 33). In fact, Pontians are granted a "visa of repatriation" from Greek consulates, and do not require residence or work permits (Petrinioti, 1993: 13). They enjoy diplomatic and legal protection, easy naturalization (thousands are naturalized every year), entitlement to social insurance benefits and vocational training and financial assistance.

The efforts of the Greek government to assist ethnic Greeks in general is extended to their place of residence. In order to sustain the Greek minority in Albania and simultaneously reduce the flow of migrants to Greece, the Government contributes to Albanian development by subsidizing Greek investment in Albania. After 1989 the Greek Foreign Affairs Ministry, being in a good position to relate to the Greek consular services in Moscow, was made responsible for dealing with Pontians wishing to come to Greece. The National Bureau for Dealing with the Pontian Issue was established, its purpose being to coordinate all efforts for the reception of Pontians. Then in December 1990, the National Foundation for the Reception and Resettlement of Repatriating Greeks was created to administer all policies relating to Pontians.

The policy framework for Pontians is the so-called "multi-stage batch processing system" (Kokkinos, 1991: 13-18). Preparation for their resettlement begins before their arrival with Greek language instruction being given by teachers sent from Greece. Upon their arrival in Greece, the Pontians are taken to "Hospitality Centres" in various parts of the country. These are either state owned, or rented hotels and student dormitories where Pontians may stay for 15 days during which they enjoy free accommodation and food and are assisted on social, professional and practical matters, including nursery and kindergarten facilities. In reality, however, guests often stay for 10-19 months because of inadequate facilities in the next "stages" of the system. At the end of 1993, the Hospitality Centres housed 1,882 persons (Hadjidimitriou, 1993).

The next stage is the Reception Village. These are located mainly in Northern Greece: four in Eastern Macedonia and Thrace and one in Thessaly. Each village of 250 houses also has a kindergarten, school, church, child care stations, infirmary and a community office. The Reception Village, in an area of 300 hectares in Evros in the Thrace region, has a capacity to host 250-300 families. Pontians may stay in villages for up to six months, during which they are subsidized and given foodstuffs to do their own cooking in their own houses. Adult Greek language courses in these villages are administered by the General Secretariat of Informal (popular) Training. They include some initiation in the structure and functioning of the Greek state as well as appropriate history courses designed to reassure Pontians of their national identity. Six months special instruction is provided by the Ministry of Education for the integration of children in the Greek educational system (Kokkinos, 1991: 15). Intensive professional training and retraining is also offered by OAED during their stay in Reception Villages. In 1991, the OAED programme was attended by 800 persons, each of whom received 40,000 drachmas (US$ 260) per month.

Following their six-month stay in a Reception Village, Pontians are normally moved to houses for which the state pays rent for two years. At December 1993, 640 houses comprising 2,563 persons were rented mostly in Thrace (Hadjidimitriou, 1993). Indeed, in November 1993, 9,197 persons were in various stages of the overall system: 1,845 in hospitality centres, 3,770 in reception villages and 3,582 in rented houses.

The next and final stage of the programme is the most difficult: permanent settlement. Although the survey showed that 78 per cent of Pontians lived in rented houses, rent payments weighed heavily on their family budgets. In Thrace, the government began a project under which it bought or built houses, or assisted Pontians to build their own houses. In Xanthi and Komotini, 145 apartments, 25 shops and 8 houses were purchased by the National Foundation for the Reception and Resettlement of Ethnic Greeks (ΕΙΥΑΠΟΕ).

Concerning education and training, a programme for Pontians aged 18-45 years was established in 19 regions of the country, mainly in Northern Greece during the period 1990-1993. Jointly executed by the GSGA and the General Secretariat of Popular Training, as well as various Pontian associations, it had a budget of 2.5 billion drachmas (8.8 million ECU). During its four years duration the programme trained 5,690 persons (Table 2, page 173). Eleven of the 26 education and training programmes for repatriating Greek migrants during 1993-1994 were specifically planned for the Pontians. These cost 200 million drachmas (707,000 ECU) for 571 beneficiaries. Pontians may also participate in other programmes provided for repatriating Greeks (GSGA, 1993b).

The integration of Pontians into the labour market is further assisted through occupational orientation, and the help of experienced social workers on personal relations, economic needs and health problems. At the same time, local populations are informed about the traditions and culture of Pontians (Kokkinos, 1991: 16). A lump sum is allocated to those who wish to begin their own business and employers who hire Pontian workers are subsidized. For those wishing to become farmers (not many, given that only one per cent of Pontians were farmers in their country of residence), the government offers agricultural land and loans under favourable conditions, as well as money for their permanent settlement.

The whole programme was envisaged to last five years and accommodate 100,000 Pontians. The total cost was estimated to be 120 billion drachmas (US$ 780 million), half of which would be covered by the Social Development Fund of the Council of Europe. In addition to the multi-phased effort for their reception and integration, Pontians are also granted some tax privileges. They are entitled to bring their household equipment and an automobile free of customs duties and other taxes although the tax free automobiles privilege has been abused, some cars having been "sold" to third parties. Pontians may also buy additional commodities and sell them in Greece in special markets, side by side with farmers in open air markets. The Foundation also distributes to Greek migrant and ethnic Greek communities abroad literature specially prepared for Greek language learning and acquaintance with the Greek

State. Videos with the repatriation programme in four languages are also distributed and 74 seminars for a selected number of Pontians were organized to train Pontian consultants to be involved in assisting Pontian children to spend their vacations in Greek camps.

In addition to government programmes, there are, according to respondents at the interviews, at least 27 Pontian associations of which thirteen are in Athens, six in Thessaloniki and eight elsewhere in the country. They assist Pontians in various ways, providing them with financial assistance, food, clothing, furniture and support in solving workforce problems. In addition, they provide information, arrange seminars on the Greek language, assist with housing, and also offer moral support (Kassimati, 1992c: 416). In contrast, government services are not very effective, as the survey shows, due to bureaucratic procedures and lack of information on Greek legislation concerning Pontians. After their first contact with Greek authorities in Moscow, only 58 per cent were satisfied, a considerable proportion having experienced delays in obtaining the information necessary to solve their problems. Once in Greece, 84 per cent contacted a variety of public services, including ministries, local authorities, public enterprises, courts and hospitals. About two-thirds of the Pontians thought that improvements were needed in order to make the system less bureaucratic and employees better behaved and more efficient (Kassimati, 1992c: 426).

Pontian associations are rather critical of the effectiveness and adequacy of Pontian integration policies. They cite many problems relating to social security arrangements, high unemployment, low wages, highly qualified persons working in petty trade jobs, the question of formal recognition of their educational degrees, inadequacy of the Greek educational system for their children and the limited number of Pontians offered Greek language instruction.

A policy for the productive integration of Pontians in the Greek labour market ought to be compatible with the more general effort of national and regional development. It should give particular emphasis to regions that possess development potential but lack the required workers,[4] such as Eastern Macedonia and Thrace (Glytsos, 1992: 376). The decision to resettle Pontians in these regions, and the measures taken accordingly, was based on an objective to increase economic growth. However, the majority of incoming Pontians are spontaneously directed to Athens and Thessaloniki, due mainly to the presence of relatives and the fact that in these cities they can more easily scrape a living by selling their home products in the special markets referred to above.

The integration of Pontians in the Greek economy and society should take account of the fact that there are two main groups: those that have already settled in Athens and Thessaloniki and do not wish to be relocated; and newcomers who, as we noted, are expected to flow at an annual rate of 10,000 to 15,000 until the end of the century. For the former, the aim should be to facilitate their employment in the two cities; for the latter, the primary policy concern should be to channel them to regions which, despite short-term problems, have unexploited resources and development potential (Glytsos 1992: 382-383).

Concerning the educational qualifications and experience related to place of residence, it seems that many Pontians belong to high unemployment risk groups. Rates of unemployment of Greeks is relatively higher for youth, women, holders of secondary education and third-level education degrees, and also for those living in the two larger cities, Athens and Thessaloniki. In addition to the problem of labour demand, there is also a problem of labour supply. For example, many Pontians do not speak Greek (which three quarters of the survey respondents considered to be their major problem for integration), and their education and experience may need some adjustment in order to fit western technology and working methods. These inadequacies make Pontians a second priority in the preference of employers unless there is compensation in the form of lower wages.

Major policy proposals have been made by the Pontian University study for the social and economic integration of Pontians, (Kassimati et al., 1992a: 533-538). In view of Greece's rapidly declining rate of natural population growth, efforts should be made to sustain the high birth rates of Pontians, attract youth in the educational system and take steps for the retirement with pensions of persons of retirement age. In view of relatively high and rising unemployment in Greece, particularly of more educated workers, who also make up a high proportion of Pontians, any discriminatory employment policy in their favour would have some negative implications for their integration. Emphasis should be on the supply side, to raise the quality of Pontian labour supply to that of the indigenous population and closer to the requirements of the Greek economy. Since the cost of the human capital investment in their education has been made by others, the cost of their adjustment to the Greek labour market would be only marginal (Glytsos, 1992: 383). Appropriate measures would be Greek language instruction, incentives for inducing at least some to move away from the larger cities, encouragement of self-employment with the provision of technical and economic assistance, subsidized loans for housing and assistance to Pontian associations. In regions with many Pontians, some appropriate adjustment in the schools would facilitate the attendance of Pontian children. Some of these measures have already been adopted but perhaps their attractiveness should be enhanced.

A number of Pontians may, after appropriate training, including Greek language courses, be employed in positions related to the reception and integration of the Pontians themselves. Worthwhile programmes of self-employment, as for instance in the framework of local employment initiatives (ILE), are an outlet explored and exploited nowadays in several countries. This may even have diffused positive effects in creating additional new jobs for both Pontians and indigenous workers alike (Glytsos, 1992: 384-385). Furthermore, potential forthcoming Pontians should be better informed on conditions of education, employment, social life and so on before they arrive in Greece.

NON-ETHNIC GREEK FOREIGNERS

Greece has openly declared that it is not an immigration country. The recent basic law (1975/1991) on foreigners, which replaced 62-year old legislation (law 4310/1929) is very restrictive in accepting foreigners for permanent stay and work. The philosophy of the new law, passed under pressure to do something about massive flows of illegal migrants, is to check the flow rather than regularize the stock of illegal migrants in the country. For this reason it was drafted mainly by the Ministry of Public Order and makes no serious effort to reach a realistic solution to the problem of illegal migration: it tries only to make the flow and integration of foreign workers more difficult.

A foreign worker may come to Greece for work only on the condition of prior approval specifying an employer, the type of work to be undertaken and the locality of employment. This approval is given only if a vacancy cannot be filled by Greeks, citizens of the EU, ethnic Greek foreigners or recognized refugees with work permits, in that order. Only one-year residence and work permits are granted to those entering Greece with a pre-authorization, renewed annually for a maximum period of five years. The permit may, under certain conditions, be renewed every two years for up to fifteen years of total legal residence, after which the foreigner is accorded a residence permit of indefinite duration.

Family reunion is allowed after only five years of legal residence by the inviting foreigner, which is the maximum duration of stay if the permit is not further renewed. Naturalization of foreigners is very difficult to achieve. Only after ten years of legal residence may a foreigner apply for naturalization, whereas the foreign spouse of a Greek national does not acquire Greek citizenship automatically, but must wait five years for his or her application to be examined. As a result, in the last two decades, only about 300 persons have acquired Greek citizenship each year (Fakiolas, 1994: 588).

This legislation has been criticized by many as being very harsh. Staying in Greece without a residence permit is a penal offence drawing prison sentences. Employment without a work permit can also lead to imprisonment, which has been denounced on grounds that the foreigner is forced to turn to illegal ways – clandestine employment or criminal activities – for his or her livelihood (Kourtovic, 1992: 4). Furthermore, the binding to a specific employer may lead to exploitation of the foreign worker. Another point of criticism is that the law itself pushes illegal foreigners to the social margin because they are prohibited from turning for assistance to government services, the police, labour inspectors, or to social services. Local authorities refuse to marry couples if the foreign spouse does not have a work permit (Kourtovic, 1992: 4).

The Greek labour movement favours regularization of illegal migrants accompanied by appropriate measures of social and economic integration to restrain clandestine employment (Linardos-Rulmond, 1993: 30 and 38). Although normally a foreign worker without a work permit cannot be a member of a labour union, some unions, for instance the construction workers union, offer them membership. Of the estimated 500,000 foreigners in Greece, 350,000 are illegal and most are Albanians. Greece is, in fact, an exceptional case because of the high proportion of illegal migrant workers in the total migration (perhaps 75 per cent) and in the Greek labour force (perhaps 8 per cent). Legalizing foreign workers runs the risk, according to some opinion, of turning worker migration to family migration and thus increasing sharply social costs in the face of financially ailing and inadequately managed social services. It would also reduce the benefits from low wages in costs of production and increase unemployment (Fakiolas, 1994: 591).

By their very nature, illegal migrant workers are enhancing the already thriving para-economy in Greece. Some persons believe that by working for low wages and in unpleasant jobs they do not displace Greek workers, except perhaps in the construction industry. Labour unions, on the other hand (and also others), hold the view that regularizing illegal migrants would solve more problems than it would create, as the government's hesitation to proceed with legalization seems to imply (for instance, Emke-Poulopoulou, 1990: 74-75).

The Greek Government has attempted to restrain the flow of illegal migrants from Albania and other countries in various ways. Apart from the ineffective and expensive measure of deporting them – 379,093 persons in 1992 costing 3.6 million ECU – due to the difficulty of adequately patrolling the extensive and inaccessible Greek-Albanian frontier, the Greek Government has reduced the maximum number of work permits (which in any case are very limited) to about 28,000 of which 17,000 are for EU citizens. Another measure is to subsidize investment for creating new jobs in Albania in the hope that this may check the flow to Greece. In 1993, Greek investment in Albania was about US$ 44 million, second only to Italy's investment of US$ 72 million.

The so-called "Mini Marshall Plan", addressed particularly but not exclusively to the Greek minority, was launched to provide technical assistance in education, rural, industrial and small-scale private initiatives. Educational assistance aims at discouraging Greek minority children from coming to Greece for school. Furthermore, OAED assists Albania with training and technical assistance, trains Albanian unemployed youth and Albanian Ministry of Labour employees.

There is also a joint Greek-Albanian programme for training the Albanian trainers. Technical assistance includes transfer of know-how for conducting labour market surveys, and organization and equipment for employment offices and training centres. The annual cost of this effort, including also some humanistic relief assistance, is about US$ 35 million.

CONCLUSION

It may be concluded from this analysis that policies adopted for the integration of various migrant groups to Greece (i.e. Greek migrant returnees, ethnic-Greek foreigners and illegal migrants) lack a central aim, orientation and strategy, as well as a long-term perspective. This could perhaps be partly explained by the different nature of population flows. The emphasis seems to be more on dealing with immediate issues, either the positive attitude of the State towards ethnic Greeks or its negative attitude towards illegal migrants. The latter's relative weight in the Greek labour market probably deters any decision for regularizing them.

No systematic evaluation has been made of the cost-effectiveness or success of policies. This study suggests a need to evaluate the extent of complementarity or substitutability of foreign workers in the Greek labour force against a medium or long-term outlook for the Greek labour market. Recent estimates point to a negative natural population growth, with great regional disparities, and potential labour shortages, by the year 2000. Evaluation of the place of foreign workers in this perspective could form the central criterion for the conception of appropriate, feasible and, if required, selective policies for integrating the different migrant groups into the Greek economy and society (Glytsos, 1993b).

NOTES

1. This is a revised version of a paper with a similar title prepared for the Andalusia Workshop on the Socio-economic Integration of Returnees (EU, ECOS-OUVERTURE Programme, DG XIV). Organizing Institute ECOTEC, Sevilla, 14-15 June 1994.
2 For the spending of Greek migrant remittances and their direct and indirect effects on the Greek economy see Glytsos, 1993a.
3. Vacancies for teachers in Greece are filled routinely by drawing from a register on which those interested place their names.
4. For an assessment of the prospects of job openings by occupation and region in Greece, and the possible opportunities of employment for Pontians, see Glytsos, 1993b.

REFERENCES

Emke-Poulopoulou, I.

1986 *Problems of Migration and Repatriation*, IMEO/ΕΔΗΜ, Athens, 1986 (in Greek).

1990 "Migrants and refugees in Greece 1970-1990", *Eklogi*, 85/86 special issue (in Greek).

Fakiolas, R.

1994 "Migration from and to Greece during the last four decades", in G. Alogoskoufis et al. (Eds), *Essays in Honor of Constantine G. Drakatos*, Papazissis Publishers, Athens: 571-592.

Fakiolas, R., and B. Dimitropoulou

1988 "The external migration in post-war period", *in George Halkiopoulos: (In Memory of)*, George Halkiopoulos Foundation, Athens (in Greek): 265-292.

GSGA (General Secretariat of Greeks Abroad)

1992 *Research Project of Emigration - Repatriation of Greek Population*, Volume B, Athens (in Greek).

1993a *Favourable Regulations for the Integration and Assimilation of Greek Migrants and Returnees in our Educational System*, Athens (in Greek).

1993b Programme 1993-1994, mimeo (in Greek).

Glytsos, N. P.

1992 "The Insertion of Pontians in the Greek Labour Market", in K. Kassimati et al., 1992a: 367-386 (in Greek).

1993a "Measuring the income effects of migrant remittances: A methodological approach applied to Greece", *Economic Development and Cultural Change*, 42(1): 131-168.

1993b *Supply and Demand for Labour in the Greek Economy, by Region and Occupation, until the End of the Century: Possibilities of Employment of Greek Political Refugees and Pontians*, GSGA and Pantheion University, Athens (in Greek). Study under Publication.

Hadjidimitriou, Z.
1993 "The ΕΙΥΑΠΟΕ and its contribution to the social and economic integration of Pontians from the ex-Soviet Union", mimeo, Athens (in Greek).
Kassimati, K., et al.
1992a *Pontian Migrants from the Ex-Soviet Union: Their Social and Economic Integration*, GSGA and Pantheion University, Athens (in Greek).
1992b "The educational level of Pontian migrants", in Kassimati et al., 1992a: 150-185 (in Greek).
1992c "Problems of Pontians – Sources of assistance – The role of Pontian associations – The extent of assistance to Pontians from government services", in Kassimati et al., 1992a: 389-432 (in Greek).
1993 *Political Refugees from Eastern Countries*, GSGA and Pantheion University, Athens (in Greek). Study under publication.
Kokkinos, D.
1991 "Inflow and integration of Greek ethnic origin foreigners from the Soviet Union and Albania", paper presented to the IOM/GSGA Seminar in Zappion, Athens (mimeo, in Greek).
Kondis, A.
1990 "Investment behaviour of Greek migrants: A theoretical and empirical approach", in GSGA, *Research Project of Emigration - Repatriation of Greek Population*, Volume A: 209-228 (in Greek).
Kourtovic, J.
1992 "The legal status of foreign workers in Greece", mimeo, Athens (in Greek).
Linardos-Rulmond, P.
1993 *Foreign Workers and the Labour Market*, Institute of Labour of the Federation of Greek Labour Unions, Athens (in Greek).
Moussourou, L.M.
1991 *Migration and Migratory Policy in Greece and Europe*, Gutenberg, Athens (in Greek).
Petrinioti, X.
1993 *Immigration to Greece*, Odysseas, Athens (in Greek)
Petropoulos, N.
1990 "Repatriation 1971-1986: Conclusions from the micro census 1985-1986, and proposals for economic policy", in GSGA, *Research Project of Emigration - Repatriation of Greek Population*, Volume A: 89-107 (in Greek).
Ragoussis, A.
1992 "The situation of employment of Greek Pontian migrants from the Ex-Soviet Union", in Kassimati et al.: 189-364 (in Greek).
Soultania, K.X.
1990 "The resettlement of repatriated Greek political refugees", in GSGA, 1990: 339-367 (in Greek).
Vergeti, M.
1992 "A brief historical account of Greek Pontians in the Ex-Soviet Union", in Kassimati et al.: 27-59 (in Greek).

TABLE 1

RETURNING GREEK CITIZENS BY SEX AND AGE DURING THE PERIOD 1971-1986

Age group	Number			Age (per cent)		
	Males	Females	Total	Males	Females	Both sexes
0-14	42,038	38,993	81,031	12.9	13.0	12.9
15-24	52,503	49,594	102,097	16.2	16.4	16.3
25-44	117,181	131,539	248,720	36.0	43.5	39.6
45-64	99,170	68,154	167,324	30.5	22.4	26.7
65 +	14,402	14,101	28,503	4.4	4.7	4.5
Total	**325,294**	**302,381**	**627,675**	**100.0**	**100.0**	**100.0**

Source: Adjusted from General Secretariat of Greeks Abroad, *Research Project Emigration - Repatriation of the Greek Population*, Vol. B. Repatriation 1971-86: Results of the Micro census 1985-1986, Athens, 1992 (in Greek), pp. 194-195.

TABLE 2

TRAINING PROGRAMMES FOR PONTIANS BY REGION, 1990-1993 (Numbers of trainees)

Regions	Greek language	Information technology	Various	Total
Eastern Macedonia and Thrace	1,002	152	-	1,154
Central Macedonia	1,411	236	174	1,821
Western Macedonia	314	47	-	361
Thessaly	253	108	8	369
Attiki	1,388	307	173	1,868
Peloponnese	91	16	-	107
Crete	-	-	10	10
Greece	**4,459**	**866**	**365**	**5,690**

Source: GSGA, "Activities of GSGA for the Greek Pontians", Athens, 6.7.93 (mimeo).

[11]

Population Movement in Zhejiang Province, China: The Impact of Government Policies[1]

Xiushi Yang and Sidney Goldstein
Brown University

China's urbanization policies include strict control of permanent migration to large cities, but encourage the growth of small cities and towns. Concurrently, temporary migration is widely permitted as a way to stimulate commerce. Data for Zhejiang province indicate that permanent mobility is largely directed toward urban places, that towns gain more than cities and that rural areas experience migration losses. Permanent migrants to urban places are selective of the better educated. Temporary migration is also urban directed but greater in volume than permanent migration, and places considerable strain on urban infrastructure. Government policies are a key to understanding the migration streams and migrant characteristics. The considerable net movement into cities suggests that strict control of city growth is more difficult to achieve than envisaged by policymakers.

As part of China's urbanization policies, strict controls have been placed by the government on migration to big cities. Chinese planners have maintained that the development of big cities should consider simultaneously the economic, social and environmental benefits of city size. If a city's size grows too large and too rapidly to be commensurate with its economy, it is argued that the city may lose most of its social and environmental benefits, which in turn will lower its economic benefits (Tu, 1985).

By contrast, because the development of small cities and towns is seen as having many advantages, their growth has been vigorously encouraged. First, small cities and towns, especially the latter, are widely dispersed over the rural countryside and provide close links with their surrounding rural areas; they usually serve as political, economic, cultural, educational and service centers for their hinterlands. Their development, it is argued by

[1] The authors would like to thank the Population Research Center at Hangzhou University, China and the Zhejiang Provincial Security Bureau for providing the data for this study. This is a revised version of a paper presented at the Population Association of America annual meeting in Baltimore, April 1989.

policymakers, may therefore stimulate rural economic development, speed the pace of rural modernization and narrow differentials between rural and urban areas, with less investment than would be necessary for bigger city growth. Second, they are viewed as bridges; their development can foster interaction between cities and rural areas, facilitate market information flows, and thereby benefit economic development in both cities and rural areas. Third, towns can help to absorb rural surplus labor, thereby helping to control big city growth. This view is embodied in the slogan: "Leave the land without leaving the township, enter factories without entering cities" (Li Tu Bu Li Xiang, Jin Chang Bu Jin Cheng).

Although China's urban policy directly concerns the problems of cities and focuses on the vertical distribution of population among urban locations of different size, to the extent that migration is a major component of urban growth, such policy must incorporate attention to population movement. Consistent with the goal of restricting big city growth and of fostering small city and town development, specific principles guiding internal migration have been developed: 1) rural to urban permanent migration must be strictly controlled; 2) movement from towns to cities and from small to big cities must be properly limited; and 3) movement from large to small urban places or from urban to rural places should be encouraged (Goldstein and Goldstein, 1985). Free permanent change in residence between different locations (referred to in this report as permanent migration) is prohibited in China, and movement must be in accord with planned economic development. All permanent changes in residence are therefore subject to control through the migration registration system, which is an integral part of the household registration system.

While urban development and migration policies have served to limit permanent migration and have tried to direct population away from cities, recent changes in economic policies have greatly stimulated population mobility and attracted population to cities. Since 1978, when the household responsibility system was introduced in rural areas, dramatic changes have taken place both in the social and economic quality of life and in population dynamics. Under the new system, land is allocated to households or individuals under contract to the collective. The ownership of the land remains with the collective, but the peasant has the right to use the land to maximum advantages or, if he decides to pursue nonagricultural activities, to transfer the land back to the collective or to another individual (Goldstein and Goldstein, 1985). Domestic sideline production was not only legalized but encouraged. Peasants are allowed to keep the domestic sideline products as well as the surplus basic agricultural produce beyond what is required by the contract. Use of these surplus products is unrestricted (for a detailed discussion of new policies, *see* Gray and White, 1982; Goldstein and Goldstein, 1985). These changes offered peasants major incentives to expand production. In addition to meeting their own needs and the contract specifications, peasants have increasingly produced surplus agricultural and domestic sideline products. These surplus products need markets to realize their economic value.

At the same time, under the newly introduced policy of "Activate the internal economy and open to the world," cities opened free markets to peasants. Peasants were allowed to enter the commercial channels and engage in long distance trade. They were even allowed to work temporarily in cities through individual or collective contracts with work units in cities. Thus, while permanent migration continued to be strictly controlled, rural-to-urban temporary migration became possible. As exchange and trade centers, cities naturally have attracted peasants who bring their surplus products for trade; as centers of extensive new construction, and lacking sufficient construction workers, cities attract rural construction teams who supplement the urban construction labor force; and facing a lack of adequate daily services, urban places attract peasants who are engaged in self-employed informal sectors such as household repairs, personal services and domestic work (Yang, 1985). As a result, temporary migration has increased rapidly. For example, Hangzhou, the capital city of Zhejiang Province, in November 1984 had about 200,000 temporary migrants, referred to as the floating population. The number had increased to 300,000 by April 1985—a 50 percent increase in less than half a year (Yang, 1985). In Beijing, on April 20, 1985, the total number of circulators was estimated at 880,000 (Du, 1986); by December 1986, they had passed the one million mark (*People's Daily*, overseas edition, December 20, 1986). Most big cities experience similar situations (Huang, 1985).

Clearly, internal population movement represents not only a response to economic development, but is also greatly affected by government policies. As a result, the low level of permanent migration suggested by the household registration statistics by no means reflects fully the actual population mobility taking place currently in Chinese society. A large proportion of rural-urban population mobility assumes the form of temporary movement. Attention to such movement is therefore essential to any assessment of changes in the social, economic and political situation in both urban and rural China and of the overall urbanization process.

China, with its low level of urbanization compared to other developing countries and its large volume of potential migrants, may therefore provide researchers a unique opportunity for the study of urbanization and migration in a centrally planned economy. The current research takes as its focus the impact of government policy on internal migration in Zhejiang province. Emphasis is given to the volume and patterns of migration, both permanent and temporary, and to the characteristics of the migrants involved. Questions about who the migrants are, their origins and destinations, and the effects of recent changes in economic policies on the type of internal migration receives particular attention.

RESEARCH SETTING AND DATA SOURCES

Similar to the situation in most of the now developing countries, the lack of appropriate data on migration has been a major obstacle to the study of internal migration in China. The only data generally available are numbers of total migrants and of in and outmigrants for different areas, which are collected by local security departments or administrative offices from the registration records for the purpose of local yearly population reports. Even these data are somewhat questionable. This is also the case in Zhejiang, on which this research focuses.

Zhejiang province lies along China's east coast. With a 1982 total population of 38.9 million and a population density of 382 per square kilometer, Zhejiang is one of the most densely populated provinces in China. As a maritime province with a 2,200 kilometer coastline, Zhejiang has superior natural conditions for economic development. The province was one of the first in China to develop modern industry and commerce. Historically, the growth of the economy and the cities has resulted in considerable rural-urban population movement. After 1949, with the transformation of the political, social and economic system of the country, previously spontaneous, free and usually urbanward migration was replaced by organized, policy oriented and usually multidirectional migration. The volume of individual free migration was greatly reduced. Since 1978, however, when the economic development strategy changed, Zhejiang, like other parts of the country, has experienced vigorous economic growth. Town and township industries are well developed, and spatial movement has increased rapidly.

Recognizing this change and reflecting its strong interest in migration and urbanization in Zhejiang, the Population Research Center of Hangzhou University organized a field investigation of permanent migration in 1985. The data collection was based on locally maintained migration registration forms. This data set is used in this research, and is supplemented by a second data set based on year-end reports from the Zhejiang Provincial Public Security Bureau (ZPPSB) on temporary migrants in six cities in the province at the end of 1984.

The field investigation of permanent migration included three cities (Hangzhou, Ningbo, and Jinghua) and eight counties. In each, two subareas were selected: for cities, one neighborhood within the city proper and one township[2] within the city suburbs; for counties, one urban town and one

[2] A township (formerly commune) is the basic administrative unit of rural areas in China. It usually consists of several natural villages, with a total average population around 10,000. The township government is located in one major village, usually the market town. Townships have rural status.

township. Of the 22 target areas, data for two of the townships were not available at the time of the data collection, and in one of the three cities—Hangzhou—two neighborhoods in the city proper were selected instead of one neighborhood and one township. Therefore, a total of 20 places were investigated, of which eight are townships (rural areas), eight are urban towns and four are neighborhoods within the cities. In all, the 20 places investigated contain a total population of 323,228, or approximately one percent of the total population of the province.

The migrants identified by the field investigation were those persons who had officially changed their residences in 1984 across either township, town or city boundaries. All were therefore permanent migrants by definition.[3] Movement between neighborhoods in the same city or between villages in the same township is not counted as migration. Information about the migrants was obtained from the original migration registration forms kept in the local security department or administrative office.

To insure that the composition of each residence type reflected the overall provincial patterns, the sample data were weighted, using the city-town-rural distributions from the 1982 Census. In the following discussion, the numbers appearing in the tables and the text will be weighted statistics. The original total number of migrants in the sample, on which the weighted statistics were based, were 13,857, of which 9,500 were inmigrants and 4,357 were outmigrants. After adjusting through weighting for areal distribution, the total number of migrants is 68,234.

The second data set used in this study covers temporary migrants in six cities of Zhejiang province—Hangzhou, Ningbo, Wenzhou, Jiaxing, Huzhou and Shaoxing—at the end of 1984. These data on temporary migrants are based on year-end reports from Zhejiang Provincial Public Security Bureau and include only temporary migrants who have spent more than three days in urban places but who are officially registered elsewhere. As such, the statistics underestimate temporary migrants for two reasons. First, only part of the total temporary migrants in cities are recorded because the records excluded those who spent fewer than three days in the cities.[4] Second, many temporary migrants, anticipating a brief stay, may not have reported themselves and therefore came and went unrecorded. We cannot be certain how serious the downward bias is but, based on

[3] According to China's statistical standards, movements that involve a change of official residence registration across clearly defined administrative boundaries are defined as permanent migration regardless of time interval. By contrast, movers who have not had their official residence registration changed at the time of the move are defined as temporary migrants regardless of how long they have been in the new residence.

[4] It can be argued that temporary migrants who stay in the city for only 1–3 days are quite properly not included in these statistics since such migrants likely disproportionately consist of visitors.

Hangzhou's experience, only a little over half of the total temporary migrants may have spent more than three days and were therefore recorded in the year-end reports from the ZPPSB. This downward bias should be kept in mind in the following discussion.

Unfortunately, for both data sets the data available to the authors are limited to simple tabulations, with only a few control variables. Because of these data limitations, neither cross-tabulations by key variables nor multivariate analyses are feasible. Despite these limitations, the uniqueness of the data sets warrants their exploitation to gain insights on the volume and character of population movement in China.

PERMANENT MIGRATION IN ZHEJIANG

In 1984, only 68,234 permanent in and outmigrants were identified among a total population of 2,883,200, yielding a gross migration rate of 2.4 percent and a net gain of only 0.2 percent. Most of the movement took place within the province. Of the 60,749 gross migrants whose origin and destination were ascertained, only 9,109, or 15 percent, were interprovincial migrants.

In addition to the fact that interprovincial migration usually involves longer distances, less information exchange and higher economic costs, the differences among provinces in cultural traditions, dialects and economic conditions all may work as social and economic barriers to interprovincial migration. Concurrently, the poorly developed transportation and communication network may further reduce the volume of interprovincial migrants because it is difficult for potential interprovincial migrants to visit or to keep close contacts with their families, relatives and friends at origin. This increases the sociopsychological costs of interprovincial movement. Moreover, as political, economic and administrative units, provinces compete with each other in achieving economic, education and employment goals and, most important in current China, in controlling their population size. Therefore, each province will strictly control the inmigration from other provinces unless it has pressing manpower needs.

Within these general constraints, differences in migration levels exist among different types of residence. In general, urban places have higher in and outmigration rates than do rural places (Table 1), but the difference is much greater for inmigration than for outmigration. As a result, the net effect of migration on urban and rural areas was quite different. Every urban place (not shown in Table 1) and only one small town showed net inmigration; in rural areas, by contrast, every location experienced net outmigration.

Within the urban category, the highest inmigration rate in Zhejiang was not to the city, but to county seats, while the highest outmigration rate

TABLE 1

IN, OUT, GROSS AND NET MIGRATION RATES[a] BY TYPE OF RESIDENCE
ZHEJIANG PROVINCE, 1984

	Residence Type in 1984									
	City		County Seat[b]		Small Town		Total Urban		Total Rural	
Migration types	No.	Rate (%)	No.	Rate (%)	No.	Rate (%)	No.	Rate (%)	No.	Rate (%)
Out	9,160	1.80	1,681	1.23	2,065	2.16	12,906	1.74	18,289	0.85
In	18,327	3.60	5,901	4.31	2,081	2.17	26,309	3.55	10,730	0.50
Gross	27,487	5.40	7,582	5.54	4,146	4.33	39,215	5.29	29,019	1.35
Net	9,167	1.80	4,220	3.08	16	0.02	13,403	1.81	–7,559	–0.35

Notes: [a] The rates are calculated by dividing the number of migrants (*i.e.*, in, out, gross, and net migrants) by the number of mid-year population in the respective type of residence. The mid-year population is the total number of official residents living in each type of residence covered by the sample during 1984.

[b] Both county seats and small towns used in this study are designated urban towns. County seats refer to those towns where the government of the county is located.

characterized small towns. On balance, while the county seats gained most from migration, small towns were almost unaffected. Whichever indicator is used—in, out, gross or net migration rates—the city category is always at a middle level. These patterns reflect both the impact of government policy designed primarily to direct population away from cities and the general differentials in social and economic environments in the various types of urban residence and their consequent different attractiveness to migrants.

Under the current urban development strategy, county seats are among those places given priority by the government, and permanent migration to such locations is less restricted than to cities. At the same time, as the political, economic and cultural center of the county, the county seat has a relatively solid economic foundation and a relatively complete social service system and urban infrastructure. The social and economic environments in county seats are, therefore, more attractive to migrants than are other towns, and they also have greater capacity to absorb migrants. As a result, county seats often become the main destination for migrants.

These differentials vary when inter- and intraprovincial movement is considered jointly. Cities have the highest proportion of gross migrants who are interprovincial (22.3%), while the county seats have the lowest proportion (8.1%). Small towns and rural areas are intermediary with 14.9 and 8.7 percent, respectively, of their migrants coming from or going to other provinces. The high proportion of interprovincial migration to cities is understandable because more information about cities than about towns would be available in other provinces. Also, the concentration of universities and other research institutes, which are both the source and the destination for longer distance migrants, may help to explain why cities have the highest proportion of interprovincial migration.

Two thirds or more of the intraprovincial inmigrants in every type of residence come from rural areas (Table 2). By contrast, with the exception of small towns, about two thirds or more of interprovincial inmigrants in every type of residence come from urban areas; in small towns less than half of the small number of interprovincial migrants are urban in origin. Within the urban category, both for intraprovincial and for interprovincial migration, the higher the category is in the urban hierarchy, the fewer the inmigrants coming from rural areas, but the differences are considerably sharper for interprovincial than for intraprovincial migration. This pattern reflects the fact that the higher an urban place is in the urban hierarchy, the stricter the government controls on inmigration. This is especially true if the movement is from other provinces.

Nonetheless, at least for intraprovincial migration, the majority of inmigrants, not only to rural areas but also to urban places, come from rural areas. Since inmigration to urban places accounts for the majority (71%) of all inmigration covered by these data, it is clear that the main stream of

TABLE 2

INMIGRATION BY TYPE OF ORIGIN, TYPE OF MOVE, AND RESIDENCE ZHEJIANG PROVINCE, 1984[a]

	Intraprovincial Migration					Interprovincial Migration				
		Origin					Origin			
		Urban		Rural			Urban		Rural	
Destination	Total No.	No.	%	No.	%	Total No.	No.	%	No.	%
City	14,095	4,754	33.7	9,341	66.3	3,793	2,758	72.7	1,035	27.3
County Seat	5,279	1,681	31.8	3,598	68.2	368	240	65.2	128	34.8
Small Town	1,841	455	24.7	1,386	75.3	230	114	49.6	116	50.4
Total Urban	21,215	6,890	32.5	14,325	67.5	4,391	3,112	70.9	1,279	29.1
Rural	4,388	583	13.3	3,805	86.7	710	482	67.9	228	32.1
Total	25,603	7,473	29.2	18,130	70.8	5,101	3,594	70.5	1,507	29.5

Note: [a] The numbers of inmigrants do not add up to the numbers in Table 1 because those of unknown origin were excluded.

intraprovincial migration and consequently overall internal migration in Zhejiang is rural-urban. On the surface, this seems to contradict the government's concerted effort to control rural-urban migration. The explanation lies, in part, in the different size of the total urban and rural populations from which these migrants come. Since the rural population in Zhejiang is almost three times as large as the urban population, rural-urban migration, which is twice as numerous as urban-urban migration in absolute terms (14,325 vs. 6,890), is, in fact, relatively smaller than urban-urban migration; the rural-urban intraprovincial outmigration rate is only 6.7 per 1,000 rural population compared to 9.3 per 1,000 for the urban-urban rate.

Except in small towns, the majority of interprovincial inmigrants do come from urban places (Table 2). This suggests that the stricter control and the greater difficulty involved in interprovincial migration have together made interprovincial migration mainly an urban phenomenon. Two additional factors may be important for the patterns observed. First, an Army Unit based in one of the small towns covered by the sample receives wives and children of the military officers every year. The considerable number of military officers who come from rural areas in other provinces may explain the exceptionally low proportion of interprovincial urban migrants to small towns. The second factor is the movement of demobilized military personnel. In China, when soldiers are demobilized most return to their places of origin. Such movement accounted for 35.7 percent of all interprovincial migration to rural areas. Since military bases are mainly located in urban places, this movement may explain the high proportion of interprovincial inmigrants to rural areas who came from urban places. Also, given the stricter control on migration to cities and county seats from other provinces, some interprovincial would-be city or county seat migrants may first move to small towns or rural areas rather than directly to cities. This may also explain why small towns and rural areas both have higher interprovincial migration than county seats.

For outmigration, a different picture emerges (Table 3). Little difference in inter- and intraprovincial migration characterizes the various types of urban residence. For both interprovincial and intraprovincial migration, the dominant stream is movement to urban places (over 70%). In rural areas, however, the percentage of outmigrants moving to urban areas is much lower for intraprovincial than for interprovincial migration (43.9% vs. 72%). Clearly, urban places are relatively less accessible to rural-origin migrants moving within the province. This may result from a combination of the small number of rural-urban migrants due to strict control of government policy and the large volume of rural-rural migrants (especially women) involved in marriage-related migration.

The major difference in destination between intraprovincial and interprovincial migrants from rural areas may be explained by the fact that the longer the distance, the more difficult the migration is—economically, psychologically and administratively. Therefore, for rural residents to decide to move out of the province, a much stronger pull force is necessary than for movement within the province. Such a strong pull usually exists in urban areas—better environment, better employment, better educational opportunities. At the same time, the differences in interprovincial outmigration from rural areas may also be partly accounted for by the much higher proportion of students but the much lower proportion of marriage-related migration, since all of the former go to urban places but almost all of the latter go to rural destinations.

TABLE 3
OUTMIGRATION BY TYPE OF DESTINATION, TYPE OF MOVE, AND RESIDENCE
ZHEJIANG, 1984[a]

	Intraprovincial Migration					Interprovincial Migration				
		Destination					Destination			
	Total	Urban		Rural		Total	Urban		Rural	
Origin	No.	No.	%	No.	%	No.	No.	%	No.	%
City	6,583	6,288	95.5	295	4.5	2,132	2,109	98.9	23	1.1
County Seat	1,458	1,056	72.4	402	27.6	223	169	75.8	54	24.0
Small Town	1,660	1,186	71.4	474	28.6	385	288	74.8	97	25.2
Total Urban	9,701	8,530	87.9	1,171	12.1	2,740	2,566	93.6	174	6.4
Rural	16,336	7,179	43.9	9,157	56.1	1,268	913	72.0	355	28.0
Total	26,037	15,709	60.3	10,328	39.7	4,008	3,479	86.8	529	13.2

Note: [a] The numbers of outmigrants do not add up to the numbers in Table 1 because those of unknown origin were excluded.

The differences in destination of outmigrants from different types of residence are, however, relatively greater than those characterizing inmigrants. Generally, urban places have a higher proportion of outmigrants to other urban areas than do rural areas. The difference is larger in intraprovincial than in interprovincial migration, and the largest difference is found between cities and all other types of residence—either urban or rural areas. Within the urban category, for both intraprovincial and interprovincial migration, the proportion of outmigrants going to rural areas shows an inverted relation with the urban hierarchy. Particularly few city residents moved to rural areas. This suggests that, in general, rural residents will as much as possible move to urban places while urban residents will try to retain their urban residence. In interprovincial migration, in both urban and rural areas, the migration streams tend to be more unidirectional—either urban goers or urban leavers.

Sex

Although most studies find that males are generally more mobile than females, the Zhejiang data show that the sex selectivity of migration is not uniform over space. While migrants to and from urban places are heavily male, migration between rural places is predominantly female, especially in intraprovincial migration (Table 4). The predominance of females is due to the large volume of marriage migration, consistent with the Chinese pattern of the bride moving to the village of her husband.

The particularly low sex ratio among migrants to and from towns may be related to some specific locational factors. As pointed out earlier, the location of an Army Unit in one of the small towns in the sample results in the movement of wives and children of the military officers every year. Another striking factor is the large proportion (though not significant in absolute number) of migrant children who moved following their adoption. Almost without exception, the children involved are female. Although most of these girls come from rural areas, the public institutions responsible for their adoptions are located in urban places, mainly county seats and cities. Since cities are relatively more distant from rural areas, most adoptions take place in county seats. For social, psychological and personal reasons, these babies are usually adopted by people from other provinces, which may contribute to the particularly low sex ratio among interprovincial outmigrants from towns.[5]

When inmigration is compared to outmigration, urban places generally have a higher sex ratio among outmigrants than among inmigrants; the opposite is true in rural places. The exceptions are interprovincial migration to and from county seats and intraprovincial migration to and from small towns. This pattern may reflect the differences in social and economic characteristics between urban and rural places and their resultant differentials in attractiveness for potential migrants. Given the great differentials in quality of life between urban and rural places, the direction of migration resulting from family reunion, in which more females (wives of urban residents) would be expected, generally favors urban places. Therefore, a higher proportion of such movement to rather than from urban places and

[5] In most cases, the biological parents of these children are unknown. They are usually brought to the public institution by other people. Therefore, at the time they are brought in, their origin is not clear, nor is their household registration available. As a result, they are usually not entered in inmigration records.

TABLE 4
SEX RATIO OF MIGRANTS BY TYPE OF MOVEMENT AND RESIDENCE
ZHEJIANG PROVINCE, 1984

Residence in 1984	Sex Ratio in Total Population	Sex Ratio in Total Migrants	Sex Ratio in Intraprovincial Migrants	Sex Ratio in Interprovincial Migrants
Inmigration				
City	107	178	170	213
County Seat	116	109	108	116
Small Town	109	124	133	73
Total Urban	110	154	148	189
Rural	107	58	52	116
Total	108	131	124	176
Outmigration				
City	107	428	510	273
County Seat	116	142	160	67
Small Town	109	122	132	87
Total Urban	110	281	311	201
Rural	107	50	47	100
Total	108	95	88	157

a higher proportion of movement from rather than to rural places may help explain the difference in sex ratio between rural and urban in and outmigration streams.

The smaller differentials in sex ratios of intraprovincial outmigrants and inmigrants from and to small towns may be explained by the argument cited above for rural areas, since small towns are similar to rural places in many respects. The lower sex ratio among interprovincial outmigrants from county seats compared to inmigrants may be due almost entirely to the large proportion of child migration.

Age

Previous migration research has consistently found evidence of age selectivity. A number of life cycle factors such as pursuing higher education, entering the labor market and first marriage account for the high percentage of migrants who are young adults. At the same time, because young adults have few well established ties at place of origin and are more able to adapt to new situations, it is easier for them to be mobile.

Regretably, the available tabulations by age provide only three categories: under 15 years, 15 to 59, and 60 and over. Among the three categories, the age group 15 to 59 approximates the working age population (the official retirement ages in China are 60 for males and 55 for females). Compared to the corresponding age composition of the total 1982 population in Zhejiang, shown in Table 5, the working age group is overrepresented among both inmigrants and outmigrants, while children and elderly people are underrepresented. The proportions of working age migrants are lower, and substantially so for most categories, in interprovincial than in intraprovincial migration in each type of residence. In each type of residence, both children and elderly people constitute a greater share of interprovincial than of intraprovincial inmigrants. This is especially true of child migrants, for whom the percentages are 18.7 and 7 for interprovincial and for intraprovincial migration respectively. This may reflect the higher proportion of attached family members moving with the key migrant in interprovincial migration which leads to a higher passive migration ratio, reflected in a higher proportion of dependent population—children and elderly people.

Urban places have a lower proportion of working age inmigrants than rural places, but the reverse is true of outmigration. Within the urban category, a positive relationship seems to exist between the proportion of working age migrants and the urban hierarchy. This is especially true for interprovincial migration. The patterns probably reflect the joint effect of socioeconomic differentials among residence and government policies regarding internal migration. While the overall socioeconomic differentials make urban places both more able to retain their residents and more attractive to potential migrants, especially these nonworking age population who need support from others, the intervention of government policies makes migration to urban places, especially cities, more difficult and hence more selective of age.

When inmigration and outmigration are compared, urban places generally have a higher proportion of working age migrants among outmigrants than among inmigrants, while rural places have a lower proportion of working age migrants among outmigrants than among inmigrants. This differential between urban and rural places again points to the role of the higher quality of urban life as a pull force both to attract potential migrants and to retain urban residents, especially the nonworking age population. But due to frequent job transfers, workers are more likely to leave involuntarily to go from one urban place to another, or even to rural areas. However, even when they do move, they frequently leave their families at urban origin, especially if the move is from urban to rural areas, or from big cities to small towns. Since men are more likely to be employed than women,

TABLE 5

DISTRIBUTION BY AGE OF MIGRANTS, BY TYPE OF MOVEMENT AND RESIDENCE IN ZHEJIANG PROVINCE, 1984

	Intraprovincial Migration					Interprovincial Migration				
	Age			Total		Age			Total	
Residence in 1984	Under 15	15–59	60 and Over	(%)	No.	Under 15	15–59	60 and Over	(%)	No.
Inmigration										
City	13.1	83.8	3.1	100.0	14,095	16.3	79.5	4.2	100.0	3,793
County Seat	17.5	79.2	3.3	100.0	5,279	29.6	66.6	3.8	100.0	368
Small Town	13.2	83.9	2.9	100.0	1,841	33.7	61.4	4.8	100.0	230
Total Urban	13.9	83.0	3.1	100.0	21,215	21.0	74.8	4.2	100.0	4,391
Rural	4.6	95.4	—	100.0	4,388	17.9	78.6	3.6	100.0	710
Total	7.0	92.2	0.8	100.0	25,603	18.7	77.6	3.7	100.0	5,101
Outmigration										
City	1.6	97.2	1.1	100.0	6,583	10.3	88.7	1.1	100.0	2,132
County Seat	13.3	84.4	2.3	100.0	1,458	45.3	51.1	3.6	100.0	223
Small Town	13.7	83.2	3.1	100.0	1,660	48.9	49.6	1.4	100.0	385
Total Urban	5.3	93.0	1.6	100.0	9,701	21.7	76.7	1.6	100.0	2,740
Rural	9.7	88.8	1.5	100.0	16,336	17.9	75.0	7.1	100.0	1,268
Total	8.6	89.9	1.5	100.0	26,037	18.9	75.4	5.7	100.0	4,008

Age Composition of Total Zhejiang Population in 1982

	Under 15	15–59	60 and Over	Total %
Cities	24.3	66.3	9.4	100.0
Total Towns	24.4	67.2	8.4	100.0
Rural	31.0	60.4	8.6	100.0
Total	29.3	62.0	8.7	100.0

particularly in government sectors which have a high frequency of promotion and work transfer, this lends further strength to the earlier explanation for the higher sex ratio among out than among inmigrants to urban places.

Education

Education also helps to account for migrant differentials. Because higher education is conducive to higher aspirations, higher education may work as a counterforce against tradition and makes its recipients more responsive to opportunities elsewhere. Data presented in Table 6 support the positive selectivity of education.

The education-specific inmigration rates shown in Table 6 indicate a clear positive relation between educational attainment and propensity to move. The inmigration rates for the college educated are especially high, and those of the middle school group are also above average. Among migrants, interprovincial migrants have a higher education level than intraprovincial migrants (measured roughly by the sum of college and middle school migrants; all references to "average education level of migrants" in this section refer to this sum, unless otherwise indicated). This general pattern suggests that internal migration streams in Zhejiang are very differentiated by education.

Among different types of residence, urban places both send and receive migrants with a higher education than do rural places; but in intraprovincial migration, those with college educations in rural areas seem to be more actively involved in outmigration than their counterparts in urban places. In addition to the fact that urban residents have, on average, a higher education level than rural residents (Table 7), government policies may be the major cause of the striking differentials in the educational composition of migrants between urban and rural places. Under the general consideration of "substituting quality for quantity" in admitting migrants to urban places, rural-urban and urban-urban migration, especially the former, are positively selective of education. At the same time, the minimum educational attainment usually required for urban employment further prevents those from the lower end of the educational scale from coming into urban places on a permanent basis. These same factors may make it relatively easier for rural residents with higher education to receive permission to move to urban places, which in turn makes them more mobile than their urban counterparts. In addition, movement motivated by pursuit of further education in urban centers is itself highly selective of the more educated.

While the proportion of college educated urban inmigrants is positively related to the urban hierarchy, it shows a negative relation to outmigration; for interprovincial migration, in both in and outmigration, the majority of highly educated migrants are concentrated in cities. This reflects, on the one hand, the fact that the degree of control of inmigration is positively related to urban hierarchy and, on the other hand, the concentration of opportunities requiring higher education in cities.

Overview of Permanent Migration

In sum, because of the restriction on free permanent migration, less than three percent of the population have made permanent moves within one year. Compared to the annual rate in other countries (Long and Boertlin,

TABLE 6

THE EDUCATIONAL COMPOSITION OF MIGRANTS AGED 12 AND OVER AND RATES OF MIGRATION BY TYPE OF MOVEMENT AND TYPE OF RESIDENCES, 1984

Type of Residence in 1984	Intraprovincial Migration					Interprovincial Migration				
	College	Middle School	Primary School	Illiterate	Total no.	College	Middle School	Primary School	Illiterate	Total no.
					Percentage Distribution					
Inmigration										
City	7.9	82.5	7.7	2.0	12,334	23.4	70.3	5.2	1.1	3,242
County Seat	6.9	75.8	13.5	3.8	4,579	6.1	69.7	21.2	3.0	278
Small Town	5.1	71.4	20.0	3.4	1,549	6.3	62.5	31.3	—	144
Total Urban	7.4	79.9	10.1	2.5	18,462	21.3	70.0	7.5	1.2	3,664
Rural	4.3	54.2	32.1	9.3	4,109	—	66.2	20.6	13.2	609
Total	6.9	75.2	14.1	3.8	22,571	18.3	69.4	9.4	2.9	4,273
Outmigration										
City	1.1	96.5	1.8	0.6	6,333	12.2	83.1	3.8	0.9	1,897
County Seat	3.5	79.9	15.3	1.4	1,289	6.7	66.7	20.0	6.7	134
Small Town	7.0	72.7	18.2	2.1	1,283	—	84.2	15.8	—	166
Total Urban	2.3	90.7	6.1	0.9	8,905	10.9	82.2	5.7	1.2	2,197
Rural	1.2	50.5	37.7	10.7	13,064	—	58.6	29.3	12.1	939
Total	1.6	65.2	26.1	7.1	21,969	7.4	74.7	13.2	4.7	3,136
					Education-specific Migration Rate[a]					
Inmigration										
Urban	97.0	52.1	7.1	2.6	24.9	55.4	9.1	1.0	0.2	4.9
Rural	82.5	4.3	1.5	0.5	1.9	—	0.8	0.1	0.1	0.3
Total	90.0	21.0	2.8	1.0	7.8	45.2	3.7	0.3	0.1	1.5
Outmigration										
Urban	14.5	28.5	2.1	0.4	12.0	17.0	6.4	0.5	0.1	3.0
Rural	73.2	12.6	5.5	1.9	6.1	—	1.1	0.3	0.2	0.4
Total	20.3	17.7	5.0	1.7	7.6	13.4	2.9	0.4	0.2	1.1

Note: [a] The education-specific migration rates are calculated by dividing the total number of migrants with a specific occupation by the number of persons with the same education for the total population for each category of residence that is covered by the sample. The denominator is based on the educational composition for the total population in the 1982 Census. For example, the intraprovincial inmigration rate for those with college education of the sample as a whole is calculated as: R=(6.9*22,571)/(0.6*2,883,200)=90.0 per 1000. The population base is the population of the sample. Therefore, for inmigration, it is the population at the destination while for outmigration, it is the population at the origin.

TABLE 7

THE EDUCATIONAL COMPOSITION OF TOTAL POPULATION AGED 12 AND OVER, BY TYPE OF RESIDENCE, ZHEJIANG, 1982

Type of Residence	College	Middle School	Primary School	Illiterate	Total (%)
City[a]	1.9	35.4	35.7	27.0	100.00
Total Towns	2.0	44.3	34.9	18.9	100.00
Total Urban	1.9	38.2	35.4	24.4	100.00
Rural	0.1	24.4	41.8	33.7	100.00
Total	0.6	28.1	40.1	31.2	100.00

Note: [a] The relatively lower education of residents in cities than in towns results from the inclusion of the outer suburbs of small cities in the statistics of city population. This part of the population accounted for 57.3 percent of the total city population in the 1982 Census. Such overbounding is not the case in towns. That is why, as reflected in the statistics, city residents have a relatively lower education than town residents.

1976; Long, 1988), Zhejiang's rate of permanent migration is low. Moreover, most permanent migration took place within the province. Nonetheless, although rural-urban migration is strictly controlled by government policy, such movement still accounts for a considerable proportion of all migration. While migrants of urban origin predominantly move to other urban places, migrants from rural places will as much as possible move to urban places. On balance, urban places gain population while rural places lose population.

The pattern of sex differentials of internal migration in Zhejiang is not uniform. While migrants to and from urban places are heavily male, migration between rural places is predominantly female. Although there are exceptions, working age persons are overrepresented while children and elderly people are underrepresented in migration streams. With respect to education, a clear positive relation between the propensity to move and educational attainment has been observed regardless of types of residence. Those with college educations from rural areas are, however, more actively involved in outmigration than their urban counterparts. The differences between types of residence are probably due more to differences in policy intervention than to individual and community socioeconomic characteristics. Overall, the intervention of government policy makes internal migration in Zhejiang more selective.

TEMPORARY MIGRATION IN ZHEJIANG

As pointed out earlier, temporary migration has increased rapidly during the years following economic reform in China. As a result, permanent migration as defined by the household registration system is no longer fully representative of population mobility in China. Available data strongly suggest that temporary migrants account for more than ten percent of the resident population in most big cities (Huang, 1985). Compared to an annual permanent migration rate of under three percent, the number of persons involved in temporary migration is far greater. Attention to such movement becomes essential, therefore, in any assessment of the impact of movement on urbanization.

If the lack of data has been the major obstacle to the study of permanent migration, the situation is even worse with respect to temporary migration. Most literature dealing with temporary migration has been largely limited to its volume and direction. With data from the Zhejiang Provincial Public Security Bureau (ZPPSB, 1985), some characteristics of temporary migrants in Zhejiang province may be examined.

In total, 106,799 temporary migrants were recorded in the city of Hangzhou at the end of 1984; they accounted for more than ten percent of the resident population (973,366). Similarly, when all six cities in the ZPPSB study are aggregated, the 205,620 temporary migrants constituted about ten percent of the approximately two million city resident population. In view of these statistics, which represent a minimum estimate of temporary migrants, the stability of the Chinese population suggested by data on permanent migration may well be a misstatement.

The increasing temporary migration resulting from economic reforms has been largely economically motivated (Table 8). In most of the six cities, economic motives were cited by more than half of all temporary migrants, and the proportion of economically motivated migration is generally higher in the cities than in the suburban counties. The exceptions are Wenzhou and Shaoxing, where the proportion of economically motivated temporary migrants in cities is less than 50 percent and where the proportion is lower in the cities than in the suburban counties. These data suggest that temporary migrants in Zhejiang are mainly responding to economic opportunities outside their origin places, and that economic opportunities are more available in cities than in surrounding counties. However, when small town and township industries (as in Shaoxing) or private businesses (as in Wenzhou) are highly developed and widely distributed, the potential migrants are also absorbed at the county level. In these places, more temporary migrants to cities are moving for reasons other than direct economic considerations.

Males generally greatly outnumber females among temporary migrants to cities (Table 9), again with the exception of Wenzhou and Shaoxing. In conjunction with the data in Table 8, the observed patterns suggest that male migrants are moving mainly for economic reasons while females are more

TABLE 8

TEMPORARY MIGRANTS BY MAJOR REASONS, ZHEJIANG PROVINCE, 1984

City/County[a]	Economic Factors	To Study	To Visit	For Health Purposes	Foster Care[b]	Other	Total Number
Hangzhou							
City	60.0	3.0	9.8	1.9	2.5	22.6	106,799
Suburban County	58.0	15.0	6.4	1.3	12.5	6.2	33,248
Ningbo							
City	55.2	4.6	18.1	0.2	7.2	14.7	35,203
Suburban County	43.7	19.5	2.2	0.1	14.4	20.0	47,818
Wenzhou							
City	33.0	4.5	23.7	0.4	24.2	14.2	23,574
Suburban County	40.2	10.3	1.1	0.02	27.7	20.7	37,553
Jiaxing							
City	78.1	9.8	3.9	0.2	7.1	0.9	10,577
Suburban County	68.8	12.9	6.6	0.1	5.3	6.8	30,696
Huzhou							
City	76.6	4.6	5.0	0.3	8.4	5.2	18,805
Suburban County	66.4	5.7	4.0	0.2	5.8	18.0	20,967
Shaoxing							
City	37.7	4.7	7.0	0.8	21.6	28.4	10,662
Suburban County	54.4	5.4	19.2	0.7	3.0	17.1	15,891

Notes: [a] Counties under the jurisdiction of the city. The statistics include only temporary migrants in urban towns.

[b] Foster care involves sending children to relatives and occasionally to friends who help to rear them. This occurs most often to the children of persons who formerly lived in the city and were sent to the countryside during the Cultural Revolution.

likely to move for noneconomic considerations. In particular, a considerable proportion of these temporary migrants are contract construction workers, almost all of whom are males. This may explain why males outnumber females among temporary migrants in general and the especially high sex ratio in Hangzhou in particular.

The majority of temporary migrants are temporary only because they have not changed their official household registration. In fact, most have

TABLE 9

SEX COMPOSITION OF TEMPORARY MIGRANTS[a]
ZHEJIANG PROVINCE, 1984

Cities	Males	Females	Sex Ratio
Hangzhou	76,948	29,851	258
Ningbo	20,485	14,718	139
Wenzhou	10,960	12,610	87
Jiaxing	7,235	3,342	216
Huzhou	12,251	6,554	187
Shaoxing	4,380	6,282	70

Note: [a] Data by sex were available only for city temporary migrants.

been living in urban places for quite a long time. Except in Hangzhou, more than 60 percent of the temporary migrants have spent more than one year at their destination, with the highest being over 82 percent in both the city and surrounding counties of Wenzhou (Table 10). This may, however, partly reflect the disproportional omission of very short-term temporary migrants from the coverage provided by these data. On the whole, cities have a higher

TABLE 10

TEMPORARY MIGRANTS BY DURATION OF RESIDENCE[a]
ZHEJIANG PROVINCE, 1984

City/Suburban County	Less Than 3 Mos.	3 Mos.– 1 Year	1–5 Years	More Than 5 Years	Total	
					Percent	Number
Hangzhou						
City	31.4	44.3	18.4	5.9	100.0	106,799
Suburban County[b]	7.1	32.5	35.7	24.7	100.0	33,248
Ningbo						
Inner City	11.8	24.6	39.3	24.3	100.0	35,203
Suburban	8.9	12.3	46.3	32.5	100.0	47,818
Wenzhou						
Inner City	2.7	15.1	30.2	52.0	100.0	23,574
Suburban	3.9	12.9	20.6	62.6	100.0	37,553

Notes: [a] Data for duration of residence were available only for these three cities.

proportion of shorter duration temporary migrants than suburban counties. This may be because economically motivated migrants move more frequently with changes in availability of opportunities. On the other hand, the pattern may reflect the stricter control on moving to cities and the greater difficulty of living there without official household registration compared to moving to and living in surrounding counties.

Finally, temporary migrants primarily come from the direct hinterlands of the urban places and the rural-urban stream is increasing in terms of both absolute volume and in relation to the urban-urban stream. For example, a report issued for Hangzhou city as of April, 1984 indicated 92,419 registered temporary residents, of whom 23,745 were either construction workers, domestic workers or repair workers (these three types of workers came mainly from rural places). There were, in addition, an estimated 100,000 nonregistered temporary migrants. By April, 1985, the total number of registered temporary migrants had increased to 134,485, of whom 52,917 were in the above three occupational categories. Within one year, while the total number of temporary migrants increased 45.5 percent, the number in just the above three categories more than doubled, and their percentage of all registered temporary migrants increased from 25.7 to 39.4 (Hangzhou Public Security Bureau, 1984 and 1985). More than 85 percent of the temporary migrants came from within the province.

In sum, these data suggest that temporary migration in Zhejiang is a major mechanism by which the labor force responds to disparities in economic opportunities in both rural and urban areas. In doing so, men seem to have clear advantages over women, probably as a result of both the nature of the opportunities (*e.g.*, construction work, instability of location) and women's stronger attachment to family and traditional sex roles. For example, women are usually more emotionally tied to children and the family; social norms usually specify that women should take care of most domestic matters, while men should be responsible for the survival of the family, economically and socially. This is clearly reflected in the standards usually used in judging men and women. A woman is respected for being a good wife and loving mother while a man is usually evaluated for his career success. However, most of the temporary migrants are temporary only because they do not officially change household registration. In fact, with the exception of the city of Hangzhou, they stay at their destination for quite a long time and are therefore de facto permanent migrants.

CONCLUSION

China's attempts simultaneously to achieve rural development and to strictly control permanent migration, especially to big cities, provide a striking contrast to other developing countries. China's concerted effort to limit urban growth by controlling and directing population movement in the face of growing rural labor surpluses has led to heavy temporary movement and commuting and to the development of small towns as alternative urban destinations.

In China, temporary movement has come to be seen as serving a two-fold purpose: 1) it minimizes the risk involved in a shift away from the production of basic crops into more diversified agriculture (*See,* Roberts, 1982) and 2) given the efficiencies in labor utilization introduced by improved technology and more effective organization, together with the higher levels of motivation for profits resulting from introduction of the responsibility system, such movement allows and stimulates growing numbers of peasants to seek the benefits of urban employment through migration. With permanent change in residence, especially to big and medium cities, still largely impossible, temporary movement provides a viable alternative for many.

It may well be, too, that the Chinese government may also be allowing such increased mobility as an experiment to assess its value for coping with the surplus rural labor, with the labor force and service needs of cities, and with rural needs for greater resources for development. Temporary migration may be favored because it helps to avoid the social dislocation and the added strain on cities that large-scale permanent migration may create (Standing, 1985). From a government point of view, the attractiveness of temporary mobility is enhanced by the ability to relax or tighten control over such movement as conditions in urban and rural places change. Permanent migration would be more difficult to reverse.

Given the considerable differentials in quality of life between urban and rural places and among different types of urban residence, analysis of the data for Zhejiang suggests strongly that the volume of permanent migration is undoubtedly less than it would have been if there were no intervention of government policies and regulations. However, the low level of population movement is only true in terms of changes in official residence, *i.e.*, those reflected in the household registration. The population is by no means sedentary, but has been actively involved in spatial movement, especially after 1978 when economic reforms were initiated. This is documented by the considerable volume of temporary migration. Even though the total number of temporary migrants is probably greatly underreported, the fact that the recorded number constitutes at least ten percent of the resident city population and that the likely number is closer to 15 to 20 percent indicates the magnitude of such movement to urban places. Even at the ten percent level, the volume of population involved in temporary migration is three times greater than the three percent recorded for permanent migration. Clearly, permanent migration has become only a small part of total movement, and temporary migration plays a particularly key role in urban places.

Within the political and economic system in China, these temporary residents will not burden the cities' educational facilities, employment and subsidized or rationed food supplies because they do not change their household registration and hence are not entitled to government assistance in these areas, as official city residents are. In reality, however, many of them are living, working and studying in the urban destinations for prolonged periods. Therefore, a substantial proportion are de facto city residents. While temporary residents provide cities with services that are needed by both the urban economy and the urban residents, they also utilize nearly all aspects of the urban infrastructure—housing, transportation, power, sanitation and general supplies of daily food and consumer goods and amenities. Therefore, in considering the impact of migration on the overall social-economic development in urban places, these de facto residents must be taken into account. Failure to do so could lead to serious problems in planning for urban services and the quality of urban life.

The analysis suggests that the intervention of migration policies and regulations generally make internal permanent urbanward migration positively selective in terms of education. Although such positive selectivity may be beneficial to economic development in urban places, it will accentuate the shortage of educated personnel and professionals who are urgently needed for the social and economic development in rural areas and even in towns. This "brain drain" is a serious problem that local governments in rural areas and towns are already facing.

While the specific approaches being used in China for channeling migration and achieving development are not unique, the scope and speed at which they are occurring and the role of the government in fostering the processes, if not actually controlling them in detail, certainly raises questions about the applicability of the experience to other developing countries. Time and fuller evaluation of all the factors are essential before reaching conclusions about the value of China's experience for other LDCs. Nonetheless, as other developing countries with no restrictions on movement also turn to rural development and a "bottom up approach" as the major mechanism for reducing urban/rural inequalities and for stemming migration to cities, the Chinese experience takes on special relevance.

Conversely, as the greater flexibility that China has allowed in its rural and urban economic systems creates pressures for more flexibility in its migration policies, China must learn from the experience of other developing countries that have already faced the distribution consequences of a much greater degree of freedom of movement than China is likely to allow in the foreseeable future. Most important is the evidence that strongly suggests that for China and other developing countries, temporary migration, whether part of official policy or not, has come to play a key role as a coping mechanism in the process of rural development.

China's experience, consistent with that of a number of other developing countries (Chapman and Prothero, 1983), teaches us that many people in these countries are, in fact, neither exclusively rural nor exclusively urban; that the dichotomies on which we have relied so heavily are artifacts of our classification scheme rather than a reflection of reality. Many persons may have bilocal or even multilocal residence patterns. The interests of these individual movers as well as of the rural and urban communities of which they are a part and to which they make important contributions can best be served by policies that take account of the needs of the resident populations in both locations as well as those who move between them. To be successful, such policies require that we recognize and give attention to all forms of population movement, including temporary movement, in our theoretical formulations, in our research and in our efforts to develop effective policies. Temporary movement may well provide an important mechanism for coping with problems of big cities and overurbanization and concurrently with efforts to achieve rural development and to reduce inequalities between rural and urban places.

Given these possibilities, the results of this analysis strongly suggest the need for a shift of research priorities to population mobility forms other than those documented by the migration registration system. The data provided by the migration registration system encompass only a small part of overall population mobility. Moreover, these data reflect more government planned involuntary migration and the differences in the ability to get permission to move, rather than individual behavior in response to opportunities. To overcome these limitations, more comprehensive data on population movement, covering both permanent and temporary movement and collected by specially designed national or provincial surveys, is urgently needed both for the scholarly insights they will provide on population movement and for policy considerations.

REFERENCES

Chapman, M. and R.M. Prothero
1983 "Themes in Circulation in the Third World," *International Migration Review*, 17:597–632. Winter.

Du, W.
1986 "Floating Population to and from Beijing City," *Population and Economics*, 1:12–14.

Goldstein, S. and A. Goldstein
1985 Population Mobility in the People's Republic of China. Papers of the East-West Population Institute, No. 95. Honolulu: East-West Population Institute. October.

Gray, J. and G. White, eds.
1982 *China's New Development Strategy*. New York: Academic Press, Inc.

Hangzhou Public Security Bureau
1985 Quarterly Population Report, 2. Hangzhou, China: Hangzhou Public Security Bureau.

____
1984 Quarterly Population Report, 2. Hangzhou, China: Hangzhou Public Security Bureau.

Huang, Z.
1985 "The Population Problem in the Urban Economic Reform," *Population Periodical*, 6:1–4.

Long, L.H.
1988 *Migration and Residential Mobility in the United States*. New York: Russell Sage Foundation.

Long, L.H. and C.G. Boertlin
1976 "The Geographical Mobility of Americans." *Current Population Reports*, Series P-23, No. 64. Washington, DC: U.S. Bureau of the Census.

People's Daily
1986 Overseas edition: Dec. 20.

Roberts, K.D.
1982 "Agrarian Structure and Labor Mobility in Rural Mexico," *Population and Development Review*, 8:299–322. June.

Standing, G. ed.
1985 *Labour Circulation and the Labour Process*. London: Croom Helm.

Tu, L.
1985 "The Population Size of Big Cities Under the Economic Reform," *Population Periodical*, 6:22–25.

Yang, X.
1985 "The City Floating Population under the Economic Reform," *Population Periodical*, 6:38–42.

Zhejiang Provincial Public Security Bureau
1985 *Yearly Reports*, Hangzhou, China: ZPPSB.

[12]

POPULATION REDISTRIBUTION POLICIES IN GREAT BRITAIN

JAMES H. JOHNSON
UNIVERSITY OF LANCASTER
ENGLAND

JOHN SALT
UNIVERSITY COLLEGE LONDON
ENGLAND

ABSTRACT

A survey of migration policy in Great Britain is presented, with special reference to labour migration. There are three strands of government policy. One is the restriction of the growth of the built-up areas of London and other large cities, with, as a result, residential population being steered into satellite towns. A second is the creation of jobs in the Assisted Areas to reduce the outward flow of population from these economically less-fortunate regions. A third is the direct financial assistance of migrants, usually unemployed, who wish to move to jobs elsewhere. In addition to government intervention, privately-financed movements, involving assistance from employers, form a fourth policy element.

During the last decade reduced levels of fertility have led to parallel falls in natural increase over many parts of the developed world. Although prediction of future birth rates has become notoriously difficult, planners now have to face the strong possibility that, at least in Britain and in most other countries in Western Europe, the period of relatively rapid population increase since the end of the Second World War is at last at an end.

An underlying concern of the planning strategies of many developed countries has been the provision of homes and jobs to accommodate population growth. This concern has not been merely national: plans for major regions within States have often assumed that regional natural increases would more than off-set migration loss. One result was that it could be quietly expected that if, for example, too many houses were placed in a particular region, this over-provision would be quite easily adjusted in the longer-term as total regional population grew. The new demographic situation, however, means that errors in the allocation of regional investment are becoming much more difficult to correct.

The demographic problems associated with planning the right levels of local investment in housing have been compounded by the new situation which is also emerging with regard to employment. The current economic recession, at first associated with rises in oil prices, is now giving way to more permanent structural changes, in which the previous relationship between economic growth and increasing employment appears to be much less firm than in the past, especially in high-wage economies. Even if economic recovery is sustained, jobs in manufacturing industry are likely to be scarcer; and it is becoming much more risky to disturb those few areas with potential job surpluses by relocating jobs in regions of higher unemployment, since any external economies that can be derived in the more fortunate locations may have to be cherished.

Population migration is thus taking on much greater significance for two reasons. First, it is becoming a more powerful demographic factor in producing changing population totals in major regions. Second, migration now has a more direct role as a positive instrument in planning policy, since the redistribution of population to take advantage of available opportunities is of growing importance. In most of the developed countries of the West, however, one looks in vain for a coherent, all-embracing national migration policy, although there is often a wide range of more limited, sometimes contradictory policies, which have a direct influence on population movements.

This paper attempts to survey the situation in Great Britain, concentrating attention on 'labour migration', that is the movement of population which involves a simultaneous change of both job and home. This is the most important type of migration for the changing map of population distribution. Migration of this kind results in relatively long-distance relocation of skills and thus has an important bearing on regional contrasts in economic change. It involves a move from one community to another, making an important impact on the social life of the families and communities involved. As a result it is the type of population migration with which government policies are predominantly concerned.

The British census does not publish the number of labour migrants, but a surrogate measure may be derived from the matrix of movements among 126 Standard Metropolitan Labour Areas (SMLAs), which are based on the larger employment centres and their surrounding commuting hinterlands (Drewett 1968; Drewett et al. 1974). In 1970–71 migration between these employment centres was 891,010, accounting for 75 % of all internal migration recorded in the census (Flowerdew and Salt 1979). The geographical pattern of moves was dominated by London; other notable migration streams linked the largest urban areas outside London; and there were a number of regions where there were more local clusters of flows (Fig. 1). One example of this is in north-west England, with much interconnection between the numerous small SMLAs around the major centres of Manchester and Liverpool (Johnson et al. 1974: 69–99).

In Britain there are three strands of government policy which have implications for this pattern of longer-distance population migration and which, in the last resort, have been inspired by ideas about desirable population distribution. First, the growth of the continuous built-up area of Greater London and other large cities has been resisted, with residential growth being steered to satellite settlements (some of them New Towns). Second, the movement of population out from the Assisted Areas* has been seen as undesirable, and as a result new jobs have been created in these areas. The measures by which these two aims have been implemented are only indirectly related to population movements, although they obviously influence them.

The third strand of Government policy is directly aimed at aiding movement of population, but has been more concerned with the problems of individual families, rather than with a grander geographical strategy. Sometimes the actual population movements produced by this have run counter to the more general geographical strategy implicit in other aspects of policy. More important, population movements which the government has directly encouraged by grants-in-aid have been quite insignificant in comparison with the broader inter-urban population movements which have been privately financed, either by employers (including the nationalized industries) or employees. These private movements form a fourth policy element, in so far as individual organisations plan the movements of their employees. This is by far the least known aspect of migration in Britain (Johnson and Salt 1980).

NEW TOWNS AND POPULATION REDISTRIBUTION

One strand of government intervention in population migration since the Second World War has

* The term includes the Special Development Areas, the Development Areas, all of which have varying levels of government assistance for the encouragement of the growth of employment.

Fig. 1. Major migration flows between S.M.L.A.'s 1970–1971.

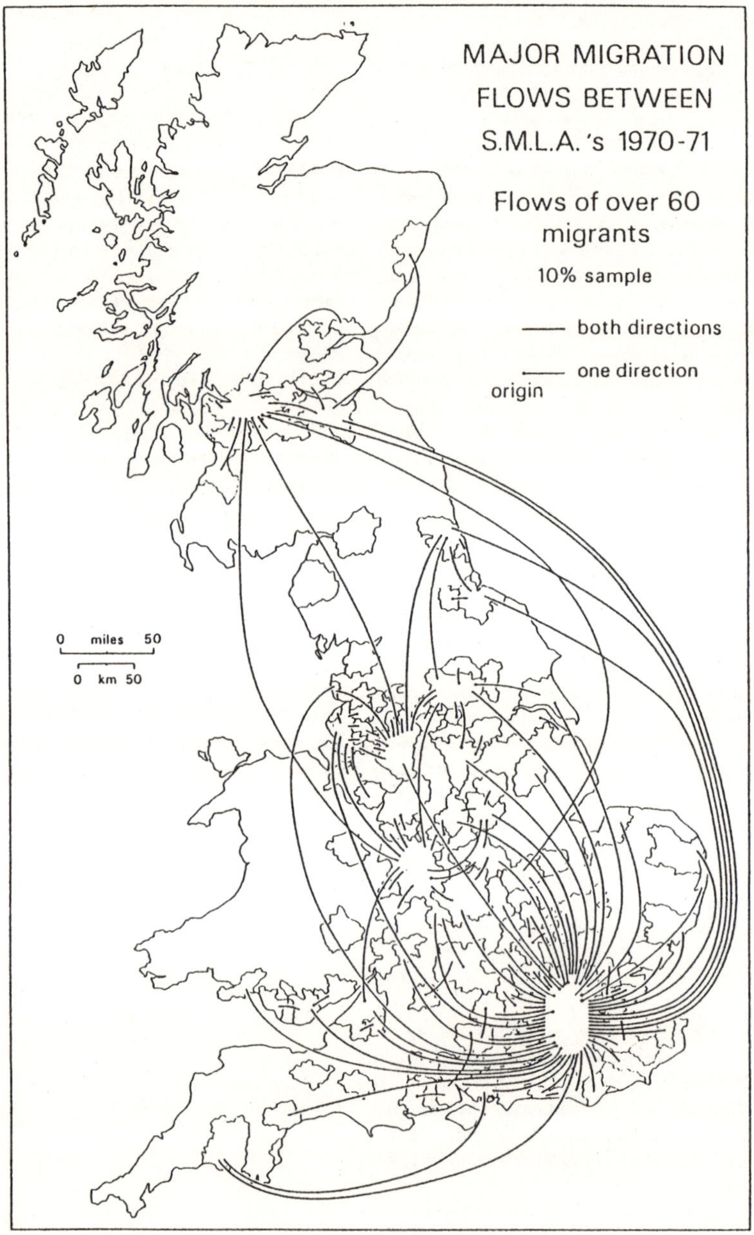
MAJOR MIGRATION
FLOWS BETWEEN
S.M.L.A.'s 1970-71
Flows of over 60
migrants
10% sample
both directions
one direction
origin
0 miles 50
0 km 50

been at the scale of individual conurbations. This is best exemplified in south-east England, where this policy of decentralization to New Towns had its beginnings. In Patrick Abercrombie's famous Greater London Plan, produced during the closing years of the War, a vital aspect was the relocation of population and employment to relieve the pressures in inner London. Abercrombie estimated that 415,000 people would have to move out of inner London to reduce residential densities to tolerable levels, but that the total for the whole metropolitan area would be over one million people. Of these, Abercrombie proposed that 383,000 should be housed in eight New Towns around London, 261,000 in additions to existing towns close to London, 164,000 in towns outside the London region but within a 50-mile radius, and 100,000 beyond the influence of London (Abercrombie 1945: 14).

During the immediate post-war years, in addition to eight London New Towns, six other New Towns were designated elsewhere in Britain, but of these only East Kilbride (associated with Glasgow in Scotland) was primarily intended as an area for overspill. A second theme was thus introduced into the motives for the establishments of new towns – the provision of an environment for economic growth in regions where older industries were in decay. In the late 1950s another batch of New Towns was designated, again aimed at fostering regional development, while also drawing surplus population from large cities. For example, Skelmersdale and Runcorn were associated with Liverpool, Redditch and Telford with Birmingham, and Irvine with Glasgow. Then in the late 1960s a further wave was initiated in which a development corporation and an existing local authority were to work together in expanding quite substantial existing towns. For example, Northampton and Peterborough were associated with London, and Warrington was expected to draw population from Manchester, During this latest period, too, Milton Keynes was designated and was intended to become a new city of 250,000 people, providing a counter-magnet for economic growth, some 80 km from London and drawing population from there (Strachan 1974: 64).

In total the New Towns now represent a shift of over one million people. Of course many of these people would have moved away from the conurbations in any case, but the movement would have been more widely dispersed and haphazard. It was a movement, too, in which people on waiting lists for local authority housing found it possible to be accommodated more rapidly by moving to a New Town, with the Industrial Selection Scheme being designed to link the changing employment needs of the New Towns with the population of London and the West Midlands. No other encouragement to move was necessary (except for a relatively small proportion of key workers), since the attraction was a new home in a location where employment was likely to expand rapidly.

Some indication of the significance of migration in the New Towns can be derived from Table 1, based on their migration experience between 1966 and 1971. In some of the recent New Towns over 40 per cent of the total population was made up of migrants who arrived during this short five-year period (Skelmersdale, 50 per cent; Cumbernauld, 41 per cent). Even in established towns the percentage arriving during this period was high. For example, over 20 per cent of the population of Stevenage, 17 per cent of the population of Hemel Hempstead and 30 per cent of the population of Bracknell were in-migrants between 1966 and 1971. Out-migration was also high, particularly in some of the less economically successful towns. During the same period, for instance, 23 per cent of the 1966 population of Glenrothes left as out-migrants, 21 per cent in Washington, and 27 per cent in Livingston. Around London out-migration was lower, but still important. Hemel Hempstead, Stevenage and Crawley had losses of between 15 per cent and 17 per cent. These London New Towns formed part of the residential system around London and this may simply represent a normal turn-over of population. In such circumstances even the most successful New Towns will have out-migrants.

The more general effects of New Towns on population redistribution are more difficult to isolate, since they embrace only a small part of migration associated with the larger conurbations. In the five years up to the 1971 census, for exam-

Table 1. Migration 1966–71 in Selected New Towns.

	In-migrants % of 1971 population	Out-migrants % of 1966 population	Net migration % growth 1966–71
Basildon	19.0	15.3	5.8
Bracknell	30.3	21.1	15.6
Carwley	16.4	17.5	0.2
Glenrothes	38.3	23.1	22.3
Harlow	17.7	12.7	6.6
Hatfield	20.2	19.5	2.2
Hemel Hempstead	17.2	15.3	5.6
Livingston	66.3	27.0	61.4
Milton Keynes	22.3	16.7	8.3
Stevenage	20.9	16.3	7.2
Washington	21.8	21.0	4.5
Welwyn	13.0	16.8	−3.1

(after Champion, Clegg and Davies 1977: 70).

ple, the 28 New Towns in Britain received only just over 12 per cent of the net migration loss from the seven official conurbations. Only 8 per cent of the gross movement from the conurbations went to New Towns during these five years, although the precise proportion varied from conurbations to conurbation (Champion et al. 1977: 73). In other words, in recent years the New Towns have not been taking an abnormal role in attracting population away from the larger cities.

The value of this observation is, unfortunately, restricted by the absence of a more recent census, but it is likely to reflect the present situation as well. Currently in Britain there is great concern over the decline of the population in the inner parts of the conurbations. What was seen in Abercrombie's time as a necessary and desirable development is now being seen as a problem, as selective outmigration removes the most active and skilled in the population from inner cities, making the provision of employment for those who remain that much more difficult. As coloured immigrants also find it more difficult to move from inner city areas, the formation of ethnic 'ghettos' in these areas often exacerbates their problems.

The evidence for selective outmigration is not conclusive. For example, a study of people involved in the Industrial Selection Scheme, which has attempted to link housing need in London with new homes and jobs in the New Towns, does not show any great bias towards skilled workers (Ruddy 1969). Twenty-three per cent of the vacancies filled by the scheme at the time of the survey (1969) were classified as unskilled and 24 per cent as semiskilled. In comparison 10 per cent were clerical and professional, 20 per cent were employed in skilled engineering, 5 per cent in other skilled work and 10 per cent in building work (Gee 1972: 33).

In fact there is evidence that Industrial Selection Scheme registrants are not identical in characteristics to those of all migrants to the New Towns. Table 2 provides some indication of this, but what emerges more clearly is that the profile of migrants to the New Towns around London is not very different from that found in Greater London as a whole. Certainly there are fewer unskilled manual migrants than in the population at large, but the similarities are much clearer than the dissimilarities.

It is now becoming part of conventional wisdom that the further growth of the New Towns is undesirable, particularly in a period during which the expansion of the total national population by natural increase appears to be halting. In terms of population redistribution the policy has created well-established towns, many of which now have a strong economic momentum of their own. As a result the growth of many New Towns (partic-

Table 2. Industrial Selection Scheme: Socio-Economic Group of Participants.

Socio-economic group	ISS registrants (1971)	Migrants to 8 new towns (1971)	Greater London residents (1971)
Professional	0.8	7.1	6.1
Managerial	3.0	10.8	13.9
Skilled manual	42.5	39.9	32.9
Non-manual and personal service	17.1	20.5	23.5
Semi-skilled and agricultural	16.8	15.5	13.4
Unskilled manual	19.9	4.7	7.2
Others	-	1.6	3.2
	100.0	100.0	100.0

(after Deakin and Ungerson 1977: 59).

ularly those around London) cannot be easily stopped, since they are growing centres of employment and form part of an outer metropolitan system of relatively frequent residential moves. Nor is it clear that the New Towns are harming the majority of inner city residents and certainly not the nation as a whole: they represent only a small proportion of total decentralisation from London: they provide better housing in an attractive setting open to a wide spectrum of the population; and they offer a location for profitable industries providing higher than average earnings.

WORK TO THE WORKERS: THE IMPACT ON MIGRATION?

The creation of the New Towns, although it was a policy which largely operated through physical land-use planning, had the expressly stated motive of relocating population within regions. Another strand of policy, in this case working through the creation of employment, also contained underlying ideas about the distribution of population, although it operated in a less direct and less precise manner. This has come to be known as the 'work to the workers' policy, as various government departments have tried to steer new employment to regions of economic difficulty in the north and west of Britian, and away from south-east England (McCrone 1969). The underlying idea was to reduce unemployment and to increase prosperity in the economically less-fortunate areas of Britain; but implicit in these policies was the restriction of migration, because of the important social and economic effects that the out-migration of the most active and skilled was having on the remaining population of the Assisted Areas, and also because of the pressures on land, housing and other social resources that were being imposed elsewhere, particularly in the south-east. It is almost impossible to assess what the movement of population would have been if vigorous regional policies had not been pursued. A.J. Brown has suggested that these policies produced 30,000 jobs a year in the development areas during the 1960s (and this would be 50,000 people if dependants are allowed for) (Brown 1972: 317–318). This calculation was based on the extra share of new industrial building going to the development areas. Using a different approach (comparing the expansion of different kinds of employment in the regions with national average changes) he found an excess of 70,000 jobs a year (between 1961–66) in the Assisted Areas which he attributed to regional policy. Moore and Rhodes used a more elaborate version of this form of calculation and concluded that regional policies produced 220,000 extra jobs in the development areas between 1963 and 1974 (27,500 a year) Moore and Rhodes 1973: 99). R.S. Howard estimated that 24,000 new jobs a year between 1966 and 1970 were brought by companies moving to the Assisted Areas, but when multiplier effects and the growth of existing firms are allowed for, he arrived at a total of 58,000 jobs a year during the late 1960s (quoted in Sundquist 1975: 71).

These calculations can be criticised on a number of grounds (see, for example, Chisholm 1976). For example, some types of development would have been attracted to areas of higher unemployment even if no government action had been taken. Or again, the multiplier effects did not necessarily produce employment in the Assisted Areas, but created jobs elsewhere. But although the figures differ, at least they are all of the same order of size. On this basis it has been estimated that, without these policies, unemployment in the development areas might have been as much as

1.8 % higher, and the outflow of migrants would have been twice as high (Brown 1972: 336–337). Such calculations, of course, represent another set of speculations, developed from data which are suspect to start with. In particular, most migrants in Britain are not unemployed; and there are dangers in supposing that a rise in unemployment would have produced a corresponding rise in out-migration. Yet the policy had as one of its aims the reduction in the need to migrate from the poorer areas of Britain; and there is no doubt that it had a considerable impact, although the exact size of its contribution is a matter for speculation.

LABOUR TRANSFER SCHEMES

In contrast to the regional economic policy which, by implication, was resisting long-distance migration, government policy directly concerned with the movement of population has consisted of a series of schemes aimed at assisting workers to move from areas of labour surplus to areas of labour shortage. Before the Second World War, mobility assistance was provided under the Industrial Transference Scheme instituted in 1928. These migrants, who averaged about 21,000 per annum between 1929 and 1938, came from those depressed areas most closely association with coal mining; and south-east England was the main receiving area (Dennison 1939: 177, 179). Thus the Industrial Transference Scheme was an element in encouraging the net transfer of labour from depressed to prosperous areas, at a level which was not approached again in peacetime until the 1970s.

Following the break of the war years, the government returned to a policy of helping the unemployed move to areas where jobs were available. In May 1946 a new Resettlement Scheme was introduced but in 1950 its scope and assistance levels were curtailed and the scheme became spatially more restricted in its operation. This, together with an improving employment situation, led to a decline in assisted migrations to a few hundreds a year. Then, against the background of a worsening economic situation in the late 1950s, greater financial assistance was again provided to encourage more movement. In 1958 the schemes were extended to cover all categories of the labour force, including lower-paid professional and executive staff. In 1962 the Resettlement Scheme was extended to cover all unemployed workers in Great Britain, not just those in employment exchange areas suffering high unemployment, and became known as the Resettlement Transfer Scheme.

The 1960s was a decade in which concern with regional problems and policies grew, and transfer schemes again came under scrutiny. A particular source of debate was the contradiction inherent in a policy of regional development that moved jobs to high unemployment areas, and a migration policy that aimed to assist movement of the unemployed to areas of prosperity. It was generally agreed, however, that the various transfer schemes served an important social purpose and made a contribution towards decreasing unemployment and mitigating the effects of redundancies. Consequently in the late 1960s levels of financial assistance were greatly increased and potentially unemployed workers as well as those actually unemployed were included in the scheme.

Because all transferees do not receive every benefit, it is difficult to provide an exact total of the numbers moving within the scheme. Table 3 records the number of settling-in grants paid under the Resettlement Transfer Scheme between 1965 and 1971. There was a gradual increase in movement under the Resettlement Transfer Scheme, although in total the numbers were really quite low. Data on origins and destinations record a general trend of movement from the less prosperous regions towards the east and south. However, movements within regions were frequently larger than exchanges across regional boundaries, and this was true for both prosperous and less prosperous regions. Hence these mobility schemes have promoted short-distance as well as long-distance labour migration.

Rising unemployment in the early 1970s resulted in substantial changes in the Resettlement Transfer Schemes, which was renamed the Employment Transfer Scheme (ETS) in 1972. Eligibility conditions were relaxed and workers were encouraged to transfer temporarily. Substantial

Table 3. Settling-in Grants Paid Under Resettlement Transfer Scheme, 1965–71.

Year	Grants Paid
1965 (March - Dec.)	3,382
1966	2,954
1967	3,636
1968	6,129
1969	6,105
1970	7,370
1971	7,860

(Source: unpublished tabulations from Manpower Services Commission).

new incentives were provided, especially a re-housing grant, initially set at £400, and a weekly allowance for single persons.

Since 1972 levels of assistance have been successively increased in response to rises in unemployment and in inflation. In 1975 and 1976 the government introduced a series of job creation and unemployment alleviation measures, which included still more finance for the ETS (the re-housing grant was increased to £1,000 for some people) and the introduction of a Job Search Scheme. This last scheme provides fares and living expenses for unemployed people, mainly in assisted areas, who travel away from home in search of a job. The Job Search Scheme may thus be regarded as complementary to the ETS.

The numbers moving during the 1970s are recorded in table 4. It is clear that with the introduction of the ETS. the numbers of transferees rose dramatically, suggesting an untapped reserve of potential migrants. This was particularly the case during 1976–77 and 1977–78, reflecting the continued high level of unemployment and a succession of emergency manpower measures introduced by the Chancellor during the preceding year. It is difficult to estimate the total number of people affected by the grants, because of the varying number of dependants of each worker, because some would have moved in any case, and because some returned home after a temporary period away. Yet the annual numbers in the past few years have at least reached the same order of size as those affected by job creation in the development areas during periods of economic success or by the decanting of population to New Towns.

From being of minor importance in the post-war years the Employment Transfer Scheme has now emerged as possibly the most important official scheme in Britain concerned with population redistribution.

Table 4. Settling-in Grants Paid Under the Resettlement and Employment Transfer Scheme, 1970–78.

Year ending March	Grants paid
* 1969–70	6328
* 1970–71	7200
* 1971–72	8437
1972–73	18557
1973–74	15237
1974–75	14333
1975–76	15701
+ 1976–77	23436
1977–78	26539

* Resettlement Transfer Scheme.
\+ Estimate.

(Source: Manpower Services Commission).

Table 5 summarises regional balances of loss and gains for 1977–78. It shows a clear pattern of net losses by the Assisted Areas, although total net gains were spatially more concentrated (in the London and Eastern and Southern regions) than net losses. The presence of Assisted Areas in some regions leads to intra-regional differences: for example, the Assisted Areas in the South-West region recorded a net loss by transfer, while the

Table 5. Regional Gains and Losses of Workers Under Employment Transfer Scheme 1977–78.

Region	Import	Export	Balance	Gross
London	4960	294	4666	5254
Rest South East	1000	391	609	1391
Eastern and Southern	4123	1350	2773	5473
South West	882	1637	– 755	2519
North West	2932	5390	–2458	8322
Wales	1104	2608	–1504	3712
Western	1239	725	514	1964
West Midlands	1111	657	454	1768
Scotland	5192	7230	–2038	12422
North East	862	2614	–1752	3476
East Pennine	1644	2323	– 679	3967
East Midlands	1490	1211	279	2701

Total movement = 26539.
(Source: Manpower Services Commission).

remainder of the South-West gained. Net movements were dwarfed by gross movements, and it is important to note the continuation from the 1960s of large flows within regions. Of the total number of 26539 transferees, 8259 (31 %) moved within their own region. This tendency for the ETS to sponsor local shifts of labour was especially marked in Scotland, where there was a net flow of 1047 from the west to the east and north. (Fig. 2).

Information on the characteristics of transferees during 1971–73 is contained in an unpublished survey carried out for the Department of Employment (Parker 1975). This examined the characteristics and experiences of a sample of 854 people who had received a settling-in grant under the RTS and ETS. Assisted movers tended to be younger than the population as a whole and 96 % were men. Nearly half of the transfers were within or into non-assisted areas. About three-quarters of movers were unemployed before transfer, and 16 % were in paid employment. Although the survey did not report skills, the sample generally contained an above-average proportion in metal industries and professional engineering, but relatively few in clerical, selling and catering occupations.

EVALUATION OF GOVERNMENT LABOUR TRANSFER SCHEMES

Despite the long history of transfer schemes, and the increasing level of government financial commitment, there is an acute shortage of evidence available to evaluate them. Criticisms of the schemes may be put in three broad categories.

Objections to the General Approach

The philosophy of moving workers to the work, rather than the reverse, has been debated since the beginning of the transfer schemes, primarily on the grounds that outmovement may unleash cumulative forces of decline; and the arguments used have economic, sociological, and political dimensions (Dennison 1939; Needleman 1965; Brown 1972; Willis 1974; Sant 1975). Economic arguments stress the possible inflationary effects of labour movement to areas where there is already pressure on housing and similar resources, and the underuse of social capital and the economic infrastructure of the origin regions. Sociological arguments refer to the disintegration of communities, a problem enhanced by selective out-migration. Political arguments include that of the Barlow committee, which stressed the strategic disadvantages of concentrating industrialisation and also the brand of local patriotism which is jealously concerned with regional population size and growth. All of these arguments are open to challenge and the debate illustrates more than anything else the marked lack of information on the role played by migration in processes of regional growth and decline. In reality the numbers involved in the government schemes have been small in comparison with the total population. Certainly the schemes have not envisaged mass exoduses of population from depressed areas, nor have these even seemed likely to take place. Critics of the selective nature of transference suggest that it is the young and skilled who move, raising potentially serious issues for the origin areas. Recent evidence has suggested that the policies may not have creamed off the labour force as might have been supposed. For example, in a study of types of movers under the ETS in Scotland, Beaumont analysed the age and skills of 395 movers for whom age information was available and 285 for whom information on skill classification was available (Beaumont 1976b). The results suggested that young workers were over-represented among movers but that unskilled workers were just as likely to move as skilled workers.

Criticisms of Specific Policy Objectives

Criticism of the specific objectives of government migration schemes centre on their basically unchanging nature since World War II, despite fundamental changes in the structure of employment and an evolving regional policy. Migration policy is intended to support regional policy but there is an inconsistency between them in that regional policy, operating mainly through industrial controls, has attempted to slow development in prosperous areas, while migration policy has encouraged people to move there. An alternative view, however, is that the two policies are complementary in a temporal sense, because migration policy can be regarded as a short-term palliative while other elements of regional policy aim at longer-term solutions.

Two other criticisms of objectives may be proposed. First, it can be suggested that the policy is too narrow in its approach. Operating primarily to relieve unemployment, it does not assist in the important adjustments in the labour market required as a result of structural changes in employment. A second criticism is that the primary objectives of the policy are concerned with movement and not with economic or social assimilation in the new area. Klaasen and Drewe (1973) argue that the schemes are more concerned with total numbers than with improving regional employment structures and that more attention ought to be paid to the type of jobs to which transferees go. The success of social assimilation is questioned by high rates of return migration within the first few months. The lack of follow-up service to help transferees settle in the new area contrasts sharply with the efforts of the National Coal Board which has been much more successful in stemming a return of miners who have been transferred to new pits.

Lack of Effectiveness

Criticism of the effectiveness of the schemes has, until recently, been muted by lack of information, since the Department of Employment does not collect follow-up information about those who have received assistance. There are three potential areas for concern: that people who are unemployed do not want to move anyway; that transfers have been characterised by impermanence and a high rate of wastage (return migration); and that many who claim assistance would have moved anyway.

In a study of the effectiveness of the schemes on workers leaving the Jarrow-Hebburn area of North-East England, Willis found a marked lack of enthusiasm (Willis 1972). Of 170 unemployed workers who requested aid during 1966–69, only 79 wanted to move permanently and for only two households were removal expenses ultimately paid. Thus, in this area of high unemployment, transfer was not popular, although it should be recorded that at that time the level of financial assistance available was comparatively low. More recently an attempt to evaluate the success of the ETS has been made by Beaumont (1976a). In analysing the wastage rate he reviewed the cases of 386 movers from four Scottish employment exchanges, 96 of whom failed to settle in the new area. The wastage rate of about 25 per cent was more or less in accord with other surveys conducted in Europe and North America in the 1960s (U.S. Congress 1966) and with that suggested by Parker (1975). A further measurement of success, however, is the number of assisted migrants who moved only because the scheme was available. Beaumont's (1976c) results show rather less success on this score than the wastage figures would suggest. Eighty-eight per cent of his sample of 220 said they would have wanted to move anyway, and 69 per cent said they would have been able to move in the absence of the ETS. Hence, assistance was being provided for a majority who would have moved in any case. The major effect of the aid was to bring about an earlier move for migrants who would eventually have moved anyway. In sum, about two-thirds of the migrants in his sample appeared to be uninfluenced by the scheme. Older, married, unskilled people were among those in the sample who could not have moved without the ETS subsidy. An implication of these findings, therefore, is that ETS assistance might better be concentrated on these sorts of people, rather than being equally available to everyone. Parker's study was somewhat more optimistic. Of his 854 informants 56 per cent said they would have found it difficult to move without the grant, and 42 per cent said they would have moved without one. He also found that more often than not the move brought financial benefit to the migrant. Earnings increased for half those finding jobs after the move, and decreased for 27 per cent. The difference between these two sets of findings may be regional. Beaumont's was a Scottish sample, Parker's was national. A clear implication, however, is the need for more information.

Fig. 2. Assisted labour migration 1977–1978.

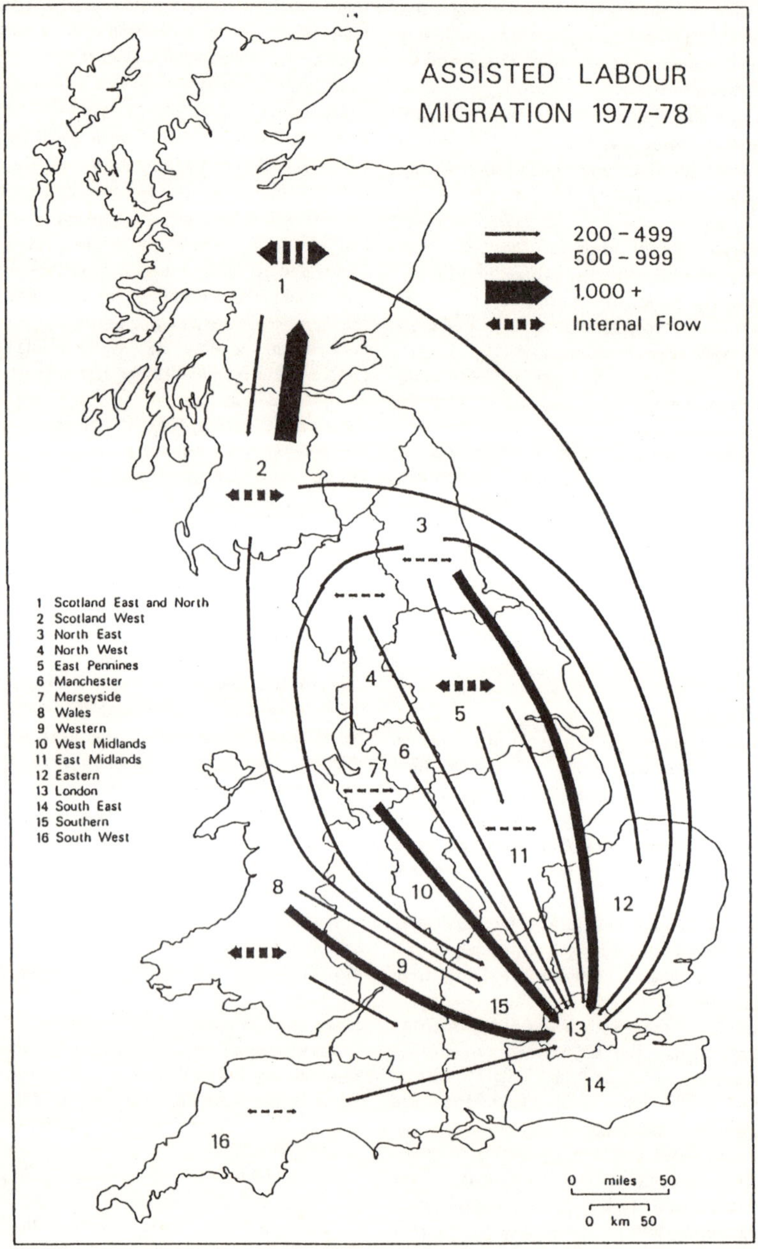
ASSISTED LABOUR MIGRATION 1977-78
200 - 499
500 - 999
1,000 +
Internal Flow
1 Scotland East and North
2 Scotland West
3 North East
4 North West
5 East Pennines
6 Manchester
7 Merseyside
8 Wales
9 Western
10 West Midlands
11 East Midlands
12 Eastern
13 London
14 South East
15 Southern
16 South West
0 miles 50
0 km 50

PRIVATE MIGRATION POLICIES

A comparison of the numbers who obtained government assistance in moving with the general level of inter-urban migration indicates the relative unimportance of formal schemes of government migration assistance. Yet, curiously, there is little systematic information about the policies of private firms and nationalised industries in assisting the movement of their employees. However, this is an aspect of migration movement of increasing importance, since in recent years advanced industrial economies have become dominated by large multi-functional and multi-locational organisations. One reason for the movement of labour migrants is related to the needs of these large companies to relocate their staff as a result of promotion or redeployment; and in order to effect these moves organisations have developed their own migration policies. The nature of the resulting movement depends on the type of organisation and the policies it adopts towards migration within its own internal labour market. McKay and Whitelaw (1977) have discussed various types of organisational structure and the migration patterns likely to be associated with them. There is, as yet, comparatively little empirical evidence on this type of labour migration, although what is available suggests that the amount of movement is considerable. Two characteristics stand out. The first is that migrants move within an environment of less uncertainty. A new job does not have to be found and frequently the company will provide information on such matters as housing and schools in the new location. Second, migrants within organisations are normally eligible for financial assistance, with benefits like removal expenses and relocation allowances.

The types of migration policy operated by employers fit broadly into three categories: (1) those dealing with plant rundown or closure and subsequent labour relocation; (2) those dealing with plant transfer and wholesale labour force shifts; (3) those dealing with normal labour mobility within a multi-location organisation.

Policies designed to cope with plant rundown or closure are not well developed in Britain. Where redundancies occur it is normal for redeployment to be left to market forces, with redundancy payments (from both employer and government) cushioning the shock. Partly, this course of action is dictated by the fact that redundancies are most likely to occur at times of recession when companies involved in labour-shedding are least likely to have alternative vacancies anyway. When redundancy is due to rationalisation, jobs at other company locations may be offered to employees but there is little evidence of how widespread this practice is. Where organisations are state-controlled there are more likely to be formal schemes. For example, the British Steel Corporation runs a redeployment scheme for its manual workers whose jobs are lost in the process of corporate rationalisation. The package of benefits available includes earnings supplementation, a training allowance, and travel, resettlement and removal grants if a move takes place to another plant within the Corporation. The National Coal Board runs a similar scheme, providing information before the movement takes place, generous benefits during the move, including help with housing. Because transferees are still working in the same industry, it is possible for the Board to look after the welfare of transferred families after the move has taken place and, as a result, there has been a very low wastage rate: the Board esimates that probably no more than 10 per cent of transferees leave within the first six months after movement.

Sometimes organisations decide on the wholesale transfer of their operatiosn from one location to another, and offer the chance of migration to their workforce. This type of movement is comparatively rare and experience suggests that not all of the labour force is willing or able to undertake such a move. In particular, moves have taken place as a result of efforts to decentralize offices from London. Occasionally industrial establishments engage in wholesale moves. Mann's (1973) study of the movements of Alfred Bird and Company to Banbury is an example.

The third type of private policy movement is probably the most important in terms of numbers involved, but is perhaps the least known. It is movement of staff between the plants or branches of multi-locational organisations as a normal element in their operations. Of particular importance is the movement of specialists, including managers and technologists, within the corporate environment. This movement may be explained in terms of two basic concepts which have been elaborated by McKay and Whitelaw. The first of these builds on Galbraith's idea of »technostructure» and Pred's model of large city growth dynamics (Galbraith 1967; Pred 1973). It maintains that large organisations engage in functional specialisation at different locations, which leads to greater interaction and interdependence between elements in the organisation, leading to transfer of managerial staff. The process of transfer gives staff wider experience and is intended to create a group of workers with high innovative capacity who will thus ensure the future expansion of the organisation. The second principle invokes the idea of »organisation man» who is also a »spiralist» (Whyte 1957; Watson 1964). It is related to the career structure of the individual as he moves through an organisation, with experience and promotion often being gained only through job mobility, which in turn leads to geographical migration. Hence, the interests of the individual in his career and the organisation in its survival tend to combine to encourage spatial movement.

Information on the details of migration policies of organisations is sparse but it is likely that in total the numbers involved are considerable. One source of evidence is a survey of 551 labour migrant households who moved into four labour markets in England in 1970–71 (Johnson et al. 1974). The details of the survey and the main characteristics of the migrants have been recorded elsewhere but some hitherto unpublished information can now be reported. This relates to those labour migrants who moved from one labour market to another, thus changing job location, but remained with the same employer. There were 157 of them, representing 29 per cent of the total sample, a substantial proportion. Particularly important were managerial, professional and executive grades who accounted for 50 per cent of those moving with the organisation, compared with only 35 per cent of the total sample of 551. Spiralist effects of movement may be seen in improvements in incomes: for example, before moving 49 per cent earned over £120 per month (1971 prices), whereas afterwards the proportion had risen to 73 per cent. An important distinction needs to be made between those who were asked by the employer to move (69 per cent) and those who asked the employer for a move (31 per cent). Members of the latter group tended to be younger, in lower socio-economic groups, earned less and were not moving to achieve promotion. This indicates that more needs to be known about the extent to which companies assist migration which is motivated more by the interests of the individual than by the obvious advantage of the company.

CONCLUSIONS

A feature of these various migration policies in Britain has been the existence of inherent conflicts, some among the various migration policies themselves, others between migration policy and other social and economic strategies. Government migration policies have been developed by different departments, including the Department of Trade and Industry, the Department of the Environment and the Department of Employment. As a result, the various policies essentially exist in isolation, each with its own specific purpose; and areas of apparent conflict among the various migration policies are not surprising. For example, the New Towns (and the associated Industrial Selection Scheme) have been taking people out of the conurbations while, at the same time, the Employment Transfer Scheme has frequently brought population in. Or again, the Key Workers Scheme of the immediate post-war years brouhgt skilled workers into the Development Areas, at the same time as the Employment Transfer Scheme was taking them out.

For similar reasons various groups of people have slipped through the net of migration assistance. Those who are unemployed, but do not live in the Development Areas, have in the past failed to benefit. In the same way there is evidence that those who live in the poorest housing in the conurbations and are unskilled find it difficult to move to the New Towns, but if they are in employment they are not covered by the Employment Transfer Scheme. The schemes operated by private employers are designed with their own particular set of priorities and usually focus on professional and highly skilled workers, but the Department of Employment schemes are aimed at the unemployed, thus leaving employed workers in 'intermediate' types of job without assistance.

Migration policies also conflict with other aspects of government policy. For example, the conflict between migration policy and housing policy is a wide-ranging one. In the New Towns the migration of population is a very directly linked with the provision of housing, with both elements forming coherent parts of the same policy, but this is an exceptional case. Elsewhere there is a need to develop housing and migration policies which are more compatible than at present. Over the years government involvement in the housing market has steadily increased. A significant result of this has been to restrict entry by labour migrants into the rented sector. This has worked in two principal ways. First, many local authorities already have long waiting lists for housing, and the priority given to those displaced by slum clearance and redevelopment means that waiting lists fall only slowly, if at all. Because of this pressure local authorities have adopted residence qualifications for the allocation of council houses which include the need for households to have lived in the local authority area for a set period – in some cases five years or more. Migrants from other areas are thus by definition, frequently barred from council housing in their chosen destination area. Second, rent controls on unfurnished private-rented housing have probably encouraged many tenants to sit tight, thus lowering turnover and hence the availability to migrants of this rented accomodation. The Housing Act of 1974 gave security for the first time to tenants in the private-rented furnished sector, an important source of accomodation for labour migrants. The result has been to reduce the availability of such accommodation, repeating the existing pattern for the private-rented unfurnished sector, and erecting a further housing barrier to labour migration. Thus it is in those sectors of the housing market where government has taken most control, and which provide relatively cheap accommodation, that there is most restriction on entry for migrants. Yet at the same time these are the sectors of the housing market most likely to provide for those workers – the lower paid and the unemployed – at whom the government's transfer schemes are aimed.

Not all these conflicts are very serious. The Key Workers Scheme involved only a very small number of workers and, after all, was designed to increase total industrial employment in the Development Areas. Some of the schemes can be seen as complementary – private schemes cover the better-off professional workers and government schemes support the unemployed. Many of the moves supported by the ETS are to destinations within the Assisted Areas as well as over longer distances, so that it would be unfair to see government migration assistance as being a strong encouragement to the downward economic spiral which some regions have experienced.

Nevertheless, it is clear from these various considerations that there is no clearly-defined national migration policy in Britain, in spite of a relatively high involvement of government in day-to-day life and the existence of various policies which have important implications for population distribution. However, migration is gaining much greater importance in changing the map of populations distribution because of the rapidly falling rate of natural increase in Britain. As a result, it can be asked whether there is a need for a more comprehensive and better-integrated policy, which has a set of much more specific population targets attached to it?

The instinctive response of geographers might be to support such a view, but there are some good reasons for taking a more negative line. First, we are not in a position to evaluate population distribution in any meaningful way. We know too little about the precise social and economic costs involved in different population distributions; and although we can nibble at this problem by assesing more carefully such matters as the locational attributes of specific types of employment, the optimum population distribution is almost impossible to specify because of the many unquantifiable elements in such a calculation. Second, it is often easier to deal individually with problems which involve population migration – a pragmatic approach possibly has little intellectual attraction, but is is the kind of approach which it is possible to implement in the real world of a political democracy. Finally, a clear view of what the population distribution of a country ought to be probably also implies, in the last resort, unacceptable restraints on individual freedom of movement, if the ideal distribution is to be fully attained.

As a result there is much to be said for favouring specific policies for specific problems, because of the flexibility that such an approach is likely to bring. British experience suggests that such pragmatism may create conflict between policies, and that individual policies with implications for migration may become fossilized, thus continuing to operate after they have reached the end of their useful lives. Yet, because there is no precisely-stated overall strategy, adjustments in emphasis have taken place without any great administrative trauma – a quality not without merit in the present British context of demographic and economic uncertainty.

BIBLIOGRAPHY

Abercrombie, P. (1945), *Greater London Plan 1944*, H.M.S.O., London.

Beaumont, P.B. (1976a), »The problem of return migration under a policy of assisted labour mobility: an examination of some British evidence», *British Journal of Industrial Relations* 14: 82–88.

Beaumont, P.B. (1976b), »Assisted labour mobility policy in Scotland», *Urban Studies* 13: 75–79.

Beaumont, P.B. (1976c), »Assessing the performance of assisted labour mobility policy in Britain», *Urban and Regional Studies Discussion Papers no. 19*, The University, Glasgow.

Brown, A.J. (1972), *The Framework of Regional Economics in the United Kingdom*, Cambridge University Press for the National Institute of Economic and Social Research, Cambridge.

Champion, A.G., K. Clegg and R.L. Davies (1977), *Facts about the New Towns: a socio-economic digest*, Retailing and Planning Associates, Cambridge.

Chisholm, M. (1976), »Regional policy in an era of slow population growth and higher unemployment», *Regional Studies* 10: 201–213.

Deakin, N and C. Ungerson (1977), *Leaving London: Planned Mobility and the Inner City*, Heinemann, for the Centre for Environmental Studies, London.

Dennison, S.R. (1939), *The Location of Industry and the Depressed Areas*, University Press, Oxford.

Drewett, J.R. (1968), »The definition of Standard Metropolitan Labour Areas», Urban Growth Study, *Working Paper no. 1*, Political and Economic Planning, London.

Drewett, J.R., J. Goddard, N. Spence, C. Connock and R. Pinkham (1974), »Urban Change in Britain: 1961–71», *Working Reports nos. 1 and 2*, Department of Geography, L.S.E., London.

Flowerdew, R. and J. Salt (1979), »Migration between labour market areas in Great Britain, 1970–71», *Regional Studies* 13: 211–231.

Galbraith, J.K. (1967), *The New Industrial State*, Hamilton, London.

Gee, F.A. (1972), *Homes and Jobs for Londoners in New and Expanding Towns*, H.M.S.O., London.

Johnson, J.H., J. Salt and P.A. Wood (1974), *Housing and the Migration of Labour in England and Wales*, Saxon House, Farnborough.

Johnson, J.H. and J. Salt (1980). »Labour migration within organizations: an introductory study», *Tijdschrift voor economische en sociale geografie* 71:277–284.

Klassen, L.H. and P. Drewe, (1973), *Migration policy in Europe: A Comparative Study*, Saxon House, Farnborough.

McCrone, G. (1969), *Regional Policy in Britain*, Allen and Unwin, London.

McKay, J. and J.S. Whitelaw (1977), »The role of large private and government organisations in generating flows of inter-regional migrants: the case of Australia», *Economic Geography* 53: 28–44.

Mann, M. (1973), *Workers on the Move: The Sociology of Relocation*, University Press, Cambridge.

Moore, B. and J. Rhodes (1973), »Evaluating the effects of British regional economic policy», *Economic Journal* 83: 87–110.

Needleman, L. (1965), »What are we to do about the regional problem?», *Lloyds Bank Review*, no. 74: 45–58.

Parker, S. (1975), »Assisted labour migration», Social Survey Division, Office of Population Censuses and Surveys (unpublished).

Pred, A.R. (1973), »The growth and development of cities in advanced economies», *Systems of Cities and Information Flows*, Lund Studies in Geography, Series B, no. 38:9-82.

Ruddy, S.A. (1969), *Industrial Selection Schemes: an administrative study*, Centre for Urban and Regional Studies, University of Birmingham, Occasional Paper no. 5.

Sant, M. (1975), *Industrial Movement and Regional Development*, Pergamon, Oxford.

Strachan, A. (1974), »The planning framework for modern urban growth: the example of Great Britain», in J.H. Johnson (ed.), *Suburban Growth*, Wiley, London.

Sundquist, J.S. (1975), *Dispersing Population: what America can learn from Europe*, Brookings Institution, Washington D.C.

United States Congress (1966), *Programs for Relocating Workers used by Governments of Selected Countries*, Joint Economic Committee Monograph, Government Printing Office, Washington, D.C.

Watson, W. (1964), »Social mobility and social class in industrial communities», in M. Gluckman (ed.), *Closed Systems and Open Minds: the limits of naivity in social anthropology*, Oliver and Boyd, Edinburgh.

Whyte, W.H. (1957), *The Organisation Man*, Cape, London.

Willis, K.G. (1974), *Problems in Migration Analysis*, Saxon House, Farnborough.

Willis, K.G. (1972), »Geographical and labour mobility», *Papers on Migration and Mobility*, no. 11, Department of Geography, The University, Newcastle-upon-Tyne.

[13]

HABITAT INTL. Vol. 13, No. 3, pp. 81–93, 1989.
Printed in Great Britain.

0197–3975/89 $3.00 + 0.00

The Transmigration Programme in Indonesian National Development Strategy

Current Status and Future Requirements

THOMAS R. LEINBACH*
University of Kentucky, USA

ABSTRACT

The transmigration programme in Indonesia is now acknowledged to be the largest voluntary land settlement scheme in the world. The programme began as an attempt to correct the population imbalance between Java and the Outer Islands. Since the inception of the programme under the Dutch in 1904 through mid-1986 over 4 million people have moved. Major emphasis in the programme has turned to regional development in the Outer Islands. Despite considerable success the programme has been plagued by numerous problems. These include inadequate income levels, improper site selection, poor matching of settlement models to the specific sites, environmental deterioration, migrant adjustment, land conflicts and financing. Several of these problems have been caused as a result of the attempt to reach unrealistic settlement targets. Given current budget constraints efforts now focus on the improvement of existing settlements and the encouragement of spontaneous or *swakarsa* migration. A secondary phase of the transmigration programme involves the development of other settlement models. One attempt involves the experiment with small enterprises some of which involve the private sector. The future success of both new and existing settlements hinges on the development of off-farm employment. In this sense, small industries and opportunities in the service sector of the settlement themselves and nearby small towns are critical. The exploration of a new basis for employment must be carried out in concert with the National Urban Development Strategy (NUDS) which identifies the functional potential of small and intermediate-sized towns in the Outer Islands.

INTRODUCTION

The ideological objectives of developing countries invariably place emphasis upon the attainment of multiple goals. In the case of Indonesia, equity, growth and stability constitute the principal guidelines. Indeed substantial progress has been made since 1970. Measures of this include an 8% average annual economic growth rate, sharp declines in infant mortality, and a general reduction in

*Address for correspondence: Department of Geography, University of Kentucky, 1477 Patterson Tower, Lexington, KY 40506-0027, USA.

poverty levels. Increases in oil prices and production levels, in part, contributed to this progress.

Coupled with this Indonesia has made good progress in terms of her *spatial development* objectives. These objectives state that spatial disparities should be reduced between local levels of population and economic activity as well as between local resources and potentials. In general terms the pace of development in the Outer Islands has accelerated. Evidence of this is seen in Java's declining share of GDP, agricultural output, manufacturing activity and transport movements. Especially important in this regard was the rapid development in Sumatra particularly in key urban regions such as Medan and Palembang, the large industrial complexes, and also the major reception areas for transmigrants.

The overall level of urbanisation in Indonesia (22% in 1980) is relatively low compared to many other developing countries and urban primacy is not a serious policy issue given the existence of numerous very large cities. A major feature of urban growth during the 1970s was the rapid development of intermediate-sized cities especially outside of Java and particularly port cities. Finally notable growth did occur also in *kabupaten* surrounding most cities of over 100,000.

The decline in oil prices, coupled with an international recession, however, has now disrupted the remarkable pattern of progress and has forced development planning into a new era. Economic growth will be considerably lower into the 1990s — perhaps on the average 4 to 5% *per annum*. While the overall population growth rate will decline to 1.8%, the labor force growth rate will be higher perhaps of the order of 2.6%. To absorb this growth an average of 1.8 million jobs per year would have to be created — a third above the actual creation rate in the 1970s. Basically urban areas will account for a much larger share of total population growth in the future. Indonesia's urban areas will possibly have to absorb 2.2 million new residents per year from 1990 to 2000. The urban population will increase from the 1980 figure of 33 million (22%) to about 76 million (36%) in 2000. These forecasts have prompted a serious re-evaluation of virtually all government policies affecting urban and regional development.

NATIONAL URBAN DEVELOPMENT STRATEGY

A nationwide strategy for urban development has recently been designed for Indonesia in consideration of the above dilemmas (Government of Indonesia, 1985; Richardson, 1981, 1987). While the clear focus is the urban pattern, indeed the broader intent is clear. The basic overall objective is to obtain a more balanced development through an appropriate and equitable allocation of resources. While there are no "urban objectives" *per se* the development of cities is to serve as a means by which various policy objectives may be carried out. A clear emphasis is to strengthen Outer Island economies. This overall plan calls for a tempered growth in the largest metro areas *while promoting growth in selected small and intermediate cities*.

In this effort all the cities have been assessed for their functional potential and subsequently assigned to a broad policy/action category. Functional potential is used here to mean potential for development in different functions rather than overall growth potential (Government of Indonesia, 1985, p. 13). The three largest cities, Jakarta (Jabotabek), Surabaya (Gerbangkertosusila), and Bandung (Bandung Raya), have been classified as Mature National Development Centres (MNDC). The intent is to slow growth by promoting more rapid growth in large lower order centres while applying indirect incentives for decentralisation. These include the reduction of business regulations, liberalising and decentralising credit provisions, and the expansion of local revenue generation and cost recovery for urban services (Government of Indonesia, 1985, p. 8).

Following the MNDC, is a category designated Emerging National Development Centres (ENDC). These nodes are places which either have currently diversified medium and large scale industrial activity or have the capacity for such development over the next decade. Appropriate centres here are most of Indonesia's cities of 200,000 population or more and the *kabupaten* surrounding them. Among the 17 central cities and 56 subcentres affected are the rapidly growing port centres outside Java, especially Medan, Palembang, Pontianak and Ujung Pandang, and slower growing but already diversified centres in Java such as Cirebon, Semarang, Yogyakarta and Malang. Below these largest cities are those nodes which qualify for attention as Interregional Development Centres (IDC), Regional Development Centres (RDC) and finally Local Service Centres (LSC).

The NUDS analysis maintains that Indonesia has a well-balanced urban structure where Jakarta's share of the urban population has not changed greatly since 1971. Given the population of 168 million the urban pattern includes a large number of intermediate-sized cities. Above all the objective is to have economic activity grow through the existing urban centres. No attempt, especially in the light of resource constraints, wil be made to create "growth poles" to draw population away from large cities.

URBAN *VS* RURAL PRIORITIES

The prominence of the NUDS in Indonesian development planning does little to deflate Lipton's (1977) eloquent argument exposing the existence of an "urban bias" which has contributed to the perpetuation of poverty among rural populations. The existence of such a bias can be explained in part by the vested interests of industrialists, policy-makers influenced by political pressures, and the employment *potential* in cities. Indeed rural poverty is, in many ways, underperceived, and rural peripheries too suffer from a series of biases. The inaccessibility of many rural areas to a variety of private and public sector change agents produces a distinct spatial bias (Chambers, 1983).

There is little doubt that the progress of the 1970s has produced a dramatic improvement in the Indonesian urban quality of life even though severe problems remain. Simultaneously the public sector must face the serious problems of rural areas. Perhaps too much concern has focused on disparities in *per capita* regional product where evidence suggests that striking contrasts exist between rural and urban *per capita* consumption levels. In Java alone, for example, rural consumption levels are half those found in urban areas (Hamer *et al.*, 1986).

Rural development in Indonesia, however, has not been neglected for planning goals have aimed to achieve balanced rural–urban development especially over the last two 5-year plans. From a "top down" perspective a variety of agricultural programmes, such as BUUD, aimed at improved access to HYVs, fertilisers, pesticides, credit and extension guidance have been implemented (Hardjono, 1983). Coupled with these have been programmes derived from the basic human needs (BHN) strategy which have improved dramatically service delivery in rural areas, especially in the education and health sectors (Leinbach, 1984).

Finally experiments to create employment in rural areas while improving infrastructure have generally been successful. The Cash Incentive Rural Works Programme (*Padat Karya Gaya Baru*) and the *Instruksi Presiden* (INPRES) programme are examples of strong efforts to develop rural public projects while generating off-season jobs at a low *per capita* cost (less than $750 per person year of employment) (Leinbach, 1983). The latter programme accounted for 40% of construction employment in 1980. The aim, in addition to the explicit purposes of creating infrastructure and generating rural employment, is to affect the urban labour absorption problem by holding more people in the rural areas (Richardson, 1987, p. 287). These efforts in rural development once again remind us of the close interrelationship between urban and rural spheres. The paradox of the urban dilemma which has been noted above is that to reverse the conditions occurring in cities we must improve the attractiveness of rural areas so that people are encouraged to remain (Todaro and Stilkind, 1981).

A final mechanism which has contributed to the growth of agricultural employment and rural development in general is the transmigration programme (Hardjono, 1977; MacAndrews, 1978). This effort has a long history in Indonesia and, despite the criticisms levelled at land settlement and population redistribution policies (Oberai, 1986), and specifically the transmigration programme (Arndt, 1983; Babcock, 1983; Otten, 1986; Secrett, 1986), it continues to command attention and resources. As a regional development strategy it utilises certain elements of the foregoing intervention measures and offers strong potential for the reduction of rural–urban imbalances.

The initial objectives of this paper are to review the basic concept, the impact, and criticisms of the programme. Another purpose and the major aim however is to focus on the future development of the programme and how it might be modified to produce results which are consistent with national development objectives. This is especially critical in light of drastically reduced development budgets which must allocate resources more efficiently in the future.

THE TRANSMIGRATION CONCEPT: A REVIEW

Nearly 65% of Indonesia's 168 million people live in Java, where population densities rise to 2,000 persons per sq. km. This basic statistic contrasts sharply with vast areas of lower population density in the Outer Islands of Sumatra, Kalimantan, and Sulawesi.

Attempts to correct this population imbalance have produced the largest voluntary land settlement scheme in the world. Beginning in 1904, the Dutch recognised the strong concentration of people in Java and the dearth of labour in the Outer Islands. From this recognition the transmigration programme was born and continues as a fundamental concept in Indonesian development planning. Essentially transmigration is a largely government planned and financed movement of landless agricultural people from Java, Bali, and Lombok to agriculture based settlements in the Outer Islands. From 1950 until 1970 approx. 424,000 sponsored people were moved (Table 1). In the first two Five Year Development Plans (Repelita I 1969/74 and Repelita II 1974/79) some 705,000 people were moved. The movement target for Repelita III (1979/84) was 500,000 families if sufficient funding were available. Actually only 1.49 million people were moved. By 1984 over 560,000 sponsored families had been resettled.

The term "transmigration", in fact, encompasses four different groups of people. The dominant group are *sponsored* or *umum* transmigrants who receive extensive support from the government during the initial 5 years of settlement in the form of transport, land, housing, and social services. In addition is a *local* transmigrant group who live in or near the settlement areas to be developed and receive the same benefits as the sponsored transmigrants. *Registered spontaneous* or *swakarsa* transmigrants move at their own expense and settle in a site

Table 1. Sponsored transmigration programme, 1950–1984

Year	Five-year plan	Total families moved	Local families	Resettled families	Total families settled	Total people
1950–1954		21,037	0	1,280	22,317	87,000
1955–1959		32,114	0	128	32,242	134,000
1960–1964		26,456	0	0	26,456	111,000
1965–1969		21,633	0	0	21,633	92,000
1969–1974	(Repelita I)	39,436	0	75	39,511	240,000
1974–1979	(Repelita II)	44,484	7,600	0	52,084	465,000
Subtotal		185,160	7,600	1,483	194,243	828,000
1979–1984	(Repelita III)	301,279	22,284	42,414	365,977	1,492,000
Total		486,439	29,884	43,897	560,220	2,320,000

Source: Ministry of Transmigration; World Bank, 1988.

of their choice. These individuals receive the same amount of land (2–5 ha of which usually only 1.25 ha is actually cleared) and benefit from the same socio-economic services. Direct government support to this group is lower and provided in the form of credit rather than subsidy. Finally *unregistered spontaneous* or *swakarsa* transmigrants move to a site on their own and are not entitled to government support.[1]

In addition to the 365,000 sponsored families who were resettled in Repelita III there were also over 169,000 spontaneous (*swakarsa*) transmigrant families who moved with little or no government assistance. This category has enlarged dramatically over the 5 year period (Table 2). Of the total sponsored families moved during Repelita III, 62% were settled in Sumatra (especially South Sumatra, Lampung, and Riau Provinces), 19% went to Kalimantan, and the remainder to Sulawesi, and Maluku, Irian Jaya, and Nusa Tenggara. The majority of the spontaneous families also settled in Sumatra.

Criteria for selection in the programme include voluntary registration, low income, knowledge of farming or a special skill, married and under 40 years old, and good health. In March 1985 the Ministry of Transmigration (MOT) had over 445,000 applications from potential sponsored transmigrant families. These applications far exceeded the absorptive capacity of the sites which were available. Many families will have to wait more than 4 years before resettlement is possible.

Table 2. Repelita III settlement, by year and island

	1979–1980	1980–1981	1981–1982	1982–1983	1983–1984	Total
Sponsored migrant families						
Sumatra	16,384	49,043	48,520	57,578	55,540	227,065
Kalimantan	565	11,976	17,378	17,488	23,207	70,614
Sulawesi, Moluccas	3,854	9,663	15,890	12,396	9,879	51,682
Irian Jaya	290	2,521	2,688	5,362	5,755	16,616
Subtotal	21,093	73,203	84,476	92,824	94,381	365,977
Spontaneous migrant families	1,985	3,359	8,961	32,445	122,747	169,497
Total	23,078	76,562	93,437	125,269	217,128	535,474

Source: Ministry of Transmigration; World Bank, 1988.

[1] The use of the term *swakarsa* has been further refined to designate settlers who are truly independent and receive no government assistance (*swakarsa murni*) and those who are partially assisted (*swakarsa berbantuan*).

Table 3. Repelita IV settlement by type of migrant family and island, June, 1987

Island	Sponsored	Partially-assisted	Spontaneous	Total
Sumatra	99,100	8,600	183,800	291,500
Kalimantan	44,900	5,800	73,500	124,200
Sulawesi, Moluccas	25,500	2,400	18,700	46,600
Irian Jaya	9,400	50	5,100	14,550
Total	178,900	16,850	281,100	476,850

Source: Ministry of Transmigration; World Bank, 1988.

Current data for the period 1984 to 1987 indicates that some 59% of the total transmigrants are of the *swakarsa* or spontaneous variety in contrast to 32% during Repelita III (Table 3). A clear MOT objective is to increase the numbers of movers in this category. Although the data shown for Repelita IV accounts for the transmigration activity only through mid-1987, it is clear that Sumatra continues as a dominant destination for both sponsored and spontaneous migrant families. Kalimantan, as in Repelita III, is the next most important destination. The intent to shift a greater proportion of transmigrants to Kalimantan and Sulawesi over the remainder of Repelita IV may be unfulfilled in light of budgetary constraints and the consequent reduced placement.

The MOT has developed a scheme of seven settlement models to insure a target income for settlers of at least twice the subsistence level. This level amounts to about 2.4 tons of rice equivalent per year and per family by the end of the 5 year period following settlement. The models are upland food crops, wetland food crops, tree crops, aquaculture, animal husbandry, industry and mining, and agro-forestry. In fact, however, only the first three models have been implemented on a large scale. Food and tree crops are clearly being emphasised during Repelita IV. Remaining models are being tested during this period.

REGIONAL DEVELOPMENT IMPACT OF TRANSMIGRATION

The transmigration programme has clearly had several positive impacts on the economy of Indonesia. In Repelita III, sponsored migration alone has created over 550,000 full time jobs and perhaps an equal number of temporary jobs through site development. Expenditures on transmigration provided from 20 to 40% of the development budget in the major receiving provinces.

It is estimated that by 1983 some 6,000 sq. km of land had been cleared and put under cultivation by settlers. In the agricultural sector transmigration has substantially contributed to the increase in food production in certain areas. Transmigration *padi* production in 1980 was estimated at 185,000 tons which was merely 0.6% of Indonesian rice production (Babcock, 1986). However in provinces such as Jambi, Riau, South Sumatra, Lampung, East Kalimantan, and Central and Southeast Sulawesi the settlements do contribute significantly to provincial rice production. Non-food crop production, such as coconuts, clove, coffee, and rubber, while important in a local sense, does not contribute greatly to provincial production.

Physical infrastructure (especially road development) related to transmigration has been important in the development of specific local areas. There is also discernibly a clear quality differential in infrastructure between the settlements and nearby rural areas. Airports and landing strips have also been upgraded in many settlement areas since considerable movement of settlers takes place by air. Surfaced access roads to transmigration sites and unsurfaced roads within settlements account for 11 and 47% respectively of the 1980 provincial networks of similar quality. Network upgrading and additions have been especially important in North and West Sumatra, Aceh, and North and South Sulawesi (Babcock, 1986). Road development in fact could be one of the most important lasting contributions of the transmigration programme.

Settlements are also provided with a host of public facilities. Schools, health posts, religious facilities and market-places, as well as extension centres are put in place in each settlement cluster. These facilities are frequently superior to those in surrounding areas and serve local non-transmigrant populations to the degree that service personnel are available and access is not constrained by distance and travel time.

Set against these positive aspects of impact are negative ones (Arndt, 1983). In this sense the impact of settlement patterns on the often fragile ecosystems of the Outer Islands is now a matter of strong national concern. Environmentalists have repeatedly pointed to the extended impact of the burning and clearing of tropical moist forests. These impacts include the destruction of certain tree species, as well as other plant and animal life. By 1984 the excessive use of forest resources, including over-cutting and inappropriate farming practices had resulted in 8.6 million ha of land which is so degraded that it is unable to sustain even subsistence agriculture or to fulfil normal soil functions such as absorbing water (Secrett, 1986).

Coupled with this is the viability of long-term food crop agriculture on reclaimed tidal swamp areas. Too often in the past, site selection with respect to soil and drainage and the matching of crops to these sites has been less than fully planned (Ross, 1980; Burbridge *et al.*, 1981). A common problem too has been prior claims on potential settlement areas by the indigenous population. In addition a matter of some considerable importance is the adjustment process of migrants (Otten, 1986).

MAJOR PROBLEMS

While the transmigration programme has enjoyed considerable success there are numerous problems which have been identified in the last few years (Arndt, 1983). Several of the major areas of deficiency are pointed up below.

(1) Many settlements appear to have failed to develop in terms of adequate income levels for the participants. A recent Indonesian Central Bureau of Statistics survey of 2,200 randomly sampled households in 22 Repelita II and III sites has produced the latest reliable evidence on income levels. The survey is especially useful for it provides data which may be compared with other surveys in rural sending and receiving areas (Table 4). Several points are clear even though there is, in connection with the survey of transmigrants, a possible understatement of home garden production used for home consumption.

Table 4. Comparison of transmigrant and non-transmigrant incomes

	Survey date	Monthly household income (Rp)	Monthly incomes below Rp 30,000* (percentage)	Monthly incomes below Rp 50,000† (percentage)	Annual household income (US$)
Transmigration sites	1985	58,300	20	50	636
Rural sending areas	1984	67,200	15	43	733
Rural receiving areas	1984	90,750	4	24	990

* Rp 30,000 (US$27) is the monthly subsistence level for a family of five.
† Rp 50,000 (US$45) is the family poverty line, estimated at Rp 10,000 *per capita*/month.
Source: BPS Transmigration Income Survey, 1985; World Bank, 1988.

Average migrant household incomes are lower than average incomes in Java and significantly lower than the incomes of households in rural areas of receiving provinces. The data show that 20% of the sampled transmigrants were at or below subsistence levels.

In drawing such conclusions however it is important to note that the lower income levels do not necessarily mean that individual families are worse off than before they moved. Clearly a large percentage of the transmigrants are above the poverty line in the receiving area. In addition assets are acquired in the movement process. These include land, a house and perhaps some livestock. Transmigrants generally have the means to meet subsistence requirements and have reduced expenses for basic needs such as housing (World, Bank, 1988).

Clearly one reason for the lower income levels among transmigrant households is the lack of adequate guidance and inputs. More important however in many cases is the intrinsic quality of the land. During the latter part of the 1970s it was already evident that only marginal land was available (Hardjono, 1986). Thus a major problem has been poor site selection. Sites associated with poor drainage, advanced erosion, excessive slope, lack of water, and poor soils have often been selected in an effort to reach targets set by the MOT. Coupled with this has been the careless and improper development of sites by contractors who are unqualified. Finally a related aspect of site situation is poor communications. Too often sites do not have adequate road infrastructure or access to service centres. Obviously this problem can be remedied as road networks are expanded. Finally transmigrant household incomes may vary considerably between those who procure off-farm employment and those who do not. This point will be developed later in the paper.

(2) The inappropriate match of settlement model to the site has also caused problems. Wet rice systems have received less emphasis in recent years and agricultural diversification has been encouraged. Tree crops have become quite important while land may still be reserved for cash crop cultivation.

(3) In the past a deficiency in the programme has been the lack of an appropriate migrant selection model. Too often willingness to move was not matched with the most enterprising and resourceful individuals. Official emphasis in selection has been on high density source areas, poor soils and natural disasters. Frequently migrants are not aware of the tasks or hardships which await them.

An important emphasis in the programme has been the steady growth of spontaneous or *swakarsa* migration. There is indeed a strong interest in encouraging this category of settlers. Yet policies regarding this form of transmigration remain inadequate. In particular unassisted families have trouble in obtaining land with some security of tenure. Special attention must be given to this group so that they may receive places in new and older transmigration sites.

(4) Ethnic relations continue to be of some concern. Generally indigenous people in the Outer Islands have not generally been eager to receive Javanese settlers. The settling in process has generally been easiest where land conflict was absent and where local people have benefited from employment or business opportunities made possible by transmigration settlements. There has however been little genuine assimilation based on intermarriage. Usually poor Javanese have very low social standing in Sumatran communities (Arndt, 1983). It will be instructive to see the progress in this obstacle as settlements develop more and more in eastern Indonesia.

THE PATH FORWARD

Even if the scale of the transmigration programme is greatly reduced, both for reasons of unattainable targets and austerity budgets in the near term, it remains an important concept in Indonesia's development planning and is therefore worthy of research focus. Within this framework, a variety of problems warrant attention. Among these are more efficient approaches to the identification of appropriate settlement sites which may reduce the backlog of registrants for the programme and enhance long-run benefits and income distribution. The World Bank, which has to date committed $439 million to the programme, is currently funding the fifth project on transmigration which focuses upon aerial photography, remote sensing and base mapping in support of the selection of new potential settlement sites. Coupled with this are ongoing efforts which are exploring various ecological issues especially the influence of transmigration settlements on erosion control and soil conservation.

In addition to these aspects of inquiry are those which focus on alternative models of development within the programme. In this respect the transmigration "effort" is in many ways at a turning point. While several basic models of an agricultural nature have been successful in part, these increasingly must be supplemented, particularly in the light of resource and other ecological constraints, by other income-generating forms. Opportunities for off-farm employment are clearly a major determinant of settlers' living standards and of income differentials between more and less successful projects. Off-season wage employment may be essential for subsistence and the only source of cash income until crops can be delivered to markets (Hugo *et al.*, 1987, pp. 358–360). Thus far the dominant opportunities have been in logging, construction, fishing and as labour on transmigration site development (Arndt, 1983). Official transmigration surveys in 1981 and 1982 showed that 75 and 85% respectively of settlers' incomes were earned from off-farm employment after 6 and 4 years respectively on the site. Many of these opportunities have very limited long-term prospects (Babcock, 1986). This is especially critical if there is a reduction in government investment in receiving areas or a shift in allocations to new regions.

The survey data from 1985 also point to the importance of off-farm employment (Table 5). With respect to type of movement, all categories derive substantial income from wages, pensions and "other" activities. Of significance are the higher amounts earned by spontaneous settlers and local resident transmigrants in these categories. Yet sponsored and spontaneous migrants earn very similar total incomes even though spontaneous farmers, in many cases, do not obtain benefits given to sponsored transmigrants. Higher incomes associated with local settlers may be attributed to additional sources of income, for example trading in Sumatra. In addition perhaps the most enterprising families have

Table 5. Monthly household income by type of transmigrant (Rp/month)

Type of migrant	Sample size	Total income	Agriculture	Wage income and pensions	Other*
Type of movement					
Sponsored	1,800	54,441	18,876	22,370	13,195
Spontaneous	152	56,741	23,533	27,113	16,095
Retired military	57	117,706	16,325	92,056	9,325
Local resident	186	74,045	20,581	33,270	20,194
Area of origin					
Transmigrants					
Java	1,856	55,757	18,490	24,319	12,988
Bali	133	60,788	18,004	23,924	18,860
Nontransmigrants					
Sumatra	117	71,224	18,252	43,522	9,450
Kalimantan	71	77,977	21,924	27,885	28,168
Sulawesi	24	82,741	23,909	24,412	34,420

*Includes home production other than agriculture (handicracts, *etc.*), transport, trade and other nonwage income.

Source: BPS Transmigration Income Survey, 1985; World Bank, 1988.

moved to the schemes and remain while others have dropped out. Finally non-transmigrants from the Outer Islands have higher total incomes than do transmigrants from Java and Bali. The source of these differences comes not only from agriculture but wage income and the "other" category as well. Among the non-transmigrants, "other" income sources in Sulawesi and wage income and pensions in Sumatra are especially conspicuous (World Bank, 1988).

Since many off-farm employment opportunities may be limited in duration, it may be possible in some situations to use local human resources to develop small industries, some of which may be ancillary in nature (Leinbach, 1987). Such small industries, if appropriate and feasible, might provide long-term employment in the transmigration scheme settings. In addition, and even more important, within the schemes and in nearby market centres, opportunities for a significant number of settlers may exist in the tertiary sector within small-scale service enterprises or as small-scale entrepreneurs. Commonly in such market centres entrepreneurs such as traders and participants in transport services come from non-transmigrant groups. However the details surrounding the question of the provision and spatial characteristics of both small industrial and service enterprises in and around transmigration areas remains sketchy and unresearched. There is therefore a critical need to explore both of these opportunities in order to examine how transmigrants themselves might participate in such activities more fully.

Recent official thinking in the transmigration programme in fact strongly supports a new phase or "second stage development" whereby previously settled areas are improved through new financial and technical support. The government has not yet developed a systematic programme for such development although efforts are being made to encourage private sector investment directed toward small-scale entrepreneurs and services provision (IDN, 1986). While service sector development has received widespread attention in the urban context of developing countries (Weeks, 1975; Richardson, 1984) and has recently received encouragement in Indonesia from a direct Presidential Instructive, little consideration has been devoted to the use of service-generated employment in non-urban settings such as the transmigration schemes. Given the population base within the schemes and access to nearby small and intermediate towns, this is a potential that must be explored (Costello *et al.*, 1987).

This idea has some validity because it has been demonstrated that the observed expansion of the tertiary and secondary sectors are an expected consequence of developments elsewhere in the economy and that productivity in the service sector is not necessarily lower than that in other sectors. The service sector is frequently treated as a source of residual employment but this view neglects the obvious point that a demand *exists* otherwise the services would not be provided. In addition this former view neglects the *growth* in demand for services as the economy develops (Squire, 1981, p. 136).

It is important to recognise that in this potential the service sector is very diversified, both in terms of productivity, income levels generated and in the motivation of the participants involved. There is in fact an *intermediate sector*, which appears in many areas as a reservoir of dynamic enterprises and entrepreneurs, and lies in distinct contrast to a large body of residual and underemployed labour in another segment of the service sector (House, 1984). It is in this intermediate sector where a strong potential exists for the accumulation of capital assets, increased incomes and employment opportunities. Investment induces significant increases in incomes and — given the labour intensity involved — improved job opportunities.

Along with the wide variety of service sector opportunities such as repair operations and trading, a critical and often assumed service in both rural and urban areas lies within the transport sector. The seminal importance of transport in fostering rural development is well known (Howe and Richards, 1984). Access to urban services and facilities is especially important (Rushton, 1984). Yet too often the supply and quality of transport services in rural areas and the access to market centres is grossly inadequate (Carapetis *et al.*, 1984). The transport sector, if programmed properly, can be a source of considerable employment particularly when such services feed densely populated rural areas. Very little hard information is at hand which allows us to assess the true depth of this potential employment source. But there are now select pieces of evidence which suggest that workers do at least as well, if not better, than those in the formal sector (Costello *et al.*, 1987). [And with respect to the transport sector, 75% of those employed in Brazil, for example, had incomes in excess of the minimum wage (Squire, 1981).] Within Indonesia recent evidence reveals too that transport services can provide above average incomes (Leinbach and Suwarno, 1985).

SUMMARY AND PRESCRIPTION

The basic legislation providing for the transmigration programme in 1972 identified numerous goals which were to be achieved. Among these were the improvement of living standards and employment opportunities, stronger and more equitable regional development, achievement of a more balanced population distribution with the alleviation of population pressure in Inner Indonesia, and increased food and tree crop production. Mentioned also were the ability of the programme to foster nationalism and ethnic harmony. Clearly a major goal which has been emphasised over the long history of the programme is that which aims to achieve an improved spatial distribution of population across the nation. Such an objective however clearly ignores the greatly varying carrying capacities between Inner and Outer Indonesia and it is now accepted that such a goal is unattainable. While other objectives of transmigration have some merit, it is regional development in the last analysis which looms as the most important (Arndt and Sundrum, 1977; Babcock, 1986). Since the early 1970s, the concept of integrated regional and area planning — in contrast to sectoral planning — has taken hold (McAndrews *et al.*, 1981). In this perspective, transmigration is viewed as an important instrument which will provide a critical developmental thrust. Ideally this should occur through a series of linked centres with local economies which can attract self-motivated (*i.e.* spontaneous) settlers.

Viewed as a policy instrument, transmigration has had reasonably good but uneven success. While clearly there are numerous problems which must be adjusted, an important concern — in order to ensure future success of the efforts both in newly developed schemes and on existing settlements — is the matter of employment for the participants. In fact the major emphasis in the coming years may shift to the consolidation and redevelopment of existing sites.

Productive enterprises and employment may be fostered through the development of service and small manufacturing opportunities in and near transmigration settlements. Yet too little is known about the nature and extent of the off-farm and non-agricultural employment of settlers. Before a prescription for the employment question is provided a thorough study must be undertaken of existing and potential employment in both services and small manufacturing which are accessible to the schemes. Within this analysis an important matter is the spatial and aspatial characteristics of services and their operations. In order to take advantage of any employment potential a thorough understanding of the availability and access to services must be accomplished. In this connection, commuting and circulation are worthy of investigation. A matter also to be investigated is the need for new services and the matching of individuals with existing and potential services. This exploration of a new basis for employment must be carried out in concert with the NUDS. The functional potential of small and middle-sized towns in the Outer Islands must be integrated with the economic readaptation of existing transmigration settlements. Two questions which have remained unanswered in the transmigration effort are the opportunity costs of the per household cost of transmigration and the implications for urban unemployment in the Outer Islands if transmigration projects fail. The results of both of these would appear to be satisfactory if indeed new employment opportunities are investigated. Needless to say, the access to these opportunities is as critical as their existence. Just as in the cases of larger settlements efficient transport can provide a useful policy instrument by allowing commuting and circulation behaviour to become an adaptive mechanism.

REFERENCES

Arndt, H.W. and Sundrum, R.M., "Transmigration: Land Settlement or Regional Development?" *Bulletin of Indonesian Economic Studies* **13** (3), 72–90, 1977.

Arndt, H.W., "Transmigration: Achievements, Problems, Prospects", *Bulletin of Indonesian Economic Studies* **19** (3), 50–73, 1983.

Babcock, T.G., "Land Settlement in Indonesia: Some Current Needs for Socio-Economic Research", *Prisma* 9, 74–79, 1983.

Babcock, T., "Transmigration: The Regional Impact of a Miracle Cure", in *Central Government and Local Development in Indonesia*, MacAndrews, C. (Editor), pp. 157–189. Oxford University Press, Kuala Lumpur, 1986.

Burbridge, P., Dixon, J. and Soewardi, B., "Land Allocation for Transmigration", *Bulletin of Indonesian Economic Studies* **17** (1), 108–113, 1981.

Carapetis, S., Beenhakker, H.L. and Howe, J.D.F., *The Supply and Quality of Rural Transport Services in Developing Countries: A Comparative Review*. Staff Working Paper No. 654. The World Bank, Washington, D.C., 1984.

Chambers, R., *Rural Development: Putting the Last First*. Longmans, New York, 1983.

Costello, M., Leinbach, T.R. and Ulack, R., *Mobility and Employment in Urban Southeast Asia: Examples from Indonesia and the Philippines*. Westview Press, Boulder, 1987.

Fachrurrozie, S.A. and McAndrews, C., "Buying Time: Forty Years of Transmigration in Belitang", *Bulletin of Indonesian Economic Studies* **14** (3), 94–103, 1978.

Government of Indonesia, *National Urban Development Strategy Draft Final Report*, T2.3/3. Directorate of City and Regional Planning, Jakarta, September, 1985.

Hamer, A., Steer, A.D. and Williams, D.G., *Indonesia: The Challenge of Urbanization*. Staff Working Paper No. 787, The World Bank, Washington, D.C., 1986.

Hardjono, J., *Transmigration in Indonesia*. Oxford University Press, Kuala Lumpur, 1977.

Hardjono, J., "Transmigration: A New Concept", *Bulletin of Indonesian Economic Studies* **14** (1), 107–112, 1978.

Hardjono, J., "Rural Development in Indonesia: The Top Down Approach", in *Rural Development and the State*, Lea, D.A.M. and Chaudri, D.P. (Editors), pp. 38–65. Methuen, London, 1983.

Hardjono, J., "Transmigration: Looking to the Future", *Bulletin of Indonesian Economic Studies* **22** (2), 28–53, 1986.

House, W.J., "Nairobi's Informal Sector: Dynamic Entrepreneurs or Surplus Labor", *Economic Development and Cultural Change* **32** (2), 276–302, 1984.

Hugo, G., Hull, T., Hull, V. and Jones, G. *The Demographic Dimension in Indonesian Development*. Oxford University Press, Singapore, 1987.

Howe, J. and Richards, P. (Editors) *Rural Roads and Poverty Alleviation*. Intermediate Technology Publications, London, 1984.

Kohli, H.S. and Sood, A., "Fostering Enterprise Development", *Finance and Development* **24** (1), 34–36, 1987.

Leinbach, T.R., "Transport Evaluation in Rural Development: An Indonesian Case Study", *Third World Planning Review* **5** (1), 23–35, 1983.

Leinbach, T.R., "Rural Services Delivery in Indonesia", in *Rural Public Services: International Comparisons* Lonsdale, R. and Enyedi, G. (Editors), pp. 297–314. Westview Press, Boulder, 1984.

Leinbach, T.R., "Economic Growth, Development Planning, and Policy Alternatives in Medan, Indonesia", *Journal of Southeast Asian Studies* **18** (1), 118–140, 1987.

Leinbach, T.R. and Suwarno, B., "Commuting and Circulation Characteristics in the Intermediate-Sized City: The Example of Medan, Indonesia", *Singapore Journal of Tropical Geography* **6** (1), 35–47, 1985.

Lipton, M., *Why Poor Stay Poor: Urban Bias in World Development.* Harvard University Press, Cambridge, 1977.

MacAndrews, C., "Transmigration in Indonesia", *Asian Survey* **18**, 458–472, 1978.

MacAndrews, C., Sibero, A. and Fisher, H.B., *Regional Development, Planning and Implementation in Indonesia: The Evolution of a National Policy.* UNRCD, Nagoya, 1981.

Oberai, A.S., "Land Settlement Policies and Population Redistribution in Developing Countries: Performance, Problems and Prospects", *International Labour Review* **125** (2), 141–162, 1986.

Otten, M., "Transmigrasi: From Poverty to Bare Subsistence", *The Ecologist* **16** (No. 2/3), 71–76, 1986.

Richardson, H., "National Urban Development Strategies in Developing Countries", *Urban Studies* **18**, 267–283, 1981.

Richardson, H., "The Role of the Informal Sector in Developing Countries: An Overview", *Regional Development Dialogue* **5** (2), 3–40, 1984.

Richardson, H., "The Goals of National Urban Policy: The Case of Indonesia", *Urbanization and Urban Policies in Pacific Asia*, Fuchs, R.J., Jones, G.W. and Pernia, E.M. (Editors), pp. 277–300. Westview Press, Boulder, 1987.

Ross, M.R., "The Role of Land Clearing in Indonesia's Transmigration Programme", *Bulletin of Indonesian Economic Studies* **16** (1), 75–85, 1980.

Rushton, G., "Planning for the Spatial Integration of Services in Developing Countries", Unpublished manuscript, September, 1984.

Indonesia Development News, "Second Stage Development: Transmigration Program Encourages Private Investment", **10** (2), 6–7, 1986.

Secrett, C., "The Environmental Impact of Transmigration", *The Ecologist* **16** (2/3), 77–88, 1986.

Squire, L., *Employment Policy in Developing Countries.* Oxford University Press, New York, 1981.

Stohr, W.B. and Taylor, D.R.F. (Editors), *Development From Above or Below? The Dialectics of Regional Planning in Developing Countries.* John Wiley, New York, 1981.

Todaro, M. with Stilkind, J., *City Bias and Rural Neglect: The Dilemma of Urban Development.* Population Council, New York, 1981.

Weeks, J., "Policies for Expanding Employment in the Informal Urban Sector of Developing Countries", *International Labor Review* **110**, 1–13, 1975.

Weitz, R., Pelley, D. and Applebaum, L., "Model for the Planning of New Settlement Projects", *World Development* **8**, 105–123, 1980.

World Bank, *Indonesia: The Transmigration Program in Perspective.* The World Bank, Washington, D.C., 1988.

[14]

SETTLING FOR WAR: SOVIET IMMIGRATION AND ISRAEL'S SETTLEMENT POLICY IN EAST JERUSALEM

JOOST R. HILTERMANN

On 2 November 1990, U.S. Secretary of State James Baker reportedly told Israel's ambassador in Washington, Zalman Shoval, that the Bush administration was now prepared to move ahead with $400 million in loan guarantees to settle Soviet immigrants in Israel. The package, to which the administration had given its fiat a month earlier, had apparently been delayed because the United States had not received sufficient assurances from the Israelis that no immigrants would be settled beyond Israel's pre-1967 borders. The main stumbling block in the U.S.-Israeli discussions on the loan guarantees was the status of East Jerusalem, to which many of the new immigrants are being directed.

Israel's annexation of the Palestinian part of the city in 1967 has never been recognized by the world community. To forestall any discussion of relinquishing East Jerusalem to Palestinian control, successive Israeli governments have provided housing for Israeli citizens in huge "new (Jewish) neighborhoods." At present, close to half of East Jerusalem's population is Jewish. The Jerusalem issue, which Palestinians consider key in any future peace settlement, has remained dormant in U.S.-Israeli relations since the

---

Joost R. Hiltermann, an editor of *Middle East Report* (MERIP), works for the Palestinian human rights organization Al-Haq. He spent six weeks in the Soviet Union and Palestine in the fall of 1990.

Journal of Palestine Studies XX, no. 2 (Winter 1991), pp. 71-85.

Carter years, with differences in opinion being glossed over or not addressed. What catapulted Jerusalem to the fore over the past year, and what made it impossible to ignore it any longer, was the Soviet Jewish immigration.

Accommodating Soviet Immigrants

On 11 September, Absorption Minister Yitzhak Peretz welcomed the 100,000th immigrant of the year 1990 at Ben-Gurion airport.[1] A few days later, the quasi-governmental Jewish Agency announced that close to 200,000 Soviet immigrants were expected by the end of 1990, and predicted that by the end of 1992 there would be one million new Israeli citizens, a number that might double by 1995.[2]

It is not fully clear what has motivated the human wave in the direction of Israel. Many immigrants have been quoted as saying that their primary stimulus was a desire to escape economic hardships and the fear of future persecution in the Soviet Union, but that they would have preferred to move to the United States or other Western countries instead of Israel, had they been given the choice.[3] However, immigration restrictions in the United States have directed the flow toward Israel which, through its "Law of Return," bestows automatic citizenship on any Jew wishing to immigrate.[4] A Jewish Agency spokesman listed in an interview four reasons, in order of priority, why Jews were leaving the Soviet Union: "they feel that there is no role for them in the new U.S.S.R."; they perceive the Soviet economy as being headed for disaster; they fear further ecological crises in the aftermath of the Chernobyl accident and the Soviet government's inadequate handling of it; and (last and apparently least) they feel an "ethnic affinity with Israel."[5] The Soviet government, for its part, has removed most restrictions on the emigration of Soviet minorities, including Jews, in the past two years.

Economic hardships in the Soviet Union thus appear to be the prime motivator behind the population exodus. Many non-Jews want to leave as well but, pending new legislation on emigration, have not been able to do so.[6] Not surprisingly, there have been reports of people obtaining fake nationality certificates affirming their Jewishness[7] or marrying Jewish women in order to emigrate. One Israeli official recalled a joke he said was currently popular in the U.S.S.R.: "To get out of the Soviet Union, your best vehicle is a Jewish woman."[8] In Israel, persistent rumors have been circulating about the high non-Jewish component of the recent wave of immigrants. One Israeli journalist referred to this as "an open secret."[9] According to one government minister, as many as 30 percent of the new arrivals are not Jewish at all.[10] This may be a misleading figure, however, because of varying definitions of what constitutes a Jew.[11] Many of the Soviet immigrants appear to be persons of Jewish ancestry who have converted to Christianity. Church sources in Jerusalem have reported a dramatic increase in Russian membership in 1990.[12]

Tensions are now emerging between secular forces in Israel, which would like to attract as many Soviet immigrants as possible regardless of whether or not they are 100 percent Jewish (and which in fact welcome the secular orientation of most of the immigrants),[13] and a segment of the religious movement that fears the impact on its own political power of a secular tidal wave.[14] Meanwhile, the rate of immigration is going up, not down.

The immigration wave of 1990 is unmatched in Israel's 40-year history, which at its core is a history of conquest through immigration and settlement. A Jewish Agency spokesman referred to it in September 1990 as an "unprecedented experience, comparable to the U.S. absorbing 60 million foreigners."[15] Initially caught by surprise, Israeli society swiftly began to mobilize in 1990 to obtain the resources necessary to take in the new immigrants. In January, the government established a committee of directors to mobilize all government offices and coordinate immigration operations. A year earlier, the government had begun to phase out its method of placing new immigrants in absorption centers in favor of a system of "direct absorption." This new method has been particularly well-suited to accommodate the huge numbers of Soviet immigrants, who are highly educated and who—unlike, for example, the Ethiopian Jews—tend to assimilate into Israeli society fairly smoothly.

Under the new system, immigrants arriving at the airport are given a sum of money to cover basic living expenses during their first year in the country. The average family of three, for example, receives as the first installment of this stipend, or "absorption basket," a check for 4,880 New Israeli Shekels (NIS) and a cash sum of NIS 750 ($1=NIS 2).[16] In addition, they receive half a year of free health insurance and generous mortgage benefits. While at the airport, they are allowed to make one free telephone call to the Soviet Union and unlimited free calls anywhere in Israel. They then receive transportation to wherever they wish to go. Many join relatives or friends already living in Israel. Once they have found temporary accommodations, they open a bank account through which they receive the remainder of the stipend, for a total of NIS 23,000 for a family of three.[17] At this point they can also begin to take out loans, which they can use, for example, to pay off their mortgage on housing.[18] They stay in Israel on a temporary identity card, valid for 12 months. During this period they cannot leave the country, since they were made to surrender their Soviet passports on departure from the U.S.S.R. Eventually, they receive an Israeli passport. Travel outside Israel remains difficult, however, because of military service and the obligation to repay loans taken out to cover housing and living expenses.[19]

Since the summer of 1990, the absorption process has been managed by a special government body, referred to in Israel as the "Aliyah Cabinet." It meets every Sunday at 5 P.M., after the regular cabinet meeting. Its chairman is Ariel Sharon, the Housing Minister, with Absorption Minister Yitzhak Peretz as vice-chairman. Sharon himself, one of the main architects of the Lebanon invasion of 1982, is popularly referred to as the "Aliyah Czar" in Israel.

The Aliyah Cabinet comprises other government ministers (Yitzhak Moda'i of the Treasury, Aryeh Deri of the Interior, Moshe Nissim of Commerce, David Magen of Labor, Avner Shaki of Religious Affairs, among others), as well as heads of major institutions, such as Simcha Dinitz of the Jewish Agency and Michael Bruno of the Bank of Israel. Although the Aliyah Cabinet was originally given special powers to circumvent the regular bureaucracy, especially in approving building plans and housing construction, the Israeli High Court limited some of these powers following an appeal by left-wing Knesset members in July.[20] The Sharon team must otherwise submit all its projects to the Treasury, which so far has rejected most of them. For its grander schemes, then, the Aliyah Cabinet could be characterized as a monster without teeth, announcing plans that it does not have the authority to implement.[21]

The Aliyah Cabinet's main task has been to find housing and jobs for the new immigrants, with housing being given the immediate priority (since the immigrants don't need jobs until they have completed language classes, which take at least half a year). In August, the government adopted an amended emergency housing plan prepared by the Sharon team, approving construction of 45,000 housing units per year for three years and agreeing to import, as a stop-gap measure, 9,000 prefabricated homes and 5,000 trailer homes. At the same time, permission was granted to private entrepreneurs to import an additional 6,000 prefabs.[22] Furthermore, homeowners have been given tax-breaks on income from rents,[23] and building contractors have been given guarantees that the government will buy any units they are not able to sell on the open market within the period of one year.[24] In September, housing was still available: the smaller apartments had all been taken, but Soviet families or individuals were still finding larger apartments that they could share.

But Israeli officials were anticipating the real housing crunch to hit at any moment.[25] By mid-September, Sharon reported that only 5,000 units of the 45,000 for which he had gained approval were under construction at that time,[26] and construction in any case takes at least two years. Newspaper reports at the end of October suggested that building was underway on only 4,000 units, and that none of the 5,000 mobile homes had yet arrived in the country. The 45,000 units approved in August were intended to house the 150,000 immigrants who the government at that time anticipated would arrive in 1990. A further 100,000 units will be needed to house a further 400,000 immigrants in 1991, but these could not possibly be completed before 1993. It is unclear where the new immigrants would stay in the meantime, but Absorption Minister Yitzhak Peretz has already alluded to the need to settle the immigrants in tents.[27]

Although by the autumn of 1990 Soviet immigrants had not faced any serious housing problems, low-income Israelis were beginning to experience the class consequences of their government's policy. The urgent demand for apartments has pushed up rents and pushed out onto the street those who were unable to pay (mostly Oriental Jews). By August, news reports referred to some 1,600 families living in tent encampments throughout Israel.[28] Tent dwellers have demonstrated in front of the Knesset and elsewhere, and violence has erupted on more than one occasion.[29] The government has had its own priorities, though. It is clearly willing to compromise social peace among Jews if Jewish immigration can tip the demographic scales, which for the last few years had been projected to tilt toward the Palestinian population in Israel and the occupied territories in the coming decades, resulting in the ultimate Zionist nightmare, an Arab majority in "Greater Israel."[30]

Soviet Immigrants and the West Bank and Gaza Strip

The issue of Soviet immigration is proving extremely explosive, especially as it relates to settlement in the occupied territories, which for most of the world community includes East Jerusalem. Palestinians have voiced strong fears that Soviet immigrants will directly or indirectly displace them, as more are expected to be enticed by the relatively cheaper housing in the occupied territories, or as congestion and high rents within Israel induce other Israelis to move eastward into the West Bank.

Israeli settlement leaders have estimated that between 6,000 and 7,000 Israelis moved to settlements in the occupied territories (excluding East Jerusalem) in the first eight months of 1990, and that demand for housing was unusually high in that period.[31] As of June 1990, a total of 94,650 settlers lived in 140 settlements in the West Bank and Gaza, according to Israeli press reports.[32] Israel has been funding the construction of settlements and infrastructure, such as roads and sewers, in the occupied territories, and has granted special benefits both to contractors and to settlers building their own homes there.[33] In 1990 alone, the Israeli government allocated $80 million for settlement funding.[34]

Figures provided by the Jewish Agency suggest that between 1 April 1989 and 1 July 1990, only 275 immigrants settled in the West Bank and Gaza, and that an additional "20-25 families moved to the West Bank. . . of their own volition after they had stayed in absorption centers." Significantly, the Agency adds: "There is no possibility of obtaining exact statistics on this; once [immigrants] no longer receive monthly absorption allowances from any source, they are free to move without reporting to anyone."[35] Settler leaders are certainly aware of this. Israeli journalist Assaf Adiv charges that a number of immigrants who are registered as residents of particular Israeli cities actually live in West Bank settlements. He also claims that absorption centers financed by the government in the settlements of Ariel, Kfar Adumim, Kiryat Arba, and others have taken in thousands of new immigrants, who are taking Hebrew for a period of six months or more. This period allows settlers to do all they can to persuade the immigrants to stay in the settlements. Whether they will stay or not will become clear in the very near future as the first graduates emerge from the *ulpanim* (language classes).

In deference to sensitivities of the U.S. government and a significant segment of the American Jewish community, the Jewish Agency—which has budgeted $2.3 billion to help finance a joint plan with the Israeli government to absorb 150,000 immigrants in fiscal year 1990-91—is on record as stating that it "does *not* finance immigrant absorption in the administered territories," that is, the West Bank and Gaza Strip.[36] Assaf Adiv claims that the Jewish Agency is skirting the question: "The benefits that are granted to an Israeli citizen who settles in the occupied territories are so extensive that they compensate for the loss the immigrant would suffer" from not receiving the "absorption basket."[37] In addition, there is the issue of "fungibility," that is, the ability of the Israeli government and Jewish Agency to earmark funding for projects inside Israel, thereby freeing other funds for use in the occupied territories.[38] They can also launder monies, acting through subsidiary agencies that are under no restrictions not to spend in the occupied territories. Israeli journalist Danny Rubinstein, for example, has reported that money is routinely channeled to Jewish settlements through the "Settlement Division" of the World Zionist Organization.[39] Moreover, the Jewish Agency openly admits that Israeli government subsidies "are given to Israelis who settle in 'development areas' *on either side of the green line.*"[40]

But the real issue is not Soviet immigrants in the occupied territories. The real issue is *settlement* in the occupied territories. At least for the time being, the vast majority of immigrants are not themselves settling across the green line (except in East Jerusalem). The fear is that the congestion and skyrocketing rents in Israel's central coastal district caused by the Soviet influx will persuade other Israelis to take advantage of government subsidies in the West Bank. Given the infrastructure and housing already in place and the pattern of settlement that has already been established, the likelihood of this happening is great indeed.

Soviet Immigration and Jerusalem

The wave of new immigrants has also given Israel a golden opportunity to escalate its demographic battle for Jerusalem. Having placed a greatly enlarged East Jerusalem under Israeli law shortly after the June war in 1967 (annexing the area formally in 1980), Israel considers the "reunified" city to be its eternal capital.[41] The vast majority of world states do not recognize Israel's claim to sovereignty over all of Jerusalem, have declared the annexation illegal, and consider East Jerusalem as occupied territory similar in status to the West Bank, Gaza Strip, and Golan Heights. Successive Israeli governments have tried to strengthen their claim by swelling the Jewish population in the eastern part of the city. Both the current government and the Jewish Agency have openly declared their intention, based on what they consider their right, to settle Soviet immigrants in East Jerusalem.[42] In 1990, of the city's 354,000 Jewish inhabitants, an estimated 120,000 lived in "Jewish neighborhoods" across the green line, that is, in East Jerusalem, as opposed to some 140,000 Palestinians.[43] The almost exclusively Jewish neighborhoods include: French Hill, Pisgat Ze'ev, Neve Ya'cov and Ramot in the north, and Talpiot Mizrah and Gilo in the south.

So far, family considerations and employment opportunities have steered most of the Russian immigrants to the center of the country: 53 percent live in the central Tel Aviv-Rishon le Zion–Petah Tikva area; 32 percent in Haifa and the north; 5 percent in Beersheva and the Negev; and 10 percent in or near Jerusalem.[44] It is not clear how many immigrants have settled in the West Bank and Gaza Strip; Israeli officials suggest that the figure is less than 1 percent.[45] But saturation in the center is bound to create outward pressures, and for the Soviet immigrants, the majority of whom are urban dwellers, Jerusalem may turn out to be the most attractive. As of late September 1990, however, the government had turned down requests by the Jerusalem Municipality to provide special subsidies to immigrants wishing to settle in Jerusalem.[46]

During the first seven months of 1990, 5,375 immigrants moved to Jerusalem, according to Municipality statistics.[47] It is not entirely clear in what part of the city most of them settled. According to the city computer, which was running behind, 1,860 immigrants (of the 3,959 for whom it had a record at the end of July) had moved to five of the six Jewish neighborhoods in East Jerusalem mentioned above, while 449 had settled in West Jerusalem. An additional 1,650 had moved to areas that are included in the category "Other," which are mostly small neighborhoods in West Jerusalem and French Hill in East Jerusalem.[48] It is therefore fair to say that during the first seven months of 1990, an estimated 50 percent of all immigrants who moved to Jerusalem (i.e., 5 percent of the national total) settled in the city's annexed eastern part. In September and October, however, the rate of immigration to Jerusalem declined.[49]

With continuing mass immigration, however, the potential for a higher rate of Jewish settlement in East Jerusalem in the coming years is great, especially since the bureaucracy needed to accommodate the new immigrants is now in place. The most powerful agency involved in the absorption process in Jerusalem is the Jerusalem Development Authority, a semi-autonomous state-funded corporation charged with promoting the city's economic growth. It is responsible for designing city plans and large economic projects, and, during the current wave of immigration, for providing housing and creating jobs for the new arrivals. The Authority works in close coordination with the Municipality and the various government ministries.[50]

In addition, in late 1989, the Jerusalem Municipality set up a special bureaucracy to regulate the flow of immigrants, the Immigrant Absorption Project (IAP). The IAP is an inter-agency forum responsible for facilitating "direct absorption" in Jerusalem. The Jerusalem Municipality, the Jerusalem Development Authority, the Jewish Agency, the Ministry of Absorption, the Ministry of Housing, the Ministry of Labor, the Jerusalem Foundation, and other ministries and voluntary organizations are all represented in the Project, the policymaking steering committee of which is chaired by Jerusalem's long-time mayor, Teddy Kollek.

The IAP does not have a great deal of autonomy; it merely has a problem-solving task in the accommodation of immigrants in Jerusalem, as opposed to the policymaking powers of the Jerusalem Development Authority locally and the Aliyah Cabinet at the national level. The Project has a dual mandate: on the one hand it addresses structural issues such as construction, employment, and development; on the other, it seeks to smooth the absorption process by providing information to new immigrants, assisting in their social problems, and helping them find housing, employment, and retraining opportunities. For the latter tasks, the forum relies in large part on volunteer efforts through neighborhood community centers that organize neighborhood absorption committees.[51] The strength of the absorption effort in Jerusalem lies precisely in this organizational bifurcation: to work through Municipality departments and government ministries in order to lay the infrastructure for absorption, while using neighborhood volunteers to help assimilate immigrants as quickly and smoothly as possible into local communities.[52]

To be ready for the thousands of immigrants that are expected in the next few years, the Municipality is also moving ahead with large-scale construction in East Jerusalem. In the span of half a year in 1990 alone, the Municipality approved six new (Jewish) neighborhoods in the northern part of East Jerusalem for a total of 16,000 apartments, which are projected to accommodate 56,000 persons. All of these are extensions of existing Jewish settlements.[53] One of them, Ras Ammar, designed to connect Pisgat Ze'ev with French Hill, can only be completed if the Palestinian village of Anata and the Shu'fat refugee camp are removed. Leftist members of the Municipal Council have charged that Kollek intends to create an "unbroken Jewish territorial continuity" in the northern part of East Jerusalem by moving the Palestinian population to other areas, including the Wadi Joz neighborhood of East Jerusalem.[54] Municipality sources assert that all "vacant" areas within the city's northern boundaries have now been planned for new Jewish neighborhoods. "Vacant land" was expropriated from its Palestinian owners for "public purposes" in two major land grabs in 1970 and 1980.[55]

In the south, the Municipality is planning to build a new settlement called Har Khoma, consisting of 4,000 units, between the Palestinian village of Sur Baher and the town of Bayt Sahur. The Municipality decided to appropriate the money to hire a planner for this purpose at the beginning of the summer, and work on the plan has begun. In September, municipal sources were predicting that the plan would be completed, presented and approved soon, outside the regular democratic channels. One of the powers given the Aliyah Cabinet was to present any town planning scheme of over 200 units directly to a special committee of the Ministry of the Interior rather than to the relevant town council. This reduces the three months of public review provided for under the law to a mere 20 days. A member of the Jerusalem Municipal Council opposed to the plan asserts that Mayor Kollek fully backs this procedure, because it allows him to implement his own ideas without opposition by circumventing the Municipal Council where on most issues he has only 11 guaranteed votes out of 31. "These new neighborhoods are all part of Kollek's policy," the official said. "He is a strategic, low-key and brilliant planner."[56] Sarah Karminker, a member of the Municipal Council for the left-wing Citizens Rights Movement (RATZ), criticized the Har Khoma plan, saying that it had originally been designated as a green zone. Kollek reportedly responded that trees had been planted in the area only to prevent Palestinian construction as long as the city did not have the means to populate the area with Jews.[57]

By November, the Har Khoma project had run into serious trouble. Palestinians from villages in the area had turned up claiming ownership to plots of land that the Municipality had said were Jewish property. Some local journalists estimated that the plan would die an early death.[58] Others predicted that more land would be expropriated from Palestinian owners.[59] An additional 16,000 units are currently envisioned to connect Har Khoma to the existing neighborhoods of Gilo and Talpiot Mizrah.

The United States, Israel, and East Jerusalem

The United States has never openly supported Israel's exclusive claim to all of Jerusalem, but neither has it opposed in any substantive way attempts to integrate the two parts of the city and build Jewish neighborhoods in the occupied section. Generally, the U.S. position is that the final status of the city should be settled in comprehensive peace negotiations. Jimmy Carter raised the issue once during his administration, but backed down in the face of a fierce Israeli response. That was the last public mention of the subject until 3 March 1990, two months after the first waves of Soviet immigrants had started to arrive, when President George Bush declared that "the foreign policy of the United States says we do not believe there should be new settlements in the West Bank or in East Jerusalem."[60] According to the *Washington Post*, the Shamir government reacted by making "a point on the Jerusalem issue," rejecting a plan that would permit a resident of East Jerusalem to participate in preliminary Israeli-Palestinian peace negotiations.[61] The Shamir government subsequently collapsed, and the Jerusalem issue remained submerged for several more months.

One of the reasons East Jerusalem had become an issue again was Israel's request that the United States guarantee $400 million in housing loans to settle Soviet immigrants. On 1 March 1990, when the loan guarantee bill was before Congress, Secretary Baker, testifying before the House Subcommittee on foreign aid appropriations, raised concerns that the money could be used, either directly or by freeing up other funds,[62] to build new settlements or expand existing ones in the occupied territories. He appeared to be linking U.S. approval of the loan guarantees to Israeli assurances to halt further settlement activity, and while he did not specifically mention East Jerusalem, President Bush did two days later, precisely in response to a question concerning Baker's statements. Thus, while Congress approved the loan guarantee bill in early summer, it languished in the administration, apparently for want of the appropriate Israeli assurances.

Then, on 2 October 1990, the Bush administration announced that it was releasing the $400 million in loan guarantees after having received what Secretary Baker told reporters were "unprecedented" assurances that went "considerably beyond" Israel's usual commitment merely not to use the funds in the occupied territories. According to Baker, Israeli Foreign Minister David Levy had pledged in a letter (the contents of which were not then made public) that "immigrants would not be settled beyond the green line"[63]—the green line being consistently defined in U.S. press reports as the 1948 armistice line separating Israel from Jordan until the June 1967 war. The Israeli assurance, therefore, was generally interpreted to include East Jerusalem.

However, the very next day, on 3 October, Israeli officials vigorously denied that new assurances had been given and stated that Israel would continue building housing units and settling immigrants in East Jerusalem.[64] As if to underline this point, Prime Minster Yitzhak Shamir on 7 October announced plans to build a new Jewish settlement near the Al-Tur neighborhood of East Jerusalem.[65] In response to these statements and actions, Baker released the text of Levy's letter on 10 October. Meanwhile, tensions between Israel and the United States had heightened considerably because of the killing of 17 Palestinians on the Haram al-Sharif on 8 October, and more particularly because of the U.S. sponsorship of a UN Security Council resolution passed 12 October condemning "the acts of violence committed by the Israeli security forces." The resolution also requested, "in connection with the decision of the Secretary-General to send a mission to the region, which the Council welcomes, that he submit a report to it before the end of October 1990 containing his findings and conclusions."*

Israel saw the resolution as undermining its claim to sovereignty over all of Jerusalem. Two days later, on 14 October, Sharon's Aliyah Cabinet announced that 15,000 new housing units would be built in East Jerusalem.[66] In fact, Sharon's move was merely a public relations exercise. Sources in the Jerusalem Municipality stress that the construction plan had been approved by the Municipality before Sharon even assumed his new post, and that in any case the Aliyah Cabinet does not have the power to approve housing plans in Jerusalem, but merely to implement them by allocating the necessary funds.[67] Meanwhile, Jerusalem Mayor Teddy Kollek declared that there were plans to build "immediately" 12,000 new housing units that had already been approved for Soviet immigrants in Jewish neighborhoods in East Jerusalem.[68]

* See Doc. IIf under Special File: The Haram al-Sharif Killings in this issue—*Ed. note.*

Baker responded to Sharon's announcement on 16 October, stating that the new construction plans would violate the assurances provided by Levy in his letter of 2 October. "The letter is quite clear, I think, in speaking about areas outside the green line," he said.[69] Meanwhile, the Levy letter had caused a stir in Israel because of the U.S. understanding of the "green line" issue; Levy came under fire for having conceded the right to settle immigrants in East Jerusalem, even if he had done so only according to the U.S. definition of the green line. In a new letter dated 18 October, Levy asserted that Israel was under no "obligation—directly or indirectly—not to build in Jerusalem, or to limit building in Jerusalem, or in any other place," but that the $400 million in housing loan guarantees "will be used in geographic regions in which Israel ruled before June 5, 1967." The U.S. media reported that Levy had "retracted" the commitments he had made in his 2 October letter.

A careful reading of the two Levy letters,* however, reveals that the second is not a retraction of the first, and that the source of the confusion is differing definitions of the term "green line," a confusion exploited by the Israelis to their advantage. On the issue of Soviet immigrants, Levy says in his 2 October letter that "the government of Israel's policy is not to direct or settle Soviet Jews beyond the green line." On the issue of U.S. funds, Levy says: "Uses of the housing loan guarantees will be restricted to the geographic areas which were subject to the government of Israel's administration prior to June 5, 1967." This second commitment is precise and therefore unambiguous: these "geographic areas" clearly include East Jerusalem. Indeed, this is not a new condition; it has been part and parcel of the annual U.S. aid package to Israel. The first commitment, however, is open to dual interpretation because of the use of the term "green line."

The "green line" was the name given after 1948 to the armistice line separating the belligerents following the war between the new Jewish state and its Arab neighbors, particularly Jordan. However, "green line" is not an official legal—but rather an informal social—designation. To most Israelis, and certainly to the Israeli government, the green line actually moved westward following the conquest and annexation of East Jerusalem and its surrounding areas in June 1967, so that the area "beyond the green line" in Israeli parlance does not include East Jerusalem: as Ariel Sharon declared on 15 October, "There is no green line in Jerusalem. We never took on ourselves a commitment not to build in Jerusalem—never."[70] Thus, what Levy, in his efforts to assuage the passions he had stirred among his detractors in Israel, in essence did in his second letter was to remove the ambiguity fostered in his first letter by the term "green line." Basically, however, the two letters outline the same positions: (1) that Israel will not direct Jews beyond the green line, as defined to exclude East Jerusalem; and (2) that Israel will not

* For the texts of the two letters, see documents C1 and C3 in this issue—*Ed. note*.

use the loan guarantees in any of the areas conquered in 1967, including East Jerusalem.

During the latter part of October, U.S.-Israeli tensions rose to new heights, particularly as a result of the continuing fallout from the Haram al-Sharif killings and Washington's vote for a second UN Security Council resolution critical of Israel. The fate of the loan guarantee agreement remained unclear during this period, despite reported assurances on 25 October from President Bush to Prime Minister Shamir that the United States had no intention of continuing the housing debate any further.[71] The next day, Sharon told visiting U.S. officials of the Jewish Agency: "We are going for a massive construction plan in the heart of Jerusalem, at least 5,000 [homes] a year for the next eight years, most of it in East Jerusalem."[72] On 31 October, Israeli officials blamed the Bush administration for holding up the loan guarantees. Israeli papers reported that the United States was still not satisfied about Israeli assurances that no new immigrants would be settled in East Jerusalem.[73] The entire matter ended on 2 November, when Baker told the Israeli ambassador that the United States had finally given the green light to the program and was sending a team from the Agency for International Development (AID) to Israel to work out details.[74]

Conclusion: Settling for War

Thus, to all appearances, the United States has essentially acquiesced in Israel's goal to "reunify" Jerusalem by settling immigrants in the city's eastern part captured in 1967. In light of continuing immigration from the Soviet Union and the United States' tendency to look the other way, the only question that remains is what strategy Israeli policymakers will pursue in their quest to settle and thereby conquer all of "Greater Israel," including East Jerusalem. The current government, with a blustering Ariel Sharon heading the Aliyah Cabinet, seems to take the approach of settling the Soviets as fast as possible (even if many are not Jews), wherever they want, and whatever the political price may be in terms of worsening relations with the United States and the European Community. Others advocate a more subtle approach, one that in the end may prove even more successful, and at a lesser short-term political expense. Their standard bearer is Jerusalem Mayor Teddy Kollek, who said on 22 October, at the funeral of one of three Israelis killed by a Palestinian in the city the day before: "The solution is to bring as many immigrants to the city as possible and make it an overwhelming Jewish city, so that they will get it out of their heads that Jerusalem will not be Israel's capital. Coexistence is a must, but they must understand they cannot go on doing as they wish while we remain restrained."[75]

The logical result of either approach, however, is another war between Israel and its neighbors, who will not accept the mass exodus of Palestinians that will be needed to settle successfully and safely Jews in the occupied territories. The United States bears significant responsibility for whatever may ensue, having in effect financed the settlement of Soviet immigrants in East Jerusalem, while failing to prevent Israel from proceeding to settle its citizens in other areas of the occupied territories.

NOTES

1. *Jerusalem Post*, 12 September 1990. By 31 October 1990, the total number of immigrants stood at 122,592. (*New York Times*, 2 November 1990). Some 90 percent of the immigrants hail from the Soviet Union.
2. *Jerusalem Post*, 18 September 1990.
3. Interview with Israeli journalists in Moscow and Jerusalem, September 1990. See also, *Jerusalem Post*, 2 August 1990.
4. For a detailed background of these issues, see Geoffrey Aronson, "Soviet Jewish Emigration, the United States, and the Occupied Territories," *Journal of Palestine Studies* 19, no. 4 (Summer 1990), pp. 30-45.
5. Interview with Yehuda Weinraub, Deputy Spokesman of the Jewish Agency, West Jerusalem, 18 September 1990.
6. From interviews in Moscow and Leningrad in September 1990.
7. See, for example, *Moscow News* (weekly), no. 34, 1990.
8. Interview, West Jerusalem, 23 September 1990.
9. Interview, West Jerusalem, 18 September 1990.
10. The Israeli Minister of the Interior, Aryeh Deri, reportedly made this claim, which has gained great currency in Israel. (*Washington Post*, 30 July 1990). Deri is a member of the ultra-orthodox Shas Party which adheres to a very strict definition of who is a Jew.
11. According to the Law of Return, a person can become an Israeli citizen if he or she has at least one grandparent who is Jewish, has converted to Judaism, or is married to a Jew. Orthodox religious forces in Israel, on the other hand, define a Jew as someone whose mother must be Jewish, and they reject certain types of conversions as illegitimate.
12. Interview, West Jerusalem, 17 September 1990.
13. *Jerusalem Post* (International Edition), 3 November 1990.
14. According to the strict, religious definition of who is a Jew, there are only an estimated 2 million Jews in the USSR. However, as many as 7 million Soviet citizens might be eligible for Israeli citizenship under the more liberal definition. (Interview with an absorption official, West Jerusalem, 25 September 1990). One official involved in the absorption process, Michael Kleiner of the Likud, who adheres to the religious definition, contends that between 5 and 12 million Soviets could possibly claim Israeli citizenship. (*Washington Post*, 30 July 1990).
15. Interview with Yehuda Weinraub, deputy spokesman of the Jewish Agency, West Jerusalem, 18 September 1990.
16. Half of this "absorption basket" is financed by the Jewish Agency. ("Immigration from the Soviet Union: Background, Facts, and Figures," document provided by the press division of the Jewish Agency, West Jerusalem, 11 July 1990).
17. Between 1 July and 1 November, immigrants received NIS 18,000 but did not have to pay import duties on belongings they brought into the country. Because this system hurt the Soviet immigrants (who tend to bring along very few of their belongings) and favored immigrants from western countries, it was changed. As of 1 November, all immigrants receive NIS 23,000, but they must pay taxes on the goods they bring into the country. (Before 1 July a family of three received NIS 21,000, and did owe import duties).
18. Immigrants receive special mortgages, and an attempt is made to induce them to move away from the center of the country, which is heavily congested. (*Jerusalem Post* [International Edition], 3 November 1990).
19. From interviews with officials at the Ministry of Absorption and the Jewish Agency, West Jerusalem, September 1990.
20. According to justice Shlomo Levine, a member of the High Court's three-judge panel, "There's no doubt that the absorption of immigrants is vital and demands unconventional means. Nevertheless, the emergency powers include extraordinary powers, and any mistake in these matters could mean that future generations would have to pay for them." Quoted in *New York Times*, 18 July 1990. The High Court ruling relates only to the Aliyah Cabinet's power to take short-cuts in providing building permits. (Telephone interview with Israeli journalist Nurit Wargaft of *Kol Ha'ir*, West Jerusalem, 10 November 1990).
21. Telephone interview with Israeli journalist Nurit Wargaft of *Kol Ha'ir*, 10 November 1990.
22. *Washington Post*, 3 August 1990.
23. Interview with Ida Ben Shetrit, spokeswoman at the Ministry of Absorption, West Jerusalem, 25 September 1990.
24. *Jerusalem Post* (International Edition), 3 November 1990.
25. *Jerusalem Post* (International Edition), 3 November 1990.
26. *Jerusalem Post*, 17 September 1990.
27. *Jerusalem Post* (International Edition), 3 November 1990.
28. *New York Times*, 5 August 1990. By the end of October, though, most of these families had found temporary shelter, and only a reported 350 families remained in tents. (*Jerusalem Post* [International Edition], 3 November 1990).
29. See, for example, *Jerusalem Post*, 31 July 1990; and *In Jerusalem* (weekly insert in the Friday *Jerusalem Post*), 3 August 1990.
30. Currently, the population of Israel and the occupied territories comprises 61 percent Jews and 39 percent Palestinians. Without immigration, projections are that by the year 2000 these figures will be 55 and 45 percent, respectively, and that by the year 2015 there will be equilibrium. Large-scale immigration will not seriously affect this trend, however. Equilibrium will come only five years later, in 2020. (Israeli demographers quoted by Assaf Adiv in "Jewish Immigration

and its Implications" [unpublished article in Hebrew, June 1990; used by permission of Derekh HaNitzotz, West Jerusalem]).

31. *New York Times*, 23 September 1990.

32. Foreign Broadcast Information Service, 29 June 1990, quoting *Ha'Aretz*, 22 June 1990.

33. *New York Times* reported that settlers who build their own home "get the land virtually for free" while more than half the amount of their mortgages is interest-free (23 September 1990). The Jewish Agency reports that the government provides "contractor subsidies" that include (1) "interim financing for construction: a grant of 50 percent of the cost of development (something like $20,000 per housing unit)," and (2) "a government guarantee of partial purchase of such apartments as are not sold." The government also provides "buyer subsidies: the average mortgage for a family of three in development areas is $32,000 ($5,000 less than an immigrant family receives under the same terms, regardless of where it settles)" (Jewish Agency, "Immigration from the Soviet Union.")

34. *Washington Post*, 4 October 1990.

35. Jewish Agency, "Immigration from the Soviet Union."

36. Jewish Agency, "Immigration from the Soviet Union." (Emphasis in the original.)

37. Assaf Adiv, "Jewish Immigration and its Implications."

38. See U.S. Secretary of State James Baker's remarks before the House subcommittee on foreign aid appropriations on 1 March 1990, reprinted in *Journal of Palestine Studies* 19, no. 4 (Summer 1990), p. 176. One telling example was provided by a Jerusalem municipal official, who declared that it was impossible to furnish a detailed budget for immigrant absorption in Jerusalem because of its complexity. His office may, for instance, receive money from the Ministry of Education to hire teachers and purchase blackboards for use in Jewish "neighborhoods" in East Jerusalem. The Ministry itself may have received the money for general purposes from, for example, the Jewish Agency or the U.S. government, which would be unable to trace the money's exact trajectory. (Interview with Shmuel Eyal, manager of the Immigrant Absorption Project of the City of Jerusalem, West Jerusalem, 23 September 1990).

39. Interview, West Jerusalem, 24 September 1990.

40. Jewish Agency, "Immigration from the Soviet Union." (Emphasis in the original.)

41. Before the 1967 war, Israel occupied only what is now referred to as West Jerusalem, an area comprising 38,000 dunums (1 dunum = 1,000 square meters). In 1967, Israel conquered and annexed what was then the Jordanian city of Jerusalem (which includes the walled Old City), an area of 6,000 dunums. At the same time, Israel expanded the Jerusalem municipal boundaries to include a number of West Bank villages, reaching almost as far to the north as the town of Ramallah, and toward Bethlehem in the south, a total area of 64,000 dunums (i.e., more than the original eastern and western parts of the city together!), which it also annexed. (Hillel Bardin in *Jerusalem Post*, 22 October 1990, reprinted in *Mideast Mirror*, 22 October 1990).

42. The Jewish Agency is on record as not distinguishing between East and West Jerusalem. (Telephone interview with Yehuda Weinraub, deputy spokesman of the Jewish Agency, West Jerusalem, 22 September 1990).

43. Figures cited by Hugh Carnegy in *Financial Times*, 25 October 1990. In an interview in September, a member of the Jerusalem Municipal Council provided slightly higher figures: 130,000 Jews and 150,000 Palestinians in East Jerusalem.

44. Interview with Ida Ben Shetrit, spokeswoman at the Ministry of Absorption, West Jerusalem, 25 September 1990.

45. *Jerusalem Post* (International Edition), 3 November 1990.

46. Interview with Shmuel Eyal, manager of the Immigrant Absorption Project of the City of Jerusalem, West Jerusalem, 23 September 1990.

47. Of these, 4,342 came from the Soviet Union, according to a statistical report prepared by the Immigrant Absorption Project of the City of Jerusalem, 26 August 1990. (Copy provided by the Absorption Project, in Hebrew). In August, an additional 1,356 immigrants moved to Jerusalem. (Interview with Shmuel Eyal, manager of the Immigrant Absorption Project, West Jerusalem, 23 September 1990).

48. "Distribution of Immigrants to Jerusalem by Neighborhood." Statistical table, based on data in the city computer, provided by the Immigrant Absorption Project of the City of Jerusalem, August 1990. Very few Soviet immigrants have settled in French Hill so far, according to local residents, though many are expected.

49. Telephone interview with Israeli journalist Nurit Wargaft of *Kol Ha'ir*, West Jerusalem, 10 November 1990.

50. Telephone interview with a member of the Jerusalem Municipal Council, 10 November 1990.

51. Flow charts provided by the IAP, September 1990. [Hebrew].

52. Interview with Shmuel Eyal, IAP manager, West Jerusalem, 23 September 1990.

53. Interview with a member of the Jerusalem Municipal Council, West Jerusalem, 24 September 1990.

54. As reported by Assaf Adiv, "Jewish Immigration and its Implications."

55. Interview with a member of the Jerusalem Municipal Council, West Jerusalem, 24 September 1990.

56. Interview with a member of the Jerusalem Municipal Council, West Jerusalem, 24 September 1990.

57. Reported by Assaf Adiv, "Jewish Immigration and its Implications."

58. Telephone interview with Israeli journalist Nurit Wargaft of *Kol Ha'ir*, West Jerusalem, 10 November 1990.

59. Hillel Bardin in *Jerusalem Post*, 22 October 1990, reprinted in *Mideast Mirror*, 22 October 1990.

60. Remarks by George Bush at a press conference in Palm Springs, CA, on 3 March 1990. Reprinted in *Journal of Palestine Studies* 19, no. 4 (Summer 1990), p. 179.

61. *Washington Post*, 18 October 1990.

62. *Washington Post*, 4 October 1990.

63. See note 38, *supra*.

64. *Washington Post*, 4 October 1990.

65. *Jerusalem Post* (International Edition), 20 October 1990.

66. *Washington Jewish Week*, 18 October 1990.

67. Telephone interview with a member of the Jerusalem Municipal Council, 10 November 1990.

68. *Jerusalem Post* (International Edition), 20 October 1990.

69. *Washington Jewish Week*, 18 October 1990.

70. In an interview on Israel army radio, as reported in *Washington Jewish Week*, 18 October 1990. The transcript in Foreign Broadcast Information Service, 15 October 1990, reads slightly differently.
71. *Mideast Mirror*, 25 October 1990. (Translated from *Al Hamishmar*).
72. Quoted in *Mideast Mirror*, 26 October 1990.
73. *Washington Times*, 1 November 1990.
74. *Los Angeles Times*, 3 November 1990.
75. Quoted in *Mideast Mirror*, 22 October 1990. Kollek had said earlier in 1990: "We Jews are the vast majority, and we must act with wisdom, and then it will take a generation or two until the city is united." (*Guardian*, 24 May 1990).

Journal of Southern African Studies, Vol. 18, No. 2, June 1992

*Comprehensive Segregation: the Origins of the Group Areas Act and its Planning Apparatuses**

ALAN MABIN
(Programme for Planning Research,
University of the Witwatersrand, Johannesburg)

In the early months of 1990, as the excitement of F.W. de Klerk's change of direction captured international attention, government television in South Africa offered its white viewers a new serial which revealed that those previously 'disqualified' people, showing an increasing tendency to move in next door, might even be 'People Like Us'.[1] This crude, if entertaining, ideological manipulation provided an extraordinary antithesis to earlier National Party contortions. Exactly forty years before, when Dr T.E. Dönges introduced the Group Areas Bill in the House of Assembly, his staff had to cast around for evidence of the popularity of generalised, compulsory urban racial segregation. In doing so they found many examples of demands for, moves towards and attempts at enforced separation of 'race groups' in urban areas. Some of these Dönges cited during the lengthy parliamentary debates on the Group Areas Bill. But what were the forces pushing for comprehensive segregation? Who contributed to the framing of the Bill? Was there a preconceived scheme to impose a master plan for internal urban apartheid?

Our inability to answer these questions stems from the fact that the creation of 'group areas', usually considered to lie at the very core of urban apartheid, has not yet been studied by scholars. The origins of the Group Areas Act have been the subject of some speculations but no serious research; the same applies to examination of the specific nature of the changes which it introduced, and to the

* Although not all would be aware of it, and some might wish to disavow the product, many people have more or less directly contributed to the production of this paper. Maria da Silva brought back an early haul from the State Archives; Ron Davies, Peter Wilkinson, Debbie Posel and Chris Saunders provided useful information and stimuli; Bill Nasson, John Lazar, Paul La Hausse and Cynthia Kros helped with conversations; Dan Smit provided ideas and reflections as well as the spark to get going; commentators at the 1990 Wits History Workshop and referees for this Journal provided direction. Financial support from the Centre for Science Development is gratefully acknowledged.

[1] This TV series portrayed the circumstances of a 'Coloured' family moving into a formerly white neighbourhood; its screening was delayed for two years according to *The Star, Tonight!* supplement, 25 January 1990, p. 10.

processes by which the superficially obvious policy of segregating towns and cities actually translated into practice. Thus two of the more substantial scholarly texts which address 'group areas', the Kuper, Watts and Davies study of Durban in the 1950s and Western's treatment of Cape Town under the Group Areas Act, both make rather glib assumptions about the Act's background. The latter accounts (without much evidence) for the Act essentially in terms of 'strategic' motives: the need for spatial separation to maintain white domination; while recognising that material gain played some role. Kuper, Watts and Davies more or less ignored developments outside Natal or even Durban which might have contributed to the 'group areas' 'solution'.[2] Studies of particular places 'before and after' the Group Areas Act tend to emphasise the results, often horrible in personal terms, of the Act's implementation, without examining in much if any detail the contested processes by which authorities achieved often partial enforcement.[3]

This article explores the roots of the Group Areas Act and the processes by which its provisions were (incompletely) applied to the urban landscape, making use of sources which may not have been accessible to previous authors, as Gordon Pirie suggested in 1984.[4] Recent work on the origins and implementation of apartheid provides a stimulus to re-examine 'group areas'.[5] Yet this work has not, so far, addressed 'group areas' in any detail. Unlike Bantu Education, for example, the Group Areas Act was not preceded by an elaborate and well-known commission, chaired by a leading figure in the framing and development of apartheid policy like W.W.M. Eiselen. Possibly this lapse on the part of the National Party government accounts for the mystery which lies behind the present implicit acceptance of 'group areas' simply as an inevitable part of apartheid. A theme of the article, then, is that 'group areas' did not follow from some master plan conceived and applied in any unilateral fashion by the Nationalist government after 1948.

A second theme lies in the close relationship which existed between the concerns of urban planning and the emergence of compulsory segregation. To pose the question of the relation between planning and 'group areas' is not original. In a largely theoretical account, McCarthy and Smit suggested the importance of ethnic zoning within the typical planning desire for efficiency and order. Dan Smit elaborated this view in his thesis on the political economy of planning, but offered little new information on specific connections between town planning and the

---

[2] J. Western, *Outcast Cape Town* (Cape Town: Human and Rousseau, 1981), pp. 74-83; L. Kuper, H. Watts and R.J. Davies, *Durban: a Study in Racial Ecology* (London: Jonathan Cape, 1958).

[3] Cf. J.G. Nel, 'The State and Residential Apartheid in Port Elizabeth', Society for Geography conference, Pretoria, 1989; A.J. Christopher, 'Apartheid Planning in South Africa: the Case of Port Elizabeth', *The Geographical Journal*, 153, 2 (1987), pp. 195-204.

[4] Cf. G. Pirie, 'Race Zoning in South Africa: Board, Court, Parliament, Public', *Political Geography Quarterly*, 3, 3 (1984), p. 211.

[5] For example, D. Posel, 'Influx Control and the Construction of Apartheid', unpub. D.Phil. thesis, Oxford University, 1987; D. Posel, 'The Meaning of Apartheid Before 1948: Conflicts, Interests and Forces Within the Afrikaner Nationalist Alliance', *Journal of Southern African Studies*, 14, 1 (1987), pp. 123-139; J. Lazar, 'Community and Conflict in Afrikaner Nationalist Politics in South Africa 1948-61', unpub. D.Phil. thesis, Oxford University, 1987.

origins and implementation of the Group Areas Act. Jeff McCarthy hints intriguingly at the close connection between planning for Durban's expansion in the 1940s and planners' perceived needs for draconian (ethnic) removal legislation;[6] but no published work yet fleshes out these ideas through careful examination of the available evidence. This article shows that procedures developed under the Act both derived from established planning practices, and enticed town planners into the implementation of comprehensive racial segregation.

Like other features of apartheid, as Nolutshungu and Wolpe have recently suggested,[7] a key to understanding the origins and early implementation of the Group Areas Act lies in defining just what changes the Act introduced. A third aspect of the present article explores the multiplicity of changes introduced by the Group Areas Act, which certainly suggests a complex genesis. That the Act was in part intended to codify and strengthen the attack on some Indian property rights in Natal is not in dispute. But the tendency to see this feature as *the* explanation of the Act and the Durban City Council as primary agitator in its cause[8] is clearly inadequate. Indeed, the Group Areas Act effectively guaranteed property rights to Indians, albeit in narrowly defined areas, reversing the legal tendency of the previous quarter century. As the Chairman of the Land Tenure Advisory Board (the original implementing body) put it in 1952, Indians were *entitled* to property rights.[9]

Other changes usually lost from view were perhaps as important. It could be argued that for the first time, the Group Areas Act at least potentially extended compulsory general segregation to 'Coloureds'; centralised control over racial segregation, effectively undermining municipal autonomy; laid the basis for long-range, wide-scale land allocation planning; opened the way to greatly expanded (though of course strictly segregated) public housing provision especially for the poorer sections of the urban population; provided for retroactive segregation; and massively interfered with concepts of property rights generally.

The article proceeds by examining, first, moves towards compulsory segregation in the period before the Second World War. It then examines the bureaucratic and

---

6 J. McCarthy and D. Smit, *South African City: Theory in Analysis and Planning* (Cape Town: Juta, 1984); D. Smit, 'The Political Economy of Urban and Regional Planning in South Africa 1900-1988: Towards Theory to Guide Progressive Planning Practice', unpublished PhD thesis, University of Natal, Durban, 1989, pp. 97-110; J. McCarthy, 'Problems of Planning for Urbanisation and Development: the Case of Natal's Coastal Margins', *Geoforum*, 17, 2 (1986), pp. 267-287.

7 S. Nolutshungu, *Changing South Africa* (Cape Town and Johannesburg, 1982); H. Wolpe, *Race, Class and the Apartheid State* (London, 1987).

8 As the Indian Congresses, the Johannesburg City Council's lawyer and Kuper *et. al.* did in the 1950s, followed by Fatima Meer in 1976 and others more recently; cf. statements by TIC and NIC in numerous documents; O.J. Frankel, representing Johannesburg at Land Tenure Advisory Board hearing, May 1955, in South African Central Archives, Pretoria (SA), Department of Planning series (BEP) 146, G7/139 'Verhoor om Groepsgebiede in Johannesburg'; Kuper, Watts and Davies, *Durban: a Study in Racial Ecology*, p. 34; F. Meer, 'Domination Through Separation', in D.M. Smith (ed), *Separation in South Africa: People and Policies*, Occasional Paper 6, Dept of Geography, Queen Mary College London, 1976, pp. 17-24.

9 Remark of G. de V. Hugo at an interview with representatives of the Pretoria City Council (29 May 1952, SA, BEP 131, G7/137).

political direction of wartime government thinking on post-war reconstruction, and shows what emerged from the resultant post-war planning ethos — with its strong zoning tendencies. The Act originated within this milieu, but new thinking also developed among powerful officials, particularly D.S. van der Merwe who chaired the crucial committees. Finally, the paper explores the development of procedures through which the Act could be implemented and their close relationship to the practice of more general urban planning.

Compulsory Segregation Before the Second World War

Quite obviously, specific allocation of land to segregated 'locations' for people other than the generally dominant whites and those whom they wanted close to their own places of residence has a long history in South Africa. Such 'planning' began to gather momentum, for example in Port Elizabeth, from the 1850s on.[10] By the early years of the twentieth century the republican government sought to demarcate areas for minority groups — Malays and Indians — resulting in numerous 'Asiatic Bazaars'. As with early public housing programmes, initiative and power resided in the colonial or republican governments. During the immediate post-Anglo-Boer War phase this situation altered, as colonial authorities began to transform the nature of local government. Thus, the Transvaal government transferred control of Asiatic Bazaars to municipalities and gave at least some of them the power to establish 'native' and 'coloured' locations.[11]

Passage of the Housing Act in 1920 created the Central Housing Board; its practice of approving only schemes for specific 'groups' enhanced already-entrenched segregation through public housing. Under the 1923 Natives (Urban Areas) Act local authorities gained the potential power to restrict most Africans to townships and compounds.[12] Yet these powers remained limited, and many urban areas remained or became more racially integrated. Successive governments contemplated legislation to provide for more substantial segregatory powers, yet with marginal exceptions each attempt was defeated or withdrawn.

Neither of the governments in power during the 1920s carried through their proposals in this regard. The Class Areas Bill of 1924, introduced by Patrick Duncan as Minister of the Interior, lapsed with the defeat of the South African

---

[10] J. Robinson, '"Progressive Port Elizabeth": Liberal Politics, Local Economic Development and the Territorial Basis of Racial Domination', *Geojournal,* 22, 3 (1990), pp. 293-304; Nel, 'The State and Residential Apartheid in Port Elizabeth'; Christopher, 'Apartheid Planning in South Africa: the Case of Port Elizabeth'.

[11] T.B. Floyd, 'Geskiedenis van Stadsbeplanning in Suid-Afrika', in E.W.N. Mallowes (ed), *Summer School of the SA Institute of Town Planners* (Johannesburg, 1959), pp. 6-19, and Smit, 'The Political Economy of Urban and Regional Planning in South Africa 1900-1988'; Transvaal Archives, Pretoria (TA), Colonial Treasurer series (CT) 152, T34/8 'Transfer of Asiatic Bazaars from Government to Municipalities', and SA, Land Tenure Advisory Board series (ARG) 10, Act 1/1/2/3/16 'Representations from public — Transvaal — Johannesburg City Council', schedule attached to D.R. Blaine to Deputy Town Clerk, 2 July 1938.

[12] T.R.H. Davenport, 'The Beginnings of Urban Segregation in South Africa: the Natives (Urban Areas) Act of 1923', Grahamstown: Rhodes University, Institute for Social and Economic Research, Occasional Paper, 1971.

Party at the polls. The new Minister, D.F. Malan, introduced essentially similar provisions in an Areas Reservation Bill in 1926, which was withdrawn to spare the government embarrassment in the course of discussions with the Indian government on 'repatriation'. Both bills sprang from a racist clamour for restriction of Indians; prominent among those demanding such action was the Natal Municipal Association, which held that 'every race should have its own area ... The local authority should have the power to compel people to reside in Class Areas'.[13]

In the 1930s legislation framed on less discriminatory lines lent itself to segregatory programmes. The 1934 Slums Act, in particular, allowed local authorities to condemn buildings or whole neighbourhoods, and move people — provided the funds were available — to new housing estates. Some did so on a grand scale: of course, segregation ruled, with different housing estates for those deemed by municipal officials to belong to different 'races'.[14] Meanwhile attempts continued to bring racial residential segregation more comprehensively on to the statute book.

To some extent the legislation of the 1930s kept local (white) demands for control over Indian property rights at bay. Frequent delay characterised the question. A 1930 select committee proposed a bill to reinforce the 1885 Asiatic Bazaar law, which became the Transvaal Asiatic Land Tenure Act (no 35 of 1932). But its toughest clause, which would have compelled local authorities to set aside 'Asiatic' areas, was postponed until after a second conference with the Indian government, and fell away when J.H. Hofmeyr replaced D.F. Malan as Minister in the new coalition government in 1933.[15]

Together, local councils and the central state had considerable if incomplete power to segregate Africans and Indians. In the Cape Province, white-dominated local authorities evidenced substantially greater concern over integration between 'Coloureds' and whites. In 1931, the Cape Province Municipal Association resolved at its annual congress — attended by delegates from many local authorities — to ask the Administrator to add powers to the existing municipal ordinance (No 10 of 1912) replicating for 'Coloureds' the location provisions of the 1923 Natives (Urban Areas) Act. Similar requests continued during the decade.[16]

---

13 *Report of the Select Committee on the Areas Reservation Bill* (S.C.9-1926), Evidence, para. 2404-2406.

14 S. Parnell, 'Racial Segregation in Johannesburg: the Slums Act, 1934-39', *South African Geographical Journal*, 70, 2 (1988), pp. 112-126; L. le Grange, 'Working class housing, Cape Town 1890- 1947', in A. Spiegel (ed) *Africa Seminar Collected Papers*, Vol. 5 (UCT, Centre for African Studies, 1985), pp. 13-37; J.P Joyce, 'Cape Town and the Origins of the Slums Act of 1934', unpub. BA (Hons) diss., UCT, 1981.

15 SA, ARG 12, Act 1/1/2/7, typescript Joint Report of the Asiatic Land Tenure Laws Amendments Committee and the Land Tenure Act Amendments Committee (hereafter t/s Joint Committee Report) para. 153-5, pp. 68-9. For more detail see A. Mabin, '"Doom at One Stroke of the Pen": Urban Planning and Group Areas c. 1935- 1955', paper presented to History Workshop conference, University of Witwatersrand, Johannesburg, 1990.

16 Cape Archives, Cape Town (CA), Provincial Secretary series (PAS), 3/171, AL39, Minutes of 24th Annual Congress of Cape Province Municipal Association, 1931; marginal notes by Provincial Secretary (PS); Town Clerk, Fort Beaufort, to PS 13 August 1938, and reply, 30 August 1938.

It may be that these requests were sparked by nervousness at the rise of militancy described by Gavin Lewis among 'Coloured' organisations in the 1930s.[17] The genesis and progress of organisations like the National Liberation League, and its effects on the politics of older, 'moderate' bodies like the African Peoples' Organisation could hardly have gone unnoticed by councils engaged in deliberate attempts to segregate 'Coloureds' in housing schemes. Probably more powerful than these fairly tame local pressures, however, was the rise of the new Afrikaner nationalism in organisations which included the Gesuiwerde Nasionale Party under D.F. Malan, and the Afrikaner Broederbond, which despite its largely Transvaal membership had significant policy stimuli from Cape circles, particularly Stellenbosch academics.[18] Given the conflicts and suspicions over economic and other matters between Cape and Transvaal members of both the Gesuiwerde Nasionale Party and the Afrikaner Broederbond described by Dan O'Meara, it is possible that evolving policy on white-'Coloured' segregation provided a unifying force within these organisations at the time. Wilkins and Strydom note that Afrikaner Broederbond policy on segregation evolved from the time of its first policy document on the subject in 1933, while the 'Afrikanerbond vir Rassestudie, under the leadership of Broederbonders, studied the concept of apartheid from 1935'.

Of course, in the mid-1930s the Afrikaner Broederbond and Gesuiwerde Nasionale Party could not simply have their way on 'Coloured'-white relations. Malan unsuccessfully sought 'Coloured' disfranchisement as an addendum to the 1936 Natives Representation Bill; J.G. Strydom lost a motion 'in favour of the introduction of legislation for determining and setting aside separate residential and business areas for certain classes of persons' in a select committee in 1937. Wilcocks, chairing the Commission of Enquiry into 'Coloured' welfare, could not gain majority support for his recommendation that 'the demarcation between European, "Coloured" and Native areas should be distinct'.[19] But 'Coloured' segregation was a developing idea, and one which touched a raw nerve in the uneasy coalition which became the United Party. Whatever the agreements arrived at in Afrikaner nationalist circles at the time, the Afrikaner Broederbond constitution of 1944 stated that 'all Broeders in their political action will strive for ... (3.) Segregation of all 'Coloured' races domiciled in South Africa ...'. The Afrikaner Broederbond was certainly capable of organising nationally in support of parliamentary action by Gesuiwerde Nasionale Party members, as Hertzog pointed out in his famous Smithfield attack on the Afrikaner Broederbond in 1935.[20]

---

17 G. Lewis, *Between the Wire and the Wall: a History of South African 'Coloured' Politics* (Cape Town: David Philip, 1987), pp. 179-192.

18 I. Wilkins and H. Strydom, *The Superafrikaners; Inside the Afrikaner Broederbond* (Johannesburg: Jonathan Ball, 1980).

19 D. O'Meara, *Volkskapitalisme* (Johannesburg: Ravan, 1983), pp. 105-106; Lewis, *Between the Wire and the Wall*, p. 178; Wilkins and Strydom, *The Superafrikaners*, pp. 190-1, 195; SA, ARG 12, Act 1/1/2/7, t/s Joint Committee Report, para 169, p. 76; *Report of the Commission of Inquiry Regarding the Coloured Population* (Wilcocks), UG.54-1937, pp. 66, 237, 240; Lewis, *Between the Wire and the Wall*, p. 167.

20 *Rand Daily Mail*, 15 December 1944, cited in Wilkins and Strydom, *The Superafrikaners*, p. 353; ibid., p. 66.

It seems reasonable to suggest, therefore, that the attempt between 1937 and 1940 to endow Cape municipalities through a provincial ordinance with powers to segregate 'Coloureds' from whites originated in policy circles in the Gesuiwerde Nasionale Party and Afrikaner Broederbond. Agitation amongst white residents' associations, particularly in Cape Town, produced enough anxiety for Smuts to speak in support of segregation between 'Coloureds' and whites, at least in public housing, in March 1938. The United Party majority in the Provincial Council referred the measure to the CPMA in 1938, and probably appreciated the breathing space provided by that organisation's request for delay. Koot Vorster, brother of the later prime minister, was active in promoting the ordinance and urging municipalities to support it at the CPMA congress in 1939.[21] Upon its debate in 1939, the CPMA endorsed the principle of segregation between 'Coloured' and white by 127 votes to 33, but not the draft ordinance.[22] When the measure again reached the Provincial Council the following year, it was opposed largely on the grounds that national rather than provincial or local policy should be developed; and to the backdrop of a public demonstration of some 15,000 people addressed, among others, by Cissie Gool, the Provincial Council defeated the measure.[23] In their actions the United Party members certainly opened the way for Dr Dönges to claim, ten years later, that the CPMA and the Cape generally wanted compulsory segregation between whites and 'Coloureds': he was able to refer to a 1948 reiteration of the desire of the CPMA for such segregation. The Cape thus provided, contrary to the protestations of United Party MPs in 1950, a strong impetus for 'group areas', specifically to segregate 'Coloureds' from whites.

The draft Cape ordinance had proposed a number of new features: it would have allowed the segregation of amenities; it defined whites married to blacks as blacks, just as the Group Areas Act did later.[24] In one crucial respect, however, it differed from the later legislation: it provided for *municipalities* to plan and execute spatial segregation. The draft ordinance went down to defeat in 1940 not because it would have allowed municipalities to determine racial zoning — indeed the rights of local authorities would probably have been strongly defended in the Cape[25] — but because the appropriate relations between national and local policies, national and local planning bodies had not yet been worked out; and because national policy on 'Coloured'-white segregation, like that affecting Indian segregation, had entered a

[21] Cf. letter of 1 December 1938 to many Cape municipalities from Ds. J.D. Vorster and 7 others for the 'Uitvoerende Bestuur van die Aparte Woonbuurte Komitees in die Kaapse Skiereiland', in, among other places, CA, East London Municipal series (3/ELN) 886, 1969, 'Segregation Ordinance 1938-40', and Simonstown Municipal series (3/SMT) 4/1/35, 300, 'Segregation of Coloured Residents Draft Ordinance'.

[22] *Cape Times*, 9 December 1937; Lewis, *Between the Wire and the Wall*, p. 189; SA, Group Areas Board series (GGR) 49, 15/10, 'Verrigtinge van die Kaap Provinsiale Munisipale Kongres 1939 en 1948 ...', extract of minutes of CPMA congress 1939, pp 43-54.

[23] Lewis, *Between the Wire and the Wall*; *Votes and Proceedings of the Cape Provincial Council*, 18 July 1940, 23 July 1940, 25 July 1940.

[24] Draft Further Powers of Local Authorities Ordinance, *Cape Provincial Gazette*, 22 July 1938, p. 276, s. 8, s. 11.

[25] For example, CA, PAS 2/1151, L 120/C/126 'Report on Housing Commission', A. Weisbecker for PS to Secretary of Government Housing Commission, 3 March 1920.

period of indecisiveness, mainly for reasons of early political paralysis in the United Party.

Hertzog's ringing declarations of the intertwined destinies of 'Coloured' and white notwithstanding, there were some moves towards a national policy of residential segregation. Responding to Malan in March 1939, Hertzog committed his government to social segregation: legislation for segregation of all new townships, and a means of segregating established areas. In May, Stuttaford, the Minister of the Interior, introduced one of the series of bills which pegged Indian ownership in the Transvaal and referred to the drafting of longer-term measures. Those, he proposed, should take the form of allowing local referenda or magisterial enquiries to determine whether three-quarters of the population of a neighbourhood wanted total segregation. If they did, it should be achieved by the blanket insertion of restrictive racial 'servitudes' in all the title deeds of the area.[26] The means, though not the trigger, reappeared in the Group Areas Bill in 1950; but in 1939, other matters precluded the introduction of national legislation.

After Hertzog's defeat on the neutrality issue in September 1939, the Smuts government did not change this policy; Lawrence, the new Minister of the Interior, repeated a commitment both to a servitudes measure and to the need for national policy in early 1940 — amongst other things contributing to the defeat of the Cape segregation draft ordinance. Accelerating ethnic change in some Durban residential areas stimulated ad hoc measures by the United Party government during the Second World War in an attempt to stem the process.[27] But servitude legislation was not forthcoming, and indeed, the general policy towards irregular settlement of the Smuts government seemed to become more permissive, with the suspension of pass laws in 1940. The material realities of proletarianising, industrialising and warring South Africa ensured that national legislation on segregation disappeared from the Smuts government's immediate agenda.

Urbanisation, War and Planning for Reconstruction

That urbanisation and industrialisation accelerated in the 1930s and 1940s, especially during the Second World War, is a commonplace. Local authorities, struggling to cope with these changes and at the same time to foster industrial development in their own areas of jurisdiction (and revenue), produced volumes of material which has only recently begun to receive the attention which it deserves, from scholars such as Bonner, Maylam and Sapire.[28] Central government departments, too, grappled with the issues; apart from the obvious importance of

---

[26] *Hansard*, House of Assembly, Vol. 33, cols. 2157-9; 4048-9.

[27] For example , the 'Pegging Act' of 1943, and the Lawrence Committee, intended to persuade Indians not to seek property in 'white' areas, and whites not to sell or let to Indians.

[28] P. Bonner, 'The Politics of Black Squatter Movements on the Rand, 1944-52', *Radical History Review*, 46/7 (1989), pp. 89-116; P. Maylam, 'The Rise and Decline of Urban Apartheid in South Africa', *African Affairs*, 89, 354 (1990), pp. 57-84; and H. Sapire, 'African Urbanisation: Struggles Against Municipal Control in Brakpan, 1920-1958', unpub. PhD thesis, University of Witwatersrand, Johannesburg, 1988.

the Native Affairs bureaucracy, others investigated, debated and recommended courses of action. Among those was the Department of Health, traditionally concerned with matters of housing and urban affairs. Its most visible act in the late 1930s was to appoint a committee to investigate what it called 'irregular' settlement on the fringes of municipal areas, a phenomenon which had become widespread. This committee, chaired by Sir Edward Thornton, chairman of the Central Housing Board, travelled widely, heard hundreds of witnesses, produced scores of interim reports on particular areas and finally reported to the Minister of Health in 1939 (its report was published in 1940). Among its concerns was the fact that few powers existed to control 'irregular' urbanisation by non-Africans: the committee identified a:

> ... need for preventing the establishment of further uncontrolled areas. The vast majority of witnesses who appeared before [the] Committee stressed the need for the prevention of further uncontrolled peri-urban settlements ... [L]ocal authorities pointed out that ... there would be nothing to prevent [irregular] settlements arising beyond [their] boundaries. Your Committee agrees ... and considers that the first essential should be to prevent the creation of similar areas in the future. As far as Natives are concerned the matter is sufficiently provided for [if s.6 of the 1923 Natives Urban Areas Act were enforced] ... As regards other classes of the community the position is not so well safeguarded ...[29]

This hint in the direction of measures to control, particularly, the activities and settlement of 'Coloured' and Indian people did not crystalise as a specific recommendation of the Thornton report, perhaps because of the delicacy of such issues in party politics at the time. But the committee's general view that all blacks, particularly 'Coloureds', should be segregated from whites found clear expression in the tone of the report, which showed horror at 'occupation of land and buildings irrespective of race with the result that Europeans were found to be occupying premises and living cheek by jowl with non-Europeans'.[30]

As the war progressed the changes identified by the Thornton committee accelerated, but the central government offered no relief. For local authorities the occupation of potentially lucrative land by irregular settlers, rapid growth of both industrially employed and unemployed population and pressure on housing meant that action seemed rather more urgent. Hilary Sapire provides an illuminating account of the Brakpan Council's attempts to persuade central government to take action, and its varied local initiatives.[31] The Durban City Council established a committee to investigate the possibilities of post-war development; Kuper, Watts and Davies noted how its report featured racial zoning based on large radial zones,

---

[29] *Report of the Committee to investigate the administration of areas which are becoming urbanised but which are not under local government control* (Thornton), UG.8-1940, p. 15, para. 47.

[30] Ibid., p. 11, para. 25.

[31] Sapire, 'African Urbanisation', pp. 208-224.

and the use of the rivers and ridges as 'buffers' between zones.[32] In Cape Town, the City Council engaged planners who recommended wholesale demolition in District Six and new roads (the progenitors of the Eastern Boulevard) to link the land thus released for commercial and industrial, as well as more salubrious residential uses, to the new foreshore — envisioned, according to Naomi Barnett, as the recreation of inner Cape Town.[33] The Johannesburg Council's planners busied themselves with plans to remove Indians to Diepkloof — vociferously opposed by the Transvaal Indian Congress and inhibited by government failure to move the reformatory made famous by Alan Paton; and, as Van Tonder shows, Johannesburg planned to 'clear the Western Native Areas', linked to the establishment of new townships on land owned by the Council such as the farm Meadowlands.[34]

Sapire, Kuper *et. al.*, Barnett and Van Tonder all point out how these plans prefigured later policies and projects carried out by the National Party government after 1948, sometimes, ironically, against the opposition of the local councils concerned. In the war years, United Party central and local governments faced the same issues of economic and social change, proposed much the same 'solutions' as did the National Party from 1947, but failed to implement them in anything but piecemeal fashion. The excuse for ad hoc policies was the war, but that did not mean a vacuum in thinking through the restructuring which would both be necessary and possible after the war's end.

From the early 1940s, the Smuts cabinet became increasingly concerned with 'reconstruction' in the post-war world. Certain figures played a key role in shaping the government mind on these matters, one of whom was H.J. van Eck, who Smuts had appointed to establish the Industrial Development Corporation in 1943. Just as the Corporation foreshadowed a more interventionist role for the state in the peacetime economy, so various state departments began to think along similar lines: the 'reconstruction' reports of several reveal the legitimacy which such thinking had achieved by the end of the war.[35] In common with other countries, a role for planning surfaced at a much wider scale than tinkering with the location of commercial activities within neighbourhoods. The trend was made explicit, among other places, in the Natal Provincial Administration's 'Post-War Works and Reconstruction Committee' report on provincial and town planning[36]; and in the addition of some planning functions to the old Central Housing Board in its new guise as the National Housing and Planning Commission. This convergence of thinking is apparent from the reports of the Social and Economic Planning Council

---

[32] *Programme of Post-War Development: Report of the Special Committee* (Durban, 1943); Kuper, Watts and Davies, *Durban: a Study in Racial Ecology*, pp. 187-8.

[33] N. Barnett, 'A Chapter in the History of Cape Town's District Six: Destruction Planned, 1940', unpub. paper, Dept of History, UCT, 1989.

[34] D. Van Tonder, 'First Win the War, Then Clear the Slums: the Genesis of the Western Areas Removal Scheme, 1940-49', History Workshop Paper, University of the Witwatersrand, 1990; SA, ARG, Act 1/1/2/3/10 'Representations from public — Transvaal — SAIRR'.

[35] See, for example, *Report of the Reconstruction Committee of the Department of Agriculture and Forestry* (Pretoria, 1944-5).

[36] *Ninth Interim Report of the Post-War Works and Reconstruction Committee regarding Provincial and Town Planning* (Pietermaritzburg, January 1945).

which Smuts set up under the direction of Van Eck to advise the cabinet. Its fifth report, on 'Regional and Town Planning', published in 1944, drew together a number of the threads stressed here: urbanisation, planning and segregation.

The Social and Economic Planning Council placed the need for expanded and better co-ordinated planning firmly in the context of state intervention:

> While it is widely accepted that the special advantages of the private enterprise system should be preserved, it is also accepted more and more widely that it is necessary and proper for the State so to control it as to make sure that important social objects will be attained. These are widening in range ...[37]

Planning, the Social and Economic Planning Council argued, needed to fulfil a number of aims: coping with 'accelerated urbanisation'; doubling the existing urban structure within a few years; guiding urban development to match the 'real economic prospects of different regions' and to 'do credit to our national aspirations'.[38] Like the Thornton committee, and perhaps for similar reasons, the Social and Economic Planning Council was a little vague on the specifics of planned segregation:

> It is further imperative that in the allocation of land for development a sound distribution, so important in a mixed community, be ensured. This will not be achieved without guidance as there is every reason to suppose that in its absence past trends will continue ...[39]

Quoting approvingly from various reports (Barlow, Scott and Uthwatt) intended to chart the course for post-war planning in the UK, the Social and Economic Planning Council adopted the contemporary British approach to urban planning: in particular, the notion of creating coherent communities separated by green belts, together with careful planning of residential and employment sites and the transport between them.[40] In the South African context, this approach translated easily into the idea of planning racially distinct, well-separated zones:

> The Union has a large and growing permanently urbanised non-European population. The Council ... therefore, urges that in the lay-out of new townships, the replanning of existing ones and the erection of state-subsidised housing schemes, full use should be made of the principle of planned neighbourhoods, protected from other neighbourhoods by 'green belts' of cultivated and park land and at the same time reasonably close to work places.[41]

---

[37] UG.34-1944, *Social and Economic Planning Council: Report No. 5: Regional and Town Planning* (Pretoria: Govt. Printer), p. 1 para. 3.

[38] Ibid., p. 2, para. 12.

[39] Ibid..

[40] Ibid., pp. 1-2, 7-9.

[41] Ibid., p. 5 para. 31.

While the public face of such reports avoided strong recommendations for a nationally-directed policy of urban segregation affecting all racial 'groups', the correspondence of the officials of the Social and Economic Planning Council leaves no doubt that this was what bureaucrats had in mind. Citing the report of the Thornton committee as evidence of the need for new segregatory planning powers, the Acting Secretary of the Social and Economic Planning Council wrote to the Secretary for the Interior in September 1945 that:

> The [Social and Economic] Planning Council has indicated in the Fifth Report that it regards the separation of residential areas of different races ... as a function of town planning in this country ... Residential segregation must be the result of a valid and accepted *National* policy ... no legal basis exists for it at the present time ...[42]

These proposals for planning to be conducted on racially-infused lines were effectively being practised at the time; for example, W.O. Backhouse, consultant to Hercules and Vereeniging among other local authorities, applied exactly these ideas of discrete and intact (racially defined) communities, separated by greenbelts. Wrongly, he, and perhaps others, thought that local councils could, 'in terms of a town planning scheme ... set aside specific areas for Europeans and Non-Europeans'.[43]

Through what agencies or departments or levels of authority a policy of residential segregation could have been implemented was left equally unspecific by the Social and Economic Planning Council report, but again, it seems fair to suggest that one of the tasks of the national department of planning, proposed by the report, would have been to undertake at least the co-ordination and probably the approval of race zone planning. The Social and Economic Planning Council argued further that

> Experience has shown that consultation between the numerous interested agencies cannot be relied upon to ensure the needed co-ordination ... A special organisation is required to test each project and so to co-ordinate them all that the best functional allocation of land between its alternative uses will occur, and that place of residence and place of work are brought into closer relation with one another without causing racial intermixing.[44]

Smuts's government did not open a national department of planning to house such a special organisation. But it did create two new agencies, one to co-ordinate

---

[42] SA, Social and Economic Planning Council series (SEC) 47, 12/5 Vol 2, Acting Secretary of SEPC to Secr. for the Interior, Pretoria, ?.September 1945, p. 8. The role of liberal members of the SEPC, in particular Senator E.H. Brookes, remains a puzzle.

[43] SA, Asiatic Land Tenure Committee series (ALTC) 5, file 'Asiatic Land Tenure Advisory Committee (General)', notes on meeting between Asiatic Advisory Committee and Vereeniging Council, 25 January 1944, p. 7. (This file contains personal papers of D.S. van der Merwe and will hereafter be referred to as 'ALTC 5, DSvdM file'.)

[44] SEPC 5th Report, p. 6 para. 41.

planning, especially regionally, of land allocation including the racial allocation of land; and the other to administer new legislation providing for stricter segregation of Indians. In the post-war phase of the Smuts government, the planners associated with these agencies laid some of the foundations on which the Group Areas Act was implemented in the 1950s and beyond, and to some degree, of the Act itself.

The Twilight of *ad hoc* Racial Planning

As the war drew to a close, the government was forced to come to grips with the political nettle represented by 'Indian penetration'. At a conference in Pretoria in April 1944 between Smuts, the Minister of the Interior, the Administrator of Natal, the Chairman of the Asiatic Land Tenure Advisory Committee (Basson) and a delegation from the Natal Indian Congress led by A.I. Kajee, agreement was reached to control ethnic change in residential occupation by licence, at least in Natal. But the ordinance drafted to provide for a body of three whites and two Indians to implement this agreement was thrown out by a select committee of the Natal Provincial Council, which substituted its own more drastic version. The new draft ordinance, passed by the provincial council, was vetoed by the Governor-General on the grounds that only the Union parliament could pass legislation affecting 'Asiatics'. The Smuts government found itself forced by this train of events to introduce new segregatory legislation.

In major respects the Natal Draft Occupational Control Ordinance of October 1944 contained the elements of the parliamentary legislation of 1946: it provided for a controlling body, the Occupational Control Board; and it proposed controls through designated areas and permits.[45] Likewise, the first Chapter of the 1946 Asiatic Land Tenure and Indian Representation Act, which applied both to the Transvaal and Natal, provided for the demarcation of Indian areas outside which an Indian could not acquire or occupy property. It also created an administrative body — the Land Tenure Advisory Board, headquartered in Pietermaritzburg — to recommend which areas should be so declared as well as performing a watch-dog function. An administrative section was created in the Department of the Interior to assist the Land Tenure Advisory Board, together with an inspectorate. These moves represented an attempt to go beyond the ad hoc motions which seemed to characterise the Smuts administration. They show that the Smuts government was inclined to respond to the urban segregation issue by providing for racial zoning and in creating a centralised body to oversee that process. In these respects, the Asiatic Land Tenure Act of 1946 was the direct precursor of the Group Areas Act, as Festenstein and Pickard-Cambridge have noted.[46]

If the Land Tenure Advisory Board's powers were limited to Indian segregation, the United Party government established a regional planning body at much the same time with far wider powers of racial land zoning. In an environment hostile to

---

45 SA, ARG 12, Act 1/1/2/7, t/s Joint Committee Report, para 214, 218-9; pp. 99-100, 101-2.

46 M. Festenstein and C. Pickard-Cambridge, *Land and Race: South Africa's Group Areas and Land Acts* (Johannesburg: SA Inst. of Race Relations, 1987).

central economic planning, Smuts hesitated to establish a national department of planning[47], or even to convene a conference to discuss ways of implementing the report of the Social and Economic Planning Council on regional and town planning.[48] But the development of an urban population on the new goldfields in the northwestern Free State, the western Transvaal (between Randfontein and Klerksdorp) and the eastern Transvaal highveld (Bethal district) demanded some sort of planning action. The government established the Natural Resources Development Council (under the Natural Resources Development Act No. 51 of 1947) in October 1947. This Council succeeded an *ad hoc* 'Advisory Committee on Development in the Northern Free State', whose chairman, F.J. du Toit, became the first chairman of the Natural Resources Development Council. One of the members of the Natural Resources Development Council's staff, T.J.D. Fair, wrote a decade later that the Natural Resources Development Council was the first regional planing body established in the country with significant, if limited powers.[49] For the Smuts government it represented a significant departure, for the Natural Resources Development Council was able not only to co-ordinate the activities of other planning bodies, but, in 'controlled areas' such as the three goldfields regions mentioned, no township development could take place without its approval. As a result, and given an energetic staff, it was in a position to initiate planning for the general allocation of land uses in those regions; it could and did exercise this power with respect to racial zoning, thereby determining the broad pattern of 'group areas' and African township positions in places like Welkom, Westonaria and Kinross.[50]

On the other hand, the Smuts government's restriction of the powers of the Natural Resources Development Council to the controlled areas meant that it offered no new grand plans for existing metropolitan areas, let alone small towns. In most of urban South Africa, decades of rapid growth, irregular urbanisation, industrialisation, small public housing schemes, property speculation and general social change left vast numbers of people without adequate shelter. Overcrowding, inadequate services and, of course, social pathologies as well as the ambitions of property developers left municipalities to confront difficult problems which were made no more tractable by the existence of the Natural Resources Development Council, Land Tenure Advisory Board and NAD bureaucracies.

In Pretoria, for example, the Asiatic Bazaar occupied valuable ground to the west of the city centre and impeded development by companies and white property interests in that direction. The question of what to do with older and extremely

---

47 Interview with T.J.D. Fair, conducted by the author, Cowies Hill, Natal, December 1990.

48 SA, SEC 47, 12/5 Vol 2, D.D. Forsyth to H.J. van Eck, Chairman SEPC, 21 August 1946.

49 SA, Natural Resources Development Council series (RNH) 279, PA3/3/5, First Annual Report of the NRDC to 31 December 1948; T.J.D. Fair, 'The Regional Approach to Planning', in E.W.N. Mallowes (ed), *Summer School of the SA Institute of Town Planners* (Johannesburg, 1959), pp. 47-67.

50 Interview, T.J.D. Fair, December 1990.

crowded 'locations' like Marabastad presented itself.[51] The government seemed incapable either of providing answers or the means to allow municipalities to deal with their problems. It certainly did not provide a lead away from segregation, while municipalities like Durban's — adhering to the ideology of segregation as solution for innumerable social ills — feared that legislation such as the 1946 Land Tenure Act would be permissively implemented.[52]

The growing cities urgently needed space for expansion, which the planning machinery seemed unable to provide. Social upheavals like the 1946 mineworkers' strike and political moves such as the self-disbanding of the Native Representative Council, with its echoes in location advisory boards, contributed to uncertainty. The environment of apprehensiveness must have been enhanced by the results of the 1946 census, which for the first time showed nervous white administrators that the cities all had majority black populations — which were increasing much more rapidly than the white minorities.

In short, the United Party government failed to deal through planning with very real urban problems; and it failed to offer any alternative at all to segregation as the prime means by which the problems of the cities would be solved. *Ad hoc* segregation did not work; planned, compulsory segregation appeared to do so, as the UP's own creations — the Land Tenure Advisory Board and Natural Resources Development Council — set about demonstrating. The United Party failed to heed the recommendations of the Social and Economic Planning Council for planning of a new order to deal with 'visible evidence of mistakes and abuse [in the absence of public control] to secure the right use of land.' Nor did it act on the realisation that with 'the advent of a road motor system, of a wider supply of electricity and of industrialisation'[53] a new order of planning had become possible. In the view of some, even liberal planners, like A.J. Cutten, the National Party government which came to power in 1948 did 'what should have been done over the previous decade' in attacking urban problems.[54]

The Herenigde Nasionale Party, Apartheid and the Origins of the Group Areas Act

When the Herenigde Nasionale Party (or National Party) came to power in May 1948 it did so on the basis of a manifesto which made clear the party's commitment to compulsory urban segregation. But there is nothing in the Sauer report of 1947, upon which the manifesto was based, nor in the works of

[51] SA, BEP 131, G7/137 'Aansoek om 'n groepsgebied in Pretoria Deel I 1950-52', Report of Manager of Pretoria Non-European Affairs Department, c.1951.

[52] Interview with R.J. Davies, conducted by the author, Cape Town, 9 January 1990.

[53] SEPC 5th Report, p. 2 para. 9.

[54] A.J. Cutten, Johannesburg City Councillor and 'well-known town planner', in debate on Western Areas removal, *Rand Daily Mail* 21 May 1952.

prominent ideologues such as G. Cronje, to suggest the means by which compulsory segregation was to be achieved.[55]

One element in Herenigde Nasionale Party ideology which had a long history and which set it apart from the United Party might be identified: that segregation should be made retroactive for everyone, therefore implying that people should be deprived of tenurial rights and bodily moved out of any 'mixed' areas they occupied.[56] Clearly, the tenor of Herenigde Nasionale Party documents prior to the election, ideological works of the 1940s and campaigns for 'Coloured' segregation in the 1930s was that this unfortunate necessity should be visited only upon black people. Even this position was not without precedent in the United Party and South African Party tradition: the 1923 Act had allowed removal of many Africans from mixed areas in towns, the Slums Act had the same effect for all, even whites, and the 1946 Asiatic Land Tenure Act had laid the foundation for retroactive deprivation and removal of Indians.[57] Nevertheless, the Herenigde Nasionale Party gave the idea if not the practice of compulsory segregation a cohesion and comprehensiveness which it had not enjoyed under the United Party; the government needed to find instruments by which that comprehensiveness could be implemented and cohesion achieved.

For guidance as to the legal means by which a process of comprehensive segregation could be set in motion, Malan's government turned to the two Committees (one each for the Transvaal and Natal but with almost identical membership) which it appointed to enquire into the future of the 'Asiatic land laws'. Both Committees, which generally sat jointly, were chaired by D.S. van der Merwe, chairman of the Land Tenure Advisory Board. Van der Merwe also drafted their joint report[58]; and he played a large role in drafting the Group Areas Bill. In some respects, therefore, this little known figure was the Eiselen of 'group areas'.

Van der Merwe was a career civil servant with legal background; he had been assistant inspector of mines in the Pietersburg district in the early 1930s but was elevated to Assistant Registrar of Mining Titles about 1935. In that capacity he was appointed to the Feetham Commission and its successor, the Asiatic Land Tenure Advisory Committee.[59] As the Smuts government procrastinated on the

---

55 Verslag van die Kleurvraagstuk-kommissie van die Herenigde Nasionale Party (Sauer Report — obtained thanks to D. Posel); G. Cronje, *'N Tuiste vir die Nageslag: die Blywende Oplossing van Suid-Afrika se Rassevraagstukke* (Johannesburg: Publicite, 1945); and G. Cronje, W. Nicol and E.P. Groenewald, *Regverdige Rasse-Apartheid* (Stellenbosch: CSV, 1947).

56 'Kort opsomming van aanbevelings uit verslag van Herenigde Nasionale Party Kaapland se Kommissie oor die kleurlinge', appendix to the Sauer Report.

57 Cf. O.J. Frankel's remarks on the 1946 Act at hearings on group areas proposals for Johannesburg, in SA, BEP 146, G7/139.

58 The draft was completed on 28 February 1950; it used to be found in SA, BEP 60, but since the reorganisation and subdivision of the records deposited by the Department of Planning it cannot be found in the Pretoria archives. The author possesses a photocopy of the original.

59 The Feetham Commission enquired into the occupation of proclaimed mining land by 'Coloured' (including Indian) people — which was illegal under the Gold Law. In 1937 a statutory committee (the Asiatic Land Tenure Advisory Committee) replaced the Feetham commission; it was in turn replaced by the LTAB in 1946; cf. *Report of the Murray Commission into Evasion of the Law*, 1939, and SA, ARG 12, Act 1/1/2/7, t/s Joint Committee Report, para 183 p. 83.

issues before this committee, its own idea of its importance expanded: the members took to calling it the 'Asiatic Advisory Committee' by the middle of the war. Promoted to Registrar of Mining Titles in 1941, made a member of the Mining Leases Board in 1942, given a joint appointment as Rand Townships Registrar and made a member of the Transvaal Townships Board, Van der Merwe sat at the centre of a network of government agencies concerned with property rights and racial matters.

D.S. van der Merwe was a stickler for complex legality, refusing to register transfers of land to British insurance companies if they could not precisely satisfy the complex requirements of legislation intended to keep urban land in white hands. He differed, sometimes sharply and in meetings with other bodies, from other members of the Asiatic Advisory Committee.[60] On a long memorandum written in 1944 by W.B. Stuart, another member of the committee, which asked 'Has the time not come for a drastic repeal of the bulk of the Asiatic Land Tenure Acts?', Van der Merwe noted a firm marginal 'NO'. To the suggestion that Indians should enjoy the same rights as other 'SA Nationals' Van der Merwe noted 'No. What about natives?' and to the suggestion that rights to acquire fixed property anywhere in the Transvaal would tend to promote South African loyalty, he replied: 'Doubtful. What about the English? They always talk of Home ... No equality possible at present'.[61]

Van der Merwe was a man of great energy and initiative. He attended a meeting organised by the Transvaal Indian Congress working committee on the housing question in January 1944, which helped to form his impression that while the Indian community was divided, there was a great deal of support within it for segregated townships as long as freehold rights were granted.[62] He formed close associations with others of his energy and persuasions, and ensured that at least one — R. Masson — was appointed to the Joint Committees in 1949. His unique position — holding multiple offices, sometimes with special arrangements to allow him to substitute for departmental secretaries and even ministers — gave him great influence and experience while maintaining public anonymity.[63] The inquiry into Asiatic land tenure laws gave him, as chairman, the opportunity to shape the planning of segregation through proposals for comprehensive, complex but superficially non-discriminatory legislation.

Following the election of the Herenigde Nasionale Party in 1948, immediate expectations of legislation for compulsory segregation arose, but the Minister of the Interior delayed, pending careful investigation and proposals.[64] Meanwhile Van der Merwe and another member of the Land Tenure Advisory Board took a tour of the Cape province to look at the 'question of land tenure' and added the new field of

---

60 For example, argument in meeting with Vereeninging Council on 25 January 1944, see Notes in SA, ALTC 5, DSvdM file.

61 Cf. marginal notes on Memorandum by W.B. Stuart, (24 January 1944), in SA, ALTC 5, DSvdM file.

62 Cf. Notes on Vereeniging meeting, SA, ALTC 5, DSvdM file, pp. 6-7.

63 Cf. D.S. van der Merwe to Secretary for Mines, 18 January 1946, in SA, ALTC 5, DSvdM file.

64 *Natal Mercury*, 6 November 1948.

'Coloured'-white segregation to their thinking on how comprehensive segregation could be justified and introduced.[65] As the acrimonious debate between 'Nat' and 'Sap' over segregation and apartheid intensified, the political atmosphere was further charged by the Durban riots and less massive 'unrest' elsewhere, pressuring several city councils to call for action.[66]

Reviewing the 'evidence' in his report — in a chapter which Dönges refused to publish — Van der Merwe opened with the carefully-orchestrated appeal[67] of the Germiston council for parliament to give local authorities power to determine areas for each 'racial group'. Evidence was marshalled to show that many municipalities and other bodies called for reserved white as well as black areas. The joint committees extracted assurances from officials of various municipalities, Johannesburg's included, that their councils would support, or at least would not oppose, the idea of separate areas for each 'race' — given provision for ownership and a clear procedure for declaration.[68] The report skated round the issue of who should control racial zoning, but did not challenge the crucial 1946 decision to place such powers in the hands of the Land Tenure Advisory Board rather than local authorities.

Even more controversially, it proposed that segregation should be retroactively applied — for which Van der Merwe relied on the representations of councils like that of Ventersdorp, as well as the inclinations of white rate-payers in Durban and other parts of Natal.[69] Disingenuously, Dönges and the state information apparatuses claimed that the Group Areas Bill which followed the Report was non-discriminatory; for Van der Merwe, it was clear that amongst other things, the process of achieving compulsory segregation required 'elimination of Asiatic ownership in European areas' and that 'trade [should] be controlled again'. To do this, in his view, required special, restricted areas for everyone.[70] Retroactivity meant that not only would new areas be proclaimed, but that old ones would be re*grouped* — the recommendation which perhaps provided the phrase which the Group Areas Act added to the political dictionary.[71]

Van der Merwe's committees finalised their internal report in March 1950. Only the last two of its five chapters were published[72] when the bill reached parliament a week later. The report proposed the replacement of the 1946 Act with a

---

65 SA, ARG 144, GEN13 'Enquiry into the question of land tenure in the Province of the Cape', Report, January 1949.

66 Interview, R.J. Davies, 9 January 1990.

67 Cf. correspondence and minutes of meetings contained in SA, ARG 10, Act 1/1/2/3/9 'Representations from Public — Transvaal Council of Germiston'.

68 Cf. SA, ARG 10, Act 1/1/2/3/16 'Representations ...', A. Blaine's remarks (as Acting Town Clerk) to Van der Merwe and others on 13 September 1949 re Johannesburg Council.

69 SA, ARG 10, Act 1/1/2/3/14, Town Clerk Ventersdorp to Secr. LTAB, 29 January 1949; see also t/s Joint Report, ARG 12, Act 1/1/2/7.

70 SA, ARG 12, Act 1/1/2/7, Memorandum on 'European Areas (provision to be made) and controlled areas' (by D.S. van der Merwe), p. 10a.

71 Perhaps first suggested by Mrs E.M. Russell, Mayor of Pietermaritzburg, in discussing 'regrouping our areas' with the select committee of the NPC, 1944; cf. SA, ARG 12, Act 1/1/2/7, t/s Joint Report, para 224, pp. 108-110.

72 UG.49-1950.

comprehensive measure, national in scope; the division of the population into racial groups, the proclamation of areas for each group and the continuation of the Land Tenure Advisory Board to undertake the task. The Group Areas Act, obviously, was drafted in concert with the production of the report, and provided for exactly these measures.

The origins of 'the group', then, had much to do with the creation of a method by which comprehensive planning could take place. The agency which would provide the wheels on which the process moved forward (or backward) had conveniently been erected by the United Party government, and its procedures, which owed much to planning models, had begun to develop prior to 1948. Thus opened a new era of spatial planning, clearly a child of the previous era, but removed from its parents and raised under the tutelage of the National Party government and its civil servants — D.S. van der Merwe in particular.

The Land Tenure Advisory Board, the Planning Process and the Seduction of Planners

'The provision of further areas for Asiatic and 'Coloured' expansion is indelibly linked up with the various town-planning schemes in the various municipalities',[73] wrote Stuart in 1944. As the Land Tenure Advisory Board initiated the process by which 'group areas' would be created, urban planners found themselves at the heart of the process. In some cases, 'group areas' planning was considered by municipal planners to form a subset of their general activities, reflected in the countless memoranda which officials produced in East London in the early-1950s headed: TOWN PLANNING: RACE ZONING: GROUP AREAS ACT.[74]

The Group Areas Act imposed two interlinked necessities on planning: allocation of racially-zoned land for new areas; and deciding on, and achieving, uniracial areas where many 'groups' lived and worked. In some respects the latter aspect fitted even better with the actual practice of town planning than the former: much of planning tended to be concerned not only with deciding what new allocations would be made and what restrictions could be applied, but with 'problems of non-conforming existing uses', as T.B. Floyd put it; or with 'eliminating' them, as the Transvaal ordinance has it.[75] Planning not only restricts the future use of private property, it sometimes tries to rearrange existing uses. But the Group Areas Act did not directly provide for planners to add racial criteria, restrictions and uses to their armoury. Thus:

---

[73] SA, ALTC 5, DSvdM file: memo. by W.B. Stuart, member of Asiatic Advisory Board, January 1944.

[74] CA, 3/ELN 1370, 50/1148/9 vol 2, Group Areas Act.

[75] T.B. Floyd, paper presented to SA Institute of Town Planners, 19 February 1960; s.44 of Transvaal Town Planning Ordinance, 1931.

> Racial reservation cannot be done under Town Planning schemes but must take place under the Group Areas Act. This means a dual set of planning schemes, each being approved by a different authority.[76]

Local authorities could initiate planning in either sense; they could find themselves approached from above by the Land Tenure Advisory Board to initiate racial planning; they could use the same or different departments or staff to undertake either task, and hire consultants (often town planners) to assist. But master zoning plans under the town planning ordinances would often be put on the shelf, awaiting approval from administrators, and be 'quietly forgotten';[77] master plans for racial 'group areas', on the other hand, would be relentlessly pursued by the Land Tenure Advisory Board and its associated bodies.

In order to undertake its mammoth task, the Land Tenure Advisory Board moved from Pietermaritzburg to large new premises on Beatrix Street in Pretoria.[78] It developed the procedures formulated for the 1946 Act; it sent out circulars to local authorities and other government bodies issuing instructions that they should undertake racial surveys of occupation and ownership, and map the results. The Land Tenure Advisory Board prescribed a code of symbols and colours for this purpose: circles on every site for ownership, with dots within them to indicate occupation. The required colours have their own ironic logic: blue for whites, brown for 'Coloureds', red for Indians, black for Africans, orange for the state; these rules could all be learnt from a booklet published by the Department of the Interior for 9d. The Land Tenure Advisory Board instructed municipalities that:

> Once the group survey is complete the local authority should have little difficulty in formulating its proposals for the demarcation of 'group areas'. These proposals should then be forwarded to the Land Tenure Advisory Board for consideration. Such proposals will be advertised in order that every interested person or group of persons may be afforded every opportunity to make representations to the Board. The Board will then hear the applicants for 'group areas' and such persons who have made representations on the application. Thereafter the Board will make its recommendation to the Minister ...
>
> [L]ocal authorities are most intimately concerned with the implementation of 'group areas' inside their own areas and ... they are the people who should primarily be consulted about the matter. They are also in a better position to assist with the implementation of the Act than anybody else ... it is advisable that in these matters the local authority concerned should take the initiative.[79]

---

[76] T.B. Floyd, *Town Planning in South Africa* (Pietermaritzburg: Shooter and Shuter, 1960), p. 204.

[77] E.A. Bouchier, 'Review of the Legislative Machinery for Planning', in Mallowes (ed), *Summer School of the SA Institute of Town Planners*, pp. 20-46.

[78] SA, ARG 1, A1 Vol 2, R. Humphreys PWD Pretoria to Secr. LTAB, 6 October 1950.

[79] CA, 3/ELN 1371, 50/1148/9 Vol 1 'Group Areas Act', Circular to all local authorities in Cape Province from Head: Administrative Section: Land Tenure, ?? 1951, 'Procedure to be adopted ...'

In many respects, bar the nature of the authority and the avowed purpose of the planning concerned, the process which the Land Tenure Advisory Board set in motion differed little from the town planning system. Provincial authorities put pressure on most municipalities to prepare town planning schemes; those schemes are subject to provincial approval; and there is strong pressure to follow the approved provincial planning model, with implied sanctions for failure to do so.[80] Just as the town planning system reveals disjunctures between central and local authority, two sources of problems greatly amplified the 'little difficulty' foreseen by the Land Tenure Advisory Board. Local authorities did not necessarily share the Board's views on how appropriate 'group areas' should be planned; and some local authorities were reluctant to cooperate or utterly opposed to comprehensive, compulsory segregation, at least under the Group Areas Act.

It has often been suggested that 'group areas' were intended to conform to a model: a radial pattern with outward growth for each group area; buffers, natural or otherwise, between them; and few, large areas for each group rather than many smaller ones in a given urban area.[81] But positive evidence is lacking in the records of the Land Tenure Advisory Board to suggest that this model was explicitly present in its policies, still less communicated to planners at local authority level. The result was a slow process of developing unique schemes of racial zoning in each town and city. Most of this process went on out of the public view, just as most urban planning does in South Africa: it was this anonymity and secrecy which led Martin Koopman of the Newclare Rate-payers Association, faced with the threat of disqualification, to condemn the power of planners to produce 'doom at one stroke of the pen'.[82]

Municipalities were gradually or, on occasion, abruptly, brought into line with the wishes of the Land Tenure Advisory Board. The powers of the Land Tenure Advisory Board did have limits, which caused its members frustration from time to time — such as the discovery that there was no power to disestablish a 'native location' formally set up by a local authority like Cape Town or Johannesburg.[83] But this lack of formal powers did not prevent the Land Tenure Advisory Board from exercising the considerable informal power which its crucial position in the state gave it, and which allowed it to insert itself ever more deeply into planning processes. One means by which this course was pursued related to the pressing problems of housing for Africans, which in 1951 began to move towards major solutions. Without a 'group areas' plan for their area, municipal officials found that they could not raise funds through the National Housing Office for housing Africans.

---

80 Cf. Bouchier, 'Review of the Legislative Machinery for Planning', p. 22.

81 Cf. Smit, 'The Political Economy of Urban and Regional Planning in South Africa 1900-1988', p. 98; Western, *Outcast Cape Town*.

82 SA, BEP 146, G7/139 Pt 1, 'Aansoek om ñ groepsgebied in distrik Johannesburg', Memorandum to the Land Tenure Advisory Board, 2 June 1955;

83 SA, GGR, 23/2 'Algemene Prosedure', correspondence between LTAB and W.W.M. Eiselen, Secretary for Native Affairs.

Given that there was a specific agreement to this end between the Land Tenure Advisory Board and National Housing and Planning Commission, the result is hardly surprising. To speed up the process of getting approval from the Land Tenure Advisory Board for 'group areas' plans, they had to formulate proposals themselves for 'group areas'. While the Land Tenure Advisory Board assured the Secretary for Native Affairs that it would move as fast as possible whenever the future of land for a 'native location' was in doubt, its staff told local authorities that they were responsible for delays since they were tardy in filing 'group areas' proposals, or group survey documents.[84] By these and similar methods the Land Tenure Advisory Board sought to persuade local authorities to change their approach to planning, captured in an official's note: '... dit is tyd dat die Stadsraad van Springs begin dink in terme van groepsgebiede'.[85]

While these pressures tended to force local planners to 'think in terms of group areas', the adoption of racial zoning and its blending into other aspects of planning occurred by no means solely through such top-down forces. Indeed, the notion that 'group areas' planning was just like other forms of spatial planning seems to have been widely accepted. For consultants, 'group areas' generated work; Floyd's report to the East London City Council shows how eagerly some town planning consultants set out their qualifications to plan 'group areas': 'It is essential that [racially mixed] areas be studied by persons with long town planning experience who understand all the implications [of group areas]'.[86]

For local authority planners, it meant activities essentially similar to their usual round: for example, drafting general plans showing features of towns, boundaries, and town planning schemes in relation to expected development and planned racial areas.[87] The implementation of the Act generated the need for exceptions, permits and so on, just as the implementation of town planning schemes tends to do.[88] For many planners, the implementation of the Group Areas Act allowed them to get on with the 'social reform' aspect of their profession which had been subject for so long to the Smuts government's stalling. It allowed an extension of the attack on undesirable activities, providing for housing, clearing up squatting and slums, sorting out geographical chaos which had begun in the 1920s and 1930s — even if they had to do so within racial zones. And when glaring mistakes were made in planning, the new procedures made it that much easier to place the blame on the

---

84 SA, GGR 64, 23/16, National Housing Office circular 1/1953, 15 October 1953; M.C. van T. Barker, Head: Administrative Section: Land Tenure, to SNA, 4 November 1953; Sec. NHO to Town Clerk Ceres, 31 August 1953 and Sec. NHO to TC Oudtshoorn 31 August 1953; and ARG, 228, NL104/R/1 'Application for Native Location: Benoni: 1951'.

85 'It is time for the Springs Council to begin thinking in terms of group areas'. (SA, GGR 63. 23/2 Bestuursliggaam vir sekere groepsgebiede, m/s note by M.C.van T. Barker, 7 June 1952.)

86 CA, 3/ELN 137, 50/1148/9 vol. 1, T.B. Floyd of Bowling, Richardson and Floyd, Town Planning Consultants, Johannesburg, in 'Preliminary Report on Proposed Group Areas' to the Mayor and Councillors of East London, 6 July 1953.

87 SA, GGR 64, 23/16 'Algemene prosedure', Sec. NHO to TC Oudtshoorn, 31 August 1953.

88 SA, GGR 64, 23/16 'Algemene prosedure', G.deV.Hugo, Sec. LTAB, to Secretary for Native Affairs, ?? July 1955.

failure of the previous government to do 'what should have been done over the last ten years'.[89]

Indeed, in some respects, despite its pressuring of local authorities, the centralisation brought about under the Group Areas Act strengthened the hand of planners *vis-a-vis* some other groups. Obviously planners who wanted racial zoning and removal of people who to them were undesirable found the Group Areas Act helpful. Amongst other things it insulated them from, for example, local branches of opposition organisations such as the Transvaal Indian Congress. Such planners found their thinking lay close to that of members of the Land Tenure Advisory Board, as minutes of their joint meetings reveal.[90]

Even in the more opposition-oriented local authorities, planners found that the centralised powers of the Land Tenure Advisory Board could be invoked to bring large corporate actors, who might otherwise defeat planning objectives, into line: as one state planner told a mining house representative, 'u verlang ... dat die myne die keuse moet hê en nie die staat nie'.[91] In this respect the powers of the Board and its associates provided the nearest equivalent to the centralised department of planning which the Social and Economic Planning Council had recommended in 1944. And, of course, planners and bureaucrats sometimes found that the threat of the Group Areas Act and the workings of the Board allowed them to defeat the objects of their councils: as the Johannesburg Town Clerk told the Board at a meeting of officials in 1951, 'we wish to cooperate fully with the Board ...'.[92] The demise of Uitenhage's initial opposition to cooperating with the Land Tenure Advisory Board owed much to the machinations of its officials.[93] Even liberal planners were subject to the need to participate in the planning procedures established by the Board, and on occasion developed their own complex schemes for 'group areas' in opposition to those advertised for comment.[94] Of course, such entry into 'group areas' planning often drew the ire of black organisations. Thus the East London Council found itself 'leaving no stone unturned' to make the lame defence that:

> the Council is in full agreement with the view that the position locally does not present a problem and is in fact opposed to the implementation of the Act in East London. It has been made unequivocally clear also that the position is that the Council is required to give effect to the requirements of the Act ... [and] that unless proposals were formulated by the Council it would result in the Government

[89] A.J. Cutten, cited in *Rand Daily Mail*, 21 May 1952.

[90] For example, see records of meetings in SA, BEP 192, G7/156, 'Aansoek om n groepsgebied in Lydenburg'.

[91] 'You wish the mining houses to exercise the power of choice, not the state.' (J.H. Moolman, at a hearing of the Mentz committee, quoted in *Transvaler*, 3 October 1952.)

[92] SA, BEP 146, G7/139, Porter, Town Clerk, Johannesburg, in minutes of informal discussion re implications of the Group Areas Act for Johannesburg, 22 August 1951.

[93] G. Adler, '"Trying Not to be Cruel": Local Government Resistance to the Application of the Group Areas Act in Uitenhage', paper presented to Southern Africa Research Program seminar, Yale University, 1988, pp. 42-57.

[94] For example , A.J. Cutten, cf. *Transvaler*, 3 October 1952.

> appointing a Committee to do so and in that even it would undoubtedly result in ... proposals ... likely to prove more severe than those formulated by the Council ...[95]

In short, planners were readily seduced by 'group areas' procedures. The ready application of their practices to the implementation of the Group Areas Act led Kuper, Watts and Davies to comment that

> If 'voluntary' segregation ... had a strong measure of compulsion, it is possible that the compulsory segregation of the Group Areas Act may be more voluntary than it appears.[96]

Opposition to the implementation of the Group Areas Act and the development of these new planning practices did exist. Southworth[97] has shown how opposition by significant bodies of whites threatened by 'group areas' proposals was usually effective; the opposition of others was only effective when it suited the broader schemes of the Land Tenure Advisory Board and, occasionally, local authorities. Local authorities on occasion proved to be dogged and temporarily effective opponents of the Board too; the Cape Town and Johannesburg cases, though partial, have been exposed elsewhere.[98] Less well-known are the cases of small municipalities' attempts to hold the line against the Board, as in Uitenhage.[99] Once the early opposition of those authorities had been broken, they seem generally to have submitted to 'group areas' planning without much difficulty; but the problems experienced by local authority planners in satisfying all the requirements of the Land Tenure Advisory Board and its successor, the Group Areas Board, led even Pretoria, by 1960, to delay and attempt to frustrate the plans of the Board to declare final dates for occupation by Indians in the city's white 'group areas'.[100]

Towards a Conclusion

How both opposition, and perhaps also commercial opportunism, affected the implementation of the Group Areas Act; how they affected its procedures, or, indeed, influenced the very drafting of the Act, awaits further research. Sources not yet readily accessible, including records concealed by fifty-year closed periods in the South African Central Archives, may yet shed light on such questions. In the interim, however, some conclusions may be formulated.

Comprehensive urban residential segregation under the Group Areas Act cannot be seen simply as part of a grand plan imposed by apartheid, along with influx

---

95 CA, 3/ELN 371, 50/1148/9 Vol 1 'The Group Areas Act', Report of the Committee ... Group Areas Act 25 March 1953, especially comments re meetings with Indian and 'Coloured' Associations of East London.

96 Kuper, Watts and Davies, *Durban: a Study in Racial Ecology*, p. 159.

97 Ibid.

98 For example, by Western, *Outcast Cape Town*. These events would sustain much more research.

99 Adler, '"Trying Not to be Cruel"'.

100 Cf. *Transvaler*, 13 July 1960.

control, Bantu education and the prohibition of interracial sex and marriage. Hindson modified that view with respect to influx control, and Posel shows that the development of policy was influenced by forces outside the Afrikaner nationalist alliance and contested within it.[101] Hyslop and Kros show that Bantu education was not an uncontested and pregiven phenomenon either.[102] This paper has sought to demonstrate that 'group areas' measures, like those affecting black 'influx' and education, emerged from a number of threads of previous segregatory measures and pressures. The practice of implementing the Act depended on the existence and growth of planning bureaucracies whose origins were wider than those of the Act itself.

The comprehensive segregation policies which emerged in 1950 and after were hardly a pure product of a grand apartheid plan, but that did not minimise the suffering caused in so many communities by its implementation. Now that the Act has finally been repealed, the danger exists that secretive planning practices could perpetuate its pernicious effects.

---

101 D. Hindson, *Pass Laws and the African Urban Proletariat* (Johannesburg: Ravan, 1987); D. Posel, '"Providing for the Legitimate Labour Requirements of Employers": Secondary Industry, Commerce and the State in the 1950s and early 1960s', in A. Mabin (ed.), *Organisation and Economic Change: Southern African Studies Volume 5* (Johannesburg: Ravan, 1989), pp. 199-220.

102 J. Hyslop, 'Social Conflicts over African Education in South Africa from the 1940s to 1976', unpub. PhD thesis, University of Witwatersrand, Johannesburg, 1991; C. Kros, '"Deep rumblings": Z.K. Matthews and African Education before 1955', *Perspectives in Education*, 12, 1 (1990), pp. 21-40.

[16]

We publish below the third Annual ERS/LSE Lecture by Akbar S. Ahmed given before an invited audience at the London School of Economics and Political Science on Thursday, 17 March 1994.

'Ethnic cleansing': a metaphor for our time?

Akbar S. Ahmed

Abstract

The intense ethnic assertion of identity often translated into violence – ethnic cleansing – can be largely explained as a consequence of the challenge to the project of modernity (economic development, justice, rule of law, the mass media, satellite technology and transport). Although ethnic cleansing itself is not a new phenomenon, developments in the mass media allow it to play a crucial role in influencing people in their perception of culture on an unprecedented scale. Hatred of the enemy, defined simply in ethnic or religious terms, is heightened through the use of television. Honour, glory, past mythology and ethnic nationalism are extolled, creating a predisposition for extreme arguments. Rape or sexual intimidation is extensively employed to terrorize and humiliate the ethnic enemy and explains the bitterness among combatants. The article considers its theoretical and methodological implications. First, all such crises need to be looked at in a global frame, those who share the religion or race of the victims of ethnic intolerance in one part of the world may be the aggressors in another. Second, we need to recognize that the discrete boundaries between academic disciplines are redundant. Third, while we need to study the ethnic death and torture camps (like those in the Balkans) we must also spot other less obvious and more subtle but almost equally tragic forms of ethnic cleansing resulting from racism and immigration policies (as in western Europe). Finally, we need to recognize fragmentation, new mutations, transformations, revivalisms and revisions. This fragmentation is both cause and effect of ethnic revivalism.

Ethnic and Racial Studies Volume 18 Number 1 January 1995

2 *Akbar S. Ahmed*

Introduction

Academic papers usually begin with a proposition or thesis; I wish to start with an autobiographical confession. My analysis and interest in the subject are not entirely of an academic nature. True, as an anthropologist, I am interested in ethnicity and ethnic boundaries, that is, how people define themselves and are defined by others on the basis of genealogy, language and customs. But I also approach ethnicity as someone who has had to come to terms with it in respect of my own identity, throughout my life.

From early childhood I was aware of the fact of ethnic differences which could lead to ethnic animosity and ethnic violence. Such differences accounted for my parents choosing to live in Pakistan when it was created in 1947. Large Indian provinces, as big as large European countries, were ethnically cleansed with all the attendant rape, torture and destruction. About 10 million people crossed each other as Hindus and Sikhs headed for India and Muslims for Pakistan; about one million died. Ethnic cleansing, clearly, is not a new phenomenon although it is disguised for us under a new term.

In Pakistan where I grew up and worked, although the vast majority of people belong to one religion, Islam, and Islam condemns discrimination based on ethnic background, it matters a great deal to which ethnic group you belong. In 1971 I was in what was then East Pakistan and which became Bangladesh in that year, and I saw, first-hand, the power of ethnic identity, how it could challenge successfully loyalty to a common religion.

Here, in the UK, I am given yet another identity, one based on colour and race: I am seen as black or Asian. Those who do not like Asians call them 'Paki', a term which denotes racial abuse. (What they perhaps do not know is that 'Paki' derives from the Urdu word pure and it is no bad thing being called pure even by swearing, snarling skinheads). Yet others learning that I am a Muslim have reservations, implying that all those with a traditional religious belief are fanatics or extremists or what the media call fundamentalists. For some Muslims, suspicious and resentful of the western establishment, I am a Fellow of a Cambridge College and therefore sullied. Multiple identities have thus been imposed on me.

Viewing the turbulence of South Asia I once envied what seemed the secure and fixed identity of being American or European. The passion generated by race and religion, I read in my American and British textbooks, was a characteristic of backward societies, those that were not modern. I now know that Northern Ireland can be as violent in its ethnic and religious hatred as the worst affected place in South Asia. In Wales and Scotland ethnic resentment against the English surfaces easily. In parts of London the colour of your skin can make you a target for abuse and assault. There are flash-points in the United States and Germany and France ready to explode into ethnic violence. To be an English-speaking male from the West in some parts of the Middle East is to know fear, to be vulnerable to the horrors of kidnapping. I no longer envied American or European identity.

Clearly I was not alone in my ethnic susceptibilities. It seemed that all of us were confronted with the same questions. What is my ethnic identity? How does the past shape it? How does it affect my life and those who are not like me? Why are the hatred and violence based on ethnic opposition so intense and so widespread? What is its relationship with the collapse of the project of modernity and the beginnings of a post-Cold War, post-Communism, postmodernity period? Is the ethnic cleansing in Bosnia a consequence of these changes and is it restricted to Bosnia alone? Has ethnic cleansing become the cognitive and affective symbol of, or metaphor for, our postmodern age?

In attempting to answer these questions my academic and personal interests in the subject coincide. I need to understand it in all its complexity to make sense of it. I therefore come to the subject with urgency and conviction and I hope with academic rigour.

Beginnings and endings

In examining the worst excesses of ethnic cleansing we are transfixed by Bosnia which has given the chilling euphemism 'ethnic cleansing' to the late twentieth century. It is the suffering of the Bosnians that challenges frontally European self-perception and self-identity, a fact not fully appreciated here in Britain (see Bell-Fialkoff 1993; Meron 1993; Mestrovic 1994; Schopflin 1993; Vulliamy 1994). Where, we may legitimately ask, are the much vaunted European liberal values – humanism, civilization and the rule of law?

The ethnic killings and hatred are a consequence of the collapse of the Soviet Union, it is argued. There is even some nostalgia for the old certainties. At least there was no mass murder, no ethnic cleansing, people say, forgetting one of the champion ethnic cleansers of history, Stalin. Others argue that the excesses of Bosnia are a reflection of the ethnic violence which took place half a century ago, of an inevitable ethnic dénouement. Some smugly talk of the conflict in the Balkans as typical of that area; they reflect cultural if not outright racial prejudice.

This is reductionism and simplification of complex historical events that are taking place on a global scale. There are many peoples facing persecution in our world – Muslims elsewhere in the Balkans especially in Kosovo, Palestinians, Kurds, Kashmiris, the Chittagong Hill Tribes, the East Timorese are examples.

However much Bosnia hypnotizes us, we need to broaden our frame of reference beyond Bosnia in order to draw universal principles and locate global explanations. We may then understand ethnic cleansing in our time. The explanations we provide are interlinked, some links strong, others tenuous, some fuelling the ethnic violence directly, others contributing to it more indirectly. Cumulatively they ensure that no society is immune, black or white, secular or religious, industrial or agricultural. Nevertheless, our exploration of those explanations is tentative and can only suggest further areas of research.

We note the collapse of the idea of Communism but we also need to be aware of another, more significant, collapse taking place, and that is the notion of modernity with its cluster of ideas, derived in the main from the Enlightenment, such as freedom of speech, humanism, rationality and secularism. To this was added subsequently economic and scientific progress. Sociologists like Max Weber placed these ideas firmly in Europe through explanations of a specifically European brand of Christianity. Because modernity was located in and spread from Europe over the last two centuries it allowed Europe to become the standard-bearer of civilization, indeed of the future. Cultural and racial superiority was implied. During the high noon of empire, authors like Jules Verne and H.G. Wells extolled the virtues of modern ways to and for all the world with the *naiveté* of enthusiastic schoolboys but its European dimension was clearly assumed.

However, modernity had its dark side even in Europe. Bauman, citing Weber (Bauman 1991, p. 14), blames it, in part at least, for the Holocaust:

> The most shattering of lessons deriving from the analysis of the "twisted road to Auschwitz" is that – in the last resort – *the choice of physical extermination as the right means to the task of* ***Entfernung*** *was a product of routine bureaucratic procedures*: means-ends, calculus, budget balancing, universal rule application . . . The "Final Solution" did not clash at any stage with the rational pursuit of efficient, optimal goal-implementation. On the contrary, *it arose out of a genuinely rational concern, and it was generated by bureaucracy true to its form and purpose* (ibid., p. 17).

Those who believed in modernity saw other systems, Buddhist, Hindu or Islamic, for example, as anachronistic. They would be obliterated in due course in the triumphalist march of western rationalism and progress. Modernity has therefore always been viewed with ambiguity by people in Africa and Asia; it is too closely associated with European colonization and the rejection of religious and traditional ways.

We cannot say with certainty when modernity began to falter – there is no dramatic equivalent to the fall of the Berlin Wall in 1989 which symbolized the collapse of Communism. But the process of collapse had been gathering momentum. It became increasingly apparent since the middle of this century that modernity could not solve all our problems. In the last decade or two the loss of optimism combined with other developments: law and order deteriorated in the cities, unemployment grew, families fell apart and the use of illegal drugs and alcoholism spread. Bosnia, and all it stands for, was perhaps the last straw.

What follows after modernity is still uncertain. Some like Anthony Giddens (1991) note continuity in modernity and use the phrase high or late modernity. Others call it postmodernity – the social condition formed by information technologies, globalism, fragmentation of life-styles, hyper-consumerism, the fading of the nation-state and experimentation with tradition (the related concept, postmodernism, is the philosophical critique of grand narratives). Some write of a post-Cold War period or post-Communism, yet others see a time of ethnic and religious revivalism. However, in noting the revivalism we point out the yearning for pre-modernity, a desire to recreate a mythical past and imagined purity. In that sense the revivalism reflects anti-modernity. It is characteristic of the age that its names are not original and reflect a relationship with the past.

What is certain is that the changes after Communism, the Cold War and the failure of western modernity have universal implications. The cement binding different peoples in the large blocs and uniting them in the grand narratives has cracked. This is most notable in the former Soviet Union. But in France, in Germany, even in Britain, we can also trace the dramatic rise of racism in the last years to the dark underside of modernity. Political opinion polls reflect the growing strength of the racist. By calling the racists neo-Nazis the media acknowledge the Nazi past. We hear louder and louder the voices of racism in Europe: 'Expel the foreigners', 'They are noisy and dirty', 'They mean disorder and drugs', 'They are not like us – cleanse our land of them'.

A similar process is also to be noted globally. Hindus and Muslims in South Asia, Muslims and Jews in the Middle East, Russians and non-Russians in Russia – those ambiguous about modernity but frozen for half a century in the Cold War structures – are falling back on an imagined primordial identity, to their own traditions and culture. People define themselves in terms of the ethnic other, usually a group that has lived as neighbours.

Importantly for purposes of our argument no one group is entirely isolated from ethnic passions. If Hindus terrorize the Muslim minority in India during communal rioting, in turn, they are terrorized in Bangladesh and Pakistan by the majority Muslims. In Kashmir Muslims have been killed and tortured by the thousand. Half a million troops are deployed in Kashmir to crush the Muslim uprising. This is a great human tragedy but there is another human tragedy also taking place simultaneously in Kashmir which is not known outside India. Hindus, who have lived in Kashmir for centuries, have fled the land out of fear; Kashmir is thus ethnically cleansed of them. Most Indians only see the plight of the Hindus, most Pakistanis that of the Muslims.

Yet in order to understand ethnicity an objective approach is needed. As an anthropologist I believe my subject has much to say about the nature of ethnic conflict. Yet somewhat to my bafflement anthropology has been conspicuous by its absence in the commentary on the major international events of the last few years like the Gulf war and the conflict in Bosnia.

Yet surely anthropologists need to explain for the general public why in some countries there is relatively little ethnic cleansing (for instance in Fiji in spite of the *coups*)? Or why it is particularly vicious in a certain period of history? Why some minorities have adjusted relatively well in an alien cultural environment (like the Sikhs in the UK), while others are less successful (consider the anti-Arab prejudice since the 1970s also in the UK)? Finally, what role does ethnicity itself play in ethnic cleansing?

Rediscovering ethnicity

The understanding of ethnicity is therefore crucial to our task. Yet despite the efforts of western social scientists the popular imagination and popular media continue to reflect traditional ignorance and prejudice when dealing with ethnicity.

Ideas and arguments about ethnicity are usually based on the assumption that ethnic identity is a characteristic of primordial and tribal societies, that only society in North America and western Europe represents modernity. Modern society has moved beyond, evolved away from, religion, belief and custom. In any case there is little nostalgia in the West for religion which is popularly associated with bigotry, superstition and intolerance. Only backward societies cling to the past. Progress, science, rationality are the key words although they are difficult to quantify; tradition, tribe and religion represent the outmoded and obsolete past. Not surprisingly western anthropologists studying African or Asian peoples once routinely classified them as 'savage', 'primitive' or 'tribal' – you only have to glace at the titles of one of the celebrated LSE names, Malinowski, for confirmation.

Those working in or on communist societies and those of a Marxist persuasion also analysed ethnicity and religion as remains of the discredited feudal and traditional order. According to their social trajectory ethnic and religious identity, although present, would in time fade away as people became equal citizens in the modern world. Clearly this has not happened for the majority of the world population and the failure of these analysts is spectacular.

Indeed, the problem of defining key concepts such as ethnicity, race, nation and tribe that has faced social scientists is symptomatic of this malaise (Barth 1969; Helm 1971; Ahmed 1976, 1980; Godelier 1977; Ahmed and Hart 1984). What, for example, is a group of Scots in the Scottish highlands? With its clans, language and customs is it a tribe, an ethnic group, a race or a nation? While the classic anthropological text on tribes, *African Political Systems* (Fortes and Evans-Pritchard 1940), restricted the definition to groups like the Bushmen and the Zulu some anthropologists like Max Gluckman (1971) included as 'tribal', along with the Bushmen and the Nuba, the Scots, the Irish and the Welsh. The debate continues.

Walker Connor (1993) contributed to the discussion by combining ethnicity and nationalism and used the term 'ethnonationalism'. He is right to underline the irrational and emotional well-springs of ethnonationalism – hence the title of his ERS/LSE lecture: *Beyond Reason* – and its capacity to influence group behaviour. But the category creates analytic problems. Surely in certain places, as in India, we need to accept the religious rather than the strictly ethnic dimension of large-scale confrontation?

Ethnicity in one place and religion in another are the central concerns of our time. Indeed, in some areas of conflict 'ethnic cleansing' is a misnomer. In most cases it is straightforward religious genocide as with the Muslims in Bosnia. So to restrict the term rigidly to ethnicity is incomplete at best and misleading at worst. When we employ the term we shall do so broadly and generally to indicate notions of exclusivity in a group, based around a cluster of symbols such as language, religion or historical memory, vehemently opposing and in turn opposed by neighbours with similar ideas of identity expressed with corresponding fervour. 'Ethnic cleansing' is the sustained suppression by all means possible of an ethnically or religiously different group with the ultimate aim to expel or eliminate it altogether.

Although we are pointing to the widespread nature and intensity of ethnic cleansing we are not suggesting it is characteristic of or exclusive to our age. Elimination, as in Bosnia, and segregation, as in the Occupied Territories of Israel, of the other (hated and weaker) group have been practised in the past: the *Reconquista* and *Inquisition* in Spain and *Glaubenskrieg* in Germany (reaching a climax with the Nazi Holocaust) are examples of the former; apartheid in South Africa and Indian Reservations in the USA for the latter.

However, the exercise of grappling with the definitions of tribe, ethnic group, race and so on may be a red herring. What we really need to analyse is why members of a group – ethnic or religious –

want to oppose members of another group with such intensity that they are prepared to inflict the most horrific cruelty on them? We are thus really examining the causes for the radicalization of mass culture and the worldwide growth in and acceptance of extremism, fanaticism and violence as a solution to the ethnic problem. It is on this that we need to focus for purposes of our analysis in the otherwise amorphous and shifting global landscape.

Ethnic hatred has a mimetic quality: the opposed groups mirror the hatred, rhetoric and fears of each other. It makes everyone an outsider; and it makes everyone a target. Everywhere – in the shopping arcade, at the bus stop, in the cinema, in your living room – you are vulnerable to sudden, random violence. Anger and hatred are easily created.

The hatred is generalized, universal and maintained at a high level. For those in traditional societies it is engendered by the dangers posed to the core unit of society, the family, whether the extended or nuclear variety. In urbanized and industrialized society this threat is exacerbated as the family is under stress externally and internally: externally from migration, immigration, unemployment; internally from divorce, drugs, alcoholism. All this creates an anger at the world around and a scapegoat is easy to locate.

Members of the neighbouring ethnic group are dirty outsiders, fifth-columnists, disloyal, speak a different language and have different customs. They must be cleansed. This argument can be heard not only in the Balkans but in one form or another in other parts of the world where ethnic clashes are taking place. The mindless cruelty takes in everyone – children, the elderly, the sick – as long as they belong to the other side. It is this combination of perceived ethnic threat and personal vulnerability that forces people to fall back on community and group. There is logic here. If formal networks fail, the more informal ones may assist.

With international structures, like the UNO, not to be trusted (as in Bosnia, Palestine, Kashmir) people fall back on their own group. The belief provides a security in an age of confusion and uncertainty, protection against the imagined or real conspiracies of the enemy. It also inures us to the stories of cruelty that we know exist. By adopting an ethnic position people simplify complex ones, and by talking of national honour and glory disguise the cruelty of their compatriots.

As a parenthesis I might point out the implications of this line of argument for Edward Said's *Orientalism* (1978; see also 1993). Said's thesis is based on the idea of the other (for Europe it is, famously, Islam). The other is out there geographically and culturally, dark, backward and mysterious to be dominated and exploited. In contrast to this external other is the internal other which we are pointing out: it is home-grown, among us, speaking our language and reflecting our customs and sometimes it is stronger than us. Said's other is only a limited tool of analysis for our post-Orientalism argument.

Ethnic cleansing in one sense has levelled the categories that divided the global community – First World, Second World, Third World or North-South or East-West. In various degrees and in different forms ethnic cleansing is in evidence everywhere, not only in Bosnia but elsewhere from Bonn to Bombay, Cairo to Karachi. Cities like New York and Los Angeles, where entire neighbourhoods are based on colour and more or less out of bounds for those of the wrong colour, are ethnically cleansed; a similar conceptual strategy to that in Bosnia is at work. Ethnic cleansing has made us all 'primitives', 'savages', 'tribals' – *pace* Malinowski.

For their insensitivity during the Holocaust many governments made the puerile excuse that they were not aware of what was taking place in Germany. The gory daily news from Bosnia – or with less frequency but equal to it in the spirit of violating human rights from Israel, Iraq or India – shown on television or discussed in print has little impact on the governments of the world; they appear to have developed compassion immunity. These stories are reduced to little more than voyeurism.

As with the Holocaust many ask questions of a deep and disturbing nature: 'Why does God – if there is a God – tolerate this suffering? Why doesn't God punish the aggressor, the rapist and the murderer? What happened to the idea that good triumphs over evil?' If there is a divine parabolic lesson in Bosnia it has escaped most people.

For a Muslim events in Bosnia are truly shocking. The holy Quran clearly preaches tolerance and understanding. Indeed, there is an anthropologically illuminating verse which talks of the wonders of the world, the diversity of races, and points to this: 'O Human Beings! Behold, We have created you all out of a male and a female and have made you into nations and tribes so that you might come to know one another – not that you may despise each other' (Surah *Al-Hujurat*, Verse 13). It is this spirit of ethnic tolerance that is under attack in our world.

Perhaps for us as academics the most distressing aspect of ethnic cleansing is the involvement of those who are educated and considered to be the pillars of modern society: the doctors, lawyers, engineers and writers. (Not surprisingly, the Jewish mass murderer who killed about fifty and wounded 200 Muslims kneeling at prayer in Hebron in February 1994 was a medical doctor). We need to be cautious here. Although ethnic loyalty tends to be a tidal wave which sweeps all before it we can cite many courageous people precisely from this class who stand up to and expose their own community (for example, Mestrovic in the Balkans in 1994; the Jewish women in Israel in 1993; Makiya in Iraq in 1993 and Padgaonkar – with too many others to name – in India in 1993. Padgaonkar, chief editor of *The Times of India*, was dubbed the chief editor of *The Times of Pakistan* in Bombay by Hindu communalists when he attempted balanced reporting of the riots after Ayodhya and published the book *When Bombay Burned*; this is the equivalent of the white liberal who earns himself the contemptuous title 'nigger lover' from his people for supporting black issues).

Unfortunately these exceptions do not disprove the ethnic rule that members of the other ethnic group are considered aliens or enemies irrespective of their merits. Let us now explore some explanations for ethnic cleansing.

The economic argument

Perhaps the most commonly cited man-in-the-street explanation of ethnic cleansing is the global economic crisis. It is directly related to modernity running its course, of the loss of confidence in the future for the world community. There is a general economic crisis in the world – call it recession or by some other jargon. Unemployment figures are high. Even educated people walk the streets looking for jobs. Prospects are poor. The long-term global forecast is pessimistic, keeping in view the continuing population explosion in Africa and Asia. Poverty turns men into beasts. It is in this context that minorities – the Bangladeshis in Tower Hamlets or the Muslims in Bombay – become targets of irrational emotions. Matters are made worse by pointing to those individuals who have prospered. 'They are taking all the jobs. They are being given all the housing. They must not be allowed to get away with this pampering.'

There is a strong argument to be made correlating economic deprivation and ethnic confrontation. Whether in Gaza or in Kashmir the government has made virtually no economic investment. The neglect is interpreted as ethnic prejudice. However, it is not only the minority that feels neglected. It is striking that each major section of society views its central problems in a similar light, casting itself as victim, and complains of injustice, blaming its misfortunes on the ethnic or religious enemy members of which are citizens and neighbours.

While the economic argument is valid up to a point it is also limited, for economic statistics or material progress are taken as a yardstick of life itself, an end in themselves. Yet poverty has never been an excuse for violence and intolerance; indeed, material austerity and spiritual development are central planks of most Asian religious thinking. This was made clear by the examples of the great spiritual messengers of history – Moses, the Buddha, Jesus and the Prophet of Islam. In our century men like Mahatma Gandhi and women like Mother Teresa have advocated the message of austerity and simplicity with success. Human beings clearly cannot live by bread alone.

Globalization and the mass media

Globalization and the mass media provide us with another explanation for ethnic cleansing. Let us explore this idea with the caution that, while globalization is a characteristic of postmodernity, it is also a direct consequence and in many significant ways a continuation of modernity. Giddens in his definition of globalization draws our attention to the relationship:

> Globalisation means that, in respect of the consequences of at least some disembedding mechanisms, no one can "opt out" of the transformations brought about by modernity: this is so, for example, in respect of the global risks of nuclear war or of ecological catastrophe (Giddens 1991, p. 22).

Globalization draws in people all over the world who willingly or reluctantly participate in a global culture (see Nash 1989; Giddens 1990, 1991; Robertson 1991; Beck 1992; Fukuyama 1992; Ahmed 1993e; Huntington 1993; Moynihan 1993; Ahmed and Donnan 1994; Turner 1994; Ahmed and Shore, in press).

Satellite TV, the VCR, communications technology and developments in transport have made this possible (for an illuminating discussion on ideology and mass communication see Thompson 1990; for the role of the media in disasters and relief see Benthall 1993). McDonald's and Mickey Mouse, 'Dallas' and 'Dynasty', Coca Cola and Levis, Toyota and Sony as much as ideas of mass democracy and human rights are now the universally recognized signs of this global culture whatever their country of origin. 'Globalization', sighs one of the pundits studying it, 'is, at least empirically, not in and of itself a "nice thing", in spite of certain indications of "world progress" ' (Robertson 1992, p. 6).

It is still early days for media studies, and the influence of the media on how people behave needs to be explored at greater length by social scientists. There is a tendency to dismiss media studies as an upstart and not take it seriously. This is a mistake because we can learn a great deal about contemporary life through media studies. Besides, it is salutary to recall the derision with which economics, sociology and anthropology – each in its turn – were greeted by fellow scientists when these subjects attempted to secure a foothold in academe.

Today TV, the VCR, satellite dishes and newspapers spread information and images more quickly and more widely than ever before in history. The consequences for our argument are enormous. For most of the population on this planet the reductive and hedonist images are a mirage, the hyper-consumerism out of reach. Envy, frustration and anger result. The need to blame someone, to find scapegoats, is great. Radicalization and violence follow.

We know that state-controlled television in Belgrade played a crucial role in manipulating and articulating Serb identity. It showed pictures of atrocities, often of Serb victims, which confirmed in people's minds the necessity to stand together against a hostile world bent on denying them dignity and statehood. Ethnic passions were aroused and ethnic cleansing appeared justified.

With its tendency to simplify complex issues the media also allow both a false and dangerous argument to circulate, one mounted by the chauvinistic and aggressive middle class, the keepers of the ethnic flame, that there is a 'global conspiracy' to keep the nation or race down and prevent it from becoming great and fulfilling its destiny, that the minorities play the role of a fifth-column in this exercise. Across the world this complaint is echoed. Let us examine the situation in India (for the recent high-quality literature on religion and the rise of extremism in India, mainly written by Indians, see Engineer 1984; Akbar 1988; McLeod 1989; Phadnis 1989; Graham 1990; Gopal 1991; Tully 1991; Das 1992; Madan 1992; Ahmed 1993b, 1993d; Basu *et al.*, 1993; Padgaonkar 1993).

The Hindu backlash was almost inevitable and needs to be explained. The vast majority of the population was Hindu but in the post-colonial rhetoric – secularism, national progress, socialism – Hindu identity was in danger of being submerged. Hindus felt justifiably aggrieved. Among India's founding fathers were men of great piety like Mahatma Gandhi and Sardar Patel but it was the first Prime Minister, Jawaharlal Nehru, who influenced independent India the most with his secular, tolerant and modern ideas. However, in the eyes of the traditional and orthodox, modernity appeared to demean, disempower and marginalize custom and belief. The Marxist vocabulary of the intellectuals added insult to injury.

By the 1970s with Nehru not long gone from the scene, Hindu revivalism began to gather momentum and Indira Gandhi, always a political animal, abandoned her father's position for an openly communal one. The globalization process and its aggressive cultural manifestation, especially of American origin, further alienated and threatened Indians – Hindus and Muslims – and forced them to hark back (a point perceptively raised by Iyer 1992; also see Amin 1994).

The political and cultural atmosphere in the 1980s was charged. The mildest reservation about or the merest hint of opposition to the Hindu cause by a Muslim would risk swift, noisy and painful retribution. It would be a feeling familiar to a Muslim Bosnian in Serb-controlled Bosnia with reservations about the battle of Kosovo, a Copt about the capacity of the Egyptian state to protect Christian churches and property, a Palestinian about the fairness of the state of Israel, a Kurd about the humanity of Saddam Hussein's regime, a Jew about the Islamic revolution in Iran and a Bangladeshi Hindu about Islamic revivalism in Bangladesh.

A glance at the long list of credits of the major and popular television series depicting a mythical Hindu past, 'Mahabharat', 'Ramayana' and 'Chanakya' (all shown in Britain) will illustrate the position of the Muslims in India today; the names are almost exclusively Hindu. It is assumed that only Hindus can make or contribute to 'religious' films. Notions of purity and exclusiveness are implied and ethnic boundaries clearly drawn. This, too, it can be argued, is a side of ethnic cleansing. (The process works both ways in South Asia: the popular Pakistani series 'Dhoop Kinarey' – also shown in Britain – has almost all Muslim names in the credit list).

This was not always so in Indian films (see Ahmed 1992b). One of the most significant contributions to the idea of a genuinely multicultural and multi-religious India was made by the Bombay cinema in the early decades of independence. It may have been an ideal but it inspired millions. One of the most famous Hindu devotional songs from the popular film 'Kohinoor' (1960) provides an example. It was sung on screen by Dilip Kumar (Yusuf Khan), written by Shakeel Badayuni, directed by Naushad and actually sung by Mohammad Rafi, all four Muslims. This was a remarkable comment on Indian tolerance and synthesis. It reflected the spirit of the founding fathers: Mahatma Gandhi, Jawaharlal Nehru, Maulana Azad. It is this spirit which is under threat and which worries many Hindus, who wish to see it preserved. The minorities are simply terrorized by the new mass violence.

Films like 'Mahabharat', 'Ramayana' and 'Chanakya' did not necessarily aim to have a contemporary political message but were watched by an estimated 600 million people every week and this, in itself a unique media phenomenon, created a highly religious atmosphere in the 1980s. It generated a nation-wide glow of pride and identity – a specifically Hindu pride and identity. The images projected an idealized Hindu past, a society in harmony, in flower.

Had the matter ended there – television as entertainment – that would have been admirable and innocuous. But a sub-text could be discerned: the ideal picture was shattered by invaders from outside India; Muslims were to blame. The series assisted in setting a chain of events in motion. Some media pundits in the BJP, a party floundering on the verge of extinction, at this point joined the emotions generated by the mass media and a political issue concerning the birth-place of Lord Ram at Ayodhya where a medieval mosque stood. Overnight its fortunes changed – from two seats in parliament to 119 – although the results of the latest State election in north India indicate the support of the BJP may have peaked.

So while Hindus thrilled at the doings of the attractive warrior-hero figure of Lord Ram on television they were angered by the mosque at Ayodhya. A vigorous campaign daubed the legend 'Declare with pride your Hinduism' on walls, posters and hoardings all over India. A not so subtle subliminal message was contained in this slogan: vote for those who identified with Hinduism (like the BJP). The BJP notably, but also the Congress, then recruited the stars from the television series, who were treated almost like gods in India, as their parliamentary candidates. They helped mobilize public opinion in demanding the mosque at Ayodhya be replaced by a temple. Widespread tension all over India resulted in frequent large-scale riots in the name of Lord Ram.

Hindu extremists were now offering Muslims throughout India the standard choices of ethnic cleansing: absorption into Hinduism by accepting Lord Ram and becoming 'Hindu Mohammedans', or expulsion (to Pakistan or Saudi Arabia or wherever). The third choice was to prepare for the destruction of life and property. From the *Reconquista* in Spain to the Occupied Territories in Israel subjugated minorities have confronted these dilemmas.

The transformation of what its devout and thoughtful followers see as a philosophic, humane and universal religious tradition to a bazaar vehicle for ethnic hatred and political confrontation saddens many Hindus. The mosque at Ayodhya was destroyed in December 1992 and an orgy of killing followed all over India in which the paramilitary and security forces were later implicated (the world saw them on television screens idly standing by as the frenzied mob in Ayodhya went about its business). Horror stories circulated of Muslims being burnt alive or raped while video recorders filmed them. In Bombay mobs stopped men and forced them to drop their trousers; those circumcised were identified as Muslim and stabbed. The link between the media and politics, between the religious-cultural assertion of identity of one group and the persecution of another, is suggested.

There were also immediate and serious international repercussions: Hindus were attacked and their temples destroyed in Pakistan and Bangladesh while angry mobs demanded a 'holy war' against India in retaliation. In Britain tension was created between the Hindu and Muslim communities and Hindu temples were mysteriously damaged. The span of responses confirms our other argument that to understand ethnic violence we need to keep its global context before us.

Although commentators singled out the BJP as the main culprit behind the ethnic violence this is incorrect and misleading; indeed, elements in the Congress had long compromised on its secular position. Others too – influential opinion-makers like bureaucrats, media commentators and academics – had been transformed and abandoned their earlier secular neutrality on communal issues. Those who were dismayed by this trend were reduced to powerless spectators.

Let us not make the mistake of the critics of the BJP by simplification of a complex phenomenon. Beneath every case of ethnic cleansing is layer upon layer of history and culture. The movement for a separate Muslim state, the creation of Pakistan (seen by many Hindus in a religious light, as sacrilege, as the division of Mother India itself), the wars between India and Pakistan, the perception of a threatening Islamic revivalism (in neighbours like Pakistan and Bangladesh and also, of course, Iran) and the continuing problems of the Muslim minority in adjusting to the new realities of India all contributed to the ethnic suppuration.

Indeed, as early as the 1930s Gowalkar (1938), one of the most influential Hindu ideologues, had argued that if Hitler could finish off the Jews in Germany then the Hindus ought to be able to do the same to the Muslims in India. Hindu extremists even today continue to use the unsavoury language of the Nazis. The tradition of virulent propaganda against Muslims disguised as scholarly research continues (Oak 1990; Elst 1992). Muslims in these books are depicted as whoring and pillaging drunks, breaking Hindu temples and buildings. These stereotypes feed into the mass media and neatly reinforce Hindu chauvinism which is calculated to win the Hindu vote.

The argument will be made that India is, after all, Asia, Third World, backward, a society stuck in the rut of religion and tradition, that the influence on society of television is a sign of such societies. It would be incorrect. Not only in India but throughout the world what we see on our television screens helps to form our ideas. The argument that the sex and violence shown on television influence people awaits long-term statistical findings but on the surface appears plausible. They inure people to cruelty. Children grow into adulthood convinced that the simple solution is to kill or maim or hurt. Not surprisingly, American pilots, on at least one carrier, about to bomb Iraq the following day during the Gulf war, were shown sadistic, pornographic films ('Dying to Please Nobody' by Marilyn French in *The Sunday Times*, 10 October 1993). Not surprisingly either, the young killers of little James Bulger here in the UK had grown up on a diet of 'video nasties'.

In December 1993 half a dozen young men raped for over an hour two young girls barely in their teens who were dragged from a McDonald's in London. About twenty other men stood round and cheered. The inspiration for this is not difficult to guess. Dozens of American films have depicted the same scene. That the gang was predominantly black gave the incident an ethnic dimension (life was also imitating art a few weeks earlier when a black – or to use the politically correct term Afro-American – gunman walked along a New York underground train shooting anyone not of his colour).

No heroes any more

The mass media are also responsible, because of their aggressive irreverence and unceasing probing, for the lack-lustre leadership of today. Our age has produced a distinctly mediocre set of leaders. Political scientists need to investigate this phenomenon further so that we become enlightened. Consider the list at random – Clinton in America, Major in the United Kingdom, Kohl in Germany, Yeltsin in Russia, Rao in India, Mubarak in Egypt. Many of us, I am sure, are not even aware of the names of the heads of government in China and Japan.

Charismatic leaders are not always the best leaders and those like Hitler and Stalin were ardent supporters of ethnic cleansing. So what makes some charismatic leaders extraordinary is their ability to stand up to majority opinion when it comes to matters of principle. We have the example of Mahatma Gandhi agreeing to the creation of Pakistan, however much it pained him, if that was what the Muslims wanted, and then starting a fast to death unless Hindus stopped killing Muslims in India. A Hindu fanatic killed him, accusing him of being too sympathetic to the Muslims. There was De Gaulle in France who took the unpopular decision of giving independence to Algeria. For many French it was the ultimate betrayal and De Gaulle's life was constantly under threat. And there was Churchill whose support for the Jews overruled the anti-Semitism at the Foreign Office.

In contrast, Rao in India, a year after promising to reconstruct the mosque in Ayodhya still vacillates. In France north African immigrants are the subject of the crudest form of racism and the prime minister's office talks openly of smelly and dirty aliens. Charles Pasqua and others have powerfully and mendaciously linked crime and immigration. Pasqua talks of returning immigrants to Africa 'by the planeload and the boatload'. He has tapped a vast reservoir of votes and added a new and dangerous dimension to both issues.

The failure of the nation-state

The failure of the nation-state to provide justice and inspire confidence, and the frustrations that it engenders is another consequence of the collapse of modernity and of the rise of ethnic identity. Modernity was expressed by the form and idea of the nation-state. 'National identity' emerged as a by-product of the formation of the nation-state, itself impelled by 'industrialization' (Gellner 1983; Giddens 1991). But in large parts of the world the nation-state itself is under challenge: in East Europe, in the lands that once constituted the USSR, in the

Middle East, in South Asia and in Africa. Boundaries are being redrawn or rejected. As old states are threatened new ones are demanded or formed.

In their haste to depart, after the international climate changed following World War II, the colonialists took little time or effort when demarcating the new nations. Tribes and villages were sometimes divided between nations (in the case of the Kurds, the tribe was divided between five nations). Half a century of living together should have cemented the new states. This is not so.

One reason is the blatant discrimination that the state practises in favour of the dominant group. It is not being suggested that the state legally supports the subjugation or the elevation of a group. On the contrary, states are based on modern notions of equality and justice and in some cases appear to favour minorities (as in India where the Constitution in this regard compares favourably to the putatively advanced countries like France and Germany). Rather, that even state functionaries are now contaminated with ethnic hatred.

Most dangerously for the health of the state the majority has developed a 'minority complex' – whether in Serbia, Israel, Iraq or India. Through a process of Alice-in-Wonderland logic it has come to believe, and proclaims for all to hear, that its population is in danger of being swamped (the minority breed like rabbits); its economy is in crisis (the minority act as a brake); it is the victim of an international conspiracy (the minority are a fifth-column) and law and order have collapsed (the minority are responsible for the drugs and gun-culture). To be a member of what is seen as the pestilential minority by the majority is almost to be a *persona non grata*, irrespective of the merits of the individual (whether Muslim in India, Hindu in Bangladesh, Palestinian in Israel or Kurd in Iraq). The minority argue that the nation-state has meant suppression of their identity usually by brute force. Torture and death are common methods. Besides, the majority monopolize economic and political power, they point out. Democracy, they rightly claim, means perpetual subordination and humiliation. Ultimately, they fear, they will be wiped off the face of the earth.

A significant ethnic lesson is drawn from Bosnia. Many are now sceptical about the plausibility of plural or multicultural societies in the future. 'If the Serbs can do this to the Muslims who even married Serbs what hope is there for integration? Is the idea of integration irretrievably lost?' There were no easy answers even by optimists. The only security, it seems, was in reversion to primordial identity, a return to the idea of the tribe, of purity in an impure and menacing world.

An important idea, widely believed, is that international organizations which should have ensured justice, law and order and the rule of law have failed. The United Nations is the primary example. It has failed the Bosnians, the Palestinians and the Kashmiris. Resolution after resolution is passed regarding the destiny of these people and blatantly ignored.

For Muslims the world over Bosnia, Palestine and Kashmir signify the hostility to Islam in our times, of the persecution of Muslim minorities in particular. Muslims are convinced that fellow Muslims are being raped, killed and uprooted because of their religion. Muslim anger and anguish echo the heart-rending cry of Shakespeare's Jew: 'Hath not a Jew eyes? hath not a Jew hands, organs, dimensions, senses, affections, passions?'

The historical past is evoked in each case. For instance, when discussing Bosnia Muslims believe that the West which is capable of stopping the genocide will not do so because it does not want a viable Muslim nation in Europe. The last Muslim kingdom was extinguished in 1492 in Granada, Spain, and Europeans, 500 years later, have not changed. Muslims, both globally and in Bosnia, suggest that European ideas of humanism, freedom and equality appear to be applicable only to white Europeans with a Christian background (Ahmed 1992c, 1993c; Mestrovic 1994; also *Impact International* and '*Q*' *News* published in London). It is in this context that commentators construct the global confrontation between Islam and the West (Ahmed 1988, 1992a, 1993a, 1993e; Huntington 1993).

Matters are complicated as ethnic groups across international borders are prepared to assist their oppressed kin (India accuses Pakistan of assisting the Kashmiris, Israel the Arabs of aiding the Palestinians, and so on). Once again the majority feel threatened and talk of fifth-columns. Unless free and fair channels of representation are available and unless the majority genuinely consider the needs of the minority, the democracy in these countries will be incomplete and the nation-state will continue to be challenged as the minorities demand their own state.

We also need to point to the nation-state and nuclear proliferation. In the context of our arguments, until a decade or two ago, the nuclear option did not exist outside the Cold War structure. Today it does. India and Pakistan have fought three wars. They are poised for a fourth. Tension is at a peak following the destruction of the Ayodhya mosque and the revolt in Kashmir. This time the war will be nuclear, a total war; it will also be total madness. No-one can win.

It is not difficult to conjecture what extremists on either side – Serbs or Bosnians in the Balkans, Jews or Palestinians in the Middle East, Hindus or Muslims in South Asia – would do if allowed to decide whether a bomb should be dropped on their enemy. It would solve all their problems, they will say enthusiastically. Holocaust solutions have always been popular with those who believe in eliminating supposedly inferior races.

Ethonocentric perceptions lull us into believing that nuclear weapons are more unsafe in the hands of the north Korean leaders than in American or British ones. However, any finger, whether yellow or white, on the nuclear button is dangerous although the safeguards are greater in a democracy. The fact is that nuclear proliferation poses a major danger to the world. The question of nuclear weapons needs to be addressed urgently on a global level.

Rape as policy in ethnic cleansing

Rape is one of the most infamous acts on man's long list of infamy, one suggesting deep psychological and emotional disturbance. Because rape is so intimately tied to ideas of honour and disgrace people are reluctant to discuss it. Yet to learn about the true nature of ethnic and religious conflict social scientists need to study rape or sexual intimidation.

We know that in Bosnia rape is used deliberately as an instrument of war, a fact confirmed by innumerable international organizations and media reports. Dogs, men affected by the HIV virus and gangs taking turns are used to rape women in what have been exposed as rape camps. Small girls are raped in front of their mothers by soldiers taking turns. Rape is known as an ugly face of battle committed by soldiers in the heat of war. But in the manner it is used in the Balkans it is chillingly sinister. Civilians, administrators, students – ordinary people – are all involved as active participants or as spectators.

Bosnia is not alone in this regard. There is also considerable evidence gathered by international human rights organizations and by Indian writers that Indian troops in Kashmir are using the same tactics. There may not be official rape camps as in Bosnia but troops have regularly surrounded villages, expelled the men and raped their women all night. After the destruction of the Ayodhya mosque the police were clearly implicated in organizing riots in Bombay and Surat against Muslims which involved rape. Iraq and Israel, the former in a crude way, the latter in a more subtle manner, also use sexual tactics to intimidate minorities we learn from the book *Cruelty and Silence* by an Iraqi expatriate writer (Makiya 1993). Iraqi soldiers force Kurd women from camps taking them to be raped; Israelis lock up Arab women in security cells for the night with threatening men. An organization of brave Israeli women risked the wrath of the authorities and documented the widespread cases of sexual abuse by the Israeli police in *Women for Women Political Prisoners*, published in December 1989 in Jerusalem.

The woman is twice punished: by the brutality of the act and by the horror of her family. Notions of honour, modesty and motherhood are all violated. Rape strikes families at their most vulnerable point especially in traditional societies where, in certain tribes, illegitimate sexual acts are wiped out by death alone (Ahmed 1980). It is thus deliberately employed by ethnic neighbours who are fully aware of its expression as political power and cultural assertion to humiliate the internal other.

The sociological implications are clear for the purposes of our argument: rape as a final line divides one group from the other; the state, through its forces, becomes the rapist, raping its own citizens, those it is sworn to protect. Bitterness is at a peak. So is the nature of hatred in the response. Blood and revenge follow. A spiral of violence is set in motion. All the key notions of modernity – justice, rule of law, rationalism, civic society – are negated by the criminal nature of ethnic rape. For the victim and her family it is no longer an age of modernity and progress but one of barbarism and darkness.

The uses of the past

Finally, to justify the acts of humiliation like rape and as a consequence of the general sense of disillusionment with international and national bodies, the collapse of law and order and the conviction that the only security lies in one's own people, is the increasingly creative use of historical-religious arguments which, in turn, support ethnic cleansing.

History is employed to buttress ethnic and religious polemics and, more importantly, to reclaim and re-construct ethnic identity by a whole range of commentators, academics and politicians (Ahmed 1993b, 1993d). Thus, Kosovo in the Balkans, Jerusalem in the Middle East or Ayodhya in India are not just neutral historical place names; they are also deeply emotive and affective symbols of identity. They rally the community as they provide it with a visible proof of the perfidious enemy by reviving bitter memories from a distant past. In the mass media such history translates itself into kitsch, sentimentality and commercialization; it also becomes popular and accessible. In the vacuum caused by the collapse of the grand narratives like Communism the indigenous becomes both relevant and inevitable. Honour, identity and the media, the past and the future, the rise of what is called fundamentalism or revivalism all relate to the historical reference points.

Historical-religious mythology feeds the ethnic passions of the Russians (like Zhirinovsky) and Serbs (like Arkan) who talk of a Christian crusade, Jews and Muslims in the Middle East and Hindus and Muslims in South Asia who view each other as enemies in a holy war. 'God is with us', the faithful pronounce with utter conviction and sincere belief.

It is this zeal which drives men in Bosnia to burn the sign of the cross on to the bodies of innocent Muslims and impale them in crucifixion (Goytisolo 1993; Yusuf 1993). This is not the spirit of Jesus but it is a crude ethnic justification for the murder and mayhem. The first target is the village mosque. The destruction of these buildings is to be condemned on religious as well as architectural grounds, for most of them are centuries old. *The Heart Grown Bitter*, the title of an anthropological account of Greek ethnic war refugees in Cyprus by Peter Loizos (1981), tellingly describes the plight of the ethnically dispossessed.

Most academics who have dismissed such historical mythology as irrelevant to our modern lives do not fully appreciate its power and influence. We are pointing to zealous supporters of ethnic superiority who number in the millions across the world and their governments which have access to nuclear weapons.

Conclusion: into the millennium

Prognosis is difficult for the post-Cold War, post-Communism, post-modern age that is forming but it is likely that the next millennium will open with limited but intensely messy ethnic conflicts – with vigorous ethnic cleansing – on-going low intensity wars in which there are no real winners or losers, no major defeats or victories, no defined battlefields or boundaries. We need to pull back from this nightmare Hobbesian scenario of the future to restore a balance between tradition and modernity, local custom and culture, respect for law and the way of others. Above all, we need more imagination and tolerance in dealing with others.

It can be done. The last year or two have provided us with some dramatic examples of a silver lining to the dark ethnic cloud. Old-standing ethnic enemies shook hands, an act symbolic of the wish to remove the vast psychological and cultural barriers that divided them and their people: Rabin and Arafat in Washington, but also the British and Irish prime ministers over Northern Ireland and the black and white leaders over South Africa. In Germany, in spite of widespread and vicious ethnic violence, Dr Ravindra Gujjula, an Indian, was elected the first Asian mayor in history. In December 1993 the Vatican reconciled with Judaism thus closing the hostility of two millennia. These significant gestures need to be more than media events and to be followed by concrete steps; the ethnic fires still rage on the ground.

Important steps need to be taken to encourage ethnic understanding. The first and most important is to underline the plurality of our world, that although people are divided by birth, language and religion they belong to the same species. To counter narrow nationalism we need to stress the extent of interdependence in today's world, growing all the time so as to encourage people to think internationally. Organizations like the United Nations, weak and ineffective in the face of ethnic crises, need urgent structural changes and larger budgets. Human rights and minority groups must be protected not only under the law but in the spirit of good neighbourliness. The idea of tolerance and understanding needs to be encouraged through the mass media. We have seen the mass media acting as a source of division, let us see its positive side (for example, see Benthall 1993 for its impact on disasters and relief). For a start, it can become aware of the stereotypes it builds up of the other and avoid them.

Education is another way to discourage ethnic hatred. Ill-defined ideas and prejudices in a student's mind easily develop into prejudice for the other. Islam and Hinduism need to be taught seriously as regular subjects in Britain; Christianity in Sudan and Pakistan, and so on. We need to call for an intensification of inter-faith dialogue. There is so much common ground; spokespersons for the different faiths should point to it and act upon it. We need more Christians and non-Christians in Europe, Jews and Muslims in the Middle East and Hindus and Muslims in South Asia sitting across tables in serious discussion.

Never before in human history have the global and the local, the high and the low, the past and the present, the sacred and the profane, the serious and the frivolous been so bewilderingly juxtaposed and so instantly available to stimulate, confuse and anger the individual. Violence is almost inevitable, the ethnic victim often at hand. Globally, the disillusioned children and inheritors of modernity, live in what the academics have termed 'a risk culture' (Giddens 1991, p. 3) or 'risk society' (title of Beck 1992; also see Giddens 1990; Ahmed 1992a; Ahmed and Donnan 1994; Turner 1994; Ahmed and Shore, in press).

In concluding, we have pointed out the links between globalization, radicalization, sexual intimidation, the mass media, the uses of religious mythology and ethnic and religious violence in the aftermath of the collapse of modernity. There is clearly cause and effect here. We have noted that victims of ethnic intolerance in one part of the world are themselves aggressors in other parts through the acts of those who share their religion or ethnicity. Every group appears to be susceptible to the ethnic virus. Ethnic cleansing, we have suggested, ranges from the outright barbarity of death and rape camps to the more subtle but also traumatic cultural, political and economic pressures brought to bear on the minority.

In ethnic cleansing the human race faces a moral collapse leading to the most diabolical acts of cruelty. Yet our world also possesses the capacity and resources to tackle other pressing problems that we face like hunger and disease. Clearly, the global community is at some kind of dramatic crossroad, a cusp, a critical point in history.

Ethnic cleansing is the dark and ugly side of human nature. To contain it and to combat it we need first to understand it. Therefore to examine ethnic cleansing is not to look at the aberrant or the marginal or the temporary – the specialist's area of interest; it is to come face to face with our age, our nature and our aspirations; it is to confront the human condition.

Acknowledgements

For their comments on this article I am most grateful to Jonathan Benthall, Martin Bulmer, Tam Dalyell MP, Anthony Giddens, Charles Keyes, Sir David Lane, Stjepan Mestrovic, Chris Rojek, Shawar Sadeque, Jon Snow and Gary Waller MP.

References

AHMED, AKBAR S. 1976 *Millennium and Charisma among Pathans: A Critical Essay in Social Anthropology*, Routledge, London

—— 1980 *Pukhtun Economy and Society: Traditional Structure and Economic Development in a Tribal Society*, Routledge, London

—— 1988 *Discovering Islam: Making Sense of Muslim History and Society*, Routledge, London

—— 1991 'Anthropology "comes out"?' in *Anthropology Today*, vol. 7, no. 3, June

—— 1992a *Postmodernism and Islam: Predicament and Promise*, Routledge, London

—— 1992b 'Bombay films: the cinema as metaphor for Indian society and politics' in *Modern Asian Studies*, vol. 26, no. 2, Cambridge University Press, pp. 289–320

—— 1992c 'Palestine revisited' in *Newstatesman and Society*, 20 November

—— 1993a *Living Islam: From Samarkand to Stornoway*, BBC Books, London

—— 1993b 'The history-thieves: stealing the Muslim past?' in *History Today*, vol. 43, January

—— 1993c 'New metaphor in the "New World Order" ' in *Impact International*, 12 March–8 April, pp. 24–27

—— 1993d 'Points of entry: the Taj Mahal' in *History Today*, vol. 43, May

—— 1993e 'Media Mongols at the gates of Baghdad' in *New Perspective Quarterly*, vol. 10, Summer

AHMED, AKBAR S. and HART, DAVID (eds) 1984 *Islam in Tribal Societies: From the Atlas to the Indus*, Routledge, London

AHMED, AKBAR S. and DONNAN, HASTINGS (eds) 1994 *Islam, Globalisation and Postmodernity*, Routledge, London

AHMED, AKBAR S. and SHORE, CRIS (eds) in press, *The Future of Anthropology: Its relevance to the Contemporary World*, Athlone, London

AKBAR, M. J. 1988 *Riot after Riot*, Penguin, India

AMIN, SAMIR 1994 'India faces enormous danger from globalization', in *Mainstream*, vol. XXXII, no. 9, 15 January, New Delhi

BARTH, F. 1969 'Introduction and Pathan identity and its maintenance' in *Ethnic Groups and Boundaries: The Social Organization of Culture Difference*, Allen and Unwin, London

BASU, TAPAN *et al.* 1993 *Khaki Shorts and Saffron Flags: A Critique of the Hindu Right*, Sangam Books, London

BAUMAN, ZYGMUNT 1991 *Modernity and the Holocaust*, Polity Press, Cambridge with Blackwell Publishers, Oxford

BECK, ULRICH 1992 *Risk Society: Towards a New Modernity*, translated by Mark Ritter, Sage Publications, London: [Originally published in 1986]

BELL-FIALKOFF, ANDREW 1993 'A Brief History of Ethnic Cleansing' in *Foreign Affairs*, Summer

24 *Akbar S. Ahmed*

BENTHALL, JONATHAN 1993 *Disasters, Relief and the Media*, I. B. Tauris and Co, London

CONNOR, WALKER 1993 'Beyond reason: the nature of the ethnonational bond', Annual ERS/LSE Lecture, 1992, in *Ethnic and Racial Studies*, vol. 16, no. 3, July

DAS, VEENA (ed.) 1992 *Mirrors of Violence: Communities, Riots and Survivors in South Asia*, Oxford University Press, Delhi

ELST, KOENRAAD 1992 *Negationism in India: Concealing the Record of Islam*, Voice of India, New Delhi

ENGINEER, ASGHAR ALI (ed.) 1984 *Communal Riots in Post-Independence India*, Sangam Books, London

FERNANDEZ, C. and FERNANDES, NARESH 1993 'A city at war with itself' in Padgaonkar 1993

FORTES, M. and EVANS-PRITCHARD, E. E. 1940 *African Political Systems*, Oxford University Press, Oxford

FUKUYAMA, FRANCIS 1992 *The End of History and the Last Man*, Hamish Hamilton, London

GELLNER, E. 1983 *Nations and Nationalism*, Blackwell, Oxford

GIDDENS, ANTHONY 1990 *Consequences of modernity*, Polity Press, Cambridge

—— 1991 *Modernity and Self-Identity: Self and Society in the Late Modern Age*, Polity Press, Cambridge

GLUCKMAN, M. 1971 *Political, Law and Ritual in Tribal Society*, Basil Blackwell, Oxford

GODELIER, M. 1977 *Perspectives in Marxist Anthropology*, Cambridge: Cambridge University Press, Cambridge

GOPAL, SARVEPALLI (ed.) 1991 *Anatomy of a Confrontation: Ayodhya and the Rise of Communal Politics in India*, Penguin, India

GOWALKAR, M. S. 1938 *We or Our Nationhood Defined*, India: Nagpur

GOYTISOLO, JUAN 1993 'Terror town' in *Newstatesman and Society*, 17–31 December

GRAHAM, BRUCE 1990 *Hindu Nationalism and Indian Politics: The Origins and Development of Bharatiya Jana Sangh*, Cambridge University Press, Cambridge

HELM, J. (ed.) 1971 *Essays on the Problem of Tribe*, American Ethnological Society, University of Washington Press, USA

HUNTINGTON, SAMUEL P. 1993 'The clash of civilizations?' in *Foreign Affairs*, Summer

IYER, KRISHNA 1992 review of Ahmed 1992a in *Economic and Political Weekly*, 7 November, Bombay

LOIZOS, PETER 1981 *The Heart Grown Bitter: A Chronicle of Cypriot War Refugees*, Cambridge University Press, Cambridge

MADAN, T. N. (ed.) 1992 *Religion in India*, Oxford, in India Readings in Sociology and Social Anthroplogy, Oxford University Press, Oxford and Delhi: [Originally published in 1991]

MAKIYA, KANAN 1993 *Cruelty and Silence: War, Tyranny, Uprising, and the Arab World*, Jonathan Cape, London

MCLEOD, W. H. 1989 *Who is a Sikh? The Problem of Sikh Identity*, The Clarendon Press, Oxford

MERON, THEODOR 1993 'The case for war crimes trials in Yugoslavia' in *Foreign Affairs*, Summer

MESTROVIC, STJEPAN G. 1994 *The Balkanization of the West: The Confluence of Postmodernism with Postcommunism*, Routledge, London

MOYNIHAN, DANIEL PATRICK 1993 *Pandaemonium: Ethnicity in International Politics*, Oxford University Press, Oxford

NASH, MANNING 1989 *The Cauldron of Ethnicity in the Modern World*, The University of Chicago Press, Chicago

OAK, P. N. 1990 *Some Blunders of Indian Historical Research*, Bharati Sahitya Sadan, New Delhi
PADGAONKAR, DILEEP (ed.) 1993 *When Bombay Burned*, UBS Publishers and Distributors New Delhi
PHADNIS, URMILA 1989 *Ethnicity and Nation-building in South Asia*, Sage Publications, New Delhi
ROBERTSON, ROLAND 1991 'The globalization paradigm: thinking globally' in D. G. Bromley (ed.), *Religion and Social Order*, JAI Press, Greenwich, CT: pp. 207–224
—— 1992 *Globalization: Social Theory and Global Culture*, Sage Publications, London
SAID, EDWARD 1978 *Orientalism*, Routledge, London
—— 1993 *Culture and Imperialism*, Chatto and Windus, London
SCHOPFLIN, GEORGE 1993 'The rise and fall of Yugoslavia' in John McGarry and Brendan O'Leary (eds), *The Politics of Ethnic Conflict Regulation*, Routledge, London
THOMPSON, JOHN B. 1990 *Ideology and Modern Culture*, Cambridge: Polity Press
TULLY, MARK 1991 *No Full Stops in India*, Viking, Penguin Books Ltd, London
TURNER, B. S. 1994 *Orientalism, Postmodernism and Globalism: Intellectuals in the Modern World*, Routledge, London
VULLIAMY, ED 1994 *Seasons in Hell: Understanding Bosnia's War*, Simon and Schuster, New York
YUSUF, FEYYAZ 1993 'Christian radicalism stirs the Serbs' in *'Q' News*, 10–17 December

AKBAR S. AHMED is Fellow of Selwyn College and Member of the Centre for South Asian Studies at the University of Cambridge.
ADDRESS: Selwyn College, University of Cambridge, Cambridge CB3 9DQ.

[17]

new **community** 23(4): 549–570 October 1997

Europe, Africa, and international migration: an uncomfortable triangle of interests

Kimberly A. Hamilton

> Perhaps the global problem of the early twenty-first century is basically this: that across our planet a number of what might be termed demographic-technological fault lines are emerging, between fast-growing, adolescent, resource-poor, undercapitalised, and under-educated populations on one side and technologically inventive, demographically moribund, and increasingly nervous rich societies on the other. (Connolly and Kennedy 1994: 62)

Abstract *Arguing that research on migration and the state has focused primarily on receiving states, this article places sending and receiving states in a dynamic historical context within which states strive to protect political, economic, and socio-cultural interests. This framework is applied to the Euro-African migration system and leads to three primary findings. First, migration flows from Africa have diversified in terms of origins and destinations and no longer necessarily follow patterns of colonial relations. Such a trend calls into question the efficacy of bilateral responses. Second, African states have clearly demonstrated interests in managing emigration and return migration and need to be considered as partners in policy responses. Third, African migrant communities are exerting greater independence vis-à-vis sending and receiving states. This diversification and growing independence poses interesting challenges for sending and receiving state policy in the Euro-African migration system.*

A few years ago, a much-touted article in the *Atlantic Monthly* (Connolly and Kennedy 1994) predicted that 'Western paradise' would soon be overrun with uncontrolled masses from the so-called South. These new 'refugees' of the twentieth century, reacting to and profiting from global technological transformations, the growing momentum of historical human diasporas, and environmental, political, and social degradation at the hands of irresponsible if not repressive leaders, would soon be gaining more than a toe-hold in the advanced industrial world. At its extreme, the overflow from the South would quickly rob the coffers of the modern welfare state and undermine the peace and security of the post-war world.

Such an outlook reflects a pessimistic view on the capacity of the states – both sending and receiving – to manage migration flows for economic and social benefit. Lack of confidence in state capacity to manage migration exists partly

Kimberly A. Hamilton is a programme officer at The Howard Gilman Foundation in New York. She is currently finishing her doctoral dissertation at Brown University on state relations, migration policy, and international migration flows. She has also been a visiting researcher at the Institut National d'Etudes Démographiques (INED) in Paris, France and at the Institute for Economic Development and Planning (IDEP) in Dakar, Senegal.

0047-9586/97/040549-22

because international migration is a broad catch phrase that embraces such diverse processes as the maintenance of political stability, economic development, demographic change, and shifting ethnic allegiances. It has quite correctly been called a symptom of 'inequality and underdevelopment' (UNFPA 1993: ii). For policy analysts, it is also the impetus for a quagmire of rules and regulations attempting to direct flows into narrower and more orderly channels.

Despite such efforts to clarify and organise flows, there is enormous ambiguity and diversity among states regarding definitions of migrants and the benefits available to different categories. Asylum channels have been increasingly used for entrée by a range of hopeful immigrants. Regularisation programmes have offered another means, shifting migrants from unauthorised to legal categories. Citizenship policies and family reunification have offered yet another strategy for access. In sum, there is a great deal of fluidity surrounding categories, strategies, and definitions. For these reasons, migration and its consequences are, in fact, the most difficult demographic processes to predict, measure, understand, and control.

Migration from Africa to Europe is one of the many regional systems that European states are striving to understand and manage. Migration from Africa to Europe has historically been synonymous with movements from the Maghreb – especially Algeria, Tunisia, and Morocco – to countries along the Mediterranean basin, including France, Spain, and Italy. Resulting partially from the decolonisation movements throughout the 1960s and the search for labour in expanding European economies, migration dynamics in the Euro-African region began to change. Most significantly, Europe has begun to witness an intensification as well as a diversification of migration from the countries of sub-Saharan Africa to Europe. The numbers are increasing and the range of origin and destination countries is expanding (Robin 1994). This trend of rising migration from other parts of Africa has been called a legacy of colonisation as well as a result of contemporary economic globalisation. Along with movements from the Maghreb, it has also fuelled concerns that Europe is becoming 'Africanised' or 'Islamicised' and that Europe's (perceived) cultural equilibrium is off kilter.[1]

This article challenges policy makers and analysts to understand international migration between Africa and Europe as a result of receiving and *sending* states' sometimes competing interests and the way these interests are cross-cut by those of migrant communities themselves. Theoretically, such an understanding augments migration literature that focuses nearly exclusively on receiving state interests and actions. Practically, it can enhance the capacity of Europe's liberal democratic states as well as African countries to manage more effectively complex international migration processes. Furthermore, an analysis of competing state interests sheds light on Euro-African relations that were once understood solely in terms of continuing colonial relations and dealt with in a primarily bilateral fashion.

This article turns first to various theories regarding the state and migration and highlights the lack of attention paid to sending state interests. It then provides an overview of emerging migration patterns between Africa and Europe with a special focus on Italy and France. After comparing sending and receiving state interests, the article concludes with a discussion of the limits of state-centred policy when dealing with migration.

State interests and migration systems

Understanding how migration touches on, rearranges, or irritates key state interests is an important step in making sense of policy success and failure. Furthermore, placing states as interested actors within migration systems – and not as passive policy screens – can dramatically change our understanding of migration flows, policy responses, and migrant strategies. Advances in state theory have pulled the state from the sidelines to centre stage in many analyses of international migration.[2] Despite the burgeoning body of literature that exhorts analysts 'to bring the state back in', however, contemporary migration theory has primarily focused on receiving states, and more specifically, on liberal democratic state interests.

If, however, international migration follows the logic of certain regional systems and processes (historical and contemporary), there is presumably an interested sending state at the other end.[3] Furthermore, if states are motivated by political, economic, and social concerns, sending states share in the risks as well as the benefits to be had from international migration. This article argues that it is this relationship that links sending and receiving states that is misunderstood and poorly theorised.

Migration theory has recently undergone a significant conceptual shift that gives greater weight to the larger political, economic, and national context in which international migration takes place (Cornelius *et al.* 1994; Hollifield 1992; Zolberg 1989). Zolberg outlines some of the common features of this new approach, noting that they are 'historical', 'structural rather than individualistic', and 'permeable to determination by transnational and international economic and political processes' (1989: 404). In essence, these theories shift the focus away from micro-level, individual-centred behaviours and look to broader economic and political contexts for explanations of migration.

Hollifield, for example, in his analysis of immigration in Western democracies, sees immigration as 'a test of economic and political liberalism'. He defines 'political liberalism as the ongoing extension of civil, political, and social rights to every member of society, whereas economic liberalism can be defined in terms of the creation and protection of relatively free markets' (1992: 6). In this sense, immigration regulations are forced to balance various sources of tension between the economy and the polity. One source of that tension – ever-present in the incentives and constraints that influence migration – may be the struggle between the inequalities associated with capitalism and the rhetoric of equality embraced by democracy.[4] A second source of tension may be derived from external forces such as various forms of economic globalisation and the creation of an international human rights regime (however controversial when viewed from a non-Western perspective). As Sassen has observed, 'a national state may have the power to write the text of an immigration policy, but it is likely to be dealing with complex, transnational processes that it can only partly address or regulate through immigration policy as conventionally understood' (1996: 74).

For some, it is this complicated interplay of social rights and market extension, increasingly viewed and acted upon as global phenomena, that has tended to erode single state autonomy despite efforts to fortify national responses. Migration flows and responses are increasingly seen as 'post-state' phenomena when viewed within this international context. European integration combined with a growing diversity of origin country citizens has opened up a lively debate about the future of the nation-state and the nature of political belonging (Brubaker 1992). Citizenship, for so long a basic building block of the nation-state, may no longer be a necessary precursor to civic rights and social benefits. In other words, universal norms have already effectively created a postnational citizenship (Soysal 1994). Hammar's (1990) distinctions between foreigners, citizens, and denizens, further highlights the nuanced gradations attached to membership within a nation. Indeed, the emergence of transnational communities has raised provocative questions about belonging, ethnic identity, and allegiance to the state (Anderson 1992; Bauböck 1996).

Despite the tendency toward convergence at the supranational level, state responses tend to dominate international migration policy. The internationalisation of migration and the rapidity of change throughout the early 1990s fed the administrative capacity of states to manage migration. In many countries, increasing numbers of legal and illegal migrants have been viewed as a failure of such state capacity, or at least, worthy of repudiation at the polls. This perceived 'failure' of state regulation may in fact represent some level of state complicity in the maintenance of certain levels of immigration – legal and illegal – to achieve other goals.[5]

Such state complicity may be due to the strength of organised interest groups and their influence on the internal dynamics of state policy-making with regard to immigration policy. Corrosive global processes are replaced by client politics and, again returning to the question of increasing numbers, the result is an expansion in migration. As Freeman asserts

> there are important characteristics of immigration politics common to the liberal democracies and these are, contrary to what most scholars seem to believe, largely expansionist and inclusive. The explanation for this convergence is to be found in features of liberal democracy itself that affect the way such regimes process migration issues. (1995: 882)

It is the structure of the liberal democratic state itself that allows well-organised interest groups to push the policy agenda through administrative channels, thus overriding anti-populist norms.[6]

Another conceptualisation of migration flows looks directly to the dominance of global capitalism. With an eye on Africa specifically, Amin (1995) argues that 'the migrations that have shaped the population patterns of contemporary Africa, brought about in close relation to the peripheralisation linked to the system of global capitalism, have their responsibility for the present "marginalisation" of the continent, its "fourth worldisation"' (1995: 37). Such an approach would limit the importance of political economy explanations and dismiss traditional migration frameworks based on rational choice or individual and family decision-making. Instead, it looks to the organisation of global capital for explanations.

States, as has been well demonstrated, may display interests other than the reproduction of capital. In fact, they may pursue goals that run counter to the interest of the capitalist classes, as they respond to global economic conditions as well as geopolitical and domestic exigencies. Herein lies the conflict between economic globalisation and the strengthening of the state, or 'renationalisation', in relation to immigration policy (Sassen 1996). Furthermore, the ability of states to achieve these goals depends on a variety of organisational and historically contingent factors,[7] leading to both anticipated and unforeseeable consequences – sometimes for other states.[8] In the parlance of Cornelius *et al.*

(1994: 3), there may be a 'gap' between the goals of states and the policy outcomes.

The key concept to grasp with regard to immigration policy and the diverse experiences among states is that state-centred theories attribute to the state *variable* autonomy in its ability to address a *range* of domestic and geo-strategic issues. In an international migration setting, this means that any one state is more or less capable of protecting its interests by addressing a variety of concerns, including but not limited to the protection of capitalist development. This broader view of the state paves the way for the inclusion of what some may call the 'soft' interests of states, such as humanitarian and human rights concerns, as well as traditional concerns about labour markets and social welfare, domestic and international security, or economic development.

But what have we to say of sending state interests, organisation and capacity? Few analysts have taken this on as a primary focus of investigation (Collinson 1996; Keely 1980). The theoretical void surrounding sending country interests is partly related to the dramatic events of 1989. The literal destruction of the most powerful symbol of the Cold War, the Berlin Wall, made the 'right to move' more than a foreign policy aphorism. European attention was riveted on mass exoduses from Yugoslavia and Albania. More importantly, it became abundantly clear that the policy instruments developed through the Cold War to manage migration were neither sufficient nor effective in this new context. And, as Europe pushed to strengthen its 'union', it was also clear that the political landscape for policy-making was much more complex.

In the post-1989 era, however, the interests and actions of the sending states themselves have been almost entirely marginalised. This is despite the growing data accumulated from the active engagement of the governments of Turkey, Morocco, Mexico, and China, among others, in migration-related issues. Most research on sending states focuses on remittances and the limited possibilities of economic development, regional integration, and employment creation to mitigate migration flows (Keely and Tran 1989; OECD 1994; Rogers 1990; Russell 1992; Tapinos 1996). Another fairly large body of literature targets the linkages between states through migrant community associations and their villages of origin. Additionally, as Collinson notes on Euro-Maghreb relations, 'the emphasis in the literature and in official reports on the issue has been on the *external* causes of migration, i.e. growing migration "pressures", such as population growth, relatively poverty, and conflict in the sending countries' (1996: 4). This genre of research generally views the state as non-present, ineffectual, or as a simple appendage of receiving state policy.[9]

Analyses of systems (Hugo *et al.* 1995; Kritz and Zlotnick 1992), when read in this light, should encourage researchers 'to bring the *sending* state back in' as it were. States (at least two) in this approach are linked in a spatial or geographical dimension as well as a time or historical dimension. They are also located within specific political, economic, social, and demographic contexts. These macro, contextual conditions are connected to micro-level migration streams by networks of legal and informal institutions and individuals as well as government institutions. The receiving state then impinges on this micro–macro relationship in the form of migration policy that may attempt both to attract certain kinds of migrants and to dissuade or prevent others. It is unclear how sending states in this conceptualisation can glean all possible benefits from emigration and return migration.

A systems approach is only of limited use in assessing the interactions between states that participate in the migration system. This is in part because the dynamics become more complex when two or more states are struggling to meet divergent goals. Similarly, all participants in the global system do not share the same capacity or authority to achieve these goals at a given time. It is useful, however, to begin to unravel how the various political, economic, social, and demographic forces that impinge on a state shape interests in sending and receiving countries. Do participating states have the capacity to protect or attain these interests? And, what facilitates this and what impedes this? The rest of this article turns to the specific situation of Euro-African migration relations to explore these questions.

The African political economy, root causes, and international migration

Despite the optimism that seemed to accompany most African countries into independence in the 1960s, the nation-states of Africa are nearly as poor today as they were 30 years ago. A long-term perspective study by the World Bank on sub-Saharan Africa outlines the disappointing results after more than three decades of various development strategies. According to the World Bank's first report *From Crisis to Sustainable Growth*, 'Africa's deepening crisis is characterised by weak agricultural growth, a decline in industrial output, poor export performance, climbing debt and deteriorating social indicators, institutions and environment' (1989: 2). The World Bank attributes the poor economic performance of Africa to losses from declining or irregular terms of trade, steady population growth of over 3 per cent, which is outstripping the GDP and declining investment.

The list of causal factors behind this economic and political decline is extensive: a reliance on primary commodities (tobacco, minerals, cocoa, etc.); burgeoning civil service sectors with guaranteed employment; large military sectors; deteriorating terms of trade with the collapse of commodities markets; high levels of debt; corruption; environmental degradation; and ethnic conflict among others. In response, the International Monetary Fund and the World Bank, in the 1980s, called for a five-point programme of structural adjustment for eligibility for development assistance. In implementing reductions in the size of the public sector, devaluation of national currencies, and other difficult measures, African governments have been faced with sometimes violent public protest.[10] In general:

> ... Several African countries have encountered severe social and economic problems, including rising unemployment, reduced real wages, and a dramatic reduction in allocations to the education and health sectors, the very sectors that are essential for human resource development. With rapidly growing population, income per capita is at its lowest. (Adepoju 1994: 4)

Creeping economic decline, increasing income inequality, and, in some minds, bitter 'World Bank medicine' have fed the 'push forces' that encourage emigration – both within the Africa continent and elsewhere.

It is not, however, only the economic situation that has created extreme 'push' conditions in the sending countries. The political structures that emerged following independence from colonial rule, the Cold War rivalry that was played out via proxies across the African continent, and, in general, the political instability that plagued many countries are, in large part, responsible for the persecution and flight of skilled elite and other sectors of the population. Davidson has written pointedly on this transition: 'while the outside world stood by and continued stolidly to take its cut of Africa's productive wealth, giving back less and less in grants, aid, or better prices, the scope for political redress correspondingly narrowed' (1992: 221). This, in part, has led to the repression, violence, and lack of human and political rights that have also created a situation ripe for ethnic conflict. Such conflict has often resulted in internally displaced and refugee populations and international migration. Liberia, Rwanda, Angola, Mozambique, Zaire, and Ethiopia, to name just a few countries, have been riddled with such conflicts.

What is interesting in this context is that 'African governments have consistently cited migration as the most important demographic phenomenon [for the state] – ahead of mortality and fertility' (Adepoju 1994: 2). This is a testimony to the complexities outlined above, to the mixed benefits and disadvantages of migration for African countries, and to the historical articulation of African economies in a post-colonial world. While this article addresses the international dimensions of migration, it is important to remember that the bulk of migration within Africa remains south-to-south. The emergence of strong economic poles such as the Côte d'Ivoire and South Africa, play an important role in shaping these continent-wide movements.[11]

Trends in African migration to Europe

In a certain sense, it is misleading to speak of one African diaspora toward Europe just as it is equally misguiding to speak of Europe as a singular entity despite the many co-operative actions at the level of the European Union to deal with migration. To be sure, contemporary migration from Africa to most European countries has been dominated by flows from Morocco. Of the Africans in Europe, Moroccans are the largest population, totalling near 1.1 million. Over half of the Moroccan population is in France; 14.7 per cent live in the Netherlands; and 12.9 per cent live in Belgium (Eurostat 1996). Sub-Saharan African migration to Europe, on the other hand, is nascent if not largely absent. Estimates of sub-Saharan migration to Europe show important increases between the early 1960s and the early 1970s. Similar levels to those of the early 1970 are also found for the 1985–1990 period (see Table 1). Although migration from sub-Saharan African has also shown increases since 1989, the overall numbers when compared to other migrant communities remain small.[12]

Despite the longevity of migration flows from the Maghreb and the relative newness of sub-Saharan migration toward Europe (with the exception of France), it is still possible to paint in broad strokes the pan-African-European migration system and its impact in Europe. For the current 15 countries of the European Union, what is most remarkable when one looks at the distribution of the population by citizenship since 1985 is the marked increase in the presence of non-nationals from non-EU countries. For all of Europe, this group made up 3.3 per cent of the population (as of 1993), compared to 2.1 per cent in 1985. Non-nationals from other EU countries make up 1.5 per cent of the population (as of 1993) compared to 1.4 per cent in 1985. Two-thirds of the non-nationals live in Germany, France, and the UK.

Table 1. *Average annual number of immigrants from Sub-Saharan Africa to the north*

Destination	Period of immigration 1960–1964	1970–1974	1980–1984	1985–1989
North America	1,900	10,254	16,973	20,284
Oceania	2,072	3,832	4,454	5,708
Western Europe	13,287	50,998	37,368	51,644
Total	17,259	65,084	58,795	77,636

Source: Findley *et al.* (1994).

Africans – including those from the countries of the Maghreb – account for 0.8 per cent of the total EU population, making this the largest non-European, non-national presence. Asians, by contrast, account for 0.5 per cent of the population. By nationality, however, Turks are by far the largest group of non-nationals resident in the EU, accounting alone for 0.6 per cent of the EU population. Of course, the percentages vary widely from country to country and depend on definitional questions within each country when disaggregated.

If one looks at the non-EU population by country, the growing importance of African migration is much clearer. What is most interesting is that African flows to Europe are developing in countries without long-standing and 'deep' colonial relationships to Africa. In addition to traditional destinations based on colonial connections, such as those in France and Belgium, destinations countries with more limited engagement, such as Italy and the Netherlands, are claiming a growing proportion of African migration. Robin's research on West African migration (1994) underscores these changes. She writes, '... essential mutations of the West African migratory space in the heart of the EEC call into question the pertinence of the symmetry between former colonial space and migratory

Table 2. *Africans as a percentage of the total population, the foreign population and the non-European Economic Area[13] foreigners by country (as of 1 January 1992)*

	% of total population	% of foreign population	% of non-EEA foreigners
Belgium	1.9	20.4	52.0
Denmark	0.2	4.8	7.0
Germany	0.3	4.0	5.7
Greece	0.2	9.8	14.4
Spain	0.2	17.4	32.8
France	2.9	45.4	71.9
Ireland	—	—	—
Italy	0.3	31.7	40.7
Luxembourg	0.3	1.0	10.2
Netherlands	1.3	27.0	36.0
Portugal	0.5	42.1	58.2
United Kingdom	0.3	9.7	16.5
European Union (12)	0.8	18.7	29.0

Source: Chrissantaki and Kuiper (1994).

space' (1994: 29, translation mine). This upholds Zartman's thesis (1995) that relations between Africa and Europe are becoming increasingly diluted and more multilateral. In other words, state-to-state relations formerly based on colonial ties are now built on relations with many states. This is further evidenced in changing migration patterns. While an in-depth analysis of each of these countries is beyond the scope of this article, it is worthwhile examining more closely how these changing dynamics have contributed to a diversity of experiences in two European countries, France and Italy.

Countries of destination: France and Italy

France and Italy are both 'advanced' industrial democracies, experiencing continuing migration from Africa – especially the Maghreb. As members of the European Union as well as the Schengen Convention,[14] both countries are moving to bring their immigration policies in line with the dictates of these larger, supranational arrangements. In light of the initial Albanian crisis that rocked Italy in the summer of 1991, and the continuing instability in Algeria, Italy and France are each in the process of re-evaluating their immigration and integration policies (Papademetriou and Hamilton 1996).

The countries differ, however, in two primary ways. First, Italy does not share the same historically-binding colonial relations with Africa that France does. Italy occupied what is now Eritrea during the late nineteenth century and, under Mussolini, held Ethiopia between 1936 and 1941. Italy also held Libya for nearly 30 years until the end of World War II. The legacy of those links, however, are much less profound than the colonisation of extensive of parts of the African continent by Portugal, France, and England.

Second, Italy has only recently become a country of immigration. Beginning in the late 1970s and continuing through the 1980s, there was a steep increase in the numbers of migrants coming to Italy partly because of the lack of legislative controls and partly because of economic pull factors, including the underground labour market. The increase in the presence of Africans may also be due to the geographical proximity of Italy as well as the growing trade and transportation links being established between Italy and Africa, including Alitalia flights to such capitals as Dakar, Lagos, Johannesburg, and Nairobi.

Between 1985 and 1991, the foreign population more than doubled from 423,000 (0.7 per cent of the total population) to 896,800 (1.5 per cent of the total population). This dramatic increase in part relates to two regularisation programmes in 1987–1988 and in 1991 that legalised the status of 118,000 and 220,000 unauthorised migrants respectively. Africans were among those most represented in the regularisations.

There has also been a significant diversification in countries of origin that send migrants to Italy. In 1985, the five primary sending countries were: the USA, Germany, Greece, the UK, and France (OECD 1993). In 1994, the five primary sending countries were: Morocco, the former Yugoslavia, the USA, Tunisia, and the Philippines (followed by Germany, Albania, the UK, France, and Senegal) (Caritas di Roma 1995). What is most notable about the Italian situation is that a growing African presence is establishing itself, along with an array of other migrant populations. This is happening despite Italy's relatively limited historical involvement with Africa, thus dispelling in part the notion that migration continues to be driven primarily by colonial ties.

Table 3. *Percentage foreign African population in France (1946–1990)*

Country	1946[a]	1954[b]	1962[b]	1968	1975	1982	1990
Algerian	01.3	12.0	16.2	18.1	20.6	21.7	17.1
Morocco	00.9	00.6	01.5	03.2	07.6	11.9	15.9
Tunisia	00.1	00.3	01.2	02.3	04.1	05.2	05.7
Other African	00.8	00.1	00.8	01.2	02.3	04.2	06.7
Total	3.1	13.0	19.7	24.8	34.6	43.0	45.4

Notes:
[a] This was the population present at the time of the census. Later censuses counted the resident population.
[b] French Muslims from Algeria are counted as foreigners. Only in 1954 are they counted as French by birth.

France, on the other hand, has a long tradition of immigration and regulations to manage it. French colonial involvement in Africa is well-documented. French contact with West Africa dates back to the mid-1600s. Its colonial presence – manifested in administrative, economic, and political control in many cases – intensified throughout the nineteenth and early twentieth centuries and continued formally until the wars of national independence throughout the 1960s. While there had been steady movements between France and its colonies, the first attempts at codified policy to regulate immigration date back to the end of World War II and are largely a response to the need for foreign labour in the aftermath of the war (Weil 1991). By 1975, more than 80 per cent of all foreigners had come to France from North Africa or the Iberian peninsula, with more than 20 per cent each from Portugal and Algeria (Horowitz 1992). It is not clear how many returned home. Based on the 1990 census, the total (legal) foreign population, around 3.6 million, made up 6.35 per cent of the population. This is a slight reduction from 6.8 per cent in 1982, and 6.5 per cent 1975. In 1992, only 36.5 per cent of the foreign population was from other countries of the European Union as compared to almost 50 per cent in the mid-1980s (Lebon 1993: 37).[15]

Until recently, migration from Africa had been steadily increasing. Tunisia, Morocco, and Algeria together comprised 30 per cent of permanent admissions in 1975, almost 50 per cent in 1981–1982 (excluding status regularisations), and nearly 40 per cent since the mid-1980s (OECD 1992). By 1990, migrants from the entire African continent comprised roughly 45 per cent of the total foreign population in France. Of this, migrants from Francophone Africa accounted for nearly 5 per cent, and those from the rest of sub-Saharan African made up nearly 2 per cent of the foreign population. However, there has been a steady decline of all permanent immigration into France since 1992. Between 1992 and 1993, for example, there was a 10 per cent decline in non-EU, permanent immigration to France from 100,000 to 90,000. Permanent immigration from Africa also shows an overall decline in this period of roughly 12.4 per cent (Lebon 1994). This trend continued through 1995. In that year 52,000 non-Europeans entered France compared with 90,000 in 1990. Table 3 shows the evolution of migration streams since the 1946 census into France from Africa.

What is evident from this table is that, after 1974, despite efforts to close off immigration channels, migrants from non-traditional (i.e. non-European) sources were on the rise. During this time period, the Italian population in France, for example, fell from nearly 25 per cent in 1954 to roughly 7 per cent of the total foreign population in 1990. Conversely, Moroccan migration rose from less than 1 per cent to over 15 per cent. More recent data, however, reveal that policy restrictions may indeed be having the intended effect of limiting permanent immigration into France. These restrictions include limitations on family reunfication based on access to suitable housing and sufficient income.

Thus, while Italy and France have different historical legacies of immigration policy, they share, in the recent period, a diversification of flows away from intra-European migration toward South–North migration, primarily from the Maghreb and to a lesser extent from sub-Saharan Africa. In Italy's case, this diversification includes a broad geographical array of other countries of origin. Given the recent downward trend of migration from Africa to France to historically low numbers, it is unclear what path future flows will follow. Furthermore, the effect of France's stringent policy changes on unauthorised migration remains untested.

Competing state interests and policies to manage migration

The most interesting point behind these flows is the ways in which sending and receiving states are organising themselves to respond to them. As has been covered extensively elsewhere (Collinson 1994; Papademetriou 1996; Widgren 1994), myriad policy changes, working groups, and international fora have sprung up to address the challenges of international migration. Furthermore, the closure of European borders in 1974 limited the negotiating power that sending states had regarding labour agreements. As a result, 'their attention shifted to the questions of return migration, of the status and treatment of migrants and their families in receiving countries, and of remittances ...' (Collinson 1996: 17). Behind the flurry of activities lie implicit if not explicitly outlined state interests. Such interests run the gamut from social and economic concerns to human rights and anti-colonial issues. Policies are the tangible expression of strategies to protect these interests. When state interests are compared, however, it becomes apparent that sending and receiving states are engaged in very different strategies to manage international migration to the benefit of the state.

Table 4 lays out the broad concerns of both sending and receiving states within the Euro-African migration system. Similar patterns of interests may be found within other systems, but the argument here is that these interests are shaped by historical relations, geopolitical arrangements, and economic arrangements – such as the Lomé Convention or the West African Franc Zone – that characterise each system. In broad terms, the interests of states can be divided into three: economic, socio-cultural, and political. These interests are manifested in various policies.

Economic interests are very closely tied to labour market issues for receiving countries. In some parts of Europe that have seen unemployment hovering near 12 per cent and even higher for migrant communities, the regulation of migration has seemed paramount. The point has been further underscored by growing populist pressures on many European countries. Thus, a variety of policies to limit and control entry of migrants have been implemented. These include stricter visa regulations, tighter security at borders, regularisation programmes, involuntary repatriation, and limits on family reunification. Such controls also aim to lessen illegal migration (although they may conversely

Table 4. *State interests and policies with regard to international migration*

European receiving states	African sending states
Economic interests	
• Regulate employment	• Benefit from remittances
• Prevent illegal immigration	• Profit from return migrants' experience
• Encourage voluntary departure	• Retain the highly skilled
Social-cultural interests	
• Facilitate integration	• Ensure protection of human rights
• Protect secularity	• Maintain religious community
• Promote women's rights	• Protect citizens against discrimination
• Limit polygamy	
• Limit drug trafficking and prostitution	
Political interests: domestic	
• Guarantee domestic security	• Maintain contacts with communities to ensure political support
• Maintain political control	
Political interests: international	
• Cooperate on Schengen, Dublin, etc.	• Limit post-colonial dominance
Resultant policies	
• Border controls: visas, patrols, involuntary repatriations, counter-smuggling initiatives	• Preferential banking, customs, and money transfer policies
• Integration schemes: language training, education, employment	• Deepened relations with emigrant communities abroad through government and private channels
• Targeted development assistance	• Predeparture education
• Return incentives	• Migration as a bargaining chip
• Conditionality of foreign assistance	

increase this as well as asylum claims by narrowing other options). Along with these policies, some countries such as Germany and France have established voluntary return programmes. In the case in France, certain migrants have been offered return packages to return to their country of origin in exchange for relinquishing their residency permit. The programme, initiated in 1984, has had variable success, has gone through several iterations, and has been met with diminishing enthusiasm over time.[16] More than 90 per cent of those taking advantage of the programme have done so between 1984 and 1989. For example, the number of Senegalese taking advantage of this programme has declined from 205 in 1985 to approximately six in 1995. According to the French representative of the *Office des Migration Internationales* (OMI) in Dakar, migrants are preferring to remain in a 'precarious situation' in France rather than return home to certain circumstances (personal interview, Dakar, 9 January 1996).

Sending countries,[17] on the other hand, are looking for ways to make the migration experience at the individual and family level more profitable for the state. One very specific goal of many states has been to bring remittances out of suitcases and envelopes and into more formal channels of exchange, including banks and post offices. In some cases, special regulations have been established for emigrants to encourage the return of money through these channels, including preferential policies at customs. For sending states, this is important since few countries have rough estimates of the magnitude of remittances. Yet, remittances remain a mainstay of many countries' GNP.

For those emigrants who do return, states would like to benefit from their experience abroad. Assistance with small enterprise development through preferential loans, for example, is one such strategy. And, while brain drain represents only a small fraction of all the emigration from most countries, it remains a concern. The most well-educated – especially those who were trained abroad – have few incentives to return home. To counter this, Senegal is creating an experts list of its technically qualified citizens throughout the world in the hope that international investors in the country will draw on Senegalese expertise.

Socio-cultural interests have proven to be among the most contentious issues in many receiving countries. These issues tend to go to the core of national identity discourse and rouse extreme sentiments among native-born and migrant communities alike. Such interests are most often couched in integration policies – especially in schools, in places of worship, and in the workplace. The most commonly heard concern is that traditional institutions of integration, including the military, are no longer fulfilling their integrating function. Migrants from Africa, as many from non-EU origin countries, are considered to pose a special challenge to state socio-cultural interests.

These interests also concern the area of crime. Two areas receiving more attention are the trafficking in drugs as well as in young women. There is evidence that increasing numbers of young women are enticed from home with the promise of a ticket to Europe. Sold as commercial sex workers, they remain under obligation to pay back the cost of their trip to the traffickers. Italy has been especially concerned with the sexual exploitation of young Nigerian women and has participated in several international meetings to raise the level of awareness on this issue.[18] Related to this is the crackdown in many receiving countries on the smugglers who facilitate illegal migration for profit.

Causing special anxiety in some corners is the increasing presence of migrants of Islamic faith, in particular, and the implications of this for integration. Despite popular perceptions, recent research (Lestaeghe and Surkyn 1995; Tribalat 1995) reveals enormous diversity among these groups, indicating that discussion of Islam as a monolithic presence throughout Europe has very little real intellectual currency. Nonetheless, Islam touches on several central nerves in many countries, such as France where Islam is now the second religion. In particular, the practice of polygamy in some households, female genital mutilation, and other religious practices such as the wearing of religious scarves by young girls have come under fire, though reactions have differed across Europe. In some cases, these events raise questions about the possibility or inevitability of multiculturalism in Europe. They are also seen as key issues on which the future of the secular nation turns. Similarly, receiving state interests in this area are often cast as the protection and promotion of women's rights.

From the side of the sending country, socio-cultural issues are also of concern but are cast in a very different conceptual framework. Concern for the protection of human rights and dignity is often voiced, especially in response to the deportations of Africans who sometimes arrive home in handcuffs. It also arises in discussions of religious tolerance. The general sentiment among many Africans is that Muslims are not free to practice openly or easily in Europe, despite rhetoric of religious freedom.

There is also great concern about the diminishing safety of emigrants abroad and the relative ease with which emigrants can be caught up in crime. Senegal has taken a two-pronged approach. First, there is an attempt to educate Senegalese at risk of emigration about the realities of emigrating, what one is likely to find, and the difficulties facing new emigrants. The government also works with Islamic religious leaders – the *marabouts* – to maintain both a practical and a spiritual contact with emigrant communities. The logic is that adherence to the tenets of Islam will keep their citizens from a more troubled path. Further, religious leaders are seen as trusted and legitimate interlocutors who can encourage migrants to return, assist with certain problems and transmit changes in state policies. They are also seen as one of the causative agents behind migration. It is widely assumed that they will support trips abroad by young followers in return for financial and political support at home.

Political interests have both a domestic and an international dimension. Domestic political interests are, in the current climate, much more pronounced for receiving countries. This has largely to do with the way by which migration has been successfully manipulated as a divisive political campaign issue through Europe. As such, the handling of immigration policy changes, such as the Basic Law 16 in Germany, France's Pasqua or Debré laws, or the Martelli Law in Italy has been viewed as a test of political strength for dominant political parties and opposition.

Beyond the quest for political party triumph has been the somewhat related tendency to see migration and domestic security as increasingly intertwined. Far-right violent reactions against migrants and electoral gains in many European countries has been increasing and receiving greater media attention. Similarly, recent bouts of terrorism such as the bombings in French metros that coincided with worrisome events in Algeria raised the level of spot-checks in the streets for proper documentation of many migrants.

For sending countries, political concerns also relate to political challenges and support from emigrant communities. There is a desire to maintain the political support of migrant communities, especially through embassies and consulates abroad. As King Hassan exhorted the Moroccan community in France in 1976, 'remain Moroccan so that your country can in time count on its sons everywhere, wherever they find themselves ...' (Collinson 1996: 23). Such an approach serves a dual role. It augments domestic political (and financial) support of the state. It also encourages the embassy to track external political activities that may threaten the dominant party's hold on power. In fact, African state and emigrant relations may be somewhat tense. In as much as embassies are seen as representatives of the dominant party, there is a great deal of mistrust by emigrants toward official state structures. This point is further underscored by the February 1997 riots in Freetown, Sierra Leone. Salpost, the national postal service, had been accused of dumping into the sea thousands of application forms destined for the US immigration lottery (*Associated Press*, 12 February 1997). This event also indicates how the pressures to emigrate and the systems to facilitate or deter emigration can quickly become heated domestic issues.

International political interests run a broad gamut of issues from the supranational to the ideological. For European receiving states, this means international migration has created a whole new set of responsibilities at the multilateral level. Performance, incompetence, or reluctance in any of these fora such as the Schengen Convention or the not-yet-ratified Dublin Convention governs the speed with which Europe is likely to move forward on co-ordination of immigration controls and integration efforts.

With regard to Africa in particular, Europe has displayed great differences of opinion as to the importance of responding to flows from Africa, and in particular, from the Maghreb. The real or perceived threat of mass migration from northern Africa has been clearly greater for Europe's southern borders. Following the events of 1989, there was growing concern by France, Spain, and Italy that Europe was going the way of Germany, i.e. listing toward an Eastern European orientation. The 5 + 4 talks in 1990 and the later 5 + 5 talks in 1991 – involving France, Italy, Portugal, Spain, Algeria, Libya, Mauritania, Morocco, Tunisia (and later Malta) – were an initial attempt to focus on the particular concerns of the Mediterranean basin on a range of political and security issues. Skillful diplomacy by Europe's southern flank transformed the migration issue from a regional concern to a European-wide concern, thus paving way for greater attention to the Maghreb in such fora as the G7 summit in Naples in 1994 (Collinson 1996). This also enabled countries such as Italy, with little money and a weak migration system, to transfer much of the responsibility to the multilateral, European Union arena (Papademetriou and Hamilton 1996).

From the sending side, one dimension of international political concerns manifests itself as a preoccupation with continued colonial domination. While this is rarely heard in official circles, intellectuals argue that the closing of Europe to Africa is fraught with colonial ideology with strong overtones of racism. It is an ideology that still sees the African as 'other' and that is characterised by exoticism and fear. Akin-Aina (1996: 39), for example, argues that South to North migration are part of a larger process that is 'an intricately intertwined unfolding and expression of complex structural dynamics and socio-economic processes embodying relations of domination and inequality'. The problem for receiving countries, one African intellectual argues, is that newly arrived migrants have not yet been subjugated by having submitted to Western and bureaucratic laws (personal interview, Dakar, 31 January 1996).

For both sides, addressing the so-called 'root causes' of migration has culminated in new strategies to protect both sending and receiving state interests. For receiving countries, this means using targeted aid and trade initiatives to assuage environmental degradation, population growth, poor health and other related problems which are believed to lie 'at the root' of decisions to migrate. Aid to address these kinds of activities is both multilateral through the European Union and bilateral between states. From the sending side, there is a seeming willingness to use migration as a sort of bargaining chip to garner increased or continuing aid. This allows sending states access to much needed development assistance to achieve broader economic and political goals in exchange for agreements to limit emigration through various interventionist policies.

Pinning migration-related 'conditions' to development aid is becoming more common. Such conditionality means that aid is contingent on efforts by the sending country to limit emigration or to encourage the return of those who have already left. A project in progress between Italy and Senegal for example was designed for just this purpose. According to one Italian government representative, the idea was that 'if we are going to give you aid, at least you could try to limit your migrants a little bit' (personal interview, 6 January 1996). Such voluntarily imposed limits by sending states may take several forms – from surveillance at the border to accepting deportations. A return agreement signed by Morocco and Spain in 1992, for example, can be viewed in this light. This 'willingness [of the Maghreb states] to play ball with the EC member states', posits Collinson:

> [does] not reflect shared interests in this context, but is indicative rather of their economic dependence on the EC and thus of a willingness to trade the migration issue off against the more critical concern to protect and improve their wider commercial, financial, and political standing within the Community. (1996: 60)

In this manner, receiving states are actively engaged in not uncommon carrot-and-stick attempts to influence migration flows by appealing to sending countries interests. Similarly, sending states are willing to use the migration issue as a bargaining chip to achieve other goals. As discussed below, it is unclear how effective such practices will be.

States and migrants: the limits of state-centred theory

Viewing the parallel and at times competing interests of states raises interesting questions about the relationship between sending and receiving states and migrants themselves. To what extent is it realistic to believe that states can actually control migrant behaviour through policies? How parallel are the macro-interests of sending and receiving states and the micro-decisions of migrants and migrant families and communities? In many sending and receiving areas, the issue of migration lay beyond the control of the state. This is precisely the key irritant for most governments. Yet, there is a certain reluctance by sending states to push too hard to reign in migrant activities given the importance of remittances. Although restrictive measures have greatly increased since 1989, European states, too, are unwilling to implement policies severe enough to dam all illegal channels. Even if they were to forge ahead with such measures, opposition from liberal constituencies would be considerable.

Moreover, migrant communities abroad play a key role in the development of some of the most remote villages in western Africa (Daum 1993; Delville 1990).[19] Accomplished largely without state intervention, community development in these regions is remarkable and includes paved roads, health centres, and post offices. There are also personal radios and mopeds. Indeed, there is much academic debate over whether remittances go toward consumer goods or toward more productive investments. As Rogers writes, 'the literature is filled with criticisms that monies are spent overwhelmingly on consumption rather than on "productive activities", that a culture of consumerism is created in the communities of out-migration, and that their availability has led some migrants' families to abandon their agricultural plots' (1990: 4). However, Russell *et al.* find that for sub-Saharan Africa 'remittances *are* used for investment, and indeed are an important source of investment financing, especially where alternative sources of funding may not be available' (1990: 35).

For good or bad, migrant communities from some regions have supplanted the state for the provision of certain services. This raises very interesting questions about the relationship of the state to its emigrant communities abroad and to the villages of origin at home. Why is it that this transnational micro-level co-operation has been so successful? Why does this happen outside the control of the state? One primary reason that emigrants have taken matters into their own hands is the inherent distrust by migrants of the ability of the African state to regulate financial matters or to implement successful economic development plans. The second reason, somewhat related to the first, is that corruption and poor management within the banks and the postal service have been the largest disincentive to emigrants to opt for formal channels for remitting. Quiminal corroborates this point in her research on the Senegal River Valley. Regarding the very well developed structure of migrant associations in France, she notes that 'the associations are looking into setting up a regional savings and loan facility, independent of the little-trusted state banking system but operating within the framework of national banking regulations' (1994: 297).

Furthermore, migrant communities in receiving countries remain the best source of information for aspiring emigrants about policy changes and strategies to circumvent them (Massey 1990; Portes and Rumbaut 1990). As is well noted by Portes and Rumbaut in their work in the USA, migration is a 'socially embedded' process (1990: 231). Migrants are more and more voicing their own interests and staging active protests against changes in European policy. Recent protests in France by Malian migrants seeking harbour from deportation in a church illustrate this point. They are becoming an increasingly organised voice and have galvanised the support of some sympathetic sectors of the host countries.

State-centred theories – even when allowing for the diverse interests of players that make up a 'state' such as parliament, various ministries, a judiciary, etc. – cannot provide the full story of the migration experience for states and migrants alike. While states do have variable interests, act on a range of issues from political to social, and are theoretically endowed with the force to achieve these goals, the state apparatus is also affected by non-state actors. These actors include migrants themselves as well as advocacy groups. At the extreme, the goals of the state may be usurped and implemented superiorly by migrants themselves, as is the case of rural economic development in the Senegal River Valley.

Thus, state interests are cross-cut by the interests, organisation, and the implicit strategies of migrants themselves. In this context, pressure from Europe on African sending states in the form of conditionality is unlikely to have a significant impact on emigration from countries of origin short of measures to implement mandatory exit visas. As long as migrants themselves are wary of government interventions – even those to their benefit – it will be difficult for sending state governments to mitigate migration flows without driving migration further underground and to portray themselves simultaneously as democratic in their outlook and practice.

Conclusion

The key finding in this discussion is that while economic, socio-cultural and political state relations have influenced migration patterns, these migration patterns are now influencing a variety of state-to-state and state-to-society relations. Colonial intervention, labour recruitment, and Cold War interests helped to shape the Euro-African migration system. Contemporary flows from Africa, however, are beginning to reveal an independence from those legacies as evidenced in the changing patterns of origins and destinations.

Migrant communities from Africa have gradually become more diverse in their destinations and represent new, permanent communities throughout Europe. The result is a changing economic, political, and cultural make-up in most of Europe that has provoked a fundamental re-questioning of state interests and strategies to protect these interests. It has also forced both sending and receiving states into new relationships with migrant communities themselves. The flows from Africa are only one small part of these changes but they, along with flows from Asia and Eastern Europe, represent the future of migration in Europe. In addition, these flows have brought so-called 'soft issues' or non-economic concerns to the forefront of policy concerns. Ethnic relations, women's rights, the division of church and state, as well as development assistance all now inform migration policy responses.

Indeed, what seems to be emerging is an uncomfortable triangle of interests in which sending and receiving states and organised migrants vie for policy dominance. The erosion of state sovereignty is not only a macro-process that blurs state boundaries in a global economy. It is also a micro-process that allows migrant communities to exert direct economic, political, and cultural influence across state boundaries. State policies are likely to be more or less successful depending on the extent to which migrant interests themselves are coincident with those of the state.

In sum, the dynamics of regionalism, multilateralism and the extension of social rights have altered our conceptual understanding of national borders. Parallel with these tendencies is the increasing inequality that separates Africa and Europe. The combination of these forces has led many migrants to diversify their selection countries of destination, thus laying the seeds for new migrant communities. As a result, bilateral responses such as those often underpinning former colonial relations are less and less appealing and probably less effective. In this regard, regional and multilateral co-operation that heeds not only the concerns of migrant groups themselves but also takes advantage of the organisation and capacity of these groups deserves greater attention. The task is to find points of state and migrant co-operation at a time when cultural misunderstanding, the rhetoric of political and economic domination, and mistrust of the state tends to taint many interactions in the Euro-African system.

Acknowledgements

This article was originally presented at a conference entitled the 'Effects of Policy on Migration Patterns and the Integration of Immigrants: Comparing Different National Strategies', held at Humboldt University, Berlin, on 1–2 November 1996. I benefited greatly from the discussion, as well as from additional comments by Charles Keely, Sharon Stanton Russell, Michael White, and James Allen Smith. The content of this article is the result of extensive interviews and archival research conducted in France, Belgium, Italy, Portugal, Senegal and Mali since 1992. I am indebted to the Population Studies and Training Centre and the Watson Institute at Brown University, the Institut National d'Etudes Demographiques (INED) in Paris, the United Nation's Institute for Economic Development and Planning (IDEP) in Dakar, and to the International Migration Policy Program of the Carnegie Endowment for International Peace for all their assistance.

Notes

1 Although the emigration from sub-Saharan Africa is on the rise, the more interesting question remains why more people do not migrate given the pressures and the growing complex of international relations.

2 In the words of Rueschemeyer and Evans: the state is 'a set of organisations invested with the authority to make binding decisions for people and organisations juridically located in a particular territory and to implement these decisions using, if necessary, force' (1985: 47). The state is vested with both the capacity and the authority to act. Both of the qualities, however, are variable across states and through time. What this article does not address is the crucial concept of 'the nation' in relation to 'the state'. As Keely discusses, the nation 'justifies the state as the concrete means to preserve a people's identity and way of life' (1996: 1051). Migration thus becomes a challenge to the perfect overlay of state and nation.

3 The absence of an interested sending state would raise equally compelling questions.

4 This polity-economy tension offers a curious twist with regard to international migration. Those in favour of an international equality, extended without regard for borders may support migration. Conversely, if the idea of equality is delimited by national boundaries, immigration restrictions may dominate depending on various political pressures.

5 Others might argue that liberal democratic states simply will not take the drastic steps necessary to curtail migration fully, since such steps would be truly anti-democratic (Brubaker 1995).

6 Freeman does not, however, tackle the obvious question of why the reach and force of client politics varies from state to state. As Brubaker states in his critique of Freeman, the more interesting question is 'the extent to which anti-populist norms actually prevail' (1995: 908).

7 Thus, *both* Freeman (1995) and Brubaker (1995) are correct.

8 Skocpol, while writing generally on state differences, suggests that '... the implementation of state policies often leads to unintended as well as intended consequences, both when states attempt tasks they cannot complete and when the means they use produce unforeseen structural changes and socio-political reactions' (1985: 16).

9 This may all be true, but it remains an assumption rather than a tested premise. Theories of the African state, while not included in this piece, could expand greatly on this point. See, for example, Sklar's discussion of the duality of the African state that allows for the coexistence of powerful traditional forms of authority behind the sovereign state (1993: 87).

10 This is despite sectoral adjustment loans to ease the impact of structural adjustment on the 'poorest of the poor'.

11 South Africa, like many of the countries of Europe, is wrestling with long queues and forged documents of hopeful applicants for permanent residency in the country. Members of the Southern African Development Community (Lesotho, Botswana, Zimbabwe, Namibia and Mozambique) are permitted legal residency if they can prove that they have been in South Africa for more than five years, i.e. from before July 1991. South Africa's Home Affairs office has received 192,422 applications since 1996 (*The Johannesburg Star*, 13 January 1997). Similarly, deportations of illegal migrants has increased from 53,418 in 1990 to 157,084 in 1995 (*Weekly Mail and Guardian*, 17 January 1997).

12 Statistical information for this section is drawn from Eurostat sources (1995, 1996). A customary word of caution is warranted. The reliability of statistics on migration flows varies from country to country on depends to a large extent on the type of 'migration accounting system' applied in each country. Similarly, there is no adequate way to account for the numbers of undocumented migrants who enter Europe from various countries.

13 The European Economic Area includes member states of the European Union and EFTA, excluding Switzerland.

14 The 'Agreement Concerning the Gradual Abolition of Controls ... at Common Borders' was first signed in Schengen, Luxembourg in June 1985. The Agreement intends to remove internal frontiers among its signatories, and thus allow for the free movement of foreign nationals. France is an original member; Italy joined in 1990 after signing the supplementary Schengen Convention. Although an independent initiative from the European Union, Schengen is widely viewed as a test-case for Community-wide efforts to remove internal frontiers.

15 A note of caution is warranted when comparing statistical sources throughout Europe. In France, the original nationality of former foreigners within France is 'lost' statistically with naturalisation. In other words, there are many more persons born outside France or born within France of foreign parents who have subsequently assumed French nationality than statistics reveal.

16 See Lebon for a discussion of the categories and qualifications (1994: 29).

17 Discussion of sending countries' interests is partly based on in-depth interviews and research in Mali and Senegal in 1996. Doubtless, sending state interests could be refined by additional qualitative research on other sending nation's interests.
18 A report to the IOM cites Albania and Nigeria as being of special concern (IOM 1996).
19 See for example the villages along the Senegal River Valley, such as Bakel in Senegal, Sélibabi in Mauritania, and Kayes in Mali.

References

Adepoju, A. (1994) 'Preliminary analysis of emigration dynamics in sub-Saharan Africa', Dakar, Senegal: African Institute for Economic Development and Planning

Akin-Aina, T. (1996) 'Ties between emigration and destination countries: historical, colonial and cultural', in A. Adepoju and T. Hammar (Eds.), *International Migration in and from Africa*, Dakar: Imprimerie St. Paul, 39–52

Amin, S. (1995) 'Migrations in contemporary Africa: a retrospective view', in J. Baker and T. Akin-Aina (Eds.), *The Migration Experience in Africa*, Sweden: Nordiska Afrikainstitutet, 29–40

Anderson, B. (1992) *Imagined Communities*, New York: Verso Press

Associated Press (1997) 'Protesters riot in Sierra Leone', 12 February

Baubock, R. (1996) 'Cultural minority rights for immigrants', *International Migration Review* Vol. 30 No. 1: 203–50

Brubaker, R. (1995) 'Comments on 'modes of immigration politics in liberal democratic states', *International Migration Review* Vol. 29 No. 4: 903–08

Brubaker, R. (1992) *Citizenship and Nationhood in France and Germany*, Cambridge, MA: Harvard University Press

Caritas di Roma (1995) *Immigrazione Dossier Statistico 95*, Rome: Anterem

Chrissantaki, P. and Kuiper, E. (1994) 'L'Afrique, Continent d'Émigration', *Revue Européenne des Migrations Internationales* Vol. 10 No. 3: 189–99

Collinson, S. (1994) *Europe and International Migration*, New York: Pinter Publishers for the Royal Institute of International Affairs

Collinson, S. (1996) *Shore to Shore: The Politics of Migration in Euro-Maghreb Relations*, London: Royal Institute of International Affairs

Connelly, M. and Kennedy, P. (1994) 'Must it be the rest against the rest', *Atlantic Monthly*, December: 61–91

Cornelius, W., Martin, P. and Hollifield, J. (1994) *Controlling Immigration: A Global Perspective*, Stanford, CA: Stanford University Press

Daum, C. (1993) 'Quand les immigés construisent leur pays', *Hommes & Migrations* No. 1165: 13–17

Davidson, B. (1992) *The Black Man's Burden: Africa and the Curse of the Nation–State*, New York: Random House

Delville, P. (1990) 'Les projets de développement initiés par les migrants', *Hommes & Migrations* No. 1131: 25–27

Eurostat (1995) *Migration Statistics 1995*, Luxembourg: Eurostat

Eurostat (1996) *Statistics in Focus: Population and Social Conditions* No. 2, Luxembourg: Eurostat

Findley, S., Traore, S., Ouedraogo, D. and Diarra, S. (1994) 'Emigration from the Sahel', submitted to the International Organisation for Migration, Committee on Emigration from Africa, 25 November

Freeman, G. (1995) 'Modes of immigration politics in liberal democratic states', *International Migration Review* Vol. 29 No. 4: 881–902

Hammar, T. (1990) *Democracy and the Nation-State*, Aldershot: Avebury

Hollifield, J. (1992) *Immigrants, Markets, and States: The Political Economy of Postwar Europe*, Cambridge, MA: Harvard University Press

Horowitz, D. (1992) 'Immigration and group relations in France and America', in D. Horwitz and G. Noiriel (Eds.), *Immigrants in Two Democracies: French and American Experience*, New York: New York University Press

Hugo, G., Arango, J., Kouaouci, A., Massey, D., Pellegrino, A., and Taylor, J. (1995) 'Contemporary international migration systems', presented at the American Sociological Association meeting, Washington, DC, 19–23 August 1995

International Organisation for Migration (1996) 'Trafficking in women to Italy for sexual exploitation', June, Geneva: IOM

The Johannesburg Star (1997) 'Home affairs immigrant check catches chancers', 13 January

Keely, C. (1980) 'Asian worker migration to the Middle East', Working Paper 52, Centre for Policy Studies, New York: Population Council, January

Keely, C. (1996) 'How nation-states create and respond to refugee flows', *International Migration Review* Vol. 30 No. 4: 1046–66

Keely, C. and Tran, B. (1989) 'Remittances from labour migration: evaluation, performance, and implications', *International Migration Review* Vol. 23 No. 3: 500–25

Kritz, M. and Zlotnick, H. (1992) 'Global interactions: migration systems, processes and policies', in M. Kritz, L. Lean and H. Zlotnick (Eds.), *International Migration Systems: A Global Approach*, Oxford: Clarendon Press

Lebon, A. (1993) *Immigration et présence étrangère en France: Le bilan d'une année 1992–1993*, Paris: Ministère des Affaires Sociales de la Santé et de la Ville

Lebon, A. (1994) *Situation de l'immigration et présence étrangère en France: 1993–1994*, Paris: Ministère des Affaires Sociales de la Santé et de la Ville

Lestaeghe, R. and Surkyn, J. (1995) 'Heterogeneity in social change: Turkish and Moroccan women in Belgium', *European Journal of Population* Vol. 11: 1–29

Massey, D. (1990) 'The social and economic origins of immigration', *The Annals* Vol. 510: 60–72

Organisation for Economic Co-operation and Development (1992) *Trends in International Migration: Continuous Reporting System on Migration*, Paris: OECD

Organisation for Economic Co-operation and Development (1993) *Trends in International Migration: Continuous Reporting System on Migration*, Paris: OECD

Organisation for Economic Co-operation and Development (1994) *Migration and Development: New Partnerships for Cooperation*, Paris: OECD

Papademetriou, D. (1996) *Coming Together or Pulling Apart: The European Union's Struggle with Immigration and Asylum*, Washington, DC: Carnegie Endowment for International Peace

Papademetriou, D. and Hamilton, K. (1996) *Converging Paths to Restriction: French, Italian, and British Responses to Immigration*, Washington, DC: Carnegie Endowment for International Peace.

Portes, A. and Rumbaut, R. (1990) *Immigrant America*, Berkeley, CA: University of California Press

Quiminal, C. (1994) 'The role of immigrants in development projects and possible forms of co-operation in the Senegal River Valley', in *Migration and Development: New Partnerships for Co-operation*, Paris: OECD, 293–98

Robin, N. (1994) 'Une Nouvelle Géographie entre Concurrences et Redéploiement Spatial', *Revue Europeenne des Migrations Internationales* Vol. 10 No. 3: 17–31

Rogers, R. (1990) 'Return migration, migrants' savings and sending countries' economic development: lessons from Europe', Washington, DC: Commission for the Study of International Migration and Cooperative Economic Development, No. 30, May

Rueschemeyer, D. and Evans, P. (1985) 'The state and economic transformation: toward an analysis of the conditions affecting effective intervention', in Evans, P. Rueschemeyer, D. and Skocpol, T. (Eds.), *Bringing the State Back In*, New York: Cambridge University Press, 44–77

Russell, S. (1992) 'Migration, remittances and development', *International Migration* Vol. 30 Nos. 3/4: 267–87

Russell, S., Jacobsen, K. and Stanley, W. (1990) *International Migration and Development in Sub-Saharan Africa* Vol. 1, Washington, DC: The World Bank

Sassen, S. (1996) *Losing Ground: Sovereignty in the Age of Globalization*, New York: Columbia University Press

Sklar, R. (1993) 'The African frontier for political science', in R. Bates, Y. Mudimbe and J. O'Barr (Eds.), *Africa and the Disciplines*, Chicago: University of Chicago Press, 83–110

Skocpol, T. (1985) 'Bringing the state back in: strategies of analysis in current research', in P. Evans, D. Rueschemeyer and T. Skocpol (Eds.), *Bringing the State Back In*, New York: Cambridge University Press, 3–43

Soysal, Y. (1994) *Limits to Citizenship: Migrants and Postnational Membership in Europe*, Chicago: University of Chicago Press

Tapinos, G. (1996) 'Development, co-operation, and international migration: the European Union and the Maghreb', paper prepared for the Council of Europe Mediterranean Conference on Population, Migration, and Development, Palma de Mallorca, 15–17 October 1996 (CONFMED(96)3), Strasbourg: Council of Europe

Tribalat, M. (1995) *Faire France*, Paris: Editions la Decouverte

United Nations Population Fund (1993) *State of the World Population*, New York: UNFPA

Weekly Mail and Guardian (1997) 'Migration policy flaws being ironed out', 17 January

Weil, P. (1991) *La France et ses Étrangers: L'aventure d'une politique de l'immigration 1938–1991*, Paris: Calmann-Lévy

Widgren, J. (1994) 'Shaping a multilateral response to international migration', in K. Hamilton (Ed.), *Migration and the New Europe*, Washington, DC: Centre for Strategic and International Studies, 37–54

World Bank (1989) *From Crisis to Sustainable Growth*, Washington, DC: The World Bank

Zartman, I.W. (1995) 'Introduction', in I.W. Zartman (Ed.), *Europe and Africa: The New Phase*, Boulder: Lynne Rienner Publishers, 1–6

Zolberg, A. (1989) 'The next waves: migration theory for a changing world', *International Migration Review* Vol. 23 No. 3: 403–30 *new* **community** 19(2): 183–199 January 1993

The impact of Western European border policies on the control of 'refugees' in Eastern and Central Europe[1]

Mike King

Abstract Much of the contemporary debate on Western European exclusionary border policies focuses on the nature of that exclusion, rather than the impact such policies are likely to have on border controls of other migrant receiving or producing states. This article addresses some of the issues of Western European border control harmonisation in the context of Eastern and Central Europe, and Hungary in particular. It suggests that the concept of 'Fortress Europe' needs some refinement as harmonisation of controls are progressively on different levels, from the Schengen group of 'inner-Europe' to the EEA 'greater inner-Europe', with perhaps the Visegràd group waiting in the wings. What is clear is that present policies and exclusionary practices, on whatever level, directed against 'refugees', are primarily framed within a notion of threat and necessary compensation for potential freedoms. So long as this persists, policies of control *per se* will outweigh prevention. What we have in Eastern and Central Europe in terms of immediate impact of policies from the West is a shifting of the border Eastwards.

That one of the major effects of the Single European Act 1986 will be to increase freedom of movement for some within the internal borders of the 12 European Community member states from 1993, while correspondingly restricting the influx of 'outsiders', is increasingly becoming common knowledge. What is still lacking, however, is informed research on the extent of this 'exclusion' and the likely impact of such exclusionist policy on the control and movement of 'refugees' and migrants from South to North and East to West. It is the intention of this article to address some of these issues.

It would appear from many of the fears that are expressed by politicians and the mass media that 'Europe' is about to be besieged by a flood of refugees. These will come from two directions, from the South (or, rather North Africa) because of increasing poverty and the rise of authoritarian Muslim-fundamentalist regimes, and out of the East, making use of new-found 'freedoms' by fleeing from economic insecurity, internal political upheaval, civil war and ethnocentricism. The remedy against this, and so protecting 'inner-Europe', would appear for some to be the building of a 'Fortress' to hold back the potential onslaught. The problem with Fortresses though, is that they can be totally impenetrable, not only being a barrier against all outsiders, but causing problems for some of those within the walls also.

What follows examines some of the main policy determining structures and

Mike King is Lecturer in Public Order at the Centre for the Study of Public Order, University of Leicester.

policy recommendations with respect to border controls, immigration and asylum. There would seem to be three trends, firstly increasing policy decision-making in this area by inter-governmental and non-EC institution accountable bodies and networks, secondly towards the strengthening of border controls and harmonisation of policies for exclusion, and thirdly increasing convergence of structures and policies towards the creation of a 'greater-inner-Europe'.

Obviously, this will have an impact on those countries that are not included within the perimeter walls, leading to processes of incorporation for some through increasing convergence, but marginalisation for others that would perhaps like to join. On this level we examine what is happening in Eastern and Central Europe, focusing on Hungary in particular,[2] suggesting that this would appear to many to constitute a 'gateway to the West'. In this respect we look, firstly, at the actual migration situation, and, secondly, the control of refugees through re-defined East–West borders.

EC border policies: structures for exclusion

The main thrust of EC border-control policy orientation is implied in the following words of John Major during the European Summit meeting in Luxemburg in June 1991: 'We must not be wide open to all-comers just because Rome, Paris and London are more attractive than Bombay or Algiers' (Cohen 1992: 332). Catherine Lalumiere (Secretary General of the Council of Europe) took up a similar call during the 4th Conference of Ministers responsible for questions of migration, also held in Luxemburg in September 1991, arguing that 'The influxes [of refugees into Western Europe] must be regulated and controlled. One cannot let in the whole world. Our aim is to regulate immigration without stopping it completely' (Arnould 1991: 43). What is happening in the EC in terms of such policy is, what Cohen has described as, 'a process of herding and sorting [which] is taking place as sheep are separating from goats, outsiders from insiders, the excluded from the included' (1992: 336). More aptly within the EC exclusionist context, perhaps, one should stress that the 'outsiders' are *being* separated from the 'insiders', or rather, the 'insiders' are subjecting themselves to a process of internal *containment*.

There are a multiplicity of interlinked and overlapping Western European structures engaged in this process under the umbrella of immigration, asylum and freedom of movement. Structures specifically relevant for the areas of concern here range from bi-lateral or multi-lateral border agreements (such as those between the Nordic Group, being Denmark, Finland, Iceland, Norway and Sweden; Germany, Austria and Switzerland; Austria and Czechoslovakia; Germany and Poland) to intergovernmental (but non-EC accountable) policy-making bodies like the TREVI Group of Ministers of the Interior. Of special importance, however, within the EC context are the Schengen Accord, the *ad hoc* Working Group on Immigration, and the Co-ordinating Committee, all established with the aim of 'harmonisation' of control. As a result of the continuing situation of immigration and asylum policies remaining outside the sphere of European Community competence, the European Parliament has now established a Committee on Civil Liberties and Internal Affairs to monitor the developments (*Migration News Sheet* (MNS) February 1992: 1). Further, the new Union Treaty (signed in Maastricht in December 1991) has provided that the question of EC powers in these respects will not be reviewed until 1996 (MNS January 1992: 1). In addition to the structures mentioned so far, and as instances of a general trend towards the strengthening of exclusionist policies, individual state legislations (such as the Carrier Sanctions Acts and the proposed UK Asylum Bill[3]) are restricting flows of refugees and determining procedures for asylum.

The Schengen treaties

The Schengen (Supplementary) Agreement was signed by Belgium, France, Germany (W), Luxembourg and the Netherlands in June 1990, and since then 3 more countries have joined, namely Italy (November 1990) and Spain and Portugal (June 1991). This leaves 4 EC member state non-signatories, Britain, Denmark, Eire and Greece. Greece, however, was granted observer status in December 1991, on the condition that it joins at a future date (MNS January 1992: 2). The Schengen Agreement is one of the primary structures with which this article is concerned. It is potentially a model for the EC generally,[4] or even for a wider Europe, in terms of both an 'open' border policy and immigration and asylum harmonisation and control. It may well be in practice, however, that only the latter, namely harmonisation and control is utilised from the Schengen model by the EC as a whole.[5] The 1990 'Supplementary' Agreement is the realisation of an earlier 'Basic' Treaty signed by the five in 1985 stating their future intention of signing a document towards implementation. The deadline for *formal* implementation of Schengen is the beginning of 1993, and will need prior ratification by the individual parliaments of each signatory state.

The Articles of the Schengen Agreement are directed towards 'open' internal borders, for goods and services as well as people, immigration and asylum control and harmonisation, closer police co-operation[6] and the establishment of a Schengen Information System (SIS).[7] Many of the provisions and practices within the Agreement, especially regarding internal border control relaxation and increased police co-operation, are simply the formalisation of the informal. That is, the formalisation of practices which have been established already through bi- and multi-lateral cross-border control and police co-operation agreements between countries. A number of Treaties existed between the respective Schengen parties which can be seen as precursors of the original Schengen Treaty. The Benelux Treaty is an example. This was an accord signed by Belgium, Luxembourg and the Netherlands in 1960 for a relaxation of internal border controls for Benelux nationals. Similar examples, however, are the Aachen Agreement signed in 1969 between North Rhine Westphalia (Germany), Belgium and the Netherlands, an agreement between Rhineland-Pfalz (Germany) and Luxembourg in 1977 and one between Saarland (Germany) and France in 1978. Other agreements exist which incorporate non-Schengen or even EC member states, such as Baden-Württemberg (Germany), France and Switzerland; that between Schleswig-Holstein (Germany)) and Denmark and already referred to above, that between Denmark and the Nordic Group (1954).

Some of the existing agreements, where they affect 'outside', countries are causing problems for an EC-wide incorporation of Schengen. Where, for example, should enhanced external border controls be sited in the case of Denmark and Sweden, or Germany and Austria or Switzerland? The present conflicting situation may ease slightly in that both Austria and Sweden are now considering the possibility of joining the EC and perhaps Schengen. Alternatively, it may result in a 'greater inner-Europe' group of countries (perhaps comprising the EEA)[8] instituting a common visa policy and enhanced policing co-operation, and further controls on immigration and asylum.

The initial agreement among EC member states for abolition of internal border controls, known as the 'Fontainebleau Declaration', was signed in June 1984. When considering the provisions of the Schengen (Supplementary) Agreement, especially on immigration and asylum, it is useful to see them as compensatory measures to offset the 'freedoms' and consequent anticipated loss of security arising from 'Fontainebleau' and the Act of Union. Kattau has effectively argued this, suggesting that 'Politicians and members of most police forces see borders as a quasi-natural strategic line in fighting crime' (1990: 2), and one may add, also in controlling unwanted immigration. Indeed, according to the analysis of statistical information from Kattau's study of border checks in Germany (W) between 1977 and 1988 it is suggested that rather than 'crime', 'the main effectiveness of border controls lies in the field of controlling foreigners and entry into [the] country' (1990: 5). Despite the notion of an 'open' border policy, under both the Act of Union and Schengen, this emphasis on control remains, indeed is strengthened. With this context in mind, we will now examine some of the specific Articles of the Schengen (Supplementary) Agreement relating to immigration and asylum.

Provisions of Schengen

The 1990 Agreement,[9] provides for a general intensification of policing controls at external borders and is particularly directed towards 'aliens' attempting to enter the Schengen territory. In this connection, Article 1 defines 'External Borders' as common 'land and sea borders and their airports and sea ports, provided they are not [otherwise defined as] internal borders', and 'Aliens' as 'any person other than a national of a member state of the European Communities'. Particular control emphasis is placed upon aliens of 'Third States', being nationals of 'any State other than the Contracting Parties'. This immediately poses a problem for freedom of movement of people who are not full nationals of member states, albeit residing within that territory. Also, in respect of border controls generally, it changes the 'internal' to 'external' for designated airports.

Article 9 provides for the adoption of 'a common policy on the movement of persons and in particular on the arrangements for visas'. Moreover, 'the Contracting Parties undertake to pursue by common agreement the harmonisation of their policies on visas'. Further, as regards:

> . . . visa arrangements relating to Third States, the nationals of which are subject to visa arrangements common to all the Contracting Parties at the time when this Convention is signed or later, may be amended only by common agreement of all the Contracting Parties.

This means in practice that a common list of countries whose nationals require visas will be drawn up by the parties. In fact, provisional lists are already in existence, and certainly incorporate almost all 'third world' countries. Spencer has suggested that the TREVI Group and the *ad hoc* Working Group on Immigration have a list of about 60 countries and the Schengen Group have one of about 115 (1990: 33). It would seem that nationals from Eastern and Central Europe, with the possible exception of those from Czechoslovakia, Hungary and Poland,[10] will also be subject to this visa requirement. One can be fairly certain that it will include nationals from Bulgaria, Cuba, Mongolia, Romania and Vietnam, since visas were introduced for these for entry (or even remaining in) the 'united' Germany on 3 October 1990 (Busch 1990: 21). Similarly, Britain has since 1985 increasingly been introducing visa requirements for 'refugee-producing' countries. In May 1985 the first Commonwealth country to be subject to visa regulations was Sri Lanka. In October 1986 others followed, namely India, Pakistan, Nigeria, Ghana and Bangladesh, in July 1989 Turkey and in April 1990 Algeria, Morocco and Tunisia. From July 1990, Somali nationals *with* visas could no longer transit through Britain (Amnesty International 1990: 26). Presumably, these countries will also be included at least in the TREVI requirements.

As a general rule, Third State aliens with visas will not be admitted to the Schengen territory for visits lasting longer than 3 months, and 'if applicable' only then on condition that they have amongst other things 'sufficient means of support, both for the period of the planned visit and to return to their country of origin or to travel in transit in a Third State, into which admission is guaranteed' and also are 'not considered to be a threat to public policy, national security or the international relations of any of the Contracting Parties' (Article 5). Article 5 (3) also provides, and this is presumably relevant too for those non-third state 'aliens' referred to above, that:

> An alien who holds a residence permit or a return visa issued by one of the Contracting Parties or, if required, both documents, shall be permitted to enter in transit, unless their name is on the national list of persons reported as not to be refused entry which is held by the Contracting Party at the external borders of which they arrive.

Otherwise, once admitted, the alien may travel anywhere within the territory on the basis of a 'uniform visa' (Article 10).

Special rules apply to those seeking asylum, and for nationals of those countries being part of 'a bilateral agreement concluded before entry into force of this Convention' (Article 20), as discussed above. As for asylum applicants and the refugee question, this Agreement has a profound impact. Article 1 stipulates that those persons seeking asylum must submit an application:

> . . . at an external border or within the territory of a Contracting Party with a view to obtaining recognition as a refugee in accordance with the Geneva Convention of 28 July 1951 relating to the Status of Refugees, as amended by the New York Protocol of 31 January 1967 and as such obtaining the right of residence.

However, as we shall argue later, the effect of 'Carrier Sanctions' (Article 26) on prohibiting the carriage of aliens without valid permits or documentation means that refugees seeking asylum are unlikely to reach external borders legally. It is also unlikely, in such cases, that those persons would be granted or even be in a position to apply for a 'tourist visa' through the 'diplomatic and consular authorities' (Article 12) in their country of origin in the first instance.

Another factor of concern regarding asylum seekers is the 'one chance only rule'. This means that an applicant can only apply for asylum to one of the signatory states, and this only to the one of initial (application for) entry (Article 30). If rejected, they 'must in principle leave the territory of [all] the Contracting Parties [to the Agreement] immediately' (Article 23). This condition was incorporated in an *ad hoc* Working Group on Immigration agreement of May 1988 (Spencer 1990:33) and confirmed by the Dublin Convention of EC Member States signed in June 1990.[11]

TREVI and other structures

The structures other than Schengen which have already been mentioned will now receive closer attention. Firstly, the non-institutional EC inter-governmental TREVI Group of Home and Interior Ministers,[12] is concerned with enhancing police co-operation among the 12 and establishing a common policy in areas that are thought to constitute a threat to stability, namely drugs, terrorism and immigration. In this connection too it is moving towards the establishment of its own Computer Information System. This will no doubt, at some stage in the future, be merged with the SIS and that of GAM 92 (Group of Mutual Assistance).

Like TREVI, the *ad hoc* Working Group on Immigration (formed in 1986) is also a non-institutional framework. Unlike the TREVI Group, however, the European Commission do have membership of this and it answers to the EC Ministers concerned with immigration. Amnesty International has suggested that since the end of 1988 it is the 'primary forum for discussion on immigration and asylum issues' (1990:38). It was this group which drew up the draft EC Convention on External Border Controls between the 12 in July 1991 (Bunyan 1991). This draft was considered at its Ministerial meeting in Maastricht in December 1991, although not signed due to continuing problems between Britain and Spain over Gibraltar (MNS January 1992).[13] The draft Convention closely follows the provisions of Schengen in terms of external border and the harmonisation of visa controls, with the exception of not requiring an 'opening' of internal borders. If Schengen were to be superseded, it would probably be through such an accord, although as we have already suggested there would in any event appear to be a process of convergence in this area.

Another important structure in this context is the so-called 'Group of Co-ordinators'. This was established at the EC Summit meeting in Rhodes during December 1988, and includes a member of the European Commission. Its main task is to co-ordinate the work undertaken by the various inter-governmental networks, such as that of the *ad hoc* Working Group on Immigration and the TREVI Group of Ministers. Indeed, it was the Group of Co-Ordinators that drew up the 'Palma Document' (Spencer 1990: 158–159), which was in turn approved at the EC Summit meeting in Madrid in June 1989. This document proposes a programme of policies required for harmonisation, and has many features in common with Schengen. Also, a number of the suggested actions are either in the process of being or have already been instituted. The document indicates which actions are 'Essential' or 'Desirable', and also suggests dates by which these should be achieved. Under 'Action at external frontiers' it suggests as Essential for 1990: the 'definition of ports and airports as external or internal frontiers', and Desirable for the end of 1992 'harmonisation of laws on aliens in general and immigrants in particular'. In respect of 'Action at internal frontiers and inside the territory of the Community', it stipulates the necessity of 'off-setting measures' on, for example, the right of asylum, refugee status and visa policy. In terms of visa policy specifically, there is an Essential necessity for the establishment of a 'common list of countries (updated every 6 months) whose citizens are required to have a visa' and the 'harmonising of procedures for granting visas (decided in 1988)'. Especially important in terms of the contemporary individual member state legislative situation is, under the heading of 'Refugees', an Essential recommendation that by the end of 1989 there be 'recourse to a simplified or priority procedure according to national legislations in the case of unfounded applications'. This emphasis is seen in the proposed British Asylum Bill currently under discussion (mentioned earlier), new Asylum legislation in Germany (MNS July 1992: 6) and also with the French 'internment' legislative proposals regarding 'illegal immigrants' (Police Review 1992). The Palma Document suggests, further, that it is Essential that by 1992 there be 'acceptance of identical international engagements with regard to asylum' and a 'Desirable' 'approximation of criteria for granting right of asylum and refugee status'. Again, the contents of this document would indicate (like the draft Convention on External Border Controls) that even if Schengen is not totally implemented by the 12, there are moves towards convergence of policy in the arena of 'refugee' exclusion.

Another worrying aspect of national legislation affecting 'refugees', and especially penal against those seeking asylum, is that regarding 'carrier sanctions' mentioned earlier. In 1987 Britain introduced the 'Carriers' Liability Act', putting the onus on 'carriers', whether airlines, shipping or other transport companies, to ensure that any passenger intending to enter the country's 'external' border have a valid permit and other relevant documentation. If that is not the case the carrier could be subject to a fine of £1,000 per inadmissible passenger. Britain, however, is not alone in instituting such legislation. Belgium under a law of July 1987 has imposed similar penalties; in October 1987 Denmark passed an amendment to its Aliens Act of 1983 imposing carrier sanctions; in January 1987 Germany (W) similarly amended its Aliens Law of 1965 and Italy passed a decree on this basis (A.3) in December 1989 (Cruz 1991: 1–7).

A problem of human rights: when is a refugee a migrant, or vice versa?

In contrast to the above EC member states, on 8th April 1991 the Dutch *Raad van State* found that Article 26 of Schengen proposing carrier sanctions contravened both Annex 9 of the 1944 Chicago Convention on International Aviation and Article 14 of the Universal Declaration of Human Rights with regard to asylum (Cruz 1991: 16). This argument, together with a more general critique of Schengen for lack of EC-institution accountability was put forward by a 'Resolution on the signing of the Supplementary Schengen Agreement' passed by the European

Parliament in December 1989. This latter argued that:

> ... the rush to sign a Supplementary Agreement on 15 December 1989 [in fact because of the situation regarding Germany (E) this did not take place until June 1990] is an attempt to avoid parliamentary and public debate on an issue which is vital for the Europe we are to create and for ... human rights.

Concern was expressed too that Schengen 'could have a detrimental effect on refugees and migrant workers' because of such severe entrance restrictions, and further that:

> ... the secret discussions, without democratic control ... on matters of ... immigration, namely those affecting refugees, by Member States acting outside the competence of the European institutions, within fora such as Schengen, TREVI and the *ad hoc* Immigration Group, violate the ... conventions [on Human Rights] and democratic principles.

Reference was also made to the question of the Commission's competence over such matters as 'the co-ordination of the rules concerning the right to asylum and the status of refugees' under the EC White Paper endorsed by member states in June 1985 and the Group of Co-ordinators 'inclusion of policies relating to internal security matters, visas, right of asylum and refugee status in the list of essential measures' referred to earlier. The Resolution concluded by calling on the Commission 'to assume its responsibility in this domain' (European Parliament 1989). Amnesty International has voiced similar concern about these breaches in human rights and in a report published in 1990 criticised the UK specifically for what it called its 'deficient policy and practice for the protection of asylum seekers' (1990: 1). However, from the restrictions and policies outlined above, one may also question EC and Schengen actual and potential practices on this basis in three main respects:

(i) that entrance permits must be obtained in the country of departure
(ii) concerning carrier sanctions
(iii) the 'one chance only' rule.

The latter especially has been highlighted in two cases of asylum seekers who fled to Britain from Germany. One involved a Lebanese woman with four children who were housed in a refugee-camp in Spandau escaping to Britain in November 1991, the other a Sudanese man held in Goster, who came to Britain during December 1991. They fled because they were subjected (in West and East Berlin respectively) to attack from neo-Fascists (Carvel 1991).[14]

The main rationale behind these restrictionist and exclusionist policies is, on the one hand, a fear concerning floods of refugees invading the West from both the South and the East, due to either internal strife or poverty or simply economic disparity. On the other hand, a 'tightening-up' of the asylum regulations and procedures is felt necessary on the official grounds of 'too many bogus applications' being made to circumvent visa restrictions. This raises two problems in particular. Firstly, if the EC member states are becoming increasingly exclusionary, what happens to the refugee 'flood'? We shall attempt to answer this question later. Secondly, when is an 'economic migrant' not a refugee, or a refugee not a migrant, or even a 'refugee' not a suitable case for asylum? For this, it is necessary to initally indicate some of the human rights provisions on refugee status and receiving-country obligations in that respect.

Article 1 of the United Nations Convention relating to the status of refugees (1951) as amended by the 1967 protocol provides a definition of a refugee as a person who is unwilling or unable to return to their country 'owing to a well-founded fear of being persecuted[15] for reasons of race, religion, nationality, membership of a particular social group or political opinion'. Further, Article 14 of the Universal Declaration of Human Rights proclaims that everyone shall have the right to 'seek and enjoy in other countries asylum from persecution'. The 1951 UN Convention also stipulates international legal obligations of receiving countries for the protection of those who qualify for refugee status, Article 33 stating that:

> No contracting State shall expel or return a refugee in any manner whatsoever to the frontiers of territories where his [or her] life or freedom would be threatened on account of his [or her] race, religion, nationality, membership of a particular social group or political opinion (Amnesty International 1990:3).

It would seem that simply on the basis of these Articles the countries instituting or proposing to institute the border policies that we have detailed are potentially in breach of human rights. Such fundamental provisions cannot be curtailed merely on the basis of a feared 'influx'. In their report, Amnesty International stress that a party to the 1951 UN Convention:

> ... is legally obliged to identify and protect all those seeking asylum ... who qualify as refugees, regardless of any pragmatic considerations such as practical and administrative demands made on resources and ... [the government concerned] cannot justify any retreat from this international obligation on grounds relating to any real or anticipated rise in the number of applicants (1990: 4).

To continue with our (second) question posed above, there does appear to be a distinction in attitude on the part of EC refugee-receiving states towards refugees trying to gain admission to 'the West' and those elsewhere. This can clearly be seen, for example, in different approaches and expectations regarding the plight of the Kurds in Iran, Iraq or Turkey compared with Albanians fleeing to Italy. Similarly, such a contradiction can be seen in the attempt of Germany to change its asylum laws (Article 16 of its Constitution) because of expected refugee pressure from the East compared with its policy of accepting those from the East of German 'stock'. Wilpert argues that the reality of this means that 'one group of foreign settlers living in Germany [being especially Turkish *Gastarbeiter*] experience institutional controls and barriers to membership, while another group has been recruited on the basis of an ethnic ideology as rightful members' (1991: 57), namely the *Volksdeutsche*. Another example of this differential distinction is that of the British government's announcement in December 1989 that it would allow a quota of 50,000 Hong Kong ethnic-Chinese into the country on condition that they are individually 'in possession of more than £150,000 and intend to use this money as capital to employ British citizens' (Miles 1991: 284).

The distinction between refugees, bona fide asylum-seekers and economic migrants, as Cohen suggests, 'rests largely on the definitions accorded to the movement by the 'host' State' (1991: 16). Further, these definitions are, in turn, primarily determined by economic and political interests. The Hungarian Central Statistical Office report on refugees similarly argues that:

> ... political refugees of a given country were [and, we would suggest, are] often treated positively or negatively [by Western developed countries] depending on

> the political purposes of the receiving country regarding its desired relationship with the country where the applicant for refugee status had arrived from (Hungarian Central Statistical Office 1991: 6).

Certainly, there was during the 'Cold War' period a marked distinction in political asylum between those fleeing the East or those from Latin America. The distinction can, of course, also be seen in the shift in attitude and policy over the last 5 years or so regarding those from Eastern Europe.

From 'inner-Europe' to 'greater inner-Europe'

We suggested earlier that the trend towards convergence of exclusionary policies for some European countries would lead to marginalisation of others. To this extent, one can depict what is happening in terms of border and immigration controls in Europe as a 'fortress', with expanding or incorporating perimeter walls. However, the notion of a fortress *per se*, needs refinement, because even taking account of a general trend towards harmonisation and convergence, one finds in the present situation different 'levels' of controls. The core, or rather what we term 'inner-Europe', is the Schengen group of 8 (presently to become 9 on the membership of Greece), moving outwards through the EC 12 to a 'greater inner-Europe' of 19, comprising the EEA.

Expansion in this direction seems very likely for a number of reasons. Firstly, the majority of EFTA countries have now applied for EC membership and the remainder are likely to follow suit. Secondly, Switzerland has already announced that it is harmonising its visa policies in line with those of EC member states 'as a result of the very severe border controls' of those states (MNS July 1992: 3), and it would seem that other EFTA countries will do likewise. Thirdly, the *ad hoc* Immigration Group at its meeting in Lisbon in June 1992 approved a convention which will run 'parellel' to the Dublin Convention, only being 'for third countries, especially EFTA member States' (MNS July 1992: 4). Fourthly, the EC intention of developing a Common Foreign and Security Policy (written into the Maastricht Treaty of Union) no longer appears to pose an obstacle for membership by presently 'neutral' nations. In this respect, Switzerland has recently declared that it 'sees no problem in reconciling its neutrality with membership of the Community' (Commission of the European Communities 1992b), and Austria's new President, Thomas Klestil, has stated that Austria's 'policy of neutrality must evolve towards a more co-operative approach . . . in Europe' (Baryli and Vernet 1992). Further, Frans Andriessen, European Commissioner for external relations, recently suggested that due to 'changing Swedish opinion . . . Sweden's traditional neutrality would not be an insurmountable problem' for membership either (Wolf 1992). It would seem also that greater inner-Europe will at some stage incorporate the Visegràd group of Czechoslovakia, Hungary and Poland. For the present, however, given Association and Readmission Agreements,[16] these are likely to act as an exclusionary 'buffer-zone' between East and West.

This leaves the 'Mediterranean group' of Cyprus and Malta, Turkey and Eastern Europe on the 'outside'. Even some of these countries are regrouping. In February 1992 a new 'Black Sea Economic Co-operation Zone' was formed (*The European*, 23/26 July 1992),[17] and Bulgaria and Romania have recently indicated that they too will be applying for Association Agreements with the EC (Michalski and Wallace 1992).

The new 'threat' from the East

Géza Jeszenszky, Hungary's Foreign Affairs Minister, stated in May 1991 that:

> The real challenge facing us today in Eastern Europe is no longer political and not only economic . . . [rather,] new threats are on the horizon . . . such as mass migration . . . [which] must be addressed before they bring down the fragile architecture of 'new democracy' in Eastern Europe (Bába and Környei 1991: 51–52).

The important point to stress here, is that the 'problem' of 'refugees' is not simply one from Eastern Europe to Western Europe, but one from Eastern Europe through Central Europe towards Western Europe. A question we posed earlier was, what would happen to the refugee 'flood' should the EC member states become increasingly exclusionary? It is conceivable that the more Western Europe pursues its exclusionist policy, as opposed to more positive policies regarding the likely situation of Eastern European refugees, the more those refugees will be trapped within Central Europe. The 'Final Communique' of an Interior Ministerial Conference held in Berlin in October 1991 (with representatives from an impressive list of countries, namely: Albania, Austria, Belgium, Bulgaria, Czechoslovakia, Denmark, Estonia, France, Germany, Greece, Hungary, Ireland, Italy, Latvia, Lithuania, Luxembourg, the Netherlands, Poland, Portugal, Romania, the Soviet Union, Spain, Switzerland, Ukraine, the United Kingdom, White Russia and Yugoslavia), appeared to take this issue on board as part of a 'long term' strategy, emphasising that:

> . . . the ever-increasing magnitude of the streams of migration from and through the countries of Eastern and Central Europe into the territories of the Western European countries. [Further,] realising that uncontrolled migratory movements in their present order of magnitude constitute a destabilising factor in all countries and place a burden on the harmonious development of relations between European peoples; [and] in view of the fact that the destination and transit countries must deploy considerable resources which could be put to better use for relieving the causes of the migrations (Interior-Ministerial Conference 1991: 1–2)

The Communique nonetheless proposed measures to control that flow. Agreement was reached on this basis for a general intensification of surveillance and monitoring of border controls including the supply of information technology equipment, the (re-)training of border guards, exchange of intelligence information and data, 'harmonisation' of visa policies and also carrier sanctions (Interior-Ministerial Conference 1991: 3–5). We must presume that such measures are primarily preventive, in that according to Eurostat Demographic Statistics 1990, only 2.5 per cent of the total population of the 12 EC member states are third-country aliens, i.e. 8.2 million (Arnould 1991: 43). These, according to *The Economist* are primarily from 'North Africa, Turkey, Yugoslavia and the Indian sub-continent' (1991: 47).

In fact, as Cohen has argued, most East–West migration falls into three categories:

(i) those returning to their 'homelands'
(ii) migrants joining communities abroad
(iii) 'refugees' attempting escape from economic, ethnocentric and political hardship (1991: 20).

What then of the realities of East–West migration projections? Since the Soviet Union declared in July 1991 a relaxation of external visa requirements for its citizens from 20 May 1993 the numbers of expected refugees to flee Westwards has been variously estimated. At the Berlin Conference of Ministers of the Interior referred to above, the expected 'exodus' was put at 5 million, whereas Simmons (1992) referred to a report by the 'Institute for European Defence and Strategic Studies' which suggested an alarmist figure of '2 million or more' people emigrating from the Commonwealth of Independent States (CIS) to Western Europe *per annum*. Gow even reported that 'there could be as many as 50 million Soviet refugees from economic collapse' (1990). The main country through which they are expected to attempt to flow is Hungary.

Hungary: Gateway to the west?

Of the Central European border-states, it is to Hungary, because of its historical and geo-political situation, that many Eastern European refugees and migrants turn in the first instance. They generally regard it as a 'gateway to the West', in a similar respect that it was for pre-unification East Germans. In this sense, Hungary constitutes for many a transitory zone.

Sík (1992) argues that migration from Romania, for example, was taking place through Hungary to Austria and then Sweden from as early as 1985. What has been happening since then, of course, is that the flow has not ceased, but large numbers are 'caught' in Hungary. This is similarly so with Yugoslav refugees now that EC and EFTA countries are increasingly instituting visa requirements. Nowhere is this problem more manifest at the moment than at the Hungarian border with what was Yugoslavia in terms of fleeing Bosnian refugees seeking temporary asylum. Indeed, rather than a 'gateway', the Head of the Hungarian Border Guard recently described Hungary as the 'waiting-room of Western Europe' (MNS June 1992:2).

In the first comprehensive study of its kind for Eastern and Central Europe, the Hungarian Central Statistical Office has compiled demographic data on refugees coming into Hungary across mainly its border with Romania between the beginning of 1989 and the end of 1990. The total number of refugees recorded from 1st January 1988 to 31st May 1990 was 31,310, 99.7 per cent of whom were Romanian citizens, being 74 per cent ethnic Hungarians and 21 per cent Romanian (Hungarian Central Statistical Office 1991: 7, 26). Of the total, 8.2 per cent declared that they wanted to transit through Hungary to the West (1991: 27). Data for the second half of 1990 shows a slightly different picture in that 6 per cent were Albanian and 3 per cent from the Soviet Union. The numbers of refugees have risen considerably since then and even more so given the situation in what was Yugoslavia. In 1991 there were 48,000 Yugoslav nationals in Hungary seeking 'temporary asylum'. Currently, tens of thousands of refugees are in refugee camps on the Hungarian–Yugoslav border territory. These figures cannot, of course, account for non-apprehended illegal immigrants. Kasriel (1992) suggests that the Hungarian authorities detained more than 24,000 illegal aliens in 1991 alone, and according to recent statistics, between October 1991 and May 1992, approximately 856,000 persons were refused entry (MNS June 1992: 5).

Controlling the border: from cold war to closed war

The agreed items of the October 1991 Berlin Conference of Ministers of the Interior included provision for:

> i) Mutual support in developing the border-securing infrastructure, in particular as regards the equipment and training of frontier protection forces, including the fields of communication and information processing (1991: 4)
> ii) Intensification of frontier surveillance between border crossing points deploying mobile forces of a strength appropriate to the situation at known or suspected weak points and, to this end, act in close concertation, which may include arrangements on the deployment of frontier protection forces at critical points, on the basis of joint analyses and up-to-date situation reports (1991: 3).

In fact what has been happening on the East–West border between Hungary and Austria is a reversal of the 'Cold War' situation. The Warsaw Pact 'Soviet Model' of border policing on the Hungarian side has from 1989 given way to a 'German-oriented *Bundesgrenzschutz*[18] model'. Previously, the border with Austria was heavily policed with a 2km 'security zone' and similarly between Hungary and Yugoslavia, which had a 500m zone. The common borders with Romania, the Soviet Union and Czechoslovakia were not policed as such. Further, illegal border-crossing was a serious criminal offence. Now, the Penal Code has been amended to make this a 'minor offence' only. However, the policing of the Eastern border with Romania has intensified, as too has that with the Ukraine (from September 1991) and Hungary's Southern border with Yugoslavia. Correspondingly, the Austrian–Hungarian border (with 16 crossing points) has been 'tightened' from the Austrian side and, as Wallace has suggested, 'Troops [are now] deployed on the Austrian border [with Hungary] . . . to stem the flow of Romanians' (Wallace 1991: 12). Now that Hungary has joined the Council of Europe, has been a party to the 1951 (UN) Geneva Convention and the 1967 New York Protocol since March 1989, and together with Czechoslovakia and Poland has applied to join the EC, one wonders whether the 'Cold War' border between East and West is being shifted further East to become a 'closed' border. As recently suggested by Mr Foltany, the Hungarian Ambassador to Vienna, 'Western Europe is benefitting most from Hungary's guarding of the borders' (MNS June 1992: 5).

Conclusion

This article has examined some of the important issues consequent upon the development of increasingly exclusionary immigration and asylum policies and structures in Western Europe. The impact of these on Southern, Central and

Eastern European migrant producing and receiving states deserves further consideration.

On the one hand there appears to be a general trend towards convergence and harmonisation of controls in Europe. On the other, this is only apparent within a presently 'layered' Europe with such harmonisation taking effect from what I have termed 'inner' to 'greater inner' Europe. This leaves some European states either on the margins and potentially subject to incorporation, such as the Visegràd three, and others as 'outsiders'. The immediate impact of such policies on refugees in Central Europe (this article has concentrated on Hungary), is not only that of exclusion from the West, but entrapment in the country of 'transition'. An alternative impact, the more that these countries are incorporated into greater inner-Europe, or conform as an expression of interest in such incorporation, or are simply left with no practical alternative because of the exclusionary policy of other potential 'receivers', may simply be for them to institute exclusionary policies too.

The October 1991 Berlin Conference of Ministers of the Interior referred to earlier, however, concluded by accepting that a long-term strategy for:

> ... social and economic progress in the home countries represents the most important precondition to give the people in those countries a new professional and social perspective, which will encourage them to stay in their home countries (1991: 6).

This represents a positive move towards recognition of the refugee problem. Similarly, in 1991 the EC proposed 4 basic principles for adoption by governments:

(i) that more effective measures be taken to curb illegal immigration
(ii) there be a 'generous application' of rights of political asylum
(iii) that the EC provide increased aid to North Africa and Eastern Europe 'to encourage people to stay at home'
(iv) that there be established a 'frontier-free [EC] market single-visa policy' for all 'outsiders' (*The Economist* 1991:47).

It is important to stress here the need for *balance* between such controls and 'freedoms'. However, from what we have outline above, through Schengen and other EC inter-governmental structures, the emphasis on control policy would seem to be dominant.

At the Conference of Ministers held in Vienna in January 1991 (attended by representatives from member states of the Council of Europe, all the states of Central and Eastern Europe and Australia, Canada and the United States of America) the Hungarian Minister of Foreign Affairs was delegated the task of developing a programme for identifying refugee needs, existing networks and collating and disseminating information about the realities of migration for intending migrants. This programme has the objective of influencing initial decision-making on the part of economic migrants especially by providing them with reliable information about labour markets, living standards, culture and, presumably, the existence of border controls. There have been a series of discussions and meetings since. Again, we see this as a more positive beginning than simply shifting the control of refugees and the Eastern border further Eastwards.

Notes

1 This is a revised version of a paper, entitled 'The Impact of EC Border Policies on the Policing of "Refugees" in Eastern and Central Europe', presented to the European Consortium for Political Research Workshop on 'Police Co-operation in Europe After 1992' held in Limerick, Ireland, 30th March to 4th April 1992.

2 Thanks are due to the Hungarian Ministry of the Interior, the Institute of Police Research, the Office for Refugees and the Border Guard in Budapest for information about Hungary used in this article.

3 This was first introduced in November 1991 under the last Parliament, but withdrawn before the General Election in April 1992. So far, despite John Major's pledge on re-election that it would be 'very soon', it has not been re-introduced pending government discussions with 'interested parties' (Knewstub 1992 and MNS July 1992: 8).

4 Boeles argues that the 1990 Schengen (Supplementary) Agreement 'serves as a model for a series of agreements on the same subject to be concluded by the twelve EC countries' (Boeles 1991: 135).

5 Baldwin-Edwards on the other hand distinguished four convergent 'policy regimes' or 'models' within the EC with respect to immigration controls, namely the Mediterranean, Schengen, Scandinavian and UK (1991: 204).

6 Trends concerning police co-operation in Europe are discussed more in King (1992).

7 This will be a computer information storage/retrieval data-base common to all Schengen member states.

8 The European Economic Area [EEA] is a proposed free-trading block comprising all EC and EFTA [Economic Free Trade Association] nations (Commission of the European Communities 1992a). The seven members of EFTA are Austria, Finland, Iceland, Liechtenstein (having observer status), Norway, Sweden and Switzerland.

9 This Agreement is entitled the 'Convention applying the Schengen Agreement of 14 June 1985 between the governments of the States of the Benelux Economic Union, the Federal Republic of Germany and the French Republic, on the gradual abolition of checks at their common borders'.

10 These countries, now known as the 'Visegràd Group', signed 'Association Agreements' with the EC on 16 December 1991 and are likely to sign an agreement between themselves in Visegràd, Hungary, later this year towards the abolition of internal border controls (Niessen 1992: 13; MNS April 1992: 5).

11 Both Boeles and Bolten suggest that this Convention, entitled 'Convention Determining the State Responsible for Examining Applications for Asylum Lodged in One of the Member States of the European Communities', is modelled on the 1990 Schengen (Supplementary) Agreement (Boeles 1991: 134; Bolten 1991).

12 TREVI was formed in 1976 and is now commonly referred to as an abbreviation of 'Terrorism, Radicalism, Extremism and International Violence'. TREVI is composed of a number of 'working groups': Anti-terrorism; public order, equipment and training; drugs and organised crime; TREVI '92 Planning for abolition of borders.

13 There is some possibility of a resolution to this in sight. The Portugese presidency has now proposed a compromise in that the Spanish authorities be allowed by Britain to 'monitor arrivals' at Gibralter's airport without their being 'physically present at the airport itself'. Kenneth Clarke, the Home Secretary, has in turn confirmed that the government would agree to this (MNS July 1992: 1).

14 The Sudanese asylum-seeker was deported back to Germany on 12th May 1992 following judicial review proceedings (MNS July 1992: 8).

15 Okojie, however, argues that in view of the problem of 'economic migration' there is now urgent need for a redefinition of the concept of refugee on the basis of 'human suffering' rather than simply 'persecution', something which the United Nations High Commission for Refugees was unsuccessful in achieving in 1977 (Okojie 1992: 27).

16 Austria has now signed 'Readmission Agreements' with both Hungary and Romania for the return of illegal immigrants from Austria to these countries of origin. The number of persons caught by Austria attempting to enter illegally from Hungary between September 1990 and February 1992 amounted to 14,729 (MNS April 1992: 3). Similar agreements were signed between Poland and the Schengen States in March 1991 (MNS October 1991: 8).

17 Namely, Armenia, Azerbaijan, Bulgaria, Georgia, Moldova, Romania, Russia, Turkey and Ukraine.

18 The *Bundesgrenzschutz* are the German Federal Border Guard, located within the police.

References

Amnesty International (1990) *United Kingdom: Deficient Policy and Practice for the Protection of Asylum Seekers*, London: Amnesty International (British Section)

Arnould, M. (1991) 'Europa auf der Suche nach neuen Lösungen' *Forum: des Europarats*, November: 40–43, Strasbourg

Bába, I. and Környei, T. (eds.) (1991) *Hungary: Democracy reborn*, Budapest

Baldwin-Edwards, M. (1991) 'Immigration after 1992', *Policy and Politics* 19(3): 119–211

Baryli, W. and Vernet, D. (1992) 'Borders of Neutrality', *The Guardian* (24 July: 25)

Boeles, P. (1991) 'Schengen and the Rule of Law', in H. Meijers *et al.*, *Schengen: Internationalisation of Central Chapters of the Law on Aliens, Refugees, Privacy, Security and the Police*, Netherlands: Tjeenk Willink: 135–146

Bolten, J. (1991) 'From Schengen to Dublin: The New Frontiers of Refugee Law', in H. Meijers *et al.*, *Schengen: Internationalisation of Central Chapters of the Law on Aliens, Refugees, Privacy, Security and the Police*, Netherlands: Tjeenk Willink: 8–36

Bunyan, T. (1991) 'EC Convention on External Border Controls', *Bürgerrechte und Polizei, CILIP* 40(3): Statewatch on-line database, October, Berlin

Busch, H. (1990) *Polizeiliche Zusammenarbeit in Europa: Grenzöffnung und 'Ausgleichsmaßnahmen für den Sicherheitsverlust'*, Report submitted to the EC Commission

Carvel, J. (1991) 'Immigration Minister Accused of "Rush to Deport"' *The Guardian*, 23 December

Cohen, R. (1991) 'East–West and European Migration in a Global Context', *New Community* 18(1), October: 9–26

Cohen, R. (1992) 'Migrants in Europe: Processes of Exclusion and Inclusion', review article, *New Community* 18(2), January: 332–336

Commission of the European Communities (1992a) Press Release WE/15/92, 16 April

Commission of the European Communities (1992b) Press Release WE/21/92, 28 May

Cruz, A. (1991) *Carrier Sanctions in Five Community States: Incompatibilities Between International Civil Aviation and Human Rights Obligations*, Churches' Committee for Migrants in Europe, briefing paper No.4, Brussels: CCME

The Economist (1991) 'The Other Fortress Europe', 1 June: 47–48

European Parliament (1989) *Resolution on the signing of the Supplementary Schengen Agreement*, Statewatch on-line database, May 1991

Gow, D. (1990) 'Kohl Wants EC To Act Over Refugees', *The Guardian*, 24 November

Hungarian Central Statistical Office (1991) *Main Demographic and Occupational Data of the Refugees who Escaped to Hungary, Between 1 January 1988 and 31 May 1990*, Budapest: HCSO

Interior Ministerial Conference in Berlin (October 1991) Final Communiqué on Measures for Checking Illegal Immigration from and through Central and Eastern Europe

Kasriel, K. (1992) 'Hungary Detains Unwanted "Aliens" in Squalid Camp', *The Guardian*, 3 February

Kattau, T.F. (1990) '1992 — Europe Without Frontiers: New Security Concepts as a Consequence of Diminishing Borders in Europe?', paper presented to 'Crime and Policing 1992: A Global Perspective' conference, Islington/London, November

King, M. (1992) 'Police Co-Operation and Border Controls in a 'New' Europe: An Indication of Trends for Change', paper presented to the *Social Changes, Crime and Police* conference, Budapest/Hungary (June)

Knewstub, N. (1992) 'Asylum Bill May be Delayed', *The Guardian*, 10 June

Michalski, A. and Wallace, H. (1992) 'Can the EC Cope with Increased Membership?' *The European*, 23/26 July: 8

Migration News Sheet Nos. 104 (November 1991)–112 (July 1992), Brussels: Churches Committee for Migrants in Europe

Miles, R. (1991) Review of A. Dummet and A. Nicol, *Subjects, Citizens, Aliens and Others:*

Nationality and Immigration Law, (Weidenfeld and Nicolson 1990), *Journal of Law and Society* 18(2), Summer: 279–286

Niessen, J. (1992) *European Migration Policies for the Nineties after the Maastricht Summit*, Churches' Committee for Migrants in Europe, briefing paper No. 7, Brussels: CCME

Okojie, P. (1992) 'The March of the Invaders: Racism and Refugee Policies in Europe', *Race Relations Abstracts* 17(1): 5–29

Police Review (1992) 'France Tightens Immigration Rules', 3 January

The Schengen (Supplementary) Agreement (1990), Statewatch on-line database, January 1992

Sík, E. (1992) 'Transylvanian Refugees in Hungary and the Emergence of Policy Networks to Cope with Crisis' *Journal of Refugee Studies* 5(1): 16–28

Simmons, M. (1992) 'East Refugees "to flood Europe"', *The Guardian*, 14 January

Spencer, M. (1990) *1992 and All That: Civil Liberties in the Balance*, London: The Civil Liberties Trust

Wallace, W. (1991) 'Tides of Crisis' *New Statesman and Society*, 17 May: 12–14

Wilpert, C. (1991) 'Migration and Ethnicity in a Non-Immigration Country: Foreigners in a United Germany', *New Community* 18(1), October: 49–62

Wolf, J. (1992) 'Sweden Gets Go-ahead on EC Membership', *The Guardian*, 1 August

Journal of Refugee Studies Vol. 3. No. 4 1990

Internal Refugee Flows and Development-Induced Population Displacement*

MICHAEL M. CERNEA
Senior sociology Adviser, The World Bank, Washington, DC

An unjustified dichotomy in the social science literature dealing with displaced populations separates the study of refugees from the study of populations uprooted by development projects. The paper argues that this dichotomy must be overcome by exploring the similarities and differences between these categories of displaced populations. Both bodies of literature, which currently do not 'speak to each other', stand to gain conceptually from overcoming their relative isolation. New trends are signalled regarding the international aid and assistance channelled during the 1980s to refugee and displaced populations. The paper discusses the worldwide growth of development-related population displacements, while in many countries domestic policies and legal frameworks to guide forced dislocation and resettlement are lacking. The differences between relief and development oriented strategies for resettling displaced people are examined with emphasis on the importance of allocating adequate resources for the sustainable socio-economic re-establishment of people displaced by development.

Introduction

Two categories of aid interventions are used by international agencies to respond to situations in which large groups of people are uprooted from their habitat, their socio-economic status is ravaged, and their human rights are jeopardized. These are first, emergency assistance projects for refugees and second, projects (or project components) aimed at resettling the people forcibly displaced by planned change (for example, dam building, highways, canals, and ports). In both categories of projects the target groups are displaced populations, even though the causes of their displacement differ profoundly.

The currently growing interest in these types of projects stems largely from the fact that they bring to the forefront two sets of key issues: on the one hand, issues related to their potential as vehicles for shifting aid from relief assistance to development goals; on the other, issues related to the increasing efforts to link development aid to human rights protection.

In the present paper, I will deal explicitly with just the first group of issues, particularly with restoring the self-sufficiency and normal productive activities of uprooted populations, even though concern for their human and economic rights is an implicit constant theme of my argument.[1] I will explore some commonalities and differences between these two categories of aid intervention and between the segments of displaced populations they address. When discussing refugee groups, I will deliberately focus on *internally* displaced people, rather than on *international* refugees; this will facilitate comparison with people displaced by development projects who, typically, also tend to remain within national borders. First, the paper will consider the causal agents of internal population displacement; second, it will provide a brief overview of World Bank involvement during the last two decades in emergency projects that assist internal refugees; and third, the paper will discuss several key issues common to refugees *and* population groups dislocated by planned development interventions. In the context of the last point, I will examine the magnitude of such induced dislocations and the policy framework that must guide projects causing displacement. For the purposes of this paper, I will generally use the term *refugees* to describe internal refugee populations and the term *oustees* to describe populations displaced by development projects.

Main Causes of Population Displacement

A Research Dichotomy

There is a visible, yet in my opinion hardly justified, dichotomy within the social science literature on displaced populations: a literature on refugees coexists side by side with a literature on development-caused involuntary resettlement. The two literatures do not usually speak to one another. With some exceptions, most of the writings on refugees, for instance, omit altogether oustee groups from the typology of displaced populations. And in turn the anthropological literature on oustees bypasses comparative analysis with refugees. As a result, the chance for more in-depth treatment by examining commonalities and differences is being missed.

There are, of course, valid reasons for discriminating between these categories. But are these reasons sufficient to justify the absence of comparative analysis? Or the lack of overarching concepts and theories encompassing both (and perhaps other) categories?

I submit that the fact that research on refugees, journals on refugees, and conferences on refugees usually overlook development-related displacement results in weakening both the theoretical conceptualizations and the practical influence of such research on government policies and programmes. Conversely, a strong case can be made, for both practical and theoretical purposes, to identify and compare the similarities and differences between the various sub-categories of displaced populations. In addition, lessons with wide applicability can be derived by comparing the different types of projects that address the needs of internally displaced populations, and by examining the behavioural strategies which the latter have adopted to regain normalcy.

There have been a handful of valuable scholarly attempts to integrate the study of both refugee relocation and development relocation under a single conceptual and analytical sociological framework. Scudder and Colson (1982) have delineated such a framework around the concept of stress and have divided the process of dislocation-relocation in stages. In a less formal elaboration, Oliver-Smith and Hansen (1982) have suggested that such population movements may be seen in the context of a migration continuum stretching from voluntary to involuntary. However promising these integrative approaches have seemed, by and large they have not been systematically followed, as could have been expected, through a subsequent body of comparative research. Such comparative investigation still remains to be done.

Internal and International Refugees

Despite the lack (or impossibility) of precise statistics, a consensus is gradually emerging that the number of internally displaced people worldwide surpasses the number of those usually encompassed by the concept of international (or external) refugees (Clark 1988; McColm 1989). The US Council for Refugees has estimated that by the end of 1987 the number of cross-border refugees worldwide stood at about 15.4 million; the same upheavals produced at least an additional 17 million people displaced internally (cf. Zolberg et al 1989). These figures do not include those displaced internally by planned development programmes. Despite the huge number of internal refugees, however, 'at present no international agency has responsibility for ensuring the adequacy of protection and assistance, including health care, for internally displaced persons' (The Georgetown Declaration 1988).

It is perhaps a telling sign of our distressed time that the simultaneous growth of both groups — internal and international refugees — is so rapid that it raises doubt about which sad category outnumbers the other. Beyond that doubt, however, the conceptual distinction between them is far from being strictly academic: it is consequential for resource allocation and assistance strategies. There are established international structures created to assist international refugees, while for internal refugees much less institutionalized support is available. While external refugees are recognized by international agencies, those who do not cross borders, namely the internal refugees, are often not recognized as such by the same agencies, even though both the triggers and the consequences of their displacement may be identical. In turn, this difference in recognition results in great differences between the levels of public and private assistance provided to these groups. It appears warranted therefore to consider that in the area of refugee assistance 'the challenge for the future is presented by internally displaced people, (where) roles and mandates are unclear' (Keely 1988).

Causal Agents of Dislocation

By seperating out types of *causal agent*, we can distinguish four sets of factors leading to population displacement:

1. wars and political turmoil;
2. persecution (or fear of) based on ethnicity, race, or religion;
3. natural disasters: floods, earthquakes, droughts, etc.; and
4. development projects that deliberately cause major changes in land and water use.

The first three of these general causes are common to *both* flows of refugees: international and internal. Indeed, when wars, persecution and/or natural calamities force people to flee their homelands, the push reasons are much the same for external refugees who cross an international border and seek shelter in a different country, and for internal refugees who cannot or choose not to leave their countries. And the trauma of being a refugee in one's own land is not necessarily less than being a refugee on foreign soil.

The last among the four causes listed above — planned change — typically results in internal rather than cross-border displacement. Major infrastructure programmes commonly require non-voluntary population relocation, imposed through state power. For want of a more adequate concept, populations forced to move are described under a variety of terms such as 'oustees' (a term widely used in India), 'evictees', 'displacees', 'resettlers', 'relocatees', and 'project affected persons'.

The oustees can be further divided into the following sub-categories:

(a) people who lose their houses;
(b) people who lose both their houses *and* their farming land or other productive assets (in full or in part); and
(c) people who lose land only (in full or in significant part), but not their houses.

People in the last subgroup, where housing is not affected, may remain in place, only if land or employment can be found nearby; otherwise, they too are compelled to resettle.

A brief comment is warranted about the last sub-category. Technical and planning agencies tend to omit these people from oustee statistics, planning, and resource allocation, on grounds that their houses are not destroyed. But the loss of even one significant part of a household's farmland may be sufficient to make that farm economically non-viable; it may cause marginalization (Cernea 1990b), defined elsewhere as the sliding of a family from barely above to below the poverty threshold.

Denying this sub-category the label of displaced people (for example of 'oustees'') is not just an innocuous semantic matter. As was correctly argued in the case of refugees (Zetter 1988; 1990), labelling (designation of status) is a powerful tool of practical policy used by governments for purposes of allocating resources to, or withholding from, certain groups. The denial (by certain government agencies) of displacement status to families falling in subgroup (c) above is a way of belittling the adverse effects of projects through the device of refusing to recognize the rights, losses, and legitimate entitlements of part of the population affected. Under the provisions of the World Bank's policy regarding involuntary resettlement (see Cernea 1988a), all three subgroups are defined as project-dislocated populations, and their socio-economic re-establishment must be carried out by the same project that displaces them.

Similarities and Differences

Some social scientists describe communities displaced by development programmes as development refugees (Mahapatra 1983). This is not a well defined and rigorous concept. Its wholesale use to define all those displaced by development programmes would blur certain essential differences between oustees and refugees, and would be misleading.

When communities are displaced by a public development project, it is incumbent upon the government to ensure that the oustees are fully compensated and assisted to resettle adequately. It is when this does not happen, however, and when development-displaced people become destitute — their assets lost, their habitat gone, and their basic human rights unrecognized and trampled on — that their situation becomes, in essence, similar to refugees. Therefore, it is conceptually useful explicitly to point out, rather than blur, both similarities and differences between refugees (from war, ethnic persecution, and drought) and oustees from planned programmes. This permits us to highlight the circumstances in which bad planning or abdication of government responsibility converts oustees into refugees. The purpose of resettlement policies must be absolutely to prevent the sliding of development-displaced people (oustees) into a refugee-like condition.

In turn, the definitions commonly accepted for the term refugees tend to be fairly restrictive. In other words, they are not open to encompass either voluntary migrants or people dislocated by planned projects (see, for instance, the definitions discussed in Zolberg et al. (1989); or the definition used by the United Nations). This is probably how it should be, for both practical and conceptual reasons. Given the special entitlements granted by many countries and international organizations to refugees, every attempt formally to define the term is underlined by the concern to avoid confusing, for instance, a migrant with a genuine refugee.

Zolberg's (1989) analysis of contemporary refugee populations distinguishes three sociological types of refugees: the activist; the target; and the victim. The characteristics that unite these types under the category (and concept) of refugees describe both causes and consequences of their condition as individuals uprooted from their habitat.

On the causal side, for instance, one common characteristic of their condition is fear of violence. As was observed with insight, 'what all three (types) have in common is fear of immediate violence — violence resulting from conflict between state and civil society, between opposing armies, or conflict among ethnic groups or class formations that the state is unable or unwilling to control' (Zolberg 1989:269). On the consequences' side, in turn, there are other sociologically significant components that these three types share as refugees: for instance, abrupt destitution, residence loss, loss of economic self-sufficiency, cultural separation, identity deprivation, and socio-psychological stress.

Carrying further the comparison between refugees and oustees, we find on the causal side essential differences, while we note many similarities in the consequences of their displacement.

Displaced people of all categories resemble each other in that they lose their houses and households; they temporarily or permanently lose their lands, water wells, workshops, vending stalls, or other assets. Their production systems are dismantled, their ways of making a living are disrupted and their very livelihood critically jeopardized. The supporting social networks of which they are a part unravel. They relocate in previously unknown places, among host populations often suspicious of them or directly hostile.

On the other hand, there are sharp dissimilarities between refugees and oustees in legal status, entitlements to assistance, and often in ethnic composition. Compared to other refugee-causing circumstances, development-related displacements inflict upon the uprooted population material losses that are often greater, or definitive. For instance, refugees fleeing their homelands because of civil war, persecution, or flooding may in some cases eventually return at least to their farming land; those displaced by dam reservoirs, however, will never get the same lands back, and simply cannot return to their earlier homes.

Referring to all these groups comprehensively as internally displaced people, but at the same time recognizing both similarities and differences between refugees and oustees, is instrumental for the comparative analyses between them, and between the operational approaches required to re-establish them to normalcy.

Emergency Projects for Refugee Assistance

Two relatively new trends emerged during the 1980s, particularly during the second half of the decade, in the assistance given to displaced populations. These trends were insufficiently grasped and analyzed by the research community. They consist of, on the one hand, a very considerable *increase in the number and diversity of emergency international aid projects* targeted to refugees and disaster victims, and, on the other hand, a significant *increase in special project components to assist development oustees*.

Relevant data documenting these trends, for example within World Bank activities, are given below. One should note, however, that the Bank's projects are only part of a larger movement. Not only have the resources been increased multifold; the approaches to the uprooted populations, the forms of technical assistance, the institutional arrangements, and so on, have been multiplied and diversified through such projects. These trends open up new possibilities: on the one hand, the practice of refugee relief aid can be informed with the experience stemming from approaches that are pursuing redevelopment, as used under oustee-resettlement projects; on the other hand, assistance given to the latter category can be informed by the experience of refugees' innovative cultural mechanisms to survive and cope (Christensen 1982), to regain self-sufficiency and to self-resettle.

World Bank Resources for Refugee Assistance

Among the international agencies involved in aid to both internal and international refugees, the World Bank contributes by financing many special assistance projects and monitoring their implementation. The most familiar category among such projects are the emergency lending operations. It should be noted, however, that a considerable number of regular Bank-financed projects also provide direct assistance to populations that consist of, or include, internal and/or international refugees.

After its establishment following World War II, the World Bank's earliest loans were post-war reconstruction projects. Between 1947–1953 such loans were extended exclusively to European countries. Those were emergency operations, addressed to a broad spectrum of populations and needs, not just to refugees. After 1953, however, the World Bank ceased this type of operations. It replaced them with investment lending.

It took almost two decades, and a serious aggravation of the worldwide problem of refugees, for emergency assistance operations to be resumed in 1970 by the World Bank. Such lending is provided in order to respond to major natural or man-caused disasters with immediate financial and technical support. These operations have benefited large numbers of refugees from natural or socio-political catastrophes, as well as other people from the same or adjacent areas (Kreimer 1989). In virtually all cases, such projects have made a massive contribution to creating the socio-economic circumstances necessary either for the return of many refugees or for their permanent re-establishment elsewhere.

Between 1970–1988, and especially in the 1980s, the frequency of such emergency loans and the amount of resources channelled through them have risen sharply (see Table 1).

Emergency World Bank assistance projects have addressed five types of situations:

1. *civil wars and other internal disturbances*: e.g., emergency projects in Nigeria, Bangladesh, Sudan, Lebanon, Nicaragua, Uganda, Zimbabwe, Ghana;
2. *droughts*: e.g., drought assistance projects in Burkina Faso, Mali, Mauritania, Senegal, Ethiopia, Somalia, Sudan, India, among others;

3. *cyclones*: e.g., emergency projects in Bangladesh, Fiji, Dominican Republic, Haiti, Madagascar, Swaziland;
4. *flood*: e.g., projects in Pakistan, Brazil, Bangladesh, Nepal;
5. *earthquakes and other disasters*, such as volcanic eruptions, forest fires (e.g. Peru, Yugoslavia, Romania, Mexico, Ecuador, China).

Altogether, 57 emergency projects were approved between 1974–1988, out of which 18 (31.6 per cent) were approved between 1984–88. The World Bank resources channelled into such projects in the last five years were 3.5 times larger than in the prior five years.

Table 1

Number and Amount of World Bank Emergency Loans by Category Between Financial Year (FY) 1969–1988*

	FY69–73		FY74–78		FY79–83		FY84–88	
	No.	$m	No.	$m	No.	$m	No.	$m
Civil War/ Disturbances	4	165.6	2	60.7	7	257.5	2	123.0
Cyclone/ Hurricane	1	25.0	—	—	5	76.2	3	25.6
Drought	—	—	8**	35.0	—	—	3	400.0
Flood	—	—	3	135.0	1	7.0	5	345.5
Earthquake	2	50.0	2	86.5	3	85.0	4	580.0
Forest Fire	—	—	—	—	—	—	1	56.9
Volcanic Eruption	—	—	1	7.0	—	—	—	—
Total	7	240.6	16	324.2	16	425.7	18	1531

NOTES: *No emergency loans are on record from FY54 to FY69. Also, this table does not include all the Bank loans and projects which had assisted refugee populations, but only those labelled 'emergency operations'. For instance, such important refugee assistance operations as the two projects targeted to Afghan refugees in Pakistan are not included in the table. The operations reflected in this table have also benefited, of course, victims of those disasters who did not become refugees.

**Includes six loans to the Sahelian countries in FY74 for a series of inter-related drought relief fund projects.

Unfortunately, no in-depth evaluation studies have been carried out on the Bank assisted projects comparable to, for instance, the kind of study undertaken in Uganda by Barbara Harrell-Bond and reported in her seminal book on aid to refugees (Harrell-Bond 1986). But a number of project audit reports and other assessments do exist, which help derive some important lessons about strategies, approaches and results.

Alternatives in Refugee Assistance

Within the type of assistance provided by World Bank emergency projects, a key strategy issue is always the trade-offs between relief measures needed immediately, on the one hand, and reconstruction investments for redevelopment in the long term, on the other.

By design, the World Bank puts the main emphasis on the latter type of programme. Considerable resources are provided for the reconstruction of physical infrastructure that has been destroyed or damaged, thus creating employment and laying the ground for the resumption of regular productive activities. In post-war or civil war situations, when production activities and trade lines have been disrupted, causing famine, unemployment and dislocation, Bank projects primarily aim at restoring production and productivity required for recovery and rebuild transportation systems.

Of course, weighing and deciding on trade-offs is a highly judgmental exercise and is vulnerable to imperfect initial information. Built in flexibility for midstream adjustments is needed. World Bank assistance needs to be complemented by short term relief programmes by other agencies and non-governmental organizations.

An example of a Bank assisted recovery programme after war and civil disturbance is the Reconstruction Credit to Uganda (FY80) which followed the overthrow of the military government in 1979. The domestic economy was devastated. Facing large scale physical destruction, the reconstruction process was complicated also by social disruption, administrative disarray and continued political strife. In response to the urgent situation, the Bank proposed a quick disbursing project to Uganda to rapidly supply inputs for the productive sectors and to meet short term foreign exchange needs. Some slippage from the original schedule reduced the overall impact, yet the quick disbursing approach did provide resources faster than was possible using regular project lending. Other comparable cases include projects in Mozambique (FY85), Ghana (FY83) and Zimbabwe (FY81), where the Bank has financed recovery programmes and imports critical to begin a long term process of rehabilitation and reform.

When Mozambique joined the World Bank in 1984, the country was confronting a huge refugee problem. Its economy was suffering from the effects of civil war, security problems, inappropriate policies, natural calamities and structural imbalances of long standing. Against this backdrop, the government developed a two year Economic Action Programme designed to institute more pragmatic policies to stem the economic decline. The Bank supported the government's emergency rehabilitation efforts by providing quickly disbursed hard currency to meet priority needs as the government began the process of rehabilitation. The initial project made possible imports of equipment, spare parts and raw materials for the key sectors of industry, agriculture and transport, and directly helped the reintegration of war displaced population into productive activities. This approach has been replicated and validated in other, smaller scale projects assisted in Mozambique by bilateral donors, like the Italian-sponsored project near Gondola (Manica province) and the Swedish-sponsored seed production unit in Chimoio. Results from these two projects (Morna 1990) confirm that production-oriented aid (inputs, seeds) enables former war-refugees to shake off their dependency upon relief-aid, re-establish themselves on a productive basis, and gradually become again self-sustaining.

The implementation quality of emergency refugee assistance programmes, however, has seldom been satisfactory. It is often suggested that the fault lies not with the programme, but with the refugees themselves. However, anthropological field research has documented that this assumption is mistaken (Harrell-Bond 1986). Analytical evaluations carried out by the World Bank tends to confirm such findings. In fact, the most neglected dimensions in such projects are usually the cultural and psychological ones, particularly the social engineering work necessary to re-establish the refugee population in new, viable settlements, with access to productive activities, some employment, and services. Indeed, as Harrell-Bond (1986:2) observed, 'establishing a rural settlement involves social engineering'. My reading of the literature produced by agencies responsible for such policy suggests that full implications of this reality has escaped attention.

One recurrent difference in the performance of emergency operations compared with conventional projects is the extent of implementation delays. According to a recent analysis, such delays occur in ninety per cent of these loans and tend to be substantial if compared to the original, usually accelerated, implementation timetable. One reason for delays in Bank assisted projects was the choice of an inadequate project model, such as the model of single-sector loans attempting to compress most of the elements of a regular project into the accelerated time frame of an emergency project. The consequence was a slowdown of the project's implementation and disbursement. Such delays are especially troubling in view of the required urgency of intervention. Delaying assistance has high human costs.

The recently re-issued, and strengthened, World Bank Operational Directives for emergency recovery assistance projects put a stronger emphasis on design adequate to speedy implementation (World Bank 1989). The new directives aim at improving the quality of both immediate and long term assistance, by focussing on restoring the self-sufficiency and autonomy of the affected population through redressing its productive capacity.

A characteristic of the Bank's approach in emergency interventions is the use of quick disbursement procedures. These are much faster compared to normal projects. Yet the use of quick disbursement should not preclude designing such interventions not just for the crisis at hand but also as measures for preventing or mitigating similar occurrences in the future. In this connection, it is worth mentioning the experience of Kenya. During a drought, no new emergency loan was made, but the Bank reallocated funds from an existing Kenya project to support a drought recovery programme it cofinanced with other donors. The reallocation was designed, appraised, negotiated and approved by the Bank's board within three months. Other donors financed complementary activities and necessary inputs. The Bank's approach encouraged subsequent planning based on 'lessons of the drought' and in so doing stimulated the government to prepare for the next possible drought. Agricultural recovery was rapid. Under the project the government started preparation of a Food Security Strategy, which includes early warning systems and contingency plans for possible future droughts.

Development-Related Displacements

Certain types of development-programmes, particularly those which entail important changes in land and water use, frequently cause forced population dislocations.

These are not benign occurrences. Such dislocations often affect large groups directly and immediately, and in addition reverberate subsequently in various indirect ways over much larger populations. For instance, the construction of irrigation and hydropower dams causes the permanent submergence of tens or hundreds of thousands of acres of land and forests, including houses, enterprises, temples, schools, shops, terraces, orchards and roads. Similarly, highway projects, strip-mining projects, the establishment of industrial estates, often necessitate the displacement of people from their habitat and work sites. Displacement required for urban improvement is already extensive and will also increase considerably, particularly in Africa and Asia (Cernea 1989).

Contradictions in Development

A profound contradiction is embedded in the very fabric of such development processes. This contradiction results from the fact that certain project-funded infrastructure is essential for national or regional development, satisfies critical needs of many direct and indirect beneficiaries, and generate immediate or long term gains unobtainable in any other way. Yet at the same time, such constructions cause forced displacement that is immediately detrimental for those affected. The fulfilment of the needs of the many clashes with the entitlements of the few. The gains do not accrue to those who bear the pains. Indeed, both the literature on refugees and that on oustees have documented in vivid detail the adverse consequences of dislocation (Scudder 1981; Appel 1985; Fahim 1988; Salem-Murdock 1989; Christensen 1982; de Wet 1991; Agreeparompil 1989; Keller 1975). Synthesizing the empirical data from many such field studies, it is clear that displacement has led in most cases to severe and all-round impoverishment, and that the typical processes of impoverishment occur along seven key dimensions: landlessness; homelessness; joblessness; marginalization; food insecurity; increased mortality and morbidity; and social disarticulation (Cernea 1990b).

Nevertheless, given the rigidity of geographical and physical parameters or the lack of comparable economic alternatives, such contradictions of the development process often connot be avoided. But the acuity and consequences of such contradictions can be mitigated and modified through good planning and appropriate resource allocations.

Displacement Size and Estimate

What is the magnitude of population displacement caused by development projects? Is it negligible, or is it significant enough to justify broad concern?

There are no hard global statistics about development-induced displacement. This absence contributes to insufficient public awareness of this issue. Yet a rough assessment can be made based on available figures. Table 2 provides an image of the magnitude of population displacement on a dam-by-dam

Table 2

Number of People Affected by Major Dam Projects

Dam	Country	No. of People
Already Built		
Tarbela	Pakistan	86,000
Srisailam	India	100,000
Akosombo	Ghana	84,000
Kossou	Ivory Coast	85,000
Kainji	Nigeria	50,000
High Aswan	Egypt	100,000
Nangbeto	Togo/Benin	12,000
Saguling	Indonesia	55,000
Danjiangkou	China	383,000
Sobradinho	Brazil	60,000
Mangla	Pakistan	90,000
Currently under Construction		
Shuikou	China	68,000
Narmada Sardar Sarovar	India	70,000
Almatti	India	160,000
Narayanpur	India	80,000
Itaparica	Brazil	45,000
Yacyreta	Argentina/Paraguay	45,000
Kayraktepe	Turkey	20,000
Under Design		
Xiaolangdi	China	170,000
Gandhi Sagar	India	100,000
Kalabagh	Pakistan	80,000
Soubre	Ivory Coast	40,000
Karnali (Chisapani)	Nepal	50,000
Three Gorges	China	750,000 to 1.2 mil.

NOTE: This table is based on data from project documents and/or public sources. Some of these projects were co-financed by the World Bank, while others were financed entirely from other sources, local and international.

basis. Some of these major dams have already been completed; others are under construction, and yet others are being planned for the future.

A study I carried out in 1986 found that all new dams to be constructed under irrigation and hydropower projects approved by the Bank between 1979–1985 would eventually displace approximately 750,000 people (see Cernea 1988b). By extrapolation, this study may also help assess roughly the worldwide magnitude of dam-caused displacement.

According to the World Inventory of Dams, the dams being constructed with World Bank financial assistance are but a small fraction of all the dams being erected in the world at a certain point in time. Of the 35,000 large dams in existence worldwide, about 11,000 were completed during the 1951–1982 period, at an overall average of 340 dams per year; for the period of 1975–1982, the average was smaller; 250 dams annually. World Bank financing for the latter period was provided to between 3 per cent to 10 per cent of the dams being completed worldwide (Mermel 1990).

Given the imprecision of the available statistics, a more conservatively adjusted estimate could be that dams constructed with World Bank assistance represented between 5 per cent to 8 per cent of the worldwide total number of dams under construction during 1979–1985. That means, again with far from definitive statistics, that the aggregate number of people affected by reservoir submergence in dams started in that period could vary between 8–15 million people. Thus, each year between 1.2 and 2.1 million people are to be displaced worldwide as a consequence of new dams only.

Despite the incompleteness of this preliminary assessment, the aggregate numbers are staggering. On a country-by-country basis, particularly in countries engaged in large hydropower programmes, the annual 'waves' of newly displaced people are continuously compounding the problem. Recent statistics from China, for instance, show that over the last three decades, from late 1950s to 1989, the number of people displaced by water conservancy projects alone exceeded 10,000,000 (Chao 1990).

In addition to the massive displacements caused by water resource development programmes, considerable forced dislocation is entailed by other types of constructions, such as industry, transportation and mining. Quite often, seemingly innocuous projects, such as establishing an agricultural research and experimentation centre, building a hospital complex in a city, or constructing a drinking water storage basin, also involve land expropriation, depriving many families of their productive units and habitat, and forcing them to relocate. The numbers of oustees are determined with more rigour in internationally assisted projects than in the ones supported from domestic sources only. Therefore, there are good reasons to believe that the real totals are much higher.

Another category of people massively displaced by planned government programmes, whose uprooting appears to closely resemble refugee floods, are the people forced to move by large state-sponsored resettlement programmes that claim to be designed to benefit primarily the relocatees. Such programmes, for instance, are the forced move of the Bulusu' of East Kalimantan (Indonesia), and of other interior Dayak groups, to government established resettlement centres, with the stated purpose of providing them with services; or the involuntary relocation of populations away from Ethiopia's droughtprone areas. Many social scientists conducting empirical studies of such resettlement programmes have concluded that in fact they are politically motivated government operations disguised by development rhetoric, but have little to do with real development (Appell 1985; Clay 1986; Kesmanee 1988; de Wet 1991; Clay, Steingraber and Niggli 1988).

In summary, both by its worldwide magnitude and the problems it engenders, population displacement caused by development programmes justifies the attention of social researchers and, in particular, justifies comparative analysis with other displaced groups such as internal refugees. Genuine development programmes that entail displacement usually produce long term benefits for a large number of people. But this in itself does not make the disruptions any less or the hardship any lighter for those who have the misfortune to be uprooted and who only rarely share in the project benefits.

Key Issues in Assisting Oustees

There are, nevertheless, some effective ways to control and reduce the extent of forced displacement and its adverse consequences. The extent of the disruptions and their short and long term effects can be corrected through appropriate *policies* and resource allocation. There are also ways and techniques to reduce the numbers of people affected and displaced.

Drawing on World Bank experience with such displacement, I will briefly refer to four important issues concerning means and solutions:

1. avoidability of displacement;
2. the need for national policies and legal frameworks governing forced displacement operations;
3. relief-based approaches *vis-à-vis* development-oriented strategies for resettling displaced people;
4. resource allocation for reconstruction and the responsibility of national governments.

Avoidability of Displacement

While development projects are and will be necessary, forced displacement of people can sometimes be fully avoided and often can be reduced. Development is not in itself a blind legitimizer of any displacement, regardless of size and consequence. On the contrary, induced development must be designed in ways that take advantage of any opportunity to minimize disruption. For instance, World Bank experience has demonstrated that if planners carefully weigh the tradeoffs between dam height and the size of population dislocation, they may reduce the latter. Small decreases in reservoir elevation may cut down significantly the number of people affected by submergence. This was demonstrated by the designers of the Bank-financed project for the Saguling dam in Indonesia, who selected a reservoir elevation of 645m instead of the initially envisaged elevation of 650m and thus reduced population displacement to 55,000 people instead of almost 100,000 people (Soepartomo and Tjiptohandojo 1988). In the same way, optimization studies for road trajectories in the Bank assisted urban improvement project in Shanghai (China) have resulted in alternatives which avoided the displacement of several thousand families.

Altogether, correct preliminary assessments of the total losses that would be caused by displacement, and the inclusion of the full costs of resettling both people and infrastructure in the estimated costs of the new project, may lead to the conclusion that one or another project is economically and socially unjustified, and therefore should either be modified or not started. It is necessary to avoid engineering biases in the design of such technical projects, to oppose the fatalistic treatment of displacement as an invariably unavoidable consequence of development, and to take into account the social dimensions in the planning of every project.

Domestic Policies and Legal Frameworks

Surprising as it may appear, most governmental agencies that are involved in projects causing involuntary resettlement do not have clearly articulated regulations or policies concerning such displacement. The absence of these domestic policy frameworks allows many abuses and infringements of peoples' socioeconomic rights to occur by default, and to remain uncorrected.

The government's responsibility *vis-à-vis* development-dislocated people is much higher, in all respects, than it is concerning refugees from natural calamities because the former displacement is initiated by the government and enforced through the state's power of eminent domain. It turns out that many countries have legal norms about expropriating and displacing people, but preserve a legal lacuna with respect to the state's role in re-establishing the living standards and self-sufficiency of oustees. Moreover, eminent domain laws and their compensatory provisions, crafted initially for small scale sporadic cases, are often unfit for situations of massive expropriations.

Even many international donor agencies, such as the regional development banks for Africa, Asia and Latin America, and many bilateral donor agencies, do not have formal policies for projects that cause displacement. As a result, when these agencies fund projects entailing displacement, they fund the new physical infrastructure and hardware but only seldom provide equal guidance and financial support for resettling the oustees. Resettlement is being left to the local/territorial agency alone, which definitely has less resources and less overall responsibility. As a consequence of the policy vacuum, relocation remains barely planned, largely underfunded, and poorly implemented.

The World Bank is, to date, the only international development agency that has adopted and published an explicit policy for addressing the social, economic, and cultural issues of involuntary resettlement, a policy rooted in social science knowledge about resettlement (see Rajagopalan 1989; Cernea 1988a, 1990a; Guggenheim 1989). Recent experiences document that the policy's existence and enforcement lead to higher standards in planning and financing involuntary resettlement. Implementation at high standards, however, does not automatically result from just adopting a policy. Departures from policy norms occur continuously, for various reasons. Consistency of implementation with the policy must be constantly monitored and enforced. The policy is disciplining not only the work of Bank staff, but it also becomes compelling for Bank borrowers when they sign a loan agreement for a project containing resettlement. In a fairly broad spectrum of projects the two major consequences of the policy have been more systematic, and advance, planning for relocation, and more adequate resource allocation (Rajagopalan 1989). The binding effects of an institutional policy are that it compels Bank staff and borrowing agencies to pursue resettlement standards of a higher quality than would have been achieved in the absence of such a policy.

The World Bank also encourages the improvement or formulation of country policies and legal frameworks pertinent to the rights of those displaced (Shihata 1991). Policy and institutional changes are widely required in many developing countries (see Paul 1988, 1991; Dhagamwar 1989). In several countries and states, the Bank-borrower policy dialogue and the lessons derived from Bank assisted projects have already led to the elaboration of improved or new domestic legislation. The Bank holds that the projects it finances should not engage in practices which violate universally recognized rights. To create legal guarantees to that respect, it supports the development of domestic legal and policy frameworks in borrowing countries.

Independent legal scholars have noted, correctly, that it cannot be said to be improper interference for the Bank or IDA to insist, as a condition of a project loan, that project-consistent law be put into practice to secure recognized rights for the people affected by the project; on the contrary, it should be inconsistent and 'unlawful to fail to insist on such protection' (Paul 1988:118). Therefore, it must be emphasized forcefully that the adoption of national resettlement policies by the governments of developing countries, together with the adoption of policy guidelines by the donor agencies of developed countries, would go a long way towards safeguarding people's human and economic rights, and speeding up the productive re-establishment of oustees.

Relief versus Development

Relief assistance to internally displaced populations is necessary, but not sufficient by far. This is, of course, true not only for oustees but also for other internal refugees. However, the resources needed to achieve such an objective for all internal refugees are scarce.

The key objective of the Bank's policy for correcting the effects of project-induced dislocation was formulated in 1986 in the following way: *because involuntary displacement dismantles a previous production system and way of life, all resettlement programmes must be development programmes as well.* When resettlement is unavoidable, the Bank's policy is to help the borrower ensure that the oustees' productive base and income-earning ability are improved, or at least restored to the level they would have achieved without relocation. More recently, in June 1990, the Bank reissued its policy operational directives (World Bank 1990). The new directives formulated this objectives in even stronger terms:

> All involuntary resettlement should be conceived and executed as *development programmes*, with resettlers provided sufficient investment resources and opportunities to *share in project benefits*. The displaced should be (i) compensated for their losses at full replacement cost prior to the actual move; (ii) assisted with the move and supported during the transition period in the resettlement site; and (iii) assisted in their efforts to improve their former living standards, income earning capacity, and production levels, or at least to restore them. Particular attention should be paid to the needs of the poorest groups to be resettled.

How can this basic objective be accomplished in the framework of a government-sponsored development project? The answer is largely dependent on the allocation of adequate resources for the re-establishment of people's productive capacity.

Reconstruction and Resource Allocation

Reconstruction strategies represent the most promising domain for experience transfers between refugee assistance projects and projects for resettling development oustees. It has been observed that 'too often the kind of agencies involved in the relief activity simply don't know much about longer term, developmental approaches' (Clarke 1989:10). The questions being asked refer to 'how can assistance be provided in ways that are as developmental as possible?'; or how can ways be found 'to build some kind of economic activity into the lives of refugees?' (Clarke 1989:10–11).

The crux of reconstruction strategies in situations of government planned displacement, as opposed to displacement caused by civil war or natural disasters, is that the government has to assume in advance financial and economic responsibility for correcting the adverse consequences of displacement. Philanthropy from the private sector and the public at large, which is so important for refugee assistance, cannot be counted upon as a resource in programme-caused dislocation. It is both a legal and ethical principle that the Government bears the primary responsibility for relocation. National governments are best placed to prevent or at least reduce, through farsighted planning, some of the causes and at least some of the effects of planned displacement.

In the case of resettlement projects, the core of the resettlement plan is a development package. It consists of provisions centred either around land-based strategies or around employment-based strategies. The most effective, and relatively less costly, are the land-based strategies. They often involve land reclamation, small scale irrigation, tree-crops development, fisheries, social forestry and similar kinds of income generating activities. Sometimes, land scarcity is a major limiting factor, given high population densities. Vocational training for jobs outside agriculture is used in employment-based strategies, but this avenue also requires investments in job creation. Vocational training alone, without actual employment in the newly acquired skills, does not restore the livelihood of those displaced.

In all such activities, it is essential to stimulate the initiative of those resettled and, whenever possible, to assist their efforts for self-resettlement as well. In fact, refugee research has, in turn, documented the effectiveness of self-resettlement, under certain circumstances. Hansen's research among Angolan refugees in Zambia found that self-resettled people achieved greater autonomy and integration in the long term than refugees that have spent an equal period of time in government controlled refugee schemes (Hansen 1990).

The Bank's resettlement policy demands borrowing agencies to recognize and allocate the financial, technical and institutional resources necessary for both the full compensation of the displaced and for re-establishing them on a productive basis. The conventional treatment of involuntary resettlement as salvage operations rather than as development opportunities has resulted in underplanning and gross underfinancing in many countries. To correct this, Bank assistance facilitates the development-oriented approach to resettlement by enabling national agencies to obtain the necessary financial resources, staff and technical expertise. The Bank is also supporting the participation of NGOs, alongside government agencies, in the planning and implementation of relocation, because NGOs are apt to express the needs and defend the rights of those displaced. Similarly, bilateral donor agencies should never finance only the construction of new physical structures without also assisting the reconstruction of sustainable livelihoods for those displaced.

Internal population displacements should not be regarded with fatalism. Their magnitude can be reduced, provided political commitment, normative policy frameworks and adequate resources are put in place. The operational approaches for re-establishing both refugees and oustees hold mutually enriching lessons. The two rather distinct social science literatures dealing with these groups could fare better by speaking more to each other, by researching and explaining both similarities and differences between 'their' populations, and by reinforcing each other in formulating policy recommendations and operational strategies.

(1) It is important to emphasize that human rights issues are becoming matters of growing concern in the allocation of international development aid. Anthropologists, sociologists and legal scholars increasingly explore the ethical and juridic links between human rights and policies for inducing development (see Paul 1988; Downing and Kushner 1988; Shihata 1988). Without elaborating here, I would like to draw attention to the fact that in designing and implementing projects, multilateral and bilateral development agencies face at least three distinct sets of human rights issues: (a) issues regarding general economic and social rights, particularly equity matters; (b) issues related to the human rights of people affected by civil war, violent ethnic persecution or natural calamities, who need protection and immediate assistance; and (c) issues

arising when development projects themselves adversely affect the economic and social rights of certain population segments. The kind of projects discussed in the present article are relevant to issues in groups (b) and (c).

APPELL, G. N. (1985) 'The Bulusu' of East Kalimantan: The Consequences of Resettlement', in Appell, G. N., ed., *Modernization and the Emergency of a Landless Peasantry*, Studies in Third World Societies, vol. 33, Williamsburg, College of William and Mary.

AREEPARAMPIL. M. (1989) 'Industries, Mines and Dispossession of Indigenous People: the Case of Chotariapur', in Fernandes, W., and Thukral, E. G., eds., *Development, Displacement and Rehabilitation*, New Delhi: Indian Social Institute.

CERNEA, M. M. (1988a) *Involuntary Resettlement in Development Projects. Policy Guidelines in World Bank Financed Projects*, World Bank Technical Paper No. 80, Washington, DC, 1988.

—— (1988b) 'Involuntary Resettlement and Development', *Finance and Development*, No. 9, September.

——(1989) 'Metropolitan Development and Compulsory Population Relocation. Policy Issues and Project Experience, Regional Development Dialogue', 10(4).

—— (1990a) 'From Unused Social Knowledge to Policy Creation: The Case of Involuntary Resettlement', Development Discussion Paper No. 342, May, Harvard University, Harvard Institute for International Development, Cambridge.

—— (1990b) 'Population Displacement and Water Resources Development: Current Practice, Issues and Policy Responses', paper presented at the Third Expert Group Workshop on the River/Lake Basin Approaches to Environmentally Sound Management of Water Resources, Otsu, Japan, February.

CHAO, L. (1990) 'State Plans New Rules for Dam Resettlement', *China Daily*, No. 2632, January 4.

CHRISTENSEN, H. (1982) *Survival Strategies for and by Camp Refugees: Report on an Exploratory Sociological Field Study in Somalia*, UNRISD Report No. 82:3, Geneva, United Nations.

CLARKE, L. (1989) 'Internally Displaced Persons: Framing the Issues', Centre for Policy Analysis and Research on Refugee Issues, Washington, DC.

CLAY, J. W. (1986) 'Research Report: Refugees Flee Ethiopia's Collectivization', *Cultural Survival Quarterly*, 10(2), 1986.

CLAY, J. W., STEINGRABER, S., and NIGGLI, P. (1988) *The Spoils of Famine. Ethiopian Policy and Peasant Agriculture*, Cultural Survival, Cambridge, Mass.

CLARK, L. (1988) 'Internal Refugees — The Hidden Half', in *World Refugee Survey — 1988 in Review*.

DE WET, C. (1991) '*Involuntary Resettlement as Imposed Transformation*', in Cernea, M. and Guggenheim, S., eds., *Anthropological Approaches to Involuntary Resettlement: Policy, Practice, and Theory*, Boulder, Colorado Westview Press (forthcoming).

DHAGAMWAR, V. (1989) 'Rehabilitation: Policy and Institutional Changes Required', in Fernandes, W., and Thukral, E. G., eds. *Development, Displacement and Rehabilitation*, New Delhi: Indian Social Institute.

DOWNING, T. and KUSHNER, G., eds. (1988) *Human Rights and Tribal People*, Cambridge, Cultural Survival.

THE GEORGETOWN DECLARATION ON HEALTH CARE FOR DISPLACED PERSONS AND REFUGEES (1988) Georgetown University, Washington, DC.

FAHIM, H. (1988) *Egyptian Nubians: Resettlement and Years of Coping*, Salt Lake City, University of Utah Press.

GUGGENHEIM, S. (1991) 'Development and the Dynamics of Displacement', paper presented at the Workshop on Rehabilitation of Displaced Persons, Bangalore, India, December.

HANSEN, A. (1990) 'Long-Term Consequences of Two African Refugee Settlement Strategies', paper presented at the meetings of the Society for Applied Anthropology, York, United Kingdom, March.

HANSEN, A and OLIVER-SMITH, A., eds. (1982) *Involuntary Migration and Resettlement*, Boulder, Colorado, Westview Press.

HARRELL-BOND, B. E. (1986) *Imposing Aid: Emergency Assistance to Refugees*, New York, Oxford University Press, 1986.

KEELY, C. B. (1988) *Foreword to The Georgetown Declaration on Health Care for Displaced Persons and Refugees*, Georgetown University, 1988.

KELLER, S. L. (1975) *Uprooting and Social Change*, New Delhi, Manohar Book Service.

KESMANEE, C. (1988) 'Hill Tribe Relocation Policy in Thailand', *Cultural Survival Quarterly*, 12(4).

KREIMER, A. (1989) 'Disasters, Sustainability, and Development: A Look to the 1990s', paper presented at the World Bank Colloquium on Disasters, June 1989.

MAHAPATRA, L. K. (1983) 'Development for Whom?' Paper presented at the International Congress for Anthropological and Ethnographic Sciences, Vancouver.

McCOLM, R. B. (1989) 'The World's Unwanted', *The Wall Street Journal*, September 28.

MERMEL, T. W. (1990) 'World Bank's Share of Worldwide Dam Construction', in Le Moigne, G., Barghouti, S. and Plusquellec, H., eds., *Dam Safety and the Environment*, World Bank Technical Paper No. 115, Washington, DC.

MORNA, C. L. (1990) 'Refugees Return to the Farm', *African Farmer*, 4, July.

PAUL, J. C. N. (1988) 'International Development Agencies, Human Rights and Humane Development Projects', in *Denver Journal of International Law and Politics*, vol. 17, No. 1.

—— (1991) *Rural Development, Human Rights and Constitutional Orders in Sub-Saharan Africa* (forthcoming).

RAJAGOPALAN, V. (1989) 'Policy and Planning in Involuntary Resettlement', *The Bank's World*, No. 9, September.

SALEM-MURDOCK, MUNEERA (1989) *Arabs and Nubians in New Halfa*, University of Utah Press, Salt Lake City.

SCUDDER, T. (1981) 'What it Means to be Dammed', *Engineering and Science*, Pasadena, Vol.54, No. 4.

SCUDDER, T, and COLSON, E. (1982) 'From Welfare to Development: A Conceptual Framework for the Analysis of Dislocated People', in Hansen, A., and Oliver-Smith, A., *Involuntary Migration and Resettlement*, Boulder, Colorado, Westview Press.

SHIHATA, I. F. I. (1988) 'The World Bank and Human Rights: An Analysis of the Legal Issues and the Record of Achievements', *Denver Journal of International Law and Politics*, vol. 17, No. 1.

—— (1991) 'Some Legal Aspects of Involuntary Population Displacement', in Cernea, M. M. and Guggenheim, S. E., eds., *Anthropological Approaches to Involuntary Resettlement: Policy, Practice and Theory*, Boulder, Colorado: Westview Press (forthcoming).

SOEPARTOMO and TJIPTOHANDOJO, P. (1988) 'Comparison between Predicted and Observed Environmental Impacts in Saguling Reservoir', in CIGB-ICOLD, *Sixteenth International Congress on Large Dams*, vol. 1, San Francisco, June.

WORLD BANK (1989) 'Operational Directive 8.50: Emergency Recovery Assistance', November.

—— (1990) 'Operational Directives 4.30: Involuntary Resettlement', June.

ZETTER, R. W. (1988) 'Refugees and Refugee Studies: A Label and an Agenda', *Journal of Refugee Studies*, vol. 1, No. 1.

—— (1990) 'Labeling Refugees: Forming and Transforming An Identity'. Paper prepared for the Program in International Cooperation in Africa, North-Western University, Illinois, February.

ZOLBERG, A. R., SUHRKE, A., and AGUAYO, S. (1989) *Escape from Violence. Conflict and the Refugee Crisis in the Developing World*, New York, Oxford University Press.

MS received February 1990; revised MS received October 1990.

* The present paper has been prepared during the author's work as Visiting Scholar at Harvard University in 1989–1990, on leave from the World Bank. Grateful thanks are expressed to both institutions for their support. The views and interpretations expressed in this study are those of the author and should not necessarily be attributed to the institutions with which he is associated. In preparing this paper, I have directly benefited from discussions with D. Maybury-Lewis, V. Rajagopalan, I. Shihata, J. W. Stanton, B. Harrell-Bond, N. Yalman, R. Cernea, Ch. Keely, S. Guggenheim, J. Clay, R. Zetter and from the comments of two anonymous reviewers. Grateful thanks are expressed to all of them. An earlier and shorter version of this paper was presented at the Georgetown University Symposium on Internally Displaced People (October 1989, Washington, DC).

[20]

Geoforum, Vol. 19, No. 4, pp. 433–445, 1988
Printed in Great Britain

0016–7185/88$3.00 + 0.00

Government Policies and International Migration of Skilled Workers in Sub-Saharan Africa

WILLIAM T. S. GOULD,* Liverpool, U.K.

Abstract: Since a central concern of the geography of international migration is to consider how and why stocks and flows of migrants are variable from country to country, the study of skilled international migration must address policies of individual governments towards local and foreign skilled workers. These policies are most evident in immigration and emigration legislation, regulations and practice, but also, less directly but often of more fundamental significance, in policies in education, manpower planning and towards wages and salaries. In Sub-Saharan Africa there is a wide range of experience of recent skilled international migration, driven by direct and indirect policies pursued by individual governments since independence. At an intercontinental scale the deleterious effects of the global division of labour have not merely been passively accepted; within the continent new patterns of skilled-labour migration have been created by increasingly differentiated economic performance and political relationships. A case study of Kenya, a country of small current net immigration of skilled workers, is used to specify some of the processes that establish the relationships between immigration and emigration policies, and how these have been mediated by conditions for skilled workers. The concluding section of this paper sets the general experience and that of the Kenyan case study in the wider context of the role of the state as a factor in the geography of skilled international migration in the Third World.

Introduction

A long-standing and unreconciled dichotomy in migration theory exists between explanations of movement that emphasize the paramountcy of macro-structural and impersonal factors on the one hand, and those that emphasize behavioural and individual factors on the other. The dichotomy is partly a matter of scale. It is clearly important for studies of internal migration, where individual choice is not normally constrained by controls imposed by the state, and especially by international boundaries, yet some recent studies of internal population redistribution [e.g. CLARKE *et al.* (1985)] have brought the role of the state firmly into the geographical analysis of migration. In studies of international migration where political boundaries as a control on movement has been much reduced, as in Western Europe, the debate over structural vs behavioural explanations of flows retains an academic vigour. However, for many countries, particularly in Africa but also in some other parts of the Third World, movement into and out of countries is now subject to more formal controls than it had been even in the recent past as countries have developed their own policies of control for immigration and emigration. Moreover, they have been more anxious to enforce them. Geographical analysis of international migration in the Third World needs therefore to devote more systematic attention to the role of the state as a major force in structuring the nature and patterning of movement.

The role of the state has particular force for the international migration of skilled workers. Individually they are more likely than unskilled workers to be required to have formal documentation for emigration and immigration; collectively, since their

* Department of Geography, The University, Liverpool L69 3BX, U.K.

movement has considerable political and economic impact at source and destination, they will be more obviously a matter of public concern. In addition skilled workers need not only formal documentation for themselves but also for their family, and they may also travel with some possessions. Therefore, they are much more likely to use formal channels and to be subject to formal controls established by individual states. While illegal and/or undocumented international migrations have been increasing almost everywhere, these have mostly concerned unskilled workers in Africa (ADEPOJU, 1983).

The literature on skilled international migration generally recognizes how migration policies and changes in these policies at source and destination have affected the migration of skilled workers from the Third World to the Developed Countries in the 'brain drain'. But the brain drain is a spatially differentiated phenomenon affecting some Third World countries more than others, due in no small measure to the range of policies for emigration and immigration of the Third World countries themselves. While individual Third World countries are somehow locked into a dependency associated with an intensifying global division of labour, there exists the possibility of some variation in policies to structure movements of skilled workers. SHAW (1986), in reviewing recent developments in approaches to the analysis of the foreign policies of African States, has shown how they have followed Latin American states by rejecting simplistic passive reactions to dependency. They have moved towards individually appropriate and differentiated positions in their relations with each other, with the World Powers and with the global economy generally. Such a perspective is as valid for migration policies as for other aspects of international relations. BÖHNING (1984, p. 32) explicitly places international migration within that wider context of interdependence between states, but argues that "interdependence does not deprive states of their inherent logic nor borders of their essentially excluding function". To identify exclusion emphasizes the negative aspects of migration policy, but the thrust of his argument can apply equally to positive and more permissive aspects of both immigration and emigration. Each state can and does impose its authority on immigration into and out of its jurisdiction.

In Sub-Saharan Africa (SSA) the importance of skilled international migration is considerable and growing. It involves brain drain movements out of the continent and also immigration of highly-skilled workers, from the Developed World in particular. It also involves movements of skilled workers between one African country and another. A recent extensive bibliographic review of intra-African migrations of skilled workers has shown that, despite severe problems of inadequate data to measure this phenomenon accurately, these have been growing rapidly (GOULD, 1985a). Governments are becoming increasingly sensitive to migrations of skilled workers and have formulated policies that seek to manage them in various ways.

This paper examines the ways in which national policies for emigration and immigration, each considered in separate sections, have affected the nature and patterning of the international migration of skilled workers beyond and within SSA. They are preceded by a preparatory section on the indirect effects of aspects of national development strategies on international migration. Thus, the discussion responds to Charles Keely's strictures for the Middle East that studies of international migration lack context to an unacceptable extent (KEELY, 1984; GOULD, 1985b). It is then complemented by a review of recent policies in one country, Kenya, and the concluding section returns to general issues of the role of the state in international migration to show that the direct and indirect roles of government in the international migration of skilled labour in SSA have been increasing and likely to remain of major significance.

Policies for international migration may be conceptualized in various ways. WEINER (1985), for example, has elaborated a 5 × 5 matrix setting a continuum of five types of entry rules (unrestricted, promotional, selective, unwanted, prohibited) against a similar five-fold division of exit rules (prohibited, selective, permissive, promotional, expulsion). AHOOJA-PATEL (1974) differentiated between restorative, restrictive and preventive measures. Other typologies, e.g. based on space and time (GOULD and PROTHERO, 1975) or historical sequence (PROTHERO, 1968), may also facilitate the setting of a conceptual basis for the analysis.

Indirect Effects on the Migrations of Skilled Workers

International migrations of skilled workers generally reflect differences in levels of economic development and job availability between countries. While specific policies for immigration and emigration attempt to control flows directly, they may do little more than

Geoforum/Volume 19 Number 4/1988 435

validate the exchanges that might have arisen without formal control; skilled workers moving to where appropriate job opportunities are available. SSA as a whole has experienced a dismal economic performance in the last quarter-century, but there is a considerable range in national experience. Whether based on agricultural activity, as in the Ivory Coast or Kenya, or on mineral wealth, as in Nigeria, Gabon or Botswana, some countries have improved their economies relatively if not absolutely. Others have experienced major economic collapse, for example Zambia as a result of severe falls in the world price of copper, and in other, rather more numerous cases, economic collapse has been precipitated by severe internal political and military disruption. The pattern of economic activity in the late 1980s is not as it was 25–30 years ago at independence, and flows of skilled labour, within the continent as well as into it and out of it, have been responsive to the changes. Such a view is fundamental to both neoclassical and neo-Marxist explanations of migration, and need not be elaborated here, even if, as is demonstrated in later sections of this paper, governments impose specific controls that distort the free flow of labour.

There are, however, more specific aspects of development where government policies can indirectly affect the supply of skilled workers, and the most important of these concern manpower and training policies, targetted primarily at the internal labour market. Independent African states, aware of the severely constrained stock of educated people in the colonial period, have devoted enormous amounts of scarce and often declining resources to educational expansion, in some instances allocating over 25% of their budgets to the education sector (*ca* 7% in the U.K.). Such high proportions are necessary for purely demographic reasons, given the very youthful age structures (GOULD, 1986), but are also felt to be necessary to sustain economic growth. Despite massive expansions in educational attainment of its formally enumerated labour force (Figure 1) (PSACHAROPOULOS and ARRIAGADA, 1986), current levels of enrolment in higher education, which are themselves highly variable from country to country (Figure 2), are also lower than elsewhere. Levels of enrolments in higher education and, by implication, the supply of skilled workers seemed to bear a closer relationship to GNP in the late 1970s [Figure 3(b)] than they did in the early 1960s [Figure 3(a)]. This is an inevitable consequence of the forging of a more direct link between higher education and the manpower requirements of the economy. However, it is also clear that the relative size of the higher-education sector changed between these periods. Enrolments in higher education have everywhere risen, but have been responsive to changing economic circumstances, with larger than average expansions in countries like

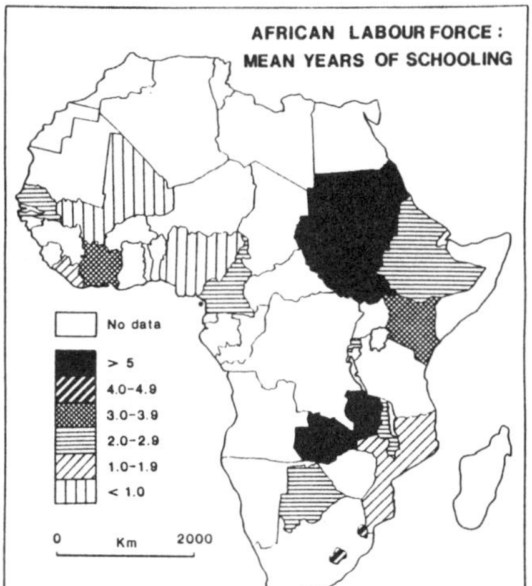

Figure 1. African labour force in Sub-Saharan Africa: mean years of schooling (*ca* 1982).

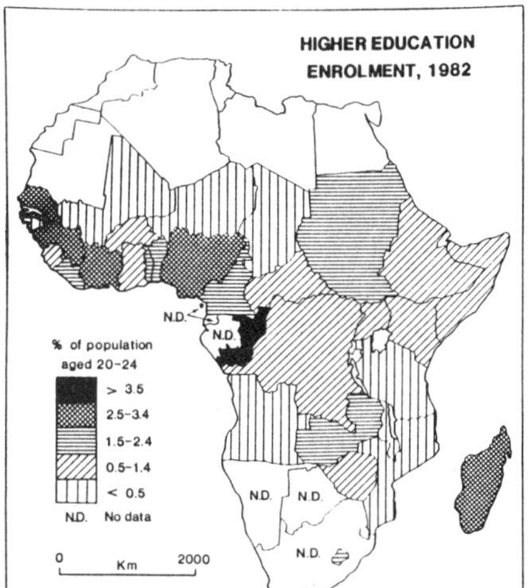

Figure 2. Higher-education enrolment in Sub-Saharan Africa, 1982.

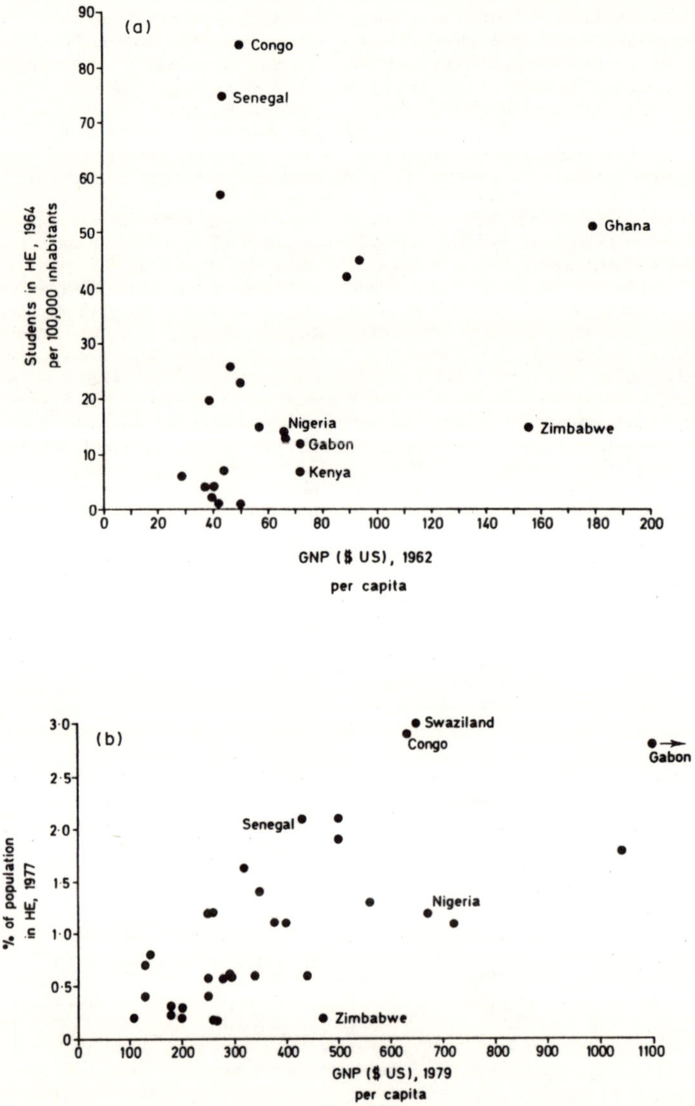

Figure 3. Higher-education enrolment and GNP in Sub-Saharan Africa: (a) early 1960s, and (b) late 1970s.

Gabon and Nigeria, both importers of labour, and smaller than average expansions in others such as Ghana and Uganda. In the latter, where there has been severe economic decline, universities have not contracted, but have maintained a steady output of graduates on to a declining market for their skills.

Manpower planning has been a prominent feature of economic management in most countries of SSA since independence. In its early days there was a fairly rigid approach to manage enrolments in education to produce *X* doctors or *Y* engineers per year. Estimates of requirements were based on what have turned out to be overoptimistic predictions of economic growth, and economies have been unable to absorb the outputs of schools or training programmes, causing either a downward escalation of individual job prospects or conversely an upward escalation of entry conditions for any given job, especially in the public service, evident manifestations of the 'Diploma Disease' (DORE, 1976). The problems of maintaining a given supply of graduates with specific qualifications are further exacerbated by the fact that typically as many students are in universities and colleges out of the country, mostly in Europe and North America, as are being educated in local universities, and engaged in courses over which government has no control (KING, 1985). Manpower planning of the traditional kind is unable to manage to match the skills needed with skilled workers available. The door is then open for emigration or immigration of workers.

The problems of manpower planning have been shown to be particularly acute throughout SSA for technical and engineering personnel. Industries have shown a low demand for skilled engineers, needing skills of a middle-order rather than those of high-level engineering graduates, yet expansion has been disproportionately of the latter rather than technicians. Furthermore where high-level skills were needed, associated with new technology, these tended to be imported with the hiring of expatriate engineers (BENNELL, 1986). Nor could the situation improve even with the more flexible approaches to manpower planning dependent on skill substitutabilities that had emerged by the 1980s (CASTLEY and ALFTHAN, 1986; YOUDI and HINCHCLIFFE, 1985). National systems of supply of engineers could not be closed, and international migration occurred at an increasing rate.

ABDIN *et al.* (1983) argue that the private sector, generally much smaller than the public sector in SSA, acts rather differently from it with respect of skill acquisition, and this too can affect international migration of skilled workers. Individual employees, whether technical or administrative, tend to be trained fairly narrowly in the ways of the company so that they are not easily transferable from one company to the other. Multinational companies (MNCs) can make up skill shortages by importing specialists from subsidiaries elsewhere, either parent-country nationals, as is the predominant pattern with European and Japanese MNCs, or third-country nationals (TCNs), more characteristic of U.S.-based MNCs. These TCN staff may in a few cases be foreign Africans, but the majority are drawn from Developed Countries. Skilled foreigners are much more likely to be found in African countries with considerable involvement of MNCs, generally the richer and more developed countries (e.g. the Ivory Coast and Nigeria) or with major mining concerns (e.g. Zambia and Botswana), than in those countries, such as Tanzania or Ethiopia, where a large component of commercial activity is undertaken by parastatal organizations or local firms. Institutional and, in the case of private businesses, family considerations militate against the hiring of expatriate specialists, even where there is adequate commercial justification.

Governments can affect individual decisions of skilled citizens who might leave the country or of foreigners who might be attracted to the country by their policies towards wage differentials. Where wages policies, for egalitarian political reasons, have narrowed the very broad span of enumeration inherited from the colonial period, the salaries of skilled workers will rise relatively slowly or even, as in Tanzania, be reduced. In other countries with less direct government involvement in the labour market the wages of skilled workers may be allowed to find their own level, often an internationally competitive salary, so that there the net effect can be a widening differential between the skilled and unskilled which can be a disincentive for skilled workers to seek a job elsewhere. Conversely, it can serve to attract skilled workers especially from those countries where high-income earners are either not given rises or are very heavily taxed.

Internal salary differentials of skilled workers are also linked to the extent to which their qualifications are internationally recognized. Those countries whose qualifications are widely recognized (e.g. by Commonwealth or international professional associations) also tend to be those with substantial salary incentives for the highly-skilled. While it is probably the case that there are too few emigrants from most African countries to have had a general effect on local salaries, this may have affected salary levels in the case of some professions in Ghana where many Ghanaians are working in Nigeria and elsewhere (ABDIN *et al.*, 1983, Chap. 8). A much more familiar effect of the international recognition of qualifications is to allow professionals to seek higher remuneration at the world level, whether they are Ugandan doctors in Saudi Arabia or Sengalese engineers in Canada.

National policies for education, manpower and wages are directed mainly towards internal labour markets as if they operated a closed system. Yet the systems are clearly not closed, though the extent of closure is highly variable. These and other economic and social policies pursued by governments can influence the emigration and immigration of skilled workers, and their effects cannot be relegated to an insignificant role in SSA.

Immigration Policies and Skilled Workers

Colonial governments were more interested in policies towards immigration than they were in policies for emigration. Skilled foreigners, whether as temporary residents on colonial service or on private-sector business or, in some colonies, as permanent settlers in rural or urban areas, were assumed to be necessary for development. Encouragement to immigration was most direct in the form of cheap land and favourable trading incentives for settlers in the colonies of Eastern and Southern Africa. This was not without problems or controversies, such as in the attitudes of the African colonies to Asian skilled artisans, where the settler interest emphasized control rather than outright encouragement, with prohibitions (with a few exceptions) on land ownership for Asians in Kenya and the Rhodesias. In West Africa, where there was very little land alienation or permanent settlement by Europeans, the colonies were less directly concerned to encourage immigration. There were major migrations of Africans across colonial boundaries that predated the establishment of these boundaries and included skilled workers in the informal sector, such as traders or builders, skill being defined in terms of individual capabilities and experience rather than modern sector and formal skills (MABOGUNJE, 1972). But these migrations could not be directly controlled through immigration policies, given the long, unpatrolled and often undemarcated boundaries that usually bore little relationship to traditional established patterns of movement.

With the coming of independence and the assumption of sovereignty by fiercely nationalistic states, policies sought to promote a sense of national identity for political as well as economic reasons. Inevitably this involved a growth of formal immigration controls, with passports and visas being required by foreign nationals who enter at formal ports of entry, affecting skilled workers rather more than unskilled workers. In the first instance immigration controls were for political and security reasons, but rapidly began to be used to effect the national composition of the labour force.

Economic control was also exercised through work permits issued by the Ministries of Economic Development or Labour rather than by immigration authorities. Policies towards the issue—and withdrawal—of work permits have been a principal factor in the extent and nature of skilled immigration. They were formulated in the wider context of 'Africanization' or 'indigenization' of the labour force, with preference given to a country's own citizens and generally reducing the numerical and economic prominence of foreign labour. They were supported by the rapid expansion programmes to train citizens to gradually, sometimes not so gradually, replace foreigners. Programmes of localization were first developed in the early 1960s when the economies of many countries were booming in the first few years after independence, and so the demand for skilled workers was sufficient to accommodate foreign as well as local people. By the end of the 1960s, however, economies were faltering but supply of trained citizens was still expanding, and feelings had grown against the continuing presence of foreigners in the workforce.

There was considerable direction by governments through expulsions (see below) as well as by tightening control of residence and work permits for immigrants. These controls continued with increasing severity into the more difficult economic conditions of the 1980s. In some countries individual foreigners require residence permits, obtainable with the assistance of the employer. In Tanzania, for example, immigration is regulated through residence permits rather than work permits, and there are three classes of permit according to job status, each issued for a period not exceeding 3 years and renewable for a period not exceeding 2 years (UNITED NATIONS, 1982, p. 45). Work permits, on the other hand, are not usually granted to individuals but to government departments and private companies who must make the case for such a permit, having first ascertained that there are no local people available for a particular job. There may also be a training requirement in the granting of the work permit, the foreign permit-holder being required to train a national who can then take over the job within a specified time.

With control of residence and work permits governments clearly operate as the principal gatekeeper and can keep the level of immigration below that felt to be appropriate by individual private companies and by some ministries. Ministries of Education, for example, are often anxious to maintain a stock of foreign teachers to maintain the quantitative expansion and quality of instruction in the schools system. A balance has to be set between the political need to place local workers into skilled positions and the economic need to have the best available people doing a particular job. Where the balance is struck varies with the ideological perspective of the government. In neocolonial, capitalist societies the economic imperative is the stronger, and work permits are the more easily obtained. For example, there were in 1985 more than twice as many Frenchmen in the Ivory Coast as there were at independence in 1960.

A system of work and residence permits also has a major effect on the geographical origins of workers who are recruited. Once a work permit for a particular job has been issued, the recruitment process reverts to the employer. For a local subsidiary of an MNC this will probably mean a transfer of an employee of the parent company. Senior technicians and managers in MNCs tend to come from a major Western country, usually that of the parent company. Otherwise the company may recruit in its home base but outside the existing staff. Subsidiaries of MNCs are increasingly managed by local staff, but most transfers are still of Europeans and North Americans, even though the possibility of international transfer of Africans from one subsidiary to another may be available. This is also true for government departments, for example where recruitment of foreign teachers tends to be in London or Paris rather than Lagos, Accra, Abidjan or Nairobi. While there are many statements of intent by governments about the value of promoting the employment of foreign Africans in the formal sector, in practice the operation of a work permit system would seem often to undermine such a stated intention. Nowhere is there evidence of any formal or even informal policy of preferring foreign Africans rather than non-Africans. 'Africanization' has been rigorously interpreted as 'localization', based on national rather than racial criteria.

Foreign African skilled workers are more likely to be in small firms in the 'informal' sector or in self-employment, but, almost by definition, this must be on a small scale to avoid formal compliance with residence or work permit regulations. Most of those Ghanaians who were expelled from Nigeria in 1983–1984 were in Nigeria without formal work permits, even though many were skilled workers in industry and service occupations. Others, however, were employed by large organizations or by government departments. (It is estimated that there were 35,000 Ghanaian teachers in Nigeria in 1982.) They had a formally accepted permit and were in general more skilled than those without formal permits, and for the most part were not expelled (ALUKO, 1985).

The irony of the Ghanaian expulsions from Nigeria is that both countries are members of the Economic Community of West African States (ECOWAS), a regional economic organization that has free movement of labour as one of its objectives. "In July, 1980, eight (including Nigeria) of the ECOWAS members ratified a protocol on the free movement of persons. One of the provisions of the protocol is that citizens of one ECOWAS country have the right to enter, reside and establish business in another ECOWAS country" (UNITED NATIONS, 1982, p. 44). Nigeria, the largest and economically strongest member of ECOWAS, is a principal destination for skilled workers from the other members, but its own political instability and current chronic economic problems have combined to make foreigners economic scapegoats, as has happened elsewhere in Africa.

One further key issue in immigration policies that is particularly apparent in SSA concerns the criteria for granting work permits and for recruiting individuals. As generally with employment in Africa, there has been an overreliance on formal educational and professional qualifications at the expense of required skills, competence and experience. This exaggerates the tendency to recruit Europeans and North Americans rather than foreign Africans, for they will normally have much longer periods of formal schooling and training of a better quality, real or perceived, with internationally transferable professional accreditation. The "paper-qualifications syndrome" can be as far-reaching in its effects on international labour markets as it is on internal labour markets (OXENHAM, 1984).

Despite the advice of multilateral agencies like UNCTAD and ILO to liberalize national immigration policies for foreign workers within Africa and to encourage mutually beneficial exchanges of skilled workers (UNDP, 1982; UNCTAD, 1983), policies for the immigration of skilled workers have been largely controlled by availability of work permits and have tended to invoke criteria that satisfy the short-term political objectives of minimizing unemployment of local educated job-seekers. In practice governments and private companies invoke recruitment criteria that maintain the patterns of international migration established during the colonial period, perpetuating dependence on the North and the established international division of labour.

Emigration Policies and Skilled Workers

Mass expulsion of foreigners has been a widely discussed feature of international migration in SSA in the last 25 years. Those expelled have been members of ethnic or national groups engaged in middle-level occupations such as trading, as in the case of the Nigerian Yoruba and Hausa expelled after the Ghanaian Aliens Compliance Order of 1969 (PIEL, 1971) or urban entrepreneurs and artisans, as in the case of the Ugandan Asians (GOULD and PROTHERO, 1981). While there were many, though not the majority, Ghanaians expelled from Nigeria in 1983 in white-collar occupations (BRYDON, 1985), the most highly skilled Ghanaians, many employed in government service with formal contracts and valid visas and work permits, were not normally directly affected. In the longer term, emigration of foreign skilled workers has been affected by less conspicuous policy and administrative decisions where contracts or trading licences are not renewed or residence permits are not extended.

More important in the context of this paper are the policies that governments have invoked towards the emigration of their own skilled nationals. Sudan has experienced considerable emigration of teachers, doctors and civil servants into the Middle East immigration system, a loss that has not been actively discouraged by restrictive emigration policies (BIRKS and SINCLAIR, 1980). A recent ILO–UNHCR study suggests that the emigration of skilled professionals has provided job opportunities for new Sudanese graduates and skilled refugees to Sudan which would otherwise not have been available (ILO–UNHCR, 1984). However, apart from Sudan with its traditional links with the Islamic World, the countries of SSA have not contributed large numbers of skilled or unskilled workers to the Middle East migration system through bilateral agreements and formal recruitment, in sharp contrast to the increasing involvement of countries and governments of South and East Asia. While individual African professionals are employed in the Gulf States, many of these have been recruited in Europe or North America. African countries have not become directly involved in promoting the emigration of their skilled professionals, and have generally adopted a fairly passive but permissive attitude to individual emigrants. Furthermore, bilateral agreements between African governments are rare. Cameroun signed a bilateral agreement with Gabon for the export of manpower in 1977, and permits recruitment for work abroad provided contracts are approved by the Ministry of Labour (UNITED NATIONS, 1982, p. 47). However, as in the case of agreements in Southern Africa between South African mine recruitment organizations and sending countries (TAYLOR, 1986), the agreements deal exclusively with recruitment and conditions of unskilled workers.

The aspect of emigration of skilled nationals in which governments have intervened most directly is in policies towards training and further education abroad. The considerable availability of scholarships to study and train abroad, from within and outside each country, often through bilateral and multilateral aid programmes, has led to the situation identified above where for many countries of SSA more students in higher education are studying abroad than at home. They acquire not only highly specialized skills for which there is no in-country training, but are also enrolled in general courses for which there are local equivalents. While the possibility of permanent emigration to work in the country where the education is acquired is readily admitted, and is a major factor in the brain drain to Europe and North America, it has not yet reached a level where governments are brought to try to stem the loss of skills by reducing the numbers going abroad for training. Despite apparent oversupply, the earnings of skilled professionals are still high in most countries of SSA, and return home remains an attractive economic option for many Africans, despite the professional and financial opportunities for skilled professionals in the North. The incentives to return are progressively reduced by continuing economic stagnation and falling living standards and quality of life, even for the highest-income earners in countries starved of foreign exchange and imported goods which high local salaries might purchase.

A recent trend in policies towards students abroad has been to diversify the range of countries to which they are sent, and particularly increase enrolments in other Third World, including African, countries. Students studying in these countries are more likely to return than if they were in Europe or North America, if only because they would be unlikely to be granted work permits for reasons discussed above. Schemes for increasing international student mobility within the Commonwealth now promote courses in countries like India, Malaysia and Nigeria rather than in Britain, Canada or Australia, taking advantage of the international accreditation promoted by Commonwealth-based professional associations as well as considerably lower costs of living, but without loss of learning or skill acquisition (BACCHUS, 1986). Although the development of intra-African student flows has been encouraged by the UN and other multilateral agencies, progress has been very limited in the face of strident nationalism within Africa and the continuing attraction of universities and other institutions in the Developed World. South–South co-operation in education has considerable potential, but achievements have generally been limited.

Where students are educated abroad, there is the increased danger of them finding work, permanently or temporarily, in the host country and therefore adding to the brain drain, at least in the short term. Some may independently return home after some time, but in general, once settled employment is found and roots put down, return becomes progressively more difficult. Since 1983, however, the Intergovernmental Committee on Migration (ICM), supported financially by the EEC, has pioneered a project to promote the return of skilled migrants in industrialized countries to their own African countries (ICM, 1987). Between 1983 and early 1987 they had had over 1000 applications for consideration and 550 vacant posts intimated to ICM by African countries, and had placed over 300 skilled migrants. Most of these (34% were women) had been in employment in industrialized countries, using their high educational qualifications (41% had a master's degree or doctorate, 26% a bachelor's degree). They are in a wide range of professions, rather more in the public sector than in private industry, but mostly in service and business sectors, with less than one in seven in manufacturing industry. The return of 300 skilled workers is small in absolute terms, but the project suggests that more systematic concern for return migration and the means to implement it could significantly reduce the rate of permanent loss of manpower.

Taken as a whole, official attitudes towards the emigration of skilled workers in SSA have been rather passive, as if this did not constitute a major issue for national development. As long as numbers remain small, it seems more appropriate to focus on policies for immigration rather than for emigration, and, for those countries where the numbers of skilled emigrants has risen rapidly, e.g. Ghana or Uganda, severe internal economic problems may persuade governments that at least in the short term the loss of skilled workers can assist political stability and provide some badly needed foreign exchange from their remittances.

The Case of Kenya

Kenya has not been greatly affected by international migration in recent years. Relatively few Kenyans are living out of the country and relatively few foreigners live in Kenya. Though numbers are particularly difficult to quantify, there is certainly a small positive net migration balance. The Kenya census of 1979 recorded 157,301 people who had been born outside Kenya. Tabulations of nationality (of non-citizens) and ethnic group (of citizens) record 71,818 non-Kenyan 'Africans', 46,046 non-Kenyan 'Asians' (separately identified from 'Kenyan Asians'), 35,456 'Europeans' (separately identified from 'Kenyan Europeans') and 20,255 'Arabs' (separately identified from 'Kenyan Arabs'), who, with 'others', totalled 183,818 non-Kenyans in a population of over 15 million. Furthermore, the foreign population is disproportionately concentrated in urban areas, particularly Nairobi. Over 75% of non-Kenyan Europeans and Asians were in Nairobi or Mombasa, and over 50% of the 'other non-Kenyans', mostly from other African countries, were in Nairobi. Since there are no large populations of unskilled foreign workers in rural areas, as is characteristic of many other countries in Africa, it is clear that the immigrant population is disproportionately skilled. Though numbers are small, the range of experience is considerable, and Kenya offers an appropriate case study for an examination of several of the principal issues surrounding the emigration and immigration of skilled labour both within and beyond Africa in the public and private sectors of the economy.

Immigration of skilled workers

The semi-official *Kenya News Digest*, reported in February/March 1987, that:

> . . . more than 23,000 work permits have been issued by the government to non-citizens since 1981. Most of these have gone to foreign investors and their staff, but have included engineers and managers of Kenya-based firms.

'Africanization', i.e. Kenyanization, programmes have been a prominent feature of employment policies since independence, and were major factors in ensuring that Kenyan citizens achieved top positions in both the private and the public sector, as foreign Europeans and non-Kenyan Asians were squeezed out of the labour market (ROTHSCHILD, 1970). The process continues and is given considerable prominence in the recommendations of the most recent Presidential Commission on Unemployment, the Wanjigi Report (KENYA GOVERNMENT, 1983, pars 264–267), even though the scope for solving the unemployment problem through Kenyanization is now small, despite these 23,000 work permits, for unemployment is concentrated among those with low levels of skill, qualifications and experience.

In the past the skilled expatriate has come from Europe or North America, seconded from or transferred by his parent MNC to a local subsidiary for a limited time, or hired directly by a local company or a government department. With increasing intra-African mobility, however, the possibility exists for attracting foreign Africans as 'Africanization', if not Kenyanization, to take advantage of Kenya's very considerable attractiveness for them. This is manifest, for example, in Nairobi now being a headquarters for international (e.g. U.N. Environment Programme) or African regional agencies, and thus the work place of large numbers of foreign African civil servants. Increasingly too it is the regional headquarters of several MNCs operating in Africa. Kenya has become attractive to 'economic' migrants from neighbouring countries, such as Tanzania or Zambia, whose economies are in serious difficulty or have collapsed altogether. This is greatly exacerbated where there is political repression and security difficulties, as in Uganda, such that the distinction between an economic migrant and political refugee is often difficult to make in practice. Kenya has certainly attracted many highly qualified Ugandans over the last 15 years of severe political strife and economic devastation in Uganda. But neither Tanzanians nor Ugandans, despite historic links and common language and economic and institutional backgrounds, have been given any privileged status; indeed many claim they have been discriminated against in the job market and that discrimination intensifies during periods of recurring political tensions between Kenya and her neighbours.

Formally recognised refugees have fared no better. A recent *Study of Employment among Educated Refugees from the Horn of Africa*, prepared for the World University Service of the U.K., states that:

> Refugees seeking employment in Kenya face a number of serious hurdles. In a survey in 1981, UNHCR estimated that, of more than 5,000 refugees registered in Kenya, those who were not students faced 50% unemployment. Refugees with education face problems as do those with few or no skills (WALLACE, 1986, p. 50).

She reports pressure on organizations and firms who employ skilled refugees to Kenyanize, and argues that efforts to establish this group in self-employment is a preferable option to finding a modern-sector job.

Clearly employment policies as pursued by the Kenyan Government do not give preference to foreign Africans—they are no more welcome that Europeans, though this is not formalized in any sense. Despite considerable potential for employing skilled Africans where local skills are in short supply, there is still a strong bias towards immigration of employees of MNCs and of those hired by European and North American employment agencies.

Emigration of skilled Kenyans

By the standards of recent African experience, Kenya's economic performance has been relatively successful, with fairly continuous growth in modern-sector job opportunities in rural and particularly in urban areas (GOULD, 1986). However, when placed against a background of annual population growth rates currently in excess of 4%, improvement has been less exceptional. Since independence in 1963, however, there have been very rapid expansions in education at all levels, to the extent that there seems to be a problem of educated unemployment, particularly for primary and secondary school-leavers with modest achievements in public examinations. Nevertheless, there is still a shortage of highly-skilled workers, and work permits are issued to non-nationals on the assumption that Kenyan citizens with appropriate qualifications or experience are not available to do these jobs.

A shortage of skilled labour nearly a quarter of a century after independence is due in no small measure to the tiny size of the African education system inherited from the colonial period. Although school and university enrolments have expanded massively, and as a result of Africanization programmes there has been permanent emigration of many non-citizens, notably Asians, the demand for highly-skilled labour has continued to outstrip supply, even though the gap is being progressively narrowed. Measures to increase the supply were implemented immediately at, or even before, independence. These included large public and private scholarship programmes for Kenyans, particularly to the U.S.A., a bias which continues in current scholarships. In 1979 the Ministry of Education estimated that there were 3500 Kenyan students in the U.S.A., with 700 in the U.K., 700 in India and 500 in Canada, the majority of whom are privately sponsored. Kenyans are studying in smaller numbers in a wide range of other countries, from 229 in the U.S.S.R. down to single figures elsewhere, Under the INTERAF Scholarship programme, administered by the Organization for African Unity there were 22 Kenyans in Nigeria, six in Ghana, six in Cameroun and three in Sudan and Zambia (KENYA GOVERNMENT, 1984). This is a minuscule number within Africa compared with those in Europe and North America. EISEMON (1986) estimated that in 1981 approximately 7000 Kenyan students were studying abroad, which compares with an enrolment of only 6200 undergraduates and 1800 post-graduates in Kenya's two universities in 1985.

Such continuing dependence on higher education overseas, and particularly in U.S.A., brings dangers of a brain-drain leakage due to the non-return of Kenyans after training (ODENYO, 1979). However, Kenya is probably less affected than many other Third World countries for both economic and political reasons. Jobs perceived to be appropriate and attractive are still available for returnees, and, despite occasional tensions, there are no major political constraints for returnees. In a relatively open economy such as Kenya's there is a range of modern consumer goods to be bought with fairly substantial salaries, so that return is certainly a more attractive proposition for the skilled person and his family than it might be for students from most other African countries. In addition, as ABDIN *et al.* (1983, Chap. 5) point out, the Kenyan Government has not pursued a strongly interventionist wages policy at the upper end of the salary scale. Salary levels in the public, and especially the private sectors, though lower than internationally competitive levels, remain sufficiently high to attract as well as retain skilled workers.

Nevertheless there are Kenyans living and working abroad, not only as international civil servants, for which Kenyans are well up to UN quotas, or representatives of the Kenyan Government or Kenyan firms, but as employees of foreign firms or on their own account. The numbers abroad are unknown, and almost certainly growing in number, but the extent to which they would consider themselves to be permanently or temporarily out of the country, whether as a matter of choice (e.g. by marrying a foreigner) or as a matter of personal or political dissatisfaction (e.g. there are certainly some political opponents of the present government though no officially recognized refugees) remains unresearched. Although Kenyans are eligible for assistance to return to Kenya, as elsewhere in Africa under programmes such as that offered by the ICM, the numbers involved have been small (GREY-JOHNSON, 1986). Perhaps of more long-term importance is the increasing integration of the Kenyan economy with the global economy and the mobility of skilled workers that occurs as a consequence of that involvement, as epitomized by an item in the *Daily Nation* (28 May 1987):

> Mr. Charles Muchene has returned to Price Waterhouse in Nairobi as an audit manager following a 27-month tour of duty with Price Waterhouse, Canada, under the firm's international exchange programme.

Conclusion: Policy Contradictions

Contemporary political and economic conditions in SSA generate international migration structures that set them apart from many aspects of international migration in other regions of the world. Many new, relatively small, but strongly nationalistic and anti-colonial states generate political circumstances that seem largely hostile to immigration of skilled workers, whether from other African countries or from the countries of the Developed World. However, economic conditions are difficult and in some countries deteriorating, and SSA as a whole is increasingly dependent on trade with and aid from Developed Countries, with all the implications that these bring for further integration of the region into the global division of labour through the internationalization of technology and production. Political factors inhibit international migration; economic factors promote it.

Policies of governments towards the immigration and emigration of skilled workers reflect these opposing factors. Direct policies of most countries have raised barriers to flows of migrants and to reduce the stocks of foreigners in order to advance the interests of the increasingly educated and skilled national labour force. Investments in education and an adherence to manpower planning, however imperfect and inflexble, in theory create conditions for an indigenous and productive labour force with only a minimal need for emigration of skilled nationals or immigration of skilled foreigners. However, in a majority of countries economic progress has been disappointing, and the demand for skilled workers is less than the local supply, and that mismatch may induce some skilled workers to seek job opportunities elsewhere in SSA or, where possible, outside Africa. By contrast, in those few countries of relatively strong economic growth the demand for skilled labour is enhanced by a secular growth in jobs that may outstrip the local skilled labour force. It is also enhanced by a greater integration into the world economic system and an introduction of new technologies that require technically experienced workers, usually drawn from Developed Countries where the new technologies have been established. Economic differentiation within Africa increases the pressure towards emigration from some countries and immigration from within and beyond SSA to others. Those countries where economic growth is strongest are also the countries which are most integrated into the world system and into which skilled migrants can be most easily absorbed without major political repercussions.

The indirect effects of general development policies on levels and types of immigration and emigration need to be weighed against direct migration policy directions for in many instances there have been contradictions between them, often resolved at an ideological level. The political economy of a state like Kenya, the Ivory Coast, Zambia or Nigeria is premissed on a continuing and growing involvement with the world economy, and a necessary price of that involvement must be immigration of some skilled workers, even though policies remain in force to minimize their number as much as possible. In other countries, including Tanzania, Zimbabwe and Ethiopia, efforts at self-sufficiency and limitations on the further penetration of MNCs give priority to political objectives, and are consistent with strong policies for restricting immigration of skilled workers, even if local labour is inexperienced or in short supply.

There is a wide divergence in practice between African countries. Despite apparent similarities in explicitly formulated policies for skilled migrants, the political and developmental context of each state sets the real limits to immigration and emigration. Approaches to the study of international migration that focus only on direct and formal policies to the exclusion of wider and less direct measures are seriously flawed. In an explicitly geographical sense, the changing patterns of national development within Africa are themselves major contributors to the changing patterns and structures of skilled migration within, into and out of the continent, and need to be central to contemporary geographical analyses.

The study of skilled international migration in SSA and in other areas of the Third World can encompass analysis of specific developmental contexts to inform policy decisions. One particular concern in several countries of SSA surrounds the possibilities for national economic reconstruction in countries affected by recurrent political instability and economic collapse. They have generally experienced major emigration of skilled workers, exacerbating the downward economic spiral. For such countries a key policy issue in national reconstruction must be the kinds of incentives that need to be available to induce the return of the emigrants. These can be political (e.g. the likelihood of stability and non-victimization of those who emigrated), social (e.g. the extent to which family factors have been important), as well as economic (e.g. the availability of attractive and appropriate jobs and perhaps even preferential availability of foreign exchange or imported goods such as a car or household goods to which the emigrant and his family might have become accustomed elsewhere). Identifying the conditions for return requires analysis of the particular circumstances in the country of current residence and the home country. The geographical particularity of places and countries is a necessary but often neglected policy presumption.

Acknowledgement—The author is grateful to Professor Mansell Prothero for helpful comments on a previous draft of this paper.

References

ABDIN, R., BENNELL, P., FAJANA, O., GODFREY, M. and HAMDOUCH, B. (1983) *A World of Differentials: African Pay Structures in a Transnational Context*. Hodder & Stoughton in association with the International Development Research Centre, Ottawa.

ADEPOJU, A. (1983) Undocumented migration in Africa: trends and policies, *Int. Migration*, **21**, 204–217.

AHOOJA-PATEL, K. (1974) Regulations regarding the employment of non-nationals in West Africa, In: *Modern Migrations in West Africa*, pp. 170–190, S. Amin

(Ed.). Oxford University Press, Oxford, for International African Institute.
ALUKO, O. (1985) The expulsion of illegal aliens from Nigeria: a study in Nigeria's decision-making, *Afr. Affairs*, **84**, 539–560.
BACCHUS, M. K. (1986) Towards a strategy for increasing student mobility between less-developed countries in the Commonwealth through third country training, *Int. J. educ. Dev.*, **6**, 275–285.
BENNELL, P. (1986) Engineering skills and development: the manufacturing sector in Kenya, *Dev. Change*, **17**, 303–324.
BIRKS, J. S. and SINCLAIR, C. A. (1980) *Arab Manpower*. Croom Helm, London.
BÖHNING, W. R. (1984) *Studies in International Migration*. Macmillan, London.
BRYDON, L. (1985) Ghanaian responses to the Nigerian expulsions of 1983, *Afr. Affairs*, **84**, 561–585.
CASTLEY, R. and ALFTHAN, T. (1986) Training for industrial development: how governments can help, *Int. Labour Rev.*, **125**, 545–560.
CLARKE, J. I., KHOGALI, M. and KOSINSKI, L. A. (Eds) (1985) *Population and Development Projects in Africa*. Cambridge University Press, Cambridge.
DORE, R. (1976) *The Diploma Disease: Education, Qualification and Development*. Unwin Educational Books, London.
EISEMON, T. O. (1986) Foreign training and foreign assistance for university development in Kenya: too much of a good thing?, *Int. J. educ. Dev.*, **6**, 1–14.
GOULD, W. T. S. (1985a) International migration of skilled labour within Africa: a bibliographical review, *Int. Migration*, **23**, 5–28.
GOULD, W. T. S. (1985b) Context, policy assumptions and theory: international migration of skilled manpower within Africa, Paper presented at the Liverpool Conference of the Population Geography Study Group of the IBG.
GOULD, W. T. S. (1986) Labour force and job creation in the Third World, In: *Planning for Population Change*, pp. 64–87, W. T. S. Gould and R. Lawton (Eds). Croom Helm, London.
GOULD, W. T. S. and PROTHERO, R. M. (1975) Space and time in African population mobility, In: *People on the Move: Studies on Internal Migration*, pp. 39–49, L. A. Kosinski and R. M. Prothero (Eds). Methuen, London.
GOULD, W. T. S. and PROTHERO, R. M. (1981) Migration between Commonwealth countries of Africa, In: *Commonwealth Migration: Flows and Policies*, pp. 170–200, T. E. Smith (Ed.). Macmillan, London.
GREY-JOHNSON, C. (1986) Measures to facilitate the return and reintegration of highly-skilled migrants into African countries, *Int. Migration*, **24**, 197–212.
INTERGOVERNMENTAL COMMITTEE ON MIGRATION (1987) Africans taking their skills back home, *The Courier* (ACP–European Community), **105**, 90–91.
INTERNATIONAL LABOUR OFFICE-U.N. HIGH COMMISSIONER FOR REFUGEES (1984) *Labour Markets in the Sudan*. ILO–UNHCR, Geneva.
KEELY, C. B. (1984) Research on Asian labour migration to the Middle East, *Int. Migration Rev.*, **18**, 367–372.
KENYA GOVERNMENT (1983) *Report on the Presidential Committee on Unemployment, 1982/83 (The Wanjigi Committee)*. Government Printer, Nairobi.
KENYA GOVERNMENT (1984) *Statistical Abstract*. Ministry of Planning and Economic Development, Nairobi.
KING, K. (1985) *Manpower, Technology and Employment in Africa: Internal and External Policy Agendas*. University of Edinburgh, Centre of African Studies, Occasional Paper No. 13.
MABOGUNJE, A. L. (1972) *Regional Mobility and Resource Development in West Africa*. McGill–Queens University Press, Toronto.
ODENYO, A. O. (1979) An assessment of the African brain drain with special reference to the Kenyan mid-career professional, *Issue*, **9**, 45–48.
OXENHAM, J. (Ed.) (1984) *Education versus Qualifications: a Study of Relationships between Education, Selection for Employment and the Productivity of Labour*. Unwin Educational Books, London.
PIEL, M. (1971) The expulsion of West African aliens, *J. mod. Afr. Stud.*, **9**, 205–229.
PROTHERO, R. M. (1968) Migration in tropical Africa, In: *The Population of Tropical Africa*, pp. 250–263, J. C. Caldwell and C. Okonjo (Eds). Longmans, London.
PSACHAROPOULOS, G. and ARRIAGADA, A. M. (1986) The educational composition of the labour force: an international comparison, *Int. Labour Rev.*, **125**, 561–574.
ROTHSCHILD, D. (1970) Kenya's Africanization program: priorities of development and equity, *Am. political Sci. Rev.*, **64**, 748–761.
SHAW, T. (1986) Peripheral social formations in the new divisions of labour: African states in the mid-1980s, *J. mod. Afr. Stud.*, **24**, 489–508.
TAYLOR, J. (1986) *The Pattern and Consequences of Declining Labour Recruitment in Botswana*. ILO, International Migration for Employment Working Paper 28, Geneva.
UNITED NATIONS (1982) *International Migrations: Policies and Programs: a World Survey*. UN, New York.
UNCTAD (1983) *Co-operative Exchange of Skills: Institutional and Policy Issues*. Trade and Development Board, Geneva.
UNDP (1983) *Report on the Conference of Governmental Experts on Technical Cooperation among African Countries on Human Resources Development and Utilization: Libreville, Gabon*. UNDP, Libreville.
WALLACE, T. (1986) *Displaced Labour: a Study of Employment among Educated Refugees from the Horn of Africa*. World University Service, London.
WEINER, M. (1985) International migration and international relations, Paper presented at International Migration Workshop, The Population Council, New York.
YOUDI, R. V. and HINCHCLIFFE, K. (1985) *Forecasting Skilled-manpower Needs: the Experiences of Eleven Countries*. International Institute for Educational Planning–UNESCO, Paris.
ZACHARIAH, K. C. and CONDE, J. (1981) *Migration in West Africa: Demographic Aspects*. Oxford University Press, London, for World Bank–OECD.

INTERNATIONAL JOURNAL OF POPULATION GEOGRAPHY, Vol. 1, 147–164 (1995)

Public Housing as a Barrier to Long-Distance Migration

Paul Boyle*

ABSTRACT

A substantial literature has developed that has considered the relationship between migration and tenure in Britain. It has been argued that while those moving into council housing are more likely to move over short distances than those moving into owner occupied housing, administrative controls restrict population mobility into council housing over long distances. Others have criticised this assumption, maintaining that those resident in council housing are typically individuals who are less likely to migrate over long distances, regardless of the administrative restrictions imposed upon them. Accordingly, it is important to control for individual characteristics before the effects of tenure on mobility may be determined. In this study, data have been extracted from the 1991 Sample of Anonymised Records to assess the impacts of tenure on long-distance migration compared with short-distance migration. Logit models are used to control for the effects of a wide range of socio-economic variables, allowing the independent impact of tenure to be identified. It is shown that long-distance migrants are less likely to move into council housing than other tenures, but it is argued that this does not support the assumption that the sale of council housing will necessarily increase labour mobility.

Key words: public housing; labour migration; logit models; Britain

*School of Geography, University of Leeds, Leeds LS2 9JT, UK.

CCC 1077-3495/95/020147-18

INTRODUCTION

There has been considerable interest, in the British migration literature, in the relationship between migration and tenure. The distribution, price and tenure of housing influences the migration of individuals and households, and it is acknowledged that residents in different tenures have different migration propensities. Those in privately rented property are generally most mobile, followed by those in owner occupied housing and those in council housing, who display roughly similar migration propensities (Owen and Green, 1992). This needs to be qualified as it has also been shown that while council tenants are less likely to move over long distances, they are more likely than owner occupiers to move within local authority areas (Gleave and Palmer, 1978; Hughes and McCormick, 1981).

Hughes and McCormick (1981, 1985, 1987) suggested that tenants are unlikely to move between local authority areas because of the administrative controls imposed upon the distribution of council housing. The policies used by local authorities to allocate council housing are designed to house those most in need of public housing, but these policies prioritise the needs of those from within their own jurisdictions above the needs of those from other local authority areas. These institutions therefore enable high levels of migration between council housing within their areas, as people's circumstances and needs for housing alter. On the other hand, migration between local authority areas is inhibited by the fact that length of residence in an area is a variable in assessing rights to tenancy.

Certain authors have interpreted these findings as evidence that a 'free' housing market, without the debilitating effect of public housing, would help to remove constraints on the mobility of labour (e.g. see Minford *et al.*, 1987). Public housing is therefore regarded as an important factor in explaining the failure of neoclassical economic theory in the British regional labour market. This theory suggests that labour should migrate to equalise imbalances in wages and unemployment levels, and seen in this light the links between tenure and long-distance migration have important policy implications, with home ownership and private renting seen as facilitating migration; for example, Black and Stafford (1988) claim that the sale of council housing will inevitably result in greater geographical mobility.

These economic arguments have been criticised by authors who suggest that residents in public housing are not necessarily immobilised solely by their tenure. Rather, these individuals are amongst those in society who are unlikely to migrate long distances because of their social and economic circumstances. It is:

> 'the combination of housing characteristics and migrant characteristics, rather than housing factors viewed in isolation, that influences the migration of labour.' (Johnson *et al.*, 1974: 224)

Various factors can be identified which may influence working class migration and these include: regional differences in house prices (Hamnett, 1992); the limited advertising of job opportunities at the lower end of the occupational hierarchy (Saunders, 1985); and cultural attachments to the origin area (Johnson *et al*, 1974; Kitching, 1990). It is simplistic, therefore, to attribute observed migration patterns to any single cause; the administrative policies of local authorities may be one of many factors influencing the mobility of council tenants:

> 'for any measured socio-economic characteristic, one would expect those with lower economic motivation, poorer health and those who have experienced more than their share of bad luck to be more likely to find themselves in council accommodation. Since such individuals are also less likely to be employable and mobile, part of the association of council house tenure with unemployment and mobility is probably due to this selection bias.' (Bover *et al.*, 1988: 12)

According to this argument, tenure is not seen as a factor restricting mobility *per se*, as those resident in council housing are less likely to migrate anyway. This proposition has gained support from Fielding (1993) who claims that owner occupiers with similar characteristics to those in council housing would also be much less likely to migrate.

> 'It is not hard to imagine, however, that people who were in every respect like council tenants except that they owned their houses, would also tend to move only very locally.' (Fielding, 1993: 198)

Hamnett (1991) tested this assumption using data for London extracted from the OPCS Longitudinal Study, which links together individual records from the national Censuses and other sources. He showed that those in council housing were more likely to move within London than those in owner occupation, but they were much less likely to move out of London than owner occupiers; these findings confirm the earlier work of Hughes and McCormick (1981, 1985, 1987). This was the case when the socio-economic group of the migrants was controlled for. However, as Hamnett admits, these differences partly reflect other characteristics of residents, such as age, which were not controlled for in the research.

This study aims to examine whether long-distance migration is influenced by tenure. Previously, it has been difficult to examine this relationship because the data sets which have been used have been too small or contained too few variables for conclusive arguments to be made. For the first time, individual-level information has been provided from the 1991 British Census and although this only includes a 2% sample, this does represent a very large sample of the British population compared with other data sets. Thus, controlling for a wide range of socio-economic characteristics, using a logit modelling approach, the independent influence of tenure on long-distance migration compared with short-distance migration within Britain can be assessed. A wide range of variables are shown to be significant in distinguishing between these two broad groups, and the significant interactions between many of these variables and tenure show the strength of the negative relationship between long-distance migration and council housing.

THE DATA SOURCE

The data analysed in this study were extracted from the 1991 Census Sample of Anonymised Records (SARs). For the first time, a sample of Census information has been provided at the individual level, rather than in aggregated tables which hinder the comparison of certain variables. Two versions have been released – a 2% sample of individuals and a 1% sample of households. All of the variables collected in the Census are available at these levels and a number of derived variables have been created from the original Census output (Census Microdata Unit, 1994).

Unfortunately, because of confidentiality measures, the information is only provided at the standard region level for the household file, although the South East is divided into Inner London, Outer London and the remainder of the South East. The individual-level data are available for 278 specially designed 'SAR areas', each of which has a population of at least 120,000. The 459 local authority districts in Britain were not divided, but when the population of a district was less than 120,000, that district was combined with a contiguous district, maintaining county and regional boundaries wherever possible.

From this source, a wide range of information about the characteristics of individual migrants who had moved over long and short distances between 1990 and 1991 could be extracted. From the individual sample, those 34,334 individuals over the age of 16 identified as being migrant heads of household, resident, rather than present, in a particular area at the time of the Census, were extracted. The result is a large migrant sample, which is especially useful when a wide range of explanatory variables are to be used in the model. As Flowerdew (1991) notes, it is important to recognise that many migrants move in small household groups and consequently cannot be regarded as being independent from one another. By choosing heads of household, rather than all long-distance migrants, the problem of non-independence among the sample is solved.

The migrants were divided into two groups, based on distance moved. Short-distance migrants were those who had moved less than 50 km, while long-distance movers were those who had moved 50 km or more, or had moved between standard regions. The distance of 50 km was chosen as a reasonable cut-off which would exclude migrants moving within districts (although it is theoretically possible that a very small minority could have moved within some of the very large local authority districts). Some of the short-distance migrants may have moved between local authority districts, but this will have a dampening effect on the final results, rather than an exaggerating effect. Also, those moving between standard regions may have moved short distances if the regions were contiguous, but such moves would have necessitated a change of local authority district. Only 6920 of the 34,334 migrants were long-distance movers, according to this definition.

This procedure distinguishes broadly between those likely to be moving short distances for residential reasons, and those moving longer distances for employment reasons, although the two groups will not be mutually exclusive. This is a crucial distinction when considering the impact of tenure on labour mobility. Finally, we should note that information about housing tenure at origin is not provided in the 1991 Census migration data. Consequently, and unfortunately, we do not know whether these individuals moved within, or between, tenures.

THE MODELLING APPROACH

Logit models were used to compare the characteristics of the long- and short-distance movers (Bowlby and Silk, 1982). These are directly analogous to multiple regression models, but the dependent variable is categorical with a value of one for long-distance movers and zero for short-distance movers. Such models allow us to test whether the characteristics of two groups (social class and age, for example) differ significantly when other socio-economic variables are taken into account. It is therefore possible to test whether tenure has any influence on long-distance migration when other socio-economic variables are accounted for in the model; as suggested above, this is the approach argued for by many authors (Johnson *et al.*, 1974; Forrest, 1987; Hamnett, 1991; Fielding, 1993).

Logit models assume that the dependent variable is binomially distributed, with the binomial parameter being related to a linear function of a set of dependent variables. The general form of the model is:

$$P_i = \frac{e^{f(X_i)}}{1 + e^{f(X_i)}}$$

where

$$f(X_i) = \alpha + \sum_{k=1}^{K} \beta_k X_{ik}$$

and where P_i is the probability of success for the ith observation, X_{ik} is the value of the kth explanatory variable for the ith observation, and α and β are parameters to be estimated. This can be fitted as a generalised linear model in GLIM. The logit transformation is used, effectively meaning that the analysis is equivalent to a multiple linear regression of the log-odds ratio (the logarithm of the odds that an individual is a 'success') on the personal, family and housing characteristics that are included as explanatory variables. In the models presented here, all of the explanatory variables are categorical, but it is possible to include continuous variables in this type of analysis.

The resulting deviance measure is useful for comparing the relative ability of different explanatory variables, although it does not tell us whether the model fitted could have generated the observed data. The reduction in deviance can be compared with the reduction in the number of degrees of freedom with the inclusion of each explanatory variable, using the χ^2 value at an appropriate significance level (95% was used in this study). The significance of individual parameter estimates can be assessed by comparing their values with the standard errors. It is common to use a 95% significance level where parameters that are over twice the size of their associated standard error are deemed significant.

Variables Used in the Analysis and Preliminary Findings

Numerous factors are likely to affect migration propensities, one of which may be the individual's residential tenure. Owen and Green (1992) drew attention to a number of these, including age, stage in the life course, and geographical location. Flowerdew and Halfacree (1994) used a specially commissioned Gallup survey to examine some of these factors, and 11 variables were assessed. In the optimal model only six of these were retained: housing tenure; age; household size; marital status; social class; and employment status. It is important, therefore, to control for as many of the potential influences on migration as possible, and in this study 20 categorical variables for each individual were extracted from the SAR (Table 1). Some of these variables relate to the individual heads of household themselves, such as their age, sex and health status; some relate to the characteristics of the family, such as the family status and the number of earners in the family; and some relate to the house in which the household resides, such as the tenure and the existence or absence of central heating.

Table 2 summarises the tenure characteristics of the long- and short-distance migrants. This shows that a far smaller percentage of long-distance migrants moved into council housing (7.3%) than short-distance movers (23.9%). Alternatively, a large percentage of the long-distance migrants moved into privately rented property (41.2%) compared with the short-distance movers (23.8%). It is also interesting that owner occupiers who had bought their property made up a higher percentage of long-distance than short-distance movers. This may be related to the fact that many owner occupiers who bought their own property will not have been one-year migrants as they will have remained in the same house for a long period of time while paying off a mortgage. Those who could afford to move into a house and buy it outright may well have been less restricted by distance than most. Table 3 disaggregates the long- and short-distance movers by age group and shows that, generally speaking, the differences are slight. Table 4 shows that those in social classes I and II and those in the armed forces were especially likely to move long distances, while those in social classes IIIM, IV and V were especially likely to move over short distances.

Modelling Long-Distance Migration

Each of these variables were modelled separately and the resulting deviances and degrees of freedom are provided in Table 5. An interesting

Table 1. Explanatory variables derived from the 1991 Sample of Anonymised Records.

Variable		Values
Tenure	1	Owner occupied, buying
	2	Owner occupied, bought
	3	Privately rented
	4	Rented local authority/new town
	5	Rented housing association
Social class	1	IIIM Skilled, manual
	2	I Professional
	3	II Managerial
	4	IIIN Skilled, non-manual
	5	IV Partly skilled
	6	V Unskilled
	7	Armed forces
	8	Inadequately described/not applicable
Socio-economic group	1	Service class
	2	Petite bourgeoisie
	3	White collar
	4	Blue collar
	5	Other
Region	1	South East remainder
	2	North
	3	Yorkshire & Humberside
	4	East Midlands
	5	East Anglia
	6	Inner London
	7	Outer London
	8	South West
	9	West Midlands
	10	North West
	11	Wales
	12	Scotland
Qualifications	1	None
	2	One or more
Household earners	1	Two or more
	2	Zero
	3	One
Cars	1	One car
	2	Zero
	3	Two or more
Employment status	1	Employed full/part time
	2	Self employed
	3	Government scheme
	4	Unemployed
	5	Economically inactive
Family status	1	Married/cohabiting couple, no children
	2	Married/cohabiting couple, dependent children
	3	Married/cohabiting couple, non-dependent children
	4	Lone parent
	5	Not in a family

Table 1. Continued.

Variable		Values
Marital status	1	Married
	2	Single
	3	Remarried
	4	Divorced
	5	Widowed
Age	1	0–29
	2	30–39
	3	40–49
	4	50–64
	5	65+
Sex	1	Male
	2	Female
Central heating	1	All or some rooms
	2	None
Limiting illness	1	Not ill
	2	Ill
Ethnic group	1	White
	2	Black
	3	Indian/Pakistani/Bangladeshi
	4	Chinese/other-Asian/other-other
Residents	1	Two to five residents
	2	One resident
	3	Six or more residents
Density	1	Less than or equal to 0.75 residents per room
	2	More than 0.75 residents per room
Water closet	1	Exclusive use of inside WC
	2	Shared/lacking use of inside WC
Bath	1	Exclusive use
	2	Shared/lacking use
Dependent children	1	No children
	2	One or more children

Table 2. Tenure characteristics of long- and short-distance movers.

Tenure	Short-distance (%)	Long-distance (%)
Owner occupied, buying	11582 (42.1)	2702 (39.0)
Owner occupied, bought	1421 (5.2)	672 (9.7)
Privately rented	6552 (23.8)	2853 (41.2)
Rented local authority/new town	6573 (23.9)	505 (7.3)
Rented housing association	1386 (5.0)	188 (2.7)

Table 3. Age characteristics of long- and short-distance movers.

Age	Short-distance (%)	Long-distance (%)
16–29	13000 (47.2)	3012 (43.5)
30–39	6403 (23.3)	1750 (25.3)
40–49	3306 (12.0)	954 (13.8)
50–64	2499 (9.1)	646 (9.3)
65+	2306 (8.4)	558 (8.1)

Table 4. Social class characteristics of long- and short-distance movers.

Social class	Short-distance (%)	Long-distance (%)
I Professional	1393 (5.1)	776 (11.2)
II Managerial	6675 (24.3)	2661 (38.5)
IIIN Skilled, non-manual	4383 (15.9)	1022 (14.8)
IIIM Skilled, manual	5696 (20.7)	780 (11.3)
IV Partly skilled	3956 (14.4)	597 (8.6)
V Unskilled	1260 (4.6)	148 (2.1)
Armed forces	275 (1.0)	250 (3.6)
Inadequately described	3876 (14.1)	686 (9.9)

Table 5. Results of fitting logit models for separate variables.

Variable	Deviance	Degrees of freedom
Grand mean	34554	34433
Tenure	32818	34429
Social class	33067	34426
Socio-economic group	33296	34429
Region	33793	34422
Qualifications	33451	34432
Household earners	34428	34431
Cars	34278	34431
Employment status	34434	34428
Family status	34277	34429
Marital status	34452	34429
Age	34513	34429
Sex	34503	34432
Central heating	34480	34432
Limiting illness	34468	34432
Ethnic group	34531	34430
Residents	34534	34431
Density	34546	34432
Water closet	34543	34432
Bath	34545	34432
Dependent children	34546	34432

initial result was that the tenure variable had the most significant impact on the deviance, reducing it by 1736 from the null deviance. The second most important variable was social class which only reduced the deviance by 1487. However, as emphasised above, this may result from the fact that the tenure variable was strongly correlated with other socio-economic variables, such as social class. It is important, therefore, to build a model incorporating all those variables that had a significant impact on long-distance migration.

Each variable was added to the model in a step-wise fashion, and Table 6 provides a list of

Table 6. Parameters of logit model for long-distance migrants compared with short-distance migrants.

Parameter	Estimate	Standard error
Base category	−2.06	0.0638
Owner occupied, bought (2)	0.5631	0.0645
Privately rented (3)	0.6389	0.0357
Rented local authority/new town (4)	−0.764	0.0605
Rented housing association (5)	−0.3475	0.0885
I Professional	0.7336	0.0679
II Managerial	0.6641	0.0491
IIIN Skilled, non-manual	0.3832	0.0556
IV Partly skilled	0.1175	0.0608
V Unskilled	−0.0269	0.0987
Armed forces	1.357	0.1015
Inadequately described/not applicable	0.1343	0.0712
North	−0.5323	0.0809
Yorkshire & Humberside	−0.4406	0.0616
East Midlands	−0.0021	0.0599
East Anglia	−0.0498	0.0722
Inner London	0.247	0.0645
Outer London	0.351	0.0551
South West	0.0104	0.0515
West Midlands	−0.5323	0.0661
North West	−0.6373	0.0611
Wales	−0.3056	0.0781
Scotland	−0.415	0.0578
Higher qualifications (1+)	0.5235	0.0375
No earners	0.4764	0.0843
Earners (1)	0.352	0.0393
Cars (0)	−0.1422	0.0401
Cars (2+)	0.1395	0.038
Self employed	−0.3823	0.058
Government scheme	0.5189	0.1547
Unemployed	0.0185	0.0789
Economically inactive	0.2806	0.075
Married/cohabiting couple, dependent children	−0.0666	0.0451
Married/cohabiting couple, non-dependent children	−0.3892	0.1062
Lone parent	−0.3589	0.0769
Not in a family	0.03	0.0475
Single	−0.1026	0.0447
Remarried	0.0141	0.0588
Divorced	−0.3115	0.0595
Widowed	−0.0792	0.0899

Table 6. Continued.

Parameter	Estimate	Standard error
30–39	0.1476	0.0407
40–49	0.2939	0.0523
50–64	0.1825	0.0646
65+	0.1609	0.0869
Female	−0.1243	0.0379
Central heating (none)	−0.1642	0.0419
Limiting long-term illness	−0.2121	0.0592

Scaled deviance is 30,744. Degrees of freedom = 34,387.
The base category parameter represents the log-odds ratio for heads of household who are buying owner occupied property, are in social class IIIM (skilled manual), reside in the South East remainder, have no higher qualifications, have two or more earners in the household, own one car, are working full or part time, are part of a married or cohabiting couple with no children, are aged 0–29, are male, have central heating and do not suffer from long-term limiting illness. The remaining parameters are expressed as differences from this base parameter.

the significant variables, their parameters and associated standard errors. The parameters provided as output by the GLIM package are expressed as differences from the base category (defined in Table 6). A great deal of information is provided about the characteristics of those who moved over long distances, but of most importance to this discussion is the tenure variable. Each of the parameters of this categorical variable were highly significant and, most importantly, those in council housing rented from local authorities or new towns were the least likely to be long-distance movers (denoted by the large negative parameter estimate). Conversely, those who rented property privately, or had bought their own property, were most likely to have moved long distances (a small fraction of the latter group could have been council house purchasers, although Forrest and Murie (1988) showed that these are unlikely to be highly mobile). Although not as large as the parameter for council tenants, the parameter for those living in housing association properties was also negative. These results are especially important given the relatively large sample size (34,434 individuals) and the large number of additional significant variables that were included in the model. The tenure effect appears to be a strong one, even when additional variables are accounted for. Removing single variables from this model showed that tenure remained the most important explanatory variable.

Summarising some of the remaining variables, the model showed that long-distance migrants were more likely to be: highly qualified; in one of the higher social classes or the armed forces; car owners, especially if they had more than one car; one of a couple with no children, married or remarried; aged 40–49; male; and well. It is apparent from this brief outline that those in privileged positions were more likely to be long-distance migrants than those at the lower end of the social ladder. Geographically, those migrants in Inner and Outer London and the South West were most likely to have moved over long distances, while those migrants in the North West, North and West Midlands were least likely to have been long-distance movers. Accounting for this wide range of social characteristics, the effect of tenure remained strongly associated with long-distance migration and this seems to support the arguments that the administrative controls imposed by local authorities may be restricting long-distance migration into council housing.

Including Interaction Effects

The models described so far have not included interaction effects which allow us to test whether the combination of categories from two or more variables produces a different effect to that achieved when the variables are fitted in isolation. Does the tenure effect vary for each of the social classes or between geographical regions, for example?

By way of example those two-way interaction effects between the tenure variable and the remaining variables which were significant were retained, resulting in a model with 179 parameters. Because of the large number of parameter estimates they have been calculated, rather than being expressed as differences from the base category, and this allows them to be compared directly (Table 7). The model deviance was reduced substantially to 30,297. Other two-way interaction terms between variables other than tenure were explored, but the broad conclusions were not altered.

This model provides us with much more information about the relationship between long-distance migration and tenure. Considering

Table 7. Parameters of logit model for long-distance migrants compared with short-distance migrants, including interaction terms[1]

Parameter	Estimate
Base category	−2.085
Owner occupied, bought (2)	−1.692
Privately rented (3)	−1.326
Rented local authority/new town (4)	−2.846
Rented housing association (5)	−1.461
I Professional	−1.289
II Managerial	−1.337
IIIN Skilled, non-manual	−1.623
IV Partly skilled	−2.111
V Unskilled	−2.334
Armed forces	−0.536
Not applicable	−1.891
North	−3.021
Yorkshire & Humberside	−2.756
East Midlands	−1.985
East Anglia	−2.079
Inner London	−2.085
Outer London	−1.878
South West	−2.109
West Midlands	−2.654
North West	−2.966
Wales	−2.632
Scotland	−2.083
Higher qualifications (1+)	−1.663
No earners	−1.338
Earners (1)	−1.616
Cars (0)	−2.209
Cars (2+)	−1.959
Self employed	−2.556
Government scheme	−1.35
Unemployed	−1.895
Economically inactive	−1.607
Married/cohabiting couple, dependent children	−2.209
Married/cohabiting couple, non-dependent children	−2.522
Lone parent	−2.511
Not in a family	−2.137
Single	−2.196
Remarried	−2.087
Divorced	−2.362
Widowed	−2.069

Table 7. Continued.

Parameter	Estimate
30–39	−1.838
40–49	−1.584
50–64	−1.652
65+	−1.793
Female	−2.214
Central heating (none)	−2.257
Limiting long-term illness	−2.284
I Professional. (2)	−0.984
I Professional. (3)	−0.713
I Professional. (4)	−2.201
I Professional. (5)	0.788
II Managerial. (2)	−1.239
II Managerial. (3)	−0.781
II Managerial. (4)	−2.065
II Managerial. (5)	−0.897
IIIN Skilled, non-manual. (2)	−1.041
IIIN Skilled, non-manual. (3)	−1.117
IIIN Skilled, non-manual. (4)	−2.573
IIIN Skilled, non-manual. (5)	−0.813
IV Partly skilled. (2)	−1.067
IV Partly skilled. (3)	−1.299
IV Partly skilled. (4)	−2.523
IV Partly skilled. (5)	−1.311
V Unskilled. (2)	−1.075
V Unskilled. (3)	−1.559
V Unskilled. (4)	−2.499
V Unskilled. (5)	−1.356
Armed forces. (2)	−1.338
Armed forces. (3)	−0.206
Armed forces. (4)	−0.302
Armed forces. (5)	2.757
Inadequately described/not applicable. (2)	−1.428
Inadequately described/not applicable. (3)	−1.382
Inadequately described/not applicable. (4)	−2.334
Inadequately described/not applicable. (5)	−1.308
North. (2)	−2.074
North. (3)	−1.413
North. (4)	−3.212
North. (5)	−3.117
Yorkshire & Humberside. (2)	−2.001
Yorkshire & Humberside. (3)	−1.479
Yorkshire & Humberside. (4)	−3.392
Yorkshire & Humberside. (5)	−1.915
East Midlands. (2)	−1.554
East Midlands. (3)	−1.389
East Midlands. (4)	−3.115
East Midlands. (5)	−1.827
East Anglia. (2)	−1.522
East Anglia. (3)	−1.504

Table 7. Continued.

Parameter	Estimate
East Anglia. (4)	−2.559
East Anglia. (5)	−1.497
Inner London. (2)	−1.349
Inner London. (3)	−0.999
Inner London. (4)	−2.529
Inner London. (5)	−1.069
Outer London. (2)	−1.982
Outer London. (3)	−0.807
Outer London. (4)	−2.499
Outer London. (5)	−0.549
South West. (2)	−1.49
South West. (3)	−1.252
South West. (4)	−3.336
South West. (5)	−1.412
West Midlands. (2)	−2.309
West Midlands. (3)	−1.613
West Midlands. (4)	−4.111
West Midlands. (5)	−1.837
North West. (2)	−2.57
North West. (3)	−1.695
North West. (4)	3.157
North West. (5)	−2.262
Wales. (2)	−1.284
Wales. (3)	−1.429
Wales. (4)	−3.259
Wales. (5)	−3.01
Scotland. (2)	−2.074
Scotland. (3)	−1.328
Scotland. (4)	−3.186
Scotland. (5)	−2.095
Higher qualifications (1+). (2)	−1.407
Higher qualifications (1+). (3)	−0.71
Higher qualifications (1+). (4)	−1.621
Higher qualifications (1+). (5)	−1.059
No earners. (2)	−0.421
No earners. (3)	−1.154
No earners. (4)	−2.086
No earners. (5)	−1.406
Earners (1). (2)	−0.984
Earners (1). (3)	−1.139
Earners (1). (4)	−2.417
Earners (1). (5)	−1.603
Self employed. (2)	−1.545
Self employed. (3)	−1.673
Self employed. (4)	−3.268
Self employed. (5)	−0.334
Government scheme. (2)	−1.227
Government scheme. (3)	−0.703
Government scheme. (4)	−3.399
Government scheme. (5)	−1.141

continued overleaf

Table 7. Continued.

Parameter	Estimate
Unemployed. (2)	−1.409
Unemployed. (3)	−1.42
Unemployed. (4)	−2.997
Unemployed. (5)	−1.822
Economically inactive. (2)	−1.402
Economically inactive. (3)	−1.019
Economically inactive. (4)	−3.153
Economically inactive. (5)	−1.307
Married/cohabiting couple, dependent children. (2)	−1.903
Married/cohabiting couple, dependent children. (3)	−1.225
Married/cohabiting couple, dependent children. (4)	−3.035
Married/cohabiting couple, dependent children. (5)	−2.545
Married/cohabiting couple, non-dependent children. (2)	−2.061
Married/cohabiting couple, non-dependent children. (3)	−1.655
Married/cohabiting couple, non-dependent children. (4)	−3.052
Married/cohabiting couple, non-dependent children. (5)	−1.987
Lone parent. (2)	−2.261
Lone parent. (3)	−1.557
Lone parent. (4)	−3.1
Lone parent. (5)	−2.947
Not in a family. (2)	−1.948
Not in a family. (3)	−1.204
Not in a family. (4)	−2.877
Not in a family. (5)	−1.711
30–39. (2)	−1.934
30–39. (3)	−0.859
30–39. (4)	−2.519
30–39. (5)	−1.821
40–49. (2)	−1.679
40–49. (3)	−1.245
40–49. (4)	−2.729
40–49. (5)	−1.412
50–64. (2)	−1.847
50–64. (3)	−1.41
50–64. (4)	−3.015
50–64. (5)	−1.793
65+. (2)	−2.147
65+. (3)	−1.252
65+. (4)	−2.87
65+. (5)	−1.387

[1] Note that to allow comparison the actual parameters have been calculated from the original GLIM output which expresses the parameters as differences from the base category.
Scaled deviance is 30,297. Degrees of freedom = 34, 255.

the single variable effects first, council housing continued to be the tenure containing those migrants who are least likely to have moved over long distances, with a calculated negative parameter of −2.846. This is much lower than any of the remaining tenure parameters; those buying owner occupied housing were the next least likely to be long-distance migrants. It is noticeable that, in comparison with Table 6, those in housing association accommodation are now more likely to move over long distances than owner occupiers. Of the remaining parameters, which do not include interaction terms, the results are reasonably consistent with those summarised from Table 6, and the large negative parameter for those in council housing remains.

Focusing on the interaction terms, it is evident that the council housing parameter (number 4) was the most negative of the tenure parameters in each of the 33 separate interactions, except for three cases. These were the interactions between: social class and tenure, where those working in the armed forces who owned, and were buying, owner occupied housing were less likely to be long-distance movers; qualifications and tenure, where those who were unqualified and were buying owner occupied housing (the base category) were less likely to be long-distance movers than highly qualified residents in council housing; and social class and tenure, where those in social class II (managerial) who were buying owner occupied housing were slightly less likely to move long distances than managers in council housing (once again, because this parameter was slightly less negative than the base category parameter). Those in the armed forces who decide to purchase owner occupied housing are probably more likely to do so when they become stationed more permanently in an area and wish to invest in property. Unqualified owner occupiers who were buying their property may have been immobilised by the down-swing in the housing market, and there are numerous examples in the literature of those who were caught up in the house buying boom in the 1980s now finding it difficult to move because of falling house prices (Forrest and Murie, 1992). Finally, managers who were buying owner occupied housing may not have been especially immobile over long distances; rather, the managers moving into council properties may have been relatively mobile (see below for a further discussion of this issue).

In the remaining 30 cases, council housing was the most negative parameter amongst the tenure parameters and this provides strong evidence that long-distance migration was restricted by this tenure. Those in council housing were less likely to have moved over long distances than those in other tenures, even when a wide range of additional socio-economic variables were accounted for.

The information derived from this model allows a more detailed examination of the relationship between tenure and migration to be made. Concentrating on the interaction between social class and council housing tenure, those council tenants in social class IIIN (skilled non-manual) were least likely to move over long distances. Alternatively, those in social classes I (professional), II (managerial) and the armed forces were most likely to have moved over long distances. Those living in council housing at the upper end of the social class hierarchy are more likely to be attracted by the offer of employment in distant places, as job opportunities in professional and managerial positions are often advertised nationally. These individuals, who are presumably amongst the better-off within public housing, were therefore the most likely ones to be taking up the limited opportunities for movement between local authority districts.

Geographically, the West Midlands, Yorkshire and Humberside and the South West regions were those where migrants into council housing were least likely to have moved long distances. Those council tenants in Inner and Outer London and the South East were most likely to have moved long distances. These areas were those where the price of owner occupied housing was highest and the employment opportunities were relatively good during the 1980s, particularly for those in lower class occupations. Thus, council housing in these areas was attractive to people who wished to move but could not afford the high costs of housing and private renting in the area. They were among the most attractive places to the professional and managerial potential migrants in council housing who aimed to move long distances. Interestingly, these are also the areas where the sale of council housing under the right-to-buy legislation has been most vigorously uptaken (Forrest and Murie, 1988). While the reduction in council housing has been greatest in these areas, the numbers moving in over long distances appear to be high and this may have serious implications for those on waiting lists.

Those households living in council housing with one earner, followed by those households with no earners, were less likely to have moved long distances than those with two or more earners. Interpreting this finding seems difficult initially, as there is an increasing awareness in the migration literature of the importance of dual career households on restricting household mobility rates (Snaith, 1990). However, it is unlikely that many households living in council housing will have two individuals with well paid careers restricting the mobility of these families. Rather, it is often the case that families are *forced* to supplement the major household income because it is low. Therefore, having two incomes is not an indication that the household will necessarily be well-off or that it is unduly restricted in its mobility by having two earners (Bonney, 1988).

The interaction terms between economic status and tenure show that those working on a government scheme were least likely to be long-distance movers into council housing. As these schemes are open to recent school-leavers and the salaries are generally small, it is unlikely that these individuals will be very mobile, particularly as these opportunities tend not to be advertised widely. Those who were self-employed were the next least likely to move long distances and this confirms assumptions that the economic success of self-employed individuals often rests upon the development of a business in a particular area where valuable contacts and business relationships evolve (Fielding, 1992). Those who were working full or part time were most likely to move over long distances, followed by those who were unemployed. Speculative migration may be important for the unemployed living in public housing. However, we should recognise that it is possible that some of these migrants may have become unemployed after they moved house.

Of those in different family types living in council housing, lone parent families were the least likely to move over long distances. These families are generally among those that are most disadvantaged because of the problem of combining work and child-rearing responsibilities and it is not surprising, therefore, that they were the least mobile over long distances. Predictably, couples with no children were most likely to move over long distances because, for couples with children, schooling is a major deterrent to migration.

Finally, those aged 50–64 were the least likely to move long distances, while those aged 16–29 were most likely to move long distances. These are individuals who probably have least restrictions on their mobility, and this relationship between age and migration is a well-acknowledged one (Bracken and Bates, 1983). The very act of leaving home and entering council housing could occur over long distances, and these are also individuals whose limited savings will mean that they rank high on local authority waiting lists.

Generally, the results presented here seem sensible, based on what we would anticipate from the migration research literature. Three-way interaction terms were also investigated. The introduction of the tenure/social class/geographical region interaction variable reduced the deviance significantly by 455 to 29,842, but this increased the number of parameters in the model to 564. Of the 385 additional individual parameters only 29 were significant, and detailed examination of the results showed that the conclusions drawn above were not altered in any way.

POLICY IMPLICATIONS

The results presented here suggest that the administrative controls that influence the allocation of council housing are hindering the migration of people into this tenure over long distances. Findings such as these have been used in the past to argue that council housing should be regarded as a major factor in the failure of labour mobility to equalise the regional imbalances in unemployment and wage levels that exist in Britain. The natural extension of this argument is that by removing this barrier, which has been pursued vigorously by the Conservative government with the right-to-buy legislation introduced in 1981, labour will be able to 'get on its bike' so that some of the regional inequalities will be redressed.

This simple argument is flawed as there are many reasons why people in other tenures do not migrate, and focusing entirely upon council housing as the only barrier to mobility is unjustified. As Forrest and Murie (1992) pointed out, the mobility of owner occupiers has been reduced significantly by various booms and busts in the housing market. Hamnett (1992) drew attention to the role of house price differentials, suggesting that the high prices in the South East are likely to be a more important factor overall in restricting labour mobility than council policies. This argument has two main elements: those wishing to move into the South East to take up or search for employment opportunities are unable to afford the higher cost of housing there; and those in the South East are discouraged from moving out because they could lose further price appreciation and may not find it possible to move back at a later date.

Detailed work by Forrest and Murie (1988) also casts doubt over the supposition that the sale of council housing will increase working class mobility. Using large samples of council house purchasers, they showed that the majority of those taking up the opportunity to buy their council property were middle- to late-aged with no children. They also tended to be from the higher social classes (Williams *et al.*, 1986) and few of these wished to move on in the near future. Indeed, a survey by James *et al.* (1991) suggested that the right-to-buy option has been used by many tenants primarily to secure their future in an area, rather than as a means of escape from 'welfare' housing.

For those who have bought council housing and now wish to move on, the problem is one of finding a buyer for a property within a council estate when the housing market has reached such a low ebb. There is also increasing evidence that lending societies are unwilling to grant mortgages to those aiming to purchase certain types of housing which were previously in the public sector (Spittles, 1994). It is important, therefore, that we do not assume that council house purchasers will behave completely differently from council house tenants; although they gain financially from the discounts offered under the right-to- buy scheme, their situation is different from traditional owner occupiers.

An alternative interpretation of the barrier effect of council housing on migration is that it is the *limited availability* of council housing, rather than council housing itself, which is the problem. Local authorities have an obligation to house those in need within their jurisdictions. Attempts to set aside small numbers of council houses for in-migrants from outside the local authority area have been largely unsuccessful and many have been abandoned. Other policies such as the National Mobility Scheme and the Tenants Exchange Scheme were designed to enable people searching for work to move more freely between local authorities, but both of them met with limited success (Green *et al.*, 1986). The administrative complexity and a lack of will amongst some authorities to encourage this movement, because of their burgeoning waiting lists, were identified as key factors in this relative failure (Munro, 1992). Also, it appears from the results in this study that the more privileged council house tenants in the higher educational and social classes are the ones taking advantage of these limited opportunities.

With the sale of large proportions of council housing, especially in the south of Britain (Dunn *et al.*, 1987), the availability is inevitably becoming increasingly restricted, while there is little evidence that the numbers in need have reduced significantly, if at all. Thus, it is hardly surprising that local authorities do not actively encourage tenants from outside their areas to apply for accommodation. Increasing the numbers of council houses and reducing waiting lists would be one way of easing pressure on this tenure, enabling local authorities to offer more of their housing to in-migrants from other areas. Clearly, this change in policy seems inconceivable given current government perspectives.

For those at the lower end of the social class ladder there are various factors which discourage them from moving over long distances. The geographically limited advertising of potential employment opportunities is a simple problem that hinders long-distance movement (Saunders and Flowerdew, 1987). Although some attempts have been made in Job Centres to advertise jobs from outside their immediate areas, few companies seem prepared to advertise lower paid jobs more widely. The attraction of remaining in a familiar cultural setting (Kitching, 1990) is a second factor that will discourage long-distance migration. Indeed, cultural attachments to an area may become especially important when individuals become unemployed, and they are unlikely to risk a speculative move to a place where they would have few friends or contacts. However, these factors should not affect those living in council housing more than those living in owner occupied housing, unless council estates are unique cultural settings where the reluctance to move away is powerful. The geographical clustering of people with similar social and economic circumstances on council estates should not be overlooked as an important determinant of (im)mobility, but consideration of this effect would require detailed interviews or surveys.

This individual-level study has utilised a series of personal, family and housing variables to identify the factors influencing long- and short-distance migration between 1990 and 1991 in Britain. Geographical location of destination was also found to be an important variable. The results suggest that council housing, or its administration, does restrict long-distance migration when these various factors are accounted for. However, this does not mean that the sale of council housing will increase the mobility of the working classes. It has been argued here that an alternative interpretation of these findings may be that *increasing* the supply of public housing, combined with more practical measures such as increasing the advertising of working class jobs more widely, may be more effective ways of increasing the migration propensities of the working classes. This, of course, assumes that this is a desirable outcome.

ACKNOWLEDGEMENT

The author thanks Robin Flowerdew for valuable comments on a draft of the paper.

REFERENCES

Black, J. and Stafford, D. (1988) *Housing Policy and Finance* (London: Routledge)

Bonney, N. (1988) Dual earning couples: trends of change in Great Britain, *Work, Employment and Society* 2:89–102

Bover, O., Muellbauer, J. and Murphy, A. (1988) Housing, wages and the UK labour markets, *Centre for Policy Research Discussion Paper No. 268*

Bowlby, S. and Silk, J. (1982) Analysis of qualitative data using GLIM: two examples based on shopping survey data, *Professional Geographer* 34.1:80–90

Bracken, I. and Bates, J.J. (1983) Analysis of gross migration profiles in England and Wales: some developments in classification, *Environment and Planning A* 15:343–55

Census Microdata Unit (1994) *SARs Newsletter No. 3 – July 1994* (Manchester: Census Microdata Unit)

Dunn, R., Forrest, R. and Murie, A. (1987) The geography of council house sales in England – 1979–85, *Urban Studies* 24:47–59

Fielding, T. (1992) Migration and social change, in J.C.H. Stillwell, P.H. Rees and P. Boden (eds) *Migration Processes and Patterns Volume 2: Population Redistribution in the United Kingdom* (London: Belhaven) 225–47

Fielding, T. (1993) Migration and the metropolis: recent research on the causes of migration to southeast England, *Progress in Human Geography* 17.2:195–212

Flowerdew, R. (1991) Poisson regression modelling of migration, in J.C.H. Stillwell and P. Congdon (eds) *Migration Models: Macro and Micro Approaches* (London: Belhaven) 92–112

Flowerdew, R. and Halfacree, K.H. (1994) *Logit Modelling of Migration Propensity in 1980s Britain* (University of Wales Swansea, Migration Unit Research Paper 7)

Forrest, R. (1987) Spatial mobility, tenure mobility, and emerging social divisions in the UK housing market, *Environment and Planning A* 19:1611–30

Forrest, R. and Murie, A. (1988) *Selling the Welfare State: The Privatisation of Public Housing* (London: Routledge)

Forrest, R. and Murie, A. (1992) Housing as a barrier to the geographical mobility of labour, in T. Champion and T. Fielding (eds) *Migration Processes and Patterns Volume 1: Research Progress and Prospects* (London: Belhaven) 77–101

Gleave, D. and Palmer, D. (1978) Mobility of labour: are council tenants really handicapped? *CES Review* 3:74–6

Green, A.E., Owen, D.W., Champion, A.G., Goddard, J.B. and Coombes, M.G. (1986) What contribution can labour migration make to reducing unemployment? in P.E. Hart (ed.) *Unemployment and Labour Market Policies* (Aldershot: Gower) 52–74

Hamnett, C. (1991) The relationship between residential migration and housing tenure in London, 1971–81: a longitudinal analysis, *Environment and Planning A* 23:1147–62

Hamnett, C. (1992) House-price differentials, housing wealth and migration, in T. Champion and T. Fielding (eds) *Migration Processes and Patterns Volume 1: Research Progress and Prospects* (London: Belhaven) 55–64

Hughes, G. and McCormick, B. (1981) Do council housing policies reduce migration between regions? *Economic Journal* 91:919–37

Hughes, G. and McCormick, B. (1985) Migration intentions in the UK. Which households want to migrate and which succeed? *Economic Journal, Conference Supplement* 95:113–23

Hughes, G. and McCormick, B. (1987) Housing markets, unemployment and labour market flexibility in the UK, *European Economic Review* 31:615–45

James, S.J., Jordan, B. and Kays, H. (1991) Poor people, council housing and the right-to-buy, *Journal of Social Policy* 20:27–40

Johnson, J.H., Salt, J. and Wood, P.A. (1974) *Housing and the Mobility of Labour in England and Wales* (Farnborough: Saxon House)

Kitching, R. (1990) Migration behaviour among the unemployed and low-skilled, in J.H. Johnson and J. Salt (eds) *Labour Migration* (London: David Fulton) 172–90

Minford, P., Peel, M. and Ashton, P. (1987) *The Housing Morass: Regulation, Immobility and Unemployment* (London: Institute of Economic Affairs)

Munro, M. (1992) Housing market restructuring: consequences for migration, in T. Champion and T. Fielding (eds) *Migration Processes and Patterns Volume 1: Research Progress and Prospects* (London: Belhaven) 41–54

Owen, D. and Green, A.E. (1992) Migration patterns and trends, in T. Champion and T. Fielding (eds) *Migration Processes and Patterns Volume 1: Research Progress and Prospects* (London: Belhaven) 17–38

Saunders, M.N.K. (1985) The influence of job vacancy advertising upon migration, *Environment and Planning A* 17:1581–89

Saunders, M.N.K. and Flowerdew, R. (1987) Spatial aspects of the provision of job information, in M.M. Fisher and P. Nijkamp (eds.) *Regional Labour Markets* (Amsterdam: Elsevier) 206–28

Snaith, J. (1990) Migration and dual career households, in J.H. Johnson and J. Salt (eds) *Labour Migration* (London: David Fulton) 155–71

Spittles, D. (1994) Under the hammer horrors, *Observer*, Sunday 4th December

Williams, N.J., Sewel, J. and Twine, F. (1986) Council house sales and residualisation, *Journal of Social Policy* 15:273–92

[22]

ANNALS, *AAPSS*, **467**, May 1983

The Commitment to Refugee Resettlement

By BARRY N. STEIN

ABSTRACT: Since 1975 the traditional refugee receiving countries have made major changes in their refugee resettlement programs and policies. They have institutionalized their refugee programs, increased the number of refugees accepted for resettlement, and broadened the range of groups that can be considered for resettlement by relying on the U.N. Convention definition of a refugee as their criterion for acceptance. Recently concern has increased about the costs and difficulties of resettlement, particularly of third-world refugees. This has led some observers to wonder if there is a diminished commitment to resettlement as a durable solution. This article concludes that if one uses 1975 as a base year for comparison, commitment to refugee resettlement has increased significantly. There are, however, present challenges to it. The numbers of refugees being resettled are dropping sharply in response to both decreased need and increased domestic pressures within the major receiving nations to limit admissions. Lower numbers by themselves are an inadequate indicator of a decreased long-term commitment to resettlement. The article suggests a range of factors to be considered in assessing this commitment.

Barry N. Stein is a senior associate at the Refugee Policy Group, an independent organization located in Washington, D.C., which does policy analysis and research on refugee resettlement, protection and asylum, assistance in developing countries, and other refugee policy issues. He is on leave from Michigan State University, where he is a professor of social science. Since 1975 he has taught the courses "Refugees, Displaced Persons, Exiles" and "Issues in Refugee Assistance." His publications include coediting a special issue of the International Migration Review *on "Refugees Today";"Refugee Resettlement Programs and Techniques," a report for the Select Commission on Immigration and Refugee Policy; and a "Refugee Research Bibliography" for the U.N. High Commissioner for Refugees.*

NOTE: The author is grateful for the comments of Dennis Gallagher and Susan Forbes of the Refugee Policy Group.

THE traditional refugee resettlement countries—such as the United States, France, Canada, and Australia—are nearing the end of an extraordinary period of resettlement. Since 1979, refugees, mostly from Indochina, have been resettled in very large numbers. At present, while these numbers have declined sharply, by more than half from their 1980 peak, they are still relatively high compared to pre-1979 levels. Is the reduction in numbers a sign that the traditional receiving countries are diminishing their commitment to refugee resettlement as a durable solution?

Many observers would answer in the affirmative. For example, a recent Canadian government report on resettlement levels stated,

> In the face of large refugee populations seeking resettlement, and increasing hardship for countries of first asylum, the situation is further exacerbated by the trend towards diminishing commitment of resettlement places by the traditional receiving countries.[1]

Those arguing that the decline is associated with diminished commitment cite some or all of the following factors:

- —increased questioning of whether people being resettled "as refugees under generous arrangements are indeed refugees;"[2]
- —increased domestic pressures to lower admissions due to high unemployment and poor economic conditions in the receiving countries;[3]
- —"compassion fatigue" and a sense of being "overwhelmed" because we "are not able to bridle" the resettlement numbers;[4]
- —"the difficulty of integrating refugees from entirely different ethnic and cultural backgrounds;"[5] and
- —an inadequately developed base of ethnic kin in the receiving countries to promote the admission of third-world refugees.

Others question the extent to which the decline in admissions numbers necessarily indicates a lessening commitment to resettlement as a durable solution. They note factors unrelated to the commitment of receiving countries that affect resettlement levels:

- —reduced numbers of refugees in the first-asylum camps in Southeast Asia;
- —the belief of the U.N. High Commissioner for Refugees (UNHCR) and other international organizations that voluntary repatriation or local settlement is a preferable durable solution; and
- —the willingness of first-asylum countries, in areas other than Southeast

1. Canada, "Refugee Perspectives 1982-1983" (Refugee Affairs, Employment and Immigration Canada, June 1982), p. 3.

2. Ian Macphee, Minister for Immigration and Ethnic Affairs, "Australia's New Policy on Refugees" (Statement to the House of Representatives, Canberra, 16 Mar. 1982,) p. 1.

3. Ambassador H. Eugene Douglas, U.S. Coordinator for Refugee Affairs, "Statement before House Foreign Affairs Committee," 16 Mar. 1982, p. 2, and "Statement before the House Judiciary Committee," 22 Apr. 1982, p. 7.

4. Alan Simpson, "United States Immigration Policy: Unsettled Issues and Emerging Policies" (Speech at an immigration seminar, Williamsburg, VA, 1 Nov. 1981), p. 5.

5. Sadruddin Aga Khan, *Study on Human Rights and Massive Exoduses,* Commission on Human Rights, U.N. Economic and Social Council, E/CN.4/1503 (31 Dec. 1981), p. 6.

Asia, to provide long-term hospitality to refugees within their borders.

It is difficult to assess the commitment to refugee resettlement, as the situation is mixed and complex. The admissions numbers are often taken as a sign of commitment, yet numbers alone are not an adequate measure. Resettlement usually occurs as a response to need and danger, not as a steady condition. Thus the history of resettlement is marked by ebbs and flows. The inevitable decline from the 1980 peak should not necessarily lead to the conclusion that there is a weakening of the commitment to resettlement.

In fact, there have been significant gains in resettlement programs in the major receiving countries. Keeping in mind that the changes are recent and the gains may be fragile, it is useful to note these indices of progress:

—substantially higher admissions levels now than for most of the seventies;

—widespread reliance on the U.N. Convention definition[6] of a refugee as the major basis for admission;

—institutionalization of resettlement programs with new legislation, administrative structures, consultation procedures, and annual resettlement plans; and

—a broadening of the range of resettled refugees with African, Asian, and Latin American refugees added to a flow that used to be predominantly European.

The next year or two may be crucial to a continued commitment to resettlement. In the United States, which has by far the largest resettlement program, the basic refugee law, the Refugee Act of 1980, is up for reauthorization by Congress this year. Past efforts, led by Senator Huddleston, to include refugee admissions under a numerical cap for all immigrants have been substantially defeated. This proposal, however, is likely to resurface in the next session of Congress, against a background of high unemployment. In other resettlement countries a mixed picture also prevails. The substantial progress that has occurred in recent years is subject to questioning and reversal.

Senator Simpson, cosponsor of the proposed Immigration Reform and Control Act of 1982, recently warned of the consequences if this bill were to be defeated:

> We shall see a change in public attitudes toward immigrants and refugees. We shall see public support for our fine immigration and refugee programs eroding as American citizens perceive that their short-term interests are being threatened by the continued uncontrolled numbers of legal and illegal immigrants competing for jobs and scarce resources.[7]

The measure of the commitment of the traditional resettlemment countries will be whether the improvements and

6. *Convention Relating to the Status of Refugees* (28 July 1951), *UNTS*, 189:137. The definition is: "the term 'refugee' shall apply to any person who: owing to a well-founded fear of being persecuted for reasons of race, religion, nationality, membership of a particular social group or political opinion, is outside the country of his nationality and is unable or, owing to such fear, is unwilling to avail himself of the protection of that country." Some countries, such as the United States, have not signed the Convention but have undertaken to apply it by signing the *Protocol Relating to the Status of Refugees* (31 Jan. 1967), *UNTS*, 606:267.

7. Alan Simpson, "Will America Control Its Borders?" *Washington Post*, 5 Dec. 1982.

mechanisms put into place are maintained or are dismantled, and whether the number of those being admitted remains adequate to meet the need for resettlement and to preserve the principle of first asylum.

DURABLE SOLUTIONS

There are three classic durable solutions to refugee problems. They are voluntary repatriation, settlement in a country of first asylum, and resettlement in a third country. A durable solution means helping the refugees to become self-sufficient, enabling them to integrate and participate fully in the social and economic life of their new country, or their homeland if they repatriate. It means more than the relief and limbo of a refugee camp, the classic nonsolution.

Repatriation means that the refugees return home; it is often referred to as the preferred solution. Repatriation should be voluntary, and the conditions at home that initially caused flight from fear of persecution should have been remedied. While a frequently used durable solution, repatriation does not always occur under optimum conditions.

Settlement or local integration occurs when refugees stay permanently in their country of first asylum and are integrated into the host country's life. Settlement is also a frequently used durable solution; it has been widely practiced in the developing countries. Even some of the traditional resettlement countries have served as countries of first asylum and settlement. The United States has settled Cuban refugees, and Australia has done the same with some of the Vietnamese boat people who sought asylum there.

Resettlement involves moving refugees from their country of first asylum to some other country. The country of resettlement is commonly referred to as the refugees' third country after their homeland and land of first asylum. The country of resettlement may occasionally also be the country of first asylum when refugees are moved directly from their homeland by means of an orderly departure program.

THE ROLE OF RESETTLEMENT

Although refugee resettlement receives more attention than the other durable solutions—resettlement occurs here rather than over there—it is the least commonly used solution. Nonetheless resettlement plays a crucial role. It represents rescue for refugees "who are in a precarious situation in their country of first asylum because of political, religious or ethnic differences with the local populace."[8]

> Resettlement . . . stands out, not as one of three practical solutions but as an exceptional measure to be pursued only for compelling humanitarian reasons or where the alternatives of voluntary repatriation and local integration do not exist.[9]

Resettlement often requires transcontinental movement, as the three major receiving countries—the United States, Canada, and Australia—are distant from most of the countries of first asylum. However, many refugees are resettled within their own continents, particularly in Africa, and Europe.

The major countries of resettlement in the post-World War II period have

8. Canada, "Refugee Perspectives," p. 9.

9. "Editorial: Resettlement: A Possible Solution," *Refugees: News from the United Nations High Commissioner for Refugees*, 4:1 (Apr. 1982).

been the United States, 1.9 million refugees; Israel, 1 million refugees; Canada, 400,000 refugees; Australia, 400,000 refugees; France, 250,000 refugees; and the United Kingdom, 250,000 refugees. All of the figures are approximate, because definitions and categories have changed over the years. Israel and the United Kingdom are not normally thought of as traditional receiving countries, despite their acceptance of many refugees. Israel has primarily taken Jewish refugees and does not generally resettle other refugees. Most of the United Kingdom's refugees entered in the first decade and a half after World War II, but since then England has taken only a modest number of refugees.

Although a few states have resettled the bulk of refugees over the years, it is important that there be a wide range of receiving states. No country of resettlement is equally open to all refugees. For political, ideological, historical, geographic, and other reasons, some resettlement states favor certain refugee groups and have little interest in others. This also works in the other direction: some refugee groups have definite preferences and dislikes regarding where they will be resettled. States rather than refugees are more able to control this situation. In cases where a refugee group is not favored by the major resettlement states, the other resettlement countries may play a key role in a group's rescue. For example, the major resettlement states took less than half of the Chilean and other Latin American refugees, although they resettle over 80 percent of most refugee flows. The slack, representing thousands of lives, largely was taken up by other resettlement countries, notably in Scandinavia and Northern Europe.

These other resettlement states have helped maintain receptivity in the major resettlement states. This is especially important for the United States, which is concerned with demonstrations of solidarity, burden-sharing, and internationalization of the refugee load by the international community. Ambassador Douglas, the U.S. Coordinator for Refugee Affairs, recently testified to a congressional subcommittee about the need "to continue strong support for multinationalization of the refugee resettlement effort so the U.S. does not carry a disproportionate share of the burden."[10]

There is also a vital link between the availability of resettlement opportunities and maintaining the principle of first asylum. Some countries, because their locations are adjacent to troubled regions, receive disproportionate numbers of asylum seekers, numbers that exceed their capacity to integrate refugees locally. These countries of first asylum expect other countries to share their burden by providing resettlement opportunities. Fearful of being left with a heavy burden, some first-asylum countries have threatened to or have *refouled* —forced the involuntary repatriation of—refugees or rejected them at the frontier.

> A dramatic example of the importance of resettlement is what happened only a few years ago when thousands of "boat people" from Vietnam were allowed to disembark on Asian shores only when other countries guaranteed to share the burden and to accept a certain quota.[11]

Recently Thailand has given ominous warnings that it has been "too merciful" and that it will not "bear an endless

10. Douglas, "Statement," 16 Mar. 1982, p. 3.

11. Ruud van Hoogevest, "The Churches and the World Refugee Crisis: A Current Summary," *Refugees: World Council of Churches,* 49:6 (Oct. 1982).

burden" of refugees much longer.[12] It is believed that this threat has been motivated, in part, by perceived reductions in the number of available resettlement slots.

THE SCALE OF RESETTLEMENT

Precise figures on refugees—whether repatriated, locally settled, resettled, or in camps—are not readily available or notably accurate. Even when the counting has been reasonably thorough, there is often confusion or disagreement regarding the category to which the refugees may be assigned. For example, many authorities list 265,000 Indochinese refugees as resettled in China when in fact these refugees fled or were expelled directly from Vietnam to China and thus are really settled in their country of first asylum.

In this century, as many as 140 million people may have been refugees. Gunther Beyer, cofounder of the Research Group for European Migration Problems, has calculated,

> Excluding the forced migrations of the Chinese in the 1930's, by 1939 approximately thirty million people were forced to leave their homes. During World War II nearly forty million civilians were forced from one place to another, and since 1945 an additional 60 to 70 million people have become victims of forced migrations.[13]

Very few of the more than 100 million refugees, displaced persons, and involuntary migrants have been resettled. Resettlement was not widely used after World War I or during World War II. Most countries had restrictive immigration policies and would not ease them for refugees. Indeed the failures of the prewar period and the Holocaust that befell many of those denied a durable solution proved to be a powerful driving force for more generous resettlement policies after World War II.

In the early postwar period, between 1947 and the end of 1951, approximately one million European refugees were resettled through the auspices of the International Refugee Organization (IRO). The IRO was a landmark experience in refugee resettlement. It represented the first large-scale, planned, international resettlement effort. Two aspects of the IRO experience are revealing with regard to the view of resettlement at that time. First, many of the countries that received IRO refugees did so only after difficult national debates about immigration policy. Second, IRO was a temporary organization—"the U.N. members had considered the refugee problem as an immediate post-war problem and assumed it could be solved in a limited time."[14] There was no permanent commitment to resettlement.

Since the end of IRO in 1952, approximately four million additional refugees have been resettled. For most of the period after 1952, Eastern Europeans fleeing communist countries represented the typical image of the resettled refugee.[15] There were exceptions, though:

12. Leo Cherne, "Closing the Doors to People in Danger," *Washington Post*, 21 Oct. 1982.

13. Gunther Beyer, "The Political Refugee: 35 Years Later," *International Migration Review*, 15(53):26 (Spring 1981).

14. Louise W. Holborn, *Refugees: A Problem of Our Time* (Metuchen, NJ: Scarecrow Press, 1975), p. 35.

15. An example of the Eastern European dominance of the resettlement flow can be seen in some figures from Canada. Between 1947 and 1967, Canada took in 242,212 refugees, displaced persons, and stateless immigrants. Of this total, 233,425 were from Eastern or Central Europe and only 931 were from outside Europe. See C.

refugees from Cuba and China were resettled in the sixties, and in the seventies refugees from Latin America, Tibet, Uganda, and, most important, Indochina were added to the flow. For most of this period, despite the resettlement of large numbers of refugees, most countries had only ad hoc resettlement programs. Some refugees were admitted through regular procedures, but any large refugee movements, such as the Hungarian exodus of 1956 and the Indochinese flight two decades later, required specific action or legislation after the crisis had developed.

RECENT RESETTLEMENT ACTIVITY

Since 1975, there have been major changes in refugee resettlement programs and policies in the overseas receiving countries. It is not easy to pinpoint a watershed event that applies equally well to Canada, Australia, and the United States, because the policy changes did not occur in an instant but were a mixture of minor and major modifications over several years. Nonetheless 1975 is used as the starting point of the current period because it is the beginning of the most significant and largest program of the past decade—the resettlement of almost one million Indochinese refugees. This influx has been a major catalyst for policy and program change. This is not to say that other refugee movements, some before 1975—Tibetans, Uganda Asians, Cubans, and South Americans—and others after—Timorese, Cypriots, Lebanese, Kurds, Soviet Jews, and others—did not either initiate or advance some policy discussions.

The impact of the Indochinese resettlement program has been to change many people's perception of refugee problems. This crisis, occurring in conjunction with a succession of other refugee emergencies—in Africa, Central America, and the Middle East—has led to increased understanding that refugees are a permanent problem and that under certain circumstances, resettlement will need to be available as part of the solution. In response to this recognition, some of the major resettlement countries have developed more permanent refugee programs, policies, and structures.

Three aspects of the current period of resettlement are noteworthy. First, the United States, Canada, and Australia—the three overseas resettlement countries that have taken the most refugees—have each developed new refugee policies. The new policies rely on the U.N. Convention definition as a major basis for admission, and each country has developed annual resettlement plans. Second, the number of refugees accepted for resettlement has increased substantially compared to admission levels prevailing before 1979. Third, refugee programs today are resettling refugees from significantly different economic and ethnic backgrounds, compared to refugees resettled before 1975. Refugees from Asia, Africa, and Latin America have been added to the resettlement flow, a flow that was almost exclusively European before 1975, with the influx of Cubans to the United States the major exception.

NEW POLICIES

For Canada, "a policy of refugee intake, *per se,* has existed formally only

---

Michael Lanphier, "Canada's Response to Refugees," *International Migration Review,* 15(53):120 (Spring 1981).

since the Immigration Act of 1976."[16] Prior to 1976, it "required special action of the federal government" to admit refugees to Canada. Until refugee situations reached sizable dimensions, they were not seen as part of the government's regular agenda but as "nonrecurring issues." Even the term "refugee" was flexible and could be adjusted to the needs of the moment.

Canada's policies changed in 1969, with acceptance of the U.N. definition of a refugee. In 1979, it formally established annual refugee admission plans. The plans set quotas for anticipated arrivals. Additionally, Canada uses a system of designated classes for certain groups of refugees. A profile and specifications for eligibility are drawn up for each designated class to facilitate their processing. The specifications vary from group to group and may depart from the strict terms of the U.N. definition.

Australia's refugee resettlement policy has been slowly evolving since 1945, but the mid-1970s provided the impetus for important changes. Australia admitted 170,000 displaced persons under IRO auspices and later took in Hungarian refugees and others from Eastern Europe. In the 1970s, Australia accepted its first resettled refugees from Asia—they were Uganda Asians who came from Africa but were viewed as Asians. As with the other overseas resettlement states, Australia, until the mid-seventies, had no general refugee policy; instead, each government dealt with new situations as they arose. The Indochinese situation brought about a reexamination of policies, and as a result Australia now uses the U.N. Convention definition as the criterion for resettlement and annually indicates its resettlement intentions.[17]

In the United States, the Refugee Act of 1980 represents the first major reform of the refugee provisions of American immigration law in nearly three decades. Prior to 1980, refugee admissions were limited to 17,400 per year under the former seventh preference of the Immigration and Nationality Act of 1952. To admit large groups of refugees, it was necessary to use the parole authority of the attorney general on an emergency basis. Parole was meant to be used for individuals, not for large groups. Despite congressional objections to the use of parole for refugee groups, the practice continued until the passage of the Refugee Act of 1980, because "existing refugee legislation was inadequate."[18] Over the years there were more than a dozen major parole programs, and over one million refugees—Hungarian, Soviet, Eastern European, Cuban, Indochinese—were admitted using this ad hoc mechanism.

The Refugee Act of 1980 includes a definition of refugee that conforms to the U.N. Convention definition. The United States had signed the U.N. Protocol in 1968, but that did not require any change in admission policies. The old law had geographic and ideological restrictions, so only refugees who fled from a communist country or a country in the Middle East could qualify for admission. The 1980 act also provides for annual consultations by the president with Congress to determine the number

16. Ibid., p. 113.

17. Charles Price, "Immigration Policies and Refugees in Australia," *International Migration Review*, 15(53):99-102 (Spring 1981).

18. Maurice A. Roberts, "The Refugee Act of 1980," *1981 World Refugee Survey* (New York: U.S. Committee for Refugees, 1981), pp. 45-46.

of refugees to be resettled. For the first three years, the act provided for a normal flow of 50,000 refugees unless the consultations set a higher figure. The first four fiscal year consultations resulted in limits of 231,700 in fiscal year 1980, 217,000 in fiscal year 1981, 140,000 in fiscal year 1982, and 90,000 in fiscal year 1983. Actual admissions have been lower—212,000 in fiscal year 1980, 159,000 in fiscal year 1981, and 97,000 in fiscal year 1982. Last, the 1980 act provides for a U.S. Coordinator for Refugee Affairs and an Office of Refugee Resettlement—both had been created previously by executive action—to coordinate and implement policy and assistance to refugees.

The reliance on the U.N. Convention definition of refugee means that Canada, the United States, and Australia are likely to be accepting a wider range of refugees than before. For example, a recent Canadian report noted, "Canada has never been so active in as many areas of the world at the same time."[19] The use of the definition, however, does not mean all refugees have an equal chance of admission, within numerical limits, because each country gives priority in resettlement to groups it considers of special interest.

Moreover use of the U.N. Convention definition is likely to lead to stricter and more legalistic procedures for determining who will be resettled. This may cause hardship for some individuals. In the past, once a resettlement program had begun, persons with the right nationality were virtually ensured resettlement if they met criteria that often had little to do with refugee status, such as family in the receiving country or past connection with its military or foreign policies. Such blanket acceptances are no longer used. Resettlement countries may decide they "will not accept people merely because they came from totalitarian countries."[20] There is a temptation to keep the Convention definition pure and to look strictly for an individual fear of persecution.

Such an approach, though justifiable, calls for a careful adjudication of claims. Those rejected for resettlement can end up in very dangerous circumstances. One critic refers to rejection as "dooming."[21] For example, an alien who has fled turmoil at home and whose claim for refugee status has been rejected by the resettlement countries may have no other alternatives. In such a case, rejection can lead to *refoulement*—forced repatriation.

HIGHER ADMISSIONS LEVELS

Admissions levels in the major refugee resettlement countries are higher now than they were for the entire decade before 1979. In 1980, worldwide refugee resettlement was at a record or near-record level of 325,000 to 350,000 refugees. This figure does not include the 140,000 Cuban and Haitian entrants who came to the United States that year and were served by the same system that resettles refugees. Reductions from that record level should not be viewed as a retreat; rather they reflect the episodic need for resettlement places.

The primary factor in lowering resettlement totals since 1980 has been the gradual but steady decline in refugee camp populations in Southeast Asia. Because of a lower influx of refugees,

19. Canada, "Refugee Perspectives," p. 1.

20. Macphee, "Australia's New Policy," p. 1.

21. Rod Nordland, "Khmer Refugees: 'Reaching for Oars,'" *Indochina Issues,* 30:4 (Nov. 1982).

governments have been able to cut resettlement numbers while still meeting the goal of camp reduction.

Compared to the levels that prevailed in the 1970s, current resettlement in the overseas countries is very high. Australia's 1982 "refugee and special humanitarian entry program is 24,500, the highest intake ever."[22] The September 1982 consultation set a fiscal year 1983 level of 90,000 for the United States, and Canada "did not deal with record numbers in 1982 but positive results were achieved."[23] The Canadian levels were 14,000 for 1982 and 12,000 for 1983.

The recent decline in admissions numbers must be seen within the context of traditional patterns of resettlement. It is likely that over the years far less than 10 percent of all refugees have been resettled. However we calculate the number of refugees, whether more than 100 million refugees in this century, or approximately 60 to 70 million refugees since World War II, the number that have been resettled might be one-tenth of the total only in the postwar period.

The crucial factor is not the total number or fraction of all refugees who are resettled, but whether resettlement is available when it is needed. In many refugee situations, all three durable solutions will be pursued and used, and resettlement usually plays a minor role. As noted before, large-scale resettlement is not normally used as a first choice but only when it is clear that the other alternatives are not available or sufficient.

EBB AND FLOW AND NORMAL FLOW

The number of refugees worldwide has stayed high for the last 20 years; since 1961 "numbers have ranged from 8 million (1964) to 18 million (1970) with the average at 14 million,"[24] yet the number of resettled refugees has been subject to sharp ebbs and flows. Just a few years before the 1980 resettlement peak, in 1976, 1977, and 1978, the worldwide resettlement total was less than 75,000 refugees per year. For 1982, the resettlement total will probably be under 150,000 refugees, and the 1983 total will drop even lower, provided conditions do not change.

Because of the episodic need for resettlement and the highly variable response of the resettlement countries to refugee crises, it is difficult to develop average or normal figures for the resettlement countries. Such figures can be misleading, because as the numbers go from peak to valley, they may never be at an average level in any given year. Resettlement in the United States averaged approximately 50,000 refugees per year between 1956 and 1974. Since 1975, the average is approximately 100,000 refugees per year, yet the total for 1976 to 1978 was less than 85,000, or about 28,000 refugees per year. In a similar vein, Canadian resettlement during the seventies ranged from a high of 27,740 in 1979 to a low of only 801 refugees in 1971.

There is a tug in refugee operations between the need to respond to emergencies and the need to regularize operations, to establish control, and to have a normal flow of properly processed refugees. It is not easy to have a neat and normal emergency response, yet as a resettlement crisis goes on, the response tends to become institutionalized, con-

22. Macphee, "Australia's New Policy," p. 1.
23. Canada, "Refugee Perspectives," p. 1.
24. U.S. Committee for Refugees, "A New Way of Reporting Statistics," *1981 World Refugee Survey*, p. 33.

trolled, and normal. High emotions recede as memories of the danger and death that require a response fade.

By establishing the concept of a normal flow, refugee programs may become measured by their divergence from the normal flow figure. This is not likely to be appropriate. In the United States, the Refugee Act of 1980, using the average refugee flow of the past two decades as a guide, established for its first three years a normal flow of 50,000 refugees per year. Since then there has been considerable public and congressional pressure on the government to control refugee admissions and to bring them in line with this normal flow. We are thus in a situation in which some people, misreading the role of resettlement, measure the success of the program by its adherence to the normal flow while others, concentrating on the number of refugees in first-asylum camps, see lower numbers as a diminishing commitment to resettlement.

REFUGEES FROM DEVELOPING COUNTRIES

Given all of this, there are indicators that recent reductions in resettlement programs worldwide have not been solely caused by a reduced need for resettlement. For example, the main European receiving countries, not including France, have cut their programs—at a time when Thailand is threatening to abandon its commitment to first asylum—from approximately 25,000 Indochinese refugees in 1979 to 6000 in 1982. Certainly domestic factors such as economic difficulties and high unemployment in the receiving states lead to a desire to protect jobs from aliens and to a focus on charity at home. Another factor is the changed perception of the refugee problem caused by the influx of refugees and asylees from outside Europe.

For the last two decades, at a gradually increasing pace, more and more resettled refugees have come from developing countries. The old flow of refugees from Central and Eastern Europe continues, but an influx of refugees from Asia, Latin America, and Africa has been added to it. Their homelands are at a different stage of development from that of the receiving country, and many of the refugees have levels of skill and education that produce prominence or success in less developed countries but do not transfer well to urban technological societies.

Third-world refugees represent a difficult challenge to those interested in providing services to refugees. Many resettlement practices that worked with European refugees have proved to be inappropriate with third-world refugees. The experience with resettlement of third-world refugees has been difficult and expensive. During an emergency, concerns about potential adjustment and cost may be overshadowed by humanitarian impulses. As the emergency recedes, though, public interest and support wanes, and the focus shifts from saving lives to the domestic implications of resettlement. In times of economic hardship this can lead, at least momentarily, to a diminished commitment to resettlement.

In addition, many people confuse refugees, particularly those from third-world countries, with nonrefugees, economic migrants, illegal aliens, and persons with weak claims to refugee status. Because of this confusion, much of the suspicion and hostility aimed at nonrefugees also strikes genuine refugees.

Refugees from poor countries are subject to suspicion that they left their homelands to seek a better way of life rather than to escape some form of persecution.

There seems to be a growing feeling that some economic migrants are being accorded the protection and benefits to which only refugees should be entitled. . . . Why then the confusion? Because in many cases the precise reasons for departure may not be clearly identifiable or may be mixed. . . . Thus persons may at first sight appear to be fleeing from poverty; on a closer examination however their situation of economic deprivation may reveal elements of persecution within the meaning of the international refugee instruments.[25]

Third-world refugees fleeing generalized conditions of insecurity, oppression, and poverty may be able only to make slight claims to a "well-founded fear of [political] persecution," which is the key to the U.N. Convention definition of a refugee. It is not clear, however, that the problem lies with the definition. In times of emergency and goodwill, flexible interpretations have occurred. In times of increasing reticence toward immigration, stricter applications of the definition can result.

To complicate matters, developing-country refugees often lack a political base in the receiving countries to support their admission. Many of the third-world refugee groups that have been resettled were the first of their nationality in the host country. One should not, however, overstate the ethnic connection to resettlement. While the lack of an ethnic political power base may delay or retard a group's prospects, the record shows that well over one million refugees from the developing countries have been resettled—even when they lacked such a base.

ASYLUM CONNECTION

Reticence about the entry of new groups, with its attendant repercussions for resettlement, has been exacerbated by the increased flow of persons seeking asylum in the developed countries. This flow of asylum seekers includes both genuine asylees—those who meet the Convention criteria—and "persons who have only very slight claims to refugee status."[26] Resettled refugees are processed and selected in their country of first asylum and then are transported to their country of resettlement. The resettlement country controls the numbers and the selection. Asylum seekers—whether genuine refugees or not—come on their own to a country of their own choice, thus reducing the receiving country's control of numbers and selection. Asylum mechanisms and systems in the developed countries have been swamped with applications. In many countries, asylum applicants can get work permits. So can those whose applications have been rejected while they appeal their rejections.

Refugees from the impoverished South Asian country of Bangladesh have begun making their way illegally into the United States by way of the Bahamas, . . . from a community of some 15,000 Bangladeshis who have been living in . . . West Germany illegally, but after years of legal appeals have been told they must leave.[27]

As a result of what is perceived to be abuse and manipulation, many Western

25. "Editorial: Refugees or Economic Migrants?" *Refugees: News from the United Nations High Commissioner for Refugees,* 7:1(July 1982).

26. Van Hoogevest, "The Churches and the World Refugee Crisis," p. 5.

27. Macphee, "Australia's New Policy," p. 10.

governments have tried to tighten and expedite their asylum procedures and to deny aliens access to them or to appeals from rejections. A recent speech by the coordinator of the World Council of Churches Refugee Service noted,

> It is not exaggeration to say that most Western governments are becoming more concerned about introducing measures that will effectively "keep people out" than about developing fair and humanitarian asylum policies and procedures.[28]

While the public hostility is principally aimed at illegal aliens, it can easily be directed at refugees and the resettlement program.

The influx of Cubans from Mariel in 1980 confused and damaged public support for refugee resettlement. The same loss of support and questioning of refugee motives, however, has appeared in almost all receiving countries, suggesting that the Mariel exodus and reaction was a visible symptom of a deeper process. In hard economic times, foreigners are seen as taking jobs from citizens. In much of Europe, the guest workers who came in better times have found that hard times lead to hard feelings. "A rise in xenophobia this year has become a primary political theme in West Germany . . . 82 percent of West Germans believed 'too many' foreigners now live here."[29] In the public mind, this creates an image of economic refugees jumping the queue to gain entry. Confused by the distinctions between foreigners, refugees, asylees, aliens, entrants, migrants, and numerous other terms, many people in these hard times simply want to keep people out. Senator Simpson has cautioned, "We might well then see all of the latent nativism, xenophobia, racism and scapegoating come fully to the surface and begin to tragically and profoundly influence public policy."[30]

On the other hand, there are strong public forces dedicated to the protection of aliens' rights, the granting of asylum, and refugee resettlement. These public forces have organized to promote public policies that strengthen the commitment to refugee resettlement. One sign of the worldwide commitment to refugee assistance is the awarding of the 1981 Noble Peace Prize to the Office of the U.N. High Commissioner for Refugees. In accepting the prize, High Commissioner Poul Hartling noted,

> Throughout history, mankind has also reacted to such upheavals and brought succor to the uprooted. . . . Through the ages the giving of sanctuary has become one of the noblest traditions of human nature and . . . nations have generously opened their doors to refugees.

SUMMARY

Since 1975, the main changes in refugee resettlement, particularly in the overseas receiving countries—Canada, Australia, and the United States—are as follows:

- —resettlement programs have become institutionalized with new legislation and administrative structures;
- —annual resettlement plans lead receiving countries to seek refugees in need rather than waiting for crises to develop;

28. "New Asian Aliens Concern Officials," *New York Times*, 20 Oct. 1982, p. 18.

29. Bradley Graham, "W. German Unemployment Magnifies Concern Over Foreign Workers." *Washington Post*, 18 Nov. 1982, p. F1.

30. Simpson, "Will America Control Its Borders?"

—the number of refugees accepted for resettlement has increased substantially and perhaps permanently; and

—use of the U.N. Convention definition of a refugee has equitably broadened the range of groups resettled, although it has also resulted in stricter criteria being applied.

Overall the current picture is of stricter but broader admissions criteria and relatively generous resettlement numbers.

At the same time, there is a growing disenchantment with resettlement and substantial political and public pressure to lower and cap refugee numbers. Thus far, such pressure has not been successful with regard to basic policies. For example, in the United States, in the last few years, several commissions, committees, and task forces have examined and reaffirmed the admissions policies embodied in the Refugee Act of 1980, and Congress to date has defeated efforts to place refugee admissions under an overall immigration ceiling.

It is necessary to take a moderately long view when assessing changes in resettlement policies and programs. Compared to the high numbers and public support of early 1980, refugee resettlement might be seen as endangered. However, measured against the ad hoc policies and temporary perspectives that prevailed into the seventies, one can perceive great strides forward.

The principal resettlement countries have been through a period of extraordinary resettlement efforts. The new institutions, policies, and programs are just that—they are new, they were developed in the midst of the crisis, and the countries are still learning to live with their new practices and legislation. It remains to be seen whether these new institutions, policies, and programs will be dismantled or will provide the foundation of a more effective resettlement system in the future. The commitment to resettlemment by the major receiving countries is strong at the moment, but it is also fragile. There is always the danger and possibility that retreats or cutbacks might occur because of public pressures, or legislative or executive action. Such retreats could leave one or more of the major resettlement countries unprepared or unable to respond if a major refugee crisis, requiring resettlement as a durable solution, were to occur in the future.

The policies of the major resettlement countries should be monitored, particularly over the next few years, to watch for developments whose presence would signal a weakening of an effective commitment to resettlement. Some of the danger signs are as follows:

—reductions in the flexibility of governments to respond in a timely manner to new refugee situations because of changes in the procedures that determine admission numbers;

—introduction of factors, such as the proposal for a single numerical ceiling for immigrants and refugees, that would put refugees into competition for admission with others;

—reduction in either annual quotas or actual admissions to levels that do not meet the need for resettlement or that do not protect the principle of first asylum;

—changes in the definition of a refugee or criteria for resettlement, by either legislative or administrative action; and

—failure to maintain, on an ongoing basis, an institutional capability to respond to refugee situations, thus leading to a return to the ad hoc policies and programs that prevailed into the mid-seventies.

[23]

new **community** 23(4): 441–460 October 1997

Admission policy, patterns of migration and integration: the German and French case compared

Wolfgang Seifert

Abstract *Different concepts of citizenship and nationality prevail in Germany and in France. These differences lead to different patterns of migration into these countries and to different policies governing the integration of migrants. The French concept of equality leads to a migration policy which is oriented towards the assimilation of migrants. Citizenship is accordingly granted more on the principle of jus soli and differences in status groups are not held to exist. Germany's understanding of citizenship has been based on descent and immigration policy has focused on groups which have German ethnic backgrounds. During the period of economic demand for foreign labour, Germany did not plan to have permanent immigration and considered the employment of foreign labour to be a temporary measure. In the meantime, even when the arrival of immigrants with no German ethnic background is accepted, there still exist enormous differences in the integration of different ethnic groups. While ethnic Germans are privileged in that they have a right to citizenship when they arrive in Germany, and are also entitled to various integration measures, other immigrant groups frequently may not be granted citizenship, even in the case of the second or third generations.*

The emergence of migration has been explained up to the present essentially through three types of variables. The approaches of neo-classical political economy for the most part used differential variables in the analysis of migration processes. Neoclassical economics focuses on differences in *levels* of income and labour markets between countries (Massey *et al.* 1993: 432). The second group of variables make reference to spatial distances[1] (e.g., the distance between region of origin and destination), costs of transportation, etc. A third path of explanation is concerned with 'variables of affinity', such as religion, culture, language, and migration networks (Weiner 1995: 116). These three types of variables form the basis of various theories of migration, but there does not exist a comprehensive approach which includes all of these concerns. Differing emphases among these variables can be found, depending upon the discipline.

The influence of migration policies upon migration behaviour has until now scarcely been considered, although it is obvious that migration flows are influenced by administrative measures. At this time, no Western industrialised country is without some form of immigration control; a willingness to receive refugees and migrant workers is more the exception than the rule, and the gates of entry in the high walls which have been built around Europe are comparatively small (Castles and Miller 1993: 23; Zolberg 1989). Controls and the establishment of admission policies express at the same time the selection of certain groups of immigrants. Immigration policy and its application thus take on a function of filtration. Since the status of prospective immigrants is also

Wolfgang Seifert is Assistant Professor at the Humbolt-University, Berlin.

0047–9586/97/040441–20

determined by admission policies, a change in the regulations of admission often causes changes in the composition of immigrant groups.

It is a fact that the Western European industrialised states have, in their recruitment of foreign workers, oriented themselves to the demands of their respective national economies. However, which workers fill this labour demand has not been determined by economic considerations, but has instead been a decision of national politics. Countries which had colonies (e.g., Great Britain, the Netherlands, and France) filled their labour demand in the main from within these dependencies. Countries without colonies recruited labour on the European periphery. During the phase of increasing restrictions on immigration since 1973, exceptions were also made for certain groups, for example for ethnic German immigrants into Germany from Eastern Europe (the *Aussiedler*).

Migration became globalised in the 1980s and 1990s. New migrants are coming from an increasing number of countries. Ever more countries are becoming involved in the system of transnational migration. The number of receiving countries has increased, and countries which in the past were often themselves emigrant-countries have become immigrant-regions as, for example, has happened in Italy and Spain. Paths of immigration have changed at the same time. Since migrant workers are accepted either not at all or only in small numbers, the area of asylum has taken on greater importance, as has illegal migration.

This article will show for the German case, but also with reference to France, how a given immigration policy leads to the establishment of a given migration pattern. Germany and France have in common the recruitment a great number of foreign workers in the period of economic prosperity after the end of the Second World War. These workers were employed predominantly in industrialised mass production and in heavy industry – in workplaces which require only low levels of qualification. Here the commonalities end. Migration patterns, and policies governing immigration and integration, varied considerably up until the freeze in recruitment of 1973 (Germany) and 1974 (France). Thereafter, immigration policies in France and Germany came to resemble each other, and to focus upon the limitation of further movement. An additional issue, therefore, is how Germany and France have reacted to the increasing globalisation of migration.

Different concepts of citizenship and integration policy in Germany and France

Historically, Germany and France have had differing concepts of citizenship and nationality. In these differences lies the foundation for different concepts of immigration and the integration of migrants. The understanding of nationhood in France has been state-centred and assimilationist, while the German understanding was *Volk*-centered and differentialist (Brubaker 1992: 1). In the French case, the second generation of immigrants has long been naturalised automatically as a result of a state centred, expansive and assimilative self-understanding of the French nation. In the German approach, citizenship was based on descent. As a consequence, German citizenship was inclusive with respect to those of German descent, but not towards other foreign immigrants (Brubaker 1992: 14). Both traditions had consequences in the respective migration policies of the two countries after World War II. The ideal of the *assimilation* of immigrants had the consequence that French migration policy was oriented towards groups which could be assimilated into French society. German borders, on the other hand, were open only for those of German descent. Germany accepted ethnic Germans in high numbers not considering them to be immigrants, and defined itself as a non-immigration country. Immigration of foreign nationals in periods of economic demand was considered to be a short term solution. Immigrants should not settle permanently. This is best reflected in the name created for this kind of foreign worker: 'guest-worker' (*Gastarbeiter*). Even when temporary migration became permanent, the ideology of being a country of non-immigration endured. The fact that Germany accepted so many immigrants despite an ideology of no immigration cannot be interpreted as a lack of control over migration. EU-citizens were entitled to come but also family members of migrants and asylum seekers. Germany was quite successful, however, in preventing further labour migration. In the period of increasing unemployment after the oil price shock of 1973, the number of foreign wage and salary earners decreased (between 1973 and 1995) from 2.6 million to 2.1 million while the foreign population increased considerably in this period from 4.0 million to 7.2 million.

The period of recruitment of foreign labour

Germany

After the end of the Second World War, West Germany was continually exposed to massive immigration. Owing to the reorientation of the political scene after the end of the war, both West and East Germany had to integrate huge numbers of immigrants into largely destroyed infrastructure. The census of 1950 gives a figure of 7.9 million displaced persons (Münz and Ulrich 1996: 8). Despite the difficult circumstances, the integration of war refugees proceeded quickly. As immigration caused by the war itself gradually came to an end, East Germany became the most important source of immigration. Between the founding of the GDR in 1949 and the construction of the Berlin Wall in 1961, East Germany lost 3.8 million people (Münz and Ulrich 1996: 11). Despite this numerically significant movement, demand for labour in West Germany soon exceeded these levels. In order to satisfy the West German economy's demand for cheap labour, the first contract for recruitment of foreign labour had already been signed in 1955, although it did not at first have great effect as the influx of workers from the GDR continued. Only 144,000 Italians were employed in West Germany by 1960 (Herbert 1986: 188). This situation quickly changed with the construction of the Berlin Wall. After the recruitment treaty with Italy there followed corresponding agreements with Greece, Spain, Turkey, Morocco, Portugal, Tunisia, and with Yugoslavia (Münz and Ulrich 1996: 15). The recruitment of foreign labour was, however, viewed as only a temporary measure to bridge periods of extreme labour scarcity (Herbert 1986). This recruitment took place according to the requirements of labour market politics and was carried out with an eye to public order (Dohse 1981).

This type of recruitment was supported by almost all social groups in Germany and found a correspondingly broad basis. While the employers were able to overcome a labour bottleneck, the unions took part in the drawing up of recruitment policies and had won equal pay for foreign workers, as well as their inclusion in the social security system. They were thus able to prevent a decrease

Figure 1. *Foreign wage and salary earners, 1960–1994*

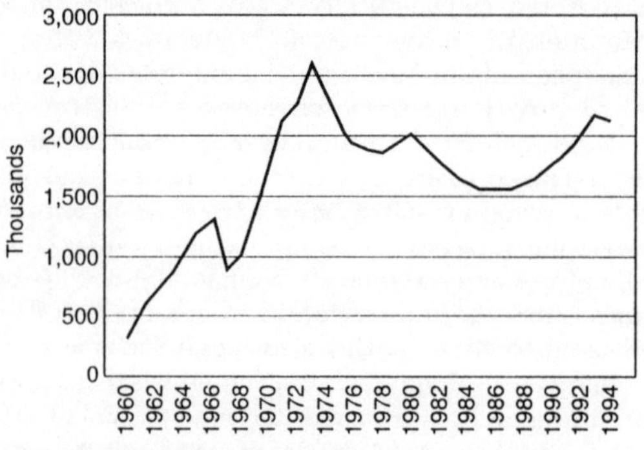

Note: 1960–1990 West Germany only.
Source: Statistisches Bundesamt.

in wages (Herbert 1986: 191ff). The employment of foreign workers was intended to function as an economic buffer for native workers, and thus to guarantee higher employment stability. The introduction of foreign workers was also intended to prevent labour-intensive sectors of production moving to low wage countries. Additionally, the employment of a foreign workforce at the lower end of the occupational hierarchy opened opportunities for occupational advancement for native workers. The state's stability and security concerns were also addressed, so that the introduction of foreign workers encountered at first scarcely any opposition.

The principle of labour force rotation, i.e., the continual exchange of employed labour, passed its first crucial test during the recession of 1966–1967. The number of foreign workers fell by half a million (see Figure 1), which amounted to 46 per cent of the foreign labour force (Angenendt 1992: 155). Thus the desired effect of being able to introduce foreign workers as an economic buffer was realised.

German workers were for the most part spared the effects of this crisis, which hit foreign workers particularly hard, and as economic prosperity returned a large number of foreign workers were still available. Between 1968 and 1973 the number of foreign workers climbed from one million to 2.6 million. The rotation of workers slowed during this phase, and foreign workers began to bring their families to Germany. In 1971, foreigners who had been living for at least five years in Germany received a five-year work permit (Angenendt 1992: 157). In this way a regulation was established which for the first time took into account humanitarian considerations. Decisive in this connection, however, were the interests of employers, who did not wish constantly to train new workers. Foreign workers were predominantly employed in sectors which did not require long training periods. Thus the slowing of worker rotation in the early 1970s, rather than being a failure in control policy, instead furthered the interests of German industry.

France

France, of all European countries, has the longest tradition of being an immigration-country. In 1931 there were already 2.7 million foreigners living in France (Hollifield 1994: 151). Before the First World War, France was already relying upon immigration to compensate for a low birth rate among the native French population compared to contemporary birthrates in Germany and Great Britain. Belgians and Italians had already immigrated to France in the nineteenth century. Poles, Czechs, and other Slavs came in the 1920s. Immediately after the Second World War France again took up this tradition, and North and West Africans, as well as Portuguese, have come since then. Permanent immigration was seen as necessary for the modernisation of the French economy. The need for an estimated 1.5 million immigrants was made official in the first plan for economic rebuilding, for the years 1946–1951 (Kubat 1993: 165). Furthermore, rather than temporary employment, the assimilation of the immigrants was envisioned. For this reason, France sought immigrants from countries such as Italy, Spain, and Portugal, which were seen as being culturally similar (Hollifield 1994).

The *Office National d'Immigration* (ONI) had already been established in 1945 for the administrative governance of immigration, and was thus responsible for recruitment, for the distribution of positions, as well as for the integration of immigrants (Angenendt 1992: 22). Yet the recruitment procedures of the ONI proved in practice to be ineffective, and many workers bypassed the ONI and came to France illegally (Silverman 1992: 41). This illegal immigration was tolerated, however, and was often legalised *ex post facto*. Legally recruited workers received a work permit limited to only one year, which was valid only for a certain position and in a certain region. It was intended that through these measures specific regions and specific industrial sectors should be supplied with labour. For foreign workers it was thus more convenient to come into France illegally, to seek out a position, and then to apply for legalisation afterwards (Moulier and Tapinos 1978: 142 ff). Eighty-two per cent of immigrants in 1968 were illegal (Castles 1987: 53). between 1964 and 1970, of approximately 65 per cent of immigrants into France were legally recognised *ex post facto* (Silverman 1992: 44). This means that during this period the French government did without any form of control over immigration and the selection of immigrants.

Recruitment of labour from the Catholic, southern European countries decreased in the 1960s, partly because of favourable economic development within these countries themselves, partly owing to competition with recruitment from other European countries. The resulting gaps were filled with immigrants from Muslim countries (Hollifield 1992: 58). Among the countries of origin which received preferential treatment were France's former colonies, in particular Algeria. Algerians were, up until 1962, French citizens with unrestricted right of domicile. Thereafter they were able to enter France with a tourist visa, and then apply later for permission to live and work in France (Kubat 1993: 168). The influx of Algerians was heatedly discussed. Some contended that they would not adequately assimilate. Therefore, the French Government made efforts to control immigration from Algeria, while for other groups scarcely any controls existed at the end of the 1960s. In 1969, an intergovernmental agreement between France and Germany fixed a quota of 35,000 immigrants from Algeria. A work permit was obligatory before entering France.

The rapid growth of the labour force led to a number of social problems. The increase in social conflicts then led the French government in the early 1970s to make its first efforts at regaining control over immigration. The freeze in foreign

Figure 2. *Foreign population in France and Germany, 1976 (%)*

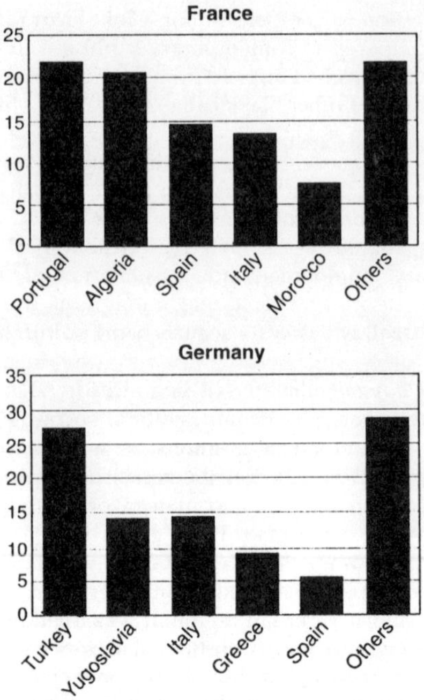

labour recruitment in 1974 was intended to win back control over immigration once and for all. In this way, French migration policies followed those of its European neighbours (Zolberg 1983: 243).

French and German industry had similarly configured needs for foreign labour in the 1960s and early 1970s, which they each filled in an entirely different manner. When France started its recruitment of foreign labour after World War II, permanent immigrants who were willing to assimilate were given preference. During the period of high demand for foreign labour, France renounced in large part political or administrative control over immigration, and restricted itself to *ex post facto* legal recognition. In contrast, German officials never planned to accept permanent immigration. A guest worker system was developed which was strictly oriented towards the demands of the labour market. Both countries thus satisfied the demands of industry, but the way in which they did so differed entirely. France developed migration relations with Portugal, Spain, Italy and its former colonies, especially Algeria. Germany recruited labour from Turkey, Italy, Greece, Spain and Yugoslavia. Where in Germany the employment of foreign workers was seen as only a temporary measure, France planned on permanently integrating at least some groups of migrants. In both countries foreign labour was predominantly employed in low-level positions in mass production and in heavy industry.

The phase of immigration restrictions

The oil crisis can be considered to be a turning point in migration politics. The introduction of microelectronics, the shift of labour intensive production in low wage countries and the entrance of the 'baby-boom generation' in the labour market caused increasing unemployment and a decreasing demand for additional labour. But a lack of cheap labour was still present in some sectors of the labour market. Migration policy in France and Germany now turned from an active position to a defensive stance which aimed at preventing further large-scale immigration.

Germany

While it is true that the system of guest-worker recruitment had fulfilled expectations in industry and politics up until the freeze in foreign labour recruitment in 1973, this changed subsequently. Illusions of 'temporary' employment of foreign workers were quickly lost. With the halt in the rotation of workers, temporary migration became permanent. Despite increasing levels in unemployment and structural change, German industry remained unable to do without foreign workers, who were concentrated in industrial sectors which were unattractive to German workers. Since renewed rotation of foreign workers was not an option, there remained no alternative to a long-term, or permanent stay for those foreign workers living in Germany. The number of foreign workers declined after 1973 through repatriations, although the number of foreigners living in Germany remained relatively constant, since as foreign workers decided in favour of a long-term stay in Germany, they sent for their families. Neither the former nor the latter had been the intended result of the freeze in recruitment, yet both were foreseeable developments. The selection of young men in the recruitment process made it reasonable to expect that they would bring families to join them when migration became permanent. It was impossible, for humanitarian reasons, to restrict the reuniting of families, and the denial of work permits to family members would have divided the foreign population into two status groups: those with, and those without work permits. At first, children of migrants were denied work permits, but a ruling was subsequently introduced, according to which work permits were to be granted to children of migrants after a waiting period of two years, and to the migrant's spouses after four years. Family reunifications were unintentionally further encouraged to some extent, as child support for children living abroad was lowered (Meier-Braun 1988: 12f), such that many foreign workers sent for their children. Family reunification has remained up to the present an important gate of entry.

After the freeze in recruitment, the possibility of legal immigration into Germany was available only to a few groups. This applied to dependants of foreigners living in Germany, citizens of other EU countries, managers, correspondents, artists, students, *Aussiedler*, seasonal and contract workers, asylum seekers, quota refugees and persons displaced by war (Münz and Ulrich 1996: 18).

As a result of the internationalisation of the labour market, the opportunity was opened for highly qualified workers to seek work without regard to national boundaries. In particular, international corporations brought in such workers (Münz and Ulrich 1996). However, science and research have also become profoundly international, as is also true of finance, commerce, and the service industries.

Entry into the German workforce is comparatively easy for foreign citizens of other EU countries, who are able to choose freely their workplace within the European community. They are entitled to a special EU residency permit (Schmahl 1995). Even so migration out of EU states showed a clear decline in the 1970s and 1980s. The opening of the labour market for persons from third countries represented a decisive renunciation of a strict, nationally-oriented migration policy. In this way an essential element of national civil administration, the control of migration, was relinquished, at least within the EU.

In the 1980s and 1990s migration became more and more a problem of legitimation. Given rising levels of unemployment among German and foreign workers, it was difficult to justify further migration. Despite public debates surrounding migration, the migration and integration of ethnic Germans from East and Central Europe (*Aussiedler*), as well as from the GDR (*Übersiedler*), were not subject to any restrictions during the 1970s and 1980s. The incorporation of these *Aussiedler* and *Übersiedler* will be examined first, and then, second, the measures which were aimed at restricting migration with particular attention to the issues of refugees and asylum claimants.

The acceptance of migrants from the GDR (*Übersiedler*) was never in question in the FRG, since citizenship of the GDR had never been formally recognised, so that East Germans were according to the West German Basic Law (*Grundgesetz*) also German, with all the attendant rights and duties. The status of *Aussiedler* was based in essence upon a *jus sanguinis* understanding of citizenship, according to which nationality is based on the principle of descent. Thus the German national is defined as an individual of German ancestry, regardless of whether or not he or she is living on German territory. While elements of *jus soli* are also embodied in German citizenship law, as for example in possible naturalisation after a certain length of stay, the general ideology remains firmly based in *jus sanguinis*. This is clear in the adherence to the motto that Germany is 'not an immigration country', as well as in the special status granted to *Aussiedler*, who are not considered to be immigrants.

The influx of *Aussiedler*, however, remained quite low in the beginning, as an effect of the Iron Curtain. In some cases the West German government made active attempts to make emigration from East European countries possible for the *Aussiedler*. In the case of Romania, compensation payments were even provided. This changed after the opening of the countries of Eastern Europe. With the passage in 1990 of a law regarding the admission of *Aussiedler* (the *Aussiedleraufnahmegesetz*), restrictions were placed on the free entrance of *Aussiedler* into West Germany. Entrance must now be applied for in advance in the country of origin, and a 50-page questionnaire which registers national affiliation must be filled in (Münz and Ulrich 1996). At the end of 1992 an administrative limit was placed upon the immigration of *Aussiedler* through the establishment of a processing capacity of 220,000 applications per year (Vogel 1994: 141). Yet it was not only the *Aussiedler* who made use of the newly won freedoms. Other groups attempted to escape the adverse living conditions in the countries of Eastern Europe by finding work in the West, and Germany was a preferred destination.

The German government reacted to this, on the one hand, with an intensification of border controls, but on the other hand legal routes of migration were also opened. The employment opportunities created for workers from the neighbouring countries to the East were exclusively temporary. Seasonal workers can pursue employment in agricultural and other sectors, such as the hotel and restaurant industries, for up to three months a year. Where in 1991 only 129,000 seasonal workers were accepted, in 1995 the numbers had already reached 193,000 (Werner 1996: 46). Contract labourers are employed by foreign firms which are active as subcontractors with a German firm. This practice is particularly common in the construction sector. In 1992 there were still 95,000 contract workers employed in Germany, but in 1995 their numbers decreased to 49,000 (Werner 1996: 47). A small quota of guest workers was also agreed upon with several East European countries. This quota totalled 9,900 people, yet it was not filled, and in 1994 it was taken advantage of by only 5,500 workers (Werner 1996: 44). One goal which was supposed to be reached through the availability of a temporary access for East Europeans to the German labour market was the avoidance of illegal employment (Sandbrink 1996).

As is the case in other countries, there are signs of an increase in the number of persons illegally employed in Germany. One can only speculate on the actual figure, since empirically reliable data do not exist. Nevertheless, there are a number of indicators. For example, the number of individuals picked up while crossing illegally into Germany increased from 7,200 in 1990 to 31,100 in 1994 (Vogel 1996: 6). Since many of those who seek work illegally enter Germany legally, for example with a tourist visa, the extent of illegal employment in Germany cannot be determined through these figures. In the same time period, however, the number of proceedings concerned with the illegal employment of foreign workers climbed from 28,800 to 71,600 (Vogel 1996: 6). This increase is not necessarily exclusively caused by rising levels of illegal employment, but might also be the result of intensified control. Other signs also point to the increasing importance of illegal employment within the German labour market.

The true arenas of conflict in immigration more generally during the 1980s and 1990s were asylum and refugee policy. The asylum procedure in Germany was complicated and became ever longer and more drawn out. In 1977, an asylum process took approximately six years to exhaust every legal recourse (Münch 1993: 73). As a result, various measures were adopted to speed up the asylum process, and finally in 1980 a visa requirement was instituted for the most important countries of origin for asylum applicants. At the same time, airline companies had, at their own expense, to return persons without visas to their point of origin (Münch 1993: 83 ff). Thus the possibility of applying for asylum at all was considerably restricted. Finally in 1982, the new law governing asylum procedure brought into force another measure for the acceleration of the process, as 'obviously ungrounded applications' were subject to a shortened procedure and to limited legal remedies (Münch 1993: 82 ff).

At the beginning of the 1990s there followed further decisive reductions of the right to asylum, which reached a high point in the so-called 'asylum compromise'. In 1993 a change in the right to asylum under the Basic Law (*Grundgesetz*) was adopted. Thus, for example, the protection against deportation was removed for certain groups under the new legal policy towards foreigners, and deportation proceedings were speeded up (Höfling-Semnar 1995: 130 ff). The possibility of applying for asylum was considerably restricted through the 'third

Figure 3. *Immigration to Germany*

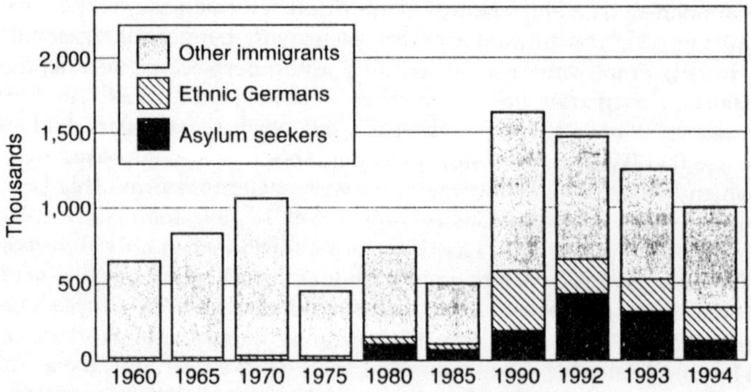

Note: Until 1990 West Germany only.

country rule' (Knipping and Saumweber-Meyer 1995). If someone enters Germany through a secure third country, he or she is not allowed to apply for asylum. Inasmuch as all of Germany's neighbours are considered to be secure third states, entry into Germany became for the most part impossible, since the way by land is ruled out, and the way by air is blocked by the carrier sanctions. Furthermore, countries of origin were classified as free of persecution under a graduated list. As a result, persons of these nationalities were not allowed to apply for asylum (Münch 1993: 133 ff). Through the influence of these measures, the number of applications for asylum declined sharply (Bosswick 1995).

In general, the right to asylum was preserved, yet the hurdles on the way there were set so high that the claim to it was made for the most part impossible. In all of this, Germany followed the lead of other countries to a large extent. This was in some cases intentional, as for example in the context of harmonising immigration policy in connection with the treaty of Schengen, but in some cases the successful policy tightening in one country had as its result rising numbers of applicants for asylum in other countries. For example, while the numbers of asylum applications declined as result of the strengthening of laws in Germany, they increased in France and Switzerland. In keeping with these negatively competitive politics, Switzerland reacted by strengthening its own laws (Santel 1995: 178).

The living conditions of applicants for asylum were consciously brought in as a means of limiting immigration. It was intended that better living conditions should never constitute an incentive to migration. For example, in 1980 the granting of social assistance was restricted, and changed to direct material assistance. The withholding of a work permit can also be viewed as being a part of these deterrence measures, yet there was a perceived danger that the cessation of recruitment could be weakened by the path of asylum. There have thus been repeated demands that applicants for asylum be forbidden to work. At the same time, however, the prohibition of work has been a considerable burden for the budgets of the municipalities.

Arguments concerning high costs were repeatedly raised against applicants for asylum. The granting of asylum was the subject of continued criticism which reached its peak with hostile activities on the part of extremists against asylum seekers and other immigrant groups. It is probable, that the federal government's refugee and asylum policies contributed considerably to less acceptance towards asylum applicants. The low rates of recognition (3.2 per cent in 1993; Velling 1995: 49) for asylum strengthened the view that a request for asylum was merely the ruse of someone who actually wanted to take advantage of the welfare state.

The structure of migration to Germany changed drastically in the 1980s and 1990s. It is now dominated by *Aussiedler*, migrants from Eastern Europe and an increasing number of applicants for asylum from the Third World. The latter have tended to enter Germany as asylum seekers. The differences in treatment towards migrants depending upon their status have been striking. Although there were fears of great waves of migration after the opening of the countries of Eastern Europe, this scenario has not come to pass. Rather than instituting strict policies of rejection towards the young democracies of Eastern Europe, Germany has opened opportunities for temporary access to its labour market.

France

After the freeze in recruitment in 1974, the French authorities took back the control of immigration which they had for a time given up. As in other countries, the authorities assumed that with the freeze in recruitment migration was at an end. The reality, however, was quite different (Garson 1992). As in the case of Germany, France was confronted after the freeze in recruitment with a significant influx of family dependants (Withol de Wenden 1994a). In 1977, a restriction in family reunification was ordered.

Despite the regaining of national control over immigration, the freeze in recruitment was not carried out categorically, so that exceptional rulings were made for certain industries such as mining and construction, and the employment of foreign seasonal workers remained possible in agriculture as well (Hollifield 1992: 76). At the same time, however, more forceful action was taken against illegal immigration. To that end, corresponding technical-administrative devices were created, and police powers expanded (Angenendt 1992: 27). With a few exceptions, the emphasis of France's migration policy until the early 1980s was on reducing the number of foreigners (Kubat 1993). A programme for the voluntarily support of repatriation came into effect in 1977 which had legal force only until 1981. During this period approximately 95,000 people applied under the programme, and 65 per cent of them were Spanish or Portuguese (Kubat 1993: 175). Whereas proceedings were liberal in the case of European immigrant groups, so that family reunification from the future EU member-states Spain, Portugal and Greece remained possible (Angenendt 1992: 28), there were perceptible attempts to reduce the number of Algerians in France (Hollifield 1994).

The immigration policy of the socialist government elected in 1981 was essentially a continuation of earlier policies and emphasised the restriction of immigration, although the position of foreigners already living in France was improved by long-term residence permits and a conditional amnesty for illegal migrants (Hollifield 1996). Measures aimed at a restriction of immigration were expanded through changes in passport regulations and through punishments for employers who hired illegal workers. The goal of restricting the number of African immigrants in France was maintained, and those returning to their country of origin received compensatory payments (Angenendt 1992: 29).

Migration into France met with resistance among the native population early on. Already in 1973 the Algerian government called a halt to the emigration of its citizens to France as a result of rising levels of xenophobia and attacks against Algerians living in France. With increasing unemployment, immigrants were increasingly made scapegoats for growing economic problems (Hollifield 1994). Tensions and xenophobic activities were above all noticeable in those cities with communist governments. It is conceivable that this was a response to the critical stance of the unions towards migration. The unions and the French Communist Party spoke out against immigration because they feared competition on the labour market and expected other negative consequences, for instance in the supply of housing (Hollifield 1992: 58). They feared wage pressures and the creation of an 'industrial reserve army'.

In the context of this xenophobic political climate, the right wing extremist *Front National*, which was advocating a programme of immigration restriction and repatriation, was suddenly able to enjoy electoral successes. For example, the share of votes for the *Front National* to the National Assembly climbed from 9.7 per cent in 1988, to 12.7 per cent in 1993 (Lambert 1995: 119). There was thus increasing pressure on the government to bring into effect a restrictive migration policy.

This can be seen in the granting of asylum. At first, France pursued refugee and asylum policies which were liberal in comparison to those of its neighbours. Until recently immediate refusal at the French border was not allowable under French law, even if applicants arrived from a safe third country. Forced return of refugees at the border was only possible if they had previously been granted asylum in another country (Lambert 1995: 115). However, with increases in numbers of applicants, the yearly percentages of recognition sank. In order to cope with the growing numbers of refugees and applicants for asylum, additional administrative personnel were trained, and the administrative guidelines were simplified in order to speed up the asylum process. This was intended to assure that applicants for asylum did not remain in a provisional situation (Withol de Wenden 1994b). In 1990 all decisions were made on the basis of written dossiers, whereas in the mid-1990s there have been hearings in roughly one third of all cases (Lambert 1995).

On the whole, French immigration policy after the oil crisis can be characterised as a period of re-institutionalisation of control over immigration. Border controls were intensified, and legal rules were created which corresponded in broad outline to those of neighbouring European countries. The opening of Eastern Europe had little effect on France. Migration policy in Germany and France had the same aims after the oil crisis of 1973. Both countries tried to reduce their numbers of foreign inhabitants and to prevent further immigration in large numbers. The opportunity for immigrants to apply for asylum has been restricted. This can be seen as a reaction to tensions in the labour market in both countries. In France and Germany the immigrants' countries of origin changed as well. Both countries had been preferred destinations for migrants from the Third World and they were both successful in the limitation of migration from the South. The commonalties in the migration policies of France and Germany since the mid-1970s did not lead to similar migration patterns. One reason for this is the exception made in Germany for ethnic Germans, and also the temporary forms of employment of Eastern European labour. Such kinds of migration can not be found in France. The influx of both ethnic Germans and of temporary workers were based on political decisions.

Integration policy

Germany[2]

The selective German migration policies, which opened different opportunities for access to different groups, were expressed in policies governing integration as well. There were essentially three tracks. First, to the *Aussiedler* were granted full integration with all rights, citizenship, inclusion in the welfare state, and access to all segments of the labour market. Second, the majority of migrants enjoyed a partial integration which, although it included a wide-ranging position of equality on the labour market and inclusion in the welfare state, did not include political and social integration. Since the members of this second group are not citizens, they cannot form an effective political lobby. The third track constitutes the opposite of integration: non-integration. Refugees and applicants for asylum are tolerated, but have no rights whatsoever, restricted access to the labour market, and receive only support for their barest subsistence. The characteristics of full integration will first be considered, and thus the integration of *Aussiedler*.

Aussiedler had a claim to German citizenship, and were able to make claims to social services to the same extent as had they been living and working in Germany. Since 1990, however, *Aussiedler* no longer receive unemployment assistance oriented to fictive income from a comparable position in Germany, but rather receive a fixed sum of money as assistance in integration. Until 1991 work done in a foreign country was credited as if it had been done in Germany. This implied a preference for *Aussiedler* in the pension insurance system, and it was in this conjuncture that accusations of over-integration were made (Heinelt and Lohmann 1992: 92) since services were granted to *Aussiedler* from state insurance, without their having made contributions for these services. In 1991 pension entitlements were reduced to 70 per cent of the pensions received by a native and were lowered again another 10 per cent in 1996 to 60. Those who arrived since 1996 receive only minimum pensions (Münz and Ohliger 1997).

Despite these restrictions, no other group of migrants have been given such favourable provisions for their integration. After the freeze in recruitment of 1973, a policy of 'consolidation' in the employment of foreigners was proclaimed, with an eye to the former guest workers. In practice this meant '... restriction of the number of foreign workers and accommodation to the social infrastructure's capacity for inclusion' (Meier-Braun 1988: 12). 'Consolidation' was also intended to include those among the foreign population who wished to remain permanently in Germany. In practice very little was done, however, to realise this intention.

In 1983 a bill was passed 'for the encouragement of immigrants to return to their countries of origin' (Bischoff and Teubner 1991). This law was valid for one year and enabled foreigners willing to return to withdraw the contributions they had paid into retirement insurance (i.e., only the worker's own part). For those who were unemployed, additional repatriation assistance of DM 10,500 was to be paid (Velling 1995). These repatriation measures achieved little success, and led for the most part to claims from individuals who were already intending to leave the country (Bade 1994; Collinson 1993; Hönekopp 1987).

One precondition to full and equal participation is access to citizenship. Although citizenship law was simplified, and in particular the fees in proceedings were reduced, decisive changes were not undertaken. The principle of *jus sanguinis* continues to apply, which means that the nationality of children born in Germany is determined by the nationality of their parents. One particular change of approach is nevertheless discernible here. In 1991, elements of *jus soli* were for the first time taken up into German citizenship law. Foreigners who were born in, or who had grown up in Germany have an entitlement to be naturalised if they submitted an application before their 23rd birthday. Expectations of ability to earn one's living were no longer put forward, and minor criminal offences were also not considered (Schmahl 1995).

One may, in general terms, distinguish between two forms of naturalisation: naturalisation by entitlement, and discretionary naturalisation. Alongside the *Aussiedler* and their families, claims to the right of naturalisation may also be made by foreigners of the second generation, as well as all foreigners who have been in Germany at least 15 years. Discretionary naturalisation, on the other hand, is contingent upon such preconditions as language proficiency, integration into German ways of life, integrity, possession of an apartment, ability to support oneself, and a continuous stay in Germany for at least 10 years. Thus discretionary naturalisation resembles more 'an administrative-technical act of grace' (Bös 1995: 182) than a claim to a right. As a rule, the former nationality must be given up in the naturalisation process. Yet this point is the subject of public discussion. With the granting of a double citizenship, the number of naturalisations could be increased, and in this way administrative equality could be achieved for the previously foreign population. Access to citizenship must especially be made easier for young men and women of the second and third generation. Yet even without a legal ruling it seems that, at least as concerns double citizenship, a liberal naturalisation policy is being applied. Of the 7,565 people from Turkey who were naturalised in 1993, double citizenship was 'tolerated' in 4,849 cases (*Die Beauftrage der Bundesregierung für die Belange der Ausländer* 1995: 126).

Foreign employees are, as a rule, integrated into the social security system. They are able to make claims, according to their contributions, to retirement, unemployment, health, and old-age care insurance. In general it presents no problem that services are granted in accordance with contributions since immigrants were young when arriving in Germany, such that over the course of a full working life a sufficient claim on retirement will have been built up. Still, the pensions of first-generation guest workers earned through employment at the bottom of the occupational hierarchy may seem comparatively low. Immigrants can also make claims to social assistance, although this can under certain circumstances lead to expulsion.

The segments of the labour market in which immigrants had been principally employed are among those most strongly affected by structural changes. Children of migrants had particular problems in finding employment. Nevertheless, in some sectors of the labour market a demand for labour still existed. Low-paid jobs in the service sector absorbed migrants, although there also existed a scarcity of skilled workers in the 1980s.

The federal government has been applying a specific non-integration policy to refugees and also to applicants for asylum. The living conditions of those groups are systematically worsened in order to direct the flow of refugees elsewhere than into Germany. This policy of scaring migrants away has had a high price. Having been moved to the centre of attention in this way, applicants for asylum have a negative image. While some have seen the German ethnic nation-state as

Figure 4. *Naturalisation in Germany 1974–1994*

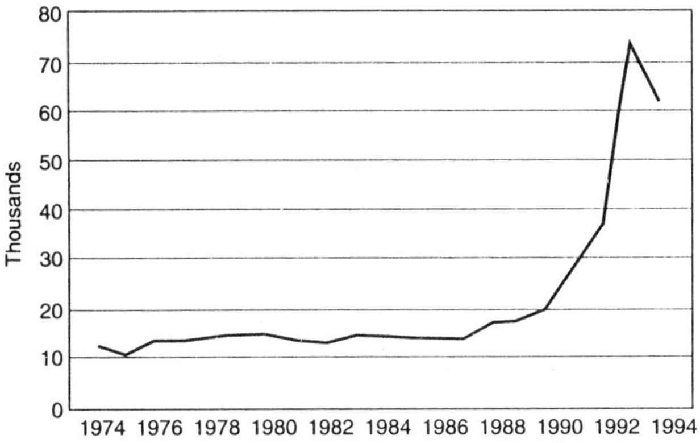

Source: Beauftragte der Bundesregierung für die Belange der Ausländer 1995.

being in jeopardy, others have complained about the high costs of lodgings and of legal proceedings.

Until the second half of the 1980s, the number of naturalisations in Germany remained rather insignificant. Until the middle of the 1980s, the natural growth of the foreign population (the difference between the birth rates and mortality rates) was greater than the number of naturalisations, such that the number of foreigners living in Germany would have grown even without additional migration. This was no longer the case at the end of the 1980s, since the number of naturalisations increased. The number of naturalisations was at a low level in the 1980s but increased in the 1990s. In particular, right of naturalisation by entitlement brought a first peak in the number of naturalisations. In 1994 the total number of naturalisations decreased, but the share of those naturalised by entitlement increased. In 1994 approximately 1 per cent of the migrant population received German citizenship. By international comparison, rates of naturalisation in Germany are extremely low (Sweden 8.3 per cent (1993); the Netherlands 5.5 per cent (1993)).

On the whole, there are signs that the long period of inaction with respect to the question of integration and the living conditions of the foreign population is gradually coming to an end. Further progress on this score must be measured against a long overdue, radical reform of German citizenship law. *De facto* nationals should also be given the status of nationals *de jure*, and equality of treatment should be the rule. The privileged status of *Aussiedler* is scarcely justifiable. More broadly, however, it can be assumed that many of the integration measures granted to *Aussiedler* are reasonable (e.g. language support). Accordingly, the extension of some of these measures to other migrant groups should be considered.

France

At the end of the nineteenth century, it was easy for migrants into France to gain citizenship. Citizenship was automatically granted to children born in France

Figure 5. *Naturalisation in France 1974–1993*

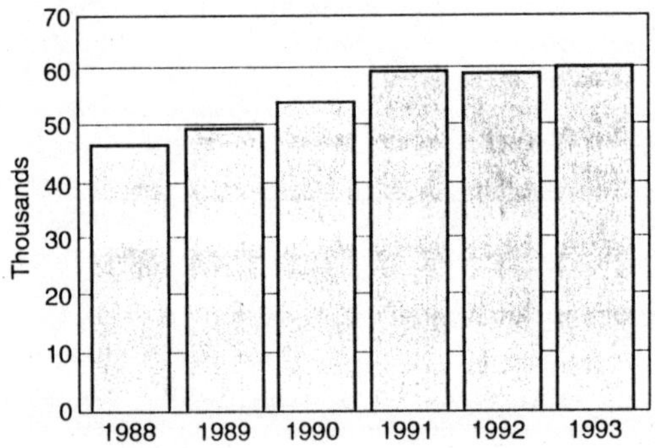

Source: SOPEMI 1995.

(Schnapper 1995: 100). These traditions of citizenship law have to some extent been maintained to the present day. After two years, the spouse of a French citizen becomes a citizen as well. The children of French citizens also receive citizenship, irrespective of where they are born. The most important ruling governing the integration of migrants, the automatic granting of citizenship to children born in France upon their eighteenth birthday, was modified in 1993. Young foreigners are now required to submit an application for French citizenship between their sixteenth and twenty-first birthdays (Withol de Wenden 1994b).

The number of naturalisations increased at the end of the 1980s (see Figure 5), and reached approximately 60,000 naturalisations per year between 1991 and 1993. This represents a naturalisation rate of 1.5 per cent. In 1988, Portuguese were still the most frequently naturalised group (8,000). In 1993 it was Moroccans (13,100). Algerians (79,000) and Tunisians (5,400) also had high rates of naturalisation, so that nearly half of the naturalisations come from North Africa (SOPEMI 1995).

Despite such liberal citizenship law there have been considerable problems in the integration of immigrants. Already in the 1950s and 1960s, owing to shortages in the supply of housing, the mass of immigrants to France lived in run-down areas. 'Bidonvilles'-self-built dwellings – which often house several thousand people – began to appear in vacant lots on the outskirts of large cities (Manfrass 1992: 103). Corrugated metal shacks, wooden settlements and overcrowded rooms in dilapidated hotels were representative of awful housing conditions. In such overcrowded slums there arose tensions between the native population and migrants, culminating in open violence (Angenendt 1992: 25). The disadvantages of the migrants continue to the present. Nevertheless, the French government has been pursuing an active integration policy for more than a decade. This integration policy is not directed exclusively towards migrants, but also towards French citizens in marginal positions. Integration within residential areas (i.e., reducing the concentration of disadvantaged people in certain suburbs), educational and occupational measures, and programmes directed at the improvement of education were measures which were intended to further the integration of migrants *and* other disadvantaged groups (Withol de

Wenden 1994b: 264). These measures have met with little acceptance among the population, however, and have continued to encounter open resistance.

In the 1980s and 1990s, the perspective from which the integration of immigrants was viewed was more socio-cultural than economic. Islam, which has become the second religion in France, met with reservations among the population: 'Islam cannot be ignored in the future, and its proponents are trying to build up and to stabilise its presence on French soil through demands for *Hallal* meatmarkets, Muslim gravestones and cemeteries, etc., and through affairs such as those surrounding Salman Rushdie, the wearing of the veil, and the Gulf War' (Withol de Wenden 1994b: 267).

It was obviously unacceptable for a large part of the French population to see veiled women in the streets. This appeared to some to be backward, while for others it was viewed as a lack of willingness to assimilate. In this way, in France, questions of migration and integration have taken on cultural and religious aspects, while in Germany, which also has a high proportion of Muslim migrants, labour market aspects were at the fore. France's longer tradition as an immigration-country is also evident in the presence of policies more directed at assimilation. Although the term 'integration' took the place of 'assimilation' in official parlance, the goal of making Frenchmen out of migrants was maintained and there was scarcely any discussion of multiculturalism (Schnapper 1995: 105). Here French immigration policy was stuck in a dilemma: On the one hand, a favourable framework for integration was created, as in the easy access to citizenship, while on the other hand expectations for assimilation were disappointed, both through the concentration of immigrants in lower social strata, and through the migrants' religion and culture, which were viewed as signifying their unwillingness to integrate into French society.

In respect of the integration of immigrants, France and Germany differ considerably. France has a tradition of *jus soli* and also a tradition of assimilating immigrants. Germany's principle of *jus sanguinis* makes it difficult for the government and the population to accept immigrants who are not of German descent as equal citizens. While in Germany the conditions for the integration of immigrants differ considerably according to different status groups (as is seen in the privileged position given ethnic Germans in particular) immigrants to France are not separated into status groups and are treated equally. In respect of citizenship, French society is more open to migrants than Germany. In both countries, however, migrants still are in marginal positions on the labour market and live in largely segmented areas in the big cities.

Conclusion

Which groups are to receive the right to migrate into France or Germany is in large part determined through political-administrative norms. Particularly in Germany, various status groups are defined, each of which has differing opportunities for access and integration. The preference for ethnic Germans cannot be explained through economic reasons, but is rather a political decision which has had a considerable role in shaping migration to Germany. The opening to Eastern European countries in the specific form of temporary migration was also a political decision. French migration policy after World War II was oriented towards permanent immigration. In the 1960s immigration was merely controlled and steered. With the lack of labour from Italy, Spain and

Portugal, the number of migrants from former colonies, especially Algeria, increased. Migration relations with other countries are less relevant.

Once a group is admitted, the migration process develops its own dynamic. Due to family unification migration processes continue even in economically weak periods in the host country. Another reason for the increasing independence of migration flows from economic developments in the host country have been the increasing numbers of refugees and asylum seekers during the 1980s and 1990s.

Both countries have reacted to the globalisation of the systems of migration with a strengthening of controls. France, for example, has introduced a particularly restrictive passport system. Both countries have aimed at closing central segments of the labour market. The mobility of highly trained workers cannot be prevented in corporations which are operating world-wide. Despite high unemployment, the lower end of the occupational hierarchy is comparatively underfilled in Western industrialised states, thanks to increasing levels of education and to occupational mobility. Migrants find economic niches and occupational opportunities most easily here. This sector is also open to illegal immigrants, since qualifications are not required for certain kinds of employment.

Comparing migration policies in Germany and France, it is obvious that both countries have reacted similarly to the challenges of migration (for example in respect to asylum) in the 1980s and 1990s. This is not only due to external pressure, but also to the political aim of harmonising policies in a united Europe. Even if immigration policies come together in France and in Germany there are still considerable differences in respect of the *integration* of immigrants. In France the tradition of equality for all migrants still grants rights which ensure an easy naturalisation. Germany by contrast still has preferences for migrants of German descent, while the integration process for all other migrant groups takes longer.

Acknowledgement

This article is based on research supported by the German Research Foundation (DFG).

Notes

1 The context of spatial differences and the intensity of migration was first discussed by Ravenstein in 1885 (Wachinger 1979).

2 For detailed analyses of social and occupational integration in Germany see Seifert 1995, 1996.

References

Angenendt, S. (1992) *Ausländerforschung in Frankreich und der Bundesrepublik Deutschland. Gesellschaftliche Rahmenbedingungen und inhaltliche Entwicklung eines aktuellen Forschungsbereiches*, Frankfurt/M., New York: Campus

Bade, K.J. (1994) *Ausländer, Aussiedler, Asyl: Eine Bestandsaufnahme*, München: Beck

Beauftragte der Bundesregierung für die Belange der Ausländer (Ed.) (1995) *Bericht der Beauftragten der Bundesregierung für die Belange der Ausländer über die Lage der Ausländer in der Bundesrepublik Deutschland*, Bonn: Eigenverlag

Bischoff, D. and Teubner, W. (1991) *Zwischen Einbürgerung und Rückkehr: Ausländerpolitik und Ausländerrecht der Bundesrepublik Deutschland*, 2nd edition, Berlin: Hitit Verlag

Bös, M. (1995) 'Migranten und soziale Ungleichheit: Soziale und politische Schließungen in westlichen Industrieländern', in W. Seifert (Ed.), *Wie Migranten leben. Lebensbedingungen und soziale*

Lage der ausländischen Bevölkerung in der Bundesrepublik, Arbeitspapier FS III 95-401, Berlin: Wissenschaftszentrum Berlin für Sozialforschung, 17–24

Bosswick, W. (1995) 'Asylum policy and migration in Germany', in F. Heckmann and W. Bosswick (Eds.), *Migration Policies: a Comparative Perspective*, Stuttgart: Enke, 305–36

Brubaker, R. (1992) *Citizenship and Nationhood in France and Germany*, Cambridge, MA: Harvard University Press

Castles, S. (1987) *Migration und Rassismus in Westeuropa*, Berlin: Express-Ed.

Castles, S. and Miller, M.J. (1993) *The Age of Migration. International Population Movements in the Modern World*, Basingstoke: Macmillan Press

Collinson, S. (1993) *Beyond Borders: West European Migration Policy Towards the 21st Century*, London: The Royal Institute of International Affairs

Dohse, K. (1981) *Ausländische Arbeiter und bürgerlicher Staat. Genese und Funktion von staatlicher Ausländerpolitik und Ausländerrecht*, Königstein: Anton Hain

Garson, J.-P. (1992) 'Migration and interdependence: the migration system between France and Africa', in M. Kritz, L. Lim Lin and H. Zlotnik (Eds.), *International Migration Systems: A Global Approach*, Oxford: Clarendon Press, 80–93

Heinelt, H. and Lohmann, A. (1992) *Immigranten im Wohlfahrtsstaat. Rechtspositionen und Lebensverhältnisse*, Opladen: Leske + Budrich

Herbert, U. (1986) *Geschichte der Ausländerbeschäftigung in Deutschland 1880 bis 1980. Saisonarbeiter, Zwangsarbeiter, Gastarbeiter*, Berlin, Bonn: Dietz

Höfling-Semnar (1995) *Flucht und deutsche Asylpolitik. Von der Krise des Asylrechts zur Perfektionierung der Zugangsverhinderung*, Münster: Westfälisches Dampfboot

Hollifield, J.F. (1992) *Immigrants, Markets, and States. The Political Economy of Postwar Europe*, Cambridge, MA, London: Harvard University Press

Hollifield, J.F. (1994) 'Immigration and Republicanism in France: the hidden consensus', in W.A. Cornelius, P.L. Martin and J.F. Hollifield (Eds.), *Controlling Immigration. A Global Perspective*, Stanford: Stanford University Press, 143–75

Hollifield, J.F. (1996) 'The migration crises in Western Europe: the search for a national model', in K.J. Bade (Ed.), *Migration Ethnizität Konflikt*, Osnabrück: Rasch, 367–402

Hönekopp, E. (1987) 'Rückkehrförderung und Rückkehr ausländischer Arbeitnehmer – Ergebnisse des Rückkehrförderungsgesetzes, der Rückkehrhilfestatistik und der IAB Rückkehrerbefragung', in E. Hönekopp (Ed.), *Aspekte der Ausländerbeschäftigung in der Bundesrepublik Deutschland*, Beiträge zur Arbeitsmarkt- Berufsforschung 114, Nürnberg: Institut für Arbeitsmarkt- und Berufsforschung, 287–342

Knipping, H.M. and Saumweber-Meyer, U. (1995) 'Basic principles of asylum law and asylum proceedings in the Federal Republic of Germany', in F. Heckmann and W. Bosswick (Eds.), *Migration Policies: A Comparative Perspective*, Stuttgart: Enke, 267–304

Kubat, D. (1993) 'France: balancing demographic and cultural nationalism', in D. Kubat (Ed.), *The Politics of Migration Policies. Settlement and Integration – The First World in the 1990s*, 2nd edition, New York: Center for Migration Studies, 164–87

Lambert, H. (1995) 'Asylum-seekers, refugees and the European Union: case studies of France and the UK', in R. Miles and D. Thränhardt (Eds.), *Migration and European Integration. The Dynamics of Inclusion and Exclusion*, London: Pinter, 112–31

Manfrass, K. (1992) 'Frankreich ein Einwanderungsland', in Forschungsinstitut der Friedrich-Ebert-Stiftung (Ed.), *Einwanderungsland Deutschland. Bisherige Ausländer- und Asylpolitik. Vergleich mit anderen europäischen Ländern*, Gesprächskreis Arbeit und Soziales Nr. 14, Bonn: Friedrich-Ebert-Stiftung, 89–112

Massey, D.S., Arango, J., Hugo, G., Kouaougi, A., Pellegrino, A. and Taylor, E.J. (1993) 'Theories of international migration: a review and appraisal', *Population and Development Review* Vol. 19 No. 3: 431–66

Meier-Braun, K.-H. (1988) *Zur Ausländerpolitik des Bundes und der Länder, insbesondere Baden-Württembergs*, Mainz: Grünwald; München: Kaiser

Moulier, Y. and Tapinos, G. (1978) 'Frankreich', in E. Gehmacher, D. Kubat and U. Mehrländer (Eds.), *Ausländerpolitik im Konflikt. Arbeitskräfte oder Einwanderer? Konzepte der Aufnahme- und Entsendeländer*, Bonn: Neue Gesellschaft, 139–52

Münch, U. (1993) *Asylpolitik in der Bundesrepublik Deutschland. Entwicklungen und Alternativen*, 2, Auflage, Opladen: Leske + Budrich

Münz, R. and Ohliger, R. (1997) *Deutsche Minderheiten in Ostmittel- und Osteuropa, Aussiedler in Deutschland. Eine Analyse ethnisch privilegierter Migration*, Demographie Aktuell No. 9, Berlin: Humboldt Universität, Lehrstuhl Bevölkerungswissenschaften

Münz, R. and Ulrich, R. (1996) 'Internationale Wanderungen von und nach Deutschland, 1945–1994', Demographische, politische und gesellschaftliche Aspekte räumlicher Mobilität, *Allgemeines Statistisches Archiv* Vol. 80 No. 1: 5–35

Sandbrink, S. (1996) 'Die Beschäftigung von osteuropäischen Werkvertrags-Arbeitnehmern in der BRD: Vorstellung des Forschungsprojekts', in T. Faist, F. Hillmann and K. Zühlke-Robinet (Eds.), *Neue Migrationsprozesse: politisch-institutionelle Regulierung und Wechselbeziehungen zum Arbeitsmarkt*, Arbeitspapier Nr. 6/1996, Bremen: Zentrum für Sozialpolitik, 94–104

Santel, B. (1995) *Migration in und nach Europa. Erfahrungen. Strukturen. Politik*, Opladen: Leske + Buderich

Schmahl, L. (1995) 'Einwanderungs- und Asylrecht in Deutschland', in M. Piazolo and K. Grosch (Eds.), *Festung oder offene Grenzen. Entwicklung des Einwanderungs- und Asylrechts in Deutschland und Europa*, München: Akademischer Verlag, 35–70

Schnapper, D. (1995) 'The significance of French immigration and integration policy', in F. Heckmann and W. Bosswick (Eds.), *Migration Policies: A Comparative Perspective*, Stuttgart: Enke, 99–111

Seifert, W. (1995) *Die Mobilität der Migranten. Die berufliche, ökonomische und soziale Stellung ausländischer Arbeitnehmer in der Bundesrepublik*, Berlin: Edition Sigma

Seifert, W. (1996) 'Occupational and social integration of immigrant groups in Germany', *New Community* Vol. 22 No. 3: 417–36

Silverman, M. (1992) *Deconstructing the Nation: Immigration, Racism and Citizenship im Modern France*, London, New York: Routledge

SOPEMI (1995) *Trends in International Migration. Annual Report 1994*, Paris: OECD

Velling J. (1995) *Immigration und Arbeitsmarkt. Eine empirische Analyse für die Bundesrepublik Deutschland*, Baden-Baden: Nomos

Vogel, D. (1994) 'Sozialpolitische Integration als zuwanderungspolitisches Steuerungsinstrument', *Forum Demographie und Politik* No. 5: 132–55

Vogel, D. (1996) *Illegale Zuwanderung und soziales Sicherungssystem – eine Anaylse ökonomischer und sozialpolitischer Aspekte*, ZeS-Arbeitspapier No. 2/96, Bremen: Zentrum für Sozialpolitik

Wachinger, H.-A. (1979) *Erklärungen und Vorausschätzungen von Wanderungen*, Göttingen: Otto Schwartz

Weiner, M. (1995) *The Global Migration Crisis: Challenge to States and to Human Rights*, New York: Harper Collins

Werner, H. (1996) 'Befristete Zuwanderung von ausländischen Arbeitnehmern. Dargestellt unter besonderer Berücksichtigung de Ost-West-Wanderungen', *Mitteilungen aus der Arbeitsmarkt- und Berufsforschung* Vol. 29 No. 1: 36–53

Wihtol de Wenden, C. (1994a) 'The French debate: legal and political instruments to promote integration', in H. Fassmann and R. Münz (Eds.), *European Migration in the Late Twentieth Century: Historical Patterns, Actual Trends, and Social Implications*, Aldershot: Edward Elgar, 67–80

Withol de Wenden, C. (1994b) 'Frankreich', in H. Heinelt (Ed.), *Zuwanderungspolitik in Europa: Nationale Politiken, Gemeinsamkeiten und Unterschiede*, Opladen: Leske + Budrich, 255–71

Zolberg, A.R. (1983) 'Patterns of international migration policy: a diachronic comparison', in C. Fried (Ed.), *Minorities: Community and Idenitity*, Berlin, Heidelberg, New York, Tokyo, 229–47

Zolberg, A.R. (1989) 'The next waves: migration theory for a changing world', *International Migration Review* Vol. 23 No. 3, 403–30

[24]

Value-Oriented Parameters in Migration Policies in the 1990s: The Israeli Experience

Tamar Horowitz*

INTRODUCTION

Immigration to Israel in the 1990s has marked a turning point in the country's history. The present wave has given the state 650,000 new citizens, half a million from the former Soviet Union (the FSU) and 50,000 from Ethiopia (Table 1, page 532). The newly arrived immigrants account for ten per cent of the country's citizens.

Recent immigrants from the FSU have several typical characteristics. They are intensive in human capital; most have post-secondary education and many are scientists, artists, doctors and teachers. Family size is generally small, with few children and many single-parent families. Their social and economic philosophy is rooted both in their socialization under the Communist regime and in their post-*perestroika* encounter with the Western world. Their motivation to emigrate to Israel is more pragmatic than ideological, wholly unlike the motives of Soviet immigrants during the 1970s. The Ethiopian immigrants of the 1990s have different characteristics: a traditional population group from a developing country with a low level of education, traditional occupational structure and family structure similar to the African family model. Motivation to emigrate to Israel was basically religious (Table 2, pages 533-534).

Immigrants to Israel during the 1990s arrived at a time when the country was undergoing changes that began with the Six-Day War and matured during the 1980s. In terms of ethnic tension, Israeli society is calmer and less schismatic today than in the 1950s and 1960s. It is also less collectivist and more individualistic than in earlier decades. The economy is less rigidly planned; large state-owned enterprises are going through a process of privatization. Israeli society is less Zionist, less idealistic and more pragmatic. The encounter between immigrants of the

* Ben-Gurion University of the Negev, Beer-Sheva, Israel.

1990s and Israeli host society has raised both practical and ideological issues that are substantive for the society at large.

Since Jewish settlement in Palestine resumed in the late nineteenth century, the newly arrived have come not as immigrants but as *olim* (sing. *oleh*, fem. *olah)*, a term denoting a combination of immigration, repatriation and ascent. *Aliya*, immigration to Israel, has always been perceived not as a demographic movement but as a value process that expresses the embodiment of Zionism. Use of the traditional term *aliya*, denoting an attitude toward Eretz Israel as a superior, lofty place, and of its converse, *yerida*, to denote emigration, reinforces this perception. When Jews move to Eretz Israel, according to the doctrine, they engage more in an ascent than in an act of immigration. In this process, the value inputs are manifested not only in the perception of Israel's centrality versus the Diaspora, in the motivation to emigrate, in the attitude toward the host country, and in the host country's image, but also in the strategies and methods of immigrant absorption.

This article focuses on value inputs at various junctures of the immigrant-absorption process in Israel and their possible implications for the future of the immigrants.

THE LAW OF RETURN

The legal framework for immigrant absorption in Israel is the Law of Return, 1950, which allows any Jew, except for one who acts against the Jewish people or is liable to endanger public health and state security, to settle in Israel. In 1954, persons with criminal records were also excluded. The law fails to define a Jew and the resulting problem, in the context of the Law of Return, has become a bone of public contention. In response to periodic litigation on the "Who is a Jew?" question, the Knesset in 1970 amended the Law of Return to provide a definition which coincided with that under Jewish religious law *(halakha)*: a Jew is anyone who is born of a Jewish mother or who has converted. This includes not only Jews but also the children and grandchildren of Jews, even if they are not Jews, and the spouses of their children and grandchildren. This amendment was offered in an attempt to solve the problem of Soviet immigrants who had intermarried.

Immigration during the 1990s brought the Law of Return back on the public agenda, this time with reference to Ethiopian Jews. Here the context of the law was collective rather than individual, as it had been in the previous immigration, and focused on the Jewishness of Ethiopian Jews who had converted to Christianity, known as the Falas Mura. A commission of inquiry established in 1992 noted:

> Experts and rabbis disagree on whether the Falas Mura are Jews. The commission did not consider itself competent to make a ruling on this historic, factual, and halakhic question... The right to immigrate to Israel is imparted by the Law of Return, 1950, first and foremost, to every individual defined by law as a Jew who wishes to immigrate to Israel. Consequently, in view of the foregoing, the Falas Mura have no general, collective right to return to Israel, and no individual has this right by virtue of his or her affiliation with the Falas Mura. This is because the commission, taking into account the evidence and testimony presented to it, cannot, as stated, act on the assumption that members of the Falas Mura come under the definition in the Law of Return.

The issue triggered public debate in Israel and focused on the limits of Jewish solidarity which, until then, had been clearly defined and included various shades of secular and observant Jews. Various positions emerged in the debate, from ultra-orthodox to secular-liberal. Those of messianic religious persuasion argued that anybody professing an affiliation to the Jewish faith is a Jew. The religious establishment chose an objective ethnic criterion: anyone born of a Jewish mother is a Jew. Their opponents argued that Israel is not an ordinary immigration country and that the Law of Return should be limited to groups that fit the general Israeli social consensus. Liberals claim that individual identity is subjective, i.e., that no truly objective definition is possible. Thus, anyone who feels Jewish is Jewish, irrespective of ethnicity. In the debate on the identity of recent immigrants from Ethiopia, the "Oriental left" (liberal intellectuals from Muslim countries) attempted to draw parallels between discrimination against the Ethiopian immigrants and the plight of the Oriental communities that arrived in the 1950s.

The debate ebbed when the Ministerial Committee on the Falas Mura (1993) stipulated that the Falas Mura's right to immigrate was individual rather than collective and set forth criteria for their admission under the Law of Entry. As the Minister of Immigrant Absorption explained in July, 1993, "Falas Mura" can be admitted into the country if (1) they argue, with evidence, that a mistake has been made and they have never been Falas Mura; (2) they describe themselves as Falas Mura who have repented and returned to Judaism, if they can back their claim with evidence; or (3) they have relatives in Israel, in which case they will be admitted under the Law of Return for humanitarian reasons.

ISRAEL-DIASPORA RELATIONS

The Law of Return issue also touches Israel-Diaspora relations and whether the Zionist solution is the one preferred by the Jewish people. This issue arises most saliently in the attitude of American Jewry toward Israel. During the late 1950s there had been academic and political debate on the question (which is not merely semantic) whether the US was a place of "diaspora" or a "dispersion." The dominant approach was that the establishment of the State of Israel had terminated the Diaspora and created a synthesis of political Jewish nationhood in Israel and Jewish life in the Diaspora.

The question of the "Zionist solution" versus development of Jewish life in the Diaspora resurfaced in the context of immigration from the FSU. In post-*perestroika* FSU, Jews are able to live Jewish lives without interference. The Israeli government has even opened Israeli centres to promote Israeli and Jewish culture. Indeed, many Jews identify with their Russian homeland as much as with Israel. By the same token, some have not emigrated because they believe that the Israeli economy would find it hard to absorb them.

In the early 1990s, over 170 Jewish organizations were active in the FSU (Ron and Medvedovsky, 1993). Some were cultural and others social and political. There are indications that this organizational activity is beginning to create a new Jewish intelligentsia (Friedgut, 1990). Even more significant is that Jews are playing a substantial role in developing Russian society. Because they are more open to the West than non-Jewish Russians, and have the skills and contacts necessary to mediate between East and West, many Jews have become entrepreneurs (Konin, 1993) or have risen to key positions in political parties. Although some of these Jews are favourably disposed toward Israel, they are not Zionists and regard Russia as their home. Gozman (1990) believes that some will make their contributions to Jewish society through participation in local Jewish community life. Chlenov (1993: 64), a Russian-Jewish leader who chairs the umbrella organization of Jews in the FSU, has declared:

> It seems to me that the Zionist philosophy of negating the Diaspora on the one hand, and arguing on the other hand that only through Israel can Judaism be fully realized, has undergone some change. Today, a new philosophy has emerged that places Israel at the centre yet asserts the possibility of interaction based on complementary relations and enrichment between Israel and other Jewish centres.

However, Rivkina (1993) presents a different view based on a survey she conducted among experts on Soviet Jewry, most of whom argued that neither a Jewish identity nor a distinct Jewish community will coalesce in the FSU. Only one quarter of the experts held beliefs to the contrary.

Israel-Diaspora relations also manifest themselves in reasons for emigration. The difference in motivation between the Soviet immigrants of the 1970s and those of the 1990s has already been noted. The former came for national and ideological reasons (Horowitz, 1994), whereas the motives of those in the 1990s were not clear cut and no single motive was dominant. Leshem (1993) identifies three factors that affect immigrants of the present decade: (1) personal and family distress; (2) existential crisis; and (3) pessimism concerning the future in their countries of residence. Leshem does point out, however, that present-day immigrants from the FSU are sensitive to anti-Semitism and Jewish consciousness.

Margolis and Singer (1993) compared the profiles of Jews who intend to emigrate to Israel with those who intend to emigrate elsewhere. Prospective emigrants to Israel share several features: unemployed, adult, pessimistic about the future in the FSU, have an affinity to Jewish culture, have relatives in and are knowledgeable about Israel. Those who wish to emigrate elsewhere have a weaker Jewish affiliation, are younger but also hold bleak expectations concerning the future in their localities. Consequently, while immigration to Israel is not ideological, it would not occur without the element of a favourable attitude toward Israel, however weak.

By implication, there is no clear-cut trend of emigration in the FSU (to Israel or elsewhere) nor liquidation of this diaspora. However, there are signs of a reawakening of independent Jewish community life that interacts with Israel and which does not consider Zionism the sole solution for the Jewish people. One cannot assume that most Jews who remain in the FSU will regard themselves as members of the Jewish community, but some will presumably have a sense of belonging and partnership. Also noteworthy is the phenomenon of Jews who shuttle between the FSU and Israel without having resolved the question of their personal identity or at least their place of residence.

The diaspora-versus-dispersion issue did not arise in the case of Ethiopian immigration because Ethiopia is perceived as a place of exile. The Falas Mura issue, however, has blurred the boundaries of this exile. Basically, this is a messianic aliya with millennial shadings.

PLURALISM VS. MELTING POT

Israel-Diaspora relations have an Israeli angle: What image should the desired new society project and what is the immigrant's place in it? In other words, will Israel evolve into a pluralistic society in which each ethnic group has equal weight and contributes equally to the social structure, but retains some of its original group identity? Or will the assimilation or "melting-pot" model prevail, in which case recent immigrants will continue assimilating into the social and value moulds that were cast in the pre-independence period and reinforced in the early years of independence and mass immigration.

The literature shows that while Israel is developing in the direction of moderate pluralism, the focus and central values of society are still those that coalesced in the early years of the state. However, Israel is far more tolerant today of group values, symbols and rights. Schools teach ethnic subjects which emphasize symbols and rituals but go no further. No attempt is being made in Israel to construct ethnic groups with a consciousness of uniqueness and separatism.

One of the important tools in the cultural integration of new immigrants is the *ulpan*, the Hebrew-language school. This setting imparts the main values and prevailing culture of Israeli society. In the past, it was assumed that "cultural absorption" was no less important than housing and occupational integration. In the recent wave of immigration, however, the concept of cultural absorption has eroded and is now given lower priority among the absorption agencies, for several reasons. First, the above-mentioned change in values has made Israeli society more tolerant and less "missionary" in the sense of inculcating the "right" values. Second, the "direct absorption" of immigrants (referral to localities without an interim period in an "absorption centre") has made it difficult to conduct organized ulpan activities beyond basic study of the language. Third, emphasis in this wave of immigration was placed, at least at the beginning, on meeting the immigrants' most urgent needs, housing and employment, in a manner similar to that which formed the integration of immigrants in the mass aliya of the 1950s.

Interestingly enough, it was the immigrants themselves who raised the issue of cultural absorption. The Russian intelligentsia stratum among recent immigrants placed the issue of "ghetto versus assimilation" on the public agenda, and several publications initiated a penetrating debate on the continued cultural distinctiveness of Russian immigrants in Israel versus the need to assimilate. On the practical level, these immigrants continue to conduct widespread cultural activities in the Russian language and culture: twenty-one Russian-language journals, a Russian theatre and Russian-language authors. FSU immigrants are rather poorly exposed to the Hebrew media (Fein, 1994). Research by Olstein and Ben-Rafael (1994) on the cultural absorption of Russian immigrants brought cultural dualism to light: on the one hand they wish to regard themselves as integrating with Israelis in various fields, chiefly those of instrumental nature, but on the other hand they seek to preserve their distinctiveness as a group. They are willing to master the Hebrew language and understand Israeli culture, but they also wish to preserve the cultural baggage that they brought with them. About one-third of the immigrants want their children to learn Russian and use it as a primary language. As for identity, they view themselves more as Jews than as Russians or Israelis.

The immigrants' attitude evidently corresponds more to the pluralistic model than to the assimilationist one, unlike that of Soviet immigrants of the 1970s, who wished to integrate into the prevailing Ashkenazi Israeli culture as quickly as possible. Olstein and Rafael (1994: 60) write:

> What we have here is a new model, strongly reminiscent of the non-Zionist model of the 1930s... We observe an unwillingness to renounce former identities and cultures in favour of new ones. However – and here is a major difference – the identity and culture that the host country emphasizes are perceived as necessary assets. The immigrants from the FSU display considerable enthusiasm in their desire to master Hebrew and in their willingness, despite all, to acquire an Israeli identity and stress their Jewishness. The findings apparently indicate that the immigrants tend neither toward a model of separatism and insularity nor toward a model of assimilation. More accurately, they wish to legitimize their Jewishness by integrating as a secular population group with a pronounced cultural identity.

Another cultural dimension is religious identity, i.e., observance versus secularism. The Russian immigrants are fundamentally secular. In several senses, this wave of immigration upset the equilibrium that prevailed in Israel between religious and secular. Although this new increment to the secular segment of Israeli society has not yet manifested itself in structural demographic change, one may assume that this will happen in the long term. Research on the voting patterns of FSU immigrants shows that only three per cent voted for religious parties compared with over fifteen per cent among the Israeli population (Horowitz, 1994).

Ethiopian immigration elicits a totally different picture. In the cultural sense, these immigrants attempt to take on the dominant Israeli social and cultural norms and values but do so very slowly because of the vast differences between the host and (their) indigenous culture. Ethiopian immigrants in Israel have not managed to disrupt the ethnic balance between "Orientals" and "Westerners" in Israel because they are totally different from both these groups, and in several respects have enriched Israel's ethnic tapestry.

In one field, religion, they did attempt to innovate. The community's clerical leaders, the *kesoch* (sing. *kes*) sought to integrate into the country's religious establishment, to function as rabbis and earn their legitimacy. Just as the religious establishment has not recognized the legitimacy of Conservative and Reform rabbis, so it refused to legitimize the *kesoch*. Following acrimonious debate on this issue after the first wave of Ethiopian immigration in 1985 (Operation Moses), the religious establishment won and the *kesoch* are not recognized as authorized rabbis for any purpose, although some of them sit on religious councils. The religious establishment has absorbed them in its own models and criteria.

The pluralism-assimilation dichotomy is determined basically at the level of policy, but no less important is the way individuals in the host society relate to the immigrants. Leshem (1993) analyses five surveys dealing with Israelis' attitudes toward newly arrived immigrants. His findings show that the value of immigrant absorption is acknowledged at the declarative level but that the favourable attitude toward immigrants has eroded steadily (to the extent of hostility) and that willingness to volunteer on their behalf has decreased markedly. The change in attitude toward new immigrants is most noticeable among Israelis of Oriental origin, secondary-school levels of education, and technical occupations. Research among teenagers presents a similar picture (Horowitz, 1994).

PERCEPTIONS OF EQUALITY, PREFERENCE AND CORRECTIVE PREFERENCE

Equality in immigrant-absorption policy is manifest on two planes: (1) equality between non-immigrant Israelis and immigrants, and (2) equality among immigrants themselves. Israel has always deemed immigrant absorption a prime objective and has urged non-immigrants to make both social and economic efforts to attain it. The preference of immigrant absorption in resource allocation, ostensibly at the expense of the non-immigrants, is refuted in research findings which show that immigrant absorption since the establishment of the state has not caused Israeli's standard of living to decline. On the contrary, each wave of immigration has led to an increase in non-immigrants' standards of living, if not in the short term at least in the middle and long terms (Simon, 1989).

The other context – equality in allocation of immigrant-absorption resources between immigrants of different origins – did not arise until the 1960s. Until then, resources were divided equally among immigrants without differentiation between "distress countries" and "affluent countries." In the 1960s, however, immigrants from "affluent countries" were defined as those able to bring resources for their initial needs (at least), whereas immigrants from "distress countries" were defined as those who lacked this initial nest egg. The first category included immigrants from Europe, North America and Oceania. The second included immigrants from Eastern Europe, South America and, to some extent, South Africa. Differentiation is therefore chiefly economic and its practical manifestation is a higher initial absorption subsidy for those in the latter group. The subsidy of immigrants from "distress countries" in earlier periods, particularly to Soviet immigrants in the 1970s, triggered a wave of protest from immigrants from "distress countries" who had arrived during the 1950s – meaning those of Asian and African origin. One government response was to initiate Project Renewal in the late 1970s aimed at rehabilitating the population of urban neighbourhoods and development towns where lived many persons of Oriental origin who had arrived in the earlier waves of mass immigration. However, despite these protests the distinction between "affluent" and "distressed" continued into the 1980s and 1990s.

Mass immigration in the 1990s did not see the issue of equality between Israelis and immigrants appear on the public agenda. Nevertheless, the aforementioned decline in willingness to help immigrants – an erosion that was particularly evident among Israelis of Asian and African origin – may be regarded as an opening shot in the battle for economic and occupational status. On the other hand, an issue that did arise in the 1990s was equality among immigrants themselves, in both economic and social contexts. Large-scale immigration from Ethiopia made an issue of their integration into modern Western society. With the change of government in 1992, absorption policy toward the Ethiopians also changed. The new Minister of Immigrant Absorption and his senior officials adopted a policy of "affirmative action" and attempted to apply it in housing and higher education. Ethiopian immigrants were allowed to purchase subsidized housing in the centre of the country through a housing loan that virtually equalled the value of the dwelling, an option that other groups of immigrants had never been given. This signalled a clear intention to encourage them to settle in the centre of the country. Ethiopians who sought admission to institutions of higher learning were also given special consideration, as reflected in doubling the duration of preparatory courses and flexibility in admission criteria for regular studies. Interestingly, this affirmative action for Ethiopian immigrants, unlike corrective preferences given to Soviet immigrants in the 1970s, met with no opposition from any group in Israeli society, immigrant or non-immigrant.

GOVERNMENT INTERVENTION VS. MARKET FORCES

Basic dilemmas in immigrant absorption concern not only the principles of immigrant absorption but also methods and strategies. Unlike other immigration countries, Israel treats absorption methods as a question of values.

The major issue in methods and strategies of absorption centres on economics. Should the government intervene in the integration process or let market forces do the job? From 1948 (when Israel was established) until the 1980s, the absorption policy was one of strong government intervention. For mass immigration of the 1990s, the government – the Ministry of Finance in particular – advocated a policy of letting market forces exert their influence. The private sector would take the lead by making whatever investments were needed to absorb immigrants; the government's role would be restricted to maximizing market elasticity, eliminating red tape and creating attractive conditions for investment so the market economy might operate without hindrance.

The Finance Ministry policy was opposed by some economists who denied the possibility of absorbing human capital by market forces alone without government intervention. Spivak (1991) likened the desired policy to the Marshall Plan under which Europe was revitalized after World War II, and attributed the secret of this successful revitalization to wise US Government intervention coupled with diagnosis of market failures that led to ongoing regulation of European economies. Zussman (1990) urged the Government to increase its selective intervention in such major fields as vocational retraining, application of new technologies, labour mobility, research and development and programmes that encourage greater activity in foreign markets.

The ideology behind free-market immigrant absorption has been implemented in several practical ways. The first is "direct absorption". On arrival at the airport, the immigrant is driven to his or her place of residence. This method, which gives immigrants more responsibility for their integration from the moment they reach Israel, has been used for 92 per cent of FSU immigrants during the 1990s. The second is the "absorption basket", a package which contains a predetermined quantity of services, allowances and entitlements:

> The absorption basket is a budgetary basket that ensures the immigrant's needs in rental housing, miscellaneous services, and a subsistence grant until work is found. This budgetary basket gives the immigrant, upon arrival, a maximum of freedom in choosing services of the nature desired, at the time desired, and in the priorities desired (Tsur, 1989).

Direct absorption and the absorption basket led to the introduction of complementary initiatives. Social networks of former immigrants were formed, particularly among Russian immigrants of the 1970s; volunteer organizations and immigrant associations began to operate in many social and material spheres; and local government, largely in the major cities, became increasingly involved in the immigrant absorption process.

Greater government intervention has been visible in the integration of scientists through the Centre for the Absorption of Scientists (established in the 1970s), and integration of doctors and musicians who have been given supplementary government support. The government has also provided Ethiopian Jews, who did not go through "direct absorption" but were taken in groups to mobile-home parks and absorption centres, with extensive welfare services.

Two years after the introduction of "direct absorption" large fringe groups of immigrants, at least one-third of the total, were unable to purchase housing and had difficulties in paying rent. These groups included the elderly, single-parent families, and the chronically ill. Furthermore, many immigrants were not learning Hebrew in an orderly way and were unable to find work in their occupations. Above all, the level of immigrant satisfaction had declined (Damian and Rosenbaum, 1993).

Findings concerning the absorption basket also showed that the value of allocation has eroded for three reasons: (1) investment in housing and high rents consumed most of the basket; (2) the general level of welfare services in Israel had declined, also affecting the immigrants; and (3) the immigrants were kept at arm's length from decision-making on welfare matters, thus rendering them unable to influence decisions affecting them. Finally, the willingness of individuals and organizations to support immigrants declined (Doron, 1991).

Following the election to government in 1992 of the Labour party, some efforts were made to moderate the prevailing government attitude concerning immigrant absorption by market forces. Yair Tsaban, the new minister responsible for immigrant absorption, termed "direct absorption" another brand of Orwellianism. It is ironic that the detachment of immigrants from a direct and immediate relationship with the absorption agencies is termed "direct absorption. Instead of providing immigrants with an array of services dealing with their needs and problems, the government had devised a set of grants that it termed the absorption basket, and instead of dealing with their housing problems, it had created a housing loan scheme" (Tsaban, 1993). Minister Tsaban prescribed more extensive government intervention and took various actions to bring it about. In addition to the operations of the Centre for Absorption for Scientists, government-subsidized jobs were made available to scientists in various fields, especially industry. The government established research funds and a think tank for scientists and began supporting entrepreneurship and small business. Vocational retraining and placement services were expanded, and the need for government support of immigrants' employers was acknowledged. Nevertheless, the assumption still prevails that government support should be granted only in the first stages of absorption and additional resources should go to special segments of the immigrant population, such as Ethiopians, scientists, single-parent families, and the elderly. Others would remain on their own, subject to market forces with no government intervention after the initial phase.

POPULATION DISPERSION VS. POPULATION CONCENTRATION

In view of the lopsided distribution of the pre-independence population – concentration of most inhabitants in the coastal region – the Government of Israel regarded population dispersion as a national goal from the start. The waves of immigration during the 1950s and 1960s helped the government achieve this goal. It was relatively easy to direct immigrants to development towns in peripheral and border areas because most of them were destitute and at the mercy of the government and the settlement agencies. At a symposium at the Hebrew University on immigrant absorption in 1966, Erik Cohen (1966) argued that the political objective of territorial dispersion clashed with the goal of social and cultural integration and that preference for the former in the 1950s alienated and isolated new immigrants (particularly those arriving from Islamic countries) from Israel's social mainstream. The arrival of today's immigrants caused these questions to resurface with a renewed dynamic, as Amiram Gonen (1990) writes:

> Who should carry out the task of settling and strengthening the border towns – immigrants or non-immigrants? Should we exploit the masses of immigrants lacking housing solutions, who will soon become part of the non-immigrant homeless, in order to direct them, almost against their will, to places where housing is plentiful, thereby ensuring and consolidating the border settlements?

Gonen answers in favour of immigrant settlement in the centre of the country:

> Mass immigrant absorption is easier to accomplish in the centre of the country, as many immigration countries have found. The centre has many advantages in infrastructure, job opportunities, and, in particular, urban conditions that were significant for the immigrants of the 1950s and even more significant for those of the 1990s, most of whom come from distinctly urban localities (Gonen, 1990: 52).

In late 1991, the government tabled for discussion the National Outline Plan (NOP) in the context of recent mass immigration. This plan shifted the focus of discussion from housing only to jobs and housing combined (Lehrman, 1991). The plan examined several alternatives for population dispersion: intensive dispersion in the south, intensive dispersion in the north, moderate dispersion throughout the country, small-scale dispersion in the centre, and continuation of existing trends on the basis of supply and demand, with emphasis on the centre. After exploring the issues, members of the steering committee concluded that distinction should be drawn between long-term and short-term solutions. In the short term, housing in the centre of the country was emphasized because this area had the infrastructure for jobs, housing and services. For the long term, emphasis was placed on the creation of immigrant-absorption infrastructure in peripheral regions. This plan corresponded with the trends that direct absorption had generated and had, in fact, resulted in a concentration of immigrants in the centre, where diverse job opportunities existed, especially for those who possessed human capital.

The centre-versus-periphery issue arose with regard to both the Russian and Ethiopian immigrant groups. As already noted, the Ministry of Immigration Absorption had adopted in 1993 a policy encouraging Ethiopian immigrants to settle in the centre of the country, as reflected in easy housing loans. The intention was to improve the Ethiopian immigrants' position at the starting line by settling where, in the opinion of absorption experts, they had the greatest chances of finding work and where services were better. This positive discrimination generated debate among researchers and within the Ethiopian community itself, one member of which actually petitioned the High Court of Justice to order the government to also subsidize housing in peripheral areas. The High Court rejected the petition on procedural grounds and acknowledged that the principle was to the benefit of the Ethiopian community.

The centre-versus-periphery issue was debated in an additional context: the rental of public housing to needy immigrants (such as the elderly or single-parent families) from the FSU. With a surfeit of houses in peripheral areas, the government decided to rent these to needy immigrants under the assumption that they would not find employment in any case; all they needed, it was thought, was a roof over their heads and social services. This allocation of housing led to protests by local government officials, especially mayors of development towns. They argued that this policy would weaken rather than strengthen their towns and would cause the stronger residents of the towns to emigrate to the centre of the country. To solve the problem, it was decided to enhance community services in localities that took in large numbers of immigrants.

Centre-versus-periphery in the context of immigrant absorption remains value-intensive and resurfaces on the public agenda on different occasions and in different contexts. It has been learned that the mere provision of cheap and subsidized housing in peripheral areas will not attract immigrants intensive in human capital if there are insufficient job opportunities. Recently there has been a perceptible "voluntary" dispersion toward the fringes of the centre of the country, or to the "outer core" of the coastal plain. This, however, should be attributed to housing-market forces (soaring housing prices) a rather than to any deliberate policy.

INTEGRATED POLICY OR INCOMPLETE POLICY?

The complexity and dilemmas of the immigrant-absorption process raise questions concerning the degree to which absorption policy is well formed. One of the guidelines of government policies since Israel was founded has been the state's commitment to immigration and to encouraging Jews to emigrate from all parts of the Diaspora. These guidelines, however, have not led to the coalescence of an integrated immigrant-absorption policy. According to Kfir and Friedberg (1992), this has been due to two groups of factors: the multifacetedness of immigration and the proliferation of agents that deal with it (especially the Jewish Agency for Israel and the Ministry of Immigrant Absorption). This situation has led to:

> ... the setting of various incomplete policies, in which one incomplete policy occasionally clashes with another; defective policymaking procedures vis-à-vis the multidisciplinary issues that characterize the immigrant-absorption system; the existence of a normative momentum that entrenches conventional approaches, concepts, and models that have taken shape over the years, thus hindering or sometimes even thwarting the formation of a comprehensive policy in this field; failure to take steps that are sometimes necessary in the modern policymaking process, such as the method of radical selectivity and inferior public consciousness. (1993: 20)

In immigrant-absorption policy, this incompleteness manifests itself not only in practical matters but also in the sociocultural sphere. Sundry government ministries, absorption agencies, and absorption plans have issued contradictory messages concerning the essence of social and cultural absorption. Some emphasize Jewish religious values, others secularism and anticlericalism. Some prescribe a traditional melting-pot model; others emphasize a pluralistic model. These contradictory messages often lead to confusion and bewilderment that cause immigrants to flee to familiar environments – those of their countries of origin.

CONCLUSION

Analysis of the value inputs in Israeli immigrant absorption in the 1990s, coupled with analysis of directions in which such policy may head, reveals the vast complexity of the immigrant-absorption process (Figure 1, page 535). For this reason, it is difficult to forecast future trends. Several factors contribute to this process:

a. Israel is now more pluralistic than it was in the past. The dominant ideology is less monolithic; the country's economy is mixed, combining the welfare state and capitalism. Previous governments' policies have differed radically, although all are similar in the sense of being incomplete and unformed. Consequently, the absorption methods themselves share these features.

b. The immigrants themselves are vastly different. The immigration of the 1990s is not driven solely by Zionist ideology; it is, at least in part, an immigration of refugees, some of whom lack the occupational skills necessary to succeed within the structure of the Israeli economy;

c. While the non-formal system of absorption (especially that of voluntary organizations) has expanded, there is also a growing sense of frustration among some segments of the Israeli population, especially the upwardly mobile Oriental population, to help integrate the immigrants.

From an historical point of view, one may differentiate three models of value inputs in the immigrant-absorption process. The first, which prevailed in the 1950s and the 1960s until the Six-Day War (1967) (the melting-pot model) had a Zionist orientation that negated the Diaspora and opened Israel's gates to all Jews with hardly any restrictions. The handling of immigrants, singly or collectively, was perceived as the state's exclusive prerogative. It was the state that planned the immigrants' social and economic integration, and it was the state that transmitted values that were meant to lead to assimilation.

The second model surfaced in the late 1960s and prevailed through the 1970s. The pace of immigration increased during this period after slumping in the early 1960s. Israeli society regarded immigration as a challenge, and the state had time to re-examine its attitudes. This is a Zionist model with a lower tendency to discredit the Diaspora. In response to the Soviet immigration that typified this period, the Law of Return was amended to include Jewish immigrants' non-Jewish spouses. The state was perceived as responsible for the immigrants' social and economic integration. When it distributed resources among immigrants, it took account of equality among the immigrants themselves (immigrants from "distress countries" versus immigrants from affluent countries) and equality between disadvantaged Israelis and immigrants (Project Renewal). As for acculturation, the need was felt to allow special groups of immigrants to express themselves culturally and preserve their own culture. The purpose, however, was more to enhance their consciousness than to legitimize differences among social groups.

The third model, first evident in the immigration of the 1990s, legitimizes the Diaspora to a much greater degree. It extended the Law of Return beyond the "umbrella of Jewish solidarity" (as defined in 1949) to include the Ethiopians. The attitude toward immigrants is less collective and more individualistic. The state intervenes less vigorously in economic integration and allows market forces to work, with the exception of the Ethiopian immigrants and special groups of FSU immigrants such as scientists and artists. For the first time in the history of immigration to Israel, the government is attempting to apply the principle of "affirmative action" to the Ethiopians. It is also less interventionist in social integration and transfers powers to volunteer organizations. With respect to acculturation, it also tends to promote pluralism.

The model of value inputs of the 1990s suggests several directions in which absorption policy may head. These are not mutually exclusive; they may even be complementary. One such direction is dominant in other immigration countries: the integration of the stronger immigrants – those whose ability to function in modern Western society is high – is left to market forces. Occupational absorption long precedes value and social absorption. However, the immigrants who "made it" are more receptive to the assimilative model than to the pluralism model; having managed to survive within the existing paradigm, they attempt to stay within it. On the other hand, this model would leave substantial numbers of immigrants on the fringes of society for a fairly long period, if not forever. An "Ashkenazi proletariat" may come into being, similar to the "Oriental proletariat" that followed immigration during the 1950s, and the group of Ethiopian immigrants may join it.

Another possible paradigm of absorption is one in which the government intervenes selectively to help especially disadvantaged groups: Ethiopians, the ill, the elderly, single-parent families, and many other immigrants who, without government assistance, would not find work in their occupations. The result would be the formation of an immigrant stratum that lives under reasonable day-to-day terms, that supports itself, but achieves no more than this, like immigrant groups throughout the world. Some members of this group will live in the margins of society, uprooted and torn between two cultures. Some will experience cultural radicalization and take shelter in extreme pluralism, to the extent of creating cultural ghettos.

A third orientation depends on the immigration trend. If immigration tapers off, the government will intervene more intensively and extensively in the integration of the 1990s immigrants, particularly at the municipal level. Attempts will be made to eradicate pockets of economic, social and cultural hardship. Most immigrants will attain a reasonable material standard of living and many will immerse themselves in the culture. However, groups will form that fail to subscribe to the prevailing cultural and social ethos of the country, and their economic and cultural deprivation will merge.

The trajectory of social processes is less obvious today than during the previous wave of immigration. The same may be said for developments in Israeli society. While this article focuses on the impact of value inputs on immigrants, it does not address directly the impact of mass immigration on Israeli society. The immigration of the 1990s will undoubtedly have far-reaching consequences for Israel in the economic, social, political and value senses.

REFERENCES

Chlenov, M.
1993 *Ha-hebet ha-tsiyoni ba-tenu'a ha-yehudit ha-leumit – haskama ve-hiluqey de'ot* (The Zionist aspect and the Jewish national movement – agreement and controversy), *Yehudey berit ha-mo'etsot* (Soviet Jewry), 16: 59-64.

Cohen, E.
1966 *Pizur ha-okhlusiya u-mizug galuyot: mesimot mitnagshot* (Population dispersion and social integration – conflicting goals), *Mizug galuyot* (In-gathering of exiles), Magnes Press, The Hebrew University of Jerusalem: 143-157.

Damian, N., and Y. Rosenbaum
1993 *Ma'aqav ahar ha-miklatim be-maslul ha-qelita ha-yeshira* (Follow-up on immigrants integrated by the direct-absorption method), Ministry of Immigrant Absorption, Planning and Research Division, April, Jerusalem.

Doron, A.
1991 *Ha-metsuqot shel qelitat ha-'aliya ha-gedola* (Hardships in absorbing the great immigration), *Ya'ad* (6)24: 28-33.

Fein, A.
1994 *Seqer hasifa li-khley ha-tiqshoret shel 'oley hever ha-'amim* (Exposure of FSU immigrants to the media), Tazpit Institute, Jerusalem.

Friedgut, T.
1990 *Tehiyat ha-tarbut ha-yehudit bi-verit ha-mo'etsot – ha-merkaz ha-yehudi la-haskala ve-tarbut be-Donczik* (Revival of Jewish culture in the Soviet Union – the Jewish Centre for education and culture in Donczik), *Yehudey berit ha-mo'etsot* (Soviet Jewry), 13: 59-64.

Gonen, A.
1990 *Geographia shel qelitat 'aliya* (The geography of immigrant absorption), January, Department of Geography, The Hebrew University, Jerusalem.

Gozman, L.
1992 *Lama anahnu lo 'olim* (Why we do not go to Israel), *Yehudey berit ha-mo'etsot* (Soviet Jewry) 13: 134-142.

Horowitz, T.
1994 *Beyn shelosh tarbuyot politiyot – oley berit ha-mo'etsot li-she'avar be-ma'avar le-Yisrael* (Among three political cultures: immigrants from the former Soviet Union in transition to Israel), The Hebrew University of Jerusalem, Davies Institute.

Kfir, A., and A. Friedburg
1992 *Qevi'at mediniyut bi-tehum qelitat ha-'aliya be-Yisrael* (Policymaking in the field of immigrant absorption in Israel), *Medina, mimshal ve-yahasim beinleumi'im* (State, governance, and international relations), 36: 5-57.

Konin, Y.
1993 *Ha-yehudim ve-ha-hevra ha-rusit* (The Jews in Russian society), *Yehudey berit ha-mo'etsot* (Soviet Jewry), 16: 76-79.

Lehrman, A.
1991 "Combined national outline plan for building, Development, and Immigrant Absorption", *NOP* 31, Vol. 2, Tel Aviv.

Leshem, A.
1993 *Ha-okhlusiya ha-Yisraelit ve-yehasa le-'oley shenot ha-tish'im* (The Israeli population and its attitude toward the immigrants of the 1990s), *Bitahon sotsiali* (Social security), 40: 54-73.

Margulies, T., and N. Zinger
1993 *Devarim she-ro'im mi-sham* (Things you see from over there), Centre for Development Studies, in Rehovot Summary.

Ministerial Committee on the Falas Mura
1993 *Recommendations to the Government*, January 18.

Olstein, Elite, and A. Ben-Rafael
1994 *Hebetim shel zehut ve-safa be-qelita* (Aspects of identity and language in immigrant absorption), The NCJW Institute for Innovation in Education (draft research paper), Jerusalem.

Rivkina, Rosalind
1993 *Arakhim yehudi'im bitequfat ma'avar* (Jewish values in a time of transition), *Yehudey berit ha-mo'etsot* (Soviet Jewry), 16: 70-77.

Ron, F., and A. Medvedovsky
1993 *Tehiyat ha-hitargenut ha-yehudit be-shetah berit ha-mo'etsot li-she'avar* (The revival of Jewish organization in the territory of the former Soviet Union), Centre for Jewish Community Studies, the Jerusalem Institute of Federal Studies, Jerusalem.

Simon, J., *et al.*
1989 "Are Russian olim good for the Israeli economy?", in T. Horowitz, *The Soviet Man in an Open Society*, Lanhan VPA: 93-99.

Spivak, A.
1991 *Rav-siah: me'oravut ha-memshala be-qelitat 'aliya* (Panel discussion: government intervention in immigrant absorption), *Reva'on le-kalkala* (Economic Quarterly), 149 (September): 325-327, 311-312.

Tsaban, Yair (Minister of Immigrant Absorption)
1993 *Remarks at a workshop sponsored by Hemdat, the Association for Freedom of Science and Religion,* Jerusalem, July 7.
1993 *A Dilemma in Setting Immigrant-Absorption Policies in the 1990s: Russian Jewry on Three Continents,* December 28, (lecture).

Tsur, Yaacov (Minister of Immigrant Absorption)
1989 *Direct Absorption – Reform in Immigrant-Absorption Methods,* Jerusalem.

Zussman, Z.
1990 *Hit'hilu liqlot bli ashlayot* (Illusion-free immigrant absorption has begun), *Yedioth Aharonoth*, financial supplement, November 20.

TABLE 1

IMMIGRANTS TO ISRAEL BY YEAR OF ALIYA, 1989-1994*

	1989	1990	1991	1992	1993	1994
Eastern Europe (Thereof: USSR)	14,624 (12,721)	187,620 (184,671)	150,012 (147,667)	66,331 (64,777)	67,312 (66,006)	68,589 (68,079)
Western Europe	2,165	2,103	2,150	2,436	3,090	2,138
North America	1,858	1,993	2,154	2,529	2,820	2,118
Central/South America	2,585	2,682	1,178	722	769	538
North Africa/Egypt	131	123	85	130	112	136
Sub-Saharan Africa (Thereof: Ethiopia)	1,639 (1,331)	4,306 (4,116)	20,206 (20,023)	3,843 (3,537)	1,372 (850)	1,792 (1,197)
Asia: Arab countries	23	36	32	201	1,141	1,719
Rest of Asia	1,064	889	1,398	2,644	2,803	-
Oceania	97	141	131	154	199	-
Other	52	73	100	92	68	1,877
Total	**24,238**	**199,966**	**177,446**	**79,082**	**79,686**	**78,907**

*Total registered (immigrants + potential immigrants)

Source: Ministry of Immigration Absorption annual reports.

TABLE 2

IMMIGRANTS BY AGE AND SEX

	1990				1991				1992				1993			
	USSR		Ethiopia		USSR		Ethiopia		USSR		Ethiopia		USSR		Ethiopia	
	Male	Fem.	Male	Fem.	Male	Fem.	Male	Fem.	Male	Fem.	Male	Fem.	Male	Fem.	Male	Fem.
0-2	293	2,843	152	129	2,080	1,986	995	902	985	957	170	171	982	965	36	33
3-5	4,740	4,460	200	153	3,288	3,163	1,224	1,053	1,402	1,325	203	205	1,480	1,343	48	42
6-9	6,467	6,262	301	297	4,614	4,282	1,574	1,419	1,925	1,848	253	239	2,025	1,835	55	50
10-14	7,299	6,999	357	310	5,265	5,036	1,626	1,445	2,208	2,009	272	200	2,306	2,155	71	56
15-18	5,336	4,719	252	225	4,346	3,770	823	821	1,988	1,600	124	162	2,244	1,837	51	29
19-24	5,600	6,512	156	160	6,112	6,039	567	724	3,311	3,177	175	191	3,575	3,550	38	41
25-34	14,662	16,472	147	158	10,686	11,612	746	1,135	4,972	5,164	253	212	5,034	5,043	42	47
35-44	16,385	16,941	124	172	11,347	12,783	761	985	4,324	4,695	126	156	4,070	4,622	33	40
45-49	3,023	3,031	52	68	2,918	3,371	348	340	1,540	1,718	54	41	1,629	1,826	8	15
50-59	4,130	6,015	51	98	3,178	8,681	551	554	2,702	3,598	71	61	2,486	3,630	14	25
60-64	7,684	9,387	76	134	7,349	4,681	234	278	1,472	2,094	32	53	1,599	2,202	14	16
65-74	5,907	9,262	142	102	5,200	8,228	491	238	2,579	3,749	53	33	2,659	3,722	24	8
75-84	2,538	4,080	28	23	2,271	4,230	58	69	943	1,881	12	11	874	1,684	5	6
85+	311	575	4	5	368	782	30	32	208	401			171	458	2	1
Total	184,676		4,076		147,667		20,023		64,166		3,533		66,005		850	

cont'd next page

TABLE 2 (cont'd)

IMMIGRANTS BY SEX AND AGE

	1994			
	USSR		Ethiopia	
	Male	Female	Male	Female
0-9	4,439	4,436	212	213
10-14	2,342	2,156	90	80
15-18	2,854	2,515	48	71
19-24	2,984	3,144	45	52
25-34	4,898	5,225	75	71
35-44	3,982	4,627	52	53
45-49	1,740	2,177	9	19
50-59	2,774	4,148	23	24
60-64	1,717	2,099	15	13
65-74	2,649	3,981	13	8
75-84	987	2,205	5	6
Total	**68,079**		**1,197**	

Source: Ministry of Immigrant Absorption annual reports.

Note: The figures cited in the table are provisional.

FIGURE 1

VALUE INPUTS AND POSSIBLE OUTPUTS

Law of Return		**Israeli Society as Host Society**			**Exile v. Diaspora**	
Liberal attitude	Formal attitude	Pluralism	Multi-culturalism	Melting pot	Diaspora	Exile
Jewish by subjective criteria Products: Pressure on gates of entry to Israel. Umbrella of Jewish solidarity widens.	Jewish by ethnic criteria Restricted immigration. Umbrella of Jewish solidarity narrows.	Creation of ghettos: Russian, Ethiopian	Awareness without legitimacy	Absorption in centre and loss of group identity	Dual identity	Single identity

Government Intervention		**Dispersion v. Concentration of Immigrants**		
Slight	Substantial	Planned dispersion	Unplanned dispersion	Concentration
Products: Creation of strong entrepreneurial class; integration of "strong" population groups; marginalization of many groups: the aged, elderly, single parents	Strengthening of the public sector; satisfactory absorption of professionals on the one hand and of weak population groups on the other; large-scale vocational retraining	Enhancing the periphery	Formation of pockets of economic and social distress in the periphery	Success of stong groups; failure of weak groups

Equality between non-immigrants and immigrants		**Equality among groups of immigrants**	
Corrective measures Project renewal	No corrective measures	Formal equality in allocation of benefits	Affirmative action
Ethnic calm	Ethnic unrest	Formation of marginal groups	Marginal groups brought nearer to centre

[25]

OUT OF PLACE IN THE COUNTRY: TRAVELLERS AND THE "RURAL IDYLL"

Keith H. Halfacree*

"History has always dismissed the nomads."
(Deleuze and Guattari, 1987: 394)

Introduction: The Criminal Justice and Public Order Act 1994

On 3rd November, 1994 a new Criminal Justice and Public Order Act received Royal Assent in the United Kingdom after over a year of parliamentary scrutiny. The Act is an extremely large and complex piece of legislation, comprising 172 sections, mostly concerned with criminal justice matters, notably the effective removal of a suspect's "right to silence" and measures dealing with "juvenile offenders." Due to the high level of interest and the contentiousness of these issues, they dominated parliamentary debate. Thus, when the original bill received its second reading in the House of Commons, only Sir Cranley Onslow spoke at length on Part V, the Public Order measures (CJB2-C: 46).[1] However, these measures have proved highly contentious, provoking demonstrations in London[2] and opposition from groups such as the civil rights organization Liberty. Included here are a variety of measures affecting England and Wales's nomadic minorities, or travellers, described in Table 1. Critical are moves criminalizing trespass in various forms and the repeal of the Gypsy site provision measures included in the Caravan Sites Act 1968.

This paper considers why travellers have been singled-out for special attention by the state in the new legislation. It is argued that they have a status as contemporary "folk devils," constructed from a number of

* The Migration Unit, Department of Geography, University of Wales, Swansea, Singleton Park, SWANSEA. SA2 8PP. U.K.

Published by Blackwell Publishers, 238 Main Street, Cambridge, MA 02142, USA, and 108 Cowley Road, Oxford OX4 1JF UK.

angles. First, they represent one of the New Right's "enemies within" in their failure to conform to the social, cultural and economic expectations of the Thatcherite agenda. This situation reinforces travellers' historically persecuted position within society. However, their folk devil status goes much further than a relatively passive failure to conform and the struc-

Table 1 Main Sections in the Criminal Justice and Public Order Act 1994 Affecting Travellers

Section	Description
61	Enables a senior police officer to direct two or more persons to leave land on which he (*sic*) "reasonably believes" they are trespassing with the purpose of residing there for any time, providing the occupier has taken "reasonable steps" to ask them to leave, **and** if either any of the trespassers has caused damage or if they have been threatening, abusive or insulting.
62	Empowers the police to seize and remove vehicles of persons failing to comply with Section 61.
70	Enhances the powers under the Public Order Act 1986 regarding "trespassory assemblies." A chief officer of police who reasonably believes that an assembly will be held on land without the occupier's permission **and** which may result in "serious disruption" to the life of the community **or** damage to a site of historical, architectural, archaeological or scientific importance, may apply for an order prohibiting all trespassory assemblies for up to four days. To organize a prohibited assembly or to incite others to take part in such an assembly is punishable by a fine and/or up to three months imprisonment. Taking part in an illegal assembly is punishable by a fine.
71	Provides a police power to direct persons "reasonably believed" to be going to a trespassory assembly, up to five miles from such an assembly, not to proceed. Ignoring the instructions of the police officer is punishable by a fine.
77	Provides local authorities with the power to direct unauthorized campers to leave land and remove their vehicles and belongings. It is an offence, punishable by a fine, for a person so directed not to comply, or to enter the land again within three months.
78	Provides for magistrates' courts to make orders authorizing local authorities to enter land to remove vehicles and other property when a direction under Section 77 has been made. Willful obstruction of such a removal makes a person liable to be fined.
79	Provides for the service of documents under Sections 77 and 78.
80	Repeals certain provisions of the Caravan Sites Act 1968 relating to Gypsy sites, including local authorities' duty to provide sites, and repeals provisions of the Local Government Planning and Land Act 1980 relating to payment of grants for sites.

Source: Criminal Justice and Public Order Act 1994 (HMSO).

tural social divisiveness of New Right politics. As nomads, travellers can subvert the spatiality of sedentary society, including the spatiality of the imagination, exposing the void of essential meaning that lies therein. Critical here is a distinction between Gypsies and "New Age Travellers" (NATs) in their positionality *vis-à-vis* the "rural idyll." Whilst Gypsies, *in an idealized form*, have acquired a place within this imaginative geography, NATs have no place within that idyll. NATs threaten to disrupt the privatized and ordered form that the commodified "post-productivist" (Lowe et al., 1993: 206) countryside is assuming.

The first section of the paper describes the broad political and historical context of the legislation. First, the contours of the New Right political agenda are outlined. Secondly, British travellers are introduced as "folk devils" for this New Right. In the second section of the paper attention is given to the threat posed by travellers to capitalist spatiality. After describing that spatiality, drawing heavily on the work of Henri Lefebvre, there is a discussion of the nomadic threat and, in particular, the challenge to the rural idyll's specific imaginative geography. Finally, the third section of the paper illustrates these theoretical issues through an engagement with recent Parliamentary debates on travellers, concentrating on the Criminal Justice and Public Order Bill 1993. Speakers in both Houses of Parliament drew on and articulated the rural idyll and the NATs' challenge to that idyll. In summary, the paper addresses Sibley's (1988: 416–17) concern that geography has failed to cope adequately with ambiguity, spatial transgressions and the State's response to such transgressions.

The New Right, "Folk Devils" and Travellers

The New Right and Thatcher's "Folk Devils"

The 1979 general election ushered in a British government committed to policies originating in the theoretical ideas of the New Right. As Andrew Gamble (1994) argues, whilst the New Right does not represent a coherent body of political thought (see Barry, 1987), being divided in particular between market libertarians and authoritarian conservatives, as expressed by Thatcherism it can be associated with, on the one hand, support of a free market economy and, on the other hand, efforts to create a limited but strong state to police and reinforce that market (see also Hall, 1983). The former thrust of policy resulted in the subsequent drive towards deregulation, privatization and the forging of a nation of petty capitalists. However, it is the efforts to build a complementary strong state which concerns us here.

A key way in which Thatcherism attempted to reestablish the authority of the state was to single out and persecute various "enemies within" through new Public Order legislation. The authoritarian wing of the Conservative Party, in particular, argued that democracy had become "decadent," creating a condition of undue permissiveness and tolerance which was leading to chaos and, ultimately, to the spectre of left-wing totalitarianism (Gamble, 1994: 65–6). This line of reasoning converged with the more libertarian wing of the Party through a joint emphasis on the sanctity of private property as the foundation of authority and order (Gamble, 1994: 62).

Throughout her period in office, Margaret Thatcher set about dealing with the disparate elements of this "enemy within." In turn, with the particular help of the tabloid press, groups such as the miners, trade unionists, students, the unemployed, football hooligans and black youth became portrayed as society's "folk devils" (Brake and Hale, 1989; Hall, 1983; Scraton, 1987), groups creating a "moral panic" within polite society (Cohen, 1987). For example, during the bitter strike of 1984–5 the miners were portrayed, in confrontations such as the "Battle" of Orgreave or personified in the National Union of Mineworkers' leader Arthur Scargill, as threatening the whole British way of life and the very bedrock of society (Green, 1990).

The concern of the Thatcher administration with Public Order (Norrie and Adelman, 1989: 113) bolstered the traditional association between the Conservative Party and "law and order" (Hall, 1983: 37). For Brake and Hale (1989: 140), this rhetoric of law and order "tacitly legitimated" attacks on those outside of "respectable life." Public Order concerns became re-presented as concerns with a "spectre of violence" (Scraton, 1987: 159), justifying the general shift towards authoritarian responses (Norrie and Adelman, 1989: 115). Threats to the state by groups such as the striking miners were metamorphosed into threats to the person.

In 1990 the fervor of the Thatcher years was replaced by the more quiescent style of John Major. However, whilst Major may not be as ideologically committed to the New Right agenda as his predecessor, there is little evidence of any substantial shift back to the "one nation" Toryism of the post-1945 consensus. For example, Major has railed against squatters and beggars in Thatcherite folk devil style (Guardian, 28 May, 1994a). Hence, we can appreciate, *a priori*, that travellers, too, may be constructed as just another New Right folk devil, another group perceived as undermining state authority and the moral community of British Conservatism.

Travellers as Contemporary Folk Devils

There are a number of reasons why travellers were well-suited to being added to the post-1979 litany of authoritarian New Right British folk devils. First, historically there is the legacy of widespread prejudice and hostility towards Gypsies and other travellers, both within Britain and in Europe more generally (cf. Cottaar et al., 1992; Okely, 1983; Rehfisch, 1975; Sibley, 1987; Sinclair, 1993). These feelings resulted in numerous British state initiatives against travellers (Adams et al., 1975: 6; Mayall, 1988: Appendix 1). This legacy had only to be tapped for travellers to move back into the limelight of popular ire.

Secondly, the opportunity for such a response presented itself in the 1980s when a new group of travellers, popularly known as "New Age Travellers" (NATs), grabbed the headlines. Emerging around 1977, these travellers first came to prominence in the media in the mid-1980s, with reports of a series of cat-and-mouse games between themselves and the police in the west and southwest of England. These minor skirmishes culminated in the infamous "Battle of the Beanfield" in Savernake Forest in 1985 (Earle et al., 1994; NCCL, 1986; Rosenberger, 1989). This confrontation between NATs, then known as the Peace Convoy (reflecting their association with the large anti-nuclear demonstrations of the 1970s and early 1980s), and police came about as the Wiltshire constabulary prevented the Convoy from going to Stonehenge for the summer solstice and attendant music festival. It was a violent encounter as the travellers tried to prevent their vehicles being impounded and themselves being taken into custody.

The state responded rapidly to the Battle of the Beanfield, and the renewed attempt the following year to reach Stonehenge (Earle et al., 1994; NCCL, 1986) resulted in incidents of trespass and confrontation with the police centered on the Yeovil area of Somerset and Stoney Cross in the New Forest, all events covered extensively in the media. By 1986 Douglas Hurd, the Home Secretary, was describing NATs as: "nothing more than a band of medieval brigands who have no respect for the law or for the rights of others" (Hansard, 1986: 733). Parliament passed, *inter alia*, Section 39 of the Public Order Act 1986 (Dixon, 1987; Driscoll, 1987), which gave the police heightened powers to control processions and public assemblies and to evict trespassers. These powers came in the wake of measures facilitating police use of searches, roadblocks and "reasonable force" contained in the Police and Criminal Evidence Act 1984 (Brake and Hale, 1989; Scraton, 1987).

A second significant event in defining the character of the NATs was the congregation of up to 50,000 people at Castlemorton Common in Hereford and Worcester in May 1992 (*NME*, 1993). This event saw the beginning of a coming-together of different strands within the traveller community, termed an "unholy alliance" by the police (Blakey, 1992: 1043). In particular, it brought so-called "Ravers" (often from the cities) into contact with the travellers proper. This introduced the latter, whom we might crudely describe as "Hippies," to rave music, whilst introducing the Ravers to the politics and the environmental values of the Hippies. A consequence of this fusion appears to be the further evolution of what have been described as "new tribes:" from the "Spiral Tribe" sound system (Dalton, 1993) to the "Dongas" environmental protestors (Fairlie, 1993; Vidal, 1992).

A third reason why travellers in general but NATs in particular were well suited to becoming New Right folk devils stems from many of their behavioral and attitudinal characteristics (see also Mayall, 1988: 89). Whilst the single name "New Age Traveller" hides a wide variety of different people and lifestyles – "Brew Crew," "cosmic hippies," "24-hour party people," "'back-to-the-land'ers" (Earle et al., 1994; Jones, 1993, Chapter Eight; Lowe and Shaw, 1993), there are a number of common traits, real or imagined, within the NAT community which contrast with the ideals of the Conservative "good society" (Gamble, 1994: 67). For example, NATs show lower levels of materialism than the settled community, reflected in a lack of concern for obtaining regular full-time paid employment. They are also less respectful of private property, especially land, and the other key institutional supports stressed by the authoritarian right, such as the nuclear family and establishment traditions.

The Material Basis of Thatcher's Folk Devils

Travellers in general but especially NATs thus have a good pedigree as potential folk devils for the New Right. The public emergence of NATs provoked a renewed growth in hostility to travellers in general (cf. Campbell, 1993; Committee of Inquiry, 1985; Sinclair, 1993). For example, resistance to the traveller sites being set up under the provisions of the Caravan Sites Act 1968 intensified (Hawes, 1987; Lloyd, 1993; Wilson, 1994). Claiming to be responding to this "cry from the shires" (Clements, 1992: 13), the Government decided to include travellers in a general clampdown on "deviant" sections of society. In other words, the measures concerning travellers contained within the new legislation represent the contemporary articulation of historical prejudices by a political regime bent on the authoritarian creation of a single nation committed to the free market economy. This drive for "consensus through conflict" (Norrie and Adelman, 1989: 112; see also Gamble, 1994: 220) contrasts with the post-1945 social democratic consensus (Barry, 1987), reflected in the Caravan Sites Act 1968, which sought to create a single nation through compromise and tolerance.

Nevertheless, this explanation is insufficient to explain why travellers have acquired folk devil status. As Jessop et al. (1984) observe, in their sympathetic critique of Hall (1983), Thatcherism was not solely a hegemonic project at the level of ideology but also had a strong material base for its concerns. Its "consensual authoritarianism" allied the ruling class with the "labour aristocracy" against:

> *déclassé* groups such as travellers, students, and peace protestors . . . It is among those who snap at the bait of private interest and wealth that we should seek the material basis of the acceptance of "authoritarian populist" ideologies. (Norrie and Adelman, 1989: 117, 122)

Norrie and Adelman go on to describe this material basis in terms of "Two Nations' politics and economics" (p. 123). The threat of the travellers is thus reflected, *inter alia*, in their violation of private property through trespass.

However, the material basis which Thatcherite politics upholds also concerns the spatiality of contemporary capitalism and the sectional interests contained within that spatiality. Returning to Gamble's summary of the New Right's need for a strong state, we can look again at the requirement for the upholding of the state's social and political authority. This requirement can be extended to encompass a need to uphold the *spatial* authority of the state; the state as guardian of capitalist spatiality. Moreover, nomads threaten this spatiality and, of British travellers, NATs threaten it most of all.

Capitalist Spatiality, Nomadism and the Rural Idyll

Capitalist Spatiality: Producing the Void

In *The Production of Space*, Henri Lefebvre (1991) charts the development of space[3] from an historical perspective, stressing its increasingly produced character (see also Smith 1984), which Soja (1985) terms "spatiality." At a greater level of detail, the establishment of capitalism is characterized by the ascendance of what Lefebvre terms abstract space over absolute space. Whilst the latter was defined largely by politico-religious forces and led to an integrated everyday experience, the former is very much guided by the market and capitalism – hence Lefebvre's concentration on the term *production* – and is characterized by fragmentation. This is not to posit a crude economic reductionism but to claim that the space we are all involved in producing must be understood in its societal context. Abstract space is intrinsically bound up with exchange.

An insight into the abstract spatiality of capitalism is given by Sack's (1986: 19) work on human territoriality, defined as:

> the attempt by an individual or group to affect, influence, or control people, phenomena, and relationships, by delimiting and asserting control over a geographic area [the territory].

Hence, Sack associates territoriality with power rather than with biology. Under capitalism, there is the:

> repeated and conscious use of territory as an instrument to define, contain, and mold a fluid people and dynamic events [which] leads to a sense of an *abstract emptiable space.* It makes community seem to be artificial; it makes the future appear geographically as a dynamic relationship between people and events on the one hand and territorial molds on the other. And it makes space seem to be only contingently related to events. (p. 78; my emphasis)

Of course, the abstract space of capitalism is only "conceptually emptiable" (Sack 1986: 37) and is always filled "on the ground." Indeed, there is a key contradiction within abstract space between its drive for homogeneity, where the universal measure is exchangeability, and its localized fragmentation (Lefebvre 1991: 287, 341–42; see also Merrifield 1993). Nonetheless, the key conclusion here is that the sheer dynamism of capitalist territoriality destroys absolute space's more inherent and established meanings. This leaves the way open for the imposition of meanings onto space.

As Sack suggests, the creation of abstract space has profound existential consequences for the individual. This appreciation also comes from Harvey's (1989) discussion of what he terms the "postmodern experience" (see also Halfacree, 1993a). Psychologically, this experience is characterized by the loss of "ontological security," defined as: "the confidence that most human beings have in the continuity of their self-identity and in the constancy of the surrounding social and material environments of action" (Giddens, 1990: 92). Lefebvre, too, acknowledges this existential inadequacy of abstract space and recognizes that: "In space needs and desires can reappear as such, informing both the act of producing and its products" (Lefebvre 1991: 348).

Capitalist Spatiality: Filling the Void

In part, the void of spatial meaning resulting from the creative destruction of capitalist spatiality can be filled from within key features of abstract space. For example, there are the three "formants" of abstract space defined by Lefebvre (1991: 285–86). First, there is the geometric formant, whereby the meaning of space is given by its Euclidean use as reference points. Secondly, there is the optical or visual formant, whereby the meaning of space is reduced to messages reaching the eyes. Thirdly, there is the phallic formant, whereby perpendicularity represents power and authority. However, whilst the latter two formants take some account of the representational spaces of experience, as compared to the formal representation of space apparent in the first formant, Lefebvre sees them as insufficient to meet the needs of human existence and community.

The need for the qualitative (Lefebvre 1991: 349) is illustrated by Lefebvre with respect to our leisure and recreational behavior (Lefebvre, 1991: 383–85). Although deeply implicated with the market and capitalist production, leisure behavior shows a tendency towards surmounting the divisiveness that characterizes abstract space. Thus, as Shields (1991, chapters 2 and 3) has demonstrated, resorts represent "liminal" zones partially liberated from everyday life. However, the liminal zones of leisure are not the only locations where the existential inadequacy of abstract space – the lack of "the celebration of lived difference, of tradition, of *jouissance,* of sensual *differential* space" (Merrifield 1993: 524; emphasis in original) – is revealed. Indeed, suppressed human needs can re-emerge in a variety of forms of revolt, some violent and others more benign (Smith 1984: 60). We can also see attempts to compensate for this inadequacy through our "social representations" of space.

Social representations are defined by the social psychologist Serge Moscovici (for example, Moscovici, 1984) as organizational mental constructs which guide us towards what is "visible" and must be responded to, relate appearance and reality, and even define reality itself. The world is organized, understood and mediated through these basic cognitive units. Social representations consist of both concrete images and abstract concepts. They are organized around "figurative nuclei," which are "a complex of images that visibly reproduce . . . a complex of ideas" (Moscovici, 1984: 38). Therefore, whilst they are partly a description of the physical material world, social representations are irreducible to it. They perform two major roles. First, they conventionalize the objects, persons and events encountered. Second, they prescribe and organize our subsequent behavior and responses. Prescription makes social representations not merely neutral and reactive taxonomic devices but also creative and transformative resources, through their usage by people going about their everyday lives.

Social representations of space refer to the application of social representational theory to everyday spatial categories. Thus, we can define "the rural" as one such social representation of space (Halfacree, 1993b; see also Shields, 1991), in contrast to attempts to define it as a "locality" (Hoggart, 1990) or a more post-structuralist category of discourse (Pratt, forthcoming). Seen this way, the rural approximates to the disembodied structures of meaning, legitimation and power proposed by Giddens (for example, Giddens, 1984). In short, "the rural" is a structure "out" of space and time which is drawn upon in discursive and non-discursive actions.

The Rural Idyll: A Selective Representation

The (historical) creation of a more-or-less distinct rural space is perceived within British culture predominantly in terms of what is known as the "rural idyll" (Halfacree 1995; Short 1991). In other words, the rural idyll is a hegemonic social representation whose meaning has overlaid a more-or-less distinct rural space[4]. The characteristics of the rural idyll are well known and described widely in the literature. For example, Short (1991) argues that the countryside is the most important landscape in English national environmental ideology i.e., "real" England is a rural "green and pleasant land." Moreover, it is a particular type of rural land, rooted in the past of the large country house and widely celebrated as "our" national heritage. Physically, "real" England consists of small villages joined by narrow lanes and set amongst small fields where cows lazily graze away the day. Socially, it is a tranquil landscape of social stability and community, where people know not just their next door neighbors but everyone else in the village; a *gemeinschaft* existence. The countryside is perceived as unchanging, and as an escape from the urban industrial society, characterized by tension, strife, pollution and general misery. In short, rural England (rural Britain?) is an escape from modernity. In this image, the city is not Jerusalem – a place of community, freedom and progress – but Babylon – a place of mob, disorder and toil.

Given the characteristics of the rural idyll, we can appreciate how it can act as a consolatory social representation and help to counter the ontological insecurity of the postmodern condition. Hence, it has been suggested that this structure is so utilized by people migrating from urban to rural Britain (Halfacree, 1995). The rural idyll provides a set of meanings for a given space – rural space – which, through its emphasis on timelessness and integration, denies the dispossessional logic of capitalist spatiality. As Harvey (1978: 26–9) noted, in respect of the similar consolatory role played by the fecund appeal of "nature," without such "mystifications" life for many people would hardly be bearable.

Nevertheless, as a "spatial code," the rural idyll is not solely an aid to perception but also serves to designate a way of understanding, operating within and producing that rural space (Lefebvre 1991: 47–8). Away from its consolidatory role, this active moment of the rural idyll demonstrates the violence of social representations of space, since they tend to be exclusive and selective in their character:

> Any determinate and hence demarcated space necessarily embraces some things and excludes others; what it rejects may be

> relegated to nostalgia or it may be simply forgotten. Such a space asserts, negates and denies . . . As a body of constraints, stipulations and rules to be followed, social space acquires a normative and repressive efficacy . . . that makes the efficacy of mere ideologies and representations pale in comparison." (Lefebvre 1991: 99, 358)

Philo has recently drawn attention to the exclusivity of the rural idyll in his criticism of rural studies's neglect of people other than "Mr. Average" (Philo, 1992: 200). In brief, the rural idyll is exclusive in its class, race and status connotations, and in the demands for conformity which it places on its adherents. In this sense it is profoundly conservative and its support by the state can be linked to the material concerns which prompt the creation of folk devils.

The Nomadic Threat to Capitalist Spatiality

Alternatives to the abstract spatiality of capitalism – "produced" difference rather than the "induced" difference internal to the system (Lefebvre 1991: 372) – ultimately must be suppressed if they are not to pose a threat to that spatiality. They must be reduced by being "forced back into the system by constraint and violence" (Lefebvre 1991: 382). This is especially true of the threat posed by nomadic challenges. In their "Treatise on nomadology," Deleuze and Guattari (1987, chapter 12) posit the nomad as being fundamentally subversive of territorialization in general (see also Mayall, 1988: 187). The nomad is concerned with "smooth" space rather than with the "striated" space of the sedentary:

> The nomad has a territory; he [*sic*] follows customary paths; he goes from one point to another; he is not ignorant of points (water points, dwelling points, assembly points, etc.). But the question is what in nomad life is a principle and what is only a consequence. To begin with, although the points determine paths, they are strictly subordinated to the paths they determine, the reverse of what happens with the sedentary. The water point is reached only to be left behind; every point is a relay and exists only as a relay. A path is always between two points, but the in-between has taken on all the consistency and enjoys both an autonomy and a direction of its own . . . sedentary space is striated, by walls, enclosures, and roads between enclosures, while nomad space is smooth, marked only by "traits" that are effaced and displaced by the trajectory." (Deleuze and Guattari, 1987: 380–81)

Nomads threaten the sedentary by threatening their spatiality; nomads are the potential conquerors of the town (Lefebvre 1991: 235). The nomadic effacement exposes the contingency of *any* physical and imaginative striations through denial of the need for such striations, at least at the social level; movement is elevated above fixity.

When smooth (nomad) space comes up against the striated (sedentary) space of capitalism it can expose the void of essential meaning that characterizes abstract space. Nomads de-territorialize and efface the meanings imposed by a sedentary society on its striated space, both on the ground and in the imagination. Hence, concern to "purify" residential space – the "urge to keep things apart" (Sibley, 1988: 409) – receives added significance under capitalism, especially during times of large-scale crisis-driven restructuring of abstract space (Smith 1984: 157), such as the present day, where capitalist spatiality is most vulnerable to exposure. Nomads are thus potentially disruptive of social representations of space unless they can be incorporated into these representations.

Travellers and the Rural Idyll

Deleuze and Guattari's discussion of nomads is pitched at a highly abstract level and must be qualified when we consider a British equivalent of the nomads, the travellers. Indeed, when we look at the specific threat posed by British travellers we see a variety of situations. Some travellers have been more-or-less successfully incorporated into the rural idyll, blunting their transgressive potential, whereas others remain firmly outside that idyll and thus pose a greater threat to it. Three broad groupings of travellers can be distinguished: tramps and vagrants, Gypsies and NATs.

Tramps and vagrants. The place of tramps and vagrants within the assorted "myths of the English" has recently been considered by Crowther (1992). She demonstrates the long-standing pedigree of vagrants within this mythology and their invocation of three powerful emotions: fear, pity and envy. Two important strands of ideas can be taken from Crowther's work for this paper's concerns. First, she is careful not to essentialize the vagrant and reduce him or her to a standard type. However, the wide variety of "real" vagrants *was* reduced in law to a distinction between "genuine" work seekers – the artisan "on the tramp" – and the "professional" tramp. Whilst a degree of sympathy was shown to the former, the latter was treated with fear and contempt. Second, the Romanticization of the tramp imbued the wanderer with a strong rural character, placing him or her firmly within the remit of the "rural idyll." In short, the tramp became a "repository of natural lore" (Crowther, 1992: 109) which, consequently, blurred the harsh realities of the tramping life. These two moments – the reduction of travellers to twin stereotypes of the "real" and the "degenerate," and the ruralization of the former – are pivotal to dominant social representations of travellers.

Gypsies. For Crowther (1992: 97), Gypsies provoked a "particular piquancy" in the myth of the tramp as they were both ethnically exotic and had their own secret language. Furthermore, as Mayall (1988), Okely (1983) and Sibley (1981, 1986, 1987) have recognized, Gypsies are associated strongly with the "rural idyll." However, theirs is a position on the margins of that rurality, always away in the distance, except in the odd encounter, perhaps in the purchasing of their craft wares. They exist hidden within the shadows of rurality, a limited assimilation finally attained after centuries of persecution (Mayall, 1988). Such a location perpetuates the ignorance of Gypsies demonstrated by Gorgio (non-Gypsy) society but it also distinguishes Gypsies from the "other" travellers.

A central issue to consider concerns *which* Gypsies are to be found in this marginal position in the "rural idyll." Whilst the term "Gypsy" covers a great diversity of different peoples, critical here is what Sibley (1981) terms the "real" Gypsy myth (see also Mayall, 1988; Okely, 1983: 30–37). In short, this myth states that "real" Gypsies are George Borrow's independent, strong, self-sufficient and exotic Romany, living out a rural existence in brightly painted caravans, selling their craft wares but largely remaining outside Gorgio (non-Gypsy) society; they are "somewhere else" (Sibley, 1986: 65). "Real" Gypsies are economically independent and their migration should be seen as: "a facet of [their] economic organization" (Sibley, 1981: 73; see also Okely, 1983; Sinclair, 1993). In contrast, actual Gypsies do not by-and-large conform to this imagery. Thus, the Gypsies of the "rural idyll" are "by definition mythical" (Sibley, 1987: 81; Mayall, 1988). This mythical exoticism is reinforced further by appeals to their distinct ethnic position, including coverage by the Race Relations Act 1976 (Liberty, 1993).

"New Age Travellers." As both the Battle of the Beanfield and Castlemorton demonstrated, migration for NATs is frequently linked to the distribution of the summer music festivals (Tucker, 1991). The importance of such festivals is paralleled to some degree by Gypsy fairs, but it draws attention to non-economic determinants of migration. In the last year or so the latter would also include migrations to protest against new road developments, such as Twyford Down (Fairlie, 1993; Vidal, 1992). This is an important contrast with Gypsies. As was shown for vagrants, tramping in search of work was a legitimate activity but "professional" tramping was unacceptable. This contrast was reinforced recently by a ruling in the Court of Appeal (*Guardian*, 28 May 1994b; see also Beale and Geary, 1994; Mars, 1989). According to Lord Justice Neill, the provisions for Gypsy sites under the Caravan Sites Act 1968 did not extend to NATs, since the latter had failed to demonstrate the economic necessity of their wandering – they were *in this respect* the "aimless" nomads described by Deleuze and Guattari (1987: 380).

Ethnicity has also been used to distinguish NATs from Gypsies, often employing Sibley's (1986: 65; see also Lloyd, 1993) split in the rural-natural between the traditional-distant-romantic (Gypsy) and the wild-no culture-uncivilized (NAT). Whilst appeals to ethnicity can be used to support the exotic location of Gypsies within the "rural idyll," there is little hope for NATs. They have not even gained a position in the shadows and their fundamentally Carnivalesque behavior, notably when they are in Tribes or teamed up with Ravers, remains an illegitimate transgression.[5] These travellers have *no* place in the rural idyll, even on its margins. Whilst historically there have always been people with mobile lifestyles who spent much of their time in rural areas, these can conveniently be lumped together in contemporary political rhetoric as ("real") Gypsies, thus becoming immunized, albeit temporarily, from criticism and attack.

This section is summarized in Figure 1, which portrays an imaginary social space for travellers, who are distinguished along two axes: degree of ethnic distinctiveness and the extent to which they are economic migrants. In order to obtain a legitimate position within the rural idyll, even if on its margins, travellers must demonstrate either an ethnic distinctiveness historically associated with migration ("real" Gypsies) or the economic necessity of wandering (artisans "on the tramp"). "Degenerate" Gypsies, "professional" tramps and virtually all NATs, in contrast, find themselves on the left-hand side of the figure, outside the social space of the rural idyll. Consequently, returning to the ideas of Deleuze and Guattari (1987), it is the nomadic transgressions of the NATs which most threaten the complacent spatiality of the rural idyll. NATs – with their "alternative" lifestyles, "alternative" cultures, "alternative" spatialities – trespass against the "idyllic" rural social representation. NATs resist the "dispossessional" logic of "enclosure" (Monbiot, 1994). Their refusal to conform to the spatial code of the rural idyll threatens to expose both the insubstantial nature of a supposedly historically-entrenched representation of rurality and the partisanship of that representation. Thus, whilst NATs may not literally possess a "war machine" (Deleuze and Guattari, 1987), they can attack sedentary society. Hence, the rigorous attempts to suppress them shown by the British State in control measures (Sibley, 1988: 419) such as the Criminal Justice and Public Order Act 1994. These measures attempt to re-striate rural space and keep it the land of Philo's "Mr Average."

Recent Parliamentary Debate on Travellers

This section illustrates some of the theoretical issues raised above through examination of the Parliamentary debates surrounding the traveller-related sections of the Criminal Justice and Public Order Bill 1993 (CJB93) which became law in the Criminal Justice and Public Order Act 1994.

However, as these sections were overshadowed by the Criminal Justice measures, analysis also includes material from other debates in the House of Commons regarding travellers from 1992 and 1993. In particular, material is drawn from an earlier proposal to amend the Caravan Sites Act 1968 (Hansard, 1993a). Two key strands of argument are identified in the analysis: travellers distinguished from Gypsies and consequently vilified, and NATs being described as having no place within the imaginative geography of the rural idyll. Concentrating on Parliamentary debates in this way follows Sibley's (1981) analysis of the Caravan Sites Act 1968. This is intentional: just as Sibley demonstrated how the "real" Gypsy myth informed the debate surrounding the 1968 Act, so the debate sur-

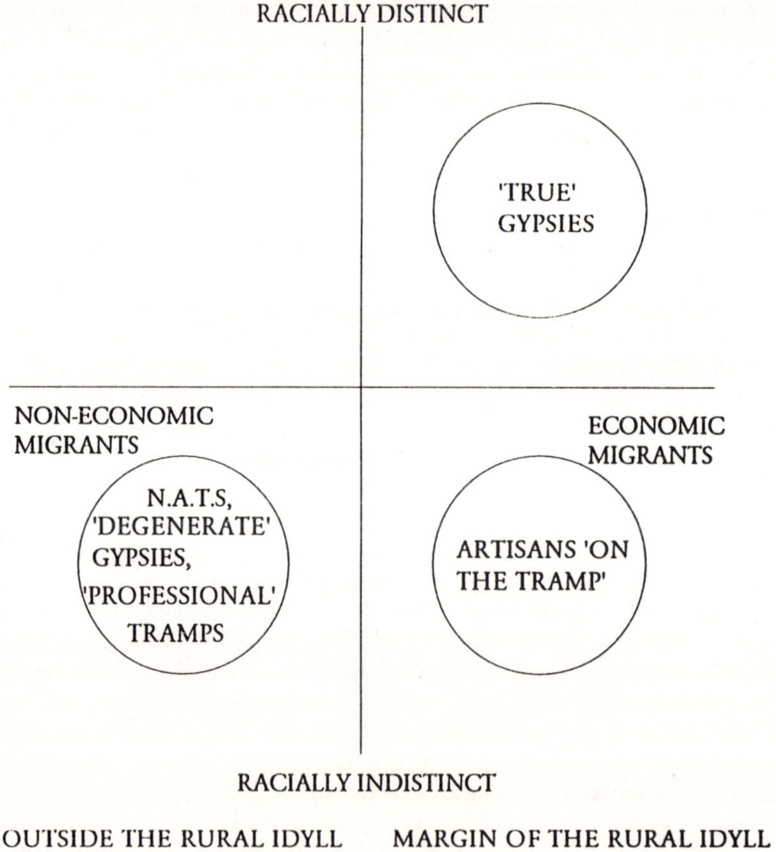

Figure 1 The place of travellers within the social space of the rural idyll

rounding the 1994 Act was heavily informed by the position of NATs *vis-à-vis* the "rural idyll." In both instances, ideologically-infused social representations of legitimacy in space are used to justify oppressive State measures against minority groups.

NATs Distinguished from Gypsies and Vilified

The need to distinguish between NATs and "real" Gypsies has featured strongly in debates in both Houses of Parliament. In particular, speakers were eager to show sympathy to the Gypsies but to attack vehemently other types of travellers. Moreover, the content of these speeches can be referred to the axes given in Figure 1, since they drew on both the ethnic distinctiveness of the Gypsies and the economic rationale for their migration, which was contrasted explicitly with the corresponding position of NATs.

The different strands within the travelling population were addressed in the debate on the Caravan Sites (Amendment) Bill 1993. First, there was an emphasis by both the proposer of the Bill, Sir Cranley Onslow and one of his opponents, Labour's Bob Cryer, that the measures being discussed were nothing to do with NATs (Hansard, 1993a: 586, 608). Secondly, there was more detailed discussion drawing on Sibley's "real" Gypsy myth. Sir Cranley Onslow got the ball rolling:

> The traditional and genuine gipsy, whom many of us remember in our childhood, is much rarer nowadays. One does not often find ladies in straw hats and long black skirts offering to sell one clothes pegs or bunches of violets that have just been picked from one's hedgerow. The pattern has changed. There are not so many opportunistic gentlemen offering to do a job and saying, "I"ve got half a load of tarmac, squire, and would be glad to do up your drive." Even that traditional gipsy activity seems to have diminished. (Hansard, 1993a: 585–6)

Onslow's speech suggests everything from the romantic mystique of Gypsy women in "straw hats and long black skirts," to an emphasis on their roguish opportunism, since the violets they were trying to sell you came from your own garden. Such genuine Gypsies were to be treasured and loved as part of the rural scene. Whilst Bob Cryer drew attention to the mythical image of "real" Gypsies as: "people in nicely painted caravans singing folk songs with guitars while a horse pulled them gently round meandering country lanes" (Hansard, 1993a: 600), it is interesting to note that this was precisely the stereotype which later contributors to the debate drew upon, some quite explicitly.

Discussion of the CJB93 also contrasted "real" Gypsies with "degenerate" Gypsies. Throughout the debate speakers referred to the great degree of sympathy and affection that they had for the "real" Gypsy. There was even considerable recognition of, and anger at, the past persecution of the Gypsy way of life (John Fraser, Labour, CJBRS-C: 318). In these debates, however, it was the contrast between NATs and Gypsies which was emphasized. First, as regards the ethnic and "traditional" character of Gypsies, attention was paid to the fact that NATs had only adopted a mobile lifestyle "recently" whereas for Gypsies it was "traditional." A brief developmental perspective was given by Lord Kenyon, who argued that the invention of the motor vehicle had corrupted the Gypsy, leading first to diddikois and then to NATs (CJBR-L: 1552).

Lord Avebury, a major contributor to the debates,[6] pleaded at length for the need to distinguish between Gypsies and NATs. A powerful advocate of the Gypsy cause, especially in respect to the proposals to reform the Caravan Sites Act 1968, proposals which he feared would criminalize the "gypsy way of life" (CJBC-L: 1117), he observed how: "New Age travellers . . . have recently adopted a nomadic way of life and . . . are causing all the nuisance" (CJBC-L: 627). He described the "evil" of NATs: "camping unexpectedly in large numbers in rural areas or near to villages and towns" (CJBC-L: 627). NATs had to be removed from the travelling community (CJBC-L: 1175–6, 1190).

Debates in the Commons on the CJB93 made less reference to the ethnic character of Gypsies compared to NATs, although the themes raised above did appear. Elsewhere, although ostensibly not focusing on NATs, discussion of the Caravan Sites (Amendment) Bill 1993 recognized a need to distinguish clearly "traditional nomads" (Bowen Wells, Hansard, 1993a: 612; Alan Haselhurst, Hansard, 1993a: 635), whilst prejudice experienced by Gypsies was blamed on the actions of the NATs (Nigel Evans, Hansard, 1993a: 641).

Secondly, as regards distinguishing NATs from "real" Gypsies, there was reference to the reasons why a mobile lifestyle was adopted. The lack of economic motivation behind the migration of NATs was stressed. Tony Baldry (Under-Secretary of State for the Environment) described the situation thus:

> New age travellers adopt their lifestyle as a matter of choice. They cannot possibly be described as true nomads . . . Furthermore, new age travellers appear to have no wish to establish themselves or reside on authorised sites, but *simply want to roam through the countryside unchecked*." (CJBRS-C: 319; my emphasis)

This accusation was repeated by Earl Ferrers in the House of Lords (CJBC-L: 1122). Drawing on the Court of Appeal decision that NATs were not covered by the 1968 Caravan Sites Act 1968, he concluded that NATs are not nomadic (CJBC-L: 1149), since: "the notion of economic independence is inherent to the idea of nomadic life" (CJBC-L: 1188). Commentators also referred disparagingly to NATs' reliance on welfare payments (Hansard, 1992a: 689; 1993a: 614), although an ignorance or vagueness concerning the NATs' lifestyle was frequently all too apparent: "These people camp in an area and then chase the sheep, rob and do other things" (Lord Stanley of Alderley, CJBR-L: 1479). Bowen Wells MP, whilst acknowledging the homelessness and the appalling urban housing conditions which encourage people to take to the road, ultimately concluded: "those who are not traditional nomads must live like the rest of us" (Hansard, 1993a: 612).

Thus, whilst David Maclean, the Minister of State at the Home Office, admitted: "I would not care to define a new age traveller" (CJBRS-C: 296), the general attitude expressed in both Houses of Parliament was one of overwhelming dislike of the NATs and sympathy for the "real" Gypsy.[7] A summary of this consensus came from Lord Kenyon:

> we are no longer talking about the same kind of gypsies as we were 16 [*sic*] years ago, when the Caravan Sites Act came into force. True gypsies have been with us for centuries. They have been tolerated – indeed welcomed – in the rural community, where they regularly assisted in the harvest and did other casual jobs around the farms and houses. But today they have acquired their parasites, the hippies or drop-outs – generically referred to as New Age travellers – who do not work, who do not want to work, but who believe that, because the gypsies have the apparent right to roam the countryside at will, they can do the same at the expense of the local taxpayer. They are the ones who are so unwelcome in the countryside . . . (CJBC-L: 1176)

This view – NATs as parasitic "bandwagon" jumpers (see also David Maclean, CJBSCB-C: 695) – was supported, notably in the House of Lords, by anecdotes concerning the bad experiences individuals had had of NATs, rather than through any more nuanced attempt to understand and tease out the varied features of the NAT lifestyle (for example, Lord Northbourne, CJBC-L: 630).

Whilst Lord Kenyon expressed the consensus view on NATs vis-à-vis Gypsies, it is also important to note some contrasting attitudes. Many MPs and peers displayed a more hostile attitude to NATs. Here are two rather intemperate but illustrative views, the first taken from the Commons:

> I am not talking about the old romantic show people – the old Romanies. I am not talking about the fortune tellers. The plain, unvarnished truth about new age travellers . . . is that . . . they

> are dirty, lazy dropouts, whose dedication to their way of life extends no further than the nearest benefit office, followed closely by the nearest pub. . . . people who stand up for travellers are standing up for loafers and spongers, hiding their position behind a veil of wishing to preserve the gipsies' way of life at all costs. (John Sykes, Hansard, 1993a: 620–21)

Secondly, we have a contribution from Lord Clifford of Chudleigh, who began to suggest why "hippies" did not belong in the countryside:

> These people [NATs] are wasters . . . if a person wants to have a mobile home . . . he must be able to afford it. Such people then get their social security and continue to afford their lives at the expense of those people whom we are supposed to be representing – . . . the majority of the country. The majority of the country knows jolly well where the hospitals and schools are. Let us not dilly dally around these people who come along and make their names with the press. (CJBC-L: 628)

Few speakers in either House had much good to say about NATs. Whilst the Labour Party was concerned with the plight of Gypsies, it did not muster front bench opposition to the Public Order measures. Thus, in the House of Lords, Baroness Mallalieu appealed for a greater level of toleration concerning "a degree of inconvenience from one's neighbours" (CJBC-L: 624) and, in response to Lord Clifford, Lord Taylor of Gryfe (CJBC-L: 628) and Lord McIntosh of Haringey (CJBC-L: 639) pointed out that democracy is about protecting minorities as well as representing the majority. However, Lord Irvine of Lairg was the only peer to elaborate on criticisms of the Public Order measures. The tone of his criticisms can be garnered from his comments in the Bill's Second Reading:

> I move from the Government's unwillingness to provide special protection for minorities who require it [legislation against racial attacks, etc.] to their willingness to persecute – and I use that word advisedly – an even more vulnerable minority. I refer to . . . gypsies and New Age travellers . . . The clauses represent a high watermark [*sic*] of repressiveness without any countervailing social policy and give the lie . . . to the Government's claim to be the party of family unity. At one stroke the provisions destroy the tradition that non-conforming minorities are not to be persecuted. . . . the Bill has a unifying theme, it incorporates every unbalanced measure that will as much guarantee ecstasy at the Tory Party conference as rejection by the responsible. (CJB2-L: 502–3)

The impact of such withering criticism was dampened by the absence of sustained support from other peers in the debates.

In the Commons, the only real sympathy voiced for NATs came from the Labour backbencher Jeremy Corbyn in the discussion of the 1993 Caravan Sites (Amendment) Bill[8]. In particular, he was skeptical of the claim made by ministers, which was repeated on numerous occasions in the debates concerning the CJB93, that: "The Government have no quarrel with the nomadic way of life" (David Maclean, CJBSCB-C: 703). Corbyn perceived a degree of disingenuousness on the part of Conservative MPs:

> surely different ways of life and lifestyles are perfectly acceptable in a pluralistic society. I do not believe that Conservative Members agree with that; they may say it, but I do not think that they believe it for one moment. (Hansard, 1993a: 626)

Other Labour criticism referred to Conservative dislike of Gypsies and travellers (Neil Gerrard drew attention to a leaflet entitled "Conservatives against Gypsies," supposedly produced in the constituency of Bowen Wells (CJBSCB-C: 703)) and concern over what Alun Michael described as the Government's "over-hasty lunge for popularity" (CJBSCB-C: 704).

NATs Do Not Belong in the Countryside

A key criticism of the NATs was that, unlike "real" Gypsies, they moved around in large groups. This is a clear violation of the social space of the rural idyll since, although there is room in the idyll's view of the countryside for village fêtes and such "traditional" merriment, this is all at the small scale. In other words, the liminality through which the Carnivalesque can emerge in the rural idyll (Shields, 1991, Chapter Two) cannot embrace large gatherings such as those associated with NATs. Moreover, the impact of such gatherings forces the travellers, albeit temporarily, into the center of the rural scene, thus violating their marginal position within that idyll; as Bakhtin recognized: "carnival denaturalized the dominant order" (Cresswell, 1994: 38). Thus, Lord Hoosen argued that movement of large numbers of travellers threatened the rural way of life (CJBC-L: 1129).

Further evidence to support this concern with scale is abundant. Michael Spicer opening an adjournment debate on Castlemorton, used an interesting military metaphor:

> new age travellers, ravers and drugs racketeers arrived at a strength of two motorized army divisions, complete with several massed bands and, above all, a highly sophisticated command and signals system. (Hansard, 1992a: 688)

This sense of invasion of "small communities, isolated farms, individuals" (Lord Congleton, CJBC-L: 1184) was repeated elsewhere, the suggestion being that NATs represented an army of marauders who were hell-bent on destroying the "peace and quiet and seclusion" (Lord Renton, CJBR-L: 1491) of rural life, disrupting both the convalescence of elderly and invalid people (Lord Boyd-Carpenter, CJBC-L: 655) but also the more general conventional rural experience, through seeking: "to trespass, molest, vandalise and . . . intimidate others" (Bowen Wells, Hansard, 1992b: 281). Thus:

> The new age travellers displayed some dreadful antics: they *invaded* peaceful countryside, *decimated* peaceful villages, went on the *rampage* and had raves lasting two or three days, showing a total disregard for the area. (Nigel Evans, Hansard, 1993a: 623; my emphases)

Similarly:

> genuine gipsies . . . do not go around *invading* private land. . . . it is the so-called new age travellers . . . They move in *droves*, *descend* on someone's land and decide to reside there." (David Maclean, CJBSCB-C: 577; my emphases)

Indeed, moving from a military to an insectivorous metaphor, Lord Kenyon described NATs as "a plague of locusts" (CJB2-L: 476) ("gNATs"?) whilst Bowen Wells moved to the avian sphere and compared travellers generally with the congregational tendency of "poultry" (Hansard, 1993a: 610). In spite of this concern with marauding hordes of NATs (see also Lord Avebury, CJBC-L: 639), one must not reduce the concern with these travellers to a concern with large numbers. Even small groups of NATs were unacceptable to many speakers (for example, Sir David Mitchell, Hansard, 1993b).

Besides the disruption of rural tranquillity, a further concern associated with large groups of NATs stemmed from a perception that they were involved in crime (Judith Chaplin, Hansard, 1993a: 616), especially "damage and destruction" (David Maclean, CJBSCB-C: 534), an extension of the perceived link between Gypsies and criminality (Lord Kenyon, CJB2-L: 476–7; cf. Mayall, 1988: 184). Indeed, such is the fear in the West Country that the spectre of revolution loomed (David Nicholson, Hansard, 1993a: 638). Thus, Earl Ferrers expressed disbelief that NATs might leave their vehicles, in order to go into town shopping, while surrounded by other travellers (CJBC-L: 641). Whilst concern with crime is prevalent within British society generally, it is an issue which surfaced readily in these debates because there is no place for crime in the rural idyll. According to the narrative of this myth, crime is an urban feature of the modern era, not of the quiet rural village.

Concern about: "converted buses arriving in convoy and planting themselves on local communities, causing them great stress and fear" (Jonathan Evans, CJBSCB-C: 530) was not just an issue of violence and crime. There was also a "visual" menace. NATs were, in short, seen as rubbish; an untidy aspect of urban life with no place in the beautiful countryside of the rural idyll – they spoilt the view (Bowen Wells, Hansard, 1992b: 281) and caused "desecration" (Earl Ferrers, CJBR-L: 1541). Hence, David Maclean can talk of "the appalling menace of [rural residents] looking out of their windows one morning to find their backyards or land have been invaded by a *pile of people* . . . [They] *despoil the landscape*" (CJBSCB-C: 534, 703, my emphases), whilst Lady Olga Maitland could "recall going to Greenham common and seeing the chaos that was caused by demonstrators, who are in effect a variation of travellers.[9] They were utterly filthy." (CJBSCB-C: 571)

To Sir David Mitchell, his constituents had three principal complaints regarding travellers in general: unsanitary conditions, the presence of rubbish and litter, and their unwashed appearance (Hansard, 1993b: 974). Thus, we can appreciate Ian Taylor's perceptive observation that: "The problem is that often there is not public disorder but merely public dismay" (Hansard, 1993a: 629). This dismay became acute when the external appearance of the travellers' encampments clashed with the experience of rural residents forced to conform to planning restrictions which bolster the visual aspect of the rural idyll (Jonathan Evans, CJBSCB: 699).

Returning to the theme of travellers near Greenham Common, Judith Chaplin summarized the clash of scale, invasion and cultural offense experienced by established rural residents as a result of contact with NATs:

> In my constituency we . . . have a large number of attractive commons, and for hundreds of years . . . itinerant workers . . . have moved around in small groups on the commons without greatly offending the local population. . . . people used to expect to see just a few travellers in the summer months; they would then move on. Not any longer. People are worried, because larger numbers are arriving, settling for longer periods and doing immense damage. The beautiful Hungerford common . . . has been the scene of great difficulties . . . Three years ago, a large convoy of travellers stopped on the common and caused great distress to the inhabitants of the town. They then

> went into the town, many of them strangely dressed, and into shops, where they offended the local people." (Hansard, 1993a: 615–16)

Once again, this account contrasts NATs with "legitimate" travellers, highlighting the position of the latter on the margins of the rural and the violation of that marginality by the former. Unlike this concern with NATs, Jeremy Corbyn observed (Hansard, 1993a: 616) how the presence of a nuclear base in the same area was accepted by Chaplin as a legitimate feature of the Berkshire countryside.[10]

The rural idyll is underpinned by a strong sense of order: there is a set social and physical landscape which characterizes this imagined countryside. Indeed, the association between the idyll and order helps explain why rural living is so appealing in "postmodern" Britain (Halfacree, 1994). It is thus unsurprising that the issue of order and the disorder created by NATs featured strongly in the debates. At one level this concern was used to attack all mobile lifestyles. Thus, John Sykes in his diatribe emphasized the "settled nature of our communities" (Hansard, 1993a: 620). Looking more specifically at NATs, the concern with order was reflected in demands to uphold the sanctity of private property and the authority of the State (Judith Chaplin, Hansard, 1993a: 616). If NATs believed that common land belongs to everyone (Jonathan Evans, CJBSCB-C: 553) then where will this appropriation of private space end, given that NATs want to be able to roam at will rather than confine themselves to select sites? For Michael Spicer: "The threat posed by new age travellers . . . is to private property and the rule of law" (Hansard, 1992a: 690), whilst for Lady Olga Maitland NATs were: "a skilful community that enjoys playing a cat and mouse game with the authorities . . . determined to leave as much chaos as they can" (CJBSCB-C: 571). Indeed, the spectre of "anarchy" in the countryside – the antithesis of the ordered calmness of the rural idyll – featured explicitly in the debates in the House of Lords (see CJB2-L: 470, 492; CJBC-L: 666). Moreover, one does not have to resort to conspiracy theory regarding NATs' organization (Jonathan Evans, CJBSCB-C: 533; Robert Maclennan, Liberal Democrat, CJBSCB-C: 538; Geoffrey Clifton-Brown, CJBSCB-C: 539; cf. Earl Ferrers, CJBC-L: 666) to perceive NATs as a threat by a minority to a (rural) majority:

> We have a long tradition of freedom in our country for all people. But freedom is easily abused, sometimes by groups of people who put forward the most bogus reasons for so-called social justice and for being a nuisance to other people. We cannot achieve freedom for the community without order. . . . *Part V breaks new ground in protecting the majority from the minority.* (Lord Alexander of Weedon, CJB2-L: 455; my empha-

ses; see also Michael Spicer, Hansard, 1992a: 690; Bowen Wells, Hansard, 1993a: 612; Lord Renton, CJBR-L: 1491).

Conclusion: Towards a New Rurality?

> I don't think it should be a crime to want to live like that, to want to live in a rural area rather than a big city. And it's impossible to go out and rent a cottage or a farmhouse or buy one. Apart from people who are born to it, rural Britain is for the rich. It's for people who can afford to buy themselves a weekend place or go and retire in the country. For me, if I want to live with space around me and trees and hills and woods, the only possible way apart from sleeping out is to buy a vehicle and live in that. (Shannon, traveller, quoted in Lowe and Shaw, 1993: 240)

> [I]f the Government's proposals are enacted, the only people free to [adopt a nomadic existence] within the criminal law will be those wealthy enough to establish sites around the country between which they may wander, as medieval monarchs were able to do. (Lord Irvine of Lairg, CJBC-L: 1194)

For Andrew Gamble, with Thatcherism "the Conservatives finally abandoned the formulas of one-nation politics . . . [and] look more than ever . . . the party of the shires and suburbs" (Gamble, 1994: 165–6). To this we can add that, with the re-construction of the traveller as a folk devil, the Conservatives have also shown themselves to be the party of the rural idyll. Yet, the post-1979 Conservative government has been unable to achieve anything like a total hegemonic consensus against social democracy, as popular support for the National Health Service readily attests. More radically, Staeheli (1994) argues that we are now in an optimistic era with respect to empowering marginalized peoples, even if the structures of oppression frequently remain.

As part of this struggle, Cloke (1993a, 1993b; see also Roberts, 1992) has appealed for rural areas to be made less exclusive and to become more welcoming for less "traditional" rural inhabitants, many of whom have been indicated by Philo (1992). Both Cloke and Philo recognize travellers amongst these currently marginalized groups, and calls for their empowerment form part of a broader radical agenda aimed at extending "mobility rights" (Blomley, 1994). Crucially, accepting travellers into the countryside requires a cultural sea-change on behalf of present-day established rural inhabitants. It requires a critical assessment and reappraisal of the cultural straitjacket provided by the rural idyll in order to give all varieties of travellers a "place" within dominant social representations of the rural. A parallel call is being made elsewhere, by, *inter alia*, critics of the gendered (Little, 1986) and racialized (Agyeman, 1990) character of the supposedly "idyllic" representation.

Arguing for a cultural political strategy which recognizes that much of the hostility to travellers stems from their alienation from the rural idyll is, of course, only part of the answer. At stake are not just conflicting representations of space but fundamental issues of power. The hegemony of the "rural idyll" was not achieved purely by chance but in part because of its amenability to capitalist spatiality. As regards this affiliation, the highly commodified and privatized character of the rural idyll is paramount (Thrift, 1989). In contrast, the social representation of rurality which travellers appear to be articulating through their actions, albeit often partially, is much less conducive to this privatized form of spatiality. These contrasts can be represented diagrammatically in Figure 2. On the left side, the "private" realm, the complementary positions of the striations of the "rural idyll" and the conceptually emptiable smooth space of "capitalist territoriality" are demonstrated. On the right, in the "public" realm, we have the space of the travellers. This ranges from the heavily striated representations of "Hippies," with their spiritual interpretation and understanding of the countryside, to the smoother transient representations of "Ravers."

Presently, travellers' ruralities do not provide a coherent anti-capitalist spatiality – and they must not be over-romanticized as a consequence – but they do provide a green shoot to be nurtured. Travellers' transgression of the rural idyll and their trespassing is not merely physical:

> Transgression depends on the pre-existence of some form of spatial ordering. . . . Transgression has limits; constant transgression is permanent chaos. . . . *Yet within transgression lie the seeds of new spatial orderings.* (Cresswell, 1994: 57, my emphases)

Whether these seeds eventually germinate remains open. Whether assimilationist (Hawes, 1987; Lloyd, 1993; Lord Irvine of Lairg, CJBC-L: 1195; cf. Earl Ferrers, CJBR-L: 1542) or merely vindictive (Lord Irvine of Lairg, CJBR-L: 1534; Vernon, 1994), the Criminal Justice and Public Order Act 1994 may succeed in removing NATs from the English and Welsh countryside. More abstractly, Deleuze and Guattari are equivocal about the nomad's revolutionary potential. Smooth space does not possess "an irresistible revolutionary calling" (1987: 387; see also Sibley, 1988: 414) and, historically, the "hesitation of the nomad is legendary" (Deleuze and Guattari, 1987: 418). Lastly, however, given the long history of "nature" and the "countryside" being used in opposition to "modern society," Mormont (1987: 11) has suggested:

> The countryside is often considered to be a place where it is possible to put into practice another way of life (from an individualistic perspective), or another model of social and economic organisation (in a social world view).

Will the "individualistic perspective" or the "social world view" prevail?

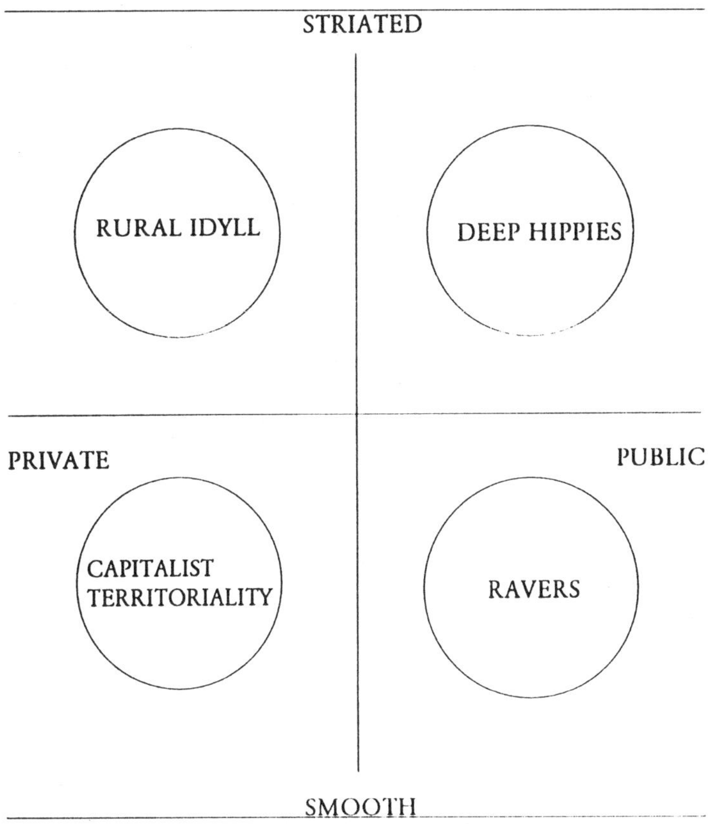

Figure 2 Alternative spatialities of the rural

Acknowledgements

I would like to thank Theresa Aldridge and Pyrs Gruffudd for their advice and encouragement during the writing of this paper, and the referees for their insightful comments and suggestions.

68 KEITH H. HALFACREE

Notes

1. Numbers next to Parliamentary proceedings refer to columns rather than page numbers. All MPs cited are Conservative unless otherwise indicated.
2. May Day 1994 saw upwards of 6,000 people demonstrating in Trafalgar Square against the proposed Act (Guardian, 2 May 1994), whilst demonstrations on 24th July and 9th October of that year each saw upwards of 50,000 participate (Guardian, 25 July 1994, 10 Oct. 1994).
3. Lefebvre's definition of space is not confined to "objective" physical geography. Instead it encompasses his "conceptual triad" (Lefebvre, 1991: 33) of "spatial practices" (practices reflecting experiences rooted in perceived space), "representations of space" (formal, academically conceived abstractions of space) and "representational space" (the symbolic imaginative space of everyday life). Whilst this triad is imprecisely delineated (Merrifield, 1993: 524; see also Harvey, 1987), it emphasizes the breadth of Lefebvre's conception.
4. For the complex and problematic link between social representations of the rural and rural space as "locality," see Halfacree (1993b).
5. Nonetheless, Cresswell's (1994) study of the Greenham Common peace camps suggests how marginal groups can quickly become incorporated into dominant representations, although it must be stressed that the Greenham women remained "unacceptable" within representations of Greenham Common.
6. As Eric Lubbock, Lord Avebury was the main instigator of the Caravan Sites Act 1968. Lord Avebury's concern with distinguishing Gypsies from other travellers mirrored the concerns of an earlier supporter of the Gypsy cause, George Smith of Coalville, who in the last century distinguished people with "Gypsy habits" unfavorably from those with "Gypsy blood" (Mayall, 1988: 79).
7. The sympathy for Gypsies expressed itself in an initially successful Lords' amendment to the CJB93, sponsored by Lords Avebury and Stanley of Alderley, for a five-year suspension of the repeal of the 1968 Gypsy site legislation (CJBR-L: 1563). This amendment was subsequently overturned in the Commons (CJBA-L).
8. Corbyn's opposition to the CJB93 was elaborated outside Parliament. For example, he contributed an article to the campaigning Green-Socialist magazine *Red Pepper* (Corbyn, 1994) and, together with other Labour MPs, such as Tony Benn, was involved in the protests cited in Note 2.
9. The issue of dirt and pollution as regards the Greenham Common women has been analyzed in detail by Cresswell (1994).
10. This brings to mind Peter Kennard's montage of cruise missiles on Constable's "Haywain" (see Daniels, 1993: 228).

References

Adams, B., J. Okely, D. Morgan, and D. Smith (1975) *Gypsies and Government Policy in England*. London: Heinemann.

Agyeman, J. (1990) Black people in a white landscape. Social and environmental justice. *Built Environment* 16: 231–36.

Barry, N. (1987) *The New Right*. London: Croom Helm.

Beale, A. and R. Geary (1994) New age gypsies? *Solicitors Journal* 138: 112–13.

Blakey, D. (1992) Our common cause. *Police Review* 100(5168): 1042–3.
Blomley, N. (1994) Mobility, empowerment and the rights revolution. *Political Geography* 13: 407–22.
Brake, M. and C. Hale (1989) Law and order. In P. Brown and R. Sparks (Eds.) *Beyond Thatcherism*. Milton Keynes: Open University Press, pp. 137–54.
Campbell, B. (1993) Travellers at the gate. *The Guardian* [Part Two] 14 April.
CJB2-C [Second Reading. Criminal Justice and Public Order Bill 1993, House of Commons] *Hansard* 11 Jan. 1994.
CJBRS-C [Remaining Stages. Criminal Justice and Public Order Bill 1993, House of Commons] *Hansard* 13 Apr. 1994.
CJBSCB-C [Standing Committee B. Criminal Justice and Public Order Bill 1993, House of Commons] *Proceedings of 12th-15th Sittings*, 8–10 Feb. 1994.
CJB2-L [Second Reading. Criminal Justice and Public Order Bill 1993, House of Lords] *Hansard* 25, Apr. 1994.
CJBA-L [Consideration of Commons Amendments and Reasons. Criminal Justice and Public Order Bill 1993, House of Lords] *Hansard* 25 Oct., 1994.
CJBC-L [Committee Stage. Criminal Justice and Public Order Bill 1993, House of Lords] *Hansard* 24 May and 7 June, 1994.
CJBR-L [Report Stage. Criminal Justice and Public Order Bill 1993, House of Lords] *Hansard* 7 and 11 July, 1994.
Clements, L. (1992) Gypsies: harsh laws no solution. *Rural Viewpoint* 52: 12–13.
Cloke, P. (1993a) On "problems and solutions." The reproduction of problems for rural communities in Britain during the 1980s. *Journal of Rural Studies* 9: 113–21.
Cloke, P. (1993b) A respect for all rural people. *Rural Viewpoint* 56: 3.
Cohen, S. (1987) *Folk Devils and Moral Panics* (3rd ed.) Oxford: Blackwell.
Committee of Inquiry (1985) *Education for All*. (The Swann Report). London: HMSO.
Corbyn, J. (1994) Unite to kill the Bill! *Red Pepper* 5: 9.
Cottaar, A., L. Lucassen, and W. Willems (1992) Justice of injustice? A survey of government policy towards Gypsies and caravan dwellers in western Europe in the Nineteenth and Twentieth Centuries. *Immigrants and Minorities* 11: 42–66.
Cresswell, T. (1994) Putting women in their place: the carnival at Greenham Common. *Antipode* 26: 35–58.
Crowther, M. (1992) The tramp. In R. Porter (Ed.) *Myths of the English*. Cambridge: Polity, pp. 91–113.
Dalton, S. (1993) You can't beat the system! *New Musical Express* 9th January.
Daniels, S. (1993) *Fields of Vision*. Cambridge: Polity.
Deleuze, G. and Guattari, F. (1987) *A Thousand Plateaus*. Minneapolis: University of Minnesota Press.
Dixon, D. (1987) Protest and disorder: the Public Order Act 1986. *Critical Social Policy* 7: 90–98.
Driscoll, J. (1987) Protest and public order: the Public Order Act 1986. *Journal of Social Welfare Law* September: 280–99.
Earle, F., A. Dearling, H. Whittle, R. Glasse, and Gubby (1994) *A Time to Travel? An Introduction to Britain's Newer Travellers*. Lyme Regis: Enabler Publications.
Fairlie, S. (1993) Tunnel vision. The lessons from Twyford Down. *The Ecologist* 23: 2–4.
Gamble, A. (1994) *The Free Economy and the Strong State*. Basingstoke: Macmillan.
Giddens, A. (1984) *The Constitution of Society*. Cambridge: Polity.
Giddens, A. (1990) *The Consequences of Modernity*. Cambridge: Polity.
Green, P. (1990) *The Enemy Without*. Milton Keynes: Open University Press.
Guardian (2 May, 1994) "It was a May Day rally a few beats removed from tradition . . ."

Guardian (28 May, 1994a) PM attacks "offensive" beggars.
Guardian (28 May, 1994b) New Age travellers fail in appeal for gypsy status and site rights.
Guardian (25 Jul., 1994) Mounted officers break up assault on Downing Street.
Guardian (10 Oct., 1994) Protest against justice bill leads to violence.
Halfacree, K. (1993a) Interpreting ruralism as the culture of counterurbanisation. Some evidence from rural England in the late 1980s. Paper presented at the First Anglo-Italian Symposium on Population Geography, Cagliari, Sardinia, 5th-7th September.
Halfacree, K. (1993b) Locality and social representation: space, discourse and alternative definitions of the rural. *Journal of Rural Studies* 9: 23–37.
Halfacree, K. (1994) Locating counterurbanization: a preliminary discussion in the context of the postmodern debate. Paper presented at the Institute of British Geographers Annual Conference, Nottingham University, 4th–7th January.
Halfacree, K. (1995) Talking about rurality: social representations of the rural as expressed by residents of six English parishes. *Journal of Rural Studies* 11: 1–20.
Hall, S. (1983) The great moving right show. In S. Hall and M. Jacques (Eds.) The Politics of Thatcherism. London: Lawrence and Wishart, pp. 19–39.
Hansard (1986) Hippy convoy (New Forest), cols. 733–9, 3rd June.
Hansard (1992a) Travellers, cols. 688–94, 29th June.
Hansard (1992b) Privatization of Gipsy sites, cols. 281–2, 4th Nov.
Hansard (1993a) Caravan Sites (Amendment) Bill, cols. 585–649, 5th Feb.
Hansard (1993b) Gipsy sites, cols. 970–6, 26th July.
Harvey, D. (1978) Labor, capital, and class struggle around the built environment in advanced capitalist societies. In K. Cox (Ed.) *Urbanization and Conflict in Market Societies*. London: Methuen, pp. 9–37.
Harvey, D. (1987) Flexible accumulation through urbanization: reflections on "post-modernism" in the American city. *Antipode* 19: 260–86.
Harvey, D. (1989) *The Condition of Postmodernity*. Oxford: Blackwell.
Hawes, D. (1987) Gypsy site policy: a failure of both carrot and stick. *Policy and Politics* 15: 49–54.
Hoggart, K. (1990) Let's do away with rural. *Journal of Rural Studies* 6: 245–57.
Jessop, B., K. Bonnett, S. Bromley, and T. Ling (1984) Authoritarian populism, two nations and Thatcherism. *New Left Review* 147: 32–60.
Jones, N. (1993) *Living in Rural Wales*. Llandysul: Gomer.
Lefebvre, H. (1991) *The Production of Space*. Oxford: Blackwell.
Liberty (1993) *The Road to Nowhere?* Report 93/4. London: Liberty.
Little, J. (1986) Feminist perspectives in rural geography: an introduction. *Journal of Rural Studies* 2: 1–8.
Lloyd, L. (1993) Proposed reform of the 1968 Caravan Sites Act: producing a problem to suit a solution? *Critical Social Policy* 38: 77–85.
Lowe, P., J. Murdoch, T. Marsden, R. Munton and A. Flynn (1993) Regulating the new rural spaces: the uneven development of land. *Journal of Rural Studies* 9: 205–22.
Lowe, R. and W. Shaw (1993) *Travellers*. London: Fourth Estate.
Mars, T. (1989) Gypsies yes, New Age travellers no. *Roof* May/June: 24.
Mayall, D. (1988) *Gypsy-travellers in Nineteenth-century Society*. Cambridge: Cambridge University Press.
Merrifield, A. (1993) Place and space: a Lefebvrian reconciliation. *Transactions of the Institute of British Geographers* 18: 516–31.
Monbiot, G. (1994) Lament for the common people. *The Guardian* [Changes Supplement], June 2.
Mormont, M. (1987) Rural nature and urban natures. *Sociologia Ruralis* 27: 3–20.

Moscovici, S. (1984) The phenomenon of social representations. In R. Farr and S. Moscovici (Eds.) *Social Representations*. Cambridge: Cambridge University Press, pp.3–69.

NCCL [National Council for Civil Liberties] (1986) *Stonehenge*. London: NCCL.

NME [*New Musical Express*] (08/05/1993) Features on the "Convoy Clampdown."

Norrie, A. and S. Adelman (1989) "Consensual authoritarianism" and criminal justice in Thatcher's Britain. In A. Gamble and C. Wells (Eds.) *Thatcher's Law*. Cardiff: GPC Books, pp. 112–28.

Okely, J. (1983) *The Traveller-Gypsies*. Cambridge: Cambridge University Press.

Philo, C. (1992) Neglected rural geographies: a review. *Journal of Rural Studies* 8: 193–207.

Pratt, A. (forthcoming) Rurality: loose talk or social struggle? *Journal of Rural Studies*.

Rehfisch, F. (1975) (Ed.) *Gypsies, Tinkers and Other Travellers*. London: Academic Press.

Roberts, L. (1992) A rough guide to rurality. *Talking Point* 137.

Rosenberger, A. (1989) One for the road. *Roof* May/June: 22–26.

Sack, R. (1986) *Human Territoriality*. Cambridge: Cambridge University Press.

Scraton, P. (1987) Unreasonable force: policing, punishment and marginalization. In P. Scraton (Ed.) *Law, Order and the Authoritarian State*. Milton Keynes: Open University Press, pp.145–89.

Shields, R. (1991) *Places on the Margin*. London: Routledge.

Short, J. (1991) *Imagined Country*. London: Routledge.

Sibley, D. (1981) *Outsiders in Urban Societies*. Oxford: Blackwell.

Sibley, D. (1986) Persistence or change? Conflicting interpretations of peripheral minorities. *Environment and Planning D: Society and Space* 4: 57–70.

Sibley, D. (1987) Racism and settlement policy; the state's response to a semi-nomadic minority. In P. Jackson (Ed.) *Race and Racism*. London: Allen and Unwin, pp. 74–91.

Sibley, D. (1988) Purification of space. *Environment and Planning D: Society and Space* 6: 409–21.

Sinclair, P. (1993) Casting out the outcasts. *Geographical Magazine* March: 14–18.

Smith, N. (1984) *Uneven Development*. Oxford: Blackwell.

Soja, E. (1985) The spatiality of social life: towards a transformative retheorisation. In D. Gregory and J. Urry (Eds.) *Social Relations and Spatial Structures*. Basingstoke: Macmillan, pp. 90–127.

Staeheli, L. (1994) Empowering political struggle: spaces and scales of resistance. *Political Geography* 13: 387–91.

Thrift, N. (1989) Images of social change. In C. Hamnett, L. McDowell and P. Sarre (Eds.) *The Changing Social Structure*. London: Sage/Open University Press, pp. 12–42.

Tucker, P. (1991) "New Age Travellers and the State: Site Provision and Mobility Patterns." BSc dissertation, University College of Swansea.

Vernon, R. (1994) In defence of the travellers. *Resurgence* 164: 4–6.

Vidal, J. (1992) The Battle of Camelot. *The Guardian* [Part Two] Dec. 15.

Wilson, T. (1994) Planning for travellers: an historical overview. Paper presented at a conference on "Planning for Travellers: Devising a Way Forward," University of Wales, College of Cardiff, 20th May.

Jnl Soc. Pol., 8, 3, 289–309

The Practice of Racial Dispersal in Birmingham, 1969–1975*

HAZEL FLETT,† JEFF HENDERSON‡ and BILL BROWN§

ABSTRACT

The possibility of using public sector housing to disperse black people across our cities in the interest of racial integration is again attracting attention. Based on an analysis of housing department records, this article examines the effects on Birmingham's black settlers of the operation of one particular policy of racial dispersal. Having described the events leading to the introduction and ultimately the termination of the policy, the article proceeds to investigate the locations in which Asian, West Indian and native white tenants were housed, their area preferences, and the housing categories from which their allocations were made, as well as their 'points' levels on allocation. The article concludes by arguing that, on these dimensions, the consequences of the policy for black people were almost entirely negative.

After the publication in 1967 of *Race, Community and Conflict*,[1] Birmingham Housing Department gained some notoriety for its alleged discrimination against black prospective tenants on its waiting list.[2] At that time the allegations of discrimination were based on the five-year residence qualification which the city's housing department imposed on all those who were seeking a council-owned dwelling.[3] Eight years later, the housing depart-

* The Research from which this article stems was funded by the Social Science Research Council (SSRC) and the Department of the Environment. The conclusions are, however, solely those of the authors and in no way represent the views of the sponsoring organizations. We are grateful to Birmingham Housing Department for its co-operation, to Ian Carr and Matt Rodger for technical assistance, and especially to Valerie Karn for her extensive comments on earlier drafts.

† Research Associate, SSRC Research Unit on Ethnic Relations, University of Bristol.
‡ Research Fellow, Centre for Urban and Regional Studies, University of Birmingham.
§ Research Associate, Centre for Urban and Regional Studies, University of Birmingham.

[1] J. Rex and R. Moore, *Race, Community and Conflict*, Institute of Race Relations and Oxford University Press, London, 1967.

[2] Throughout this paper the term 'black' will be applied to peoples both of West Indian and of Asian origin.

[3] The residence qualification has subsequently been reduced to two years.

ment again received attention for its alleged discriminatory practices, but this time not as a result of sociological research, nor because of its residence qualification. On this second occasion, the Race Relations Board considered that the department's denial of access for blacks to certain council dwellings, which was a consequence of its practice of dispersing black tenants across the city, contravened the *Race Relations Act* 1968.

The existence and operation of a dispersal policy has been a key organizing feature of Birmingham's council housing allocations in the past decade, and this article sets out to examine specifically the impact of that dispersal policy on the allocations made to black applicants. It is based on a comparison of the allocations made to black applicants with those made to white applicants. The article begins with a brief outline of the background within which a dispersal policy came to be perceived as a possible means of avoiding potential racial conflict. It goes on to indicate the mechanics of the policy's operation as well as the events which led up to the Race Relations Board's ruling, and the consequent abandonment of dispersal in October 1975. The article then examines the impact of the policy: the settlement pattern to which it gave rise and the categories of people who were the most affected. A section follows on area preferences and the extent to which they were met. The next section explores whether the dispersal policy meant that blacks were presented only with alternative disadvantages: a location which they did not want or a longer wait for housing. The implications of the policy for black people are underlined in the conclusion. What we are not able to examine here is whether the 'quality of life' of black tenants was altered, be it positively or negatively, as a result of dispersal. That investigation is part of an ongoing research project.[4]

THE BACKGROUND OF DISPERSAL

In May 1968 a conference of chief officers and committee chairmen in Birmingham discussed the problems which the city faced in education, welfare, and housing – problems which they considered to result from black immigration and settlement in the city. Individual reports were submitted by the chief officers, and a conference report was submitted to the General Purposes Committee of the City Council. The main observations and recommendations of the report were accepted by the council in July 1968.

The report was primarily concerned with stressing the extensive 'additional' burden on local authority services, in terms of extra staff and buildings, caused by the presence of 82,000 West Indians and Asians in Bir-

[4] 'Race and Council-Housing Allocation', funded by the Department of the Environment and based at the Centre for Urban and Regional Studies, University of Birmingham.

mingham.[5] Although the report indicated that greater financial support to cope with these additional burdens should be forthcoming from central government, it argued that, even in the absence of such support, the local authority was itself in a position to spread the burden on services in areas of black concentration by a policy of dispersal of black people out of them. Such a policy was seen as desirable for other reasons, principal among which was that it would facilitate racial integration by spreading black people thinly amongst the white population. The report did say that the aim of dispersal would also in part be the improvement of housing conditions for the blacks, but this was not its main focus. Given this lack of emphasis on improving housing, it is not surprising that, in subsequent debate, the possible connection between dispersal and improved housing conditions was obscured. Analysis of this phenomenon, and indeed the ideological context within which dispersal policy arose and was applied, is the subject of another article.[6]

The report of the General Purposes Committee suggested that the numbers of black households that would have to be housed by the local authority would increase as areas with large black populations fell within the clearance programme or within improvement programmes proposed by the 'Old Houses into New Homes' White Paper.[7] On the basis of this, and the figure of 250 per annum being housed at that time, the report estimated that by 1975 10 per cent of council tenants would be black – as it turned out, a vast overestimate.[8]

The report was well publicized in Birmingham, and both the leader of the Conservative administration, and the chairman of the housing committee showed themselves well aware of the danger of predicting the increased entry of black people into council housing at a time when the housing department's waiting list was believed to contain in excess of 30,000 applicants. The chairman of the housing committee was at pains to stress that there would be neither negative nor positive discrimination for blacks relative to whites. After all, he suggested, the white population had already benefited because the five-year residential qualification had in the past protected them against competition over access to council housing.[9] Paralleling these statements of 'equivalence of access', there were calls from

[5] General Purposes Committee, *Report on Immigration*, Birmingham City Council, 1968. There was only a passing reference to the contribution being made to local authority services by black residents.

[6] J. Henderson, H. Flett and B. Brown, 'Racial Dispersal as Ideological Practice', forthcoming.

[7] *Old Houses into New Homes*, Ministry of Housing and Local Government, Cmnd 3602, HMSO, London, 1968.

[8] H. Flett, *Black Council Tenants in Birmingham*, Research Unit on Ethnic Relations Working Papers, University of Bristol, forthcoming, 1979.

[9] *The Birmingham Post*, 15 July 1968.

Conservative and Labour councillors alike for a restriction of further black immigration into the city.

It is against this background that a threatened rent strike by a group of white tenants precipitated the introduction of a method of distributing black households in council property on the basis of a set ratio. In February 1969, nine white tenants in a block of twelve maisonettes in the Ladywood area of the city signed a petition objecting to the allocation of one of the maisonettes to a black family. The allocation would have meant that there were two black families in the block. They threatened a rent strike if the second black family actually moved in. The rejection of the petition by the chairman of the housing committee – on the grounds that he could not accept a complaint based solely on racial prejudice – received all-party support, support which was accompanied by the assertion that dispersal of the black population was the best way to achieve racial integration.[10] The white tenants backed down in the face of threatened eviction, and predictably the event was well publicized by the local press. The decision to produce a set-ratio dispersal policy for black tenants was not, however, made public.

The policy, though not the method, of racial dispersal instituted by the Birmingham Housing Department in the summer of 1969 seemed to have considerable support in principle at the national level via the report of the Institute of Race Relations, the Cullingworth Report, and the *Report of the Select Committee on Immigration and Race Relations*.[11] All three reports advocated dispersal as a means of improving housing conditions, assisting integration, easing the pressure on education and welfare services, and circumventing the possibility of racial conflict. However, the reports did emphasize that dispersal of black tenants by housing departments must be voluntary and not forced, but they failed to specify how this could be effected. In particular this discussion failed to give adequate recognition to the importance of ethnic cultural infrastructure to the quality of life of Britain's black settlers. In this all the reports revealed an ethnocentric bias, which continues to pervade discussion of dispersal policies.

THE MECHANICS OF DISPERSAL AND ITS TERMINATION

The immediate aim of Birmingham's policy was to prevent the concentration of black people in any block, street or area of local authority housing.

[10] *The Birmingham Evening Mail*, 14 February 1969.

[11] See E. J. B. Rose, in association with N. Deakin, M. Abrams, V. Jackson, M. Peston, A. H. Vanags, B. Cohen, J. Gaitskell and P. Ward, *Colour and Citizenship*, Institute of Race Relations and Oxford University Press, London, 1969; *Council Housing: Purposes, Procedures and Priorities* (Cullingworth Report), Ministry of Housing and Local Government, HMSO, London, 1969; and *Report of the Select Committee on Race Relations and Immigration: Housing*, HMSO, London, 1971.

In other words, concentrations of blacks were in themselves seen as undesirable because it was felt that integration could best be effected where very small numbers of blacks were dispersed amongst overwhelming numbers of whites. Both central and local government at this time seemed to assume that social integration would necessarily follow from spatial integration.

The concern of housing committee members about black concentrations (undoubtedly exacerbated by the 'Ladywood revolt') resulted in the institution of a mechanical dispersal policy. In any block of flats or maisonettes and in any street of houses, a maximum of one in six properties could be allocated to blacks (interestingly, the same ratio that pertained in the Ladywood maisonette block after the revolt of the white tenants). The five properties on either side of the one allocated to a black tenant were automatically reserved for whites by the coding of property cards (the housing department's record cards, which carried the details of each property). The ultimate aim was that, in time, the black population would be dispersed from the inner-city ghettos. With the eligible properties in familiar areas already full, blacks, it was hoped, would accept dwellings on suburban estates.

In 1975, six years after the implementation of this policy, the housing department allocated a 'white-designated' property to an Irish woman. Only when she collected the keys to her new home did it emerge in conversation with the lettings clerk that her husband was Jamaican.[12] At that point the clerk indicated that there had been a mistake, and the offer was withdrawn. With the assistance of a housing aid centre, the case was referred to the Race Relations Board, which subsequently ruled that discrimination had occurred. This case of individual discrimination cast doubt on the dispersal policy as such, despite protestations from both the housing committee and the housing department that dispersal was in tune with the spirit (to foster integration) if not the letter of the 1968 *Race Relations Act*. In subsequent negotiations between the Race Relations Board and the local authority, the board, while conceding that a voluntary dispersal policy was perfectly acceptable and possibly desirable, regarded a set-ratio policy as problematic. As a result of these negotiations, Birmingham's dispersal policy was formally suspended in October 1975.[13]

[12] The only personal contact which most prospective tenants have with the housing department before allocation is their interview with the housing visitor. As this takes place at home during working and school hours, the wife is frequently the only person present. Hence, in this case it was easily understandable that the family was categorized as white rather than black, which is the department's normal practice with 'mixed' marriages.

[13] See *The Birmingham Evening Mail*, 6 January 1976.

PATTERNS OF DISTRIBUTION

Our analysis of the impact of the dispersal policy on settlement patterns and on different categories of prospective tenants is based on a division of the city into rings, sectors and segments (see Figure 1) and on samples of

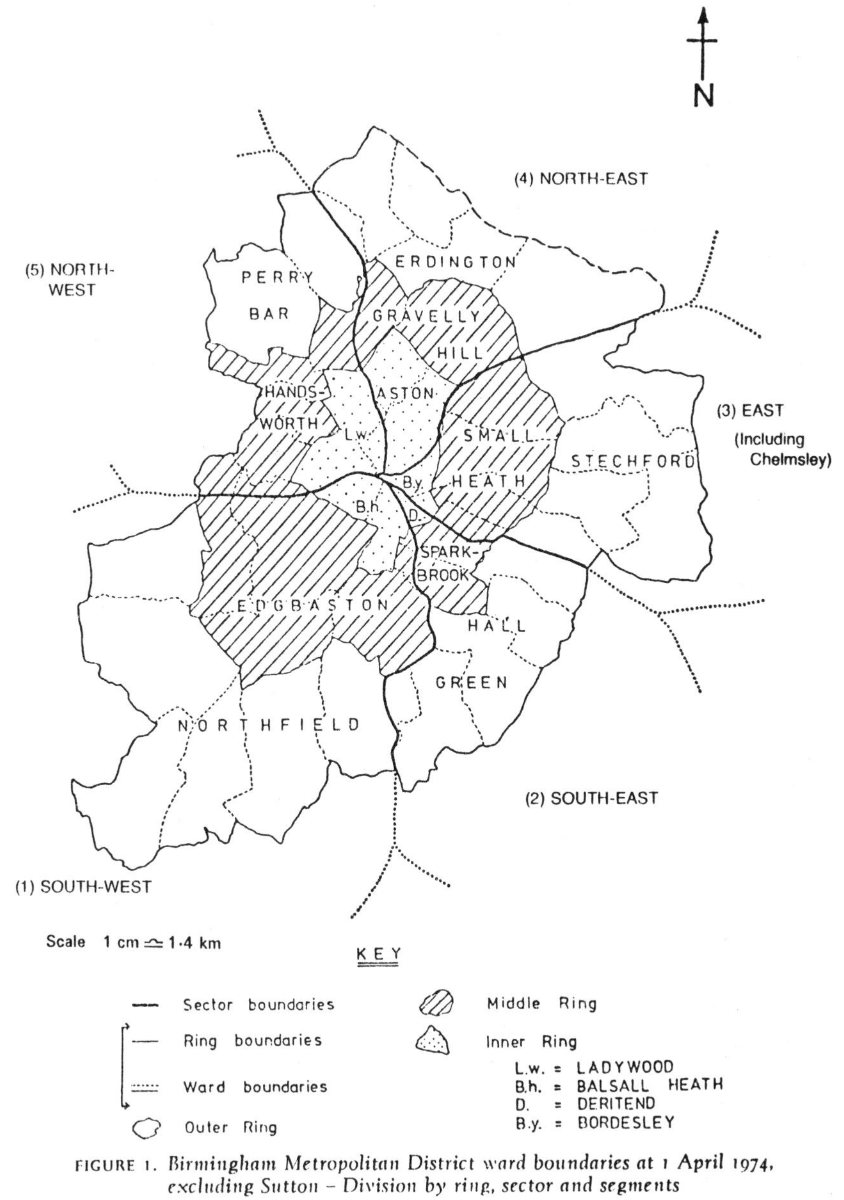

FIGURE 1. *Birmingham Metropolitan District ward boundaries at 1 April 1974, excluding Sutton – Division by ring, sector and segments*

the respective allocations made to black and white households in 1971, 1974 and 1976. 1971 was taken as a period representative of allocations prior to the full impact of dispersal, 1974 as a year in which the policy was operating at its height, and 1976 as the first year of allocations after the formal abandonment of dispersal.[14] The inner ring comprises the five central wards. The middle ring, fourteen wards, includes four wards in the south-west which are surburban in character: the other ten, together with the central wards, conform to current notions of the inner city. The outer ring is surburban, having been developed since 1919. The only exceptional ward there is Sandwell, whose southern end is an extension of the Handsworth and Soho wards, and like them it has considerable multi-occupation and a large black population. Since few people in our samples were housed in the four south-west wards of the middle ring, we can in general equate suburban housing with the outer ring.

At the time of the 1971 census the outer ring contained 68 per cent of council-owned dwellings in the city: the figures for the middle and inner rings were 20 per cent and 12 per cent respectively. Predictably the black population was housed mainly in the inner city – 85 per cent in the inner and middle rings – where local authority dwellings were fewer and housing conditions were poor. Table 1 illustrates that on three measures of housing stress the inner and middle rings were substantially worse off than the suburbs.

TABLE 1. *The quality of housing in the inner, middle and outer rings of Birmingham (all tenures), 1971*

	Proportion of all households in each ring		
	In shared dwellings %	*Lacking exclusive use of amenities* %	*At a density of over 1.5 persons per room* %
Inner ring	4	32	6
Middle ring	9	35	5
Outer ring	1	13	3

Source: Office of Population Censuses and Surveys, 1971 *Census*, England and Wales, HMSO, London, 1971.

After discussion with the housing department's allocation officers, we

[14] We had hoped to study allocations for a year prior to the introduction of dispersal in 1969, but all the housing department's registers for lettings prior to 1971 had been destroyed, though a list of lettings to black tenants had been kept since 1968. In the event, 1971 proved to be the first year in which comparative white and black samples could be generated. This did not, however, constitute a major problem for our analysis, since, by 1971, dispersal had hardly begun to bite.

also divided the city into sectors. In their experience, direction was generally more important in defining the area acceptable to an applicant than was distance from the city centre. They suggested five sectors, using radial roads as boundaries: south-west (1), south-east (2), east (3), north-east (4) and north-west (5). The cross-cutting of rings by sectors produced fifteen segments. Much of the analysis uses these fifteen segments, which are individually named in Figure 1 on the basis of a ward or area by which the segment may be identified.

Random samples were taken of approximately 200 of the allocations made to black households and 200 of those made to white households in each of the three years 1971, 1974 and 1976. Transfers, direct exchanges, referrals to housing associations and overspill were excluded, as were allocations to elderly persons, who were overwhelmingly white.

An analysis of the location of applicants' addresses before and after rehousing (see Table 2) generates the following observations:

(1) Housing by the local authority tended to produce suburban migration. The proportion of households housed in the outer ring by Birmingham's housing department in the three sample years for both blacks and whites was higher than the proportion previously living there.

(2) The proportion of whites who were already living in the outer ring (mainly in Stechford and Erdington in 1971 and Stechford and Northfield in 1974 and 1976), and the proportion rehoused in the outer ring (in Stechford, Northfield and Erdington), were in each case much higher

TABLE 2. *Distribution of old and new addresses*

	1971		*1974*		*1976*	
	Blacks %	*Whites* %	*Blacks* %	*Whites* %	*Blacks* %	*Whites* %
	Old		*Old*		*Old*	
Inner ring	34	26	20	17	23	10
Middle ring	58	39	70	43	65	44
Outer ring	6	35	10	39	13	46
N =	230	230	230	205	226	203
	New		*New*		*New*	
Inner ring	43	19	21	15	36	8
Middle ring	37	22	36	15	34	13
Outer ring	20	59	44	70	30	78
N =	230	230	230	205	226	203

than the proportions for blacks. A third of all white allocations were to the eastern suburbs in 1971 and to the south-west suburbs in 1974 and 1976, corresponding with the construction of new estates. The period covered by the samples saw settlement in the outer ring by an increasing majority of new white tenants – 59 per cent in 1971, 70 per cent in 1974, and 78 per cent in 1976. In 1976 very few whites settled in the inner or middle rings. Although nearly half the whites housed in that year were already resident in the suburbs, there was also a substantial white exodus from the inner city.

(3) A substantial majority of black people were previously living in the middle ring (in Handsworth and Small Heath especially). Fewer were rehoused into this ring than from it. Both 1971 and 1976 saw movement inwards as well as outwards, but in 1974 virtually all the black migration from the middle ring was to the outer ring (primarily to Northfield and Stechford).

In 1971 blacks were rehoused mainly in the inner and middle rings (in Balsall Heath, Ladywood and Handsworth), because, although a dispersal policy was in operation, there was still 'room' on central estates. The policy became effective as the 'eligible' properties in the inner city were filled. By 1974, when the policy had been operative for five years, the proportion of blacks rehoused in the outer ring had increased from 20 per cent in 1971 to 44 per cent. After the policy had been dropped the proportion fell, though not to the 1971 level.[15]

An analysis of the distribution by category of applicant and by race will enable us to establish more precisely which people among the black population were most likely to be housed in the suburbs. The claims of prospective tenants to the housing of their choice vary in strength according to the category to which they belong, with clearance area residents having the strongest claim and homeless families the weakest. This variation was to some extent offset by the grading of their housekeeping standards:[16] if they received a poor housekeeping grade, even those with the strongest claim might, in fact, only qualify for poor-quality properties in certain areas of the city. Table 3 indicates the levels of allocation to the outer ring from each of the three categories of applicant.

[15] It might have been possible that the fall in the proportion of blacks housed in the outer ring in 1976 resulted not from the abandonment of dispersal policy, but from an increase in the availability of properties in the inner city. This, however, was not the case. Analysis of our total samples suggests that there was no significant change in the proportion of available properties in the inner city between 1974 and 1976. Inner-city lettings were to 15 per cent of available properties in 1974 and to 16 per cent in 1976.

[16] This practice was formally abandoned by the housing department in 1975.

TABLE 3. *Allocations to the outer, middle and inner rings from each application category*

Proportions allocated to:	1971 Blacks	1971 Whites	1974 Blacks	1974 Whites	1976 Blacks	1976 Whites
			Waiting-list applicants			
	%	%	%	%	%	%
Inner and middle rings	78	12	43	19	68	19
Outer ring	22	88	57	81	32	81
N =	125	158	90	113	140	150
			Clearance applicants			
	%	%	%	%	%	%
Inner and middle rings	83	56	82	46	84	(36)
Outer ring	17	44	18	54	16	(64)
N =	93	59	73	50	63	28
			Homeless applicants			
	%	%	%	%	%	%
Inner and middle rings	(92)	(85)	46	40	(43)	(24)
Outer ring	(8)	(15)	54	60	(57)	(76)
N =	12	13	67	42	23	25

TABLE 4. *Settlement pattern of West Indians and Asians by new address*

	1971 West Indians	1971 Asians	1974 West Indians	1974 Asians	1976 West Indians	1976 Asians
	%	%	%	%	%	%
Inner ring	46	38	24	19	44	22
Middle ring	30	55	26	56	21	61
Outer ring	24	6	51	25	34	17
N =	138	55	149	57	140	76

Waiting-list applicants were more often housed in the suburbs than clearance area residents. Even so, race was a better determinant of location than was category of applicant. The figures for the allocation of white people to the outer ring rose over the three years for all categories. The figures for the allocation of black people to the outer ring remained stable over the three years for clearance area residents but for those on the waiting list they fluctuated in line with dispersal policy. In other words, the brunt of the effects of dispersal policy fell on those who were on the waiting list.

The typical form of housing allocated to the homeless has changed over time. In 1971 the normal offer was that of a pre-clearance house in the inner city. With continuing clearance and renewal, this stock was depleted: the normal offer became that of a flat in one of the less popular estates in the outer ring. The system, effectively ignoring preferences, produced similar patterns for blacks and for whites. Thus, for 1976, after dispersal policy had been abandoned, the proportion of black homeless people housed in the outer ring was far higher than the corresponding waiting-list or clearance figures. Even without a dispersal policy, the local authority could direct a proportion of black tenants to the outer ring – the homeless families which had no choice.[17]

Dispersal hit West Indians more than Asians (see Table 4). Half the West Indians in the 1974 sample were housed in the outer ring, compared with only a quarter in 1971 and a third in 1976. By contrast, almost 60 per cent of Asians were housed in the middle ring in each year, even with the dispersal policy in full operation. These ethnic differences in suburban migration are partly, but not entirely, explained by differences in the categories under which the two groups were housed. Most Asian tenants were housed under the clearance or renewal programmes and hence had the strongest claim to those inner-city properties for which blacks were eligible under the dispersal policy. West Indians occupied a weaker position, coming chiefly from the waiting list or as homeless, and hence they could be coaxed or directed to the suburbs.

REGARD FOR PREFERENCES

In an assessment of the impact of choice on the areas in which housing was allocated to the various applicants, the two crucial questions are whether the area preferences of blacks differed greatly from those of whites, and whether the set-ratio policy meant that preferences had to be overridden. The answer to both questions is yes.

As far as the first question is concerned, the black and white populations in the total samples voiced very different preferences when they were

[17] Since the number of the homeless in our 1976 sample was small, we checked the allocations to all black homeless people (94), and to one in five of all white homeless people (a sample of 147 whites). We found that 62 per cent of the blacks and 67 per cent of the whites had been housed in the outer ring. Since 1976, with the decline of clearance and a smaller total allocation programme, homelessness has come to represent a larger proportion of total allocations. In 1978, for instance, allocations to the homeless represented 22 per cent of those to incoming tenants. As blacks tend to opt for housing in inner-city areas (see the following section of the article), homeless policy in Birmingham has operated as a dispersal mechanism. This contrasts with the situation in London, where the homeless have tended to be housed in the inner city - see J. Parker and K. Dugmore, *Colour and the Allocation of GLC Housing: The Report of the GLC Lettings Survey, 1974–75*, Research Report 21, Greater London Council, 1976.

questioned by housing visitors.[18] Blacks generally named inner-city areas, and whites suburban areas. The ten commonest preferences given by blacks were all for inner-city areas; those given by whites were all for suburban areas. There was no overlap. Outer-ring estates comprised only 19 per cent of all preferences stated by the blacks (1971 and 1974), rising to 25 per cent in 1976, compared with 57 per cent (1971) rising to 70 per cent (1974 and 1976) of those stated by the whites. Proponents of voluntary dispersal may be pleased that as many as a fifth of black preferences were for outer-ring estates, and that the figure has risen. One outer estate, Northfield, narrowly missed the top ten for blacks in 1976. But the figures are no greater than the proportion of blacks housed in that ring in 1971 and 1976, and they are far below the figures housed there under the involuntary dispersal policy in 1974.

As regards the second question, the housing department matched preferences exactly in any one year for between a third and a half of the total sample, black and white. As preferences include estates added after the housing visit, often to enhance the chance of an early offer, and since most applicants named at least two estates and some of them more than ten, the success rate was scarcely satisfactory for prospective tenants.

The black waiting-list applicants, however, did much worse than their white counterparts. Although in 1976, the year after the termination of the policy, blacks were almost as likely as whites to be housed in the areas they preferred (52 per cent and 54 per cent respectively), in the years during the operation of dispersal, the situation was markedly different. In 1971, 37 per cent of the blacks, compared with 54 per cent of the whites, were allocated homes in the areas of their choice. In 1974, only 22 per cent of the blacks attained their preferred areas, compared with 38 per cent of the whites.

Although the preferences of the blacks in the total sample were met to a lesser extent than those of the whites, Table 5 indicates that it was particularly the West Indians who were housed in unsolicited areas. Asians, overwhelmingly housed from clearance areas, more often had their preferences met, for reasons indicated earlier.

We can make allowance for any lack of success in matching preferences precisely by taking account of whether the estates on which people were housed lay in the same segment of the city as the preferred estate (although this constitutes a loose criterion of success for some of the large outer-ring

[18] Our analysis is of applicants' area preferences initially recorded on their application forms and subsequently amended or supplemented after an interview with a housing visitor. After discussion with a housing visitor, some applicants alter their preferences in order to secure an early offer. Under such circumstances, it is likely that a proportion of the recorded preferences bear little relation to the areas in which applicants would actually prefer to live. This fact would appear to enhance our argument in the present section of the article.

segments). In fact this test magnifies the race differential. Again the lowest figure (ignoring the homeless) is for black waiting-list applicants in 1974. Only 40 per cent were housed even in the desired segment of the city, let alone the desired area (see Table 6).

TABLE 5. *Proportion of West Indians, Asians and whites housed in a preferred area (all categories of applicant)*

	1971 %	*1974* %	*1976* %
Whites	49	39	49
West Indians	39	23	49
Asians	44	63	57

The chance of a segmental match varied between segments. For the whites, success rates were the highest among those housed in segments of the outer ring. The reverse, however, was true for the blacks. Only one in five of the blacks housed in outer-ring segments in 1974 had asked for an estate in the segment concerned. Only one in three of them had named *any* estate in the outer ring. In that same 'dispersal' year only 42 per cent of the blacks were housed in the segment of their choice, compared to 60 per cent of the whites.

TABLE 6. *Percentage of people housed in each ring who were housed in their preferred segment (all categories of applicant)*

	1971		*1974*		*1976*	
	Blacks %	*Whites* %	*Blacks* %	*Whites* %	*Blacks* %	*Whites* %
Inner ring	58	38	52	37	69	65
Middle ring	55	49	63	53	82	44
Outer ring	51	84	22	65	53	75
All rings	55	68	42	60	69	71

Detailed work on matches and approximate matches further illuminates the operation of the policy. The samples were divided into four groups – those with exact matches; those housed on estates close to the ones requested; those whose achieved estate bore no relationship to preferences; and those with no preferences or with preferences so general (for example 'anywhere') that one cannot speak of an exact match. This group was 'not applicable' for our purposes.

Between 80 per cent and 90 per cent of the black and the white clearance-area residents in each year obtained exact or rough matches. For the homeless the figures were large enough to permit analysis in 1974 only, when an exceptionally high proportion of allocations went to homeless families.[19]

Preferences were rarely stated, and even when they were stated they were rarely met. The blacks' preferences were for the inner city, the whites' for the suburbs. For all the homeless, however, allocations were mainly to the outer ring, as we have already shown. The interesting point is the high proportion of black homeless families compared with white ones, which were already registered and had been given quite high 'points' on the waiting list. Imminent or actual homelessness precipitated an offer of housing; it effectively drove applicants to accept offers in the outer ring which in other circumstances they might have refused. Homelessness, then, allowed the housing department to retain some scope for dispersal regardless of preferences.

It is in the waiting-list samples that the impact of dispersal is again most clearly marked. Without a dispersal policy (1976) the distribution of our four groups in the black and white samples was very similar. In 1971, during the early stages of dispersal, exact matches were more common in the white sample, but this was offset to some extent by more approximate matches in the black one. About a quarter of each sample in that year accepted offers which did not match the preferences. In the case of the blacks, half of the mismatches were in the outer ring.

The 1974 waiting-list sample, however, was quite distinctive. Matches were rarer on the black sample (21 per cent) than on the white one (34 per cent). A third of the blacks took offers not resembling their preferences, compared with 23 per cent of the whites. This disparity is only partly reduced by the smaller number of rough matches for whites. Black matches were mainly in the inner ring: rough matches included more suburban offers. However, 90 per cent of the black mismatches were in the outer ring, and 75 per cent of those who had expressed no preference or only a vague one were also housed there. In other words, the result of the city's policy was that the blacks were dispersed by being given housing which took little account of their preferences.

DELAYS IN ALLOCATION

All waiting-list applicants for a council dwelling are allotted a number of 'points' which reflects the housing department's assessment of the degree of their housing need together with the length of time during which they

[19] Approximately 25 per cent of allocations went to homeless families. The proportions for 1971 and 1976 are 6 per cent and 15 per cent respectively.

have been on the waiting list. The actual level at which allocations are made varies greatly according to the area and the type of property. However, one would expect these variations to even out over a population group, with the result that average points at allocation would be comparable for blacks and whites.[20] A complication, here, is the bed queue (or property size), in which applicants are located according to the size of their families. Points levels required for allocation to the larger properties tend to be higher. This is a reflection of both greater need (more points are awarded for overcrowding, and so on) and the scarcity of properties with more than three bedrooms. Blacks, because of either family size or family structure, are disproportionately found in the queues for larger properties. However, controlling for these differences in queues, we found that the blacks were in fact housed at higher points levels than the whites. This, however, has been examined elsewhere.[21]

Our interest here is in the differential points levels of those housed in different rings. Our investigations indicate that:

(1) The whites had lower median points than the blacks in each ring, in each bed queue, in each of the three years.
(2) The median points level on allocation was generally a little lower for the outer ring than for the inner ring. (Hardly any waiting-list applicants were housed in the middle ring.)
(3) This was most pronounced for the blacks at the height of dispersal, in 1974.[22]

The blacks rehoused in the inner ring in 1974 had on average thirty-six more points than the blacks housed in the suburbs. Blacks were housed in the inner ring at levels fifty-five points higher on average than whites in the same ring.[23] In theory, those in the greatest housing need, that is, those

20 This assumes that neither group is concentrated in highly popular property. The validity of this assumption for our sample is demonstrated elsewhere – see H. Flett, 'Disadvantage and Dispersal', Research Unit on Ethnic Relations, University of Bristol, forthcoming, 1979.

21 See Flett, *Black Council Tenants in Birmingham*.

22 The cells are too small to prove the point statistically, but for black applicants in 1974 median points were higher for the inner ring than for the outer ring for both the main (two- and three-) bedroom queues (and no applicants were housed from the one- or four-bed queues into inner-ring properties). This was not the case for the whites, or for either sample in 1971.

23 Some small part of the black-white disparity here is explained by the bedroom queue. As a guide to the significance of these points disparities, thirty-six points can be taken as roughly equivalent to an extra two years on the waiting list, and fifty-five points as roughly equivalent to an extra three years on the waiting list. This is not to say that blacks actually spent these longer periods on the waiting list; their waiting time and waiting points in fact were close to those of the whites. Rather the disparity stems mainly from the greater housing need that blacks were in relative to whites, and hence the higher housing-need points they were allotted.

with the most housing-need points, are housed soonest. However, blacks, in fact, waited just as long as whites, who had fewer points and therefore waited longer than the degree of their housing need warranted. This was especially true for the inner ring, where the wait was artificially lengthened, because, as a result of the dispersal policy, blacks did not qualify for properties near to existing black tenants. These properties were reserved for white applicants, who had a weaker claim (that is, fewer points) than waiting blacks. Had the dispersal policy continued, the wait for inner-city properties would have lengthened even further, because, as more blacks obtained tenancies there, this would proportionately have reduced the vacancies for which black applicants were eligible. To put it concretely, if every sixth property already contained a black household, blacks on the list could only be housed by waiting for these tenants to vacate the property. All other vacancies on the estate had to go to whites. One possible explanation for the black tenants' higher points levels at the time of allocation is that more of them refused earlier offers. This, however, can easily be refuted: points levels at the time of the first offer show a similar disparity.[24]

Examining the whole samples, we see that more blacks than whites refused properties. This raises questions about the properties refused: why were they refused and what was gained by refusal? In other words, how did refused offers differ from accepted offers, and was the disparity greater for blacks than for whites?

One of the reasons for which blacks refused offers was that they wanted to hold out for properties in inner Birmingham. Those who refused their first offer were more likely to be housed eventually in the inner and middle rings than were those who accepted their first offer. Blacks refusing suburban offers normally settled in the inner or middle ring. The reverse, how-

TABLE 7. *First-offer refusals and eventual location at which applicants were housed*

Percentage of:	*1971*		*1974*		*1976*	
	Blacks	*Whites*	*Blacks*	*Whites*	*Blacks*	*Whites*
Those refusing the outer ring who were housed in the inner or middle rings	72	35	58	16	71	18
Those refusing the inner or middle rings who were housed in the outer ring	12	37	19	38	21	41

[24] See Flett, *Black Council Tenants in Birmingham.*

ever, does not hold, namely, that blacks refusing offers in the inner or middle ring were eventually housed in the suburbs.

The implication is that location was the reason for applicants' refusing suburban properties but not generally for their refusing inner-city properties. This is supported by the reasons which applicants gave for refusal. 'Too far out', 'too far from work' and 'wrong area' figure prominently as rationales for outer-ring refusals. Those refusing inner-city offers, in contrast, commonly objected to the size, storey (height) or condition of the dwelling.

The white 'norm' was for suburban first offers to be accepted more frequently than inner-city offers and for those who refused a suburban offer to accept another suburban offer subsequently. For instance, in 1976, of all white refusers, 71 per cent rejected suburban offers and 70 per cent accepted suburban offers made later. Those who refused suburban offers were not rejecting a suburban location. Few of them returned offers as being 'too far out' or 'too far from work', even though whites were just as likely as blacks to work in the inner or middle rings. Most of them later settled in the suburbs – but it was in *better property* than that previously offered. A large minority of those refusing inner-city offers (the numbers are small) also settled in the suburbs. Their refusals were frequently based on their assessment of the area as such.

This analysis has revealed a tendency for blacks, depending on circumstances (including their housing category), to refuse suburban properties and to hold out for inner-city areas. It was least marked in 1976, when the abandonment of the dispersal policy allowed the housing department to pay more regard to preferences. Suburban first offers were most common in 1974, constituting over half of all first offers to black families, even though only 30 per cent of them had listed any suburban estate as a preference. With a high incidence of homelessness, and the likelihood of long delays for inner-city estates, the pressures to accept were greatest in this year, at the height of dispersal. Constraint rather than choice drove the black applicants to the suburbs.

CONCLUSION

The purpose of this article has been to investigate to what extent the housing needs of black people can be satisfied under dispersal schemes introduced in the hope of facilitating racial integration. What we have not touched on is whether a housing department, even under 'normal' circumstances, is able to satisfy the housing needs of its tenants or prospective tenants, be they black or white. That, of course, would involve a much broader investigation than the one which we have undertaken, and, among other things, it would have to include a critical appraisal of the concept of housing need. Our concern, rather, has been to assess the impact of a particular dispersal policy on the housing allocations made to West Indians and Asians. As there is likely to be continuing concern at both central and local government levels with ways in which racial integration can be effected, and as *laissez-faire* housing policies have been shown to result in the segregation of black tenants into the worst estates,[25] dispersal as a possible facilitator of integration will continue to attract attention. In these circumstances our investigation should prove to have more than just historical relevance as an analysis of a policy abandoned in one particular city. The experience in Birmingham must provide strong ammunition against the introduction of similar policies elsewhere.

In concluding it is important that we emphasize the key features – all largely negative for blacks – of the practice of a racial dispersal policy. The first point is that the policy, as operated in Birmingham, did, at its height, effectively disperse black people, and particularly West Indians, across the city. However, inevitably, it did so at the cost of creating a massive disruption in the normal settlement pattern of blacks moving into the public sector. That this disruption was effected only by the dispersal of blacks *against their wishes* can best be seen in the fact that, after the abandonment of the policy, the black settlement pattern reverted towards the pre-dispersal situation.[26]

West Indians were less able than Asians to resist dispersal. One reason for this was their relatively weak position in the housing system. Most West Indians were housed from the homeless or waiting-list categories, which, in the context of a policy that effectively discriminated against the homeless and to a lesser extent against the waiting list, meant that they were in a more vulnerable position, with less bargaining power. As Asians were housed primarily as a consequence of slum clearance (75 per cent in each year) they were able to hold out for better properties in the areas which they found more desirable.

More crucially, however, it was the estates which were popular with West Indians which were becoming 'full' under the one-in-six rule, and therefore allocations for West Indians were scarce in the areas which they

25 The evidence is from Greater London – see Runnymede Trust, *Race and Council Housing in London*, London, 1975; and Parker and Dugmore, *op. cit.* – from Islington – see Directorate of Housing, *Allocation of Islington Housing to Ethnic Minorities*, Research Report no. 12, London Borough of Islington, 1977 – and from a survey of seven unnamed cities in England and Wales – see D. Smith and A. Whalley, *Racial Minorities and Public Housing*, Political and Economic Planning, London, 1975.

26 What is more, analysis of the preferences of black transfer applicants who were originally allocated suburban housing in 1974 indicates their marked desire to return to the inner city – see Flett, *Black Council Tenants in Birmingham*.

preferred. Asians, a much smaller proportion of whom were applying for council housing at the time, were to some extent opting for different areas, particularly in the eastern and south-eastern parts of the city, where there is a large Asian community in the private sector. As these areas were becoming less and less popular with white tenants, there was not, up till then, a serious problem, either from the dispersal policy or from competition with other applicants. Had the dispersal policy continued, however, there would soon have been severe problems because there is very little council-owned and even less council-built property in, say, Sparkbrook, and the set-ratio policy would soon have started to bite hard.

Although even under normal circumstances only about half the people housed by the city received accommodation in the area of their choice, the black dispersal policy could only be implemented by systematically ignoring the preferences of blacks more than those of whites. Those who refused to be housed other than in areas of their choice were forced to remain, often for considerable periods, in bad housing conditions. The premise on which housing allocation is based is that those with the greatest need are housed first. The operation of dispersal, however, in effect negated this basic premise. Blacks, with generally greater housing need than whites, had to wait for longer periods of time, relative to the bad conditions in which they lived.

In terms of both the greater disregard of preferences and the longer delays in allocation to which blacks were subject, the impact of dispersal was compounded over time. Just as it only began to bite when the black-designated housing in the inner city became filled, so, had the policy continued, and assuming that blacks would maintain their preference for inner areas, their situation would have deteriorated sharply, particularly with regard to delays in allocation.[27]

Birmingham's dispersal policy operated not through directing black people to particular areas, but rather by constraining them from being housed in certain areas. As a result the appearance of tenant choice remained in the allocation system, and hence dispersal could be upheld as an

[27] Although dispersal was a policy that specifically affected black people, it must be remembered that the department's policies with regard to homelessness and housekeeping standards discriminated against people, both black and white, on grounds of class. Such policies adversely affected (and in the case of policy for the homeless still affect) the so-called 'disreputable poor' – see D. Matza, 'The Disreputable Poor', in R. Bendix and S. M. Lipset, *Class, Status and Power*, Routledge and Kegan Paul, London, 1967; C. Valentine, *Culture and Poverty*, University of Chicago Press, Chicago, 1968; and R. Means, *Social Work and the 'Undeserving' Poor*, Occasional Paper no. 37, Centre for Urban and Regional Studies, University of Birmingham, 1977. The existence of such policies is but one indication that ultimately the connection between race and housing policy can only be fully understood when it is theorized in terms of the dialectical interface between race and class.

expression of liberal values. Two important consequences resulted from the operation of the policy in this way. Firstly, if black people with greater housing need remained in poor housing conditions, then they alone could be blamed for their situation; it was they, after all, who had refused to move to the outer estates. And, secondly, by maintaining a semblance of choice within the allocation system, city councillors and housing department officials could claim, as indeed they did, that the dispersal policy was in the spirit of the *Race Relations Act*. Had the policy been directive, such a claim would have been on weaker ground, and furthermore it would surely have generated complaints to the Race Relations Board and would therefore have become public knowledge much earlier than was in fact the case.

Birmingham's claim to have been operating a liberal policy is also difficult to reconcile with the fact that the policy was never made public, so that black applicants were left in ignorance of its existence. If the policy had really been intended for the welfare of blacks, why were they not told of it?[28] Instead they remained unaware that their white neighbours were being allocated inner-area properties on points levels much lower than their own.

'Voluntary' dispersal schemes, though dependent on a greater openness than was evident in Birmingham's policy, must still be regarded with scepticism. 'Voluntary' dispersal policies could succeed only if those with control over housing allocation could persuade the people subject to their control that it was in their interests to accept properties in areas to which they originally, for perfectly rational reasons, had little or no desire to move. To call such policies 'voluntary' is to ignore the unequal power relationship which exists between housing officers and prospective tenants.

There are other charges, however, that can be laid against dispersal policies of all forms. Such policies are suspect because they take no account of, and make no reference to, one of the main reasons why racial ghettos are created – namely, the exodus of white people from areas that progressively come to be stigmatized as 'slums', as 'violent', and as 'black'. Furthermore, in assuming that the area preferences of black people are illegitimate or irrational, dispersal policies necessarily express the same ethnocentric bias that we identified in the central government's housing and race reports of the late 1960s and early 1970s. In other words, such policies by implication are based on the devaluation of the importance of ethnic

28 Although the then chairperson of the city's housing committee had indicated as early as November 1970 that a dispersal policy was in operation – see *The Birmingham Evening Mail*, 23 November 1970 – its existence was not widely known – and certainly not to tenants and prospective tenants – until the results of the Race Relations Board's investigation began to emerge in 1975.

cultural and community life to the identity and happiness of Britain's black settlers.

Criticisms such as these point to the need for a fuller examination of the political and ideological construction of dispersal policies than we have attempted in this article. Here we have done no more than to study the available evidence of the impact of a dispersal policy in Birmingham, but we believe that in so doing we have vindicated the Race Relations Board's decision to contest the operation of Birmingham's dispersal policy. Furthermore, we have raised serious questions as to whether *any* dispersal policy can be anything but racist in practice, if not in intention.

[27]

Up the creek without a paddle? Britain's boat people ten years on

It is now almost ten years since Britain agreed to receive and resettle two quotas of Vietnamese refugees, totalling 11,450 people. Most came from the camps in Hong Kong which had acted as temporary homes whilst families applied to various host countries for acceptance. Several of these countries specified minimum qualifications without which refugees would not be accepted, whilst others demanded fluency in English. Britain was less selective since, in part, its decision to accept quota migrants was motivated by the developing crisis in its Crown Colony. Resentment against the Vietnamese was growing in Hong Kong and the 'open' camps there were becoming increasingly overcrowded. The same reasons have ensured that Britain has continued to accept smaller numbers of Vietnamese each year since 1979, although most new arrivals are now dependants of earlier quota migrants. This continued immigration (467 people in 1987 for example), and the natural increase of those refugees already here, have ensured that the Vietnamese community in the UK now numbers between 22,000 and 25,000. This number will grow further during 1989 and 1990 as the government receives the further quota of 1,000 Vietnamese which they agreed to accept in December 1988.

Little geographical research has yet been completed on the Vietnamese in Britain. This is surprising given the size of the community and the media interest in their arrival. It is also surprising because the government resettlement programme designed for the Vietnamese is one of the few examples of official state intervention in patterns of ethnic settlement that we have yet seen in this country. Traditionally, ethnic groups in Britain have been left to determine their own settlement patterns across the nation and within cities, and although segregation has been frowned upon, it has never actually been discouraged. However, in the late 1960s and early 1970s official thinking began to move in favour of both direct state intervention and the dispersal of ethnic minorities. It was argued that this would assist both society as a whole and the migrants. The former would benefit from the spreading of the 'costs' and 'burdens' of ethnic settlement, whilst the latter would gain greater opportunities for 'assimilation'. Government reports made it clear, however, that there would be problems dispersing established ethnic minorities such as Asians and Afro-Caribbeans. Forced dispersal would be seen as unacceptable infringement of their civil liberties and dispersal of groups such as these could therefore only be achieved through voluntary means. The same logic was not applied to refugee groups who were thought to possess neither the power nor the will to oppose forced dispersal.

The Vietnamese were not the first refugee group to have their settlement patterns determined by the British state, but they are certainly the group which has experienced the greatest degree of spatial engineering. The Home Office established guidelines which sought to disperse the Vietnamese widely across the country in clusters of 4 to 10 families. Communities of this size were felt to be sufficient to prevent problems of isolation, but were also thought to be small enough not to overtax the local volunteer support groups charged with the day to day responsibility of resettling individual families (Jones, 1982).

The remainder of this paper reports on research in progress currently which assesses the policy of dispersal against two different criteria. Firstly whether dispersal was ever achieved in practice. And secondly whether Vietnamese refugees regarded dispersal as desirable or whether they sought to reverse it by voluntary secondary migration into areas of nascent concentration. Initially the research is addressing these questions using a data-set assembled from the records of Ockenden Venture and Refugee Action, the two charities most centrally

Table 1
Addresses of Vietnamese households in Britain at time of resettlement

Economic region	% of Vietnamese	% of total population	Vietnamese location quotient
South East	45	31	1.5
East Anglia	3	3	1.0
South West	8	8	1.0
West Midlands	9	9	1.0
East Midlands	4	7	0.6
Yorkshire/Humberside	6	9	0.7
North West	9	12	0.7
North	4	6	0.7
Wales	6	5	1.2
Scotland	5	9	0.6
Total	99%	99%	

Location quotient = % sub group ÷ % total population; where 1 = under-representation, 1 = over-representation, 1 = parity.

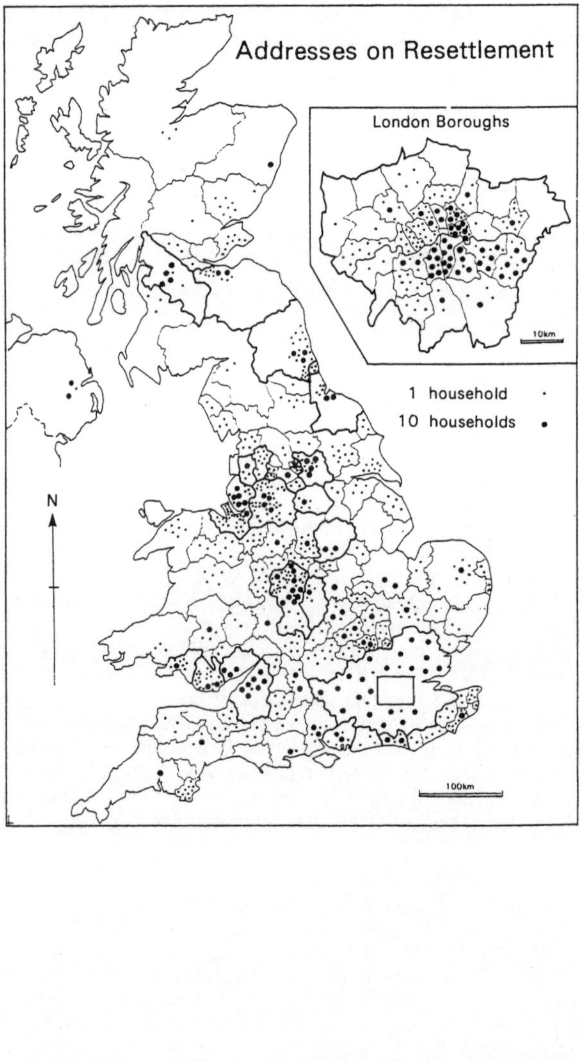

Fig. 1. — The national distribution of Vietnamese households at resettlement.

involved in the resettlement programme. The national data-base thus created contains 8,426 chained addresses for some 3,101 households over the period 1978-88. Although there are omissions within the data, records exist for almost all of the original quota migrants in the UK, and it is unlikely that a better data-base will ever be assembled.

Table 1 shows the spatial distribution by economic region of the Vietnamese at the time of their resettlement. At this spatial scale the data suggest that dispersal was a good deal more successful than earlier reports and data indicated (see, eg. Robinson's 1985 analysis of 1982 Home Office data). The Vietnamese were over-represented in the South East and Wales and under-represented in the East Midlands and Scotland, but the overall national distribution was not dissimilar to that of the population as a whole. However, Fig. 1 qualifies this conclusion somewhat and also indicates how distributions across large spatial units can be deceptive. It is clear that *within* economic regions the Vietnamese *were* concentrated and that the largest agglomerations of households occurred in urban areas. Few Vietnamese were dispersed to truly rural areas. This finding is underscored by Table 2 which lists the 22 local labour market areas which had the greatest number of Vietnamese households at resettlement. Again conurbations and cities predominate, with almost 1 in 3 of all Vietnamese households located in London or Birmingham. Other centres such as Basildon, Milton Keynes and Folkestone recorded gross over-representation with approximately 4 or 5 times more Vietnamese than might have been expected given their total populations. Clearly then, dispersal was not wholly successful. Concentrations were allowed to develop in Britain's largest and, in some cases, poorest cities. Within London, for example, the main areas of resettlement were the relatively deprived boroughs of Southwark, Tower Hamlets and Lambeth.

Dispersal was never as extensive as the government hoped, for the simple reason that it failed to requisition housing. Instead it chose to rely upon voluntary and unrewarded offers of accommodation from local authorities and housing associations. The location of these offers was out of the control of the Home Office and this meant that, in turn, they relinquished control of the pattern of resettlement. The government had therefore sought dispersal but

Table 2
The 22 leading centres of Vietnamese population at the time of resettlement in the UK

Rank	City	% of Vietnamese	% of total population	Vietnamese location quotient
1	London	27.6	14.4	1.9
2	Birmingham	4.2	2.7	1.6
3	Bristol	2.5	1.4	1.8
4	Manchester	2.1	2.1	1.0
5	Liverpool	1.9	1.7	1.1
6	Leeds	1.9	1.4	1.4
7	Newcastle	1.6	1.7	0.9
8	Basildon	1.5	0.3	5.0
9	Glasgow	1.4	2.2	0.6
10	Luton	1.3	0.6	2.2
11	Aldershot	1.2	0.6	2.0
12	Cardiff	1.2	0.8	1.5
13	Milton Keynes	1.1	0.3	3.7
14	Edinburgh	1.0	1.3	0.8
15	Swindon	1.0	0.5	2.0
16	Northampton	1.0	0.4	2.5
17	Newport	1.0	0.4	2.5
18	Peterborough	0.9	0.4	2.3
19	Portsmouth	0.8	0.7	1.1
20	Bradford	0.8	0.7	1.1
21	Derby	0.8	0.6	1.3
22	Folkestone	0.8	0.2	4.0

All data relate to local labour market areas as defined by Champion *et al.* (1987).

had failed to provide any mechanism by which this could be guaranteed. In other European countries, governments wishing to disperse refugee groups have often requisitioned a proportion of all new properties under construction and then reimbursed their public sector owners.

The data suggest that the forced dispersal policy was not only a numerical failure but also a social failure. Approximately 51 per cent of those Vietnamese households for whom we have a relatively complete record of mobility changed their address during the nine year study period. When the quinquennial rate of Vietnamese household mobility (43 per cent) is compared with that of the total population over a similar period it is clear that Vietnamese mobility is one-third higher (see Robinson and Hale, 1989). Indeed, one in six Vietnamese households were found to have engaged in multiple mobility during this period and one household had even changed its address nine times. What is equally revealing is that a good deal of this mobility occurred shortly after resettlement. Thirty one per cent of movers left their resettlement address within twelve months of arriving there, and fully 54 per cent had left within two years. This suggests that dispersal failed to provide many Vietnamese with accommodation which they wished to retain in the long term. However, it is equally true

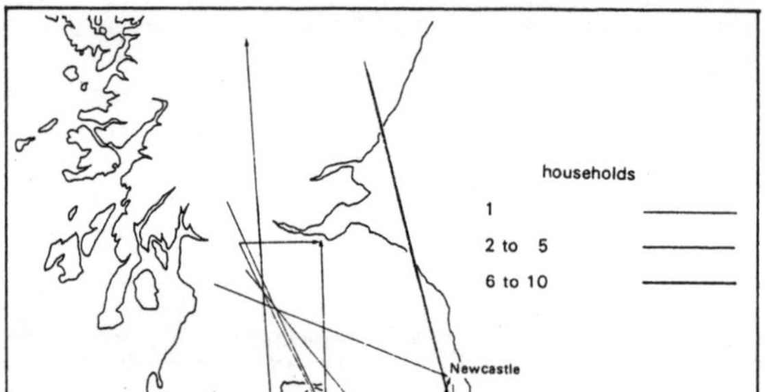

Fig. 2. — Cross country migration of households from first to last known address.

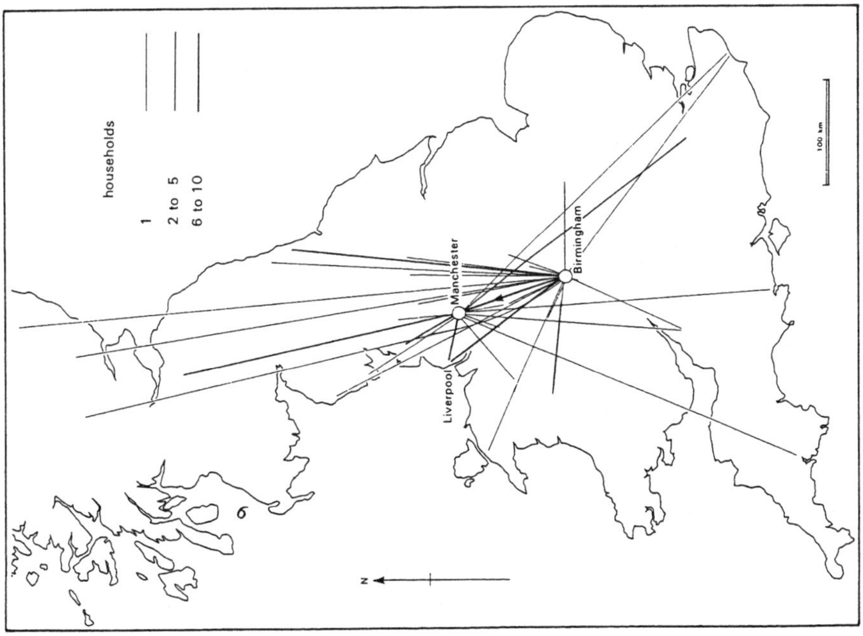

Fig. 3. — Migration from first address to last in Birmingham or Manchester.

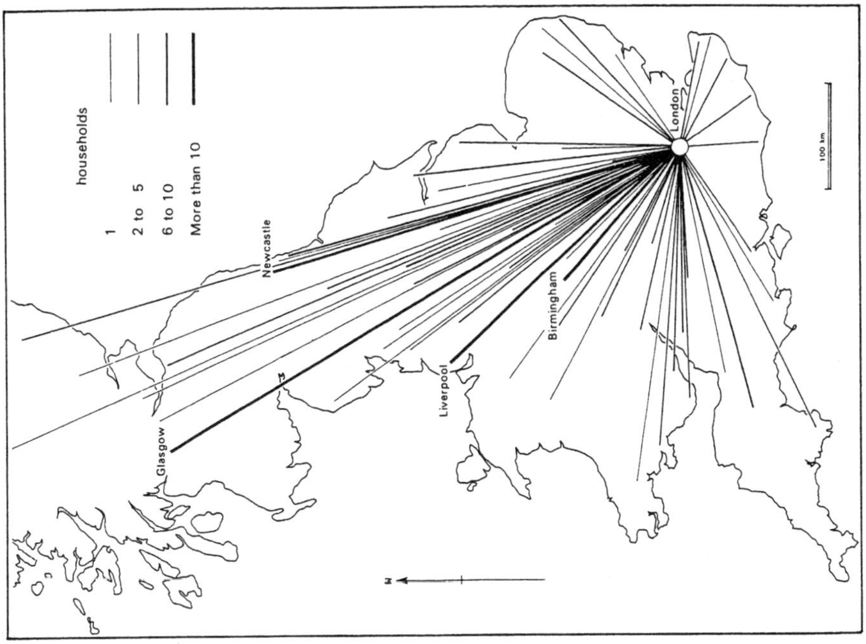

Fig. 4. — Migration from first to last address in London.

that mobility might have been between a rented flat in one street and an owner occupied house in the next. Mobility, in itself, cannot therefore be used as direct evidence of the failure of forced dispersal.

Figs 2 to 5 provide more conclusive evidence of that failure by investigating the direction of Vietnamese secondary migration over the period from resettlement to last recorded address. Fig. 2 shows a pattern of movement of Vietnamese households from outlying areas into urban centres with small existing Vietnamese communities. These include Cambridge, Bristol, Southampton and Leeds. Fig. 3 isolates movement over the same period into the larger existing concentrations of Birmingham and Manchester. Such movements have not only been over short distances but have also included long distance inter-regional migration. The map shows, for example, the drift out of Scotland and the North East. Fig. 4 is perhaps the most dramatic of all, since it shows the major movement which has taken place from all parts of the country into London. Again this includes direct movement from areas of dispersal as well as mobility up the hierarchy of Vietnamese settlement (eg. from Liverpool, Birmingham and Leeds to London). Finally, Fig. 5 shows the destinations of in-migrants to London. It is clear that certain boroughs have been particularly attractive and that these are predominantly in Inner London (eg. Lambeth, Southwark, Tower Hamlets and Islington).

The net effect of these flows of migration has been four-fold. First, the South East has gained Vietnamese at the expense of other regions. Whereas it contained 45 per cent of all Vietnamese at the time of resettlement, by 1984 this had risen to 57 per cent. Second, remote or peripheral areas have lost their Vietnamese population. Wales saw its share of the Vietnamese fall from 6 per cent at resettlement to less than 1 per cent by 1988. The South West's share fell over the same period from 8 per cent to 3 per cent. And nationally, the proportion of the country's local labour market areas which contained Vietnamese households declined from 81 per cent at resettlement through 63 per cent in 1982 to 56 per cent in 1984. Third, the Vietnamese population are becoming increasingly concentrated into the major conurbations (particularly London, Birmingham and Manchester) at a time when the white population is abandoning those cities. The proportion of Vietnamese households found in the six

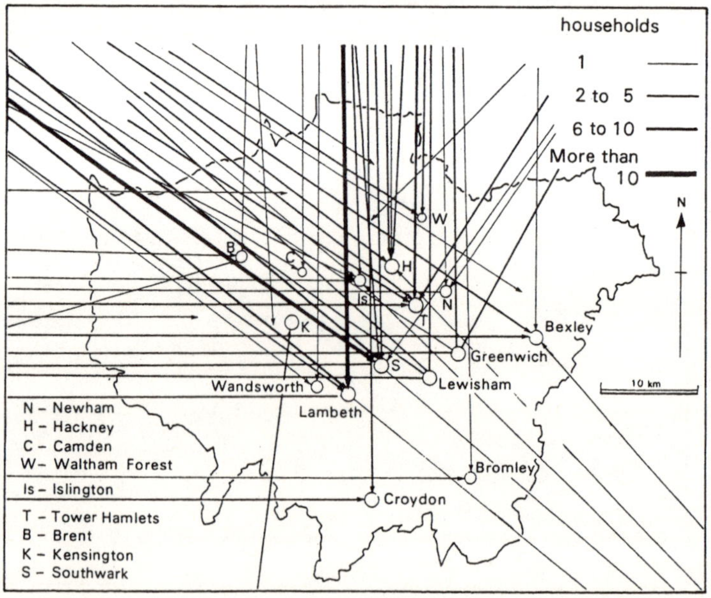

Fig. 5. — Migration into and between London Boroughs.

Table 3
Local labour market areas containing the largest number of Vietnamese households: resettlement to 1988

	Resettlement	1980	1982	1984	1985-88
1	Birmingham	Bexley	Birmingham	Southwark	Birmingham
2	Southwark	Birmingham	Lambeth	Tower Hamlets	Manchester
3	Tower Hamlets	Bristol	Tower Hamlets	Lambeth	Southwark
4	Lambeth	Lambeth	Southwark	Birmingham	Lambeth
5	Bexley	Southwark	Greenwich	Leeds	Greenwich
6	Bristol	Greenwich	Hackney	Greenwich	Bexley
7	Greenwich	Basildon	Bristol	Hackney	Tower Hamlets
8	Manchester	Manchester	Manchester	Manchester	Islington
9	Liverpool	Lewisham	Bexley	Bexley	Lewisham
10	Lewisham	Aldershot	Leeds	Bristol	Waltham Forest
11	Leeds	Leeds	Camden	Wandsworth	
12	Hackney	Liverpool	Lewisham	Basildon	
13	Newcastle	Newport	Wandsworth	Bradford	
14	Basildon	Edinburgh	Basildon	Northampton	
15	Glasgow	Glasgow	Glasgow	Lewisham	

1985-88 is last known address after 1985. The ranking is truncated at ten because of small sample size.

conurbations or conurbation dominants (as defined by Champion *et al.*, 1987) consequently rose from 25 per cent at resettlement to 73 per cent of last known addresses after 1985. And fourth, the Vietnamese are becoming more concentrated into particular boroughs in London, and these tend to be the more deprived inner areas. Southwark and Lambeth have remained within the leading five centres of Vietnamese settlement throughout the study period; Bexley, Greenwich, and Tower Hamlets have stayed in the top ten; and the total number of London boroughs in the top ten has risen from five in 1980, to eight at the close of our study period (see Table 3). In short, the Vietnamese are becoming increasingly polarised in their spatial distribution and are migrating to localities characterised by deprivation.

The speed with which secondary migration developed and the direction of that migration strongly suggest that forced dispersal was neither appropriate to the Vietnamese nor accepted by them. Over half of all households have now moved from their resettlement address, and the overwhelming destinations for these migrants are those cities which have sizeable Vietnamese communities. This surely indicates a desire for concentration as well as the importance of those services which can only be provided when a migrant community exceeds a certain 'critical mass'. This, and the earlier failure of a similar policy designed to disperse the Ugandan Asians (see Robinson, 1986), suggests that the entire notion of dispersal should now be re-evaluated and employed only in circumstances where there is both a clear demand for it, and also an obvious need. In the meantime, the government perhaps ought to consider introducing a much enhanced programme of targetted aid for the Vietnamese who have so clearly been the victims of a social experiment which was not of their own making.

Acknowledgements. I am grateful to the Nuffield Foundation who funded the research reported here, and to Samantha Hale who assisted with the collection and collation of charity records. Guy Lewis drew the diagrams.

REFERENCES

Champion, A.G. *et al.* (1987) *Changing Places: Britain's Demographic, Economic and Social Complexion,* London: Arnold.

Jones, P. (1982) *Vietnamese Refugees,* Home Office Research Paper 13, London.

Robinson, V. (1985) "The Vietnamese reception and resettlement programme in the UK; rhetoric and reality", *Ethnic Groups,* 6, pp. 305-330.

Robinson, V. (1986) *Transients, Settlers and Refugees; Asians in Britain,* Oxford: Clarendon Press.

Robinson, V. and Hale, S. (1989) *The Geography of Vietnamese Secondary Migration in the UK,* Warwick: University of Warwick, Centre for Research in Ethnic Relations.

University College Swansea VAUGHAN ROBINSON

[28]

The development of policies for the resettlement of quota refugees in the UK, 1945–91

Vaughan Robinson

Introduction

Until recently, Britain has had an international reputation as a safe haven for refugees. Groups as disparate as the Huguenots and the Russian Jews have fled to the UK in the hope of experiencing the tolerance and freedom denied them in their countries of origin. Of late, however, changes in both the nature of the international refugee crisis and the UK's international status have combined to produce a new set of policies towards refugee admission and resettlement (see Box and Figure 1). This section of the atlas seeks to chart these changes through three case studies which have been selected to contrast the fortunes of European and non-European refugees, recent and less recent arrivals, and self-settled and government-resettled refugees. The three groups which have been selected for study are the Polish Catholics displaced to this country by the onset of the Second World War, the British Asian passport holders expelled from Uganda in 1972, and the quota of Vietnamese admitted between 1979 and 1981. Their movements to the UK are set in the context of recent migration history by Figure 1, which demonstrates the changing scale of total immigration into the UK, the number of refugee admissions by year, and the number of quota refugees admitted.

The Poles

Unlike the other groups under discussion, the Poles were not motivated to leave their country by persistent persecution but were driven out by a very short armed conflict. They then continued to fight for the liberty of their homeland from bases elsewhere in Europe and the Middle East. Because of the new geopolitics forged at the Yalta conference, the end of hostilities did not see Poland again becoming a free democratic country and, as a result, the overseas Polish military were faced with the option of returning to a communist Poland or remaining as exiles elsewhere in the world.

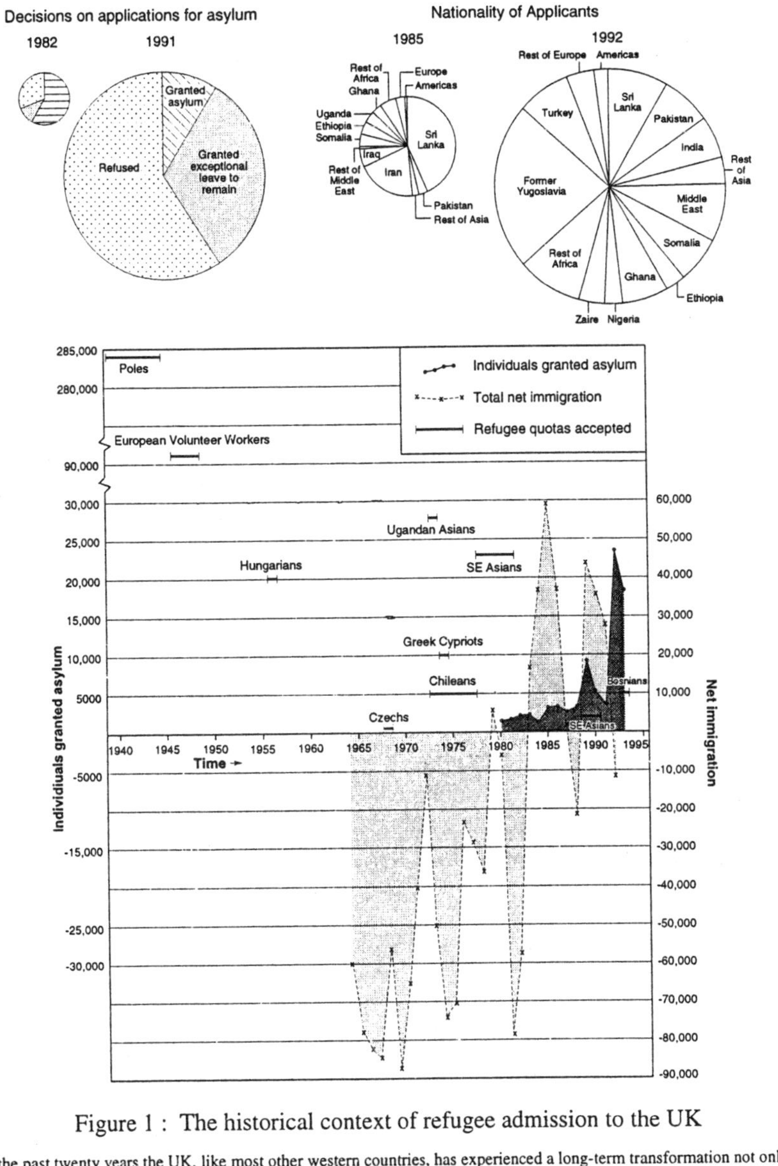

Figure 1 : The historical context of refugee admission to the UK

Over the past twenty years the UK, like most other western countries, has experienced a long-term transformation not only in the number of people applying for asylum, but also in the regions of the world from which its refugees come. Overlaid upon this secular trend have been short-term fluctuations resulting from specific refugee crises. The graph demonstrates how asylum applications have increased from only 1563 as late as 1979 to 66,000 by 1991. The first pie chart demonstrates how the present Yugoslavian crisis has added considerably to these numbers but it also shows that the main sources of the UK's asylum seekers are the countries which were former colonies in the Indian subcontinent and several former African colonies. In response both to public opinion, which has hardened against further non-white immigration to the UK, and also the fear of extreme right wing groups, the refugee determination decision has also undergone a profound change. As the second pie chart shows, increasing numbers of applicants are being refused, whilst a growing percentage are being offered quasi-refugee status through Exceptional Leave to Remain.

Box 1 : UK refugee policy in context

The Poles in Britain thus began life as a classic example of a military exile community (Sword, Davies and Ciechanowski, 1989). The fall of France in June 1940 led to the remnants of the Polish Army, Navy and Air Force fleeing across the Channel to the UK, along with the pre-war Warsaw government and its officials. In total, 84,000 Polish military personnel and 21,000 civilians found their way to Britain during the war. Others were scattered around the Commonwealth and alternative theatres of war, with sizeable numbers of civilians being dispersed to India and Africa, and the Second Army Corps ('Anders Army') being billeted in Iraq, Palestine and later Italy. Churchill's parliamentary 'pledge' of 27 February 1945 to offer British citizenship and the right of abode to the dispossessed Poles who had fought under British command led to many of these satellite populations being brought to the UK at the end of the war. The exact number involved is unlikely ever to be accurately ascertained, but estimates suggest that 33,000 military dependants and 146,000 military personnel arrived in the UK between May 1946 and April 1948. The European Volunteer Workers scheme, established by the British Ministry of Labour in 1946 in order to provide labour for essential post-war reconstruction, attracted a further 12,500 displaced Poles between 1947 and 1950 (Tannahill, 1958). A Polish refugee population of nearly 300,000 had thus arrived in the UK in a period of less than a decade.

Britain's response to the arrival had to take account of several factors. These included reported hostility towards the settlement and employment of Poles in parts of the country; the unusual nature of the refugee flow, which consisted largely of young military men; the delicate relations which existed with the new communist regime in Warsaw; the devastation of Britain's housing and industrial base wrought by German bombing; and the need to receive the Poles over a relatively short period of time (around three to four years).

The imaginative response to these constraints was to create the Polish Resettlement Corps (PRC), a non-operational unit of the British Army funded by the War Office. Enlistment in the PRC was voluntary, and while it offered recruits a guaranteed salary and accommodation, as well as assistance with finding work on demobilization, it did also ensure that the Poles were under British military jurisdiction. This was thought to be particularly important by the British, who feared that the presence of over 200,000 Polish soldiers, many of whom felt betrayed by the Allies in general and Britain in particular, posed a threat to national security. The PRC also gave the Poles the opportunity to become involved in their own resettlement, since it was to be led by Polish officers, and it also allowed the government to phase demobilization over a number of years. There was, however, doubt as to whether the PRC could receive and resettle such a large number of people, so the government embarked upon a parallel policy of encouraging the repatriation or onward migration of the Poles. This concept of smoothing the acceptance of permanent settlers by encouraging others either not to come to Britain or to re-emigrate has since become a central tenet of British immigration and 'race relations' policy, with most administrations in the last 25 years linking 'community relations' with tough admission criteria.

The government opted to resettle the Poles from military bases that were given over to the PRC, thereby establishing a precedent followed in subsequent refugee episodes. Undoubtedly the idea of using camps resulted both from the post-war housing crisis and the Home Office's belief that uncomfortable reception facilities would encourage many Poles to consider repatriation or onward migration. Two hundred and sixty-five camps were eventually opened in the UK (see Figure 2 for the distribution of those belonging to the Second Army Corps),

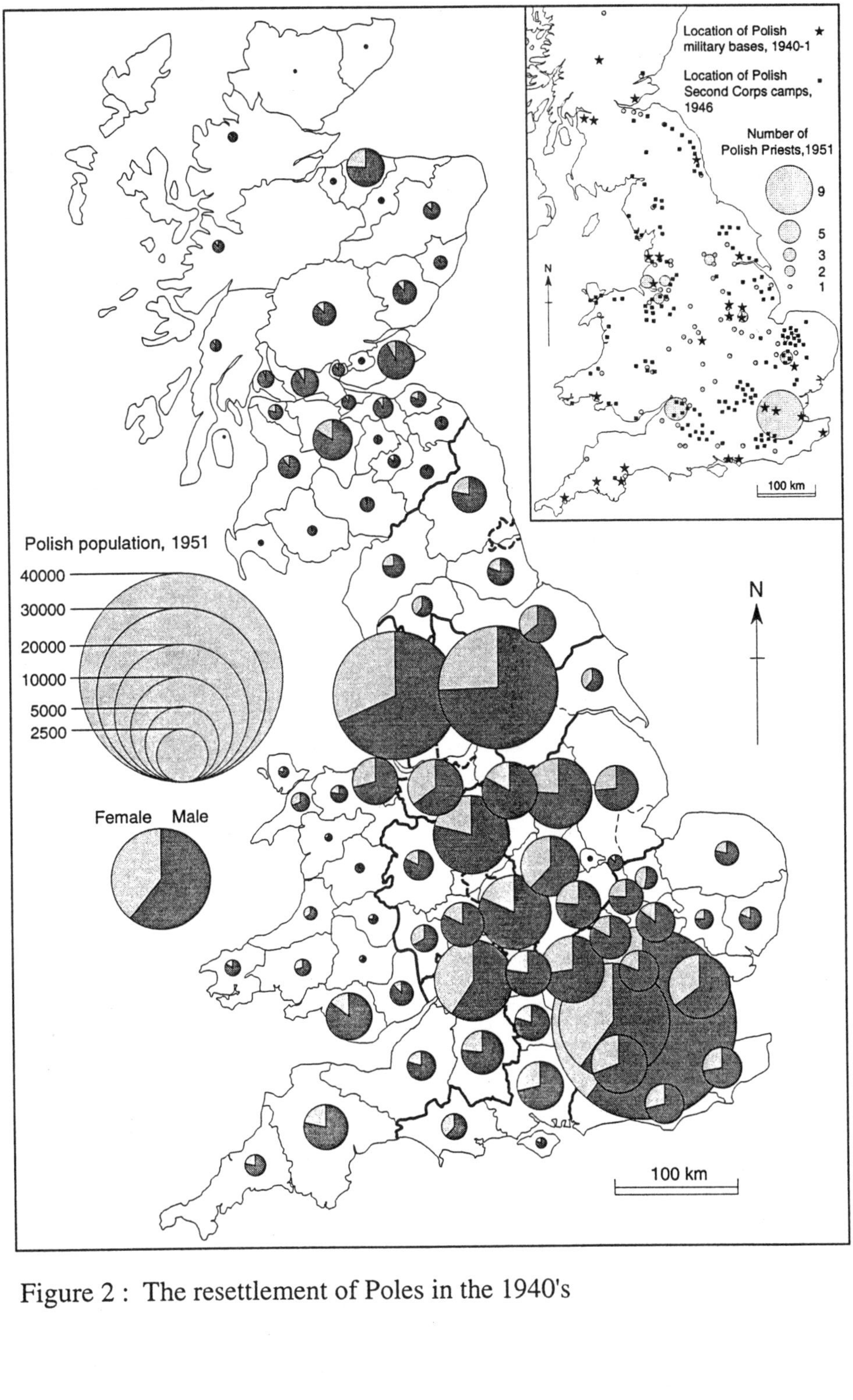

Figure 2 : The resettlement of Poles in the 1940's

their distribution being determined by two factors: the location within the UK of the main Polish military units during the war (Figure 2) and the Foreign Office's desire to disperse the Poles as widely as possible. The contrary view of the Ministry of Labour that camps should be sited near the main centres of industry and population was ignored. Instead, dispersal was preferred since it was seen as a way of forestalling ghettoization, avoiding any threat of mass disobedience by Polish troops and of breaking the grip of Polish military HQ over their men. The decision to opt for dispersal provides a third example of how the Polish programme established guiding principles of refugee reception and resettlement which have been employed with most subsequent quota arrivals (see Robinson, 1993a). The same can also be said of the decision to concentrate funding on the early stages of reception rather than on long-term resettlement. Of the £122 million spent on Polish resettlement between 1945 and 1950, over half was spent in the first two years.

Figure 2 also charts the distribution of the Polish-born population by administrative county using data derived from the national census of 1951. The distribution can be accounted for by four factors. The first was the importance of the community's wartime past. London and Middlesex contained over one-third of England and Wales' Polish born, a proportion heavily influenced by the role of the capital as the centre of Polish wartime government, education and military influence: Zubrzycki (1956) notes how for these reasons the number of Poles in London trebled between 1945 and 1949. The second factor was the location of wartime military bases. Lancashire and the West Riding of Yorkshire became important areas of Polish concentration because they had been centres of military activity during the war, possessing both training camps and operational bases. The same was also true of Nottinghamshire. The third factor was the scattered distribution of the post-war resettlement camps, with Poles simply diffusing out of the camps into adjacent areas. As a result, even relatively isolated counties such as Anglesey, Merioneth, Northumberland and Cornwall possessed resident Polish populations in 1951. And fourth, the government's attempts to steer Poles towards particular industries that were short of labour were also a contributory factor. Lancashire, Yorkshire, Staffordshire and Nottinghamshire offered opportunities in their coalmining industries (the third largest employer of Poles by 1949), while the former two counties also possessed sizeable textile industries (the sixth most important industry for Poles). Bedfordshire could offer work in the brickmaking industry (seventh). And London was an important centre for construction (first), hotels (fourth) and government administration (fifth).

The regional concentration of Poles is also reflected in the distribution of their associations and institutions. Figure 2 shows the location of Polish Roman Catholic priests. Not surprisingly, this follows the distribution of population closely.

Research on the more recent history of Poles in the UK (Patterson, 1977) has described how they have gradually shed their exile status and become more accommodated to the notion of permanent settlement in the UK. With this shift in self-perception have come other changes. Although many Poles experienced a loss of socio-economic status immediately after the war, having to take unskilled manual employment even if previously professional workers in Poland, in the longer term they have acquired upward social mobility. Patterson describes the growing band of Polish professionals in the UK and the movement of manual workers from unskilled positions to skilled work. She also charts the expansion of self-employment, particularly in London, and the growth of these businesses into sizeable enterprises. Alongside this socio-economic mobility there has also been spatial mobility. London proved to be a magnet to mobile Poles, as did other cities with existing Polish communities (e.g. Manchester, Bradford, Birmingham and Nottingham), but Patterson argues that once the Polish distribution had recrystallized around these nodes, it ossified. Movement after the 1950s tended to be residential mobility within cities for status or life-cycle reasons, rather than inter-regional movements.

Figure 3 bears out these generalizations since it demonstrates the continuing importance of London and the other conurbations for Poles in the 1990s, and the withdrawal which has taken place from more remote areas. Anglesey, for example, has seen the number of Polish born drop by two-thirds, while the rural Welsh county of Radnor experienced an 85 per cent fall. The map also shows the location of branches of the ex-combatants association (the SPK) and Polish Catholic priests, and indicates how these are closely aligned with the major population concentrations, especially London.

The Poles thus provide an excellent example of a group that had its resettlement geography shaped directly by external forces, most notably central government intervention. The billeting of troops in particular parts of the country during the war, the attempt to disperse the resettlement camps around the nation and the steering of PRC members into particular industrial niches have all had a profound impact upon the present-day distribution of the Poles, and one only partially modified by individual action. What is perhaps more pertinent is that the Polish example provides an early and clear indication of how important the location of resettlement camps is in shaping subsequent patterns of permanent settlement. In South Wales, for example, nearly all the current Polish residents came through two nearby resettlement camps and simply found the nearest available employment (with British Steel) and accommodation. Many of those people still live in towns such as Newport 45 years later.

The Ugandan Asians

The Ugandan Asians provide a case study that has several similarities to the Poles but also some significant differences. Similarities include the fact that neither group was drawn from an uneducated peasant background, both groups were admitted as a matter of honour by a Conservative government and both arrived during periods of economic recession. However, there were also marked differences. The Ugandan Asians, who arrived late in 1972, were a much smaller group than the Poles, were more conversant with the English language and could have no 'myth of return', given the circumstances of their expulsion. But above all, they were black and they were British citizens. The issue of race is critical, since the arrival of Ugandan Asians in Britain came some ten years after the peak of West Indian and South Asian labour migration, by which time the issue of 'coloured' immigration had become highly contentious and highly politicized. The speeches of Enoch Powell MP had warned of civil war between whites and non-whites and 'rivers of blood'. Race and immigration policies had become vote-winning issues and extreme right-wing groups had started to make local electoral progress in particular parts of Britain's inner cities. Public opinion against further 'coloured' immigration was being expressed not only through the ballot box, but also through opinion polls (Kohler, 1973) and racial violence on the streets. Thus while the British government felt it had an international moral obligation towards the Ugandan Asians, it also had to pander to its (white) domestic constituency. This had profound implications for the reception

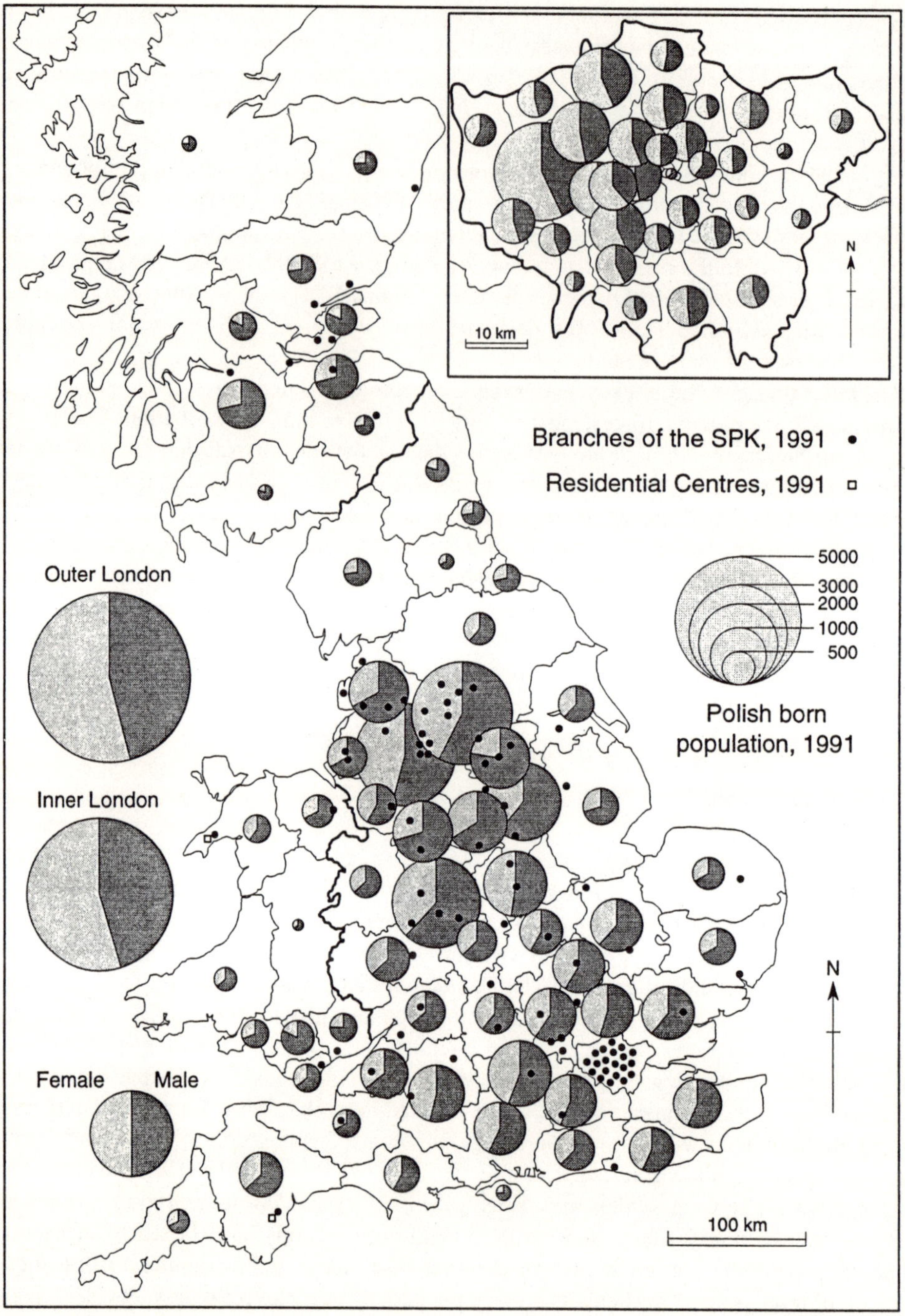

Figure 3 : The contemporary distribution of Poles and their associates in the UK and resettlement programme and also, again, established precedents which have now become an integral part of refugee policy.

Historical accounts of the settlement of Asians in East Africa describe how the group had become successful middlemen, many of whom were relatively affluent and had taken the opportunity to use their wealth to educate their children for professional employment (Delf, 1963). The progressive spread of Africanization policies after independence in the ex-colonies of East Africa had already started to threaten the position of Asians by the late 1960s, and a steady flow of Asians chose to leave Kenya and Uganda from 1967 onwards. However, by 1972 President Amin had further increased the pressure on the Asian community in Uganda by excluding them from public employment, limiting their right to own businesses and restricting their trading activities to specified products. When Amin finally announced on 4 August 1972 that he was giving the 80,000 Asians thought to be in Uganda 90 days to leave the country there was an international outcry, although other groups in Uganda had experienced similar treatment without Amin garnering international opprobrium (Mamdani, 1993). The chronology of the expulsion has been well documented elsewhere (see Marett, 1989; Robinson, 1995), as have the conflicting claims about the treatment of Asians during the last 90 days in Uganda (Adams and Bristow, 1979).

Britain's response to the challenge of resettling the 29,000 Ugandan Asians who came to the UK was in some ways predictable. The government again opted to distance itself from reception and resettlement activities by establishing the Uganda Resettlement Board (URB). It again chose to establish reception camps to process refugees and hold them while attempts were made to find accommodation and employment. It used military camps for this purpose, as it had with the Poles, and it made little attempt to plan the location of these camps so that they coincided with areas of economic potential (see Figure 4). It opted for a dispersal policy, designed to steer the Ugandan Asians away from areas of existing Asian settlement (see Robinson, 1995). And again the government refused to provide purpose-built accommodation for the new arrivals.

In some respects the Ugandan programme marked a new departure. While the Conservative government made it clear that it would honour its moral obligations to the Ugandan Asians, it did so only within the context of international burden sharing. Strenuous diplomatic efforts were made to ensure that other members of the Commonwealth and historic allies would also resettle Ugandan Asians. Eventually India accepted some 15,000, Canada 8000, the USA 3000, Malawi 1000, and Australia and New Zealand 600. This left Britain with about half the Ugandan Asians (28,600) to resettle in the UK, although it was known that a good number of these would subsequently migrate to join relatives in Canada and the USA.

In response to the government's fear of a white backlash if it were seen to be doing too much for 'coloured' refugees, it further distanced itself from resettlement by only *requesting* that local authorities supply public housing for Ugandan Asians. Local residents who felt aggrieved by the use of public accommodation for 'coloureds' would direct their criticism to local, not central, government. A further voluntaristic element was introduced through the charities and their volunteer helpers who ran the reception camps. The Women's Royal Voluntary Service was particularly active, as was the Red Cross and St John Ambulance (Swinerton, Kuepper and Lackey, 1975). In some cases, camps also appealed directly for individual volunteers. The government also drew back further from direct intervention by relying upon the natural workings of the labour and housing markets to ensure successful long-term

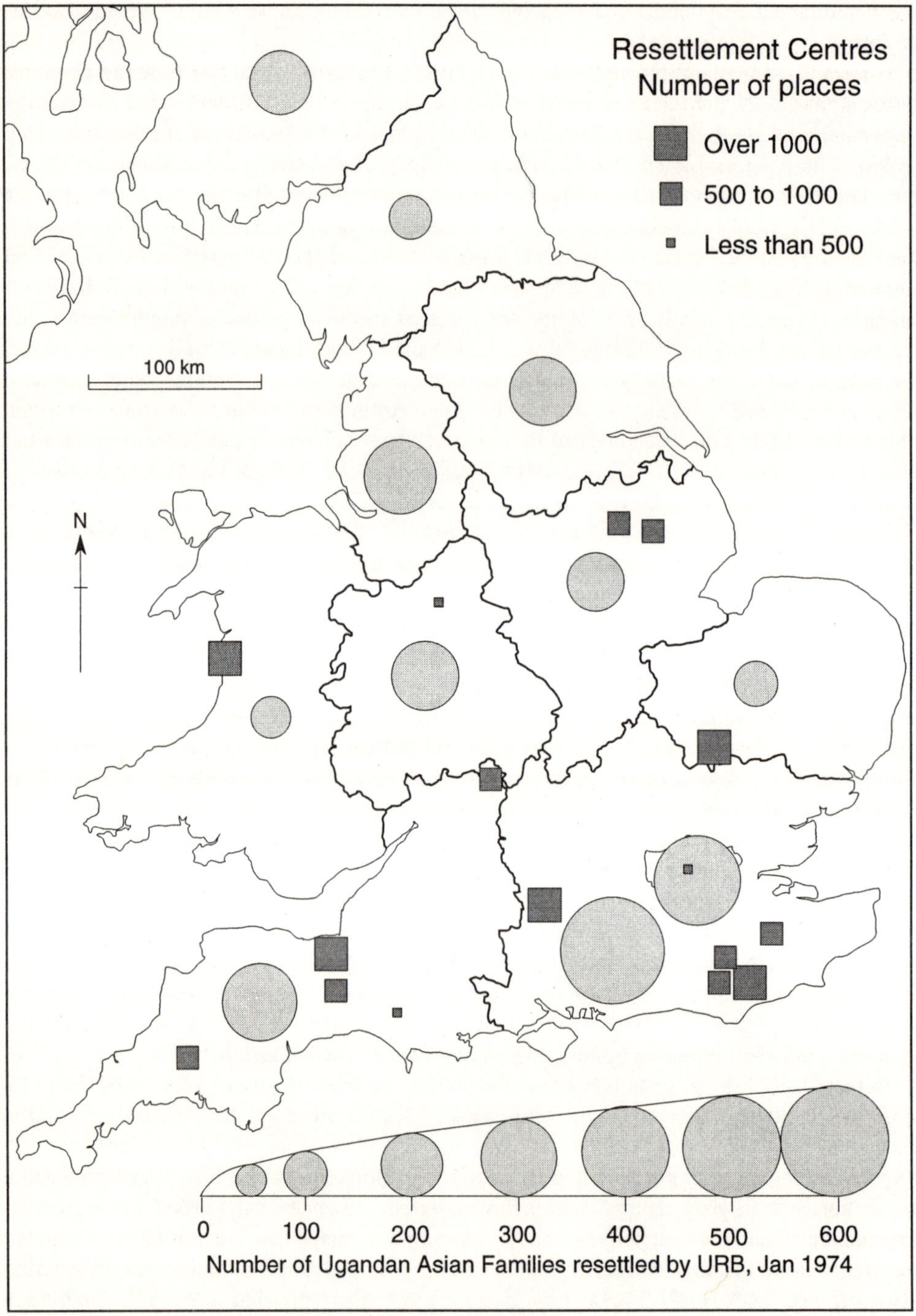

Figure 4 : The resettlement of Ugandan Asians in the 1970's

resettlement: Ugandan Asians were not directed to specific industries or offered bespoke retraining opportunities, the government persistently declined to assist the self-employed with short-term loans to re-establish businesses, and there was never a concerted attempt to ensure the recognition of qualifications acquired in Uganda (e.g. teaching certificates). In fact, the government relied to a much greater extent with the Ugandan Asians on what has since become known as 'mainstreaming', where support and welfare services are provided to refugees to the same level and through the same administrative channels as would be the case for indigenous residents. Bespoke or additional assistance was denied, and the 'headline' cost of resettlement was reduced (the PRC spent perhaps £160 on each Pole whereas nearly 25 years later the URB spent around £210 on each Ugandan Asian).

There was one further element in the government's effort to ensure the smooth acceptance of the Ugandan Asians. This was positive stereotyping of the Ugandan Asians and continual reporting of the circumstances of their expulsion. It is not clear whether this was deliberate media manipulation by the government or a Conservative-biased press supporting their party during a time of electoral danger. Nevertheless, Adams and Bristow (1979) comment upon the widespread reporting of the atrocities allegedly experienced by Asians as they tried to leave Uganda, and Swinerton, Kuepper and Lackey (1975) describe how the press focused upon the middle-class background and occupational skills of the Ugandan Asians, and television emphasized the basically British way of life the Asians had experienced in East Africa. Amin's widely reported admiration for Adolf Hitler and his treatment of the Jews scaled the stereotyping of the Asians as innocent and helpless victims of the actions of an irrational despot.

The final area of difference between the Ugandan Asian and earlier programmes was the new emphasis upon the acquisition of housing as the pre-eminent measure of successful resettlement. For the first time, resettlement agencies had as their main objective getting refugees out of reception camps into houses. Once housed, refugees could be supported by mainstream welfare benefits. This was in sharp contrast to the Polish programme, where refugees were found work and often then remained resident in the camps for extended periods until they eventually decided that they wished to move out on their own. This new emphasis on housing has remained a central feature of resettlement policy in the UK ever since.

Once the URB was established and the Ugandan Asians were arriving regularly, the Board turned its attention to the geography of resettlement. As stated above, it committed itself to a policy of voluntary dispersal in which Ugandan Asians would be steered away from 'red' areas and towards 'green' areas. The criterion for defining areas as red or green was ostensibly pressure upon local services, but some commentators feel that the presence of an existing Asian community was a more potent factor behind the list of red areas. In practice, the zoning of the country was somewhat academic since refugees could only be resettled where housing had been offered and families could not be compelled to move against their wishes. Many Ugandan Asians had relatives or friends already settled in the UK who were in a position to help with accommodation or employment. As a result, some 23 per cent of the refugees who passed through the hands of the URB made their own arrangements for accommodation without entering a camp: most of these went straight to red areas. In addition, a further 39 per cent ultimately found their own accommodation despite a period of residence in a resettlement camp: again, this would probably have been in red areas. Bristow (1976) thus argues that, despite the public utterances about dispersal, only 38 per cent of Ugandan Asians were actually found accommodation in green areas. As

Figure 4 demonstrates, the net geographical impact was to ensure that the East African Asians were more concentrated within the UK than either the Indian or Pakistani labour migrants which had preceded them, with particular concentrations in London and Leicester (Robinson, 1986).

The use of longitudinal data has allowed commentators to chart the socio-economic progress of the East African Asians in the UK. A number of pieces of research assessed their status within the UK immediately after resettlement. Their assessment was decidedly pessimistic. McCart (1973) noted that 25 per cent of household heads in Wandsworth were still unemployed, 75 per cent were housed unsatisfactorily and three-quarters were living below the poverty line. Dines (1973) commented on the social isolation of those who had been dispersed. And Kumar (1973) described how almost all the Ugandan Asian businessmen in Manchester were still looking for work and how those few refugees who had found work had experienced considerable loss of status.

As is often the case with refugee migrations, the immediate public and academic interest in the Ugandan Asians soon waned and as a result there has been little longitudinal analysis of the progress of the group over the medium term. However, Robinson (1994) undertook such a piece of work using national data-sets measuring standard indicators of socio-economic status for the whole East African Asian minority in the UK. His findings were that, despite the powerful forces of racial exclusionism at work in every facet of life in Britain and the deepest recession the country had seen since the 1930s, the national profile of the group had changed considerably between the early 1970s and the mid 1980s. East African Asians had acquired better formal qualifications than their Indian or white British counterparts, were over-represented in self-employment, had transformed their socio-economic profile more rapidly than either of the other two groups, were found in better accommodation than Indians, and had achieved all of this without wholesale secondary migration. Thus by the time of the 1991 national census, Asians born in East Africa (the nearest census category) had maintained the patterns established 18 years previously, albeit with increasing concentration into the two main cores of Leicestershire and London (see Figure 5).

The Ugandan Asian case study allows us to see the gradual refining of refugee resettlement policy in the UK. Housing took precedence over employment, dispersal was still seen as desirable, voluntarism was preferred to state intervention, mainstreaming replaced tailored provision, and central government distanced itself even further from the procedures of reception and resettlement.

The Vietnamese

The Vietnamese are the most recent of the large quota groups to have arrived in the UK. Again, the details of the circumstances leading up to their expulsion and their subsequent arrival in the UK (via camps in Hong Kong) have been covered elsewhere (Robinson, 1993b). Suffice to say that the initial quota of 12,500 arrivals came to the UK only after prolonged periods in open or closed camps in Hong Kong and that British criteria for admission were a good deal less selective than those of many other Western countries, which succeeded in attracting refugees with occupational skills, qualifications and good spoken English or French. The British entrants were thus very youthful, largely uneducated and often illiterate

Figure 5 : The contemporary distribution of East African Asians in the UK even in their own languages, and were predominantly Chinese Vietnamese from erstwhile North Vietnam. They had few transferable skills and were largely ignorant of Western ways (Robinson, 1993b).

The process by which Britain became involved in a refugee episode with which it had little direct connection bears out some of the emerging generalizations made above. Britain did not respond to the first wave of South Vietnamese refugees who fled Vietnam with the capture of Saigon in 1975. As other entries in this atlas no doubt make clear, many of these refugees were received and resettled in the United States. However, during 1978 and 1979 the second wave began to flee persecution in the north of the country as Sino-Vietnamese relations continued to deteriorate. Once the overland route to China was cut, the Chinese Vietnamese turned to the sea and the international phenomenon of the 'Boat People' came into being. Hong Kong proved to be a significant destination for the Boat People, and as numbers in camps there increased and public sympathy fell away, it became clear that the rate of arrivals was far exceeding the number of acceptances for resettlement being made by third countries. Britain was also at this time considering the future of the colony and the refugees threatened to complicate relations with the Chinese authorities during negotiations about its return. Britain thus only became involved out of necessity and was reluctant to do so; it did not act out of any moral imperative. The first initiative taken by the British government was to suggest an international conference on the plight of the Vietnamese refugees throughout South East Asia. This took place under UN auspices in Geneva and was simultaneous to a British diplomatic campaign that sought to extract offers of resettlement from other nations. The meeting eventually produced some 250,000 resettlement places, and against this background of international 'burden sharing', Britain offered to take 10,000 Vietnamese from the camps.

Despite independent research that had demonstrated the weaknesses of the Ugandan Asian programme, the Vietnamese programme was clearly modelled upon it. The government distanced itself from both reception and resettlement through the creation of an intermediary body, the Joint Committee for Refugees from Vietnam (see Robinson, 1985). Voluntarism was again a central policy imperative, with charities being responsible for the camps and for the administration of resettlement, with each being given a territory within which to operate. Local authorities were not required to offer public housing for resettlement, and it was made clear to them that, if they did, funds would not be forthcoming to cover any additional long-term costs arising from the needs of Vietnamese families in their locality. Housing was again taken to be the main barometer of successful resettlement, with the result that very little attempt was made to match the employment skills of individual refugees with local labour markets. Front-end loading was also practised again, with £21 million out of a total expenditure of £23 million being assigned to reception, which was operationalized through reception camps which were, again, old military bases, often in isolated areas (see Hale, 1993). And, finally, the government committed itself firmly to mainstreaming rather than group-specific policies.

The Vietnamese programme did, however, mark the further development of policy in at least two respects. First, the day-to-day responsibility for resettlement was delegated even further to volunteer support groups made up of individuals drawn from charities, religious groups and other voluntary associations. It was they who often decorated houses and acquired furniture for refugees before their arrival and then undertook unofficial liaison between the family and school authorities, social services, benefit agencies and the health services. They also provided emotional support and friendship in the critical first months after arrival, but they were expected to do all this without training, payment or knowledge of Vietnamese culture or languages. Second, the Vietnamese programme marked a further extension of policy towards dispersal (Robinson, 1993a). Since the Vietnamese were acute refugees, had little spoken or written English and no prior knowledge of Britain, and had no pre-existing ethnic community to which they could turn for advice (Jones, 1982), they were particularly manipulable. In addition, the Conservative government had just been elected with a party manifesto which committed them to further reductions in (non-white) immigration. The combination of a political imperative and a manipulable group produced one of Britain's most extensive experiments in spatial engineering, matched only by wartime evacuation (Zelinsky and Kosinski, 1991) and recent legislation on gypsy mobility (Sibley, 1981). The Home Office recommended that the Vietnamese should be dispersed throughout all parts of the United Kingdom in small and separate clusters of between four and ten families per locality (Robinson, 1993a). As with the Ugandan Asian programme, the government's failure to requisition or build homes for the refugees meant that the Vietnamese could only be resettled in local authorities where housing had been offered. The geographical distribution of the group immediately after resettlement, shown in Figure 6, therefore evidences a dualism, with refugees located in isolated and far-flung parts of the country, as well as in parts of larger cities such as London, Birmingham and Bristol.

Vietnamese unemployment levels of up to 85 per cent in parts of Britain and the psychological toll of isolation were clear indicators of the failure of policy, as was the scale and speed of secondary migration (Robinson and Hale, 1989). As Figure 7 demonstrates, this was overwhelmingly towards (selected parts of) London, with refugees moving not only directly from parts of Wales and Scotland but also stepwise up the urban hierarchy. As Figure 8 shows, the long-term effect of secondary migration and the subsequent additions to the Vietnamese population through family reunion and a small second quota of arrivals, has been to solidify the group's distribution around London, where access to employment is at its greatest and where the rental market is well developed. Community associations and community infrastructure are now starting to reflect this.

Conclusion

Many commentators argue that episodes of refugee resettlement are isolated and individual events that by their very nature defy attempts to develop long-term or standing policy responses. Rather, each episode has to be treated as a unique event requiring *ad hoc* responses tailored to specific circumstances. As a result, one is rarely able to discern a progressive evolution in a country's policy.

This brief review has demonstrated that, in Britain's case at least, such an assumption is false. Over the last 50 years Britain has developed and progressively refined policies of refugee reception and resettlement which are based upon a continuity of implicit assumptions about what the British public will accept and what Britain's contribution to the international refugee crisis should be. These continuities far outweigh the specifics of policy towards any one group. Furthermore, as the nature of the refugee crisis has changed in the more recent period, policy has been increasingly shaped by a new political ideology, based more upon markets, voluntarism and – some would say – meanness of spirit, than upon morality.

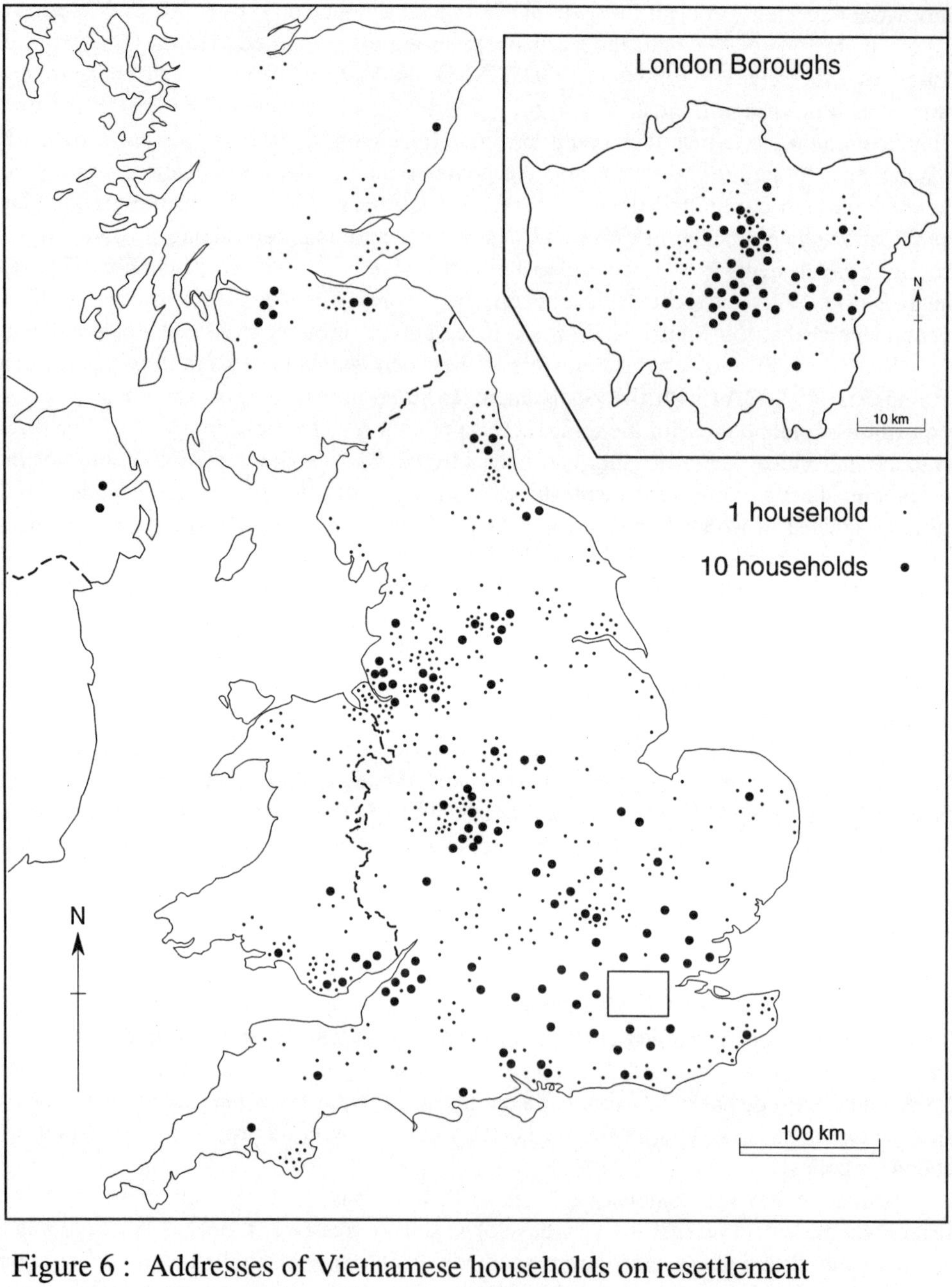

Figure 6 : Addresses of Vietnamese households on resettlement

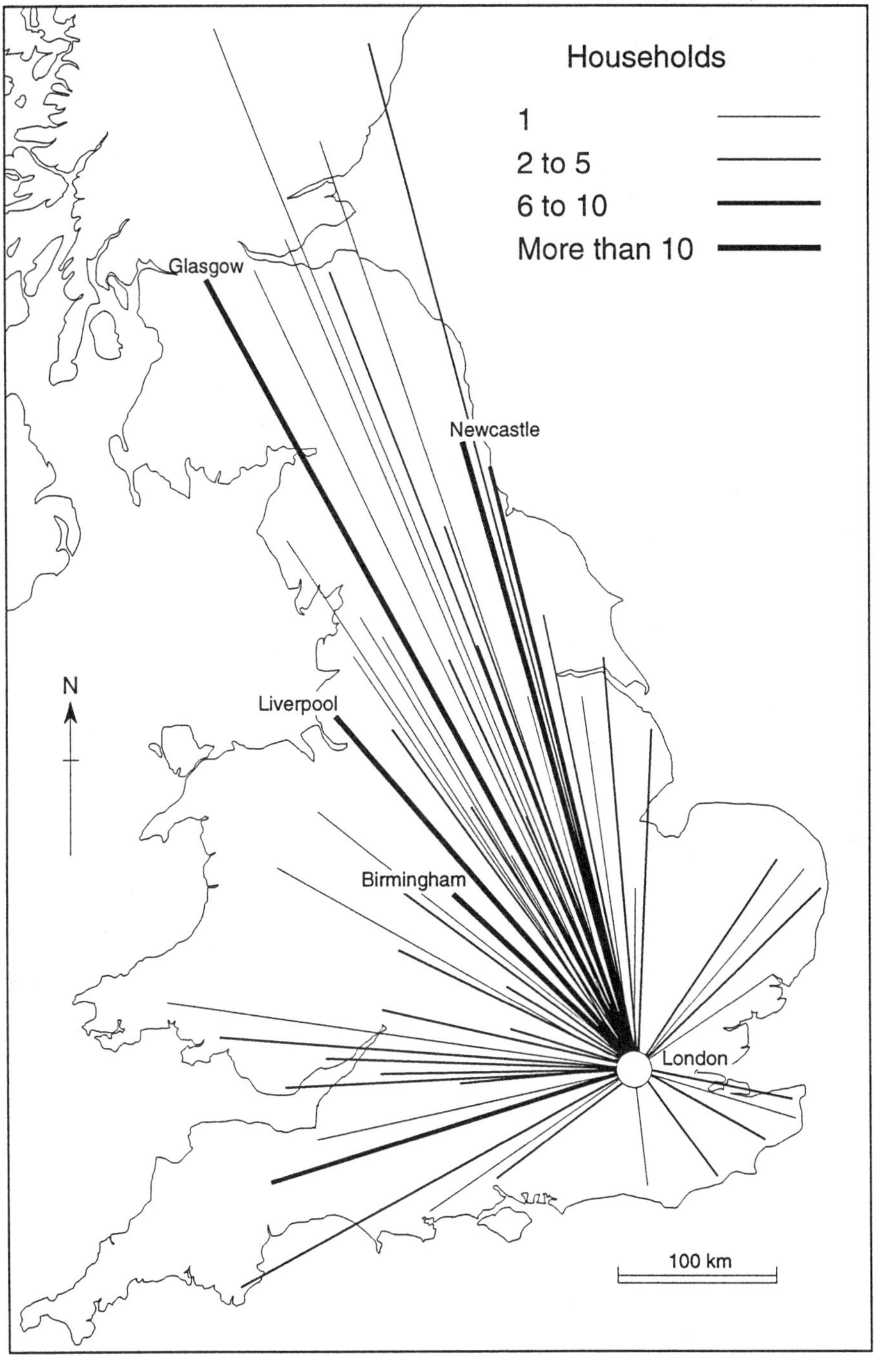

Figure 7 : Movement of Vietnamese first resettlement address to last address into London

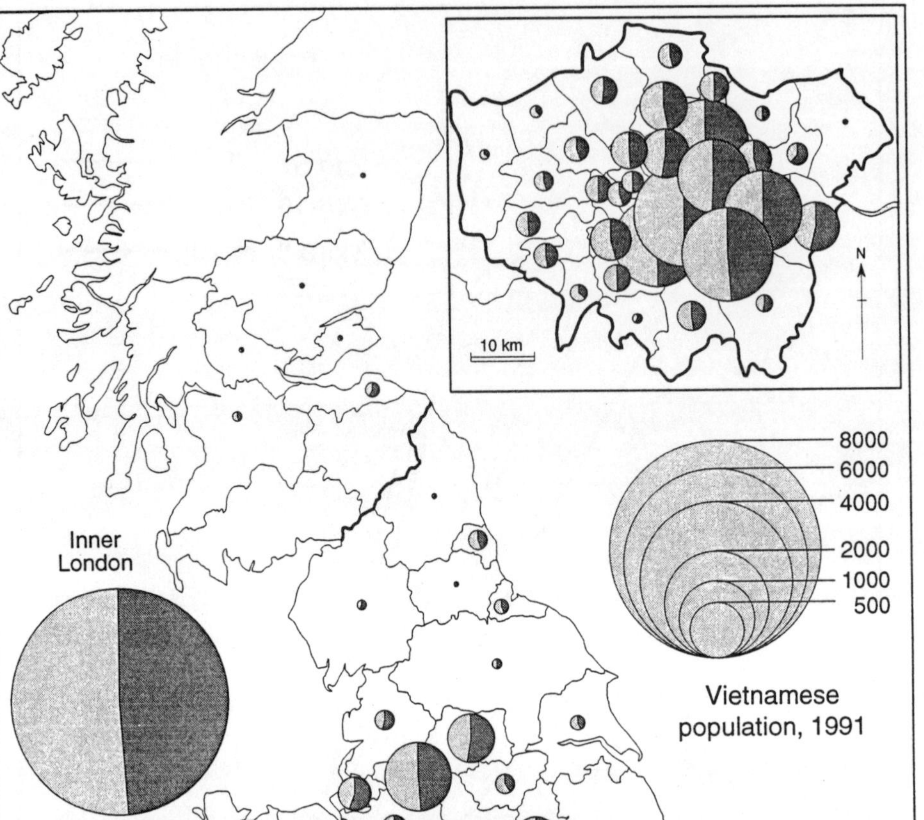

Figure 8 : The contemporary distribution of the Vietnamese population in the UK

References

Adams, B.N. and M. Bristow (1979), 'Ugandan Asian expulsion experiences: rumour and reality', *Journal of Asian and African Studies*, **14** (3), 191–203.
Bristow, M. (1976), 'Britain's response to the Ugandan Asian crisis: government myths versus political and resettlement realities', *New Community*, **5** (3), 265–79.
Delf, G. (1963), *Asians in East Africa*, London: Oxford University Press.
Dines, M. (1973), 'Ugandan Asians: one year later', *New Community*, **2** (4), 380–83.
Hale, S. (1993), 'The reception and resettlement of Vietnamese refugees in Britain', in V. Robinson (ed.), *The International Refugee Crisis: British and Canadian Responses*, Basingstoke: Macmillan.
Jones, P. (1982), *Vietnamese Refugees*, Research and Planning Unit Paper 13, London: Home Office.
Kohler, D. (1973), 'Public opinion and the Ugandan Asians', *New Community*, **2** (2), 194–7.
Kumar, S. (1973), 'Ugandan Asians one year later: Manchester report', *New Community*, **2** (4), 386–8.
McCart, M. (1973), 'Ugandan Asians one year later: Wandsworth. Unsettled Ugandan refugees', *New Community*, **2** (4), 383–6.
Mamdani, M. (1993), 'The Ugandan Asian expulsion: twenty years after', *Economic and Political Weekly*, 16 Jan., pp. 93–6.
Marett, V. (1989), *Immigrants Settling in the City*, London: Leicester University Press.
Patterson, S. (1977), 'The Poles: an exile community in Britain', in J.L. Watson (ed.), *Between Two Cultures: Migrants and Minorities in Britain*, Oxford: Blackwell.
Robinson, V. (1985), 'The Vietnamese reception and resettlement programme in the UK', *Ethnic Groups*, **6**, 305–30.
Robinson, V. (1986), *Transients, Settlers and Refugees: Asians in Britain*, Oxford: Clarendon Press.
Robinson, V. (1993a), 'British policy towards the settlement patterns of ethnic groups: an empirical evaluation of the Vietnamese programme', in V. Robinson (ed.), *The International Refugee Crisis: British and Canadian Responses*, Basingstoke: Macmillan.
Robinson, V. (1993b), 'North and South: resettling Vietnamese refugees in Australia and the UK', in R. Black and V. Robinson (eds), *Geography and Refugees*, London: Belhaven.
Robinson, V. (1994), 'Marching into the middle classes? The long term resettlement of East African Asians in the UK', *Journal of Refugee Studies*, **6** (3), 230–47.
Robinson, V. (1995), 'The migration of East African Asians to the UK', in R. Cohen (ed.), *The Cambridge Survey of World Migration*, Cambridge: Cambridge University Press.
Robinson, V. and S. Hale (1989), *The Geography of Vietnamese Secondary Migration in the UK*, Warwick: Centre for Research in Ethnic Relations.
Sibley, D. (1981), *Outsiders in Urban Society*, Oxford: Blackwell.
Swinerton, E.N., W.G. Kuepper and G.L. Lackey (1975), *Ugandan Asians in Great Britain*, London: Croom Helm.
Sword, K., N. Davies and J. Ciechanowski (1989), *The Formation of the Polish Community in Great Britain, 1939–50*, London: University of London.
Tannahill, J.A. (1958), *European Volunteer Workers in Britain*, Manchester: Manchester University Press.
Zelinsky, W. and L. Kosinski (1991), *The Emergency Evacuation of Cities*, Savage: Rowman and Littlefield.
Zubrzycki, J. (1956), *Polish Immigrants in Britain*, The Hague: Martinus Nijhoff.

[29]

Migrant Remittances and Development

Sharon Stanton Russell*

INTRODUCTION

Remittances - the portion of migrant workers' earnings sent back from the country of employment to the country of origin - are central to the links between migration and development. The forces affecting remittance flows are multiple, complex, and diverse.[1] These may include the number and characteristics of workers abroad as well as of other household members; levels and types of economic activity in sending and host countries; differential wage, exchange, and interest rates; political risk; and the facility for transferring funds. These exogenous factors in turn shape the personal decisions made by migrants and their families regarding remittances: whether to send funds home or keep them abroad; how to remit (through official or informal channels); and how to use remitted earnings (for consumption or for savings and investment). Only then can the longer range development consequences of remittances - if any - begin to occur.

As the evidence below suggests, there continues to be considerable and often heated debate concerning the effects of remittances on development. This paper reviews selected issues in the measurement of remittances and presents recent findings on the volume and direction of flows. It then considers evidence concerning the uses of remittances and their consequences for development, and finally discusses policy options for increasing and channeling remittance flows.

* Center for International Studies, Massachusetts Institute of Technology, United States of America.

GLOBAL TRENDS IN REMITTANCE FLOWS

Remittances are private transfers, and as such only a portion flow through official channels; those sent informally are particularly resistant to measurement and can be sizable. For the Sudan, Galaleldin (1979) found that only 24 per cent of migrants sampled in 1980 transferred hard currency through the banking system, while Choucri estimated that in 1983 only 11 per cent of remittances flowed into the country through official channels (Choucri, 1985:1-10,5). In some countries, remittances are repatriated in the form of goods; in Swaziland, for example, non-cash transfers have been reported as high as double the cash amounts (M. Russell, 1984).

Estimates of official remittances are generally derived from the International Monetary Fund's (IMF's) *Balance of Payments Statistics Yearbook*, which compiles data from individual country sources. While these remain the best available data, they are not without serious flaws: e.g. data are not reported for all countries; some record and report remittances in different categories of the balance of payments (BOP) statistics; and reporting requirements or conventions differ amongst countries.[2]

Measurement of official remittance flows is further complicated by definitional issues. Three categories in the BOP detailed current account statistics are of relevance: "workers remittances", "migrant transfers", and "labour income".[3] By definition, "worker remittances" are the value of transfers from workers abroad for more than one year; "migrant transfers" include the flow of goods and financial assets associated with migration; and "labour income" is factor income of migrants working abroad for less than one year.

In practice, however, it is extremely difficult (if not impossible) for reporting authorities, or even migrants themselves, to know a migrant's intended length of stay abroad. For this reason, a number of World Bank studies include all three categories when estimating remittance flows (Swamy, 1981; Russell and Teitelbaum, 1992). But not all researchers follow this convention; some use only one category, others use total "private unrequited transfers" as a proxy for remittances, and others confine their analyses to selected countries (e.g. Keely and Tran, 1989). Others eschew the IMF statistics altogether and rely on data from individual country sources. Extreme care should therefore be taken when comparing results of remittance studies.

In a recent estimate of official global flows (Russell and Teitelbaum, 1992), the three categories were combined to calculate remittances for all countries reporting to the IMF and it was found that nominal remittance credits increased from US$ 43.3 billion in 1980 to US$ 65.6 billion in 1989. Since publication of this study, Canada has announced downward adjustments in the "migrant transfer" category and, as shown in Table 1 (page 284), the 1989 figure for global remittance credits[4] has now been revised downward to US$ 60.9 billion. We now also have an estimate for 1990: adjusted global credits rose to US$ 71.1 billion, a nearly 17 per cent increase over the preceding year. The value of remittances remains second only to trade in crude oil and significantly larger than the value of trade in coffee, the most important non-oil primary commodity[5] (Russell and Teitelbaum, 1992: 29).

For many labour-sending countries, remittances also constitute sizable proportions of GDP, exports, and imports. In 1989, total remittances were over 8 per cent of GDP in Portugal, over 14 per cent in Yemen and Jordan, and nearly 170 per cent in the extreme case of Lesotho. In selected countries, remittances can be 25-50 per cent of the value of merchandise exports and 10-33 per cent of merchandise imports (Russell and Teitelbaum, 1992: 31 and Tables 4, 5, and 6). There are both positive and negative implications of these figures. Remittances (like international migration itself) are notably volatile, and countries that rely heavily on them may experience economic shocks when the flow is disrupted, as was the case in Jordan and Yemen following the recent Gulf War.

The global volume of remittances also reflects the fact that international migration has become central to international trade in services: in 1989, remittance credits were roughly 8.5 per cent of what has become the very substantial total value of world trade in services -US$ 770 billion in 1990. There is also evidence that remittances constitute an increasingly important mechanism for the transfer of resources from developed to developing countries (Pagaran, 1992). Table 3 (pages 286 and 287) shows that nominal net transfers (i.e. credits minus debits) to developing countries rose from US$ 21.1 billion in 1980 to nearly US$ 31 billion in 1989.[6] The latter figure (which does not include the value of informal transfers) is over half the total value of official development assistance in 1988 (US$ 51 billion), a sobering fact for those who look to development aid as a means to reduce migration pressures.

USES AND CONSEQUENCES OF REMITTANCES

Once remittances are repatriated (by whatever means), migrants and their families make key decisions as to how these resources are used. The contradictory nature of empirical evidence on this point results in part from the fact that few studies distinguish patterns of use according to types of migration, types of households, or characteristics of the countries and regions into which remittances flow. Further, conclusions about remittance uses are often based upon limited evidence that fails to view expenditures of migrants in comparison with those of non-migrants, or to trace patterns of use over time. Findings may also be affected by the definition (including currency denominations) of remittances as well as by categories of use employed in a given survey or analysis.

At the broadest level, migrants must choose between consumption and investment expenditures. Distinctions between the two are often blurred (as in the case of spending for education or housing) and evaluations of the relative merits of such expenditures depend on the perspectives of the analyst. One school of thought argues that remittances are used primarily for the purchase of land and housing, jewelry, and general household consumption, rather than "productive investments" and concludes that remittances thus do little to stimulate development on a regional or national level. The alternative view counters that migrants do save and invest, that expenditures for land, housing, and jewelry are rational under prevailing conditions (they frequently offer better rates of return or are better stores of value than available investments in agriculture or industry), and that expenditures on housing and consumption not only have positive multiplier effects in the wider economy, but also reduce the need for government spending or infrastructure, subsidies, and services.

There is ample empirical evidence to support both points of view, even for a given country.[7] For the Sudan, whose stock of migrants abroad has included many highly educated and skilled workers, researchers have reported the principal uses of remittances to be (variously): land purchase, construction, purchase of consumption goods, and establishment of small business enterprises (Galaleldin, 1979); housing construction, "business transactions", and agriculture (Al-Ghul, 1982); and the purchase of houses, land, taxis, and canteens (Abu Gabal, 1984). Choucri (1985: 2-6, 9), on the other hand, found that approximately two-thirds of remittances were allocated to consumption, including basic needs; the remaining one-third (a non-trivial rate of savings) was apportioned between liquid and non-liquid assets. She found little evidence of lavish expenditures for weddings and luxury items.

The ongoing "consumption versus investment" debate is fuelled in part by different methodological approaches. Most studies of remittance use tend to report on the proportional distribution of total remittances amongst alternative uses. In a microeconomic analysis of survey data for rural Egypt, Adams (1991: 67ff) examined *marginal* propensities to spend. He found that, for all but the lowest income quintile, marginal budget shares for consumption are relatively low (less than 32 per cent) and are lower for migrant than for non-migrant households, while incremental expenditures for "durables" are higher (60 per cent for migrant households compared with 50 per cent for non-migrant households). The most important "durable" expenditure is housing - the replacement of mud brick with red brick dwellings. Adams' study also found that migrant households invested a larger share of marginal budget increments than non-migrant households (19 per cent versus 6 per cent).

Evidence for the Sahel[8], where the stock of migrants includes many less well educated than in the Sudan, underscores the fact that education and income levels affect remittance use, and that observed patterns of use can vary depending upon the unit of analysis. Sahelian migrants in France generally hold low- or unskilled jobs there; yet they save 18 per cent of their average monthly wage and remit another 20 per cent. A significant proportion of their savings accumulated abroad are channelled through migrant associations to finance social undertakings in the home village, including construction of schools and health facilities (Condé *et al.*, 1986: 108).

Sahelian migrants' households at home, however, use remittances primarily for consumption, spending over three-quarters of remittance income on basic necessities such as food, clothing, and toiletries. Surprisingly, the third major expense for this group is tax payments (on average, over 10 per cent of remittance income). Overall, miscellaneous expenses such as health care, school fees, wages for labour to replace absent males, improvements to housing, and religious observances combined absorb just over 3 per cent of remittance income. New construction and savings in the Sahel account for less than 3 per cent each (Condé *et al.*, 1986).

Similar patterns have been found in Lesotho, where Mueller (in Palmer, 1985: 20) notes that remittances tend to flow in two ways: small, regular sums, and less frequent, larger, lump sum transfers. The uses of these streams are distinct. The smaller sums are allocated between basic necessities (soap, candles, tea, sugar) and farming expenses; lump sum transfers are used for education, acquisition of livestock, improved housing and household effects, and clothing. Spending for consumption can have positive effects on the wider economy: for Greece, Glytsos (1990: 21ff) found that consumption spending of remittances had a multiplier of 1.8 on domestic production.

The extent to which remittances are used for agricultural improvements is a particularly contentious subject of debate in the literature. A number of studies imply that investment of remittances in agricultural production is all too infrequent. One World Bank study of Lesotho asserts that the inflow of remittance income "explains... the prevailing stagnation of agricultural production and sharp decline of area under cultivation" (World Bank, 1984: 1). Others suggest, however, that the agricultural uses of remittances are shaped by a complex and diverse set of underlying factors, including land tenure patterns, producer pricing policies, rates of return to alternative investments, and sexual divisions of labour in agriculture.

For Lesotho, massive soil erosion and the fact that expansion of herds is a more reliable form of investment are more likely to account for crop neglect than are inflows of remittances *per se*. For Egypt, Adams (1991: 67ff) confirmed that migrants' investments were primarily in land, as opposed to agricultural equipment. However, he points out that in the period analysed, real rates of return on land averaged 9.5 per cent, while returns on small-farm crops were negative. A government survey in Swaziland found that returns from increasing maize production cannot be retained by women as their own income, and accordingly women invest remittance income in non-agricultural activities that yield income over which they do have control (Palmer, 1985: 40).

Other studies suggest that where agriculture is profitable, migrants do invest. In the Sahel, remittance income has been linked to the feasibility of irrigated agriculture: remittances are necessary to pay water fees and purchase agricultural inputs (Findley, 1989: 7, 16). Similarly, in some areas of Turkey, returned migrants have used remittances to purchase agricultural machinery and for expansion of irrigation and thus the land under cultivation (Martin, 1991: 46-47).

Remittances have been an important source of financing for agricultural inputs in Zambia, accounting for nearly 14 per cent of all capital for the purchase of fertilizer, and nearly 6 per cent of capital for buying or hiring oxen ploughs and tractors. For both types of input, remittances constitute a proportionately larger source of capital for women than for men, since women are less readily granted government-sponsored agricultural loans (Chilivumbo, 1985: 78ff).

Evidence on the consequences of remittances for development is as mixed as that concerning remittance uses. In their aptly titled book, *The Unsettled Relationship: Labor Migration and Economic Development*, Papademetriou and Martin (1991) have stressed that there is no automatic mechanism by which international migration and remittances result in development, and few would dispute this conclusion. However, for a given country, analysts differ in their assessments of migration's development consequences. Papademetriou and Emke-Poulopoulos (in Papademetriou and Martin, 1991: 98) found only a "tentative relationship" between Greek migration, return and development. Glytsos (1990: 29), however, came to a different conclusion in his comparison of East Macedonia (with high emigration) and Thessalia (with low outmigration). Before emigration (1961), the two regions were comparable with respect to population growth, ageing and proportion of employment in agriculture, but differed in per capita income, which was lower in East Macedonia. After migration (1971), remittances to East Macedonia had effectively closed the 16 per cent income gap with Thessalia; further, non-agricultural employment, agricultural productivity, standard of living, and general economic performance were higher in East Macedonia.

The effects of migration on poverty depend on the extent to which the poor participate in the migration process, and it is seldom the poorest who have the means to emigrate. When poorer members of a society do migrate, however, limited available evidence suggests a positive effect on poverty. Burki (1984: 680-682) has concluded that international migration played a decisive role in alleviating absolute poverty in many poor regions of Pakistan. This is consistent with Oberai and Singh's (1980) finding that remittances from internal migration in Pakistan raised the average income of migrant households by nearly 31 per cent. When remittances were included in estimates of household income in Egypt, the number of poor households decreased by nearly 10 per cent and Sen's poverty index declined by 12 per cent (Adams, 1991: 37ff).

To the extent that migrants come from above-average income households, remittances may exacerbate income inequality. Indeed, Adams observed a sharp increase in the Gini coefficient and Theil's entropy measure of income inequality in Egypt, and noted that this was primarily because upper income households had the largest share of still-abroad migrants in the survey period; but compared with the effects of agricultural income, remittances made only a small contribution to overall inequality. For Pakistan, it has been argued that "no other net inflow of resources... has historically been as equally distributed over the national population as remittances" (Gilani *et al.*, 1981: 40). A more recent study of Pakistan (Adams, 1992: 16ff) confirms that both internal and international migrants are distributed fairly equally through the income order (e.g. only the lowest and highest income groups have less than their quintile share of international migrants) and in both cases remittances had a neutral effect on income distribution.

The contention that remittances fuel inflation persists in the literature, but few studies have undertaken the complex task of disentangling the role of remittances from other inflationary pressures, and empirical evidence remains contradictory. Martin (1991: 57) notes that remittances may not have had the alleged inflationary impacts in Turkey because they increased the supply of, as well as demand for goods: remittances permitted the importation of spare parts and new machinery that facilitated increased domestic production. Papademetriou and Emke-Poulopoulos (in Papademetriou and Martin, 1991: 102) argue that demand for building materials generated by remittance-financed construction played a "leading role" in fueling inflation in Greece. On the other hand, Glytsos (1990: 3, 21ff) contends that between 1960 and 1972, when remittances were over 30 per cent of the commercial balance deficit and over 20 per cent of imports, Greece experienced rapid economic growth without substantial unemployment or inflation. Further, his analyses indicate that spending on housing had a multiplier of 2.0 on domestic production and induced virtually no imports. There is some evidence that remittances can contribute to inflation in land and housing prices, as in Yemen and Egypt (Serageldin *et al.*, 1981; Adams, 1991: 72).

The effects of remittances on many other aspects of development are relatively unexplored. Few studies have examined systematically the effects of migration on international trade (see Russell and Teitelbaum, 1992) but limited evidence suggests they may be substantial. The presence of Turkish migrants abroad has increased demand for transport, banking, and communications services and stimulated business and tourist travel between Turkey and EC countries (Martin, 1991: 58). The presence of Indian migrants in the Arab Gulf and elsewhere has promoted the export of Indian goods and agricultural products. Cooperation between developing countries in construction and engineering services is thought to have benefitted from providers' links to their emigrant populations in countries purchasing such services (OECD, 1989: 29).

In many instances, remittances have had positive (and largely unmeasured) effects on investment in human capital through expansion of education. These are particularly notable in Sub-Saharan Africa, where literacy and enrolment rates have remained low, government resources for extending educational services are limited, and individual households and communities face significant education expenses. In villages of Kenya's Western and Nyanza provinces, nearly half of remittance income is used for school fees, while elsewhere in Kenya (as in the Sahel) remittances have been crucial to financing expansion of educational facilities in rural areas (Gould, 1988: 4.1.49; Bradshaw, 1988). In Zambia, migrants are substantially more likely than non-migrants to invest in education beyond the secondary level (Adepoju, 1984: 35-36), while in Greece comparison of expenditures before and after migration show a 180 per cent increase in spending for education (Glytsos, 1990: 21ff).

WHAT CAN GOVERNMENTS DO?

It has been stressed that remittances flow into a country as private transfers and that their uses are largely the result of decisions by migrants and their households. What, then, are the policy options for governments that want to increase official remittance flows and promote their uses for development? Most assessments agree that special programmes to increase remittances (e.g. special deposit accounts, two-tier exchange and interest rates, etc.) have had only limited effects. It would appear that macroeconomic, political, and institutional factors in the labour-sending country are far more influential.[9]

Straubhaar (1986) concluded, for example, that the level of remittances to Turkey have been determined by the stability of the Turkish exchange rate and the economy, not by special programmes. Wide divergence between formal and informal exchange rates has been implicated by a number of observers as a disincentive to repatriation of remittances through official channels.[10] Choucri (1985: 7, 6-22-25) postulated that, while only a small fraction of remittances to the Sudan in the 1980s were on the formal record, there was a large and effectively organized informal monetary market; her prescription was to adjust the official exchange rate and thereby promote the transfer of transactions from informal to official markets.

Similarly, Wahba (1989: 31-32) projected for Egypt that a 1 per cent decrease in the ratio of the parallel rate to the official rate would yield a 1.18 per cent increase in remittances, while a 10 per cent devaluation of the Egyptian pound would increase recorded remittances by at least 9 to 12 per cent. Empirically, the 37 per cent devaluation of the pound in May 1987 was followed by a 211 per cent increase in cash remittances. Devaluation of the Turkish lira in 1980 was also observed to increase remittances (Martin, 1991: 33).

A comparison of historical remittance flows to countries of southern Europe and North Africa also suggests that those countries with low rates of inflation and low black market exchange rate premiums were more successful in attracting official remittances than countries with high inflation and high black market premiums. Econometric analyses for these countries estimate that a 10 per cent increase in the black market premium results in a 3 per cent decline in official remittances per capita (Elbadawi and Rocha, 1992: 19, 30).[11]

There are also indications that expansion of national banking services to migrants abroad can effectively increase official remittance flows. In 1990, for example, the Philippine National Bank extended its services in Italy, Amsterdam, Germany, and Madrid and per capita labour income from Europe more than doubled over 1989 levels (Russell, 1991: 20). Expansion of the Portuguese banking system is also credited with observed increases in remittances and with capturing 90 per cent of remittances.

While it is increasingly clear what governments must do to attract remittances, the prescriptions for transforming these repatriated funds into effective development at home are less apparent. As Martin has noted, there are few empirical examples of successful schemes to promote remittance-financed development. After an extensive study of the subject, the US Commission for the Study of International Migration and Co-operative Economic Development (1990) concluded that, in addition to establishing mechanisms for the safe and rapid transfer of remittances, the most promising measures include targeting migrant-sending regions for investment; developing small businesses; and establishing national and regional development banks to channel remittances into productive investments.

There is still much to be learned from more careful analysis of those few countries that appear to have successfully incorporated migration into their rapid development strategies (e.g. Korea), as well as those where the contribution of migration to development has evolved over a much longer period of time (e.g. Italy, Spain). In the final analysis, the effects of migrants' remittances on development will probably be determined by many of the same factors that shape the decisions of foreign investors and development generally: a stable political environment; sensible macroeconomic policies; adequate investment in human capital; and the availability of institutional mechanisms for investment in activities with attractive rates of return.

The author wishes to thank Ms. Lourdes Pagaran, World Bank Graduate Scholar at the Massachusetts Institute of Technology, for her invaluable research assistance in organization and analysis of the remittance data files and preparation of the final tables.

NOTES

1. For a fuller discussion of these factors, see Russell, 1986.

2. For example, some countries report "worker remittances" in a separate line; others aggregate "private unrequited transfers". Some include only cash transfers; others include the value of in-kind transfers. Remittances below a certain amount may not be reported, or reporting may be limited to transactions with selected countries. To illustrate, labour income credits for the US include only receipts from US residents employed temporarily in Germany, Canada, and the United Kingdom, while debits reflect only earnings of Mexican, Canadian, and West Indian residents employed temporarily in the US, together with estimated wages of foreign students in the US (Pagaran, 1992).

3. Workers' remittances (reported in lines 35 and 36 of the BOP statistics) and migrant transfers (lines 33 and 34) are subsets of "unrequited transfers"; labour income (lines 27 and 28) is reported under "goods, services, and income".

4. Credits are inflows of financial assets. These are offset by debits (outflows), the adjusted global values of which are shown in Table 2 (page 285) for purposes of comparison. The reasons why credits do not equal debits are complex, poorly understood, and beyond the scope of discussion in this paper.

5. Petroleum exports in 1984 were valued at US$ 240 billion; the total average annual value of worldwide coffee exports in 1982-84 was US$ 9 billion (World Bank estimates).

6. The data in Table 3 have been adjusted as discussed above. Net transfers to developing countries were US$ 36.7 billion in 1990, but this figure may be skewed by incomplete reporting of debits. For this analysis, 25 out of 193 countries are considered "developed" based upon their classification as high income countries in the World Bank's 1991 *World Development Report*. The remaining 168 countries are considered "developing".

7. This section draws upon findings reported in Russell *et al.*, 1990 and Russell, 1992.

8. Aggregate averages are for migrants and migrant households surveyed in Mali, Senegal, and Mauritania. Data for certain expenditures (notably taxes and school fees) vary significantly by individual country.

9. Levels of and fluctuations in economic activity in host countries have also been shown to be important determinants of remittance flows, but

these are not under the control of sending country policy makers. Migrants' length of stay abroad is also an important determinant of remittance levels, which tend to decline over time (Swamy, 1981; Elbadawi and Rocha, 1992). However, unless labour-sending governments are willing or able to promote short-term, rotational migration, this factor, too, may be beyond their control.

10. Generally, interest rate differentials between host and home countries have not been demonstrated to have a significant impact on remittance flows. Elbadawi and Rocha (1992: 10; 34) discuss evidence on this point and note one possible exception: a scheme by which deposits of Turkish workers to the Dresdner Bank in Germany were transferred to Turkey through the capital account and may have succeeded in mobilizing remittances. They caution, however, that the result may be to divert resources from the current to the capital account, with adverse results for debt repayment capacity and creditworthiness.

11. Elbadawi and Rocha define the black market premium as the percentage difference between the black market exchange rate and the official exchange rate. Their analyses are of Algeria, Morocco, Portugal, Tunisia, Turkey, and Yugoslavia.

BIBLIOGRAPHY

Abu Gabal, A.
1984 *Migration of Sudanese: Causes and Effects on Sudan's Economy*, Faisal Islamic Bank Publications.

Adams, R. H.
1991 The Effects of International Remittances on Poverty, Inequality, and Development in Rural Egypt, Research Report 86, International Food Policy Research Institute, Washington, D.C.

1992 The Effects of Internal and International Migration and Remittances on Income Distribution in Rural Pakistan, International Food Policy Research Institute, Washington, D.C., Report prepared for the U.S. Agency for International Development, mimeo, June.

Adepoju, A.
1984 "Migration and Rural Opportunities in Nigeria", *Labour and Society*, 9(1): 29-49.

Al-Ghul, A. al-Sharif
1982 *Mulahathat an al-Higrat al-Kharagiyya* (Observations on External Migration), Council on Economic and Social Research, Khartoum.

Bradshaw, Y. W.
1988 "Urbanization, Personal Income, and Physical Quality of Life: The Case of Kenya", *Studies in Comparative International Development*, 13: 15-40, Winter.

Burki, S. J.
1984 "International Migration: Implications for Labor Exporting Countries", *The Middle East Journal*, 38(4): 668-684.

Chilivumbo, A.
1985 *Migration and Uneven Rural Development in Africa: The Case of Zambia*, University Press of America, Lanham, Maryland, USA.

Choucri, N.
1985 A Study of Sudanese Nationals Working Abroad, unpublished, Massachusetts Institute of Technology, Cambridge, Massachusetts.

Condé, J., P. Diagne, *et al.*
1986 "South-North International Migrations, a Case Study: Malian, Mauritanian and Senegalese Migrants from Senegal River Valley to France", Development Centre of the OECD, Paris.

The Economist
1991 "GATT and Services: Second Best", August 3rd.

Elbadawi, I. A., and R. Rocha
1992 Determinants of Expatriate Workers' Remittances in North Africa and Europe, The World Bank, Washington, D.C., draft, June.

Findley, S. E.
1989 Choosing Between African and French Destinations: The Role of Family and Community Factors in Migration in the Senegal River Valley, Paper presented at Département de Démographie, Université de Montréal, March 14.

Galaleldin, M. al-Awad
1979 Migration of Sudanese Abroad, Council on Economic and Social Research, Khartoum.

Gilani, I., M. F. Khan and M. Iqbal
1981 Labor Migration from Pakistan to the Middle East and its Impact on the Domestic Economy, The World Bank, Washington, D.C.

Glytsos, N.
1990 Measuring the Income Effects of Migrant Remittances: An Empirical Analysis for Greece, Centre for Planning and Economic Research, Athens, mimeo, September.

Gould, W.T.S.
1988 Urban-Rural Return Migration in Western Province, Kenya, African Population Conference, sponsored by the International Union for the Scientific Study of Population (IUSSP), Union for African Population Studies (UAPS), and the Central Statistical Office, Dakar, Senegal, November 7-12.

Keely, C., and B. N. Tran
1989 "Remittances from Labor Migration: Evaluations, Performance, and Implications," *International Migration Review*, 23(3).

Martin, P. L.
1991 *The Unfinished Story: Turkish Labour Migration to Western Europe*, International Labour Organisation, Geneva.

Oberai, A. S., and H. K. M. Singh
1980 "Migration, Remittances and Rural Development: Findings of a Case Study in the Indian Punjab", *International Labor Review*, 19(2): 229-241.

OECD
1989 *Trade in Services and Developing Countries*, Organization for Economic Cooperation and Development, Paris.

Pagaran, L.
1992 Remittances from International Migration, mimeo, Massachusetts Institute of Technology, Department of Political Science, Cambridge, Massachusetts.

Palmer, I.
1985 *The Impact of Male Out-Migration on Women in Farming*, Kumarian Press, West Hartford, Connecticut.

Papademetriou, D. G., and P. L. Martin, eds.
1991 *The Unsettled Relationship: Labor Migration and Economic Development*, Greenwood Press, New York.

Roberts, A.
1976 *A History of Zambia*, Heinemann, London.

Russell, M.
1984 "Beyond Remittances: The Redistribution of Cash in Swazi Society", *Journal of Modern African Studies* (U.K.), 22: 595-615.

Russell, Sharon Stanton
1986 "Remittances from International Migration: A Review in Perspective", *World Development*, 14(6): 677-696.

1991 Population and Development in the Philippines: An Update. The World Bank, Asia Country Department II, Population and Human Resources Division, Washington, D.C.

Russell, Sharon Stanton; K. Jacobsen and W. D. Stanley
1990 International Migration and Development in Sub-Saharan Africa, Volume I, Overview, World Bank Discussion Paper, No. 101, The World Bank, Washington, D.C.

Russell, Sharon Stanton, and M. S. Teitelbaum
1992 International Migration and International Trade, The World Bank, World Bank Discussion Paper No. 160, Washington, D.C.

Serageldin, I., *et al.*
1981 Manpower and International Labor Migration in the Middle East and North Africa, The World Bank, Technical Assistance and Special Studies Division, Washington, D.C., June 30.

Straubhaar, T.
1986 "The Causes of International Migration - A Demand Determined Approach", *International Migration Review*, 20(4): 835-855.

Swamy, G.
1981 International Migrant Workers' Remittances: Issues and Prospects, World Bank Staff Working Paper No. 481, Washington, D.C., August.

US Commission for the Study of International Migration and Co-operative Economic Development
1990 *Unauthorized Migration: An Economic Development Response*, U.S. Government Printing Office, Washington, D.C.

Wahba, S.
1989 Workers' Remittances as a Source of Foreign Earnings: A Study in the Determinants of Recorded Remittances in Egypt, International Monetary Fund, Middle Eastern Department, Washington, D.C., mimeo, October.

World Bank
1984 *Fourth Education Project in the Kingdom of Lesotho*, The World Bank, Washington, D.C.

TABLE 1

DISTRIBUTION OF REMITTANCE CREDITS, WORLD TOTAL, 1980-1990 (in million current U.S. dollars)

Inflows	1980	1981	1982	1983	1984	1985	1986	1987	1988	1989	1990
Workers' remittances	29,095	27,908	27,822	27,710	27,728	26,385	28,876	31,775	32,264	36,510	43,811
Migrants' transfers	2,176	2,529	2,281	2,108	2,063	1,938	2,528	3,515	4,525	5,543	5,437
Labour income	11,079	10,651	11,282	11,422	10,735	10,699	13,470	16,108	17,971	18,831	21,892
Total	42,350	41,088	41,384	41,240	40,526	39,021	44,874	51,399	54,761	60,884	71,141

PER CENT SHARE OF EACH COMPONENT IN WORLD TOTAL REMITTANCE CREDITS, 1980-1990

	1980	1981	1982	1983	1984	1985	1986	1987	1988	1989	1990
Workers' remittances	69	68	67	67	68	68	64	62	59	60	62
Migrants' transfers	5	6	6	5	5	5	6	7	8	9	8
Labour income	26	26	27	28	27	27	30	31	33	31	31

Source: World Bank International Economics Department.

N.B. Percentage share columns may not total to 100 because of rounding.

TABLE 2

DISTRIBUTION OF REMITTANCE DEBITS, WORLD TOTAL, 1980-1990 (in million current U.S. dollars)

Outflows	1980	1981	1982	1983	1984	1985	1986	1987	1988	1989	1990
Workers' remittances	19,592	19,641	19,608	18,897	17,633	17,104	18,066	19,535	21,696	23,452	28,304
Migrants' transfers	1,231	1,320	1,274	1,148	1,272	1,228	1,310	1,698	1,809	2,014	2,067
Labour income	11,792	11,289	11,573	11,574	11,317	11,628	14,976	18,785	21,414	23,038	29,212
Total	32,615	32,250	32,455	31,619	30,222	29,960	34,352	40,019	44,919	38,504	59,583

PER CENT SHARE OF EACH COMPONENT IN WORLD TOTAL REMITTANCE DEBITS, 1980-1990

	1980	1981	1982	1983	1984	1985	1986	1987	1988	1989	1990
Workers' remittances	60	61	60	60	58	57	53	49	48	48	48
Migrants' transfers	4	4	4	4	4	4	4	4	4	4	4
Labour income	36	35	36	37	37	39	44	47	48	48	49

Source: World Bank International Economics Department.

N.B. Percentage share columns may not total to 100 because of rounding.

TABLE 3

A. NET GLOBAL REMITTANCES (US$ millions)

	1980	1981	1982	1983	1984	1985	1986	1987	1988	1989	1990
Net Global Credit	9,735	8,838	8,929	9,621	10,304	9,061	10,522	11,380	9,842	12,380	11,558
Global Credit	42,350	41,088	41,384	41,240	40,526	39,021	44,874	51,399	54,761	60,884	71,141
Global Debit	32,615	32,250	32,455	31,619	30,222	29,960	34,352	40,019	44,919	48,504	59,583

DIRECTION OF REMITTANCE FLOWS: DEVELOPING AND DEVELOPED WORLD 1/ (by category)

B. NET WORKERS' REMITTANCES

Region	1980	1981	1982	1983	1984	1985	1986	1987	1988	1989	1990
Developing	20,110	19,325	19,239	19,444	20,461	19,387	21,650	24,195	24,251	27,958	33,737
Credit	25,336	24,698	24,682	24,787	24,882	23,444	25,420	27,898	27,990	31,884	38,599
Debit	5,225	5,374	5,443	5,343	4,422	4,057	3,771	3,703	3,740	3,926	4,862
Developed	(10,607)	(11,057)	(11,026)	(10,631)	(10,366)	(10,107)	(10,840)	(11,955)	(13,682)	(14,900)	(18,230)
Credit	3,760	3,210	3,140	2,923	2,846	2,941	3,455	3,877	4,274	4,626	5,213
Debit	14,367	14,268	14,166	13,554	13,211	13,047	14,295	15,832	17,956	19,526	23,442

1/Includes 24 countries classified as high-income economies plus Saudi Arabia. Until 1991, Saudi Arabia falls under the high-income category but has been reclassified as upper-middle-income economy in 1992 (see World Development Report 1992). It seems more realistic, however, to include Saudi Arabia under the high-income category in light of substantial remittance flows from the country to several labour-exporting economies in Asia and the Middle East.

Source: World Bank International Economics Department.

continued overleaf

TABLE 3 (continued)

C. NET MIGRANTS' TRANSFERS

Region	1980	1981	1982	1983	1984	1985	1986	1987	1988	1989	1990
Developing	(147)	(176)	(189)	(197)	(145)	(94)	(46)	38	208	130	43
Credit	230	247	182	151	155	131	205	254	437	346	212
Debit	377	424	371	348	300	225	251	216	228	216	168
Developed	1.092	1.385	1.195	1.156	936	804	1.264	1,779	2,507	3,400	3,326
Credit	1.946	2.281	2.098	1.957	1,908	1.807	2.323	3,261	4,088	5.197	5,225
Debit	854	897	903	800	972	1,003	1.059	1,482	1,581	1,797	1,899

D. NET LABOUR INCOME

Region	1980	1981	1982	1983	1984	1985	1986	1987	1988	1989	1990
Developing	1.161	1,693	2.016	2.360	2.130	1.756	2.001	2.222	2,502	2,910	2,923
Credit	3.713	4.019	4.283	4.688	4,332	4.056	4.562	5.237	5,654	6,161	7,144
Debit	2.551	2.326	2.267	2.328	2,202	2.300	2.561	3,015	3,152	3.251	4,220
Developed	(1.874)	(2.330)	(2.307)	(2.512)	(2.712)	(2.686)	(3.506)	(4,899)	(5,944)	(7.117)	(10,243)
Credit	7.366	6.632	6.999	6.733	6.403	6.642	8.909	10,872	12.317	12.670	14,748
Debit	9.240	8.963	9.306	9.245	9,115	9,328	12.415	15.770	18,261	19,787	24,992

E. NET TRANSFERS TO DEVELOPING COUNTRIES, 1980-90

Region	1980	1981	1982	1983	1984	1985	1986	1987	1988	1989	1990
Developing	21.125	20.841	21.066	21.607	22.445	21,049	23.604	26,454	26.961	30.998	36.704
Developed	(11.389)	(12.003)	(12.138)	(11.986)	(12.141)	(11.988)	(13.082)	(15.074)	(17,119)	(18.618)	(25,147)

Source: World Bank International Economics Department.

[30]

Environmental Concerns and International Migration

Graeme Hugo
University of Adelaide

This article focuses on international migration occurring as a result of environmental changes and processes. It briefly reviews attempts to conceptualize environment-related migration and then considers the extent to which environmental factors have been and may be significant in initiating migration. Following is an examination of migration as an independent variable in the migration-environment relationship. Finally, ethical and policy dimensions are addressed.

Migration on a permanent or temporary basis has always been one of the most important survival strategies adopted by people in the face of natural or human-caused disasters. However, our knowledge of the complex two-way relationship involving environmental change as both a cause and consequence of migration remains limited. Moreover, how migration and environmental concerns interact and impinge upon economic development, social change, and conflict is little understood. In a context where global environmental stress and degradation have accelerated and unprecedented numbers of the world's population are seeing migration as an option, the need for research in this area is considerable. In recent years there has been an increase in the attention directed at the relationship between migration and the environment among both researchers and policymakers, especially in the lead up to, and aftermath of, the United Nations Conference on Environment and Development (UNCED) held in Rio de Janiero in 1992 (*e.g.*, Kibreab, 1994; Suhrke, 1992, 1994; Richmond, 1993; United Nations, 1994; The Population Institute, 1993; IOM, 1992). Chapter 5 of Agenda 21, which was adopted by UNCED, recognized the need to develop and disseminate knowledge of the links between changes in demographic processes like migration and achievement of sustainable development (United Nations, 1993).

Historically, the vast bulk of migration caused by environmental change has occurred within national boundaries, as have the environmental effects initiated by population movements. Nevertheless, the international dimensions of this relationship have been neglected until recently. Moreover, it is argued here that this dimension is of increasing scale and significance in concert with the accelerating pace of globalization processes. Accordingly, the present paper focuses upon international migration occurring as a result of environmental changes and processes and the implications of increasing levels of population movement between countries for the environment. We begin with a brief review of some attempts to conceptualize environment-related migration and then consider the extent to which environmental factors have been, and are likely to be, significant in initiating international migration. This is attempted through a consideration of the environment as both a direct and a contributory factor in causing such migration, especially South-North international migration. Attention is then focused on migration as an independent variable in the migration-environment relationship, and the environmental consequences of international population movements are discussed. Finally, some of the ethical and policy dimensions of emerging international migration-environment trends and processes are addressed.

CONCEPTUALIZING THE RELATIONSHIP BETWEEN MIGRATION AND ENVIRONMENTAL CHANGES

The migration literature is replete with typologies which differentiate migrants and migrations according to the relative permanency of the move, the distance traversed, the nature of the boundaries crossed, the causes of the move, the characteristics of the movers, etc. One of the pervasive distinctions made between types of population movements is that between voluntary and forced migrations which dates back 60 years to Fairchild's (1925) migration classification. Perhaps the most frequently quoted typology of migration is that of Peterson (1958), in which one of the most fundamental divisions employed is the degree to which a move is "forced." However, the distinction between voluntary and involuntary migration is not as clear cut as it would appear at first glance. As Speare (1974:89) points out,

> In the strictest sense migration can be considered to be involuntary only when a person is physically transported from a country and has no opportunity to escape from those transporting him. Movement under threat, even the immediate threat to life, contains a voluntary element, as long as there is an option to escape to another part of the country, go into hiding or to remain and hope to avoid persecution.

On the other hand some scholars of migration argue that much of the population mobility which is conventionally seen as being voluntary occurs in situations which in fact the migrants have little or no choice. Amin (1974:100), for example, in his discussion of migration in Western Africa states that

> A comparative costs and benefits analysis, conducted at the individual level of the migrant, has no significance. In fact it only gives the appearance of objective rationality to a 'choice' (that of the migrant) which in reality does not exist because, in a given system, he (sic) has no alternatives.

Indeed the early typology developed by Peterson recognized this degree of overlap between voluntary and involuntary movement and distinguished an intermediate category. He differentiated between ". . . *impelled* migration when the migrants retain some power to decide whether or not to leave and *forced* migration when they do not have this power" (Peterson, 1958:261). These, in turn, are separated from free migration in which the will of the migrants is the decisive element initiating movement.

Population mobility is probably best viewed as being arranged along a continuum ranging from totally voluntary migration, in which the choice and will of the migrants is the overwhelmingly decisive element encouraging people to move, to totally forced migration, where the migrants are faced with death if they remain in their present place of residence (*see* Figure 1). The extremes in fact rarely occur, and most mobility is located along the continuum. The present paper is concerned with moves toward the forced end of this continuum.

There is also some diversity in the literature with respect to what particular types of involuntary migration can be identified. Much of this centers around the issue of defining the term refugee. While the term refugee migration in some cases is used as a synonym for involuntary migration, others apply it only to a very restricted subset of all such movements. The 1967 United Nations Protocol on Refugees considers a refugee as "every person who, owing to a well-founded fear of being persecuted for reasons of race, religion, nationality, membership of a particular social group or political opinion, is outside the country of his nationality and is unable or, owing to such fear, is unwilling to avail himself of the protection of that country" (Keely, 1981:6). However, this has been modified and extended in practice by both the United Nations High Commission for Refugees (UNHCR) and individual Third World countries and regions. Nobel (1985:44), after an exhaustive discussion of contemporary refugee determination in Third World countries concludes that the common elements can be listed as follows:

1) Cases of well-founded fear of being persecuted for any of the reasons mentioned in the Geneva Convention and/or the Statute for the Office of UNHCR.
2) Cases where lives, safety and freedom are threatened by events seriously disturbing public orders like external aggression, occupation, foreign domination, massive violations of human rights or generalized violence in the whole or part of the country of origin.

This definition, however, still only recognizes migrants who are forced to move because of political pressures or conflicts. Other commentators have adopted wider definitions of refugee and forced migrations. A good example of such a definition is that provided by Olson (1979:130).

> Refugees differ from other, spontaneous or sponsored migrants, largely in the circumstances of their movement out of one area to another, and the effects these have on them in the settlement and adjustment phases of their relocation. Refugees are forced to leave their homes because of a change in their environment which makes it impossible to continue life as they have known it. They are coerced by an external force to leave their homes and go elsewhere.

This definition stresses the involuntary, forced nature of the move, the 'uprooting' suddenness of most refugee moves and the externality to the mover of the force or forces impelling the move. It also implies a substantial degree of powerlessness among the movers in the decision to move and selection of

FIGURE 1. A Simple Continuum of International Migration

destination. There is no consideration in this definition of the distance the refugees move or whether or not they cross an international boundary, although Olson points out "these spatial factors do affect refugees' adjustment after flight." This definition is clearly more holistic and sees refugee moves as a subset of all population mobility rather than of international migration.

Olson's definition is also broader than that of the UNHCR with respect to the nature of the external force or forces, the threat or presence of which impels refugee movements. Again the UNHCR definition is somewhat restrictive in that it refers only to persecution, or fear of persecution, as initiating refugee movement. Keely (1981:6) points out that this excludes people fleeing the ravages of war, and who are usually considered refugees, although the broader definitions in wider use usually include such groups. More commonly, persons who are displaced by civil conflict or war are also categorized as refugees. Some writers, however, have extended the recognition of forces which create refugee movements even further and go beyond the conflicts created by human agents to include people displaced from their home areas by natural disasters. Olson (1979:130), for example, identifies the following five types of external compulsions that alone or in concert create refugees:

- physical dangers (*e.g.*, floods, volcanic eruptions, etc.);
- economic insufficiency (*e.g.*, drought, famine);
- religious persecution;
- ethnic persecution;
- ideological persecution.

More recently the term environmental refugee has gained wide usage (Hinnawi, 1985; Jacobsen, 1988) to refer to people who have been forced to leave their home area because of environmental disruption. Such refugees, however, are not officially recognized by national governments or international agencies, and hence the term environmental migrants would seem preferable. This includes migrants who are forced to flee their home areas by the onset of (or fear of) a natural calamity or disaster, would incorporate the first two categories of Olson's classification of external compulsions to migration listed above, and covers not only the migrations initiated by the sudden and violent onset of floods, earthquakes, volcanic eruptions, etc., but also the "silent violence" (Spitz, 1978) of drought, famine and the onset of severe food shortage associated with the gradual degradation of environments.

Refugees, as conventionally defined, are distinguished from environmental migrants by the fact that the overt force impelling migration is conflict or the threat of conflict (Zolberg and Suhrke, 1984:2) – it has human rather than environmental origins. It must be stressed, however, that we are referring here to the immediate cause which triggers the forced migration, not necessarily the deeper underlying long-term determinants. For example, many natural disasters have their root causes in long- term political, social, economic or agricultural practices or policies. Nevertheless, in both types of forced movement, external pressures are paramount in initiating moves – without the sudden introduction of particular external forces the move would not have occurred. As Kunz (1973:130) points out,

> It is the reluctance to uproot oneself, and the absence of positive original motivations to settle elsewhere, which characterizes all refugee decisions and distinguishes the refugee from the voluntary migrants.

In fact, Kunz goes on to recognize two distinct "kinetic" types of refugee movement in which the chief distinction is the strength of the external forces impinging upon the potential refugee: 1) anticipatory refugee movements involve people moving before the deterioration of the military or political situation becomes overwhelming, preventing an orderly departure; and 2) acute refugee movements, where the emphasis is on unplanned flight en masse or in bursts of individual or group escapes in which the overwhelming objective is to reach a haven of safety. This differentiation is equally applicable to environmental migrants, and Richmond (1993) has divided environmentally induced migration into "proactive" and "reactive" movement on similar grounds.

Some have argued that it is best not to refer to migrants forced to move for environmental reasons as refugees, given the specific legal connotations of the term refugee (*e.g.*, Hugo and Chan, 1990). Nevertheless, as Richmond (1993:2) correctly points out, "the reality of external and internal migration induced mainly, or partly, by environmental factors cannot be denied." One major difference between migration induced by political and civil conflict and that caused by environmental factors is that it is rare that the latter affects an entire nation, so environmentally displaced persons can usually find refuge within their national boundaries. On the other hand, people fleeing persecution often are forced to flee from the entire jurisdiction of national governments. Another significant difference is that while political refugee movement is often an uncomplicated response to fear of persecution, environmental migration is often the result of a complex set of multiple pressures of which an environmental event is only the proximate cause.

Richmond (1993:11) argues persuasively that it is necessary to go beyond more descriptive typologies of environmentally induced migration and to understand the dynamic interaction of the multiple causal factors that can generate such movement. Whether or not environmentally induced migration occurs, the scale and composition of the movement and where it is directed will be shaped by many elements: predisposing conditions such as the nature of the biophysical environment; structural constraints; facilitating factors; precipitating events; and feedback effects of the migration.

Richmond's model, a simplified version of which is presented in Figure 2, recognizes first of all that certain contexts are more susceptible to environmental disruptions likely to force outmigration than others. These, for example, would include: ecologically fragile ecosystems which, when subject to excessive cropping, forest removal or other human use impacts, become less productive; areas at high risk of natural disaster – earthquake zones, low lying areas subject to inundation, etc.; marginal agricultural or pastoral areas subject to frequent drought; and areas of poverty where the residents do not have the accumulated reserves to prevent, ameliorate, or cope with the onset of a natural disaster.

Hence the predisposing factors for environmental migration can be environmental but also are related to population pressure upon natural resources, the way in which the environment is being exploited by people, and the wealth of the occupants of the area. In general, these predisposing conditions are more likely to occur in less developed than in more developed countries.

Environmentally induced migration is likely to be precipitated by a particular environment-related event which effectively forces people to move. Table 1 is a list of factors identified by Richmond (1993) as being likely to precipitate reactive migration which has direct or indirect environmental implications. He stresses that these factors are not independent of one another. Whether or not an event-producing disruption to the environment actually produces migration, however, is partly influenced by the predisposing conditions mentioned earlier. It also will be shaped by a range of constraints and facilitators to migration which exist in the area affected. These include the existence or lack of escape routes not only in the form of transport networks but also kinship and social networks which mean that some environmental migrants can move to an area where they have relatives and friends who can support them. The presence of such networks undoubtedly acts as a facilitator to such movement while their absence would constrain movement.

Richmond (1993) stresses the importance of feedback effects in consideration of environmentally induced migration. The migration itself may have positive effects on the origin area through reduction of pressure of population on the local environment and hence reduce the likelihood of the occurrence of an environmental disaster. Similarly, environmental policies introduced as a result of those disasters may influence migration. Hence, in Indonesia the erosion of uplands causing flooding and siltation in lowlands has resulted in a policy of sedentarization whereby people who have practiced a type of slash and burn, shifting cultivation in the upland areas have been resettled in sedentary agricultural communities in lowland areas. This has affected some 4 million people (Hugo, 1988).

Conceptualizing environmentally induced migration as a subset of forced migrations draws attention to the neglect of this type of movement by

FIGURE 2. A Simple Model of Environmentally Induced Migration

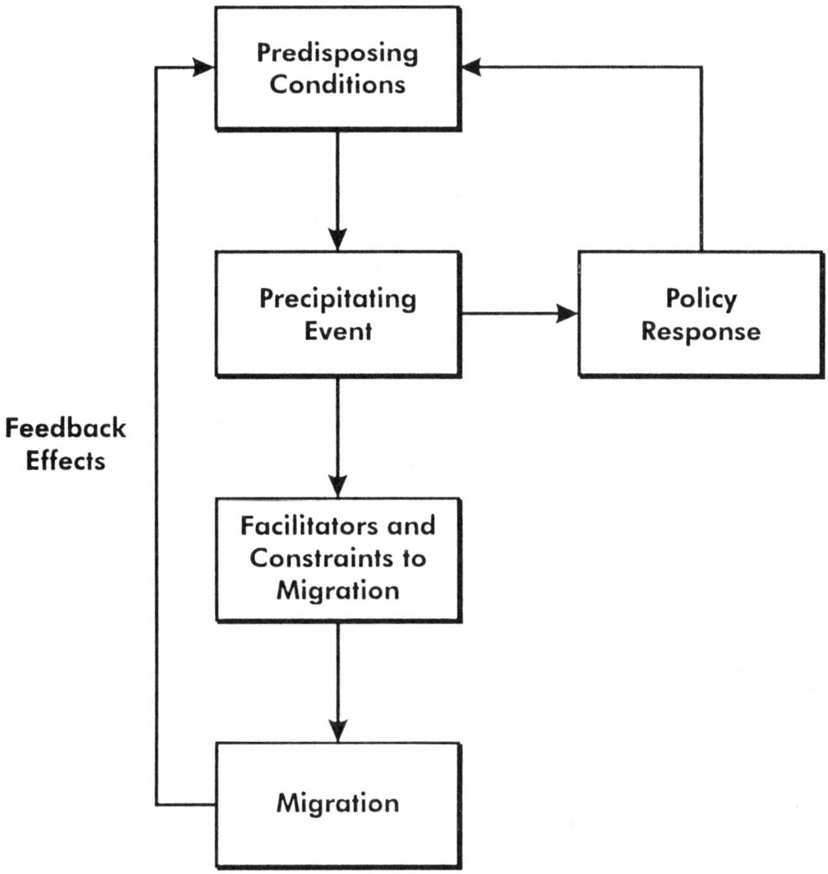

Source: Modified and simplified from ideas in Richmond (1993).

researchers and policymakers alike. Jacobsen (1988:6, 1989:30) summarizes the situation thus:

> Most governments do not recognize environmental decline as a legitimate cause of refugee movements, choosing to ignore the issue. Neither the U.S. State Department nor the UN High Commissioner for Refugees for example collects data on this problem. Yet the number of environmental refugees – estimated by the author to be at least 10 million – rivals that of officially recognized refugees and is sure to overtake this latter group in the decades to come.

While the last point may well be overstated, the thrust of these strong remarks must be accepted – researchers and policymakers have neglected the signifi-

TABLE 1
TYPOLOGY OF ENVIRONMENTALLY RELATED DISASTERS

Naturally Induced Disasters (NIDs)		
Hurricanes	Tornadoes	Whirlwinds
Earthquakes	Volcanic Eruptions	Avalanches
Floods (freshwater)	Floods (saltwater)	Hail and Snow Storms
Fires	Electric Storms	Lightning
Droughts	Famines	Plagues
Technologically Induced Disasters (TIDs)		
Chemical	Nuclear	Oil Spills
Pollution (air)	Pollution (water)	Pollution (soil)
Explosions	Building Collapse	Rail or Airplane Crash
Dams (floods, etc.)	Mining Accidents	Power Cuts
Factory Accidents	Soil Exhaustion	Urban Dereliction
Economically Induced Disasters (EIDs)		
Deforestation	Crop Failure	Fishery Exhaustion
Mineral Exhaustion	Species Extinction	Human Redundancy
Population Clearances	Relocation	Structural Adjustment
Politically Induced Disasters (PIDs)		
War (external)	War (internal)	Terrorism
Apartheid	Ethnic Cleansing	Holocaust
Exile	Persecution	Rights Violations
Totalitarianism	Anarchy	Extremism/Intolerance
Socially Induced Disasters (SIDs)		
Ecological Extremism	Animal Rights Activism	Green Crusaders
Fanaticism	Excommunication	Jihad
Class War	Shunning	Boycott

Source: Richmond (1993).

cance (both in numerical and human suffering terms) of environmentally forced migrations.

Obviously one of the major barriers to research in environmentally induced migration is the lack of available relevant data. This is understandable since collection of data is accorded low priority in societies experiencing environmental crises. As Dirks (1980) has pointed out:

> While the biology of starvation has been analyzed in considerable detail, there exists little systematic knowledge about social behavior. The imbalance has been attributed to certain stumbling blocks impeding field study: chaotic conditions, the priority of the relief missions, the repugnance of seeking data amidst human suffering.

As has been reviewed elsewhere (Hugo, 1984:12–14) a number of studies have employed innovative, imaginative and sensitive approaches to collect data in such crisis situations where conventional sources have been absent or severely deficient. Nevertheless, it is important that due consideration be given in areas susceptible to such movement to inclusion of relevant questions regarding environmentally induced population mobility in censuses and other large-scale data collection initiatives. Too often the questions included reflect international recommendations and not the specific local conditions and needs of local people.

ENVIRONMENTAL FACTORS AS A CAUSE OF MIGRATION

The response of leaving an area on a permanent or temporary basis in the face of a life threatening environmental crisis is, of course, eminently rational and has been a most important survival strategy throughout human history. However, the situation in the mid-1990s with respect to such movements would appear to differ somewhat from the historical experience in a number of ways: the scale and pace of environmental change has increased substantially; differences between countries in ability to cope with these changes have increased; whereas in the past the migration destination options for environmental migrants have overwhelmingly been to move within their country of origin, international destinations are of increasing significance. These propositions will be expanded upon in this section.

Considering first the environmental forces impelling acute or reactive migration, a global survey of natural disasters for the period 1947 to 1980 found that the overall number of disasters is increasing over time and that a disproportionately large share of all lives lost (86%) in such disasters occurred in Asia (Shah, 1983). Since 1980 environmental pressures have continued to increase due to increased population growth leading to greater consumption of resources, pressure on agricultural land, pollution, etc., increased industrialization, and massive technological changes increasing the capacity of people to reshape environments. While it is true that global awareness of the need to adopt sustainable development policies and practices has also increased, there can be no doubt that the incidence of environmental disasters also has increased as have the associated population displacements.

To substantiate this contention we focus on the Asian region, which contains more than half of the world's population and is experiencing rapid economic and social change. The *United Nations Disaster Research Organization News* for the period 1976–1994 was scanned for reports of all major environmental catastrophes that occurred in Asia over the last two decades along with the volume of associated environmentally induced migration. While these data are far from comprehensive, they are indicative of the scale of the phenomenon of such population movement, although it must be reiterated that the vast bulk of the refugees were resettled or otherwise accommodated within their own nations. The data are summarized in Figure 3 and show that over the last two decades there has been a trend toward increasing numbers of people displaced by environmental disasters in Asia, although there is considerable variation from year to year in the numbers involved. Figure 4 shows the numbers of Asian environmental refugees by country. As would be expected, the largest

FIGURE 3. **Asia: Population Displaced by Natural Disasters, 1976–1994**

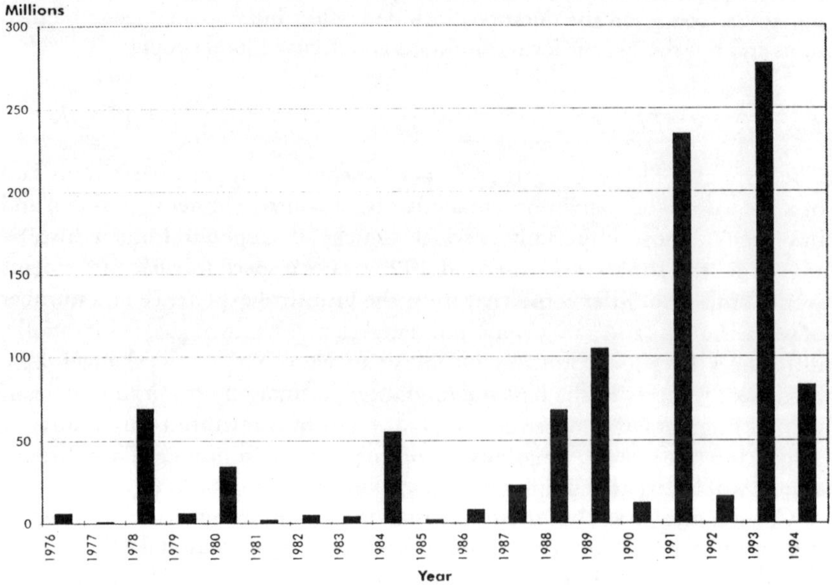

Source: Compiled from *UNDRO News*, 1976–1994.

nations of China and India (with 37.8% of the world's population) dominate, although the incidence in the much smaller nation of Bangladesh (1995 population of 119.2 million) is very substantial.

Nevertheless, some of the largest displacements of environmental refugees occurred in the largest countries in Asia. In 1976, China experienced its worst earthquake since 1556. Centered on Tangshan, some 730,000 people were rendered homeless (Breeze, 1980:103). In 1994, one-fifth of China's uplands were idled by floods and drought, creating a mass migration to urban areas (Kaye, 1994). The construction of China's Three Gorges Dam will displace 1.3 million people (Huus, 1994). In Bangladesh, frequent cyclones, floods and tidal surges have taken considerable toll of human life as well as causing massive population shifts.

> Whenever natural calamities like floods hit Bangladesh, people migrate from the countryside to urban areas. An unusual increase of beggars and people looking for work in cities and towns is part of the aftermath of drought and floods. This year, five successive floods submerged nearly 14 million acres, destroying the homes and hopes of over 30 million people. They claimed 900 lives, 85,000 head of cattle, and washed away half a million homes. (*Population: UNFPA Newsletter*, 10, II, November 1984:2)

In India alone it is reported (Kayastha and Yadara, 1985:79) that 15 million people are affected by natural disasters each year. This involves some 2.5 million being rendered homeless and 4 million having to migrate elsewhere to seek food and shelter.

It is apparent that environmentally induced migrations are especially marked in Africa. As Jacobsen (1988:11) has pointed out:

> Of all the continents, Africa, a land where poor soils and variable rainfall pose a harsh climate for agriculture, has spawned the most environmental refugees. Most came from the Sahel, a belt that spans several agro-ecological zones and stretches west to east across some nine countries from Mauritania and Senegal on into the Sudan. Desertification is accelerating in the Sahel, the world's largest area threatened by the wholesale loss of arable land.

The droughts of 1968–1973 and 1982–1984 led to millions of environmental refugees. In the first of these, there were a million environmental refugees in Burkina Faso alone. Table 2 shows the numbers displaced by the end of the second drought.

With reference to the simple model depicted in Figure 2, there are a number of developments in contemporary less developed countries (LDCs) which have exacerbated the predisposing conditions and increased the incidence of precipitating events for environmentally induced migration:

- Population growth has continued to increase pressure on agricultural land although significant fertility declines have occurred in Asia and Latin America and in limited parts of Africa. This has forced more people to settle in and cultivate marginal areas, making them more subject to flooding, erosion, desertification and other environmental degradation.
- Continuation of high incidence of poverty has meant that both individuals and nations have not the resources to initiate environmentally sustainable practices. For many there is a total preoccupation with survival.
- Concerted efforts to increase food production through the green revolution have seen some spectacular increases in output, but often at the expense of environmental concerns. Hence, clearing practices, heavy use of fertilizers, herbicides and pesticides have all often had undesirable environmental outcomes.
- Many LDCs have liberalized their economies to encourage foreign investment, especially in manufacturing, and multinational companies have taken advantage of cheap labor to establish factories. In many cases, environmental controls on such developments are less comprehensive than in more developed countries (MDCs), and certainly the policing of existing regulations is usually weaker so that environmental pollution from such activity can be considerable.
- In many LDCs the ability to enact legislation for environmental sustainability and to police existing legislation is restricted by limited infrastructure and corruption. Accordingly, it is difficult to control deforestation, air pollution, water pollution, land degradation, etc., in the face of increasing pressures on exploitation of the environment created by growing population, increasing involvement of foreign enterprises, etc.

FIGURE 4. **Asia: Number of Persons Displaced by Environmental Disasters, 1976–1994**

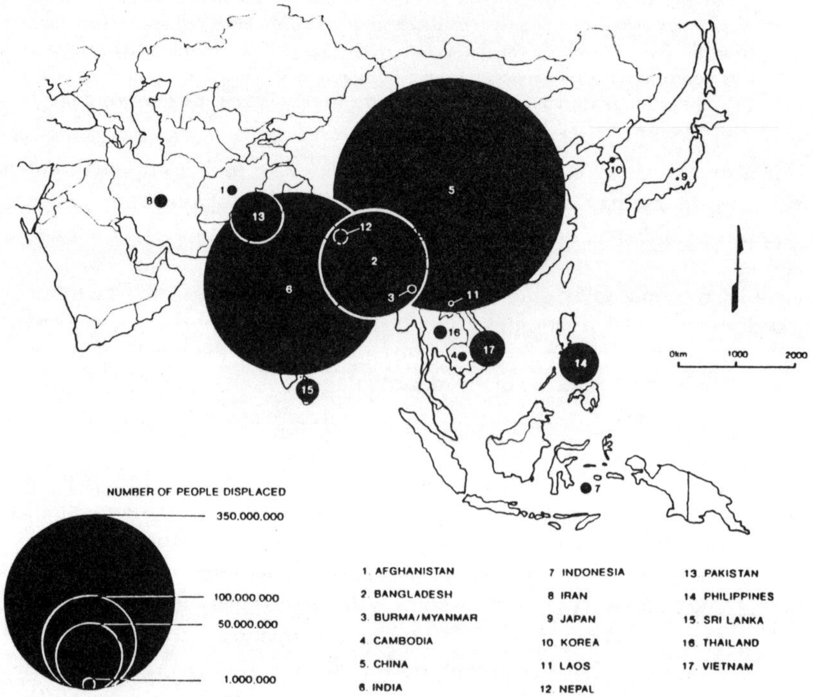

Source: Assembled from *UNDRO News*, 1976–1994.

TABLE 2
DISPLACED POPULATION IN SELECTED AFRICAN COUNTRIES, SEPTEMBER 1985

Country	People Displaced (*N*)	Share of Population (Percent)
Burkina Faso	222,000	3
Chad	500,000	11
Mali	200,000	3
Mauritania	190,000	12
Niger	1,000,000	16

Source: Jacobsen (1988:13).

- Climate change may become a significant factor in impelling environmental migration. The expansion of the hole in the ozone layer, global warming, and anticipated increases in sea levels would have significant population displacement implications. For example, a report by the U.S. National Academies of Sciences and Engineering and Institute of Medicine (1991:24) concludes that while understanding of complex global climatic systems is limited, some radical changes which will increase global temperatures must be considered plausible:
  - As high altitude tundra melts, CH_4 would be released, increasing greenhouse warming.
  - Increased freshwater runoff in high latitudes and reduced differentials in temperature between poles and equator could radically change ocean currents, leading to altered weather patterns.
  - There could be a significant melting of the West Antarctic Ice Sheet, resulting in a sea level several meters higher than it is today.

  The report concludes that, while migration is likely to be an important response to climate change, in the United States it is unlikely that climate-driven migration will be on a scale that cannot be managed.

However, it is not sufficient to consider the migration-environment relationship only in terms of migration induced as a response to the occurrence of particular environmental events. As Suhrke (1992:5) points out:

> From a broader development perspective, environmental degradation appears as a proximate cause of migration. The underlying causes are found in increasing population pressures on land and the patterns of resource use. Demography and political economy, in other words, are most salient causal factors. Yet these obviously interact in critical ways with specific environmental variables. Sometimes the result is stress of a kind that leads to massive outmigration. But to understand why, it is necessary to focus on the broader development process.

Similarly, Richmond (1993:8) argues

> . . . when environmental degradation leads to migration itis generally as a proximate cause linked to questions of economic growth, poverty, population pressure, and political conflict.

Bilsborrow (1991), in his case studies of Indonesia, Guatemala, and Sudan, depicts environmental degradation as one of a cluster of causes of outmigration. He suggests that environmental changes induced migration through their "social" effects by 1) reducing income; 2) increasing the risk of income reduction in the future; 3) making the environment less healthy.

The model outlined in Figure 2 emphasizes the fact that although a particular environmental event may be the trigger that actually initiates a substantial population displacement, it is the predisposing conditions which are often crucially important in determining one or more of the following: the nature and severity of the actual precipitating event, which is usually some form of environmental disaster or disruption; whether or not migration results; the nature and scale of that migration. Hence in many cases, especially in LDCs, the deeper underlying causes of environmental migration are not environmental but related to political, economic, social and demographic processes. Thus policy interventions need to address the more fundamental causes of the movement rather than the triggering event which initiated the migration.

It would seem that environmental degradation is increasingly becoming a contributory cause of population mobility in LDCs. It is linked to the economic push being exerted by poverty, population pressure on resources, unemployment, underemployment, lack of access to services, etc. in rural areas of many LDCs. Migration is usually not simply a response to a single cause or event but to a constellation of often interlinked forces. As agriculture becomes more commercialized and mechanized in LCDs, declining demand for and displacement of labor is exerting considerable outmigration pressure, and this is being exacerbated by increasing environmental disruption.

ENVIRONMENTALLY INDUCED MIGRATION – INTERNAL VERSUS INTERNATIONAL

The bulk of migrants displaced by environmental disruption move within national boundaries, and international environmental migration has been very limited. However, there are a number of arguments which could be advanced to suggest that over the next decade environmental factors will become more significant in impelling international movements.

The first such argument would point to the increasing strength of environmental push factors in LDCs, especially the nonmetropolitan sectors of those countries. As was made clear at UNCED and in a number of comprehensive reviews (e.g., Suhrke, 1992, 1994; United Nations, 1994; Green, 1992), the signs of environmental stress are continuing to increase in LDCs. A few examples will suffice to make this point (Green, 1992:12–17). Each year . . .

- 17 million hectares of tropical forest vanish;
- a billion tons of topsoil are lost due to soil degradation which has seen 1.2 billion hectares of land losing much of their agricultural productivity since 1945;
- if water pollution continues at current rates, as much as one-fourth of the world's freshwater supply could be unsafe for human consumption by the end of the 1990s.

Air pollution, desertification and loss of biodiversity also are increasing their impacts in LDCs. Despite global action following UNCED, there are few signs of a reversal in trends of environmental degradation in LDCs.

Particular attention has been focused on global warming and its inevitable corollary – rising sea levels (Birdsall, 1992). While there is some debate, it is anticipated that sea levels may rise one meter by the year 2100, affecting

360,000 kilometers of coastline (Suhrke, 1992). Since almost two-thirds of the world's population lives within 100 kilometers of the coast and 30 of the world's 50 largest cities are located on the coast, the potential for population displacement from a significant rise in sea level is considerable. Indeed, some commentators have painted future scenarios of millions of people being forced to move by sea level changes (Gleick, 1989; Kaplan, 1994). Kritz (1990:110) has reviewed the impacts of climate change and migration and concludes:

> While historical and contemporary cases can be cited of climate exerting a major influence on migration, climate per se is seldom the root cause of migration but rather one more factor that exacerbates the already difficult conditions under which poor people attempt to cope with their changing environments.

It is apparent that while significant population displacement is a likely result of climate change, the effects have been exaggerated in the literature. As Suhrke (1993:11) points out:

> The social impact is indicated by estimates that over the next 60 years, 13–15 percent of Bangladesh's population would be displaced in a worst case scenario (Jacobsen, 1988:34). If the displacement occurs at a steady rate, the first 'installments' would be of the order of 200,000–300,000 persons annually. While a sizeable figure, it is less than one-quarter of the new arrivals who annually enter Bangladesh's labor market due to popular increase alone.

Moreover, in most such cases, it is within countries that the bulk of population displacement is likely to occur. This is not possible, however, in small low lying island nations such as the Maldives and especially in several of the island nations of the Pacific (Connell, 1987). The scope for internal population redistribution within such countries is limited, so there will be pressure for resettlement in another country. In many such nations there are strong existing social networks set up with destination countries along which displaced populations may travel (Moore and Smith, 1995).

There are other emerging developments in international migration which in the future may lead to environmentally displaced persons considering international as well as internal destinations. These relate predominantly to the forces identified in Figure 2 as facilitators – elements which, rather than cause movement, make that movement possible or channel it in a particular direction once the decision to move has been made. The sheer increase in the scale of international migration, especially South-North migration in the last decade, has meant that the social networks linking potential migrants in LDCs with family and friends in MDCs have proliferated exponentially. This has meant that the destination options for people in LDCs pushed out of their homes by environmental disruptions are increasingly including international destinations.

Another factor here and an often neglected element in the acceleration of population movement between nations over the last decade is the emergence and development of an international immigration industry. This is an increasingly large group of agents, recruiters, travel businesses, lawyers, etc., operating both within and outside legal structures to facilitate international migration of one kind or another. As with the strengthening and spread of international social networks, the development of the immigration industry has acted as an important facilitator (Figure 2) of international migration.

Hence it could be argued strongly that environmental pressures will continue to increase in LDCs over the next decade and that such pressures will become increasingly important in pushing people out of rural areas in LDCs. Environmental factors will become a more significant cause of migration out of LDC rural areas, but mainly as a proximate and contributory factor among a range of pressures on people seeking to survive in such contexts, although the increasing incidence of sudden environmental disasters will also periodically produce significant displacements of population. It is likely too that while most environmentally induced migration will take place within nations, a greater proportion will occur between nations in line with globalization trends and proliferation of migration networks and increasing numbers of institutions, businesses and people facilitating international migration.

While the bulk of our attention here has focused upon environmental pressures and disciplines as a push factor initiating or contributing to migration, it should also be mentioned that environmental factors can be a pull factor in attracting population movements toward destinations perceived to have favorable environments (Svart, 1976). Such movement predominantly affects MDCs, and the bulk of it occurs within nations, as with the movement to the Sunbelt in the United States and from the southeast to northeastern Australia. However, such movement also occurs internationally, especially among retirees, as is the case with the flow of northern and western Europeans to some Mediterranean nations.

ENVIRONMENTAL IMPACTS OF INTERNATIONAL MIGRATION

In considering the role of international migration as an independent variable impacting upon the environment, a useful starting point is the equation developed by Ehrlich and Holdren (1971) and Ehrlich and Ehrlich (1990:58)

$$I = P \times A \times T$$

Where I = Environmental Impact
P = Population Size and Growth
A = Affluence – per capita consumption of goods and services
T = Technology – quantity of resources consumed, environmental damage sustained and pollution generated during production and consumption per unit of goods and services.

While this formula has been subject to criticism (Bartiaux and van Ypersele, 1993; Hogan, 1992), it does emphasize the point that although population growth is an important element shaping the extent of environmental impact, it is not the only one. Hence control of population growth does not offer a "quick fix" for environmental problems. Clearly, although reduced population growth can assist in reducing environmental pressure, there is no simple linear relationship between population density and growth and environmental degradation.

International migration plays a role in influencing population growth and size in the areas of origin and destination of migrants. Other things being equal (which of course they rarely are), emigration will reduce environmental pressures at the origin and increase them at the destination. However, it is unlikely that international migration can occur on such a scale to be any long-term solution to environmental pressure problems in LDCs except in relatively restricted localized areas (Keyfitz, 1991).

In the traditional immigration nations such as Canada, the United States and Australia, debates about immigration have generally raged around the issues of ethnic composition of the intake and the economic consequences of the immigration. However, there are some indications of the environmental effects of immigration becoming an increasingly important element in that debate. To take the case of Australia, in the 1980s there were a few commentators who argued that Australia should dramatically reduce immigration levels because of environmental concerns that an expanding population will have detrimental effects upon the native environment, flora and fauna and upon the capacity of the nation's resource base to accommodate that expansion (Birrell, Hill and Nevill, 1984; Day and Rowland, 1988). However, in more recent times, concern about the environmental consequences of immigration has seen this issue emerge as one of the dominant arguments against expanding immigration levels.

- The National Population Council (1992:109) report on Population issues and Australia's future stated, that "... the Committee has concluded that national ecological integrity would be best served by an active population policy which resulted in a reduced rate of population growth."
- A report by the House of Representatives Standing Committee for Long Term Strategies (Parliament of the Commonwealth of Australia, 1994:149) on Australia's population carrying capacity recommended that the nation develop a population policy which explicitly takes into account environmental costs of population growth.
- Environmental arguments against immigration are being increasingly addressed in the Australian literature on population and environment (Smith, 1991; Bierbaum, 1991; Boyden, Dovers and Shirlow, 1990; ABS, 1992; Clarke *et al.*, 1990; Fincher, 1991; Industries Assistance Commission, 1989).
- A symposium of the Australian Academy of Science (1994) emphasized the environmental limitations of Australia and the pressing need to

reduce population growth as part of the development of a policy of Ecologically Sustainable Development.
- In 1995, the Premier of New South Wales called for a moratorium on immigration to Sydney (the destination of more than half of the immigrants arriving in Australia) because of the environmental infrastructure and service delivery costs imposed (*The Australian*, May 24, 1995).

It is apparent, therefore, that in Australia the argument that immigrants exacerbate environmental pressures is gathering strength in the ongoing national debate about immigration levels. It is suggested that high levels of immigration:
- through enhancing population growth, increase consumption levels of scarce national resources (especially nonrenewable natural resources which have a limited finite supply such as oil) and increase overall levels of environmental degradation;
- through concentrating population distribution, in particular ecologically sensitive or fragile subareas within the nation, exacerbate environmental pressures and problems in those areas. Immigrant settlement in Australia is extremely concentrated in a few parts of the nation (Hugo, 1995).

Obviously there is a great deal of scapegoating of immigrants in such arguments. They ignore the reality of the environmental impact equation provided above which indicates that sheer population numbers are only one of the variables impinging upon the environment, along with per capita consumption levels and the way in which the people use the environment in which they live. Limitation of population growth or immigration levels is obviously of its own not a solution to such environmental problems. They cannot substitute for the development and adoption of policies and practices which reduce per capita consumption levels and which ensure that urban and rural environments are managed and exploited in ways that are compatible with ecological sustainability. On the other hand, it is crucial that environmental considerations be factored into the decisions made by the Australian government about immigration levels because population growth is one of the factors impinging upon the environment. It is clear that in the traditional immigration nations like Australia, the environmental consequences of immigration are coming under much greater scrutiny by government – and the community more generally – and that they will increasingly be a factor in shaping policy about the level of international migration gains for the nation.

Suhrke (1992:2) points out that the body of research on the impact of migration on the environment is considerably greater than that on the environment as a cause of migration. Again, however, the bulk of the evidence relates to internal migration, with little examination of the ecological and environmental consequences of international migration. There are many case studies where expanding land settlement into marginal and fragile ecosystems in LDCs have led to desertification, deforestation and other environmental degradation (Suhrke, 1993; Bilsborrow, 1991, 1992; Allen and Barnes, 1985; Bilsborrow, 1987; Bilsborrow and DeLargy, 1991; Blaikie and Brookfield, 1987; Cruz, Zosa-Feranil and Goce, 1988; Georges and Bilsborrow, 1991; Hafner and Apichatvullop, 1990; Pichon and Bilsborrow, 1992). The expansion of agricultural settlement into hitherto untilled areas in some LDC contexts has led to severe environmental deterioration. This occurs both in government organized and sponsored land settlement programs and especially where the settlement occurs outside of government controls and involves squatters. In Indonesia, for example, the ecological impact of the government's Transmigration Program has been substantial (Secrett, 1986).

One type of international migration which has attracted attention because of its environmental impacts is refugee movement. The sudden unplanned influx of large numbers of people into a generally spatially restricted area, often already vulnerable to environmental degradation, can have devastating environmental impacts (Stevens, 1993). Ghimire (1994:561) has recently summarized the situation:

> Deforestation is one of many environmental problems facing refugees in developing countries. Others include the depletion and contamination of water, overcrowding, poor sanitation, soil erosion and pasture degradation. In some cases, forest coverage and other environmental problems existed prior to the arrival of refugees; in others the problems have been exacerbated by the refugees. Dwindling resource base has also led to increasing conflict with local populations and much hardship for refugees.

There are a number of studies which depict situations in Africa, and to a lesser extent Asia, where refugee settlement has resulted in environmental degradation (Ek and Karadawi, 1991; Simmance, 1987; Christensen and Scott, 1988; Utting, 1992; Aguayo *et al.*, 1987; Hugo, 1987).

While it is apparent that international migration can and does have negative environmental consequences, in some contexts there are considerable dangers that the migrants involved can become scapegoats for a general failure to adopt sustainable policies of land and other resource use in the destination areas. In Australia, a review (Clarke *et al.*, 1990) of literature concerned with immigration, population growth and the environment, concluded that Australians will be better off in general using resource management policies targeted to deal with specific resource and environmental concerns, rather than using immigration policies. This should not be taken to mean that population growth and immigration are not of relevance in discussion about Australia moving toward a sustainable development strategy but rather as Toyne (1990) has pointed out,

> It is vital the immigration debate is moved directly into the broader debate over ecological sustainability in Australia. No long-term resolution to the question of appropriate net immigration levels can be found until the broader questions are settled.

Toyne makes the important distinction between short-term and long-term considerations:

> A much more sophisticated approach to the question of population and sustainability is needed than has been evidenced in the debate to date. It must be acknowledged that in the short run over the next 20 years or so, environmental decline in Australia can only be

addressed through changing our lifestyles, consumption patterns and improving our waste disposal and minimization technologies. In the long term the number of people we wish to accommodate in Australia will play a significant role in determining the level of environmental impact and demand for scarce natural resources.

SOME ETHICAL AND POLICY IMPLICATIONS

The causes and effects of environmental deterioration in LDCs cannot be quarantined within the national boundaries of individual nations. It is clear that much contemporary environmental degradation in LDCs has its real roots in historical processes such as colonial exploitation which produced different modes of agricultural and pastoral activity to meet the needs of the colonial power and different patterns of population growth and distribution from those which prevailed in precolonial times. Similarly, international inequalities in power, access to resources, unequal terms of trade, etc. have all been influential in shaping patterns of land use and settlement in LDCs, as have the interventions of international companies and agencies. Moreover, the consequences of deforestation, pollution, etc. are not confined to single nations. The rapid depletion of rainforests in a few countries like Brazil and Indonesia, for example, has climate change and loss of biodiversity implications which are global. The clear message, not only from the 1992 UNCED but from as far back as the 1972 Stockholm Conference on the Human Environment and the 1987 publication of the World Commission on Environment and Development report, *Our Common Future*, is that achieving ecologically sustainable development demands action at the global level as well as the national and individual levels. Successfully tackling many of the environmental problems of LDCs and MDCs will require a global approach, and central to this is the pressing need to eradicate poverty so that people can have access to the resources to live sustainably. This will demand several redistributions from MDCs to LDCs through changes in international power, trade and aid relationships. In short, the environmental pressures which are increasingly the cause and consequence of population movements in LDCs should not be seen as exclusively the problems of the individual countries involved since those pressures have been caused partly by forces outside of the country and they have consequences which extend beyond the borders of those countries.

Migration is a logical and common immediate response to environmental degradation and disaster, but it is rarely a medium or long-term solution to environmental problems. This will only be attained via lower levels of population growth through substantial and sustained fertility decline and adopting ecologically sustainable ways of using the environment. Both of these goals are only going to be achieved through overcoming poverty and powerlessness among the people living in regions subject to environmental disaster and degradation. Only through improving employment opportunities for men and women, health, education, human rights and enhancing the status and roles of women within such societies can long-term sustainability be achieved. Just as international processes have contributed to the creation of environmental problems in LDCs, long-term solutions will only be possible with significant involvement of the international community.

Environmental pressures are undoubtedly an increasing element initiating outmigration from many rural areas in LDCs. However, environmental factors are more significant as contributory and proximate causes of such migration, although "environmental refugee" migration is significant. The bulk of such movement is intranational, but just as other forms of migration in LDCs are increasingly involving crossing international borders, it is likely that a larger proportion of environmentally displaced persons will move to other countries. However, such migration cannot be generally seen as a solution to environmental problems in LDCs because:

- The vast scale of such movement is such that the sheer logistics of moving and establishing such refugees in other nations is many times larger than any previous global migration (Keyfitz, 1991).
- It does not represent a real and lasting solution to environmental problems, which can only come through eradicating poverty, reducing fertility, and adopting environmentally sustainable practices.

International relocation may provide an enduring solution only in very specific circumstances such as in small island nations influenced by a significant rise in sea levels or in small regions devastated by an environmental disaster.

The fact remains, however, that there are significant displacements of population occurring in LDCs as a result of environmental disasters or deterioration. Most of this displacement occurs within the boundaries of nations and there is certainly no indication of a lessening of the numbers of environmental migrants in LDCs. Hence it is imperative that the international community look to short-term measures as well as the longer-term solutions discussed above. As was indicated earlier, the people involved are certainly not covered by international refugee protocols, and there is a pressing need for this group of forced migrants to be systematically incorporated into an expanded international regime to assist people who are uprooted involuntarily from their home areas (Rogers and Copeland, 1993:132).

CONCLUSION

The growing appreciation of the global implications of environmental problems is occurring at a time of a rapidly changing context in which international exchanges of population, goods, capital and information are accelerating at an unprecedented rate. Our understanding of the nature and significance of the complex linkages between migration and environmental change remains very limited (IOM, 1992). It is clear, however, that the international dimensions of the migration-environment relationship are assuming increasing significance. This presents a considerable challenge to both policymakers and researchers. Rogers and Copeland (1993:135), in examining emerging policy issues related to forced migrations associated with political conflict, conclude:

> The 1990s is a time of uncertainty, change and opportunity. While the challenges that confronted the international community with respect to forced migration were more predictable during the Cold War, certain opportunities for prevention activities and for the creation of solutions which present themselves today were not available even a few years ago. Our paper expresses the hope that governments – working with a UN system that is itself undergoing changes, and with regional bodies and NGOs – will find the political will and the necessary resources to realize the considerable opportunities for dealing creatively with the new and old challenges posed by forced migration due to war and persecution.

It is the contention here that the world is facing a comparable situation with respect to forced migration due to environmental disruption and there is a need for international involvement. This should be both in the short term in dealing with environmental migrants displaced by the sudden onset of disasters, but more importantly in the longer term in working to eradicate poverty, reduce population growth and encourage the adoption of sustainable ways of using the environment which, if successful, will obviate the need for such migration.

REFERENCES

Aguayo, S. *et al.*
1987 *Social and Cultural Conditions and Prospects of Guatemalan Refugees in Mexico.* Geneva: UNRISD/Colegio de Mexico.

Allen, J. C. and D. F. Barnes
1985 "The Causes of Deforestation in Developing Countries," *Annals of the Association of American Geographers*, 75(2):163–184.

Amin, S.
1974 *Modern Migrations in Western Africa.* London: Oxford University Press.

Australian Academy of Science
1994 *Population 2040 Australia's Choice.* Proceedings of the Symposium of the Annual General Meeting of the Australian Academy of Science, Canberra.

Australian Bureau of Statistics (ABS)
1992 *Australia's Environment: Issues and Facts.* Canberra: AGPS.

Awanohara, S.
1982 "In the Shadow of Death," *Far Eastern Economic Review*, pp. 42–43. Oct. 15.

Bartiaux, F. and J. van Ypersele
1993 "The Role of Population Growth in Global Warming." In *International Population Conference, Montreal 1993, Volume 4.* Liege: IUSSP. Pp. 33–54.

Bierbaum, ed.
1991 *Towards Ecological* Sustainability. Prepared for the Planning Committee, Centre for the Environment and Sustainable Development, Flinders University of South Australia, Adelaide.

Bilsborrow, R. E.
1992 "Population, Development and Deforestation: Some Recent Evidence." Paper presented at the U.N. Expert Group Meeting on Population, Environment and Development, New York. January.

______
1991 "Rural Poverty, Migration and the Environment in Developing Countries: Three Case Studies." Background paper presented for World Bank, World Development Report 1991, Chapel Hill, North Carolina.

______
1987 "Population Pressures and Agricultural Development in Developing Countries: A Conceptual Framework and Recent Evidence," *World Development*, 15(2):183–203.

Bilsborrow, R. E. and P.F. DeLargy
1991 "Land Use, Migration and Natural Resource Deterioration in the Third World: The Cases of Guatemala and Sudan." In *Resources, Environment and Population*. Ed. K. Davis and M. Bernstam. Belgium: IUSSP. Pp. 125–147.

Birdsall, N.
1992 "Another Look at Population and Global Warming." Policy research working paper, Country Economics Department, The World Bank, New York.

Birrell, R., D. Hill and J. Nevill, eds.
1984 *Populate and Perish? The Stresses of Population Growth in Australia.* Melbourne; Fontana/Sydney: Australian Conservation Foundation.

Blaikie, P. and Brookfield
1987 *Land Degradation and Society.* London: Metheun.

Boyden, S., S. Dovers and M. Shirlow
1990 *Our Biosphere under Threat: Ecological Realities and Australia's Opportunities.* Melbourne: Oxford University Press.

Breeze, R.
1980 "The Building of a New Tangsham," *Far Eastern Economic Review*, p. 103. March 7.

Christensen, H. and W. Scott
1988 *Survey of the Social and Economic Conditions of Afghan Refugees in Pakistan.* Geneva: UNRISD.

Clarke, H. R., A. H. Chisolm, G. W. Edwards and T. O. S. Kennedy
1990 *Immigration, Population Growth and the Environment.* Canberra: AGPS.

Clarke, J. I., P.Curson, S. L. Kayastha and P. Nag, eds.
1989 *Population and Disaster.* Oxford: Basil Blackwell.

Connell, J.
1987 "Paradise Left? Pacific Island Voyagers in the Modern World." In *Pacific Bridges: The New Immigration from Asia and the Pacific Islands.* New York: Center for Migration Studies. Pp. 375–404.

Cruz, M. C. J., I. Zosa-Feranil and C. L. Goce
1988 "Population Pressure and Migration: Implications for Upland Development in the Philippines," *Journal of Philippine Development*, 26(1):15–46.

Day, L. H. and D. T. Rowland, eds.
1988 *How Many More Australians? The Resource and Environmental Conflicts.* Melbourne: Longman Cheshire.

Dirks, R.
1980 "Social Responses During Severe Food Shortages and Famine," *Current Anthropology*, 21(1):21–44.

Ehrlich, P. R. and A. H.
1990 *The Population Explosion.* New York: Simon and Schuster.

Ehrlich, P. R. and J. P. Holdren
1971 "Impact of Population Growth," *Science,* 171:1212–1217.

Ek, R. and A. Karadawi
1991 "Implications of Refugee Flows on Political Stability in the Sudan," *Ambio,* August.

El-Hinnawi, E.
1985 *Environmental Refugees.* Kenya: United Nations Environment Programme.

Fairchild, H. P.
1925 *Immigration: A World Movement and Its American Significance.* New York: Putnam.

Fincher, R.
1991 *Immigration, Urban Infrastructure and the Environment.* Canberra: AGPS.

Georges, M. E. and R. E. Bilsborrow
1991 "Deforestation and Internal Migration in Selected Developing Countries." Paper presented at Annual Meeting of the Southern Demographic Association, Jacksonville. October.

Ghimire, K.
1994 "Refugees and Deforestation," *Internal Migration Quarterly Review,* 32(4):561–568.

Gleick, P.H.
1989 "Climate Change and International Politics: Problems Facing Developing Countries," *Ambio,* 18(6):333–339.

Green, C. P.
1992 *The Environment and Population Growth: Decade for Action.* Population Reports, Series M., No. 10. Baltimore, MD: Johns Hopkins University.

Hafner, J. A. and Y. Apichatvullop
1990 "Migrant Farmers and the Shrinking Forests in Northeast Thailand." In *Keepers of the Forest.* Ed. M. Poffenberger. West Hartford: Kumarian Press. Pp. 187–219.

Hardjono, J.
1986 "Transmigration: Looking to the Future," *Bulletin of Indonesian Economic Studies,* 22(2):28–53.

Hinnawi, E. E.
1985 *Environment Refugees.* New York: United Nations Development Program.

Hogan, D. J.
1992 "The Impact of Population Growth on the Physical Environment," *European Journal of Population,* 8:109–123.

Hugo, G. J.
1995 *Understanding Where Immigrants Live.* Canberra: AGPS.

———
1988 "Population Movement in Indonesia Since 1971," *Tijdschrift voor Economische en Sociale Geografie,* 79(4):242–256.

———
1987 "Postwar Refugee Migration in Southeast Asia: Patterns, Problems and Policies." In *Refugees: A Third World Dilemma.* Ed. J. R. Rogge. New Jersey: Rowan and Littlefield.

———
1984 "The Demographic Impact of Famine." In *Famine as a Geographical Phenomenon.* Ed. B. Currey and G. Hugo. Dordrecht: D. Reidel. Pp. 7–32.

Hugo, G. J. and C. K. Chan
1990 "Conceptualizing and Defining Refugee and Other Forced Migrations," *Southeast Asian Journal of Social Sciences*, 18(1):19–42.

Huus, K.
1994 "More Dam Trouble," *Far Eastern Economic Review*, pp. 70–72. Oct. 20.

Industries Assistance Commission
1989 *The Environmental Impacts of Travel and Tourism.* Canberra: AGPS.

International Organization for Migration (IOM)
1992 *Migration and the Environment.* Geneva: IOM and Refugee Policy Group.

Jacobsen, J. L.
1989 "Environmental Refugees: Nature's Warning System," *POPULI*, 16(1):29–38.

———
1988 "Environmental Refugees: A Yardstick of Habitability," *Worldwatch Paper 86.* Washington: Worldwatch Institute.

Kaplan, R. D.
1994 "The Coming Anarchy," *The Atlantic Monthly*, 273(2):44–76.

Kayastha, S. L. and R. P.Yadara
1985 "Flood Induced Population Migration in India: A Case Study of Ghaghara Zone." In *Population Redistribution and Development in South Asia.* Ed. L. A. Kosinski and K. M. Elahi. Dordrecht: D. Reidel. Pp. 79–88.

Kaye, L.
1994 "The Reckoning," *Far Eastern Economic Review*, pp. 24–30. Oct. 27.

Keating, M.
1994 *The Earth Summit's Agenda for Change.* Geneva: Centre for Our Common Future.

Keely, C. B.
1981 *Global Refugee Policy: The Case for a Development Oriented Strategy.* New York: The Population Council Public Issues Papers on Population.

Keyfitz, N.
1991 "Population and Development Within the Ecosphere: One View of the Literature," *Population Index*, 57.

Kibreab, G.
1994 "Migration, Environment and Refugeehood." In *Environment and Population Change.* Ed. B. Zaba and J. Clarke. Belgium: IUSSP. Pp. 115–130.

Kunz, E. F.
1973 "The Refugee in Flight: Kinetic Models and Forms of Displacement," *International Migration Review*, 7(2):125–146.

Moore, E. J. and J. W. Smith
1995 "Climatic Change and Migration from Oceania: Implications for Australia, New Zealand and the United States of America," *Population and Environment*, 17(2):105–122.

Mortimore, M.
1989 *Adapting to Drought: Farmers, Famines and Desertification in West Africa.* Cambridge: Cambridge University Press.

National Academy of Sciences, National Academy of Engineering, Institute of Medicine, U.S.
1991 *Policy Implications of Greenhouse Warming.* Washington, DC: National Academy Press.

National Population Council
1992 *Population Issues and Australia's Future: Environment, Economy and Society.* Final Report of the Population Issues Committee. Canberra: AGPS.

Nobel, P.
1985 "Refugee Determination in the Third World." Paper prepared for United Nations Research Institute for Social Development's Project on People Affected by Uprootedness.

Olson, M. E.
1979 "Refugees as a Special Case of Population Redistribution." In *Population Redistribution: Patterns, Policies and Prospects.* Ed. L. A. P. Gosling and L. Y. C. Lim. New York: United Nations Fund for Population Activities. Pp. 130–152.

Oucho, J. O.
1995 "International Migration and Sustainable Human Development in Eastern and Southern Africa," *International Migration,* 33(1):31–54.

Parliament of the Commonwealth of Australia
1994 *Australia's Population 'Carrying Capacity': One Nation – Two Ecologies.* Canberra: AGPS.

Peterson, W. A.
1958 "A General Typology of Migration," *American Sociological Review,* 23(3):256–266.

Pichon, F. J. and R. E. Bilsborrow
1992 "Agricultural Colonization and the Social Dimensions of Deforestation in the Ecuadorian Amazon." In *The Social Dynamics of Deforestation in Developing Countries.* Geneva: UN Research Institute on Social Development.

The Population Institute
1993 "Desparate Departures: The Flight of Environmental Refugees." Paper prepared for Expert Group Meeting on Population Distribution and Migration, Santa Cruz, Bolivia. January.

Richmond, A.
1993 "The Environment and Refugees: Theoretical and Policy Issues." Revised version of a paper presented at the meetings of the International Union for the Scientific Study of Population, Montreal. August.

Rogers, R. and E. Copeland
1993 *Forced Migration-Policy Issues in the Post-Cold War World.* Massachusetts: Tufts University.

Ruzicka, L. T. and A. K. M.A. Chowdhury
1978 *Demographic Surveillance System – Matlab Volume 4. Vital Events and Migration 1975.* Dacca: Cholera Research Laboratory.

Secrett, C.
1986 "The Environmental Impact of Transmigration," *The Ecologust,* 16(2):77–86.

Shah, B. V.
1983 "Is the Environment Becoming More Hazardous? A Global Survey, 1947 to 1980," *Disasters,* 7(3):202–209.

Simmance, A.
1987 "The Impact of Large-Scale Movements and the Role of UNHCR." In *Refugees: A Third World Dilemma.* Ed. J. R. Rogge. New Jersey: Rowan and Littlefield.

Smith, J. W., ed.
1991 *Immigration, Population and Sustainable Limits to Australia's Growth.* Adelaide: Flinders Press.

Speare, A.
1974 "The Relevance of Models of Internal Migration for the Study of International Migration." In *International Migration: Proceedings of a Seminar on Demographic Research in Relation to International Migration.* Ed. G. Tapinos. Paris: CICRED. Pp. 84–94.

Spitz, P.
1978 "Silent Violence: Poverty and Inequality," *International Social Science Journal*, 30(4).

Stevens, Y.
1993 "UNHCR and Environmental Issues." Paper presented at Refugees and Environmental Change Conference, University of Oxford, London. September.

Suhrke, A.
1994 "Environmental Degradation, and Population Flows," *Journal of International Affairs*, 47(2):475–496.

———
1993 *Pressure Points: Environmental Degradation, Migration and Conflict.* Occasional Paper No. 3, University of Toronto and the American Academy of Arts and Science, Toronto.

———
1992 "Pressure Points: Environmental Degradation, Migration and Conflict." Prepared for a conference organized by the American Academy of Arts and Science at the Brookings Institution, Washington DC, May 11–12.

Svart, L. M.
1976 "Environmental Preference Migration: A Review," *Geographical Review*, 66:314–330.

Toyne, P.
1990 "Damage Control the No. 1 Priority," *The Australian*, June 1.

United Nations
1994 "Population and the Environment in Developing Countries: Literature Survey and Research Bibliography." Paper prepared for the Population Division of the Department for Economic and Social Information and Policy Analysis. U.N. Secretariat, New York.

———
1993 *Report of the United Nations Conference on Environment and Development.* Rio de Janiero, June 3–14, 1992, 1, Sales No. E.93.I.8.

United Nations Population Division
1994 "Population and the Environment in Developing Countries: Literature Survey and Research Bibliography." New York: United Nations Secretariat.

Utting, P.
1992 *Trees, People and Power: Social Dimension of Deforestation and Forest Protection in Central America.* Unpublished UNRISD Report. July.

Zolberg, A. and A. Suhrke
1984 "Social Conflict and Refugees in the Third World: The Cases of Ethiopia and Afghanistan." Paper presented at the Center for Migration and Population Studies, Harvard University, March 22.

[31]

Indochinese Refugees in Canada: Sponsorship and Adjustment

Gertrud Neuwirth
Lynn Clark

In July 1979, the government of Canada issued a new policy which raised the quota of Indochinese refugees to 50,000 and introduced the one-to-one matching formula between privately and government sponsored refugees.[1] Since the admission of the total target number of refugees was made dependent upon the prior initiative of civic groups to sponsor their share of 25,000, the private sector was, in effect, invited to enter into partnership with the government in the settlement of refugees.

The new policy met with overwhelming success; private sponsorship groups were formed across Canada overnight. In addition, volunteer organizations, such as Project 4,000 in Ottawa, were set up in several cities with the explicit objective of assisting Canadians in the formation of sponsorship groups and providing them with whatever services they could muster. By the end of August 1979, 1,420 groups across Canada had applied to sponsor refugees; by the end of January 1980 the number of sponsorship groups came to 5,457.

Under the new policy, the refugees' introduction to, and initial settlement experiences in, Canadian society will differ significantly depending on whether they are government or privately sponsored. Government sponsored refugees are aided in their settlement by local Employment Centers and traditional Immigrant Service Organizations. The former provides the refugees with financial assistance during the six months full-time language training and until they can place them in available jobs. The latter conduct orientation programs in which refugees are acquainted with basic aspects of the Canadian urban way of life and

[1]The government made use of a little known provision in The New Immigration Act of 1978 which made it possible for local groups of at least five Canadian citizens (or permanent residents) and local legally incorporated organizations to sponsor refugees. The Act also enabled national organizations with humanitarian traditions to enter comprehensive sponsorship agreements with the federal government in order to underwrite the commitment of their local member groups. Up to summer 1979 several church organizations had already signed so-called umbrella agreements with the government.

which are available for any other services the refugees may require, such as assistance in finding housing or enrolling children in schools. Privately sponsored refugees are placed, upon arrival, in the care of a sponsorship group which assumes "financial and moral responsibility" for them during their first year of residence in Canada. The sponsorship group usually finds accommodation before the refugee has arrived and provides clothing and furniture. If it is decided that the refugees should be enrolled in the official language training program the sponsors support them financially during this period and continue to do so, in all cases, until the refugees find work or the sponsorship year expires. The refugees learn about the Canadian way of life directly from their informal interactions with sponsors; rarely, if ever, are any agencies involved in this orientation.

THE "CAREER" OF SIXTEEN SPONSORSHIP GROUPS AND REFUGEES

In the first phase of this study,[2] sixteen sponsorship groups and their respective refugee families were closely studied and monitored since the beginning of August 1979. All of these groups were scheduled to receive "their" refugees on August 6, 1979, on the only direct flight from Hong Kong to Ottawa.[3] Owing to the small number of cases, the findings concerning the facilitating role of sponsors and the initial resettlement experience of refugees can only be tentative; they are, however, supported by interviews with additional sponsors and refugees.

By and large the sixteen sponsorship groups included the range of characteristics which are normally found among sponsorship groups in general, particularly as far as the *loci* of group formation, the group's size, resources and division of labor are concerned.

Generally speaking three different *loci* or bases of group formation can be distinguished. First, groups can be organizationally affiliated, that is, formed among members of established organizations, such as churches; second, groups without organizational affiliation can be recruited at their place of work; or, third, groups can be formed on the basis of residential propinquity. Of the sixteen groups under study, seven were church-based

[2]This phase of the study was made possible by a contract from the Ethnic and Cultural Relations Program of the Institute for Research on Public Policy.

[3]Of the sixteen groups, fourteen indeed received the refugees as scheduled and the remaining two a few weeks later. The contact person of most of these groups was interviewed three times and the head of household of the refugee's family once. The first interview with sponsors was conducted in most cases a few days before the refugees arrived, the second interview about three weeks after their arrival and the third, four to five months later. Refugees were interviewed roughly at the same time as the third interview with sponsors was conducted.

groups, five were generated from the work place and four were residentially-based groups. The sixteen groups ranged in size from the minimum of five persons to seventy or more members. Naturally, groups that are larger have greater potential to generate human and financial resources. However, there is no consistent relationship between the size of the group and the money they have at their disposal (*e.g.*, one group of seventeen and another group of sixty members each had the same financial resources of $9,000). Larger groups tended to meet regularly and have a more strictly defined division of labor. Members were typically organized into committees with specific responsibilities such as finding accommodation for the refugees or looking after their medical and educational needs. Highly organized groups tended to be more cohesive than less organized groups; members of the former met regularly and enjoyed frequent social contact with other group members, while in the latter group meetings tended to be infrequent.

The *locus* or basis of group formation appears to be an important characteristic, since it is related to other group attributes as well. Organizationally affiliated church groups, not unexpectedly, were large, had considerable human and financial resources and were highly organized and cohesive. Work-based groups, on the other hand, were small, had few human and limited financial resources, a looser organizational structure and little cohesion. Residentially based groups varied in size; however, they seemed to have made certain they had the human and financial resources to accomplish their task. They tended to be well organized and, with one exception, were quite cohesive.

It is interesting to note that groups with the fewest financial and human resources, the least organization and cohesion (work-friends groups) tended to take responsibility for larger families. In other words, they over-extended themselves from the beginning. However, it should be emphasized that in some instances groups were asked to take and accepted larger families than had they originally applied for; thus the strain on their resources was aggravated.

In all groups a core group of "special friends" took the leading role in orienting the refugees to the new society. They interacted frequently, in the beginning almost daily with the refugees, identified problems which had to be dealt with and had a major voice in decision-making concerning refugees. Interviews with core group members revealed some consistency in their social background. Most had university education, and most had combined family incomes of over $25,000 per year.[4] It is also in-

[4]However, this finding should not be generalized to the other members of the group who show considerable variation in terms of income and occupation. Uniformity of socioeconomic status only seems to apply to those sponsors who act, as it were, as the spokesperson for the group as a whole. Data concerning the socioeconomic composition of members of sponsorship groups will be obtained by a short mailed questionnaire.

teresting to note that the majority had either worked in or traveled to other countries.

The sponsorship program generally appeared to have tapped a desire in people to experience personal involvement. However, the sponsors differed somewhat in terms of how this desire was articulated. Some regarded their involvement as a spontaneous act of compassion, *e.g.*, "I'm doing it out of love, gratitude and compassion". Others emphasized the active role the sponsorship program enabled them to fulfill. As one respondent noted, "It's available, an opportunity, and I don't have to fight the system". The same respondent compared involvement with refugees to involvement in the plight of Native Canadians and said "There's not much I can do about them". A few contact people expressed their motivation for sponsoring in terms of personal growth saying "I thought it would be a good experience". Some individuals characterized their sponsorship as a moral imperative, *e.g.*, "We have an obligation to do what we can, even though we can't solve the world's problems". Although our preliminary findings are tentative, it appears that those individuals who sponsor out of spontaneous goodwill or reasons of personal growth are much less likely to follow through on their responsibilities than those who sponsor from a feeling of moral obligation based on religious or humanitarian principles.

The refugees sponsored by the sixteen groups were somewhat atypical in several respects. The proportion of white collar workers was higher than that of refugees as a whole; in fact, they were equally divided between white and blue-collar workers. As far as the country of origin and ethnic background are concerned, eleven escaped from North and five from South Vietnam, twelve were ethnic Chinese and four ethnic Vietnamese, although of the latter not all came from South Vietnam. The number of dependents in their families ranged from two to nine, with an average family size of about six.

In the absence of any specific guidelines concerning the sponsors' obligations,[5] it should come as no surprise that sponsorship groups differ greatly in how they defined their role as social facilitators, that is, the way they discharged their material obligations and introduced the refugees into Canadian society.

Monthly allowances ranged from $33 to $117.00 per person. However, the actual allowance given did not appear to be related to the financial

[5]In a paper issued by *Employment and Immigration, Canada*, sponsors were told that they had to provide material assistance, such as furnished accommodation and household effects, food, clothing and incidental expenses for one year. It was only recommended that a group set aside at least $1,200 per refugee but no specific guidelines were given as to the amount of financial assistance a family, depending on its size or composition, should receive per week or month.

resources of the group. While most refugees found their allowances to be sufficient and some were even able to save a little, those refugees in particular whose money for food was near the lower end of the range expressed difficulties in making ends meet and stressed the need to budget very carefully. Nearly all the refugees compared the allowance and other kinds of assistance they received from their sponsors with other refugees—indeed this seemed to be a frequent topic of conversation among refugees attending language classes. Although quite a few of them admitted that they were getting less than others they knew or had heard of, they were not necessarily dissatisfied and often stress that their sponsors were not very affluent themselves. Several refugees also seemed to place a high value on the kindness of, and social contact with, sponsors which, in their opinion, compensated for the comparatively lower level of material assistance they received. One respondent, however, remarked: "We wish all the sponsoring groups would get together and agree on the same amount. That would prevent ill-feeling among the refugees." It is also worth noting that the dissatisfaction which the few refugees expressed was not necessarily related to the actual amount received but, not surprisingly, to their previous social status in Vietnam.

As far as English language training is concerned, the sponsors discharged their function well. The heads of household of all sixteen families were eventually placed in English Secondary Language Training (E.S.L.). Women with children, who, by their own account, were potential wage earners could not take the regular full-time E.S.L. program because of the difficulty of finding child care.[6]

Those refugees who had completed their language training were, by and large, satisfied with the progress they made, particularly since they stressed that upon arrival they did not know any English. However, when they were asked whether they knew enough English to get by in everyday life, they were equally emphatic that their knowledge of English was still really insufficient. They could, at best, make themselves understood when they went shopping and in turn were able to understand simple sentences when they were spoken slowly. They were also acutely aware that their occupational mobility was limited unless they improved their linguistic skills. Women, who as a rule had much less formal education than their husbands, did not seem to be able to cope with learning a new language.

Sponsorship groups were also divided whether to encourage refugees to work while in language training. Furthermore, considering the low earning capacity of those in full and part-time work, sponsors had difficulty in reaching a consensus as to whether they should adjust the refugee's allowance once employed. In some groups, one dollar was

[6] Since they are privately sponsored, women are not eligible for any kind of day care subsidies and the cost of day care is prohibitive even for sponsors.

deducted for every two dollars earned; in others no adjustment was made.

Of the refugees who completed English language training, none is now unemployed, although one works part-time. Moreover, with one exception, sponsors were instrumental in finding them jobs. Only three groups, however, were able to find jobs which were related to the refugee's previous occupation and these refugees earn approximately $4 per hour. The others found employment as dishwashers or other unskilled work at a rate of $3 to $3.50 per hour. It is significant to note that the few wives who were able to work part-time, because their children were at school, earned more money per hour than did their husbands.

As a rule, sponsors continued paying the rent after the refugee held a full-time job but, with few exceptions, they no longer did so once the year of sponsorship was ended. Many refugees with large families expressed spontaneously their anxiety that their present income would not be sufficient to cover the rent as well. Project 4,000 encouraged sponsors to find accommodations in their own neighborhood to facilitate the refugees' integration process. As a result, only four families were initially placed in the low rent district of Centretown where yearly leases are not required. Refugee families who lived close to the sponsors' residences were introduced to accommodations which were not only beyond their perception of what they required but also beyond their projected earning capacity once they would become totally self-supporting. Thus, at the end of their first year of residence in Canada many families would be likely to relocate to Centretown and a second exodus from the suburbs could well occur. The situation may be further aggravated by the fact that refugees saw their future housing as a potential source of cutting down expenses. They would like to move into smaller and simpler quarters or share a larger apartment with another family. However, the prevalent social definition of what constitutes adequate housing and, more importantly, an acceptable occupancy ratio, will prevent them from making any substantial savings in this regard.

In their role as social facilitators, sponsors, with few exceptions, adopted a strictly instrumental and short-term approach. They tried to make the refugees self-sufficient as soon as language training was completed and helped them in locating whatever work happened to be available, sometimes with the promise to look for better paying jobs. Only two sponsorship groups, neither organizationally affiliated, have planned for the long range. One group insisted that the refugee, a white collar worker, enroll in a second language course to become proficient in English as a prerequisite for finding a job related to his previous occupation. Members of the second group found the refugee employment where he could get on the job training in the former occupation and enrolled the refugee in a night class to upgrade technical skills.[7] The few other sponsors who investigated the possibilities for retraining and upgrading were discouraged by the fact that, with their present level of English, refugees could not qualify for retraining, even if the sponsors could support them during this period. Employment Center officials have similarly suggested to sponsors that occupational training is "premature at this point".

Thus, refugees were caught in a double bind. They needed to improve their knowledge of English; yet, considering the type of jobs they were holding and the hours they work, the chances of doing so either at work or in night courses were slim. Without qualifying for any retraining or skill upgrading programs, these refugees would not be able to raise their present occupational status and would remain in marginal jobs. The exception was three watchmakers, who, as members of a traditional craft, could readily transfer their skills and even found it much easier to repair watches in the West than in their own country.

As expected, upgrading of skills may be more easily achieved in the case of blue collar than in the case of white collar workers. For blue collar workers such upgrading may be essentially confined to improving their skills and technological knowledge. All of them reported that they had acquired their skills in Vietnam by having been trained on the job or by simply observing others; they also admitted, without exception, that they did not have the necessary technical skills to resume their old occupation in Canada. White collar workers constituted a rather heterogeneous category ranging from businessmen and managers to teacher and middle-level administrator. The two businessmen—one a peddler of watches and the other a former owner of a small restaurant—had limited education and, according to North American criteria, did not belong in this category at all. Since they also had no technical skills, at present they could only accept unskilled work and hope for some occupational training in the future. Of the four plant managers only one appeared to be an expert in his craft and would be able to qualify as a skilled worker in the same industry if such a job were available. The remaining three had limited technical qualifications and were bound to remain occupationally downwardly mobile. The former administrator was realistic enough to hope for some occupational training as a skilled worker which would give him a steady income, while the teacher would have liked to have been able to use his knowledge of mathematics once proficient in English.

[7] It is worth noting that after he had been certified as "being capable of working in an auto-mechanic's job", the refugee started work in a garage for $3.50 an hour, but received a raise to $4.00 three days later and was promised further increases in the future.

Findings concerning the social adjustment of refugees as perceived by sponsors and refugees themselves were rather complex and required extremely careful interpretation. The definition of what constitutes successful adjustment was vague among sponsors; their understanding of it was influenced by an implicit model of integration which ranged from assimilation to adaptation.

We asked sponsors, "In your opinion, which of the family members has made the best adjustment"? The responses were quite consistent. Younger children were preceived to have made the best adjustment, followed by older children, fathers and, lastly, mothers. The very ranking and reasons given for it suggest that adjustment is assessed on two dimensions, language proficiency and an implicit model of assimmilation. The two dimensions are associated, but at this point cannot be isolated conceptually and empirically. For instance, the high ranking of children and the low ranking of mothers is based, as sponsors admit, on their respective level of English. Yet, mothers are also seen as being unwilling not only to learn English but to integrate into the larger society as well; in addition, they are most frequently reported to have emotional and health problems. While sponsors were worried about the wife's adjustment and had some sympathy for her situation, they also expressed surprise and a little resentment at what they perceived to be her powerful position within the family and her unwillingness to make an effort to adjust.[8]

However, sponsors clearly had an assimilation model in mind in regard to the children. Sponsors often mention the children as being the most gratifying and enduring benefit of sponsorship. As one sponsor put it, "The children integrate so quickly; in a couple of months they'll be like normal Canadian kids". It seems that children are the focus of sponsors' efforts in a large part because their rapid assimilation is "rewarding". Sponsors tended to act *in loco parentis* at schools, at social functions and on outings in the community. Thus sponsors may inadvertently contribute to the intergenerational conflict of refugees which is an inevitable consequence of tension between preserving cultural identity and the pressure to assimilate into the larger society.[9] Refugees did not

[8] Sponsors were told in orientation sessions that the head of household acts as spokesman for his family and that the wife and children have a subordinate position. The finding as to the role of the wife within the family is at this point difficult to interpret; however, the fact that in Vietnam all women contributed to the family income by working mostly as street peddlers and fruit and fish vendors may be related to it.

[9] Among others, *See*, S.N. Eisenstadt's *The Absorption of Immigrants*, 1954, F.L.K. Hsu, *The Challenge of the American Dream: The Chinese in The United States*, 1971, S.W. Kung, *Chinese in American Life*, 1975.

feel any resentment against the attention their children received by the sponsors, particularly since most had already transferred their hopes and aspirations to them and expected little for themselves.

Differences in models of integration held by the sponsors were clearly discernable in reply to the question as to how they would feel about the development of a Vietnamese community in Ottawa. Some sponsors with an assimilationist approach were remarkably candid in their responses: "They're not at home anymore, they shouldn't segregate themselves from us", or "I'd rather see refugees merging in with the rest of the community". Others simply stated that they had not given any thought to the development of an ethnic community since they defined their own task as resocializing the refugee family. However, it appears that in some groups sponsors suspended the assimilationist model for the older generation, since they saw a role for the ethnic community in the short-term. Thus, depending on their implicit integration model, they saw moral support as a task to be shared with the ethnic communities, and felt that these communities and particularly other refugees could give subtler kinds of emotional support which sponsors could not provide because of language barriers and cultural differences. In the sponsor's words: "Refugees need the support of their own group . . . to facilitate adjustment . . . in that way they are less of a burden on the sponsors" and "on the general society".

Although we did not ask the refugees directly how they view their own adjustment process, replies to other questions showed that they have not yet found their social anchorage in Canadian society; in view of their relatively short stay in Canada this should not be surprising. North Vietnamese, particularly, seem to be overwhelmed by the high standard of living and material wealth in Canada compared to their home country, and all of them have difficulty in adjusting to the cold climate in winter. Many mention that their time is consumed with learning English or making enough money to support their families and as a result they had little time for finding out more about the Canadian way of life.

Sponsors act, as it were, as the direct representatives of the new society; apart from providing material help, they, ideally, should also guide the refugees in their initial social and cultural adjustment. It is reasonable to assume, therefore, that the refugees' ability or willingness to integrate will depend, to a significant extent, on the nature of their interaction with sponsors. We asked refugees to characterize their relationship with sponsors as "adopted parents, relatives, friends, or acquaintances they have to get along with for a year". In most cases refugees saw their sponsors as either adopted parents or friends and expressed satisfaction with the amount of social contact. The few sponsors who were seen by refugees as "acquaintances" belonged to work and residentially based groups. These refugees also reported that their contact with sponsors was infrequent and irregular.

In other words, the majority of refugees viewed their sponsors as persons whom they could trust, and, more importantly, as equals in their social interaction. This finding would suggest that, despite cultural differences and communication problems, sponsors were able to prevent or overcome any feeling of personal dependence and hence of social inferiority on the part of the refugees which the very nature of sponsorship can easily give rise to.

Since our last interviews were conducted midway through the sponsorship year and the number of groups studied was small, any findings concerning sponsorship groups and refugees have to be cautiously interpreted. For instance, it would seem that organizationally affiliated groups, by virtue of their high level of organization and cohesion, are more successful in fulfilling their obligations. However, we cannot say as yet which of the structural characteristics are more important contributing factors as far as this success is concerned: the *locus* of group formation or the group members' ability to develop a well defined division of labor and social cohesion among them regardless of whether the group was formed within or outside an organizational context.

Moreover, the fact that, irrespective of their structural characteristics, sponsorship groups on the whole have adopted a strictly instrumental, short-term approach toward refugees may defeat the very purpose of facilitating the refugees' social adjustment. Most of the refugees have been placed in unskilled, deadend and low paying jobs. As a rule sponsors also have not made any provisions to further improve or upgrade the refugees' linguistic and occupational skills. In absolute terms the refugees' occupational downward mobility is less than it would be if they had been professionals in Vietnam; however, they seem to feel their status loss keenly, particularly since all of them had high occupational aspirations when they first came to Canada, the preferred employment being "work in the electronics industry". We cannot say at this stage to what extent these high expectations have inadvertently been fostered by the refugees' exposure to the middle class way of life of their sponsors. We can also only conjecture that in some cases this exposure may ultimately become a source of frustration once they realize that such a way of life is beyond their reach. These questions can only be answered by a comparative study of government and privately sponsored refugees after they have been in Canada for a longer period of time. It is hoped that the main project will produce findings which will give us greater confidence in the viability of the conjectures and inferences raised by the preliminary results discussed in this paper.

[32]

Journal of Refugee Studies Vol. 4. No. 1 1991

Labelling Refugees: Forming and Transforming a Bureaucratic Identity

ROGER ZETTER*
Editor, Journal of Refugee Studies

This essay examines how and with what consequences people become labelled as refugees within the context of public policy practices. Conceptual and operational limitations to the existing definition of refugees are noted. These, the paper contends, derive from the absence of a systematic study of labelling processes in the donative policy discourse associated with refugees.

The paper outlines the conceptual tools of bureaucratic labelling – stereotyping, conformity, designation, identity disaggregation and political/power relationships. These tools are then deployed to analyse empirical data collected from a large refugee population in Cyprus, supplemented by selective secondary research data on various African refugee populations. The analysis proceeds in three parts. First the formation of the label is considered in which stereotyped identities are translated into bureaucratically assumed needs. The label thus takes on a selective, materialist meaning. Alienating distinctions emerge by the creation of different categories of refugee deemed necessary to prioritize need. Next, reformation of the label is considered. The evidence shows how latent and manifest processes of institutional action and programme delivery, reinforce a disaggregated model of identity; in this case disturbing distinctions are made between refugee and non-refugee. Third, the paper considers how labels assume, often conflicting, politicized meanings, for both labelled and labellers.

The paper concludes by emphasizing: the extreme vulnerability of refugees to imposed labels; the importance of symbolic meaning; the dynamic nature of the identity; and, most fundamentally of all, the non-participatory nature and powerlessness of refugees in these processes.

'You don't feel a second class citizen except with other people – then the housing is a label' – Greek-Cypriot Refugee

Introduction

Within the repertoire of humanitarian concern, refugee now constitutes one of the most powerful labels. From the first procedures of status determination -who is a refugee? – to the structural determinants of life chances which this identity then engenders, labels infuse the world of refugees.

This paper is concerned with labels as a conceptual metaphor. It considers as a general aim, the conceptual language of labelling in the context of refugee studies. Then, using empirical data mainly from Cyprus but also from research literature on refugees in Africa, the specific tasks are to explore how and with what consequences people become labelled as refugees - how an identity is formed, transformed and manipulated within the context of public policy and especially, bureaucratic practices.

A popular conceptualization of the refugee is readily to hand. To the extent that some 14 million or so forced migrants are categorized - labelled - as refugees with an internationally recognised legal status, given credibility by an international agency specifically charged to safeguard their interests, endorsed most powerfully of all by spontaneous philanthropy - the meaning of the label seems self evident. Refugees are, like the places described in Waugh's first travel book, 'fully labelled' in people's minds (Waugh 1930).

Despite a widely recognised universal condition it remains the case that there is great difficulty in agreeing an acceptable definition of the label refugee. This is more than a taxonomic problem because, far from clarifying an identity, the label conveys, instead, an extremely complex set of values, and judgements which are more than just definitional (Zetter 1988:1).

There are a number of major difficulties in sustaining the popular assumptions. First, the interventionary and definitional practices of states, and their political interests, illustrate that the apparent simplicity of a *de minimis* legal label very quickly evaporates. (Montes 1988; Loescher and Scanlon 1986; Zolberg et al. 1989; Zucker and Zucker 1987). In practice there are many interpretations of the definition and, like currencies, they have fluctuating values and exchange rates.

These operational considerations co-exist with a second set of difficulties. There is extensive empirical evidence to illustrate that refugees conceive their identity in very different terms from those bestowing the label (Harrell-Bond 1986; Mazur 1986; Waldron 1988).

Third, there are severe conceptual difficulties in establishing a normative meaning to a label which is a malleable and dynamic as refugee. It is contingent upon notions of persecution, and sovereignty (Adelman 1988; Shaknove 1985) about which there is little concensus, a situation clearly recognised by the OAU Convention of 1969, for example, with its much broader conceptualization of refugee status (Kibreab 1985). Then there are internally displaced people, enduring physical and social trauma equal to that of refugees (Gersony 1988); but they are not officially labelled as refugees. More generally sociological distinctions between concepts of refugeehood and concepts of migration remain lacking in precision (Mazur 1988: 44–5).

Any conceptualization of the label refugee must contend with a fourth problematic area; it is this which forms the specific concern of this paper. Refugees inhabit an institutionalized world of NGOs, intergovernmental agencies and governments, in which a highly developed framework of public policy exists to provide emergency and developmental assistance. Given this conjuncture, there remains, in my view, an important lacuna in any attempt to define the label. There exists the need to establish more precisely the extent to which bureaucratic interests and procedures are themselves crucial determinants in the definition of labels like refugee. The challenge is a significant one because our concern is fundamental - processes by which refugees are socialized with certain identities and the structural impacts (control, regulation, opportunities) of these identities (Wood 1985:5).

There is a substantial literature on managerialism and patron-client relationships to which this concern relates. Yet within public policy discourse there has been little systematic development of a theoretical framework of labelling which might help to explore in more detail how bureaucratic labels are formed. It was to address this concern that together with colleagues (Wood 1985), we attempted to construct a language and a framework of conceptual tools of labelling target groups in public (especially development) policy. These theoretical developments, it is contended, offer a potentially rich vein of exploration of the refugee phenomenon. It is this framework which I deploy to examine the interaction between bureaucratic policy and procedures on the one hand and refugees' reactions on the other. The conceptual tools of labelling allow us to explore this interplay of interests at their 'point of organizational connection' (Schaffer 1975:7). Simultaneous examination of both the meaning of the institutional label and the reactions of the labelled, sheds new light on the ambivalent and disjunctive responses which refugees frequently display towards assistance programmes. This is the forming and transforming of a bureaucratic identity.

The Refugees

My own entry point to this problematic analytical situation was in trying to understand the reactions of Greek-Cypriot refugees to their newly acquired identity. In 1974 after a long period of intercommunal conflict between Greek- and Turkish-Cypriots, Turkey invaded and still continues to occupy northern Cyprus - approximately 40% of the land area. Some 180,000 Greek-Cypriots (from an ethnic population of about 500,000) became labelled as 'refugees', fleeing from the north to the south of the island. This was paralleled by a reverse flow of 50,000 Turkish-Cypriots from a total ethnic population of 120,000. *De facto* partition and the mass movement of people created an entirely new political and bureaucratic context for public policy. Of the many responses to this crisis, the one that is particularly significant for this paper, concerns the mobilisation of an extremely large rehousing programme for the Greek-Cypriot refugees in the southern part of the island, and the impact which this had on them.

There are three main components in this programme. First, there are comprehensively planned contractor built estates on the periphery of the three main towns in the south of the island. About 14,000 units have been built and those eligible for these houses are the poorer and larger refugee families. Second there are self-build schemes where refugees, with concessionary government grants and loans, build their own homes to prescribed plans on serviced government land. Again these are located, by and large, on the urban periphery but in some village locations.

Popular because this method mirrors pre-1974 housing processes, nonetheless, like the estate houses, the regularity of form and layout provides a dramatic contrast to the pre-existing morphology of towns and villages. About 12,500 units have been built in this fashion. In the larger self-build and government estates, schools, shopping centres and other community facilities have been built. Third, similar assistance is available for those fortunate refugees who owned or who have been able to buy their own plots of land freehold and a further 12,000 units have been built in this way. A range of smaller scale initiatives exists: By 1990, some 150,000 Greek-Cypriot refugees had been rehoused and over 40,000 houses constructed. Progress has thus been made towards rehousing a very large number of refugees in good quality housing. The programme is detailed elsewhere (Zetter 1986:108–109; 1987:117–196).

Closely linked to the housing programme have been far reaching programmes for reconstructing and restructuring the shattered economy, from an agricultural to an urban-industrial base and to achieving virtually full employment (Zetter 1987:173–184). Disaster as development (MEED 1981; Lewis 1980; UNDRO 1987), the response to the severe economic disequilibrium created in 1974, has been remarkably successful.

By many conventional evaluative measures, this appears, therefore, to be a remarkably successful programme and indeed there is much in the experience which is relevant elsewhere. The speed, quality and volume of housing output, the number of families rehoused, the organizational capability of the public sector, the equity-based allocative mechanisms, the rapid absorption of refugees into the productive economy, the evident achievement of many programme targets - these and many other criteria highlight what in many respects is an astonishing accomplishment. Over 40% of the *total* population has been rehoused in a decade and a half.

Many enabling conditions prevailed in Cyprus which do not occur in most refugee stricken countries - capital and material resources; technological, administrative and professional capability; ethnic, religious and linguistic solidarity; monopolistic control of the reconstruction by the government, for example. Thus the refugee housing is unlike the stereotyped image in other countries similarly struggling to respond to refugee influxes.

Despite these factors the Cyprus situation displays many of the complexities of other refugee situations to suggest that this is not a limited case. For, despite the effectiveness of the programme in these terms, there remains a series of outcomes, now displayed by the refugees and arising from the programme, which cannot be satisfactorily explained or understood by utilising orthodox forms of public policy evaluation. What has meaning to the refugees cannot be interpreted by the kinds of data which focus on programme output and normative policy assumptions. Rather, these indices, amongst others, are themselves indicative of highly instrumental, though not necessarily intentional, components of the programme which need to be more precisely revealed.

In the pre-crisis situation public sector housing scarcely existed. Now, confronted by a government-dominated programme located on easily identifiable 'refugee estates' at the urban periphery, the refugees simultaneously display a number of paradoxical responses. There is both client-group compliance yet also alienation in the refugees' reactions to the programme. They, paradoxically, appear to accept yet also to reject the label and differentiation which the housing gives to their situation. There is dependency assertively employed to maintain a separate identity. They are indifferent to, yet draw political solidarity and status from the programme. Many responses to housing, particularly in the self-help projects, seem to indicate settlement in the south; yet the refugees retain a profound belief in 'repatriation' to the north as a paramount and still achievable objective – a decade and a half since the crisis and with little immediate prospect of achievement. By and large there are few indicators now of temporariness. In part attributable to the physical characteristics of the housing, there are severe and disturbing changes in cultural norms, kinship patterns and family structure. Yet, confusingly, though widely replicated, these changes are rationalised by refugees as progressive.

From a number of complementary perspectives therefore, the dilemmas of refugee identity are now derived not so much from the legacy of exodus and the diaspora, movingly portrayed in the Cyprus case by Loizos (1977, 1981). Rather, it is differentiation and 'identity by programme' (de Voe 1981), which, through a process of incorporation, appears so clearly to label their status.

Labelling

The ambivalent and apparently incongruous outcomes, like those displayed in Cyprus, are widely documented features of refugee communities. They are well established phenomena consistent with the dilemmas and tensions generated by the relief and development programmes of most governments and NGOs responding to the assumed needs of refugees (eg Shawcross 1984; Harrell-Bond 1986; Waldron 1988; Hirschon 1989).

Because of the pre-eminence both of the government and of the post-partition housing policies, the institutional and bureaucratic characteristics of this programme, constitute an important arena for examining the reactions of the Greek-Cypriot refugees. A framework of analysis is needed, however, which allows the interrelationship between institutional action on the one hand and the apparently incongruent responses of the refugees on the other, to be more precisely observed and explored.

The literature on the general set of relationships between institutional action and refugee behaviour is now substantial; concepts of dependency and control figure highly (Harrell-Bond 1986; Shawcross 1984). So far as conceptualizing these relationships in terms of labelling, however, the literature is tangential. That there has been little systematic treatment of the conceptual framework of labelling in this context is surprising. Labels pervade both social and development policy discourse, donative discourses to which, I contend, refugees are particularly subject.

'Labelling is a way of referring to the process by which policy agendas are established and more particularly the way in which people, conceived as objects of policy are defined in convenient images' (Wood 1985:1). This conceptualization is predicated on a series of propositions; those more relevant to this paper are now briefly summarized (see Wood 1985:5–31; Schaffer 1985:33–66).

First, to the extent that my concern is to explore how and with what effects designation takes place, then it is the *processes* of labelling as much as the labels themselves which are of significance.

Next, labelling is a process of *stereotyping* which involves disaggregation, standardization, and the formulation of clear cut categories. In the institutional setting these characteristics assume considerable power, for labelling simultaneously defines a client group and prescribes an assumed set of needs (food, shelter and protection) together with appropriate distributional apparatus. With this symmetry, especially in the context of humanitarian assistance, institutional action acquires its own legitimacy and apparent benevolence. It is, precisely through this prescriptive process that an institutional identity is being formed.

> What is being exchanged . . . is the way in which people can present themselves as applicants and present their wants and needs for the items and privileges of institutional services. That is . . . a disaggregation into programme terms . . . It reduces the whole man and family into formal sets of compartmentalised data . . . a sort of individuation and alienation of a man from a large part of his being (Schaffer 1977:32).

Thus, in this separation of an individual's needs from their context, and the process of reconstruction into a programmatic identity, there is created the important distinction between 'case' and 'story' (Wood 1985:13). Delinkage takes place whereby an individual identity is replaced by a stereotyped identity with a categorical prescription of assumed needs. These categories are usually absolute not relative or comparative. Labels replicate the professional, bureaucratic and political values which create them; but a story is thus reformed into a case, a category. I examine in some detail, in the next part of this paper, how the formation of a refugee stereotype in this way took place in Cyprus.

The counterpart to stereotyping is *control*, since a considerable degree of client loyalty and conformity with the stereotype is required (Hirschman 1970), not uniqueness and individuality. Such control, though not physically enforced in Cyprus as in many refugee situations, has been nonetheless instrumental in determining the meaning of the label refugee. These processes of categorization and differentiation have been significant factors in forming a stereotyped identity for the Greek-Cypriot refugees. Further, I argue that the need to conform to an institutionally imposed stereotype can both reinforce control and transform an identity.

Fourth, labelling is a process of *designation*, for it involves making judgements and distinctions; crucially, it is *non-participatory*. The process of labelling, by its very familiarity and ubiquitousness in bureaucratic activity, may almost go unnoticed or unquestioned. It suggests neutrality; the very conformity it produces conveys, 'a substantive objectivity . . . ', (Wood 1985:7). But bureaucratic procedures, resource distribution and the underlying political interests they represent, suggest that the labelling of target groups and their needs is not neutral or precise (Rosenblat, 1984). These implicit values need more critical review. Refugee relief programmes, because of their self-evident humanitarian derivation, are particularly prone to the neutralising conformity which the label conveys about refugees' status and their situation. Labels then reveal 'the political in the apparently non-political' (Wood 1985:6) and the power displayed through administrative procedure and practice. Subsequent connections with theories of the state are considered but are not the main issue here.

Finally, and by extension, labels are not only political but also *dynamic*. A programme's goods and services acquire a status; a client group, like refugees does not necessarily remain acquiescent and 'loyal'. Accordingly, the label may not only be the consequence of, but also the cause of further policy development, institutional activity and demands by the labelled group. These may be factors in restructuring further, the political interests. I examine this characteristic in the last parts of my analysis.

Although much research into refugees, as I have indicated, makes significant contributions to my concerns with institutional labelling, the treatment is peripheral. There are in the literature, however, two rather more clearly exposed perspectives on labelling to which this paper connects.

Studies by Stein (1981), de Voe (1981), de Waal (1988) and Centlivres and Centlivres-Demont(1988) implicitly draw on the concept but do not specifically deploy it. Stein draws attention to the effects which stigma and identity have on assumptions about status and the potential success or otherwise of resettlement schemes. Although suggesting that these factors may be institutionally determined, the conceptual basis of his analysis concerns processes of assimilation. De Voe studied the way relief agencies formed Tibetan refugees as clients. Her interest in ambiguous benefactor-beneficiary relationships focuses, however, on psychological anxiety in individual adjustment to agency intervention. Finally, studies by de Waal (1988; 1989) and Centlivres (1988) are closer to my own. Both illustrate how the superimposition of institutionally determined refugee status greatly destabilizes the co-existing ethnicities of hosts and refugees. Ambiguous identities emerge which, in the former study, are disastrous.

A second conceptual reference point has a bearing on this approach. It derives from Shacknove's question - who is a refugee? (Shacknove 1985). Here the label is painted as a minimal social bond of rights and obligations between a citizen and a state 'the negation of which engenders refugees' (Shacknove 1985:275). Defining a refugee in these terms is predicated on the argument that a 'theory and policy of entitlements' (Shacknove 1985:277) is separate from and subsequent to the former, although frequently, and erroneously in his view, the concepts are reversed. I deploy this distinction in my initial evaluation of the Cyprus data in the next section. Nevertheless, much of my paper, though not proposed as an examination of Shacknove's thesis, leads me to question whether such a distinction holds.

Our starting point is a concern with policy shortfall expressed in disjunctive outcomes of the kind found in the Cypriot refugee population. These outcomes - misconceived identities - we take as evidence of institutional failure. Although our explanations of this evidence are complementary, there are important differences of emphasis. These studies argue that the problem is attributable to the preconceived objectives and assumptions which institutions hold about their tasks and clients and an unwillingness to observe and enlist the resources, capabilities and views of the refugees. These factors, in some senses, I take as given: the attributes of institutional ideology. My emphasis is on what happens *within* the institutional arena. More specially, I contend that what is crucial to an understanding of how institutions (mis)conceive a refugee label, is an examination of the bureaucratic practices which are intrinsic to any public institution concerned with resource distribution. It is through the apparently normal, routine, apolitical, conventional procedures of programme design and delivery that identity is determined. For the instrumentality of these procedures lies in the conformity they demand from refugee clients to gain access to the resources and label. This is the 'political significance of organizational analysis' (Batley 1983:5).

Who Is a Refugee? — Forming an Identity

Many aspects of the situation in Cyprus were consistent with what the label, in conventional usage, implied. Ethnic conflict and persecution which were widely documented, accompanied the forcible removal of the Greek-Cypriots. Substantial UNHCR assistance, although not mandated, conferred added legitimacy. Contained within a small island, with a short migratory time period, easily controlled 'borders' and with sophisticated data collection, these factors eliminated the difficulties that have occurred elsewhere of documenting who was a refugee.

The label appears clear cut. But who was a refugee? Whilst conforming to some aspects of what Vincent (1989) terms the 'narrow band' of convention refugees (persecution was undoubtedly a well founded fear) they were not outside their country of origin. They were protected by their (albeit emasculated) *de facto* government. In these terms they constituted the rather less evocative category of displaced people. These contradictions and their precise consequences constitute an interesting subject for political and legal analysis. My concern, however, is not that of legal norms and sovereignty - who was a refugee? Rather, it was an issue of entitlements, in particular housing, and the institutionalization of those entitlements - who was a refugee for housing purposes? In this rather different formulation, two sets of principles can be seen in operation, often confusingly together. First there was a general set of equity-based assumptions designed to provide most for those in greatest need - families considered to be under greatest threat of destitution or breakdown. These substantive considerations - difficult enough to determine in themselves - then became translated into managerial requirements. Given the extreme scarcities that accompany most refugee crises, queues form, needs have to be prioritized and managed in relation to the general principles. Accordingly, access and allocation criteria were established, some categorical, some discretionary, based, in the first instance on family size and income thresholds.

To conform to the label refugee defined in these terms, putative beneficiaries adopted different strategies often simultaneously. Some, the reconstructors, altered their family circumstances to fit the criteria; reticulists sought assistance from contacts; optimisers who clearly understood rather more about bureaucratic procedures, judiciously sought to exercise some choice. Whilst different levels of pragmatism underpin these strategies, two conclusions are relevant to the general argument. Whether a strategist or a compliant client the objective was to be included. Because of the symbolic importance of housing (discussed in the next sections) exit or self settlement were not perceived as options. Second, and more fundamentally, inclusion, being labelled a refugee, required conformity; circumstances of 'story' had to be relinquished to the bureaucratic dictates of 'case'.

By and large, though, the criteria have ensured that it was the rural farming families and the urban poor who were suddenly unwaged in the diaspora, and those with larger dependent (though, significantly, not extended) families who were thus housed in the early phases - since their economic status was highly location specific to the north of Cyprus. Civil servants, salaried income earners, and wealthier families with perhaps more spatially diffuse land holdings and varied income sources were, initially, excluded although all were refugees. To this extent the criteria determining access to the tangible physical identity of the refugee label, a house, have been remarkably progressive, although even the first category families may have waited four or five years for an estate house. But in Cyprus, as elsewhere there is evidence of paradoxical outcomes from the distributional features of the policy. The label refugee now conveys a disturbing identity.

It may indeed have been advantageous, early on, to be labelled a poor refugee with a large family. In this way, with a rent free house and perhaps then a job in the rapidly reconstructed economy, these refugees became, in the short term at least, materially better placed than many of those originally excluded by higher income and smaller family status. The latter category have endured many difficult years perhaps in shared accommodation, almost certainly in unsatisfactory temporary shelter.

Yet, the equity intentions embodied in the label, have engendered unwanted and disturbing outcomes within the refugee community. Those who had least have become incorporated most by initial opportunities. Restricted mobility constrains the choices now available from the much more sophisticated range of housing options which currently exists. More disturbingly, it is the housing estates built in the early phases which are perceived as problem or 'ghetto' estates. They are inhabited by a population of uniform demographic and socio-economic characteristics (larger families and poorer means). This image is underpinned by physical characteristics as well, since the oldest estates are, generally, much larger, housing designs are more monotonous, maintenance problems with the then new technology are greater. But these outcomes are of course the precise image of the definitional criteria applied to the label refugee. Obviously unintended, these outcomes derive from more than one's self-perceived status as a refugee. It is the stereotyping of an identity; it is imposed not elective, and the more stigmatizing and alienating as a result.

Conversely the newer estates are smaller and more attractively laid out; the houses are better finished. Self build opportunities - replicating the traditional cultural processes - came later and increasingly generous grant/loan packages together with rising prosperity, have permitted much higher quality to be achieved. Paradoxically the queue for the label has thus been beneficial. Those towards the end of the queue; those in the pending category because of smaller families or higher levels of disposable income; those initially excluded from the label as less deserving by the stringently progressive criteria; these categories now have access to the label as the programme reaches its goal of housing all the refugee families from 1974. But unintentionally, of course, they are better housed in the popular image. Reflecting, then, on the spatially heterogenous structure of pre-1974 towns and villages, a new form of social stratification is evident in the refugee housing estates.

A second set of data reinforces this evidence of disjunctive and alienating outcomes which derive from the bureaucratic response. For rehousing purposes, refugees were classified according to marital status pre- and post- 1974 and their locational preference. Families which were constituted before 1974 (so called first generation) have had unconstrained access to housing. For the latter group (so called second generation), access was at first resisted. It was however conceded, though severely circumscribed, some years later. Dowry house provision was the reason for this concession since refugees no longer had land or finance available which would have been used in their past to carry out this cultural obligation. Only women (second generation) refugees were eligible and at first their spouses too had to be refugees although this was later relaxed. In addition to this major change, the general access criteria (income and family size) were also relaxed, to a small degree, in some districts. So, additional and more precisely defined categories obtained. At issue though is not just a response to changing needs. Compartmentalizing the refugees into these categories, was also, I contend, a bureaucratic way of fulfilling a set of managerial objectives. Widening eligibility helped to diversify the demographic and social character of the estates. It helped also in tackling the lumpiness of the construction process, since leads and lags were endemic in Cyprus as elsewhere. In any case, fluctuating refugee preferences accentuated shortfalls and overruns.

In much the same way as the primary criteria, these additional categories too, have reinforced a bureaucratically formed meaning for the label. In the government's terms, income, birthplace, marital status and family size, generation and age of children would, understandably, have appeared to be equitable, uncontentious and above all practicable criteria for defining refugee housing needs. But they embody concepts of time, family status and organizational structure rooted in a bureaucratic language quite unfamiliar to the refugees. From their point of view, they were refugees having fled the invasion in which the politico-historical antecedents to their situation were much more significant. Their identity was not, in their perception, predetermined by thoughts of housing programmes, eligibility and access rules. Rather it was constructed with a social language drawing on past norms - community, village, extended family, dowry house provision for daughter upon marriage. This point is well documented in African refugee studies (Harrell-Bond 1986; Christensen 1982, 1985).

These familiar kinds of attachments - re-establishing the pre-existing identity one might say - have been replaced by a bureaucratically imposed identity, often with perverse consequences. The state now provides dowry housing for a substantial proportion of the Greek-Cypriot population.

Most disturbing for all the refugees is the breakup of the pre-1974 village groupings, made fragile anyway in the diaspora. Many villages fled as entities, initially retained their cohesion in temporary accommodation and aspired to sustain their village communities intact in the rehousing programme. Re-establishing 'community', as noted above, is widely documented in refugee populations. By disaggregating the label in order to form it into bureaucratically manageable individual cases, the criteria have thereby prevented village re-formation. If practicable, a programme which rehoused them comprehensively village by village, might have removed the most profound consequences of their social trauma. Village fragmentation more than many outcomes, now dramatizes for the refugees the ambiguity of their changed identity. On balance, though, they paradoxically rationalise that the fragmentation of village life has consolidated their new identity of displacement, temporariness and abnormality. Ambiguity of the kind displayed here demonstrates, as Goffman observed, how even with a reformed identity, individuals seek to balance the complementary parts of the 'normal-deviant' drama (Goffman 1963:158).

Who is a refugee therefore, especially since housing is the most dramatic indicator of the label has assumed a socially divisive meaning. In being relabelled by bureaucratic requirements, refugee is differentiated from refugee - hence the continuing sense of alienation and anomie. This 'spoilt identity' is not how the group would choose to perceive itself. But they deploy the co-existing yet contradictory languages to pursue their own agendas and interests – the need for shelter at one level; pressure for repatriation at another.

A review of several recent studies of the situation of African refugees endorses both the evidence and utility of these findings. Reference is now made to three studies with a thematic focus on food aid.

De Waal's study (1988; 1989) reminds us of the dangers of reacting to involuntary migration with stereotyped categories. He presents a disturbing explanation of how 'conceptual blunders' of this kind (1988:128) led to a famine disaster in Western Sudan (Dar-el-Masalit) in 1984/5. The disaster was preventable but for the crude categories by which the refugees were designated. Based on the false belief that the 120,000 Chadian refugees were drought migrants, assistance was withheld. Having precipitated the famine the error was reversed but compounded by a food distribution programme contingent upon a very prescriptive categorization of the refugees. Largely ignorant of indigenous and subtle cultural and ethnic resonances, the agencies created conflict between hosts and refugees thereby accentuating the crises. As in Cyprus so too here, who was a refugee was crucial. The extent to which bureaucratic needs create too simple a conceptualization of identity and the consequential and often traumatic results are the crucial points here.

Waldron too (1988) adds to this evidence in his work amongst encamped Somali and Oromo refugees from Ethiopia in Somalia. Three problematic situations – a severe firewood shortage, a food provisioning crisis and cyclical patterns of supplementary feeding programmes – are discussed. There were rather obvious explanations for what, superficially, appeared to be perverse patterns of behaviour in which aid, imposed for survival, was rejected. Necessarily summarising the detail, all three issues illustrate how a failure to look beyond inappropriate, stereotypical categories, led to misrepresentation or even non-recognition of the three problems and thus misconceived programmes. The bureaucratic label failed to articulate the salient factors which made up the refugee identity.

A third study concerns declining nutritional status of refugees. This formed the stimulus for a detailed assessment of food provisioning (commissioned by WPF) to the 850,000 Mozambican refugees in Malawi (Wilson 1989). A rather different reading of this consultancy shows it to be a significant reappraisal of refugee food aid concepts, which has direct relevance to my own concerns. Wilson contends that the singleminded emphasis on sustaining the basic ration is not so much wrong as misplaced and defective. It ignores context. He demonstrates that a proper understanding of feeding strategies and needs can only derive from a study of the livelihood strategies of the refugees themselves; this embraces matters as diverse as comodification of wild resources, family feeding patterns, wage and bartered labour, ecological impacts and so on. In short, as with housing, so with food aid: conventional bureaucratic practice disaggregates one identity and replaces it with a designated stereotype, shorn of variety and individuality. If we return to our original question - who is a refugee? - it is one who conforms to institutional requirements.

Labels, like refugee, appear benign in their attempt to embrace many potential beneficiaries. But being labelled a refugee can come to mean a number of things over time, as we saw in the Cyprus data for example. These meanings are more than a simple materialistic eligibility for a house, a plot, food and so on. These examples show that in the institutional setting, labels assume a much more powerful significance. They serve as a linguistic shorthand for policies, programmes and bureaucratic requirements - practices which are instrumental in categorizing and differentiating between facets of an identity. Labelled with an identity in one conceptual language, refugees in all these cases have had imposed on them a radically different language. Whether deliberately or in ignorance, this imposition dominates the behaviour of refugee societies.

Transforming an Identity

Identities are not only formed by bureaucratic action, they are also transformed by it. Programmes develop their own momentum, rationality and continuing legitimacy in servicing perceived needs. It is these attributes of bureaucratic practice, frequently remaining unexplored, which need to be tested. By distinguishing between what the label implies is needed and what is actually provided through institutional action, we can highlight how contrasting images of identity are reinforced, and explain how alienation and ambivalence are the outcomes.

In Cyprus, two kinds of evidence from the housing programme sustain the significance of this distinction between manifest and latent intentions - economic reconstruction and housing morphology.

Post-disaster studies frequently emphasize the destructive costs and the aggravation of development constraints. A different conceptualization is relevant in examining the economic impact of the 1974 invasion in Cyprus. Here, by no means entirely pragmatically, the disaster has been engaged as a developmental disequilibrium to which the response has been a restructuring of the economy both sectorally and spatially away from its rural agrarian base. In the decade and a half post-invasion, the economy demonstrated strong yet stable growth; virtually full employment was restored and GNP far exceeded pre-1974 levels. The pursuit of these goals stands, in part, by itself; but these outcomes also have a direct bearing upon the phenomenon of refugee labelling. A reconstructed economy, as the emergency development plans make clear, was a central component in government policy for the 'reactivation and reintegration of the refugees' (Republic of Cyprus 1977:5). To this end, these remarkable achievements have been contingent on the housing programme as the leading sector and government-led investment as the dynamic force, certainly in the first decade after the invasion. In so far as this set of relationships holds, the configuration can equally well be reversed. Reconstruction of the economy could only have been achieved by deploying the refugees as a structural and spatial resource. They were a structural resource as producers and consumers. On the supply side they provided the wage labour essential for the housing construction programme and for rebuilding and extending the manufacturing and service base of the economy. On the demand side they have provided the market for light industrial/consumer goods which predominate in the relatively small economy. This structural reconstruction has been underpinned by spatial determinants. An economy dominated by the urban sector depended on mass urban housing to attract labour - exactly what the refugee housing programme has provided. Far from a burden, the refugees have literally and metaphorically rebuilt the economy.

What was being provided though, was not simply good quality housing for refugees, although the humanitarian objectives and achievements are undeniable. Simultaneously the housing programme was formulated to achieve an effective model of economic reconstruction and development. In short, one conceptualization of the label - housing need - legitimised the assertion of a rather different one, incongruent with the refugees' own perceptions. Incorporated from a rural setting into an urban economy and in a form of housing which reflected pragmatic interpretations of need - not individual requirements family by family - the meanings and outcomes of the label refugee assume distinctive yet divergent characteristics.

Evident in the physical design and location of the housing, is a second set of ambiguities. Large scale housing estates were a radical departure from the pre-1974 urban morphology - characterized by a piecemeal and incremental process of plot by plot development by individual owners. Motivated by the desire to provide material compensation, perceiving the overriding priority to be shelter provision and assuming total responsibility, these requirements became translated, by the government, into bureaucratized mass-housing solutions - functional designs, uniform styles, standardized layouts. These acknowledge nothing of the preceding cultural and vernacular characteristics. Designed for small nuclear families, they fail especially to reflect the prevailing requirements of the extended family. They are incapable of extension or adaptation to changing needs. Moreover programmes mean leads and lags and thus sub-optimal allocation - a wrong sized house, a less preferred estate, a longer wait in the pending category. The resulting discontinuities, between expectation and outcomes - an accentuated sense of alienation and deprivation, overcrowding, loss of privacy - are a clear and sharp reflection of an institutionalized definition embodied in the label refugee. Needs and aspirations became structured into technocratically manageable programmes with unwanted effects on the lives of the refugees

Underlying these perceptions, it is the location of the estates which is more significant. Effectively a predominantly rural population (60% of the refugees) has been urbanised. Located adjacent to, but not contiguous with, urban areas and with easily identifiable characteristics (layout, form, size of schemes), the housing estates give a distinctive physical identity to the label.

This again has accentuated the development of a 'refugee consciousness' which is expressed in various contradictory ways. Solidarity and compliance are counterbalanced by pathological attempts to delabel – refusing all but the last, most isolated, house on an estate, for example – and adoption of Goffman-like metaphors to describe feelings: prisoners, foreigners.

Refugees do not necessarily complain that they did not participate in the shaping of policy. Housing is accepted with gratitude yet, ambivalently, the refugees feel stigmatised. Despite showing identical cultural norms with their hosts, they believe the housing, the obviously recognisable symbol of their status, may have encouraged enmity by non-refugees. There is continuing anomie and resentment at the control and conditionality which the housing represents. Conversely, it is recognised that policy failure is important. Were assimilation to be successfully achieved, a label would be blurred and pressure for repatriation would thus be lost. The refugees have managed to avert this marginalization of their interests, so far.

For the refugees their designation was instrumental in gaining access to important resources. In this process, their aspirations were filtered into the housing programme which became characterised by a particular formula of professional and technocratic assumptions. This lack of congruence has had dramatic consequences. Just as the access criteria have differentiated between refugee and refugee, so too, the form and location of housing, set within the context of economic reconstruction, have also tended to differentiate. In this instance though, it is a categorical distinction between refugees and non-refugees. The pattern of housing provision has created fundamental contrasts between what by other criteria would seem to be similar identities. The label has become, through powerful institutional processes, a potent tool of prescription and differention far removed from the initial premise that refugees need shelter.

Many of these themes are replicated in the findings of studies on refugees in Africa. In this context, perhaps the most significant demonstration of the confusing interaction between latent and manifest meanings of the label, relates to settlement schemes and self-settlement. These touch closely on issues of transitory or protracted status.

There is now, abundant evidence in the continent, documenting refugee preference for self-settlement, in so far as this exists in a pure sense (Hansen 1981, 1989; Harrell-Bond 1986;). The more obvious conditions conducive to this preference are documented in the sociological and anthropological literature (Mazur 1988; and above). And yet, it is conceded that scheme settled refugees are better provided for materially in the short term and evidently, too, in the long term (Hansen 1989). Moreover a substantial proportion of aid to African refugees is for settlement schemes (hereafter called schemes). Why therefore should only a quarter of Africa's refugees live in schemes? I contend that these paradoxical findings can, in part, be clarified by considering them in the context of labelling. The negative findings for schemes derive, I suggest, from the transformations which take place in the label's meaning.

Because schemes are established upon important misconceptions (Kibreab 1989), they tend to create, often simultaneously, false or confusing labels. On the one hand they purport to be a long term and durable solution. And in protracted refugee situations coordinated investment of this kind makes sense, as in Cyprus, to institutional 'investors' and the managerial requirements of their bureaucracies. As a solution however they are fallacious, since neither for host nor refugees can the implied meaning of the label - large scale first country asylum - be a durable solution to the African refugee crisis.

On the other hand, schemes are often validated on the again false premise that they offer potential for integration, itself often further confused with assimilation (Kibreab 1989). These terms denote important characteristics in the bureaucratic designation of a refugee. For in practice, either by accident or intention, schemes frequently marginalize refugees and undermine long term objectives. At worst they prevent integration by controlling the extent of social and economic interaction with host communities, as in Cyprus. At best they are devices to remove long term burdens by targeting assistance with the aim of attracting aid and promoting self-sustaining development. Even in the latter case the results are disillusioning. Armstrong (1988) notes in Tanzania a predilection, evident elsewhere, for physical investment as a demonstration of schemes' credibility, with little regard given to less tangible community building investment - precisely the conditions observed in Cyprus. Rogge's disturbing evidence in Sudan suggests that one objective of the label has been achieved - integration - but only at the perverse price of a local agricultural economy dependent on the extremely low wages for which refugees are prepared to sell their labour (Rogge 1985:86–98).

Karadawi (1983) cites a contingent issue in the confusion between integration and long term needs. He demonstrates how the government's long term commitments to integrate refugees in schemes (*pace* Kibreab), were undermined by UNHCR and donors' policies which were unwilling to embark upon comprehensive programmes and projects beyond emergency and rehabilitation phases. One set of labelling objectives were destabilized by another.

Most disturbing of all, schemes are mechanisms for control and, fundamentally, are a non-participatory vehicle for assisting refugees, as we saw in Cyprus. Whether it is the powerful interplay between food distribution and protection as a control mechanism in Zimbabwe (Zetter 1991) or controlling refugee food distribution in a drought (de Waal 1988) or the more pervasive processes of disaggregation and reformulation which underpin institutional management of organized schemes (Harrell-Bond 1986), or the identification of political interests of agencies and donor governments (Mazur 1989), control has a profound influence on definitions of label and identity.

From this albeit cursory evidence from the conceptual approach of labelling, what conclusions might be drawn? Clearly settlement schemes in Africa, as in Cyprus, have been vehicles for differing interests and objectives - although these have not always been coherently expressed. Schemes are instrumental in transforming identity. Founded upon ambiguity, they impart an ambiguous status to refugees.

Schemes purport to offer long term autonomy; but, in effect they ambiguously create environments of control and dependency. Not necessarily intended, these are the concommitants of institutionalised distribution of assistance – food aid, building materials, income-generating start-up facilities. Moreover, with an emphasis on material provision, schemes require disaggregation of stories and conformity as cases. Transformation of an identity thus takes place.

Furthermore, proposed integration goes hand in hand with attempts, sometimes explicitly, to enforce segregation and inhibit interaction between refugees and hosts. Again these are mutually conflicting aspirations which confuse an identity. Next, whilst orientated towards developmental (and thus long term) aspirations, neither refugees nor host countries in Africa see schemes as a viable durable solution. They fear the implied permanency which long term programmes might impart to the label.

In short, the perceived advantages of settlement schemes are often illusory. They arouse hostility and rejection by refugees and uncertainty in the operational stance of governments. Schemes create a category of refugees, with an identity ostensibly based on development and integration as priorities. The reality however is a somewhat contrasting model of problem containment and management. In this alternative configuration, schemes become a vehicle for transforming an identity where refugees are marginalized into a segregated and permanently transient and dependent status. In contrast to Cyprus, exit becomes a popular option, in Africa, perversely accentuating the severe problems of self settlement which schemes are designed to alleviate.

These outcomes suggest that a labelled identity is being formed and transformed in ways unacceptable to refugees.

Politicizing an Identity

Refugees, more than many target groups suffer from the dilemma of policies which seek to integrate and to create independence, yet which exclude, sustain dependency and differentiation. The labelled may not necessarily be unwilling victims of such discrimination and cooptation. A 'refugee consciousness' maintains an identity, and the enhanced solidarity may be turned to advantage as a lever on governments and agencies.

An initially bureaucratic meaning, therefore, gradually assumes a distinctive, politicized identity, It expresses the strength of the target group's influence on policy. Deployed as a tool to create marginalization, the political outcomes of the label may become dominant features in the refugees' responses, accentuating the contradictions they seek to reduce. The evidence accumulated so far to illustrate the formation and reformation of an identity, is now brought together to demonstrate some aspects of the politicized identity

In Cyprus, the stance of both the government and the refugees is a commitment to 'repatriation'. Nevertheless, as the prospects for this recede, and as the material and economic provision designed to satisfy short term needs take on the appearance of a long term permanent solution, the physical identity of the label has gradually acquired a more explicit, politicized meaning as well.

The refugees have exploited the ambiguities of the programme to enhance their political profile in a number of ways. Extracting from the government the rights to second (and eventually third?) generation housing is one example. Proposals to charge rent or to impose maintenance charges are vigorously opposed. Dependency means that the providers have to adopt new responsibilities and widen existing provision, generation by generation. These provisions may well extend beyond the initial interpretation of the refugee label - a house

Each year the progressive extension of housing support obtained by the refugees, is consistent with an extension of dependency too. These outcomes of institutionalized provision are essential features sustaining the 'refugee consciousness' vis à vis the government. Moreover, despite growing internal debate about open-ended commitments, sustaining the label is important for both the government and its dependent clients in order to sustain an international identity of an unresolved international issue. In this way the refugees resist the countervailing tendencies of the programme which are creating an emerging sense of assimilation. For, even presupposing a diplomatic solution, the mass housing provision and the substantial economic disparity between the prosperous south and poorer north consolidate *de facto* division and undermine the broader political objectives. To maintain repatriation as a central commitment, the refugees cannot exit from dependency on the refugee housing label: rather they have to use their voice to sustain a dependent and differentiated identity (Hirschman 1970). The price is heavy. Despite the identical social characteristics of hosts and refugees, the refugees feel stigmatized. Prejudice though often understated and subtle is painful. Some refugees feel that their hosts begrudge the housing provision, despite their losses. Attempts to conceal the label become, as we have seen, pathological.

These paradoxical outcomes are dramatized by what is perhaps the most tangible indication of temporariness - the refusal of the refugees to accept property title. Title would imply permanency, the *status quo* partition, manifestly a softening of the negotiating position was the Turkish Cypriots. Conversely the lack of title maintains a powerful commitment to the refugees that their situation is still temporary, that they are not, despite appearances, becoming assimilated and that they will be repatriated. Refusal to accept title maintains, again, a label and special status of dependency and it is deployed as a stratagem to legitimize a continuing commitment to their political objectives. Even, perhaps especially, in a country so firmly adhering to the precepts and status of private property ownership, refugees say they would refuse the gift of title even if their houses were gilded - 'these are not ours'. With a programme so comprehensive, this is perhaps the last clear vestige of the temporariness of the situation. Title would remove an uncomplicated image of dependency - this would mean permanency of division. Encapsulated here are all the dilemmas of refugee identity as it has come to be expressed in the outcomes of the housing programme.

Proposals to curtail support, merely strengthen the refugees' tendency to display a politicized identity vis à vis state interests, although these interests are not articulated by a particular political party. This position is consistent with the general conclusions so far: that is the retention of specific identity but located centrally within a national political context of displacement. From the refugees' point of view this prevents marginalization into a single issue party which, though large, would be a minority.

From the state's point of view these outcomes can be interpreted rather differently. Politicization of refugee identity cannot yet be described in terms of class interests. It is too soon to conclude whether a proletarian political class has been created on the housing estates and whether this presages a state/capital, refugee/left wing class struggle. Left parties have always been strongly supported in Cyprus. The salient difference now is the spatial consolidation of a poor working class on the estates. A 'refugee' consciousness exists and one might expect this to be mobilized as class consciousness if repatriation remains a frustrated option; particularly might this be the case as the interests of capital have benefited so widely from the successful economic and housing policies on the divided island. Again the paradoxical position of state interests is evident. For, to diminish support for refugees might reduce the burden on public revenue; but simultaneously it might intensify the development of the identity of a class under threat. Conversely, classified as refugees waiting to return - this has an apolitical and less threatening implication for state interests.

Although housing is no longer the explicit need, its symbolic value is inestimable. It is manoeuvred by the refugees as a negotiating device because of the things that go with it: special interest group status; proxy for repatriation - housing in Cyprus gives the label a link, albeit tenuous and convoluted, with this dominant aspiration.

These entangled political interests help to explain the contradictory responses of the refugees. The state, incorporates, in part intentionally, yet it wants to disengage. The refugees acquiesce in the creation of dependency; but they wish also to disengage from the unwanted outcomes of the policy. Dependency and independence, integration and the wish for the repatriation occur, ambiguously, together.

Turning briefly to the African situation, as might be expected, given the very different contexts, there are significant contrasts with the Cyprus case. Nonetheless, case specific issues apart, the general proposition holds. Displayed in different ways, there is, in the research literature, demonstrable support for the evidence on the politicization of the refugee label.

Familiar in Tanzania is the response of refugees to the withdrawal of assistance (Armstrong 1988) that we have already seen in Cyprus. Though this research suggests a concern primarily with the consequences for material well-being, conceivably the underlying concerns of loss of political status are equally significant. Certainly the unwillingness to accept Tanzanian citizenship would seem to confirm that that is the case.

Salient differences in the way political identity is perceived and utilized are as follows. Whereas in Cyprus I have argued that a balance currently exists between refugee politicization and the state's growing interest in depoliticizing refugee status, African studies seem to confirm, as Karadawi tellingly asserts in his work on Sudan, 'pacification and depoliticization may be the prerequisites for humanitarian action' (Karadawi 1983:540). In deploying political solidarity, African refugees are inevitably in a weaker position vis à vis the interests of their hosts. They are less able to lever their hosts and command the kind of solidarity which is evident for the refugees in Cyprus. If a political identity is deployed then it is more likely to be by the host countries. The symbolism of settlement schemes is much more a political tool to attract international assistance (Harrell-Bond 1986; Karadawi 1983) than a policy instrument to serve refugee interests. Moreover this category may be tightly conceived to ensure that it remains sufficiently small in order not to threaten the *status quo*. Conversely it is reasonable to suppose that the essentially diffuse nature of self settled refugees in Africa creates *de facto* a diffused political identity. Despite material deprivation, conditions of self settlement, as we have seen, are conducive to a more integrated pattern of life with hosts. Moreover, the threat of detection, and thus encampment or repatriation, reinforces a tendency to merge with the landscape and not to declare a political identity, as Hansen's study demonstrates was the case with early Angolan influxes into Zambia (Hansen 1981). Caution should be exercised in driving this supposition too far. It is a matter of degree and circumstances.

These formulae point to the political marginalization of African refugees as a major objective and outcome of government and agency policies. Deploying the label in this way, however, need not always produce negative conditions. Preliminary research in Malawi hypothesizes that the state adopts a mediating role between different interests in its attempts to coordinate refugee assistance (Zetter 1991). In this instance the label refugee has achieved an important political currency (for the state at least), invested to encourage considerable assistance of a developmental nature for both refugees *and* hosts. This I suggest is a positive outcome, facilitated by an open door policy which, significantly, has not yet sought to create clear cut categories of self settled and scheme settled refugees. This is an important precondition; it removes the labelled distinctions, so powerful in Cyprus for example, between refugee and non-refugee, and also between refugee and refugee.

There is probably no more telling example of the refugee label concealing the 'political in the apparently unpolitical' (Wood 1985:6) than in the matter of food aid and in close proximity agreeing census figures for the number of refugees (Journal of Refugee Studies 1989; Clay 1989; Cuny 1989). Waldron (1988) demonstrates precisely this configuration in the study earlier cited. For the Eritrean refugees in the camps, the principal meaning of their label was a basic one – access to food. For the various institutional factions the same debate sought to deploy the label in rather different ways. The issue was not one of declining food delivery and rising malnutrition (only some 59% of prescribed daily intake was available), even presupposing that logistical constraints in supply could be overcome. It was instead an issue of overall identity. With census estimates varying by as much as 200,000 (low 500,000, high 700,000), the real purpose of enumerating who were refugees was not to determine food provisioning but the 'total investment in the Somali relief effort, which was a major component of the Somali economy', (Waldron 1988;160).

Labels, then have powerful political meanings. They are a crucial index of differing assumptions and contradictory political interests surrounding the designation refugee. The process of 'delinking' case from story, in order to achieve conformity with institutional and ultimately state interests, represents control and the designation of certain kinds of acceptable political status. Programmes, like rehousing refugees, food provisioning and so on, potentially become both policy means and ends. They conceal more difficult political aspirations and needs, like repatriation or integration. In this way a label is delinked from what, in extreme conditions and large-scale unmet needs, may be potentially revolutionary circumstances. It is reformulated into a status, which helps to remove challenges to the prevailing ideology and structures. Labelling legitimized this kind of action. Precisely, this can occur because labels like refugee appear benevolent, neutral and obvious.

Conclusions

Labelling matters so fundamentally because it is an inescapable part of public policy making and its language: a non-labelled way out cannot exist. A theory of labelling provides some constructs with which to observe the way bureaucratic procedures and practices form a refugee identity. It is the instrumentality of these procedures, in creating an official status and in establishing the asymmetrical relationship between power and powerlessness, which this paper has explored. By reinforcing actions of designation, labelling means conditionality and differentiation, inclusion and exclusion, stereotyping and control. To summarize, there are a number of conclusions relevant to policy-based perspectives on refugee labelling.

First there is the vulnerability of refugees to imposed labels. Refugeehood, contingent on accepting a bureaucratized delivery of basic and familiar needs, may not differ from the experience of non-refugee groups. Nor may it, in every case concerning refugees, be a fundamental change from pre-existing conditions – although it was in Cyprus. Where refugees differ, crucially, from most other client groups, is in two respects. First conditions of extreme scarcity prevailing in refugee situations create new procedures, rules and categories – familiar experiences of designation become substantially changed. Most significant however, is the fact that the modes of designation occur rapidly, in traumatic and unfamiliar circumstances. It is this that makes refugees extremely vulnerable to institutionalized perceptions, an imposed crisis-based identity and a prescriptive programme of needs. Given this turbulence, ambivalent and non-compliant responses should not be surprising.

Second, designation is not an end in itself. Labels create their own momentum especially where transitory situations become protracted. This momentum is not independent of the label but preconditioned by it. We have seen evidence of this in second generation housing and refusal of title in Cyprus and in cases in the African situation where dependency and non-integration are displayed by refugees. In this way they can sustain an image of a transitory status. In Cyprus this was especially important where permanent housing has been increasingly identified with permanency of settlement in the south. These dynamic characteristics of the label again help to explain how patterns of alienation and politicization emerge.

Third there is an important element of symbolism in labels. Clearly the symbolic, to have credibility, must have some material representation - housing, food distribution and so on. But, these material provisions may also be deployed as a proxy for other more important institutional statuses - refugees wanting repatriation, greater political representation. Again identities become transformed and quite distinct from the initial assumptions, for example that refugees need housing, and the bureaucratic procedures to achieve them.

Fourth concealed within a label are several co-existing but contrasting identities, as the cases in this paper have demonstrated. There are distinctions: between refugee and non-refugee; between different categories of refugee; between agency, government and the refugees' own perspectives; between manifest and latent components. Rarely are these co-existing identities compatible. There is no normative identity which can be agreed. The conceptual tools of labelling seek to disaggregate these identities. For it is only in this way that a clearer account can be given of why disjunctive and confusing outcomes accompany virtually all refugee assistance. The point is not that one model of identity is necessarily superior to another. 'Rather, three things are crucial: how identities are defined and adopted; who controls them; and how the different categories complement or conflict with each other' (Zetter 1988:105–106).

Finally, we have seen how labels have been instrumental in forming a political identity. The debate about labelling in public policy, therefore is ultimately one about empowering the powerless, like refugees. In short, it is about participation in forming an identity and thus in enabling greater access to and control over decisions about their own lives. Arguably, it is the failure to recognise this fundamental issue, which, in the end, inhibits manifestly humanitarian intentions being achieved.

Careful observation of how the label refugee is constructed is essential. The alternative is predetermined stereotypes, inappropriately applied models from other cultures, crisis-imposed identities of powerlessness and dependency which 'tend to destroy much of what they wish to support and undermine the identities they wish to sustain' (Zetter 1988:106).

ADELMAN, H. (1988) 'Refugee or Asylum: A Philosophical Perspective', *Journal of Refugee Studies*, 1:1, pp. 7-19.
ARMSTRONG, A. (1988) 'Aspects of Refugee Wellbeing in Settlement Schemes: An Examination of the Tanzanian Case', *Journal of Refugee Studies*, 1:1, pp. 57-73.
BATLEY, R. (1983) *Power Through Bureaucracy*, Aldershot, Gower.
CENTLIVRES, P. and CENTLIVRES-DEMONT, M. (1988) 'The Afghan Refugees in Pakistan: An Ambiguous Identity', *Journal of Refugee Studies*, 1:2, pp. 141-152.
CHRISTENSEN, H. (1982) *Survival Strategies for and by Camp Refugees*, Geneva, UNRISD.
—— (1985) *Refugees and Pioneers: History and Field Study of a Burundian Settlement in Tanzania*, Geneva, UNRISD.
CLAY, J. W. (1989) 'Ethiopian Famine and the Relief Agencies', in *Nichols and Loescher (eds)*.
CUNY, F. (1989) 'Politics and Famine Relief', in *Nichols and Loescher (eds)*.
GOFFMAN, E. (1963) *Stigma: Notes on the Management of Spoiled Identity*, Harmondsworth, Penguin.
—— (1982) *Asylums*, London, Penguin.
GERSONY, R. (1988) 'Summary of Mozambican Refugee Accounts of Principally Conflict-Related Experiences in Mozambique', *Bureau for Refugee Programs, Department of State*, Washington.
HANSEN, A. (1981) 'Refugee Dynamics: Angolans in Africa 1966-1972', *International Migration Review*, 15:1, pp. 175 -194.
—— (1989) *Preliminary Report on The Long Term Consequences of Two Different Settlement Options for the Security, Rehabilitation and Sustainable Development of Refugees Based on a Case Study of Angolan Refugees (1966-1989) in Zambia*, Unpublished Mimeo, RSP, Oxford.
HARRELL-BOND, B. E. (1986) *Imposing Aid: Emergency Assistance to Refugees*, Oxford, OUP.
HIRSCHMAN, A. O. (1970) *Exit, Voice and Loyalty*, Harvard, Harvard UP.
HIRSCHON, R. (1989) *Heirs of the Greek Catastrophe: The Social Life of Asia-Minor Refugees in Piraeus*, Oxford, Clarendon Press.
JOURNAL OF REFUGEE STUDIES. (1989) Special Issue on Food Aid and Refugees, containing a paper by James Ingram (WFP Director) and Responses by researchers, *Journal of Refugee Studies*, 2:3, pp. 329-353.
KARADAWI, A. (1983) 'Constraints on Assistance to Refugees: Some Observations from the Sudan', *World Development*, 11:6, pp. 537-547.
KIBREAB, G. (1985) *African Refugees: Reflections on the African Refugee Problem*, Trenton, NJ, Africa World Press.
—— (1989) 'Local Settlement of African Refugees: A Temporary Measure or a Durable Solution', *Journal of Refugee Studies*, 2:4, pp. 468-490.
LEWIS, J. et al. (1980) *Disasters as Opportunities, Disaster Preparedness Seminar*, (USDSA), Manila.
LOESCHER, G. and SCANLON, J. A. (1986) *Calculated Kindness - Refugees and America's Half Open Door 1945 to the Present*, New York, Free Press/Macmillan.
LOIZOS, P. (1977) 'A Struggle for Meaning: Reactions to Disaster Amongst Cypriot Refugees', *Disasters*, 1:3, pp. 231-239
—— (1981) *The Heart Grown Bitter: A Chronicle of Cypriot War Refugees*, Cambridge, CUP.
MAZUR, R. (1986) 'Linking Popular Initiatives and Aid Agencies: The Case of Refugees', *Refugee Issues* Vol 3, No 2, pp. 1-16, Refugee Studies Programme, University of Oxford.
—— (1988) 'Refugees in Africa: The Role of Sociology on Analysis and Praxis', *Current Sociology*, 36:2, pp. 43-60.
—— (1989) 'The Political Economy of Refugee Creation in Southern Africa: Micro and Macro Issues in Sociological Perspective', *Journal of Refugee Studies*, 2:4, pp. 441-467.
MEED (Middle East Economic Digest). (1981) *Cyprus A Special Report*, London, MEED.
MONTES, S. (1988) 'Migration to the United States as an Index of the Intensifying Social and Political Crisis in El Salvador', *Journal of Refugee Studies*, 1:2, pp. 107-126.
NICHOLS, B. and LOESCHER, G. (eds). (1989) *The Moral Nation: Humanitarianism and US Foreign Policy Today*, Notre Dame, Indiana, University of Notre Dame Press.

REPUBLIC OF CYPRUS. (1977) *Second Emergency Action Plan 1977-78*, Planning Bureau, Planning Commission, Nicosia, Cyprus.

ROGGE, J. R. (1985) *Too Many, Too Long: Sudan's Twenty Year Refugee Dilemma* New Jersey, Rownan and Allenhead.

ROSENBLATT, R.(1984) 'Who Cares? (Review of Shawcross (1984))' *New York* Review of Books, 16.8.84.

SCHAFFER, B. B. (1975) 'The Problems of Access to Public Services', *Development and Change*, 6:2, pp. 3-11.

—— (1977) *Official Providers - Access Equity and Participation*, Paris, UNESCO.

—— (1985) 'Policy Makers Have Their Needs Too', in *Wood, G* (ed), 1985.

SHAWCROSS, W. (1984) *The Quality of Mercy: Cambodia, Holocaust and Modern Conscience*, London, Andre Deutsch.

SHACKNOVE, A. E. (1985) 'Who is a Refugee?', *Ethics*, 95:2, pp. 274-284.

STEIN, B. N. (1981) 'The Refugee Experience: An Overview of Refugee Research', *International Migration Review*, 15:1, pp. 320-330.

UNITED NATIONS DISASTER RELIEF ORGANISATION. (1982) *Shelter After Disaster, Guidelines for Assistance*, New York, UN.

VINCENT, R. J. (1989) 'Political and Economic Refugees: Problems of Migration, Asylum and Resettlement', *Journal of Refugee Studies*, 2:4, pp. 504-512.

DE VOE, D. M. (1981) 'Framing Refugees as Clients', *International Migration Review*, 15:1 pp. 88-94.

DE WAAL, A. (1988) 'Refugees and the Creation of Famine: The Case of Dar-el-Masalit, Sudan', *Journal of Refugee Studies*, 1:2, pp. 127-140.

—— (1989) *Famine That Kills, Dafur, Sudan, 1984-1985*, Oxford, Clarendon.

WALDRON, S. (1988) 'Working in the Dark. Why Social Anthropological Research is Essential in Refugee Administration', *Journal of Refugee Studies*, 1:2, pp. 153-165.

WAUGH, E. (1930) *Labels, A Mediterranean Journey*, (Reprinted by Penguin, 1985), London, Harmondsworth.

WILSON, K. et al. (1989) 'Food Provisioning Amongst Mozambican Refugees in Malawi. A Study of Aid, Livelihood and Development', *Report Prepared for WFP*, Refugee Studies Programme, Oxford/WFP Rome.

WOOD, G. (ed). (1985) *Labelling in Development Policy*, London, Sage.

—— (1985) 'The Politics of Development Policy Labelling', in *Wood G* (ed) 1985, pp. 5-31.

ZETTER, R. W. (1985) 'Refugees, Access and Labelling', in *Wood, G* (ed), 1985, pp. 87-108.

—— (1986) 'Rehousing the Greek-Cypriot Refugees from 1974: Assimilation, Dependency and Politicization', pp. 106-125, in *Cyprus in Transition 1960-1985*, *Koumoulides, J* (ed), London, Trigraph.

—— (1987) *Rehousing the Greek-Cypriot Refugees from 1974. A Study of Institutional Access and Labellings*, DPhil (unpublished), University of Sussex.

—— (1988) 'Refugees and Refugee Studies: A Label and an Agenda', *Journal of Refugee Studies*, 1:1, pp. 1-6.

——(1988b) 'Refugees, Repatriation and Root Causes', *Journal of Refugee Studies*, 1:2, pp. 99-106.

—— (1991) 'Coordination or Interest Mediation? Governments, NGOs and Humanitarian Assistance to Mozambican Refugees in Malawi and Zimbabwe', *Work in Progress*.

ZOLBERG, A. R. et al. (1989) *Escape from Violence: Conflict and Refugee Crisis in the Developing World*, Oxford, OUP.

ZUCKER, N. M. and ZUCKER, N. F. (1987) *The Guarded Gate. The Reality of American Refugee Policy*, San Diego, Harcourt, Brace, Jovanovich.

MS received March 1990; revised MS received December 1990.

*Earlier versions of this paper were prepared for the Program in International Co-operation in Africa, Northwestern University Illinois, March 1990 and the Institute of Social Studies, the Hague, August 1990. Thanks are given to referees of this paper.

Name Index